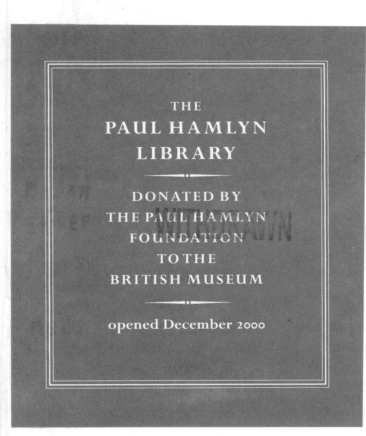

ATLAS OF THE
CLASSICAL WORLD

Κτῆμά τ'ἐς ἀεί

A possession for all time

MONUMENTUM
AERE PERENNIUS

*A monument
more lasting than bronze*

HORACE, ODES, iii, 30

ATLAS
OF THE
CLASSICAL WORLD

EDITED BY

A. A. M. VAN DER HEYDEN, HIST. DRS.

AND

H. H. SCULLARD, M.A., PH.D., F.B.A.

READER IN ANCIENT HISTORY, KING'S COLLEGE,
UNIVERSITY OF LONDON

NELSON

1959

THOMAS NELSON AND SONS LTD
LONDON AND EDINBURGH

THOMAS NELSON AND SONS
NEW YORK

THOMAS NELSON AND SONS
(CANADA) LTD
TORONTO

THOMAS NELSON AND SONS LTD
JOHANNESBURG
MELBOURNE

SOCIÉTÉ FRANÇAISE D'ÉDITIONS NELSON
PARIS

N.V. Uitgeversmaatschappij ELSEVIER
© 1959   Thomas NELSON and Sons Limited
Originally published as ATLAS VAN DE ANTIEKE WERELD (AMSTERDAM ELSEVIER)

Foreword

It is a pleasure to introduce to English readers this ATLAS OF THE CLASSICAL WORLD. Those who already know and have enjoyed the *Atlas of the Bible* (1956) and the *Atlas of the Early Christian World* (1958) will know what to expect, but new-comers to the series will be pleasantly surprised to find the wealth of treatment that is included by the generous interpretation of the word 'Atlas'. The material is three-fold. Maps of course there are, covering a wide range of interests, beyond the strictly geographical. They vividly illustrate many aspects of the classical world, religious, economic, military, literary, and artistic, as well as political history; and by the use of a system of colours, symbols, and over-printed legends they help to relate historical facts and monuments to the geographical setting. The second chief feature is a series of magnificent illustrations, many of which are air-photographs taken specially for this work. Their range is wide, their impact impressive. It is most valuable, for instance, to be able to see the topographical setting of Mycenae and then, as it were, with a television camera lens to 'zoom' forward and survey in accompanying photographs the royal citadel in ever-increasing detail, or again to look down on the heart of Rome from some 40,000 feet, and then to swoop lower and regard the Palatine, Capitol, and Forum directly from above, and yet again to get a still lower oblique view of the same scene. Some of the illustrations are arranged in accordance with subject-matter rather than chronology: for example, many dealing with the Roman army are placed together to show in one series the development of the military system. The third main feature of the work is the text which sketches the development of the world of Greece and Rome and touches upon many cultural as well as the political achievements.

The whole work is infused with a lively and sincere appreciation of the value of the achievement of the classical world and of its importance for the world of today. Much is said in these days about the values of Western civilisation, and it is important that all who share in this civilisation should become increasingly conscious of and familiar with the origins of the ideas and influences upon which their ways of thought are based; and many of these are rooted and grounded in the world of Greece and Rome. This Atlas offords a unique introduction to that world, its achievements, its remains, and its lasting importance.

Although the book is not intended primarily for professional scholars, few of them surely will fail to find interest in the maps and value as well as delight in the photographs. Geographical factors, while not the ultimate force in man's development, have clearly exercised a dominant influence on the form that this has taken, and therefore a work that presents to the eye so many of these factors with such vividness must help student, teacher, and general reader alike. But besides portraying much of the geographical setting of ancient history and many individual landscapes and sites, the work also illustrates the everyday life and occupations of ordinary men who helped to shape the classical world, and the text discusses many aspects of the intellectual, artistic and cultural achievements of the Greeks and Romans, although the field is naturally too wide to allow more than a selective treatment in a book that is primarily designed to present a general view of the Graeco-Roman world.

The ATLAS OF THE CLASSICAL WORLD, it should be said, deals exclusively with pagan antiquity. For the development of Christianity and its influence on art in the later centuries of the Roman Empire, reference should be made to the *Atlas of the Early Christian World*.

In general, to aid ease of reference from map to map and from maps to text, Latin spelling has been adopted in the transliteration of names in order to secure consistency. This system has not been rigidly adhered to, however, and well-known place names (e.g. Athens, Rome) appear in their English form, and many Greek names in the forms which are commonly used in this country (e.g. Delos rather than Delus). If any difficulties arise, reference to the very full Index will avert confusion.

Without the helpful co-operation of many people this book obviously could never have been completed. Their names are given elsewhere. Special acknowledgment, however, is due both to the Greek Government, which by making an aeroplane available enabled a great number of new photographs to be taken, and to the Italian Air Ministry, which opened its archives. I should like to express my thanks for the helpful co-operation of Dr. K. Davies and Mr. W. T. McLeod, both of Messrs. Thomas Nelson & Sons Limited, and to the latter also for having added a few paragraphs on classical art.

UNIVERSITY OF LONDON, KING'S COLLEGE, 1959   H. H. SCULLARD

CONTENTS

The heritage of classical culture

Legend

MAPS

Maps dealing with general subjects (e.g. Map 57, Distribution of the tribes within the Empire) show the Empire at its greatest extent, in the time of Trajan.

Brackets signify modern place-names unless otherwise stated. Where a place-name between brackets stands by itself, it means that the ancient name is not known. Years B.C. and A.D. are specified as such only where it is necessary to avoid misunderstanding.

Signs and abbreviations are explained in the keys to the individual maps in which they occur. Some in general use are given below.

▣	Place of special importance	I.	Insula (island)
✕	Battlefield	Iae.	Insulae (islands)
S.	Sinus (gulf)	M.	Mons (mountain)
Pr.	Promontorium (cape)	Mon.	Monumentum (monument)

On the maps names are for the sake of consistency and ease of reference mostly given in the forms commonly used in Roman times (except for Maps 13, 24, 25 which retain Greek spellings); but in the text and captions for the reader's convenience conventional English spellings are adopted where these exist. Both forms appear in the Index.

ILLUSTRATIONS

In order to avoid overburdening the captions with names and dates, details of fact concerning the objects shown (artists, time and place of origin, present location, etc.) are assembled in a separate list after the Index. References to illustrations in the text are indicated by the sign →.

Contributors

A. A. M. van der Heyden, hist. drs.	*General editor*
H. H. Scullard, m.a., ph.d., f.b.a.	*English editor*
Mary F. Hedlund, m.a.	*Translator*
dr. K. Sprey	*Greek and Roman history*
dr. A. R. A. van Aken	*Roman maps, co-ordination of maps and Index*
p. dr. Calasanctius	*Greek maps*
dr. M. A. Schwartz	*Classical literature*

dr. M. Broshi	*Jerusalem*	J. Lassus	*Algiers*
prof. F. Castagnoli	*Rome*	dr. M. Marriën	*Brussels*
dr. L. Cozza	*Rome*	prof. P. de Pallol	*Valladolid*
M. Euzennat	*Rabat*	P. Stathacos	*Athens*
dr. J. M. H. Fernhout	*Den Helder*	dr. M. J. Vermaseren	*Amsterdam*
dr. G. Forni	*Rome*	dr. S. Yeivin	*Jerusalem*
R. G. Goodchild	*Cyrene*		

Co-operating organisations and institutions

Archaeological Institute	Utrecht
Air Ministry	Rome
Royal Hellenic Air Force	Athens
North Atlantic Treaty Organisation	Paris

Algeria	*Direction des Antiquités de l'Algérie, Algiers*
Austria	*Österreichisches Archäologisches Institut, Vienna*
Belgium	*Museum voor Schone Kunsten, Brussels*
Britain	*British Museum, London*
	Society of Antiquaries, London
Denmark	*Carlsberg Glyptothek, Copenhagen*
France	*Bibliothèque Nationale, Paris*
Germany	*Landesmuseum, Trier*
	Archäologisches Institut, Mainz
	Staatliche Museen, Berlin
Greece	*American School of Archeology, Athens*
	École française d'Athènes, Athens
	Museum, Chaironeia
	Museum, Corinth
	Museum, Delphi
	Museum, Heraklion
	Museum, Nea Anchialos
	Museum, Olympia
	Museum, Sparta
	Museum, Tegea
Hungary	*Budapesti Történeti Muzeum, Budapest*
Israel	*Ministry of Education and Culture, Jerusalem*
Italy	*Istituto Storico Olandese, Rome*
	Museo Capitolino, Rome
	Museo dei Conservatori, Rome
	Museo Lateranense, Rome
	Museo delle Terme, Rome
	Museo Etrusco di Villa Giulia, Rome
	Uffizi, Florence
Jordan	*Palestine Archaeological Museum, Jerusalem*
Lebanon	*Institut française d'Archéologie, Beirut*
Libya	*Department of Antiquities, Sjahhat (Cyrene)*
Morocco	*Inspection des Antiquités du Maroc, Rabat*
Netherlands	*Museum Kam, Nijmegen*
	Museum voor Oudheidkunde, Leiden
Spain	*Instituto de Arqueología, Madrid*
	Seminario de Aarte y Arqueología, Valladolid
Vatican State	*Monumenti Musei e Gallerie Pontificie*
United States of America	*Metropolitan Museum of Art, New York*
	Museum of Fine Arts, Boston

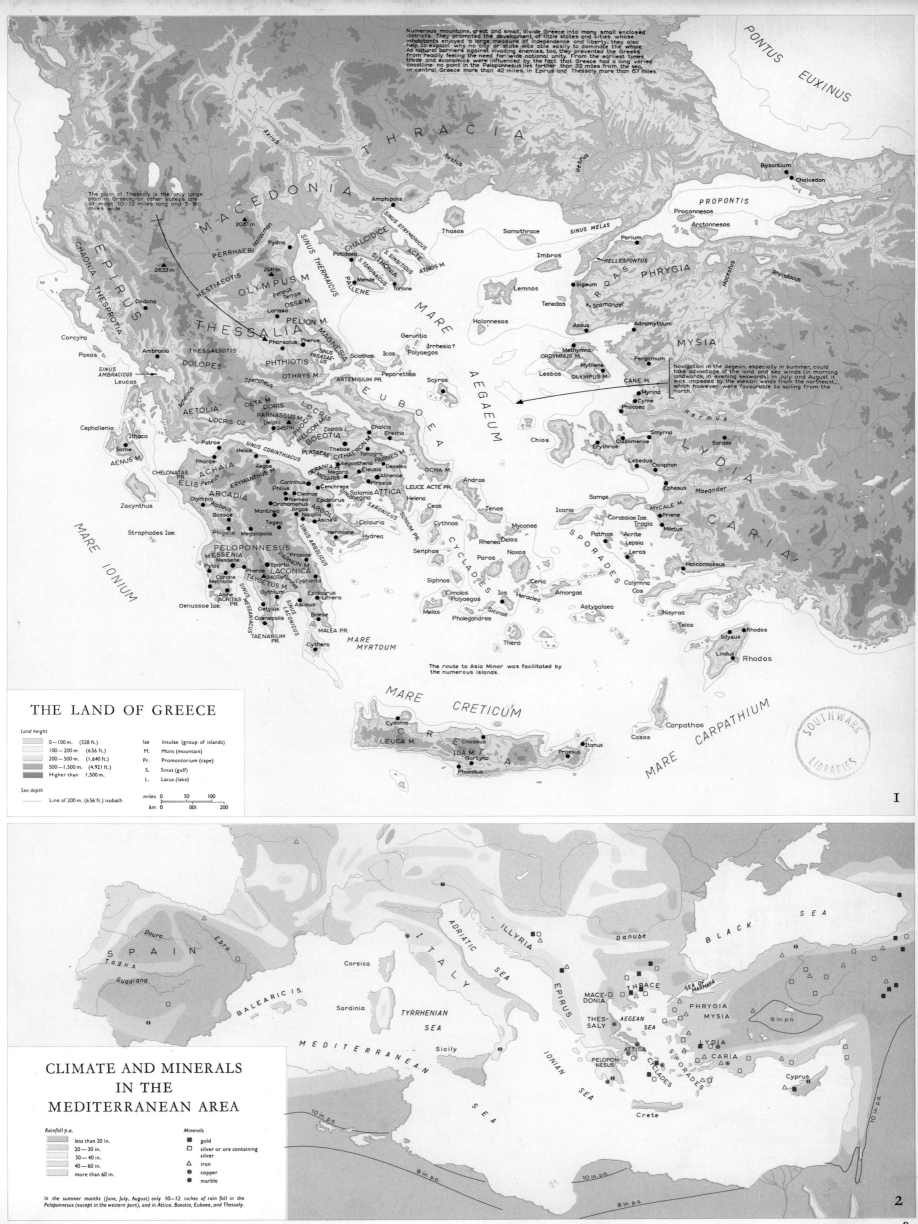

THE LAND OF GREECE

Land height
- 0—100 m. (328 ft.)
- 100—200 m. (656 ft.)
- 200—500 m. (1,640 ft.)
- 500—1,500 m. (4,921 ft.)
- Higher than 1,500 m.

Sea depth
- Line of 200 m. (656 ft.) isobath

- Iae Insulae (group of islands)
- M. Mons (mountain)
- Pr. Promontorium (cape)
- S. Sinus (gulf)
- L. Lacus (lake)

miles 0   50   100
km 0   001   200

I

CLIMATE AND MINERALS
IN THE
MEDITERRANEAN AREA

Rainfall p.a.
- less than 20 in.
- 20 — 30 in.
- 30 — 40 in.
- 40 — 60 in.
- more than 60 in.

Minerals
- gold
- silver or ore containing silver
- iron
- copper
- marble

In the summer months (June, July, August) only 10—12 inches of rain fall in the Peloponnesus (except in the western part), and in Attica, Boeotia, Euboea, and Thessaly.

2

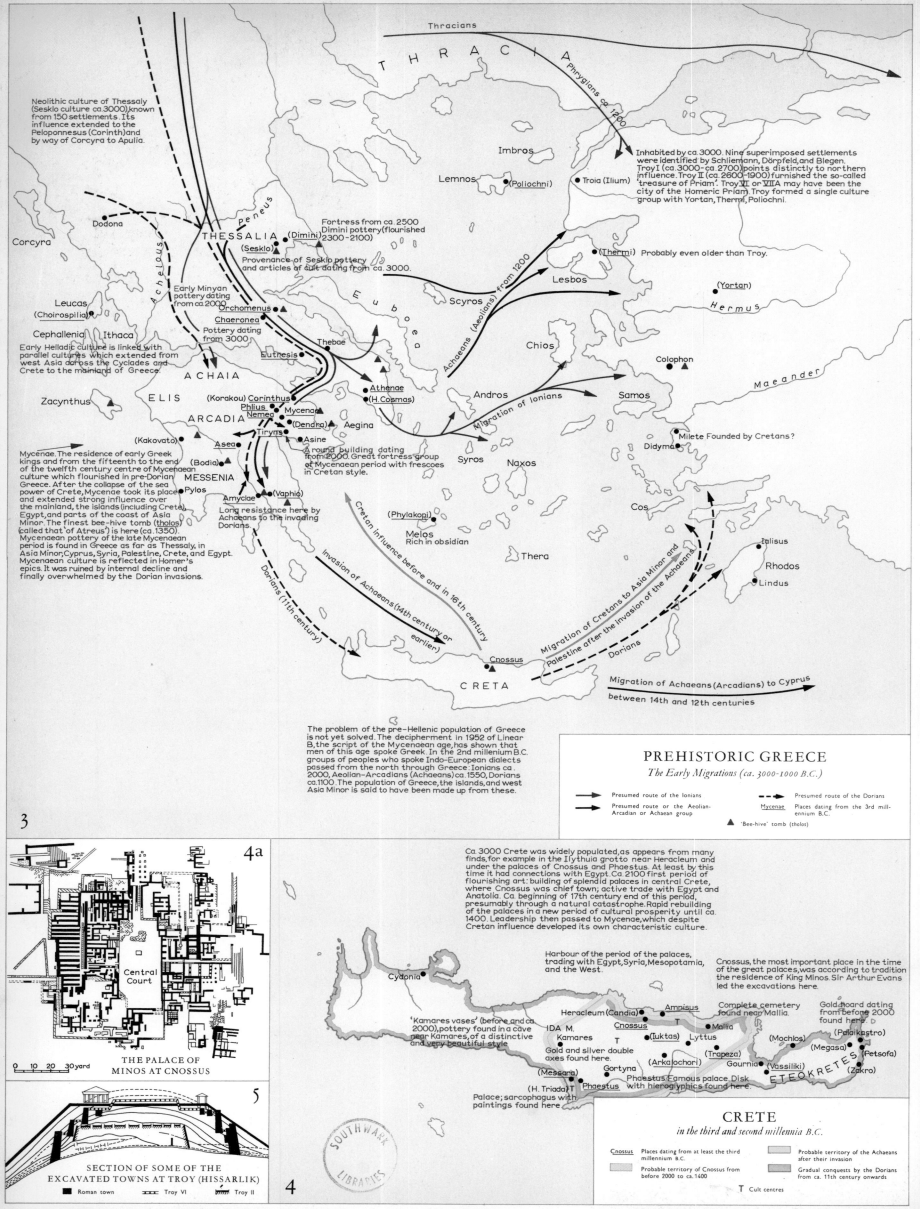

The land of the Greeks

THE HOME OF THE GREEKS WAS THE LANDS AROUND THE AEGEAN SEA, TOGETHER WITH THE ISLANDS SCATTERED THROUGHOUT IT. It was formed then as now by the southern spurs of the mountain ranges of the Balkan peninsula where mountain chains running from north to south are crossed by ridges running from east to west. The landscape is extremely broken, with many small valleys which are separated from each other by mountain formations and constitute numerous independent cantons. Only a few of the wider river valleys are suitable for agriculture and cattle breeding on a larger scale. The rivers are not navigable, and their estuaries, blocked by silt from the mountains, are not suitable for ports. The largest plain, that of Thessaly, has only one outlet, through the narrow vale of Tempe, a cleft worn in the mountains by the waters of the Peneus. Yet on the other hand the sea everywhere cuts deep inlets into the land, which continues, as it were, in countless islands that form a natural link with the coast of Asia Minor.

In classical times the land was more wooded than now and abounded more in game. Even in recorded times lions were said to be found in the mountain forests of the Balkans; wild goats and wild boars lived in Attica, upon the slopes of Cithaeron. The mountain slopes, now eaten away by erosion, were covered with woods and brush. But it was always a rather poor country, offering little possibility for development. The Greeks praised it highly for its productivity and climate, but, when the voice of patriotism was not speaking, admitted that toil and poverty had always been the mothers of Greek life. The stony fields were usually tilled with the hoe. Horses were used only for military purposes and were a luxury confined to the very rich. Goats were the most usual livestock, and mules and donkeys were the only means of transport along the steep mountain paths which linked the various settlements by land. Land travel was always slow and difficult, but the sea was never far away and, in summer at least, allowed men to travel from coast to coast. Thus from the very earliest times the inhabitants of this land had made their way cautiously across the water. Mythological tales bear witness to the monsters and perils that menaced these early seafarers, and navigation always remained a dangerous undertaking. But even for men in small primitive ships the numerous islands made it possible always to keep land safely in sight, where a narrow sandy beach offered shelter from storm and darkness. Whenever a bold seafarer lost sight of the shore or a skipper was driven from his course by foul winds, the starry sky, which was normally clear, served to guide him home. Necessity drove many Greeks from their land; its limited possibilities compelled the inhabitants to seek means of subsistence across the sea. Although olive groves, vineyards, marble quarries, and silver mines later brought wealth to their owners, Greece provided food for only a limited population.

Navigation thus became the dynamic factor in the development of the Greeks; the sea, far horizons, adventure, set their seal upon the Greek spirit. The inland states were always considered conservative and soon as backward, while contact with the sea, with distant lands, with foreign peoples on the islands and other coasts, drove the inhabitants towards ever new possibilities and transformed them from primitive tribes into the bearers of a culture which was to dominate the then known world. Greek culture became the school of Europe.

1. The temple of Sunium, built on a promontory and dedicated to Poseidon, was a landmark for Greek sailors on their journey to the mainland. The Doric temple was built in the time of Pericles, a little later than the Parthenon, after an earlier sanctuary had been destroyed by the Persians. In the background the coast of Attica and near-by islands (→ 5). 2. The modern as well as the ancient Greek farmer has to work hard on his unrewarding ground. Cornfield in Attica, full of large scattered stones.

THIS IS HOW THE COASTS of the Ionian and Aegean islands appeared to the Greek seafarers upon their wanderings. They travelled at first in small sailing ships and later in large rowing vessels. 3. The coast of mountainous Ithaca. 4. The rich island of Siphnos, a link in the great island chain, famous for its silver and gold. With its many bays it shows how sailors could easily find a beach upon which to drag their ships at night. The amount of precious metals found here enabled the former inhabitants of this now almost deserted rock to build a treasury at Delphi of which the beauty can still be admired thanks to the extensive remains (→ 101, 102, 107-9). 5. The geographical make-up of Greece played an important rôle in the development of the city-states. The sea, which penetrated the land in many deep inlets, formed in summer a safe route to the many islands which, one in sight of the next, formed a visible bridge both to Asia Minor and the west. These conditions strongly encouraged emigration and the formation of extensive trade links. The southern coast of Attica, from Piraeus to the steep promontory of Sunium, crowned by a temple, gives an idea of the fantastic coastline with precipitous rocks and wide bays. Now, many centuries after Sophocles' description of the 'wooded, sea-sprayed crag at the tip of Sunium's plain', the mountains are weather-beaten and bare. Yet such superficial changes in landscape, introduced over the centuries by natural causes or man's occupancy, have not fundamentally modified the character of the country, and it still largely conditions the life of the inhabitants.

3

4

THE RIVERS OF GREECE ARE of little importance since they are useless for navigation. They are dry torrent beds in summer (when they are frequently used as tracks or foot paths) and in winter the rushing current is too swift. One of the largest rivers is the Peneus (now Salamorias), which flows through the plain of Thessaly, now, as in classical times, one of the most fertile districts of Greece. Herodotus describes how many rivers of the plain joined together and then flowed by way of the Peneus to the Gulf of Salonica. **6.** The course of the Peneus in the mountain-fringed plain of Thessaly where nowadays good roads run from north to south. **7.** Before reaching the sea the Peneus flows through the mountain ranges of Ossa (right) and Olympus (left), by way of the narrow vale of Tempe, already famous in antiquity for the beauty of its landscape. Claudius Aelianus (A.D. 200) writes of the many attractions granted this valley by bountiful nature: oleanders, plane-trees, poplars, and shrubs of many kinds overshadowed the 'slow, oily-flowing river'. Today the railway line from Athens to Salonica runs along the Olympus side of the valley. **8.** Mount Olympus, on the borders of Macedon and Thessaly, was sacred in the eyes of the Greeks. This mountain is almost 9,600 feet high and is covered with snow for much of the year. Its summit was thought to reach the upper air. Here Zeus had his throne, surrounded by the gods and goddesses of Greek mythology. In the *Iliad* they have no other abode; in the usage of later poets "Olympus" sometimes denotes some vague idea of a more aetherial heaven.

9

10

TWO REGIONS, ATTICA AND LACONICA, PLAYED A PREDOMINANT RÔLE IN THE HISTORY OF GREECE. THEY FORMED the bases of the two most important city-states: Athens and Sparta. Attica is a rather infertile peninsula where the rocky stratum just below the soil has always hindered cultivation. Farmers still guide their ploughs over rocky reddish soil (→ 2). Now, as in earlier times, the olive is the only important agricultural product. **9.** The plain of Marathon (→ 94), lying between the bay, Mt. Pentelicus, and the other mountains of Attica, was one of the four plains of the region. Formerly marshy, it has now been rendered suitable for cultivation by drainage. **10.** The adjacent region of the Megarid resembles Marathon in many respects, with stretches of hills and mountain ranges, formerly partly wooded but now growing little else than phrygana, the low brush so characteristic of Mediterranean countries. The photograph shows the Gulf of Corinth where it forms a deep bay near the former Aegosthena (modern Porto Germano). A large part of the walls and some towers of this small town still stand upon the hills (see white line, and cp. Plates 113, 114).

16

11

12

IN A LONG VALLEY, BOUNDED ON THE EAST BY THE PARNON AND ON THE WEST BY THE TAYGETUS RANGE, LIES 'HOLlow Lacedaemon' (as Homer called it), a region so surrounded by mountains that its centre, Sparta (→ 131) needed no walls. Thucydides tells us that the city was not built all crowded together, nor did it possess large buildings and temples. Following ancient Greek custom, it consisted of separate village settlements. **11.** The former city area of Sparta seen from the low acropolis. In the background the steep eastern side of the Taygetus range, only a few miles from the city. **13** (following page). Modern Sparta and, to the right, the former city area. This forcefully illustrates how the mountains formed a wall of defence. In the foreground the river Eurotas in its summer bed (→ 69). **12.** On the other side of the Taygetus range lies the great plain of Messene, coveted by Sparta when land became short on its own side of the mountains. The photograph shows the extremely fertile plain, viewed from the north. It is now thickly planted with olive trees. In the background the Gulf of Messene, with the mountains running down both the encircling promontories.

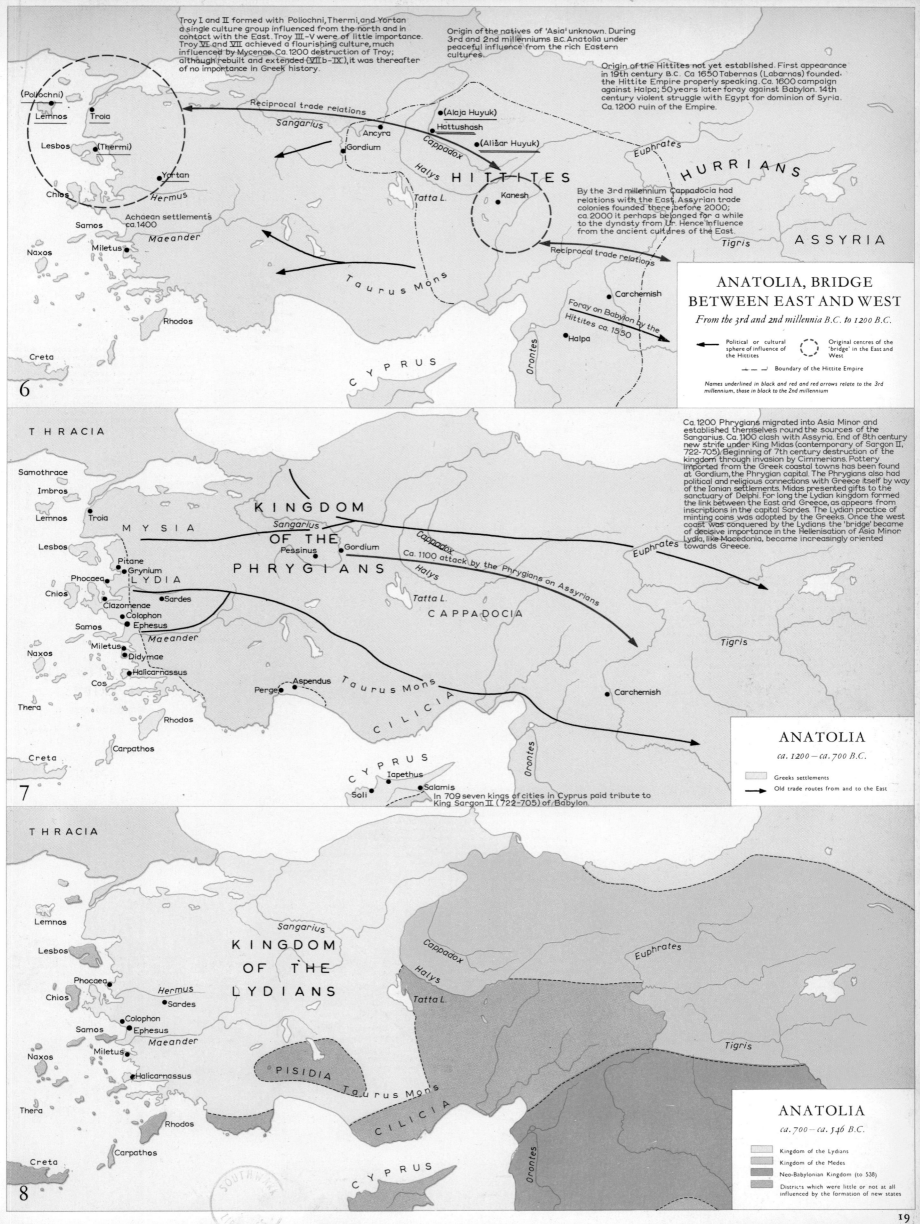

6

Troy I and II formed with Poliochni, Thermi, and Yortan a single culture group influenced from the north and in contact with the East. Troy III–V were of little importance. Troy VI and VII achieved a flourishing culture, much influenced by Mycenae. Ca.1200 destruction of Troy; although rebuilt and extended (VIIb–IX), it was thereafter of no importance in Greek history.

Origin of the natives of 'Asia' unknown. During 3rd and 2nd millenniums B.C. Anatolia under peaceful influence from the rich Eastern cultures.

Origin of the Hittites not yet established. First appearance in 19th century B.C. Ca 1650 Tabarnas (Labarnas) founded the Hittite Empire properly speaking. Ca. 1600 campaign against Halpa; 50 years later foray against Babylon. 14th century violent struggle with Egypt for dominion of Syria. Ca. 1200 ruin of the Empire.

By the 3rd millennium Cappadocia had relations with the East. Assyrian trade colonies founded there before 2000; ca. 2000 it perhaps belonged for a while to the dynasty from Ur. Hence influence from the ancient cultures of the East.

Reciprocal trade relations

(Poliochni)
Lemnos
Troia
Lesbos
(Thermi)
Chios
Yortan
Samos
Miletus
Maeander
Hermus
Sangarius
Ancyra
Gordium
(Alaja Huyuk)
Hattushash
Cappadox
(Ališar Huyuk)
Halys
Tatta L.
Kanesh
HITTITES
HURRIANS
Euphrates
Tigris
ASSYRIA
Naxos
Achaean settlements ca.1400
Taurus Mons
Rhodos
Creta
Reciprocal trade relations
Carchemish
Foray on Babylon by the Hittites ca. 1550
Halpa
Orontes
CYPRUS

ANATOLIA, BRIDGE BETWEEN EAST AND WEST

From the 3rd and 2nd millennia B.C. to 1200 B.C.

→ Political or cultural sphere of influence of the Hittites

◯ Original centres of the 'bridge' in the East and West

–·–·– Boundary of the Hittite Empire

Names underlined in black and red and red arrows relate to the 3rd millennium, those in black to the 2nd millennium

7

Ca. 1200 Phrygians migrated into Asia Minor and established themselves round the sources of the Sangarius. Ca. 1100 clash with Assyria. End of 8th century new strife under King Midas (contemporary of Sargon II, 722–705). Beginning of 7th century destruction of the kingdom through invasion by Cimmerians. Pottery imported from the Greek coastal towns has been found at Gordium, the Phrygian capital. The Phrygians also had political and religious connections with Greece itself by way of the Ionian settlements. Midas presented gifts to the sanctuary of Delphi. For long the Lydian kingdom formed the link between the East and Greece, as appears from inscriptions in the capital Sardes. The Lydian practice of minting coins was adopted by the Greeks. Once the west coast was conquered by the Lydians the 'bridge' became of decisive importance in the Hellenisation of Asia Minor. Lydia, like Macedonia, became increasingly oriented towards Greece.

THRACIA
Samothrace
Imbros
Lemnos
Troia
MYSIA
Lesbos
Pitane
Grynium
Phocaea
LYDIA
Chios
Clazomenae
Sardes
Colophon
Ephesus
Samos
Miletus
Didymae
Halicarnassus
Cos
Naxos
Maeander
Thera
Rhodos
Carpathos
Creta
KINGDOM OF THE PHRYGIANS
Sangarius
Pessinus
Gordium
Cappadox
Ca. 1100 attack by the Phrygians on Assyrians
Halys
Tatta L.
CAPPADOCIA
Euphrates
Tigris
Carchemish
Taurus Mons
Perge
Aspendus
CILICIA
Orontes
CYPRUS
Iapethus
Soli
Salamis
In 709 seven kings of cities in Cyprus paid tribute to King Sargon II (722–705) of Babylon.

ANATOLIA

ca. 1200 – ca. 700 B.C.

▨ Greeks settlements

→ Old trade routes from and to the East

8

THRACIA
Lemnos
Lesbos
Phocaea
Chios
Sardes
Colophon
Ephesus
Samos
Miletus
Halicarnassus
Naxos
Thera
Rhodos
Carpathos
Creta
Sangarius
Hermus
KINGDOM OF THE LYDIANS
Maeander
PISIDIA
Taurus Mons
CILICIA
Cappadox
Halys
Tatta L.
Euphrates
Tigris
Orontes
CYPRUS

ANATOLIA

ca. 700 – ca. 546 B.C.

▨ Kingdom of the Lydians
▨ Kingdom of the Medes
▨ Neo-Babylonian Kingdom (to 538)
▨ Districts which were little or not at all influenced by the formation of new states

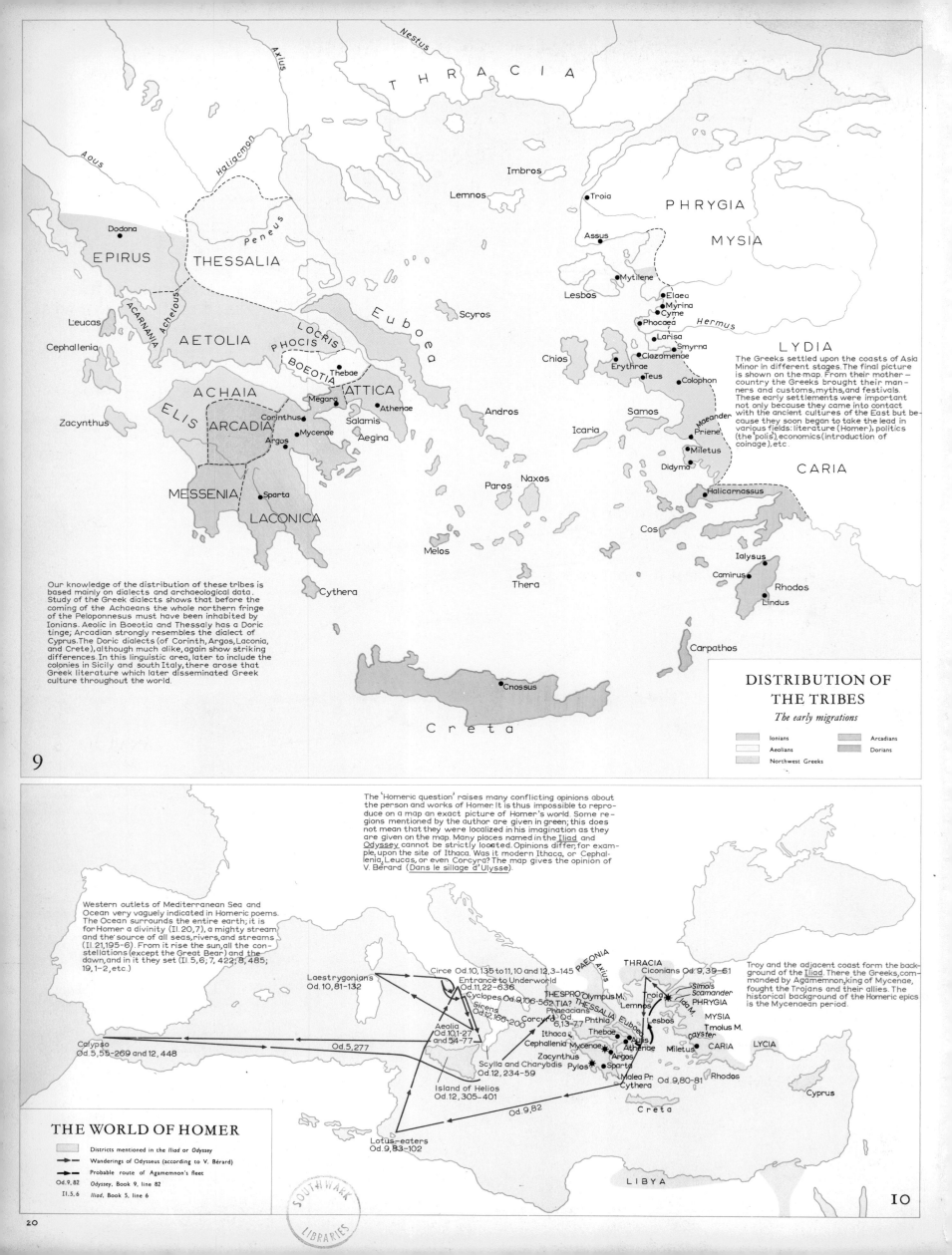

Our knowledge of the distribution of these tribes is based mainly on dialects and archaeological data. Study of the Greek dialects shows that before the coming of the Achaeans the whole northern fringe of the Peloponnesus must have been inhabited by Ionians. Aeolic in Boeotia and Thessaly has a Doric tinge; Arcadian strongly resembles the dialect of Cyprus. The Doric dialects (of Corinth, Argos, Laconia, and Crete), although much alike, again show striking differences. In this linguistic area, later to include the colonies in Sicily and south Italy, there arose that Greek literature which later disseminated Greek culture throughout the world.

The Greeks settled upon the coasts of Asia Minor in different stages. The final picture is shown on the map. From their mother-country the Greeks brought their manners and customs, myths, and festivals. These early settlements were important not only because they came into contact with the ancient cultures of the East but because they soon began to take the lead in various fields: literature (Homer), politics (the 'polis'), economics (introduction of coinage), etc.

DISTRIBUTION OF THE TRIBES
The early migrations

Ionians
Aeolians
Northwest Greeks
Arcadians
Dorians

The 'Homeric question' raises many conflicting opinions about the person and works of Homer. It is thus impossible to reproduce on a map an exact picture of Homer's world. Some regions mentioned by the author are given in green; this does not mean that they were localized in his imagination as they are given on the map. Many places named in the Iliad and Odyssey cannot be strictly located. Opinions differ, for example, upon the site of Ithaca. Was it modern Ithaca, or Cephallenia, Leucas, or even Corcyra? The map gives the opinion of V. Bérard (Dans le sillage d'Ulysse).

Western outlets of Mediterranean Sea and Ocean very vaguely indicated in Homeric poems. The Ocean surrounds the entire earth; it is for Homer a divinity (Il. 20,7), a mighty stream and the source of all seas, rivers, and streams (Il. 21,195-6). From it rise the sun, all the constellations (except the Great Bear) and the dawn, and in it they set (Il. 5,6; 7, 422; 8, 485; 19, 1-2, etc.)

Troy and the adjacent coast form the background of the Iliad. There the Greeks, commanded by Agamemnon, king of Mycenae, fought the Trojans and their allies. The historical background of the Homeric epics is the Mycenaean period.

Laestrygonians Od. 10, 81-132
Circe Od. 10, 135 to 11, 10 and 12, 3-145
Entrance to Underworld Od. 11, 22-636
Cyclopes Od. 9, 106-562
Sirens Od. 12, 166-200
Aeolia Od. 10, 1-27 and 54-77
Calypso Od. 5, 55-269 and 12, 448
Od. 5, 277
Ciconians Od. 9, 39-61
Scylla and Charybdis Od. 12, 234-59
Island of Helios Od. 12, 305-401
Lotus-eaters Od. 9, 83-102
Od. 9, 80-81
Od. 9, 82

THE WORLD OF HOMER

Districts mentioned in the Iliad or Odyssey
Wanderings of Odysseus (according to V. Bérard)
Probable route of Agamemnon's fleet
Od. 9, 82   Odyssey, Book 9, line 82
Il. 5, 6   Iliad, Book 5, line 6

FROM TRIBAL STATE TO CIVILISED NATION

THE HISTORY OF ANCIENT GREECE AND ROME IS PART OF OUR OWN HISTORY. HOWEVER MUCH THE PEOPLES AROUND THE ATLANTIC may differ in origin, historical development, and fortunes, one element continues to unite them down to the present day — a cultural unity which owes its origin, first to the continued influence of Christianity, and secondly to its common derivation from the school of Greece and Rome; thus there has arisen a characteristic difference between them and the peoples who have not passed through this school.

Other cultures and cultural spheres have existed before and after the Graeco-Roman, cultures which have attained great intellectual and material achievements. They have left behind them monuments which we view with respect and admiration, and which are capable of fascinating our Western minds by the attraction of their distinctive character. We can study them and to some extent understand them. Nevertheless they remain alien to us.

On the other hand, in the culture which first developed after 1000 B.C. in the region round the Aegean Sea, and afterwards extended over the entire Mediterranean area, organised and united by the Roman Empire, we see the foundations upon which our Western civilisation still continues to build. This culture ceased after A.D. 300 to exist as a distinctive, independent manner of life and thought and was replaced by Christian and national structures. It did not, however, perish entirely. Ideas inherited from this world survived, whether consciously preserved or not, and set their seal upon its heirs, and these cultural heirlooms remained in the keeping of the Western nations as irreplaceable treasures, serving as models and as incentives to further achievement. Even down to the present day they form part of cultural and scientific training in the Atlantic world. Although it may sometimes appear that the foundations of our thoughts, desires, and feelings are natural possessions, they are in reality inherited. We are largely following the path and the direction determined by choices made many centuries ago in Greece. So long as our culture clings to the ideals and ideas which determine our present manner of life and thought, the Greek and the Roman, whether we realise it or not, will continue to live on in us all.

The prehistory of Greece

THE CRETAN AND MYCENAEAN WORLDS

From about 2500 B.C. a distinctive culture flourished in the eastern Mediterranean, with the relatively large and fertile island of Crete as its centre. It had some connections with the cultures of the near East and of Egypt, but nevertheless displayed a wholly individual character. This Minoan civilisation, so called after the legendary king Minos who, according to Greek tradition, was ruler of the sea in prehistoric times, was revealed in 1900 by Sir Arthur Evans, who excavated the palaces at Cnossus. Here and at Phaestus we can still see the wealth and art of Minoan palaces with their halls and throne-rooms, their frescoes and magnificent pottery, often as delicate as porcelain, the painted scenes of the games in which male and female acrobats vaulted over bulls, and the refined luxury and fashions of the women.

The people themselves were not Greeks and they did not speak Greek; they were of non-Indo-European stock, belonging perhaps to the so-called Mediterranean race, and their language also was almost certainly not Indo-European. In many respects they attained a very high level of culture. They developed the natural resources of their island and their own skill in the arts and crafts. Their religion was a form of nature-worship, with a Mother Goddess as a central object of worship and the double-axe as a cult-symbol. Their prosperity depended largely upon seafaring and trade, especially with the East and Egypt, as a result of which they built up great wealth and their rulers enjoyed a refined and civilised court life centred on the palaces. That of Cnossus, which covers an area of five acres, had so many rooms and passages that it gave rise to the legend of the Labyrinth, where Theseus finally slew the Minotaur; it was not merely the residence of the king and his court but also the administrative centre of an empire.

Unlike the Pharoahs of Egypt, the kings of Cnossus did not decorate the walls of their palace with long inscriptions describing their exploits in peace and war, nor has any Minoan literature survived, so that the lack of historical records robs us of any detailed knowledge of their history. But the archaeological discoveries can be dated fairly accurately and show that the palaces at Cnossus and Phaestus were arising about 2000 B.C., after which life became increasingly more civilised. Widespread destruction was caused about 1700 by an earthquake, but thereafter the palaces were

rebuilt and entered upon an even more prosperous period; by the sixteenth century Crete had become a worldpower, administered by a highly centralised bureaucracy and governed from the royal city of Cnossus. About 1400 B.C., however, the palace was sacked and this brilliant civilisation sank quickly into oblivion.

Even in the early period writing was known in Crete: it took the form of a pictorial script not dissimilar from Egyptian hieroglyphics. Sometime about 1800 B.C. this gave place to a syllabic script, which modern scholars call Linear A; this has not been deciphered and its language remains unknown. During the fifteenth century this script in turn was modified in a form known as Linear B, which remained equally obscure until it was brilliantly deciphered in 1952 and revealed as an early form of Greek. The surviving documents, some 2000 clay tablets from Cnossus, are chiefly lists and inventories of goods in the palace; they throw much light on the life of the period, though naturally not on its political history in detail. Above all they have revealed one fact of great importance: during its last phase before 1400 B.C. Cnossus had been forcibly occupied by Greeks from the mainland - the Achaeans of the Greek epics or, as modern historians tend to call them, the Mycenaean Greeks.

Minoan trade and Minoan skills had spread to the mainland of Greece and to the Indo-European tribes who penetrated into Greece from the north after 2,000 B.C. Since these invaders conquered Crete sometime before 1400 B.C., the fame of Minos' kingdom lived on in Greek legend. Although they learned some of their technique from the Minoans, their own life and customs were very different. Instead of undefended palaces they built impregnable fortresses which bear witness to the might of their warrior kings. They, too, sailed the seas, but often more like Vikings than merchants. To these centuries belong the sagas of the great expeditions, of the Argonauts, of the Seven against Thebes, of the war of the Achaeans against Troy, which furnished the material for the later Greek epics. In a 'corner' of the Argive plain mighty Mycenae commanded a strategic position. The excavations conducted there by Schliemann in 1876 fully confirmed its Homeric epithet of 'rich in gold' (→ 27, - 44).

In the shaft-grave tombs he found the skeletons of the kings, with their gold masks and breastplates and their swords ornamented with gold.

14

15

16
17
18

14. At the foot of the mountains of sea-girt Crete lie the ruins of the earliest European civilisation, the Minoan culture, revealed by the pioneering work of Sir Arthur Evans. From ca. 2100 kings began to build undefended palaces. One of the largest was that of Minos at Cnossus. 1. Main entrance with southern propylaeum, 2. throne room, 3. theatre, 4. central court, 5. storehouses with large vessels, 6. sacred horns, 7. megaron of the queen (→ 16), 8. hall of the double axes, 9. royal storehouses, 10. north entrance, 11. pillar hall. **15.** The horns, a sacred symbol. **16.** Megaron of the queen with reconstructed wall paintings with dolphins. **17.** Costly materials such as gold and ivory were used for statuettes of snake-goddesses or priestesses; these statuettes contribute greatly to our knowledge of rites, dress, etc. **18.** North entrance with partly restored columns, thinner towards the base.

The wall paintings of Cnossus give a vivid picture of the lively, luxurious life of the court. **19.** Scene from a bullfight, perhaps of religious significance: stages of a daring somersault on the back of a bull. **20.** Fragment of a female portrait sometimes called 'La parisienne'. **21.** Restored fresco, displaying the lively, naturalistic style. **22.** Jar painted with cuttle-fish; example of decorative art. **23.** The appearance of the houses is also known from these little clay models. **24.** Striking scene of Cretan life, on a vase; probably represents a harvest festival with singing men. **25.** Fresco of a man carrying a drinking cup. **26.** In the south of Crete, sheltered by a mountain ridge along the coast, lie the ruins of the palace of Phaestus; the monumental staircase and walls still survive. The palace overlooked the formerly thickly-populated plain of Messara where many ancient objects have been found, including pottery.

27. Between the mountains of the prophet Elijah (left) and Zara (right), in a strategic yet hidden position dominating the plain of Argos, lies the citadel of Mycenae, strikingly described by Homer as 'lying in a corner of horse-rearing Argos.' The photograph, taken from Argolis, shows the position of the fortress protected by a mountain ridge. **28.** The triangular citadel, of which the walls disappear in the folds of the terrace-like landscape: 1. Lion Gate (→ 31-33) protected by bastion (2) and slightly higher wall (3). 4. Staircase leading to the palace. 5. So-called shaft-grave A (→ 34) where many gold objects were found (37-44). 6. Palace with megaron and other buildings about 150 ft. higher than the Lion Gate; in the 7th century and in the Hellenistic period a temple was built right across the palace. 7. 'Tomb of Clytemnestra'. 8. Mycenaean houses. 9. 'Lion Tomb', of which the dome has disappeared. 10. To the 'Tomb of Atreus'.

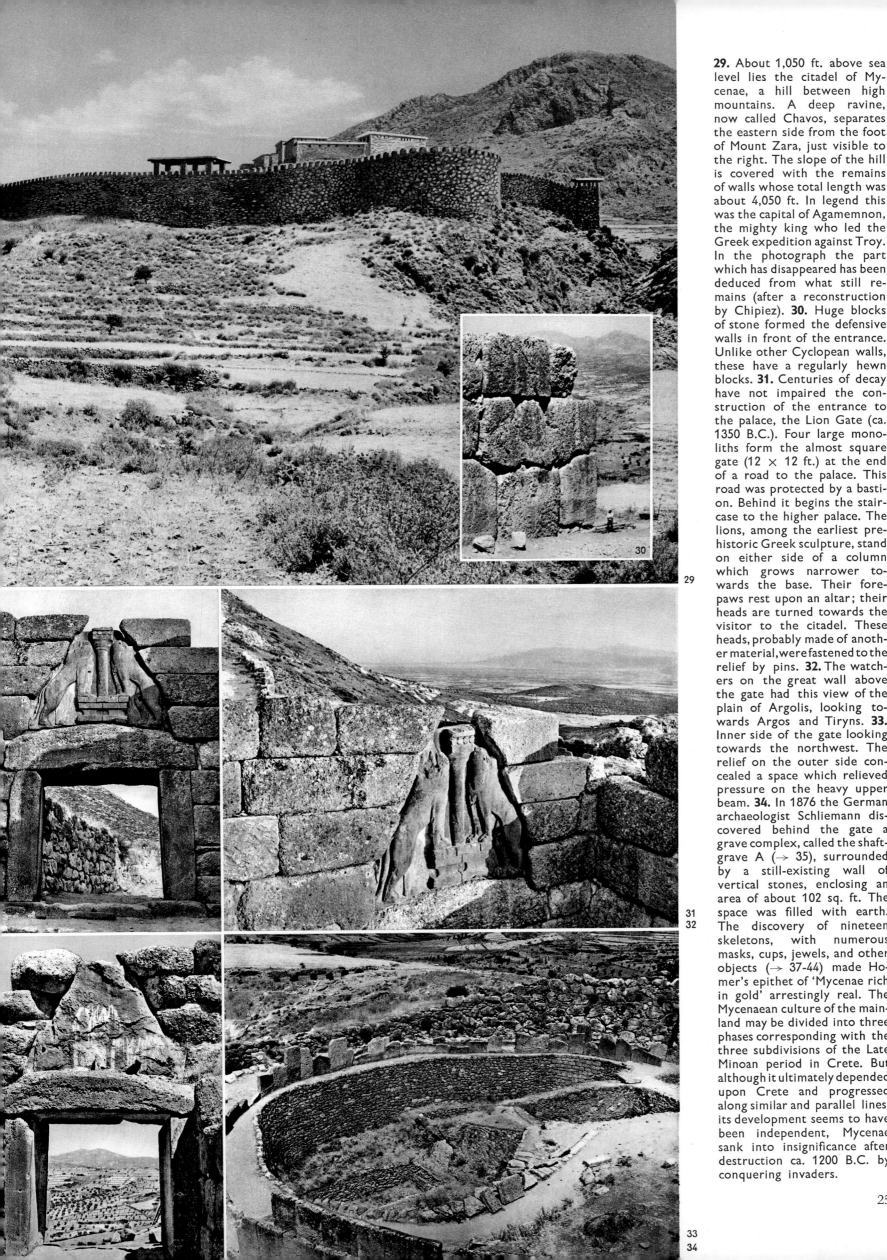

29. About 1,050 ft. above sea level lies the citadel of Mycenae, a hill between high mountains. A deep ravine, now called Chavos, separates the eastern side from the foot of Mount Zara, just visible to the right. The slope of the hill is covered with the remains of walls whose total length was about 4,050 ft. In legend this was the capital of Agamemnon, the mighty king who led the Greek expedition against Troy. In the photograph the part which has disappeared has been deduced from what still remains (after a reconstruction by Chipiez). **30.** Huge blocks of stone formed the defensive walls in front of the entrance. Unlike other Cyclopean walls, these have a regularly hewn blocks. **31.** Centuries of decay have not impaired the construction of the entrance to the palace, the Lion Gate (ca. 1350 B.C.). Four large monoliths form the almost square gate (12 × 12 ft.) at the end of a road to the palace. This road was protected by a bastion. Behind it begins the staircase to the higher palace. The lions, among the earliest prehistoric Greek sculpture, stand on either side of a column which grows narrower towards the base. Their forepaws rest upon an altar; their heads are turned towards the visitor to the citadel. These heads, probably made of another material, were fastened to the relief by pins. **32.** The watchers on the great wall above the gate had this view of the plain of Argolis, looking towards Argos and Tiryns. **33.** Inner side of the gate looking towards the northwest. The relief on the outer side concealed a space which relieved pressure on the heavy upper beam. **34.** In 1876 the German archaeologist Schliemann discovered behind the gate a grave complex, called the shaft-grave A (→ 35), surrounded by a still-existing wall of vertical stones, enclosing an area of about 102 sq. ft. The space was filled with earth. The discovery of nineteen skeletons, with numerous masks, cups, jewels, and other objects (→ 37-44) made Homer's epithet of 'Mycenae rich in gold' arrestingly real. The Mycenaean culture of the mainland may be divided into three phases corresponding with the three subdivisions of the Late Minoan period in Crete. But although it ultimately depended upon Crete and progressed along similar and parallel lines, its development seems to have been independent, Mycenae sank into insignificance after destruction ca. 1200 B.C. by conquering invaders.

25

35

36

37 38

39 40

41 42

43 44

In 1876-7 Schliemann excavated the citadel of Mycenae; photographs were taken which were used for Plates in his publications. **35.** Excavation of the shaft-tombs behind the Lion Gate (1) where the treasures were found. This photograph was composed of several snaps: Schliemann appears twice (2). 3. Schliemann's wife. **36.** The bee-hive tombs give an idea of the achievement of Mycenaean architecture. Entrance of the 'Tomb of Atreus' (54 ft. across, 51 ft. high). The heavy stones, disposed with admirable skill in thirty-three layers, were internally decorated with stars. **37-44.** The objects found upon skeletons include golden masks, which, although representing unknown people, bring us surprisingly close to the inhabitants of the world of the Homeric epics. **37-9.** Gold masks. **40.** Gold beaker. **41.** Silver utensil in the shape of a bull's head. **42.** Figures with Cnossus motifs. **43-4.** Ornaments representing lion and butterfly.

45

46

Ten miles south of Mycenae, amid flat farmland, lies the citadel of Tiryns, built upon an isolated hill about 1,125 ft. long. It was excavated by Schliemann and Dörpfeld. They found a number of palaces built one upon the other, dating from 1600 to 1200 B.C. The city was divided into two enclosures, an upper towards the south and a lower towards the north. **45.** The site of the citadel near the bay of Nauplion and the eastern side of the palace. Reconstruction superimposed upon the ruins. **46.** The city viewed from the sea side: 1. north corner of the great wall (→ 49), 2. lowest section, which served among other purposes as a place of refuge for the subjects living around the citadel, 3. entrance gate protected by a bastion (→ 47), 4. foundations of the palace and megaron, 5. staircase between bastions, leading to a western sally-port, formerly partly covered over, of which sixty-five steps survive (→ 65), 6. covered gallery of heavy stones, with pointed roof, part of the defences.

47. The main entrance to the citadel of Tiryns was formed by a wide avenue flanked by walls of heavy stones. At the end of this avenue was the gate, roughly the same size as that at Mycenae, and flanked by towers. The hinges can still be seen in the stones. **48.** Staircase, formerly roofed, which led from the palace to the foot of the acropolis. **49.** The northern corner of the fortress wall was built of heavy stones piled in the Cyclopean manner. The section shown is about 38 ft. high. **50.** Orchomenus in Boeotia is one of the oldest cities of Greece. There is preserved part of the 'Treasury of Minyas', a tholos tomb built in the Mycenaean style. **51.** One of the great Mycenaean citadels was Gla, in a situation of great natural strength upon a rock 263 ft. high, near Lake Copais. A Cyclopean wall with entrance gate (1) and towers ran around the edge of the rock. The photograph, taken from the palace, shows the triangular fortification.

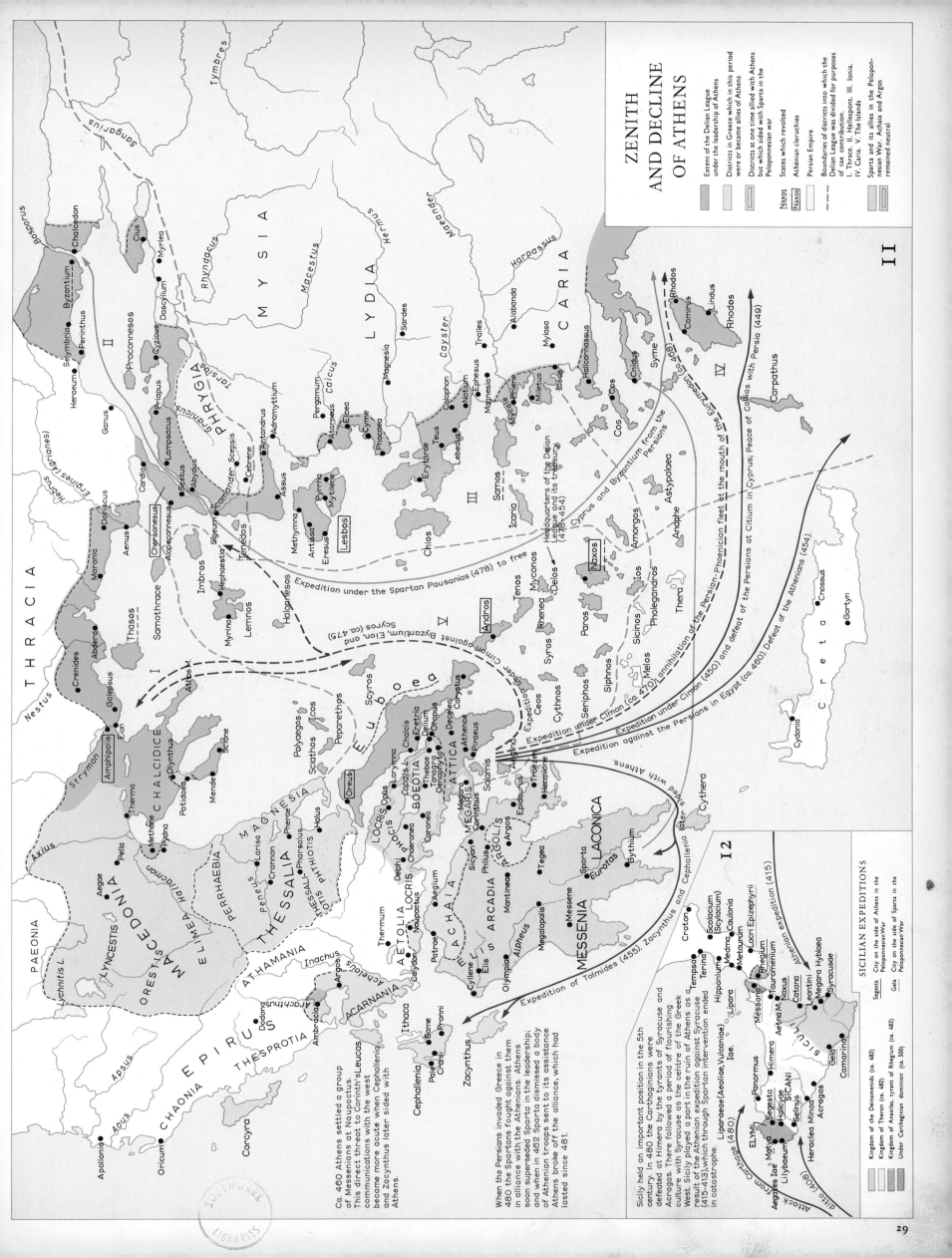

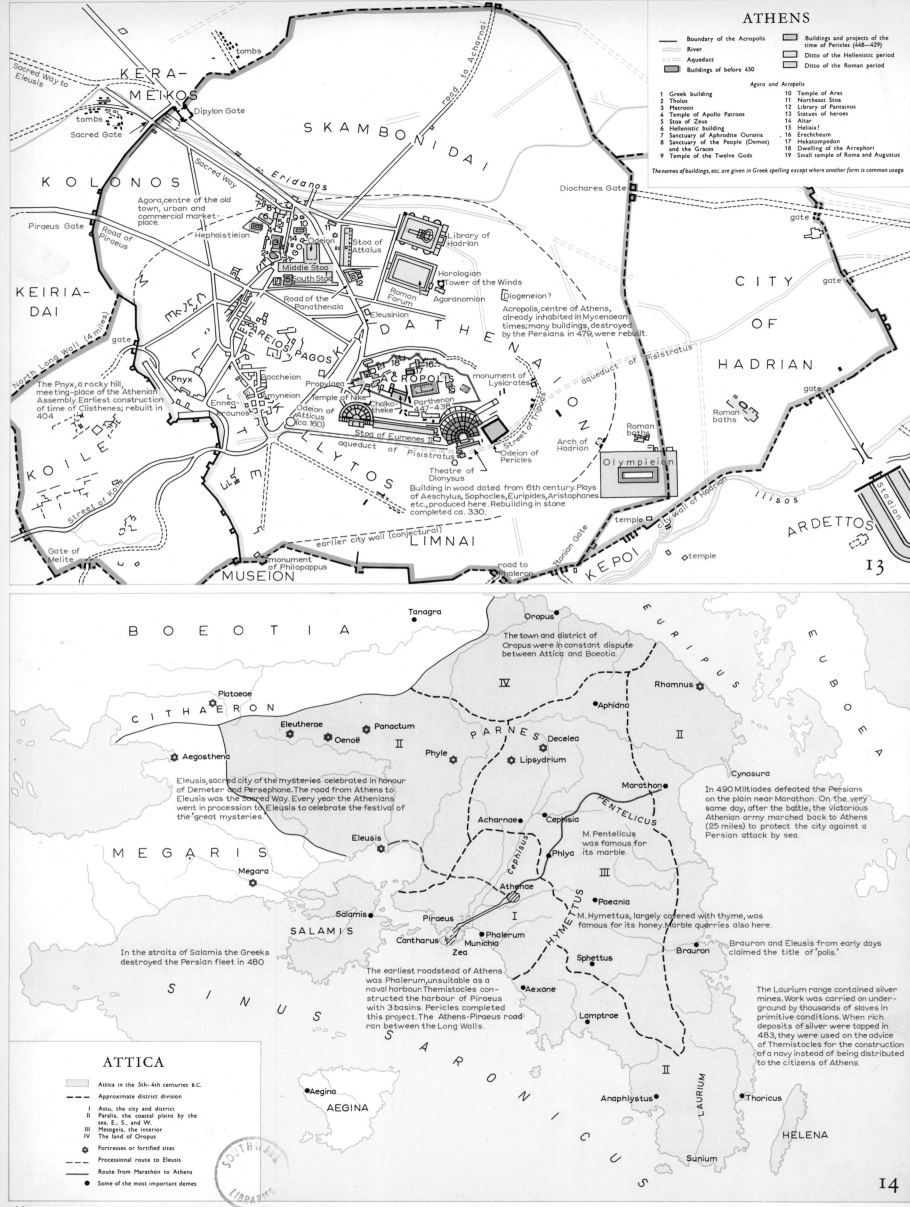

ATHENS

KERA-MEIKOS

tombs

Sacred Way to Eleusis

KOLONOS

Dipylon Gate

Sacred Gate

tombs

SKAMBONIDAI

road to Acharnai

Sacred Way

Eridanos

Piraeus Gate

Road of Piraeus

KEIRIA-DAI

Agora, centre of the old town, urban and commercial market-place.

Hephaistieion

Odeion

Stoa of Attalus

Library of Hadrian

Middle Stoa

South Stoa

Road of the Panathenaia

Roman Forum

Horologion Tower of the Winds

Agoranomion

Diochares Gate

CITY OF HADRIAN

gate

gate

Eleusinion

Diogeneion ?

Acropolis, centre of Athens, already inhabited in Mycenaean times; many buildings, destroyed by the Persians in 479, were rebuilt.

AREIOS PAGOS

Pnyx

The Pnyx, a rocky hill, meeting-place of the Athenian Assembly. Earliest construction of time of Clisthenes; rebuilt in 404

Baccheion

Amyneion

Enneakrounos

ATHENAION

aqueduct of Pisistratus

Roman baths

gate

North Long Wall (4 miles)

Street of Koile

Gate of Melite

Odeion of Atticus (ca. 160)

Stoa of Eumenes

Odeion of Pericles

Theatre of Dionysus

Building in wood dated from 6th century. Plays of Aeschylus, Sophocles, Euripides, Aristophanes etc., produced here. Rebuilding in stone completed ca. 330.

Propylaea

Temple of Nike

Chalko-theke

Parthenon 447-438

ACROPOLIS

monument of Lysicrates

Street of Tripods

Arch of Hadrian

Roman baths

aqueduct of Pisistratus

ILLYTOS

Olympieion

Ilisos

city wall of Hadrian

ARDETTOS

Stadion

earlier city wall (conjectural)

LIMNAI

Itonian Gate

KEPOI

temple

temple

MUSEION

monument of Philopappus

road to Phaleron

13

ATTICA map

BOEOTIA

Tanagra

Oropus

The town and district of Oropus were in constant dispute between Attica and Boeotia.

EURIPUS

EUBOEA

Plataeae

CITHAERON

IV

Rhamnus

Aphidna

Eleutherae

Oenoë

Panactum

II

Phyle

PARNES

Decelea

Lipsydrium

Aegosthena

Eleusis, sacred city of the mysteries celebrated in honour of Demeter and Persephone. The road from Athens to Eleusis was the Sacred Way. Every year the Athenians went in procession to Eleusis to celebrate the festival of the 'great mysteries'.

Cynosura

Marathon

In 490 Miltiades defeated the Persians on the plain near Marathon. On the very same day, after the battle, the victorious Athenian army marched back to Athens (25 miles) to protect the city against a Persian attack by sea.

Acharnae

Cephisia

MEGARIS

Eleusis

PENTELICUS

M. Pentelicus was famous for its marble.

Phlya

Cephisus

Megara

Athenae

III

Paeania

M. Hymettus, largely covered with thyme, was famous for its honey. Marble quarries also here.

Salamis

Piraeus

I

SALAMIS

Cantharus

Phalerum

Munichia

Zea

HYMETTUS

Brauron

Brauron and Eleusis from early days claimed the title of 'polis.'

In the straits of Salamis the Greeks destroyed the Persian fleet in 480

The earliest roadstead of Athens was Phalerum, unsuitable as a naval harbour. Themistocles constructed the harbour of Piraeus with 3 basins. Pericles completed this project. The Athens-Piraeus road ran between the Long Walls.

Aexone

Sphettus

Lamptrae

The Laurium range contained silver mines. Work was carried on underground by thousands of slaves in primitive conditions. When rich deposits of silver were tapped in 483, they were used on the advice of Themistocles for the construction of a navy instead of being distributed to the citizens of Athens.

SINUS

SARONICUS

II

LAURIUM

Aegina

AEGINA

Anaphlystus

Thoricus

II

HELENA

Sunium

14

Another dynasty of rulers was buried outside the walls of the citadel in the impressive beehive tombs whose solid vaulted structure has defied the centuries. Not far away upon a low hill in the plain of Argos lay Tiryns (→ 45-9), rendered impregnable not by its position but by its enormous walls.

This Mycenaean civilisation spread widely in Greece. Excavation has revealed that it extended far in the Peloponnese, where Pylos was an important centre, and northwards to Athens, to Thebes and Orchomenus (→ 50) in Boeotia, and to southern Thessaly. It is not known to what extent Mycenae exercised political control over other centres; but, if not the dominant mistress of a widespread empire, it at least probably predominated in prestige and power in a large area which was bound together by a common culture and probably by some kind of political union. In fact Greece was more united and richer between 1400 and 1200 B.C. than during the next five hundred years. Nor was this culture confined to Greece itself. As already said, the Mycenaean Greeks captured and occupied Cnossus late in the fifteenth century, and particularly after this date their contacts with the East increased. Their vases and pottery have been found over a wide area, and it would appear that Greek traders settled in Rhodes and Cyprus, in north Syria, on the southwest coast of Asia Minor, and to some extent on the west coast, as at Miletus. Here they must have come into contact with the great Hittite empire. One later episode in their expansion was the Trojan War, when they besieged and sacked Troy about 1200 B.C.; many details of this epic story may be fictitious, but the fact of their expedition cannot reasonably be denied.

Fresh light has been thrown on the organisation of Mycenaean society by the decipherment of documents in the so-called Linear B script. This script, which is not alphabetic but syllabic (some 87 signs represent different syllables, not letters), and is known, as already mentioned, from clay tablets at Cnossus, has also been found at many places in Greece itself, on tablets at Pylos and Mycenae and on inscribed jars at Tiryns, Thebes, and Orchomenus. It is a development of the older script used by the Minoans and was clearly taken over and adapted by the Mycenaean Greeks as a medium in which to record their own language. Thus not only has it been revealed that the Mycenaeans spoke Greek, but our knowledge of the Greek language has been extended backwards for a period of more than five hundred years, and it is not to be wondered at that the language is as different from classical Greek as Chaucerian English is from the speech of the present day. The bulk of the documents from the Greek mainland come from Pylos, where they reveal a much more highly organised and bureaucratic society than the organisation of the later Greeks would have led one to expect. The king (*wanax*, not *basileus*; a *basileus* was rather a local mayor), the Leader of the Host (a commander-in-chief) and a group of aristocratic barons seem to have been the chief land-holders. At the other end of the scale, there were slaves, although their precise status and origin are not known. The tablets reveal the complex organisation and administration of the royal palace and show the specialisation of labour that had been reached: they refer to gold-smiths, masons, fullers, potters, bow-makers, unguent-boilers, weavers, and spinners. The tablets chiefly comprise inventories of stores, especially war equipment, as swords, spears, arrows, and armour, but they also record foodstuffs (wheat, barley, spices, cheese, figs, oil, and honey) and list the tribute exacted from subject villages. They also record some offerings to the gods, and reveal that Zeus, Hera, Poseidon, Hermes, Artemis, Athena, and probably Dionysus were all worshipped at this very early period in the history of Greece. Unfortunately none of the literature of this period, if it ever existed, has survived, but many echoes of this Mycenaean world are reflected in the Homeric poems.

The Greek themselves attempted to reconstruct history from their epics. But this was not really possible, because, like all epic poetry, they mingle fact and fantasy, magnifying the insignificant, making the great small, and bringing together in one story heroes from many centuries. It is, however, certain that princes like Agamemnon really did exist and that expeditions like that against Troy did take place. Yet finally even the mighty kings of Mycenae and the culture centred on their citadel were wiped out by a new invasion of fierce tribes from the north, the Dorians. These invading Greeks destroyed the older citadels and after bitter struggles drove the Achaeans across the sea or to the fringes of Greece. They brought with them iron weapons which gave them superiority over the 'bronze-clad' Achaeans.

Lack of reliable sources reduces speculation about the course of this Dorian invasion to little more than guesswork. We may, however, assume that it was not unconnected with the widespread migratory movements which overthrew the great empire of the Hittites in Asia Minor and led to attacks by the 'Peoples of the Sea' on the Egyptian coast. Archaeologists have made it clear that the great citadels of the wealthy kings of Mycenae, of the rulers of Tiryns, Pylos, and other strongholds were destroyed and that much more primitive pottery, the 'geometric' type, began to predominate in a much poorer and less developed milieu. The Greeks were largely unconscious of this gap in history. They saw their own period as an uninterrupted development, unjustifiably, although the epics prove that a connection survived in their memory. The Greek people emerged from the melting-pot after the Dorian invasion. The Achaeans had already assimilated certain sections of the pre-Greek population, and although other sections fled from Greece, some certainly remained and mingled with the newcomers. Place-names and religious sites bear witness to this intermingling. The language of the epics clearly betrays that it originated in different dialects, and its content is a fusion of many traditions. In the later art of the Greeks it is tempting to discern the realism and elegance of the Minoans and the monumental quality of the Mycenaeans. But although the Greeks undoubtedly inherited from many sides they set their own stamp upon this inheritance.

The formation of the Greek people

THE RISE OF THE GREEKS

Minos and Mycenae belong to the dim world of legend in which the gods and heroes still walked the earth with men. Thence we move into a period which is recorded with increasing fulness in the historical tradition of the Greeks; this recording was made possible when they adopted the Phoenician alphabet and adapted it as a medium for their own language (by the eighth century B.C. at least).

Under pressure from the invading Dorians, many people fled from Greece to seek new homes in other countries. The Achaeans were scattered, some to Arcadia and others overseas to Cyprus. The Dorians themselves occupied southern Greece, the Peloponnese, Crete, and the southwest coast of Asia Minor. The Ionians crossed from Attica by way of the Cyclades to the central part of the coast of Asia Minor (which thereafter was called Ionia). The Aeolians from Thessaly and Boeotia crossed to the coast of northwest Asia Minor, including (later) the Troad.

These scattered Greeks, who felt separated from their neighbours because of their differing dialects and customs, usually retained some traces of their common origin in their cults, but they developed little or no political unity among the various tribes. Each group lived apart and considered itself independent of even neighbouring groups which spoke the same dialect. On the other hand, they gradually acquired a common name, that of Hellenes; this in the usage of Homer had been merely the name of a small tribe in Thessaly. Although there is no indication of how it came to be adopted as the name of a people, the fact of its adoption shows that the Greeks felt themselves to be a coherent whole, probably because they could understand one another and because their manner of life, especially their religion, was essentially the same.

The surrounding tribes they called *barbaroi* ('people speaking an incomprehensible language'); but the word had little pejorative meaning or suggestion of Greek superiority over 'barbarians'. On the contrary, the Greeks were glad and quick to learn much from the more highly developed peoples with whom they came into contact. Thus they derived their script from the Phoenicians, who during the ninth and eighth centuries sailed throughout the Mediterranean in their trading ships. Early Greek art, clothing, and jewellery show influences from the East. Later Greeks were conscious of owing scientific ideas and techniques also to the East. Yet it is striking that from the very beginning they infused their own spirit and ideas into all that they borrowed, so that their cultural pattern immediately diverged from that of the surrounding peoples.

THE DEVELOPMENT OF THE CITY-STATE (POLIS)

The various tribes forming the Greek people established themselves in groups. The invaders, in communities of family or clan, chose favourable sites for their new homes, which would be centred at first in villages but soon around a citadel, a *polis* (→ 56, 73, 78). The mountainous and very broken nature of the country encouraged this establishment of isolated groups. On and around the citadel, often the former dwelling of a local ruler, the chief of the tribe settled, together with the heads of the families, who formed the aristocracy (*eupatridai*). These were the warriors who, serving as cavalrymen and equipped with bronze armour, shield and spear, assured the safety of the community. The training demanded by the use of arms excused them from common daily tasks, which after the community had settled down were performed by the ordinary citizen. In the stronghold justice was administered by the elders, the gods were honoured, and festivals were celebrated. Here, too, lived the craftsmen, carpenters, smiths, soothsayers, and priests needed by the community. All felt themselves citizens (*politai*) of this city-state.

31

This form of settlement was widespread and in early times was found everywhere in the East. The distinctive feature of the Greeks was that, whereas elsewhere these small cities were absorbed into a larger unit of tribe or state, in the Greek world this form of life became permanent and the natural form of society. For the Greeks the city was the state and the highest sovereign unit, claiming for itself the 'power of the sword' in order to maintain internal justice and freedom from external attack.

In these small communities the chief could never become overbearingly strong. From the beginning he had to rely on the leaders of the noble families, who with him formed the Council which possessed the real power. Where the king (*basileus*) survived, he was generally chosen, sometimes from a certain family, for life or for a shorter period, in order to personify the community and to act as its supreme representative at religious ceremonies. Thus he developed into a mere magistrate with limited powers, alongside other magistrates with other functions who were appointed by the nobles (*aristoi*). Thus monarchy developed into another form of government, aristocracy.

An assembly of the free citizens existed; but the commoner was occupied by his work and moreover was bound to his clan and its leaders by strong ties of blood and tradition. Thus the Assembly was dominated by the heads of the families.

Almost inevitably, the world of these small city-states was full of feuds and frontier skirmishes. Nevertheless bonds existed between different cities. People might know one another, they understood one another's language, felt themselves Greeks and not barbarians, and met at some common religious festivals and at the oracles where the gods could be consulted. From this world the Greeks always retained a strong 'agonistic' tendency to compete with others in an *agon* or public festival. At the feasts in honour of the gods not only were possessions, such as cattle or precious objects, offered as gifts; athletic feats were also performed in races and games. Thus the festivals acquired the character of competitions.

Consciousness of unity and solidarity was maintained by the panhellenic festivals at Olympia, Delphi, and the Isthmus of Corinth, and by the oracles. It was also strengthened by the common myths and legends recited everywhere by itinerant singers. From this sense of unity there developed a code of honour which bound every noble. But all this never fused into a national feeling which might serve as the basis for political union. Hellenism always meant cultural affinity and lacked any political significance, which was associated exclusively with the *polis*.

COLONISATION AND TRADE

As a result of the Dorian invasion, Aeolians, Ionians, and Dorians themselves had occupied the islands and parts of the coast of Asia Minor and established city-states there. The art of seafaring had already been practised by the Minoans and Mycenaeans; the Greeks could also learn much in this respect from the Phoenicians. In Asia Minor they found themselves in a land where trade and crafts had been carried on for centuries, and they quickly followed suit. Although the economic basis of their cities remained agricultural and the possession of land their essential form of wealth, they soon learned to exchange their products for those of other regions and cities. Trade developed, and markets arose within the cities where the citizens sold their products to merchants and traders who travelled along the coast in small ships seeking for gain.

Meanwhile on the mainland of Greece, where the available land was extremely limited, economic difficulties grew. An increasing population created a land shortage, and this in turn occasioned fierce quarrels between cities and tribes for small areas of fertile soil. Then came stories told by bold seafarers, who sometimes differed little from pirates, about fertile land which was to be had for the asking in distant countries. This led to a vast colonising movement. Unlike the earlier streams of random refugees who had migrated from Greece across the Aegean, various cities now organised groups of their members who sailed off to seek land and new homes overseas. Although the founding of these colonies was sponsored by the 'mother-city', once established, they became independent sovereign states. Thus from the eighth to the sixth century a great number of Greek cities were established along the coasts of the Mediterranean and Black Sea (see Maps 9, p. 20, and 16, p. 35) and introduced the Greek way of life there. In places where the coast was controlled by powerful rulers it was naturally impossible to establish independent cities, and here immigrants could come only as merchants (as to Etruria) or mercenaries (as in Egypt).

This geographical expansion had far-reaching economic and social results. The earliest colonists sought land, for example in southern Italy, which received the name of Magna Graecia (see Map 29, p. 93); but the development of communications and the exchange of goods gave increasing importance to trade and commercial interests, so that later colonists sought places suitable for harbours and markets. Industry in the cities of the mother country was stimulated by demand from the colonies. These, in their turn, began to produce the raw materials which were manufactured in the mother country. After two centuries the movement found its logical conclusion. Industry provided the mother country with the means to import foodstuffs,

and thus one centre could support a greater population than before. The need for emigration lessened. Colonies founded after the sixth century usually had a different, often a political, cause for their establishment.

This development, however, seriously menaced the autarky of the city-state. Many cities had to turn to trade and commerce in order to exist, that is, they had to seek their salvation 'abroad'. Markets and ports began to compete, and trade wars ensued. Further, piracy created the need for a law common to all states; so many of the autonomous city-states began to negotiate treaties with each other. Then a few of the favourably situated and flourishing cities tried to force smaller places into subjection. This gave rise to 'hegemony', the recognised leadership of certain cities, maintained by force. For example, in the sixth century Miletus, Samos, and Corinth became of more than local importance. But although considered great and rich by the Greeks, they remained small by our standards, with at most 30,000 to 40,000 inhabitants.

The internal structure of the city-state was also radically altered. Its agrarian basis remained unchanged, with land and cattle as the basis of existence; but trade and industry gained in importance until the possession of land was only profitable so long as the workers continued to produce and the traders to require their products. In Miletus, for example (→ 214), the famous wool of the local sheep was woven into materials which were exported to the region around the Black Sea where they were exchanged for skins, corn, and slaves.

Despite their aristocratic traditions many Greek nobles appreciated these new possibilities. In many cities a rich middle class did not grow up alongside and separate from the aristocracy, as it did in the Middle Ages, but the aristocracy itself, which had always been based upon birth, took advantage of the new commercial opportunities, so that many newly-enriched nobles and non-nobles developed into a new plutocracy. *Chremat' aner* became a proverb — 'Not birth (alone) but money makes a man.' At the other end of the scale the people, the *demos*, was composed of the small farmers, land workers, craftsmen, and traders.

These external and internal developments had a drastic influence upon the pattern of political life, when the early independent economy of the city-state was complicated by trade interests and the formation of new groups within the old social framework of heads of families and their dependents.

Economic development was further complicated by the introduction of coinage. This useful device was invented in the Lydian kingdom, which was rich in gold, and was soon adopted throughout Greece. The city-states mainly used silver coins, owing to the large deposits of silver in Greece.

THE ECONOMIC CRISIS AND ITS EFFECTS

The development of trade and communications thus turned the landed nobles and chiefs in many cities into wealthy capitalists. They were able to exploit the possibilities of import and export and to employ traders and craftsmen. The habit of thinking in terms of money soon spread even to the traditionally minded agrarian sections of the community.

From the earliest times members of a clan will have helped one another and worked for their chief in return for the lease of land, seed, or other forms of payment in kind. This traditional relationship was now imperceptibly replaced by one of creditor-debtor. Help given, now in the form of money, was reclaimed with interest. Coined money not only served as a standard of value and exchange but could also be kept and accumulated in unlimited quantities. The rich with their money could withstand the disasters of a bad harvest or a war, whereas their dependents, if their harvest failed or their huts were burned or their cattle driven off, were obliged to borrow. Such loans, since they were mostly intended for immediate use and the interest demanded was exorbitant, could never be repaid, and thus led to permanent dependence. The rich could also use their land to cultivate such crops as vines and olives which took years to show a return but which ultimately were much more profitable than arable farming, which in any case suffered from competition from imported corn. In short, the small man often became either a tenant-farmer, a serf, or even the slave of his creditor. He had little chance of redress, because the administration of justice and the harsh laws of debt (which were based upon oral tradition from an earlier society) were entirely in the hands of the nobles and consequently were often biased.

Such developments naturally did not occur only in Greece. There are indications that the crisis was felt also in the East. There, too, we hear of rich men and nobles who abused the law, oppressed the weak, and appropriated what little land they possessed. But reactions differed in East and West, and this accentuated the difference in the manner of life and thought of Greeks and barbarians. In the East protests were heard, for example from the prophets of the Old Testament, but they confined themselves to appeals to divine authority and the conscience of the ruler; at most, if their prayers remained unheard, the people might have recourse to arms and choose a better king. But the Greeks demanded another system and other laws. Their deeply-rooted craving for reason prevented them from accepting a development as if it were inescapably imposed by some super-

53. The city of Athens in Attica developed from a settlement around and on a limestone rock 512 ft. high. The rock, first the dwelling-place of a king, became later a sanctuary and the religious centre of the city. In the time of Pericles temples were built which, although now in ruins, have remained a symbol of Western civilisation. Even in its heyday ancient Athens was not a large city. 1. Acropolis; 2. Parthenon; 3. Propylaea and temple of Nike; 4. Theatre of Dionysus; 5. Agora; 6. Hephaesteum; 7. Areopagus; 8. Theatre of Herodes Atticus; 9. Stoa of Eumenes; 10. Dipylon cemetery and Sacred Way to Eleusis; 11. Olympieum. **52.** Coin of the city of Athens with owl, sacred to Athena. **54.** Nike, goddess of victory, a symbol found also on the hand of Athena Parthenos, the statue of the city goddess. **55.** Noble Athenian youths on the way to the Acropolis in the procession of the Panathenaea, the yearly feast in honour of Athena, the tutelary goddess.

human power. The citizen demanded his rights and sought them in the law. The fact that in the foundation of the colonies the Greeks were continually being obliged to devise some form of rational organisation in the absence of any hallowed tradition undoubtedly had some influence on this. They began consciously to demand a more democratic system which would offer freedom and justice to every citizen.

These changes were not effected without bitter struggles. We hear of the murder of the rich and the partition of their land, of debt redemption extorted by force, and also of the savage suppression of such risings by the nobles and their armed supporters. The first demand of the oppressed, that for written laws to which the citizen could appeal against the rich, was virtually everywhere granted. But this guarantee of justice was soon not sufficient for the Greeks. They had the deep inner conviction that law without power to maintain it was merely a favour granted by authority. They considered as slaves the subjects of the Eastern kings, who although they might call themselves free were in fact dependent upon the favour of their lord. The Greek demanded his individual rights as the counterpart of the autonomy which each city-state was prepared to defend to the last man.

In principle this freedom did not mean lack of restraint. Even in a democracy the citizen was bound by the laws and customs of the state in a way scarcely comprehensible to us. But it was law which now ruled, not private individuals. To uphold the law, said the philosopher Heraclitus, the citizen must fight as he would to defend his city-wall. Government was no longer the prerogative of those of noble birth, no longer the natural right of a ruler, but a function granted by law. In general, in the more conservative agrarian communities on the mainland this function remained in the hands of the landowners, the *eupatridai*. This form of government continued to be called aristocracy (its opponents spoke of oligarchy or plutocracy, the rule of the few or of the wealthy), while the trading towns, with their population of artisans, seamen, and merchants, often developed into democracies where the magistrates were elected and controlled by a popular assembly.

This period of crisis produced popular leaders (*prostatai*), usually discontented or ambitious noblemen who in the rôle of protectors of the people set themselves up as 'tyrants'. This word merely meant an unconstitutional ruler and originally had no unfavourable suggestion. The tyrants were often energetic men who governed their cities ably and promoted the material welfare of the people, upon whom they relied for support. This form of government, however, did not long survive. It was precisely during periods of increased prosperity and knowledge that the Greeks refused to remain subject to a ruling house which was essentially unconstitutional. The second generation usually saw a popular rebellion, and any attempt by a tyrant to retain power by force and oppression inspired such a hatred of tyranny that tyrannicide might be regarded as a patriotic duty.

This political development is paralleled by that in the fields of art, learning, and literature. There, too, we see a breaking with tradition and a search for forms which would allow scope for the individual personality. Mythology, the authoritative story based upon inspiration, was replaced by reasoning and speculation. The impersonal epic made way for the expression of individual feelings in the lyric. Architecture aimed at design which was logically justifiable. Statues of the gods became statues of idealised man. The history of lands and peoples was treated critically. But the Greek was not yet an individualist. By every fibre of his being he was still bound to the community of his city-state, although he had become more independent within that community. The sixth century was a period of material and intellectual development in all spheres of life.

THE POSITION OF GREECE AS A BORDER STATE: THE BASIS OF POLITICAL AND CULTURAL EXPANSION

The basis of the general material prosperity of Greece in the sixth and fifth centuries which paved the way for the intellectual flowering often called 'the Greek miracle' was its position as a border state between the ancient cultures of the East and the primitive world about the Mediterranean and the Black Sea. Profiting by their geographical position, the Greeks exploited their raw materials and manufactured and supplied goods of high quality. Greece itself produced olive oil, wine, honey, and fish; it imported corn (this was essential for the feeding of the growing population, but a weakness in time of war), slaves, wood, wool, skins, pitch, and metals. These imports provided the materials for the export of articles made by hand: applied art, cloth, weapons, bronze work, objects of art, and above all pottery, which found its way throughout the whole of the ancient world.

In this manner Miletus, Corinth, and Athens acquired their wealth, or rather what they themselves considered wealth, although it was extremely modest compared with the riches of the East. The Minoans, Phoenicians, and Carthaginians before them, and Venice, Genoa, and the United Kingdom, among others, after them, made their fortunes in the same way. Real estate, lands and houses, still formed the core of a fortune; but the products

of such property had to be exported. The seamen who hazarded long journeys in their little ships were classed among the lower sections of the population and served the rich, who financed their voyages. The rich also owned the 'factories' which worked for the market. These factories were not large buildings with machinery but merely workshops, mostly in the house of the owner, where a few trained slaves manufactured products such as furniture, weapons, and pottery. The lead of the Greeks in this field is to be attributed not to better tools or equipment but to personal skill and technical ability. It was not their ships which outclassed those of the Phoenicians but their seamen, not their tools but their artisans.

This personal human element became the essential characteristic of Greek life and culture. It was already evident in the domain of politics and most strongly in the democracies, where the citizen increasingly demanded his share in the government. Liberty was guaranteed by the law, which admittedly was compiled by legislators, but at the command of the community. Greek literature began with the epic, strongly traditional in style and metre, yet already ordered by the vision of the poet, who created an artistic unity from an abundance of material. The lyric developed a form of poetry in which the poet considered the expression of his personal feelings worthy of publication, yet not in any free form but restrained by intricate metres. Architecture produced the temple, derived from the simple *megaron* which housed the image of the god, but logically extended with entrance and colonnades. Beauty was sought not in ornamentation but in line and proportion. The plastic arts also gradually abandoned ornament and decoration in order to attain a sublimated reproduction of forms which expressed the ideal rather than the real. Personal, yet not individual, each pupil in seeking for a synthesis of freedom and discipline always observed the rules of his art and did not aspire to an individual style. He followed the teaching of his master and strove only to surpass him. Thus Greek art developed with that logic found today only in science. Not without reason was it called *techne* (skill). The consistency of form which we call the Greek style arose from this. In its greatest period this style offered the masters the opportunity of nearing perfection in their own limited field, in firm lines yet without rigidity.

The sixth century saw the same conflict between freedom and tradition in the realm of thought as men sought for order and discipline. The Greeks could learn something of mathematics and astronomy from the Egyptians and Babylonians, but so far as we know they were the first to use this scientific thought in an attempt to discover the essential nature and structure of the world. They explained the universe no longer by myths but by theories which at first sight seem primitive but on closer examination prove surprisingly acute. These theories form the beginning of Western scientific enquiry, which attempts by observation and reason alone to solve the riddle of the universe. The Ionian 'hylozoists', who postulated a living first principle, flourished in the sixth century. Thales postulated water as the first principle. Anaximander, however, took the infinite as the first principle, and thus sought for the origin of all things (*arche*) in a principle which can be apprehended only by thought. So rationalism was born. Pythagoras, an eminent mathematician, saw the essence of things in numbers, and interpreted the world as a whole through numbers, which he systematically studied. These thinkers are all typically Greek in the logic and audacity with which they drew the most extreme conclusions from their limited and inadequate basis of facts.

Towards the end of the sixth century the power and glory of the great kings of the East were undoubtedly objects of envious admiration to the comparatively small Greek states. The Greeks were impressed by the mighty monuments of Egypt and Babylon. Yet they felt themselves different from the barbarians and considered that their own forms of freedom and justice were possessions which they were prepared to defend at all costs.

THE TWO LEADERS, SPARTA AND ATHENS

The two states that were to assume a position of leadership owed this possibility to the fact that in each case a single city-state had expanded to include a large portion of the neighbouring country. Thus their powers of resistance and farther expansion were considerably greater than those of perhaps more brilliant states like Miletus, Argos, and Corinth.

Sparta (→ 11, 13, 69), the capital of Laconia and the state of the Lacedaemonians, displayed remarkably archaic forms. The double kingship of the houses of the Agiads and Eurypontids clearly perpetuated an origin from the union of at least two Dorian tribes, while the country population of serfs betrayed in the name *Helots* ('captives') the fact that they were the descendants of the subjected original inhabitants of Laconia. The *Perioikoi* ('surrounding inhabitants'), although regarded as free Lacedaemonians, still possessed no influence upon the government; this suggests that at some early period all the able-bodied conquering Dorians concentrated themselves in the city and became the masters of the state.

This precarious position of a ruling minority and the stern need for self-preservation drove Sparta to adopt the legislative reforms which are attributed to Lycurgus. From archaeological evidence Sparta appears to have begun as a 'normal' aristocratic state. It enjoyed poetry and music, it

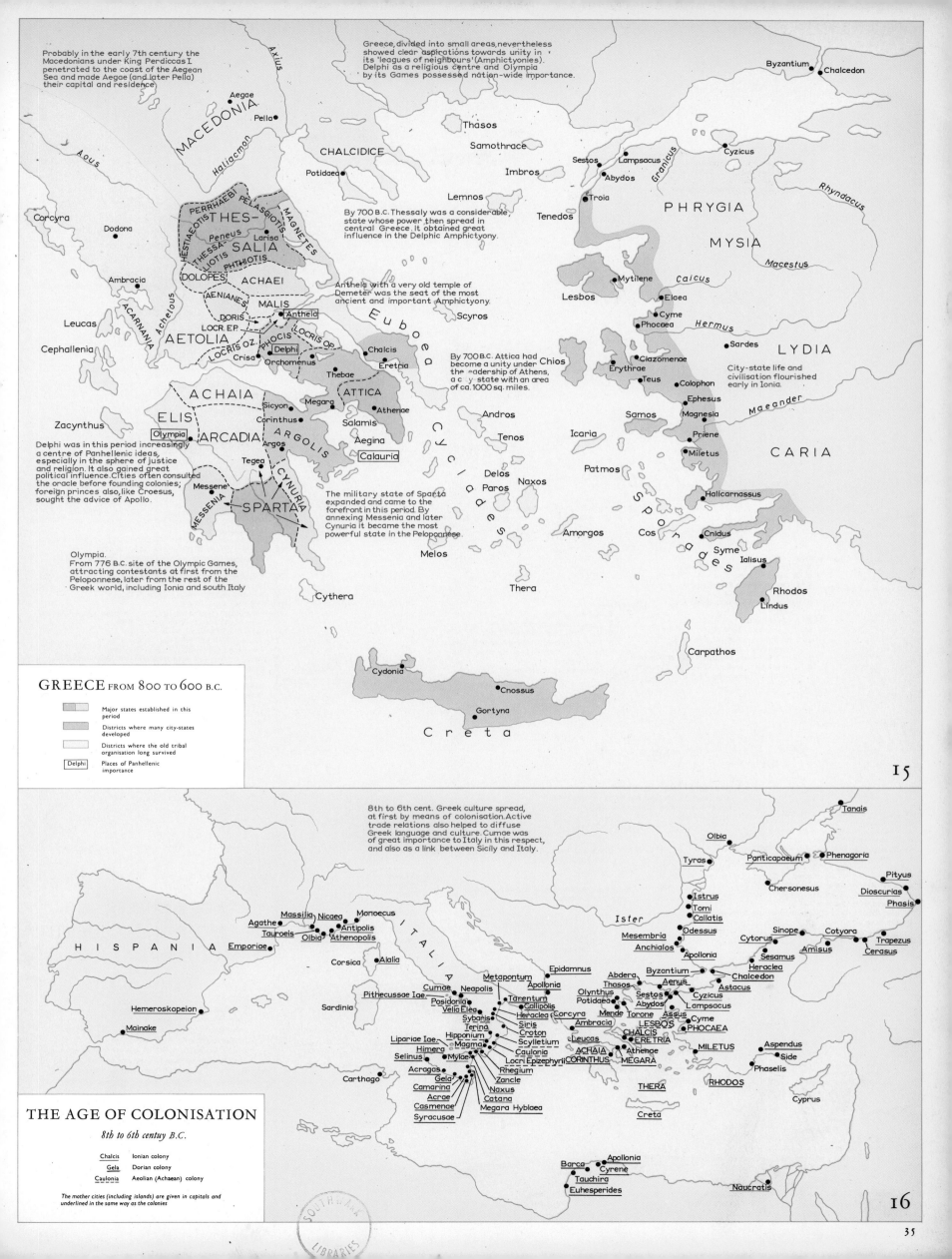

GREECE FROM 800 TO 600 B.C.

THE AGE OF COLONISATION — 8th to 6th century B.C.

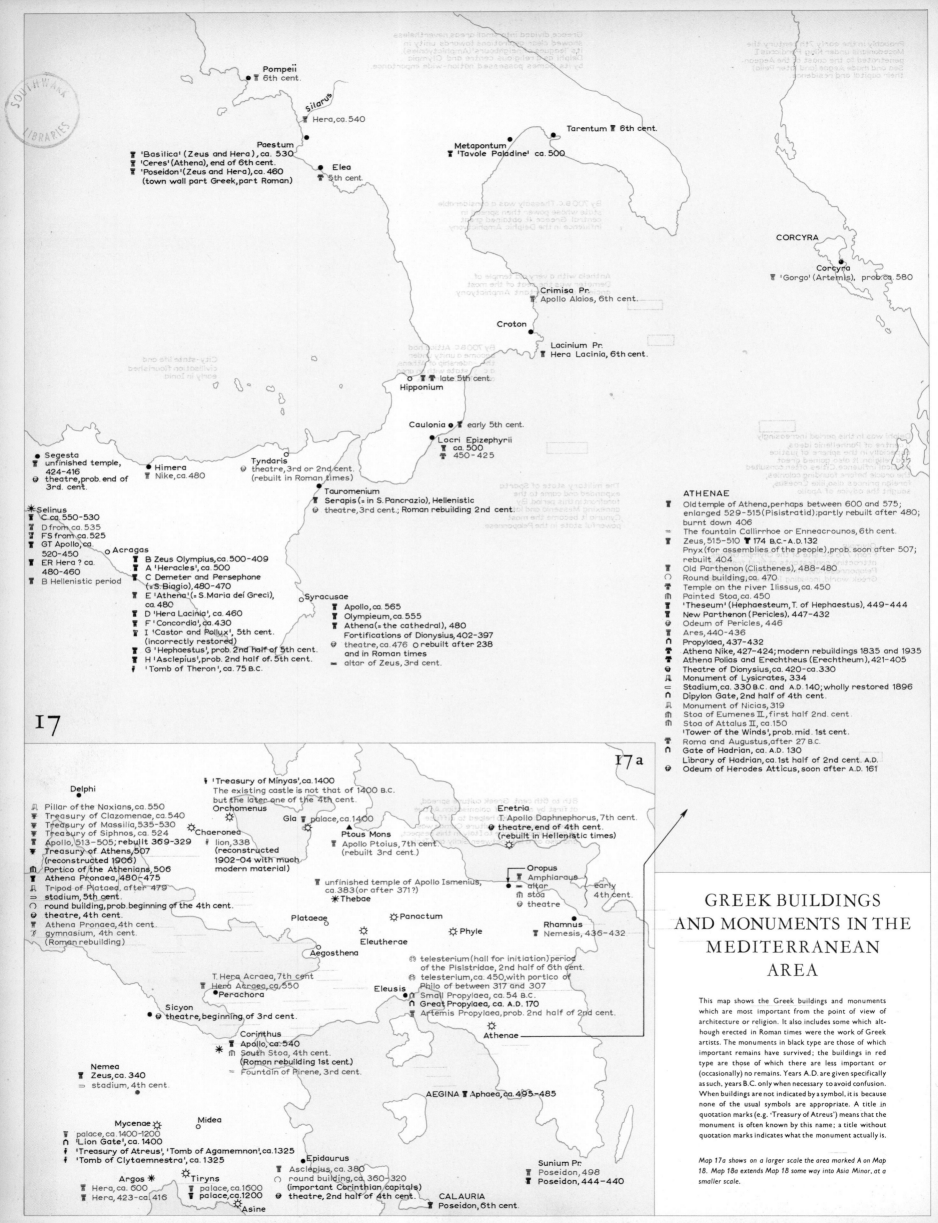

Pompeii ⊤ 6th cent.

Silarus
⊤ Hera, ca. 540

Paestum
⊤ 'Basilica' (Zeus and Hera), ca. 530
⊤ 'Ceres' (Athena), end of 6th cent.
⊤ 'Poseidon' (Zeus and Hera), ca. 460
(town wall part Greek, part Roman)

● Elea
⊤ 5th cent.

Tarentum ⊤ 6th cent.

Metapontum
⊤ 'Tavole Paladine' ca. 500

CORCYRA

Corcyra
⊤ 'Gorgo' (Artemis), prob. ca. 580

Crimisa Pr.
⊤ Apollo Alaios, 6th cent.

Croton

Lacinium Pr.
⊤ Hera Lacinia, 6th cent.

○ ⊤ ⊤ late 5th cent.
Hipponium

Caulonia ● ⊤ early 5th cent.

Locri Epizephyrii
⊤ ca. 500
⊤ 450–425

● Segesta
⊤ unfinished temple, 424–416
⊕ theatre, prob. end of 3rd. cent.

● Himera
⊤ Nike, ca. 480

Tyndaris
⊕ theatre, 3rd or 2nd cent. (rebuilt in Roman times)

✳ Selinus
C ca. 550–530
⊤ D from ca. 535
⊤ FS from ca. 525
⊤ GT Apollo, ca. 520–450
⊤ ER Hera ? ca. 480–460
⊤ B Hellenistic period

○ Acragas
⊤ B Zeus Olympius, ca. 500–409
⊤ A 'Heracles', ca. 500
⊤ C Demeter and Persephone (= S. Biagio), 480–470
⊤ E 'Athena' (= S. Maria dei Greci), ca. 480
⊤ D 'Hera Lacinia', ca. 460
⊤ F 'Concordia', ca. 430
⊤ I 'Castor and Pollux', 5th cent. (incorrectly restored)
⊤ G 'Hephaestus', prob. 2nd half of 5th cent.
⊤ H 'Asclepius', prob. 2nd half of. 5th cent.
ᛁ 'Tomb of Theron', ca. 75 B.C.

Tauromenium
⊤ Serapis (= in S. Pancrazio), Hellenistic
⊕ theatre, 3rd cent.; Roman rebuilding 2nd cent.

Syracusae
⊤ Apollo, ca. 565
⊤ Olympieum, ca. 555
⊤ Athena (= the cathedral), 480
Fortifications of Dionysius, 402–397
⊕ theatre, ca. 476 ○ rebuilt after 238 and in Roman times
⊶ altar of Zeus, 3rd cent.

ATHENAE
⊤ Old temple of Athena, perhaps between 600 and 575; enlarged 529–515 (Pisistratid); partly rebuilt after 480; burnt down 406
≈ The fountain Callirrhoe or Enneacrounos, 6th cent.
⊤ Zeus, 515–510 ⊤ 174 B.C.–A.D. 132
Pnyx (for assemblies of the people), prob. soon after 507; rebuilt 404
⊤ Old Parthenon (Clisthenes), 488–480
○ Round building, ca. 470
⊓ Temple on the river Ilissus, ca. 450
⋔ Painted Stoa, ca. 450
⊤ 'Theseum' (Hephaesteum, T. of Hephaestus), 449–444
⊤ New Parthenon (Pericles), 447–432
⊕ Odeum of Pericles, 446
⊤ Ares, 440–436
⊓ Propylaea, 437–432
⊤ Athena Nike, 427–424; modern rebuildings 1835 and 1935
⊤ Athena Polias and Erechtheus (Erechtheum), 421–405
⊕ Theatre of Dionysius, ca. 420–ca. 330
⊓ Monument of Lysicrates, 334
= Stadium, ca. 330 B.C. and A.D. 140; wholly restored 1896
⊓ Dipylon Gate, 2nd half of 4th cent.
⊓ Monument of Nicias, 319
⋔ Stoa of Eumenes II, first half 2nd cent.
⋔ Stoa of Attalus II, ca. 150
⊤ 'Tower of the Winds', prob. mid. 1st cent.
⊓ Roma and Augustus, after 27 B.C.
⊓ Gate of Hadrian, ca. A.D. 130
Library of Hadrian, ca. 1st half of 2nd cent. A.D.
⊕ Odeum of Herodes Atticus, soon after A.D. 161

I7

I7a

Delphi
⊓ Pillar of the Naxians, ca. 550
⊤ Treasury of Clazomenae, ca. 540
⊤ Treasury of Massilia, 535–530
⊤ Treasury of Siphnos, ca. 524
⊤ Apollo, 513–505; rebuilt 369–329
⊤ Treasury of Athens, 507 (reconstructed 1906)
⋔ Portico of the Athenians, 506
⊤ Athena Pronaea, 480–475
⊓ Tripod of Plataea, after 479
⊶ stadium, 5th cent.
○ round building, prob. beginning of the 4th cent.
⊕ theatre, 4th cent.
⊤ Athena Pronaea, 4th cent.
✗ gymnasium, 4th cent. (Roman rebuilding)

ᛁ 'Treasury of Minyas', ca. 1400
The existing castle is not that of 1400 B.C. but the later one of the 4th cent.
Orchomenus
✺ Gla ⊤ palace, ca. 1400

Chaeronea
⊤ lion, 338 (reconstructed 1902–04 with much modern material)

Ptous Mons
⊤ Apollo Ptoius, 7th cent. (rebuilt 3rd cent.)

⊤ unfinished temple of Apollo Ismenius, ca. 383 (or after 371?)
✺ Thebae

Eretria
⊤ Apollo Daphnephorus, 7th cent.
⊕ theatre, end of 4th cent. (rebuilt in Hellenistic times)

Oropus
⊤ Amphiaraus
⊶ altar
⋔ stoa
⊕ theatre

Plataeae

✺ Panactum

✺ Phyle

Rhamnus
⊤ Nemesis, 436–432

Eleutherae
Aegosthena

early 4th cent.

telesterium (hall for initiation) period of the Pisistridae, 2nd half of 6th cent.
telesterium, ca. 450, with portico of Philo of between 317 and 307
⊓ Small Propylaea, ca. 54 B.C.
⊓ Great Propylaea, ca. A.D. 170
⊤ Artemis Propylaea, prob. 2nd half of 2nd cent.

T. Hera Acraea, 7th cent
⊤ Hera Acraea, ca. 550
Perachora

Sicyon
⊕ theatre, beginning of 3rd cent.

Corinthus
⊤ Apollo, ca. 540
⋔ South Stoa, 4th cent. (Roman rebuilding 1st cent.)
= Fountain of Pirene, 3rd cent.

Eleusis

Athenae

Nemea
⊤ Zeus, ca. 340
⊶ stadium, 4th cent.

AEGINA ⊤ Aphaea, ca. 495–485

Mycenae ✺
⊤ palace, ca. 1400–1200
⊓ 'Lion Gate', 1400
ᛁ 'Treasury of Atreus', 'Tomb of Agamemnon', ca. 1325
ᛁ 'Tomb of Clytaemnestra', ca. 1325

Midea

Argos ✳
⊤ Hera, ca. 600
⊤ Hera, 423–ca. 416

Tiryns ✺
⊤ palace, ca. 1600
⊤ palace, ca. 1200

Asine

Epidaurus
⊤ Asclepius, ca. 380
○ round building, ca. 360–320 (important Corinthian capitals)
⊕ theatre, 2nd half of 4th cent.

Sunium Pr.
⊤ Poseidon, 498
⊤ Poseidon, 444–440

CALAURIA
⊤ Poseidon, 6th cent.

GREEK BUILDINGS AND MONUMENTS IN THE MEDITERRANEAN AREA

This map shows the Greek buildings and monuments which are most important from the point of view of architecture or religion. It also includes some which although erected in Roman times were the work of Greek artists. The monuments in black type are those of which important remains have survived; the buildings in red type are those of which there are less important or (occasionally) no remains. Years A.D. are given specifically as such, years B.C. only when necessary to avoid confusion. When buildings are not indicated by a symbol, it is because none of the usual symbols are appropriate. A title in quotation marks (e.g. 'Treasury of Atreus') means that the monument is often known by this name; a title without quotation marks indicates what the monument actually is.

Map 17a shows on a larger scale the area marked A on Map 18. Map 18a extends Map 18 some way into Asia Minor, at a smaller scale.

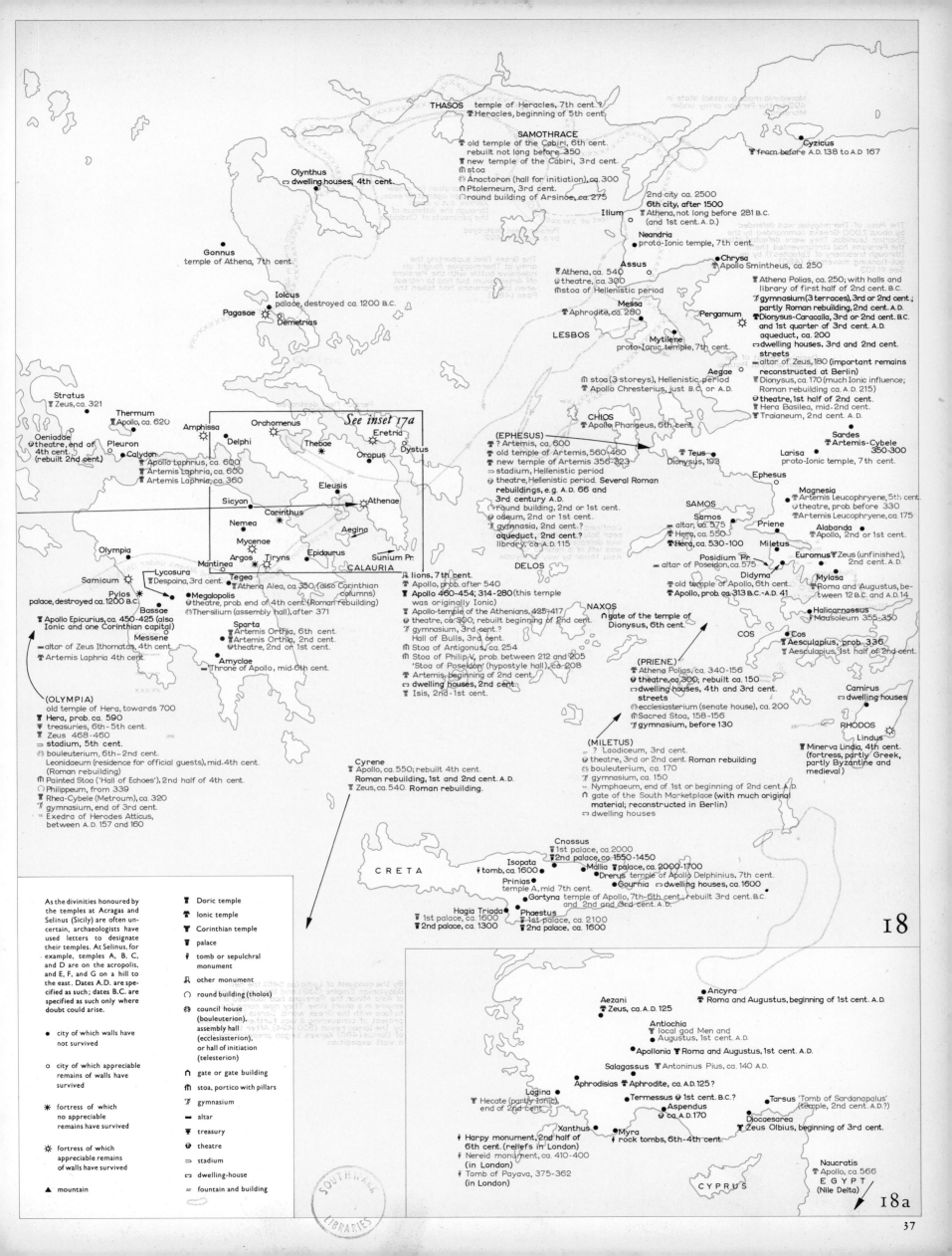

THASOS temple of Heracles, 7th cent. ?
⊤ Heracles, beginning of 5th cent.

SAMOTHRACE
⊤ old temple of the Cabiri, 6th cent.
  rebuilt not long before 350
⊤ new temple of the Cabiri, 3rd cent.
ffi stoa
ᴖ Anacoron (hall for initiation), ca. 300
ᴖ Ptolemeum, 3rd cent.
ᴖ round building of Arsinoe, ca. 275

Cyzicus
⊤ from before A.D. 138 to A.D. 167

2nd city ca. 2500
6th city, after 1500
Ilium
⊤ Athena, not long before 281 B.C.
  (and 1st cent. A.D.)

Neandria
  proto-Ionic temple, 7th cent.

Chrysa
⊤ Apollo Smintheus, ca. 250

Assus
⊤ Athena, ca. 540
ᴼ theatre, ca. 300
ffi stoa of Hellenistic period

Messa
⊤ Aphrodite, ca. 280

Pergamum
⊤ Athena Polias, ca. 250; with halls and
  library of first half of 2nd cent. B.C.
♀ gymnasium (3 terraces), 3rd or 2nd cent.;
  partly Roman rebuilding, 2nd cent. A.D.
⊤ Dionysus-Caracalla, 3rd or 2nd cent. B.C.
  and 1st quarter of 3rd cent. A.D.
∾ aqueduct, ca. 200
ᴼ dwelling houses, 3rd and 2nd cent.
  streets
᎓ altar of Zeus, 180 (important remains
  reconstructed at Berlin)
⊤ Dionysus, ca. 170 (much Ionic influence;
  Roman rebuilding ca. A.D. 215)
ᴼ theatre, 1st half of 2nd cent.
⊤ Hera Basilea, mid-2nd cent.
⊤ Traianeum, 2nd cent. A.D.

LESBOS
Mytilene
  proto-Ionic temple, 7th cent.

Aegae
ffi stoa (3 storeys), Hellenistic period
⊤ Apollo Chresterius, just B.C. or A.D.

CHIOS
⊤ Apollo Phangeus, 6th cent.

(EPHESUS)
⊤ ? Artemis, ca. 600
⊤ old temple of Artemis, 560–460
⊤ new temple of Artemis 356–323
⇒ stadium, Hellenistic period
ᴼ theatre, Hellenistic period. Several Roman
  rebuildings, e.g. A.D. 66 and
  3rd century A.D.
ᴖ round building, 2nd or 1st cent.
ᴼ odeum, 2nd or 1st cent.
♀ gymnasia, 2nd cent.
  aqueduct, 2nd cent.?
  library, ca. A.D. 115

Teus
Dionysus, 193

Sardes
⊤ Artemis-Cybele
  350–300

Larisa
  proto-Ionic temple, 7th cent.

Ephesus

Magnesia
⊤ Artemis Leucophryene, 5th cent.
ᴼ theatre, prob. before 330
⊤ Artemis Leucophryene, ca. 175

SAMOS
Samos
᎓ altar, ca. 575
⊤ Hera, ca. 550
⊤ Hera, ca. 530–100

Priene
Alabanda
⊤ Apollo, 2nd or 1st cent.

Miletus

Posidium Pr.
᎓ altar of Poseidon, ca. 575

Euromus ⊤ Zeus (unfinished),
  2nd cent. A.D.

Didyma
⊤ old temple of Apollo, 6th cent.
⊤ Apollo, prob. ca. 313 B.C.–A.D. 41

Mylasa
⊤ Roma and Augustus, be-
  tween 12 B.C. and A.D. 14

NAXOS
ᴖ gate of the temple of
  Dionysus, 6th cent.

Halicarnassus
⊤ Mausoleum 355–350

COS
Cos
⊤ Aesculapius, prob. 336
⊤ Aesculapius, 1st half of 2nd cent.

(PRIENE)
⊤ Athena Polias, ca. 340–156
ᴼ theatre, ca. 300, rebuilt ca. 150
ᴼ dwelling houses, 4th and 3rd cent.
  streets
ᴼ ecclesiasterium (senate house), ca. 200
ffi Sacred Stoa, 158–156
♀ gymnasium, before 130

Camirus
ᴼ dwelling houses

RHODOS
Lindus
⊤ Minerva Lindia, 4th cent.
  (fortress, partly Greek,
  partly Byzantine and
  medieval)

(MILETUS)
⊤ ? Laodiceum, 3rd cent.
ᴼ theatre, 3rd or 2nd cent. Roman rebuilding
ᴼ bouleuterium, ca. 170
♀ gymnasium, ca. 150
∾ Nymphaeum, end of 1st or beginning of 2nd cent. A.D.
ᴖ gate of the South Marketplace (with much original
  material; reconstructed in Berlin)
ᴼ dwelling houses

Stratus
⊤ Zeus, ca. 321

Thermum
⊤ Apollo, ca. 620

Oeniadae
ᴼ theatre, end of
  4th cent.
  (rebuilt 2nd cent.)

Pleuron
Calydon
⊤ Apollo Laphrius, ca. 600
⊤ Artemis Laphria, ca. 600
⊤ Artemis Laphria, ca. 360

Amphissa
Delphi
Thebae
Orchomenus
Eretria
Dystus
Oropus

See inset 17a

Eleusis
Sicyon
Corinthus
Athenae
Nemea
Aegina
Mycenae
Sunium Pr.
Argos Tiryns
Mantinea Epidaurus
Tegea CALAURIA

Gonnus
temple of Athena, 7th cent.

Iolcus
palace, destroyed ca. 1200 B.C.

Pagasae
Demetrias

Olynthus
ᴼ dwelling houses, 4th cent.

DELOS
Ⴈ lions, 7th cent.
⊤ Apollo, prob. after 540
⊤ Apollo 460–454; 314–280 (this temple
  was originally Ionic)
⊤ Apollo-temple of the Athenians, 425–417
ᴼ theatre, ca. 300; rebuilt beginning of 2nd cent.
♀ gymnasium, 3rd cent.?
  Hall of Bulls, 4th cent.
ffi Stoa of Antigonus, ca. 254
ffi Stoa of Philip V, prob. between 212 and 205
  'Stoa of Poseidon' (hypostyle hall), ca. 208
⊤ Artemis, beginning of 2nd cent.
ᴼ dwelling houses, 2nd cent.
⊤ Isis, 2nd–1st cent.

Olympia
Samicum
Pylos
palace, destroyed ca. 1200 B.C.

Bassae
⊤ Apollo Epicurius, ca. 450–425 (also
  Ionic and one Corinthian capital)

Messene
᎓ altar of Zeus Ithomatas, 4th cent.
⊤ Artemis Laphria 4th cent.

Lycosura
⊤ Despoina, 3rd cent.

Megalopolis
ᴼ theatre, prob. end of 4th cent. (Roman rebuilding)
ffi Thersilium (assembly hall), after 371

Sparta
⊤ Artemis Orthia, 6th cent.
⊤ Artemis Orthia, 2nd cent.
ᴼ theatre, 2nd or 1st cent.

Amyclae
᎓ Throne of Apollo, mid-6th cent.

Tegea
⊤ Athena Alea, ca. 350 (also Corinthian
  columns)

(OLYMPIA)
old temple of Hera, towards 700
⊤ Hera, prob. ca. 590
⊤ treasuries, 6th–5th cent.
⊤ Zeus 468–460
⇒ stadium, 5th cent.
ᴼ bouleuterium, 6th–2nd cent.
  Leonidaeum (residence for official guests), mid-4th cent.
  (Roman rebuilding)
ffi Painted Stoa ('Hall of Echoes'), 2nd half of 4th cent.
ᴖ Philippeum, from 339
⊤ Rhea-Cybele (Metroum), ca. 320
♀ gymnasium, end of 3rd cent.
᎓ Exedra of Herodes Atticus,
  between A.D. 157 and 160

Cyrene
⊤ Apollo, ca. 550; rebuilt 4th cent.
  Roman rebuilding, 1st and 2nd cent. A.D.
⊤ Zeus, ca. 540. Roman rebuilding.

Cnossus
⊤ 1st palace, ca. 2000
⊤ 2nd palace, ca. 1550–1450

Isopata
⊤ tomb, ca. 1600

Mallia
⊤ palace, ca. 2000–1700

Prinias
  temple A, mid 7th cent.

Drerus temple of Apollo Delphinius, 7th cent.
Gournia ᴼ dwelling houses, ca. 1600

Gortyna temple of Apollo, 7th–6th cent., rebuilt 3rd cent. B.C.
  and 2nd and 3rd cent. A.D.

CRETA

Hagia Triada
⊤ 1st palace, ca. 1600
⊤ 2nd palace, ca. 1300

Phaestus
⊤ 1st palace, ca. 2100
⊤ 2nd palace, ca. 1600

18

As the divinities honoured by
the temples at Acragas and
Selinus (Sicily) are often uncertain, archaeologists have
used letters to designate
their temples. At Selinus, for
example, temples A, B, C,
and D are on the acropolis,
and E, F, and G on a hill to
the east. Dates A.D. are specified as such; dates B.C. are
specified as such only where
doubt could arise.

● city of which walls have
  not survived

○ city of which appreciable
  remains of walls have
  survived

✳ fortress of which
  no appreciable
  remains have survived

✲ fortress of which
  appreciable remains
  of walls have survived

▲ mountain

⊤ Doric temple
⊤ Ionic temple
⊤ Corinthian temple
⊤ palace
⊤ tomb or sepulchral
  monument
Ⴈ other monument
ᴖ round building (tholos)
ᴼ council house
  (bouleuterion),
  assembly hall
  (ecclesiasterion),
  or hall of initiation
  (telesterion)
ᴖ gate or gate building
ffi stoa, portico with pillars
♀ gymnasium
᎓ altar
⊤ treasury
ᴼ theatre
⇒ stadium
ᴼ dwelling-house
∾ fountain and building

Ancyra
⊤ Roma and Augustus, beginning of 1st cent. A.D.

Aezani
⊤ Zeus, ca. A.D. 125

Antiochia
⊤ local god Men and
  Augustus, 1st cent. A.D.

Apollonia ⊤ Roma and Augustus, 1st cent. A.D.

Salagassus ⊤ Antoninus Pius, ca. 140 A.D.

Aphrodisias ⊤ Aphrodite, ca. A.D. 125?

Lagina
⊤ Hecate (partly Ionic),
  end of 2nd cent.

Termessus ᴼ 1st cent. B.C.?

Aspendus
ᴼ ca. A.D. 170

Tarsus 'Tomb of Sardanapalus'
  (temple, 2nd cent. A.D.?)

Diocaesarea
⊤ Zeus Olbius, beginning of 3rd cent.

Xanthus
⊤ Harpy monument, 2nd half of
  6th cent. (reliefs in London)
⊤ Nereid monument, ca. 410–400
  (in London)
⊤ Tomb of Payava, 375–362
  (in London)

Myra
⊤ rock tombs, 6th–4th cent.

CYPRUS

Naucratis
⊤ Apollo, ca. 566

EGYPT
(Nile Delta)

18a

37

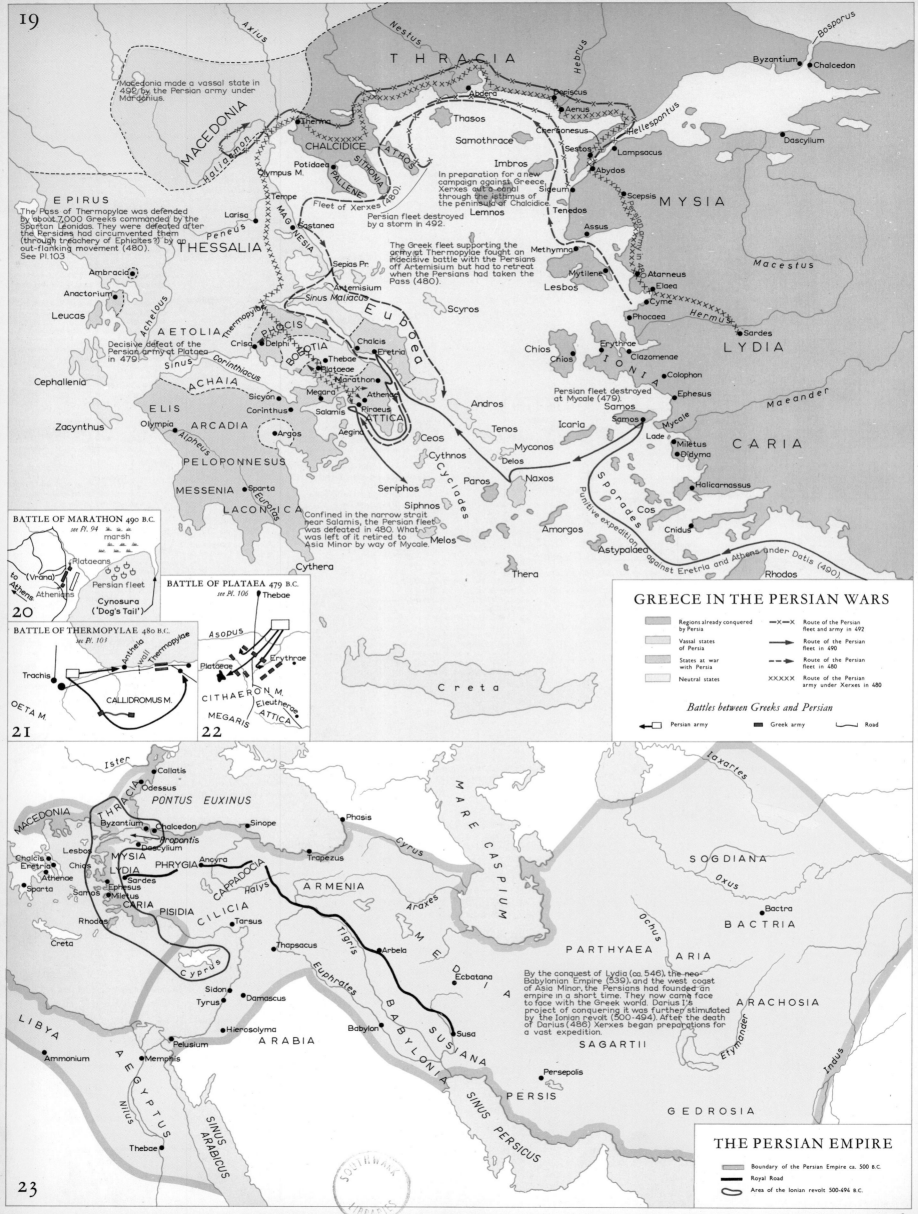

19

Macedonia made a vassal state in 492 by the Persian army under Mardonius.

THRACIA

Byzantium ● Chalcedon

Bosporus

Nestus

Abdera ● Doriscus

Axius

Aenus

Chersonesus

Hellespontus

Dascylium

MACEDONIA

Therma ●

CHALCIDICE

Thasos

Samothrace

Sestos

Lampsacus

Sigeum

Abydos

Scepsis

MYSIA

Haliacmon

SITHONIA

PALLENE

Imbros

Potidaea

Olympus M.

In preparation for a new campaign against Greece, Xerxes cut a canal through the isthmus of the peninsula of Chalcidice.

Fleet of Xerxes (480)

Macestus

EPIRUS

The Pass of Thermopylae was defended by about 7,000 Greeks commanded by the Spartan Leonidas. They were defeated after the Persians had circumvented them (through treachery of Ephialtes?) by an out-flanking movement (480). See Pl.103

Larisa ●

Tempe

Castanea

Persian fleet destroyed by a storm in 492.

Lemnos

Tenedos

Assus

Atarneus

Elaea

Cyme

Methymna

Mytilene

Lesbos

Phocaea

LYDIA

Sardes

Hermus

THESSALIA

Peneus

MAGNESIA

Sepias Pr.

The Greek fleet supporting the army at Thermopylae fought an indecisive battle with the Persians off Artemisium but had to retreat when the Persians had taken the Pass (480).

Ambracia ●

Anactorium ●

Leucas

Artemisium

Sinus Maliacus

Scyros

Chios

Chios

Erythrae

Clazomenae

IONIA

Colophon

Ephesus

AETOLIA

Thermopylae

PHOCIS

Crisa

Delphi

BOEOTIA

Chalcis

Eretria

Euboea

Maeander

Decisive defeat of the Persian army at Plataea in 479.

Sinus

Corinthiacus

Thebae

Plataeae

Marathon

Persian fleet destroyed at Mycale (479).

Samos

Mycale

ACHAIA

Sicyon

Megara

Athenae

Lade

Miletus

Didyma

CARIA

Cephallenia

ELIS

ARCADIA

Corinthus

Salamis

Piraeus

ATTICA

Aegina

Andros

Tenos

Samos

Olympia

Argos

Icaria

Zacynthus

PELOPONNESUS

Ceos

Myconos

Sporades

Cos

Halicarnassus

MESSENIA

Sparta ●

Eurotas

LACONIA

Cythnos

Delos

Cyclades

Seriphos

Confined in the narrow strait near Salamis, the Persian fleet was defeated in 480. What was left of it retired to Asia Minor by way of Mycale.

Siphnos

Paros

Naxos

Punitive expedition against Eretria and Athens under Datis (490)

Cnidus

Melos

Astypalaea

Rhodos

Cythera

Thera

Amorgos

Creta

BATTLE OF MARATHON 490 B.C.
see Pl. 94

marsh

(Vrana)

Plataeans

to Athens

Athenians

Persian fleet

Cynosura ('Dog's Tail')

20

BATTLE OF PLATAEA 479 B.C.
see Pl. 106

Thebae

Asopus

Erythrae

Plataeae

CITHAERON M.

Eleutherae

MEGARIS

ATTICA

22

BATTLE OF THERMOPYLAE 480 B.C.
see Pl. 103

Anthela

wall

Thermopylae

Trachis

CALLIDROMUS M.

OETA M.

21

GREECE IN THE PERSIAN WARS

Regions already conquered by Persia	×—×—× Route of the Persian fleet and army in 492
Vassal states of Persia	Route of the Persian fleet in 490
States at war with Persia	Route of the Persian fleet in 480
Neutral states	××××× Route of the Persian army under Xerxes in 480

Battles between Greeks and Persian

◄—▭ Persian army   ■ Greek army   ◠ Road

Ister

Callatis

THRACIA

Odessus

PONTUS EUXINUS

Iaxartes

MACEDONIA

Byzantium

Chalcedon

Propontis

Sinope

Phasis

Dascylium

Lesbos

MYSIA

Chalcis

Chios

LYDIA

PHRYGIA

Ancyra

Sardes

Trapezus

Cyrus

MARE CASPIUM

SOGDIANA

Eretria

Athenae

Sparta

Samos

Ephesus

Miletus

CARIA

Rhodos

PISIDIA

CAPPADOCIA

Halys

ARMENIA

Araxes

Oxus

Ochus

ARIA

Bactra

BACTRIA

CILICIA

Tarsus

Thapsacus

Arbela

Ecbatana

MEDIA

PARTHYAEA

Creta

Cyprus

Sidon

Tyrus

Damascus

Tigris

Euphrates

Babylon

Susa

SUSIANA

ARACHOSIA

By the conquest of Lydia (ca. 546), the neo-Babylonian Empire (539), and the west coast of Asia Minor, the Persians had founded an empire in a short time. They now came face to face with the Greek world. Darius I's project of conquering it was further stimulated by the Ionian revolt (500-494). After the death of Darius (486) Xerxes began preparations for a vast expedition.

LIBYA

Hierosolyma

ARABIA

BABYLONIA

Persepolis

PERSIS

SAGARTII

Efymander

Indus

Ammonium

Pelusium

Memphis

AEGYPTUS

Nilus

SINUS ARABICUS

SINUS PERSICUS

GEDROSIA

Thebae

23

THE PERSIAN EMPIRE

Boundary of the Persian Empire ca. 500 B.C.	
Royal Road	
Area of the Ionian revolt 500-494 B.C.	

produced sculptors and architects who built temples, it manufactured an attractive pottery and took part in the panhellenic festival at Olympia, where a Spartan was victorious in 628 B.C. But in order to maintain their independence and their sovereign position over the common people, the ruling class, the *Spartiatai*, who called themselves the Peers (*homoioi*), later found themselves constrained to transform their constitution and social structure into a more rigid system. A secret police was instituted, particularly to spy on the Helots. Trade was forbidden and foreign contacts ceased. Thus Sparta turned in upon itself and the whole of life was subordinated to producing fine soldiers in a completely militarised state.

When shortage of land made itself felt and the number of *kleroi* (the parcels of land cultivated by Helots for their Spartan masters) became too small, the Spartans adopted a policy of conquest. Unwilling to diminish the number of warriors, who had to live from these *kleroi*, by the sending out of colonies, they seized land from their neighbours. After a prolonged struggle they succeeded in conquering Messenia (→ 12, 67). But by thus increasing the number of their Helots they intensified the latent danger of a revolt, and in consequence the military preparedness of the Spartiatai had to be permanently maintained. They became professional soldiers, serving the state throughout their whole life. This in the long run rendered them incapable of any normal forms of cultural expression. Magistrates called ephors enforced this new discipline and gained great authority, holding kings and people alike in subjection to the immutable laws. The other Greeks regarded this isolated police-state, which Sparta became, with wonder, mingled with a certain respect. Such an institution, which sacrificed the liberty of the individual to the liberty of the whole, was in any case not entirely inconsistent with the Greek character.

The supremacy of Sparta was founded not on numbers but on quality. Later theorists even glorified this *eunomia*, this sovereignty of the law, and although not blind to the one-sidedness of the Spartan ideal spoke of this collective discipline with approval. In the sixth century, when the superiority of their professional soldiers became obvious, the Spartans united the entire Peloponnese under their hegemony. The weaker states were offered an alliance in which they retained full independence but had to promise to help Sparta in time of war and to accept its command. These terms entailed so many advantages that almost the whole Peloponnese became members of this league. Although only an assembly of all the allies could declare war, Sparta exercised a great influence upon its discussions and decisions. This league might seem to contain the seed of a Hellenic or at least a Peloponnesian-Dorian 'nation', and undoubtedly a sense of solidarity did develop among the Peloponnesians. But the principle of the hegemony in fact proved to be one of the greatest stumbling blocks in the way of Greek unification. Any real assimilation was prevented by the guaranteed independence of the allies and the unbridgeable gulf between the leader (*hegemon*) and the ally. A Spartan could never become a Corinthian nor a Corinthian a Spartan, for the difference of *polis*, which appeared to be unchangeable and founded in nature, forbade any absorption into a higher unit. It was nevertheless of the greatest importance that in time of danger a powerful bloc of states was united under trained and skilled leadership, at least so far as military matters were concerned.

While thus in Sparta the law guaranteed the unchangeableness of the state and the status of the citizens, in Athens (see Maps 13, 14, p. 30) the law became the guarantee of the citizens' right to liberty, that is, to responsibility and personal participation in governing the state.

From before 700 the city-state of Athens included the whole of Attica. Every inhabitant of Attica was an Athenian citizen. Until the sixth century Attica (→ 9) was an agrarian region, conservative and old-fashioned, such as for example Thessaly was and always remained. The coast was overshadowed by the trading city of Megara and the island of Aegina. Noble families held power and vied with each other for supremacy. But an economic crisis soon brought about changes. The small farmers and craftsmen (for example the potters) were threatened with extinction and rebelled against the existing state of affairs, and a situation developed which might allow a popular leader to set himself up as tyrant. In these critical conditions it was

decided to elect as archon for the year 594 B.C. a man with powers to arbitrate. The choice fell on Solon, a noble, a merchant, a poet, and a thinker. The people expected him to introduce cancellation of debts and redivision of the land, and with this in view they were prepared to accept him as head of the state under any title which he might choose. But he confined himself to introducing reforms which were intended to safeguard the rights of both the governing classes and the people. Measures were taken to alleviate existing abuses. Debts were reduced, the law of debt was made less harsh, enslavement as a means to settle a debt was forbidden for ever, the possession of large estates was rendered more difficult. The guarantee that these reforms should be permanent, however, lay in the political power which Solon conferred on the people. He published a code of laws, before which all men should have equal rights, and he enabled the people to defend their rights by establishing a new Council of 400, which gradually superseded the older aristocratic Council of the Areopagus, and by creating popular law-courts (*Heliaea*) where his code of laws could be administered by all the people. Though Solon was primarily seeking to give the people protection rather than political power, his reforms opened up the path to democracy.

It was evident that an élite must rule, but it was no longer based exclusively upon privilege of birth or rank but rather upon service to the state. The people were divided into four classes. The wealthiest class, which contributed the most to the state, held the most important offices. The second class was the Knights, who served their country as cavalry. The third comprised the citizens who served in the army as hoplites (heavy-armed infantrymen). The fourth class, those who owned little or no property, were allowed to vote but could not themselves be elected magistrates. Every magistrate, from the highest to the lowest, owed his authority to the choice of the people and must render account of his stewardship to them.

Such constitutional reforms could only be perfected by time. Much discontent remained, and a few years later Pisistratus, an able nobleman, succeeded in setting himself up as tyrant. He established his peasant supporters as small farmers, improved the city by new buildings, promoted art and culture, encouraged trade and industry, and weakened the influence of his rivals, the other nobles. His recension of the Homeric poems effectively preserved them for posterity in their present form. He retained the laws of Solon, but took care that he and his friends occupied key positions. Colonies were sent to the Hellespont, which lay on the vital corn route from Scythia to Greece. Athens flourished as never before. While Solon may be considered as the founder of Athenian democracy, Pisistratus was undoubtedly the founder of Athenian trade and sea power.

When he died in 527 his sons at first succeeded in taking over his firmly-established rule. But Hipparchus was assassinated in 514, and the oppressive measures of the other son, Hippias, aroused fresh opposition. He was expelled in 510 with the help of Sparta and the Delphic oracle. Clisthenes, the leader of the rebellion and a member of the powerful family of the Alcmaeonidae, introduced democratic constitutional reforms. He broke the power of the noble clans by reorganising the tribal system. This now comprised ten tribes which were artificially constituted so that each tribe included members from different parts of Attica; this prevented the domination of any local faction. He also reorganised the Council; it now consisted of fifty representatives from each of the ten tribes and became the lynch-pin of the whole constitution. Membership was open to every citizen over thirty years of age. Its main function was to render the Popular Assembly (*Ecclesia*) workable by preparing business for it; but it was also designed to control the magistrates. Thus the people were given authority over the executive power and it was made impossible for a single man to obtain excessive authority. Another check against would-be tyrants was the introduction of ostracism. By this institution anyone whom the citizens considered to be too powerful could be banished out of hand for ten years. It served later to settle conflicts between rival politicians by proclaiming as it were a vote of no-confidence against one of them. Although the chief magistracies continued to be reserved for the rich, the basis of a full democratic system was established and every citizen had a say in the government of his city.

The classical period

THE PERSIAN WARS
Up till the middle of the sixth century the Greeks had been able to develop undisturbed by foreign powers. After 600 the kings of Lydia began to reduce the Greek cities of Ionia to subjection. When Croesus king of Lydia was defeated by Cyrus of Persia in 546 these cities passed under Persian rule. The Persian Empire, which extended from the Indus to the Aegean, was consolidated and reorganised by King Darius (521–486). It formed a well-regulated system of provinces, linked by a network of roads with Susa

(see Map 23, p. 38), the court of the Great King, who in the eyes of the distant Greeks appeared as the supreme embodiment of earthly power and glory.

The Greek cities at first offered little resistance. The yoke of the Persians was light. They usually allowed their subjects to keep their own institutions and internal government so far as possible, while a link with so enormous a hinterland could have been profitable to the Greeks. The Phoenicians

56

57

56. In the fifth century B.C. Pindar wrote: 'Glorious Athens, shining and crowned with violets; renowned in song, bulwark of Greece, city of the gods.' In the period of its greatness (460-435) it was embellished by the care of Pericles with monuments of unsurpassed beauty. The photograph shows the city viewed from the hill of the Muses, 482 ft. high. In the centre, rising high above the surrounding city, stands the Acropolis with the Parthenon. Behind the Parthenon, and separated from it by a broad valley, lies Lycabettus, in ancient times outside the city, now its highest point (911 ft.), **57.** The southwestern side of the Acropolis; in the foreground the Agora, the centre of the classical city. The many public buildings, stoas, shops etc., have been excavated by the American School of Archeology. Part of the area was bought and a large number of modern houses were pulled down in order to expose the ancient ruins beneath.

58. The centre of Athens seen from the east. In the middle, the Acropolis; behind, the Agora and the temple of Hephaestus (1). On this side modern Athens has covered the site of the old city. The site of the temple of Zeus in Corinthian style (the Olympieum), first included in the city when the Emperor Hadrian extended its boundaries, has remained free (2). Sixteen columns some 56 ft. high give an idea of the majestic building that once stood here. Hadrian also built the gate named after him (3) which indicated the limits of the old and new city. **59.** The oval Acropolis surrounded by the wall dating from the time of Cimon, seen from above. The longest part of the rock is about 920 ft., the widest 230 ft. 1. Propylaea; 2. temple of Nike; 3. Erechtheum; 4. Parthenon; 5–6. Theatre of Herodes Atticus and Stoa of Eumenes, buildings from the Roman period; 7. modern museum containing many treasures found on the Acropolis.

by their privileged position as sea-carriers for the Empire achieved great prosperity, and similar opportunities lay open to the Greeks. Their ships rendered valuable services during the campaigns of Darius against Egypt and the Scythians, and some of their leaders won the king's favour. But the Ionians gradually became discontented. One of the main causes of rebellion was the fact that the Persians often supported local tyrants, who ruled their fellow-citizens with Persian help. Thus Persian rule meant their domination and the hated satrap of Sardes who kept them in power. Greece itself also may have felt threatened now that Persian power extended across the Hellespont into Thrace and Macedon.

In 499 B.C. Ionia revolted. The tyrants were driven out and Sardes was set on fire. Athens and Eretria half-heartedly sent a little help to the Ionians (see Map 22, p. 38). It transpired, however, that the rebels had little idea of the real might of Persia; they thought that they would be able to return immediately to the old life of free city-states. Feeble voices pleading for unity and organisation were ignored. So it is in no way surprising that when in 494 the full power of the Persian forces was exerted the disunited Ionians were crushingly defeated. Horror ran through the whole Greek world when the mighty city of Miletus was razed to the ground.

In 492 the satrap Mardonius advanced into Macedon, but the wreck of his fleet by a storm near Mount Athos (→ 100) prevented an attack upon Greece itself. In 490 a punitive expedition against Athens and Eretria crossed directly to Greece. Eretria was destroyed, but at Marathon the Persian army was defeated by the Athenians under the effective command of Miltiades (→ 94, 95; also Map 20, p. 38). The heavy-armed Greek hoplites proved superior to the Persian light infantry and bowmen (→ 93, 97ff). At one blow Athens had become the champion of Greece, with the right to share with Sparta the command in the new encounter by which it was obvious that the Persians would attempt to avenge their defeat. Only the death of Darius in 486 and the fact that his successor Xerxes had to deal with internal disturbances gave the Greeks ten years' respite.

Under the threat of approaching danger Athens and Sparta did little to unite or organise Greece. But in 483 the more far-sighted Themistocles persuaded the Athenians to devote the proceeds of some new silver mines to the construction of a fleet. He realised that the Persian menace could be overcome only by sea power. On the very eve of the renewed invasion the Greeks at last met to arrange their defence (481–480). Sparta naturally undertook the conduct of the war, and the Athenians accepted this decision for the sake of harmony, although their fleet was now the largest in Greece.

The Persian preparations were extensive: two bridges across the Hellespont carried the army to Europe, while a large fleet with provisions to support the army sailed along the coast. The long march by difficult roads was accomplished without any considerable losses. The traditional numbers of the Persian army are undoubtedly much exaggerated; but nevertheless it was the greatest force ever seen in Greece. Since the number of men that the Greeks could put into the field and the number of their ships were so small in comparison with the forces of the Persians, they had to try to make use of geographical features to counteract their weakness. They must try to force the Persian land army and navy to fight in narrow positions where their vastly superior numbers could not be fully used. They therefore sent their fleet to Artemisium in the narrow waters between northern Euboea and the mainland, while their land forces marched to the vale of Tempe. When, however, they found that it was impracticable to hold this position, the infantry retired to the pass of Thermopylae, a narrow plain between sea and hills (much narrower then than now). Here the Spartan king Leonidas attempted to check the advance, but was outflanked by the Persians (→ 103, 104; also Map 21, p. 38). The Spartans, who fought to the last man, were overwhelmed, and the Persian army could resume its advance southwards. In consequence the Greek fleet, which had fought with some success at Artemisium, was obliged to retire. Central Greece fell into the hands of the enemy.

Athens could not be held, and the population was therefore hurriedly evacuated, chiefly to the island of Salamis. The Greek fleet, which was now stationed at Salamis, could see the flames of the burning city. As Themistocles had foreseen and planned, the decisive battle was fought at sea. Autumn was approaching, and without the support of their fleet the Persians could not attack the Isthmus of Corinth, which was being fortified by the Peloponnesians. Xerxes therefore gave the order to attack the Greek fleet, which was blocking the way at Salamis. But the Greeks were not taken by surprise. The Persian fleet, which had approached under cover of night, was crushingly defeated in the narrow channel of the straits of Salamis (→ 105). This meant the failure of Xerxes' attempt to defeat Greece in a single campaign. He returned to Asia leaving his brother-in-law Mardonius with a strong army to finish the war. In the following year (479), however, after Mardonius had again ravaged Attica and Athens, the Peloponnesians took the field in full force. In a great battle at Plataea the allied Greeks defeated Mardonius, thanks largely to the leadership of the Spartan commander Pausanias and the courage of the Spartan soldiers (→ 106). Greece was saved and could now proceed to the offensive. At the same time a powerful attack on eastern Sicily by the Carthaginians was repelled at Himera by

Gelo, the tyrant of Syracuse. Thus the Greeks maintained their freedom also in the west. In the same year the Greek fleet began an attack on Ionia (479). The remains of the Persian fleet were destroyed at Mycale; the Ionian crews revolted, and opposition collapsed when the Greeks attacked by land. From Byzantium to Caria the coastal towns deserted from Persia, and the Persian garrisons were mopped up during the following years.

At the beginning this liberation of the Ionian Greeks had been conducted under the leadership of Sparta. But the authoritarian behaviour of Pausanias led the ephors to suspect that he was aiming at making himself tyrant, and it also aroused hostility among the Ionians. He was recalled, and Sparta abandoned the leadership of the naval war for which it lacked men and materials. The hegemony was transferred to Athens, who organised the coastal towns and islands into a league, the Delian Confederacy, with headquarters at Delos, in order to carry on the struggle against the Persians. The allies provided either ships or money for the maintenance of the land and sea forces of the league. Since this money was in practice at the disposal of the *hegemon*, who used it to maintain a permanent fleet under its own command, this meant that Athens soon dominated the league and became supreme at sea, as Sparta was on land.

Athens, hastily strengthened by Themistocles with massive walls and, under Pericles, linked with the port of Piraeus five miles away by the famous Long Walls, was safe so long as the navy kept the sea open for supplies, and it was determined to preserve its naval supremacy at all costs. When the Persian danger seemed less threatening some members of the league wished to resume their independent existence, but Athens refused to recognise the right of secession and reduced the deserters by force.

Thus within a few decades Athens grew to be the political and economic centre of the entire Aegean region. But once again the Greeks' deeply-rooted belief in the natural freedom of the city-state prevented any fusion into an Attic-Ionian nation. The allies counteracted any such tendency by struggling harder to free themselves from the Athenian yoke. The contrast was accentuated by the fact that Athens, unable to allow the allies equal rights, attempted to hold its satellites by ideological ties.

THE ATHENIAN DEMOCRACY

The power of Athens was founded on its navy, manned by oarsmen and sailors from the poorest classes, and its economy was based largely on trade and shipping. Thus the working class of the city and port developed into a powerful influence in the sovereign Popular Assembly, and the constitution was further democratised. Offices were declared open to all and even, for the sake of equality, filled by lot. One after another the prerogatives of the nobles were suspended. The ancient Council of the Areopagus lost all power. In order that the poor might take their part in public administration payment was given for the holding of office and later even for attendance at the Popular Assemblies. Only the office of commander in army and navy (*strategos*), for which obviously candidates had to possess special qualities, was still filled by election. These generals became the leading figures in democratic yet imperialist Athens, the trusted representatives of the people (*demos*) in the city and the upholders of Athenian supremacy over the allies.

The Athenians also encouraged democracy among their subject-allies, since they saw in this ideology a means of consolidating their control. And in fact in most of these cities the *demos* and the government based on it felt that their destiny was linked with the Athenian democracy, without which their own 'liberty' seemed endangered. On the other hand, the conservative elements turned more and more towards Sparta as the head of the conservative country states and their only saviour from the Athenian yoke and from what they called 'the domination of the populace'. Opposition was so strong that in a revolt against Athens even Persian help was not refused. Thus Greece began to split into two hostile camps.

So long as military command in Athens was retained by the conservative general Cimon, who called Athens and Sparta the yoke of oxen which together must draw the plough of Greece, peace was preserved. After his downfall the democratic noble Pericles came to power and retained the confidence of the people for thirty years. Under his guidance Athens reached its pinnacle of glory. But the latent rivalry with Sparta led to open conflict which dragged on indecisively for years and ended by both parties recognising each other's sphere of influence (445 B.C.). Thus the division in Greece was openly acknowledged.

Meanwhile the Delian Confederacy had fulfilled its function and *raison d'être*. It had been formed to secure effective defensive and offensive action against Persia. About 467 B.C. the allied forces under Cimon's leadership had defeated the Persian navy and land forces at the river Eurymedon in southern Asia Minor. Less successful was the attempt by Athens to help Egypt in its revolt against Persia: that led to serious naval losses (ca. 455). But Cimon, who meantime had been ostracised, returned to Athens in 451 and again led an expedition against the Persians which culminated in great naval and land victories off Salamis in Cyprus. In consequence Persia negotiated a peace, and thus the purpose of the Delian Confederacy had been gloriously vindicated.

Since Cimon died in the hour of victory, political leadership at Athens fell

60. Corinth, situated at a point favourable for trade, was one of the most important cities of Greece. It lay between two harbours on the Isthmus, linking the Peloponnese with the north. It controlled the dragging of ships across the Isthmus along a prepared way and had also the power to sever trade between north and south. Most of the original Greek city has disappeared. Only the temple of Apollo (1) dates from the 6th century: its seven heavy columns still dominate the ruins, most of which date from the Roman period. Caesar rebuilt the city one hundred years after it had been completely destroyed by Mummius; 2. basilica; 3. road to Lechaeum (→ 61); 4. spring of Pirene; 5. Julian basilica; 6, 7, and 8. various stoas; 9. the odeum hewn out of the rock; 10. theatre. **61.** The street leading from the centre to the port of Lechaeum. **62.** View of Corinth and the gulf from Acrocorinth; 1. temple of Apollo.

63

64

65 66

63. The landscape around Corinth is dominated by Acrocorinth (1,857 ft.), a steep rock with a flat top which from the earliest times formed the acropolis, the fortified citadel. Apart from a few stone blocks from a temple and a fountain, no classical ruins remain. The temple (1) was dedicated to Aphrodite, who was served by a thousand courtesans and priestesses living in the city. This gave Corinth the name of being one of the most immoral towns in Greece. **64-6.** Corinth was a centre of trade and industry. A number of votive plaques found in a temple of Poseidon, near Corinth, show scenes of the city's activity and reflect the importance of the pottery industry. **64.** Ship with earthenware jars. **65.** Miners at work in an open mine. One hacks the stone loose with a pick and others pass it up in baskets. In the middle an amphora hangs in a sling. **66.** Potter's oven filled with amphorae and other pots to be baked.

Argos, situated on the hill of Larissa and encircled by the river Inachus (now Panitsa), dominated the Argive plain. **70.** Modern Argos covers to a large extent the area of the classical city. **68.** The theatre of Argos (see circle on 69). **69.** Sparta lies on the broad, usually sluggish Eurotas. Along the bank still grow the reeds and rushes with which Spartan youths were flogged in the 'Contest of the Whips'. **71.** Tegea, a smaller town, possessed in the Doric temple of Athena Alea one of the largest sanctuaries in the Peloponnese. **72.** In eastern Arcadia lie the remains of Mantinea, which followed its own policy, especially in the Peloponnesian War. It was surrounded by a wall 15,000 ft. long, of which the foundations (foreground) still survive (→ 116-17). The photograph shows the acropolis. **67** (previous page). In the 4th century Messene was an important centre in the Peloponnese. The walls and towers of the city are well preserved (→ 111-12).

73. Lindus was the most important city in the island of Rhodes before the city of Rhodes was founded ca. 400 B.C. by three older cities. The rock upon which it is built, rising steeply from the sea – a striking example of the Greek acropolis – still bears magnificent ruins, including a temple and propylaea. **75.** In 407 B.C. Rhodes was founded by Lindus, Caminus, and Ialissus on the northern point of the island. The city prospered as participator and middleman in the commerce of the eastern Mediterranean. The photograph shows, left: the old city surrounded by a wall built by the Knights of St John; 1. probable site of the bronze colossus of Helios (the Sun-god) (90 feet high) standing upon a jetty which divided the harbour into two; 2. remains of the temple of Aphrodite dating from 3rd century B.C. **74.** Bench hewn from the rock upon which a 3rd-century artist has executed a trireme, a ship which was seen often in the city harbour. To the right begins the steep, heavily walled stairway which leads to the lofty acropolis of Lindus (→ 73).

73

74

75

Already in the 8th and 7th centuries B.C. the Greeks swarmed across the seas and founded many cities in coastal regions. **76.** Ephesus in Ionia was one of the earliest foundations. The site has been altered by alluvial deposits. The dotted line roughly indicates the former coastline. **77.** Of Metapontum (S. Italy) there remain ruins of a 5th-century temple. **78.** The acropolis of Cumae near Naples, the earliest Greek colony in Italy. **83.** Probable site of the fourth Sybaris in southern Italy. **79-82.** Beautiful coins were struck in Sicily. From Syracuse (**79-80**) with four-horse chariot and head of Arethusa. **81.** From Gela, with river god Gelas. **82.** From Naxos, with head of Dionysus. **84** (following page). Posidonia (Paestum), founded ca. 530 from Sybaris, flourished as a link between Magna Graecia and Etruria. 1. Temple of Ceres; 2. excavated parts of the city; 3. Roman forum; 4. temple of 'Neptune'; 5. 'basilica'; 6. gate and city wall. **85-6.** Metopes from temple of Hera near Paestum. **85.** Dancing girls. **86.** Hoplite.

85

86

Ca. 631 Dorian emigrants from the island of Thera founded Cyrene on the African coast. It developed into a large city and remained so up to the Roman period. It derived its prosperity from the export of silphium, a spice much used in Greek cooking. **89.** A 6th-century Spartan kylix gives a striking picture of this trade, showing the spice being weighed and loaded in the presence of King Arcesilaus of Cyrene. **87.** The city is partly excavated. 1. Greek agora with rectangular street plan; 2. theatre (not yet excavated); 3. Hellenistic Forum of Proculus (1st century A.D.); 4. temple of Isis; 5. part of the Sacred Way; 6. sanctuary and temple (7) of Apollo; 8. Greek theatre, transformed into amphitheatre. **88.** Western part of Cyrene with: 1. theatre; 2. temple of Apollo; 3. temple of Isis; 4. temple of Artemis. **90-1.** The 'Venus of Cyrene', dating from ca. 50 B.C. and found in the Thermal in 1913. The goddess has arisen from the sea (supported by a dolphin) and was probably shown wringing her wet hair.

to Pericles, who by his democratic reforms had already gained great popularity. His policy was to strengthen the power and extend the glory of his beloved city. If the allies could not be held by loyalty, they must be held by force. Thus the Delian Confederacy continued its existence as an Athenian empire, and Athens enforced stricter measures of control. One of these was the establishment of colonies of Athenian citizens (*cleruchies*) at strategic points, not least on the shores of the Propontis and Black Sea in order to safeguard the vital corn supply from this area. Athens must also be made a worthy capital of the empire, so that the unfortunate allies now saw their annual contributions, which they had sent for the maintenance of the common fleet against Persia, diverted by Pericles to a lavish building programme at Athens, which included the construction of the Parthenon, begun in 447. His policy towards the other Greeks also led to tensions. An attempt to build up a land empire in central Greece, which Athens had held in alliance for ten years, had failed (447), but Athenian interests were widespread: as already seen, Sparta was alienated, but Corinth also became increasingly anxious at the spread of Athenian power and not least of Athenian trade into markets which Corinth itself had hitherto dominated.

THE CULTURE OF THE FIFTH CENTURY

Whereas Greece appeared unable to achieve political unity, Greek culture although with some local divergences, developed a unity whose distinctive features were recognisable through the whole Greek world from East to West. This is the classic form which has left an indelible mark upon the culture of the West. The foreign influences to which Greece had been and still was subjected were entirely absorbed into the Greek pattern.

THE MONUMENTAL ARTS. In contrast to the sixth century, in which an Oriental influence can still clearly be detected, Greece after its victory turned to its own style in which ornament was completely subordinate to form and line.

The Athenian sculptor Phidias in his statues of Athena and of Zeus at Olympia created types which continued to be regarded as the personification of majesty and divinity. But beside statues of the gods sculptors tried now to represent the ideal man. Myron and Polyclitus created an image of the Athlete which became the ideal for the contest-loving Greeks. The remains of the Parthenon frieze (→ 55, 180), from the school of Phidias, are like an epic in marble. Each figure and each group is a masterpiece in itself, but they are linked together by the motif of the procession in honour of the goddess at the Panathenaic festival. This art is not one of quantity or supernatural size but of quality, perfect technique, a style which is firm yet allows great flexibility and freedom of composition, a whole which supports all its parts.

The prosperous Greek beautified his city and his gods rather than his house. From Sicily to the Black Sea temples arose in the new style (see Maps 17, 18, pp. 36, 37), of which there were two variants, the Doric and Ionic. The former was stiff and severe, the latter lighter and more graceful. This however is merely a difference of emphasis; the basic principles remain the same. Marble was used for the temple itself, gold, silver and bronze for the statues; and friezes and metopes, decorated in warm colours which have now faded, adorned the walls and façades. Yet what is moving about these buildings is not the materials or the magnificence but the beauty of line and proportion which still survives even in ruined temples from which the ornamentation has disappeared. There are splended ruins in Sicily and Italy (Paestum, → 84) and at Delphi (→ 145, 147, 153); but for the Greeks themselves their crowning achievements were the temples at Olympia (→ 161, 172) and on the Acropolis of Athens (→ 56-9, 174), where Ictinus built the Parthenon, embellished by Phidias, and Mnesicles adorned the entrance with the Propylaea. The architectonic beauty of the whole is striking, but for the Athenian it had an even greater significance. It was the dwelling-place of the tutelary goddess of the city, looking out over Salamis where she had granted her citizens the victory over Persia.

INTELLECTUAL CULTURE. Greek culture was still deeply religious. Everywhere — at Eleusis, Corinth, Delos, Delphi — the great temples surrounded by treasuries testified to the care lavished upon the cult of the gods (→ 101-2, 137, 151-4). For it was the cult, the sacred ceremony, and not a doctrine, which was the essence of Greek religion. The mysteries of Eleusis, in honour of the earth goddess Demeter, represented the annual death and rebirth of vegetation and the constantly renewed fertility of the earth. The

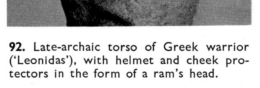

92. Late-archaic torso of Greek warrior ('Leonidas'), with helmet and cheek protectors in the form of a ram's head.

initiates took part in the ceremonies and were promised a better fate after this life. The mythological stories of the gods and heroes were little more than an imaginative game for the Greeks, who found a poetic explanation for every ancient traditional custom or practice, for every marvellous phenomenon that caught their fancy. Every poet was free to interpret the tales as he pleased and to choose from the countless variants the one which seemed to him most probable. Greek poets were never obliged to come into conflict with the traditional religion.

From this freedom of interpretation grew Attic drama. It developed from the Dorian custom of celebrating in chorus an episode from the life of a god or hero, with the leader of the chorus replying as soloist to the choral song. In Attica in the sixth century an 'answerer' was added, thus enhancing the dramatic effect. This addition of a second and later a third actor was the beginning of Attic drama. Every year, with modest accessories, three successive plays were produced at the festival of Dionysus in the theatre at the foot of the Acropolis. The subjects were still linked with the myths, but in the hands of the poet they took on a broader and deeper significance and extracted from the old grim tales of the heroes a more profound understanding of man and his fate. The work of the great Attic tragedians is dealt with in the chapter on Literature. Here we merely notice that one must not underestimate the culture of an entire population which, at the expense of the state, that is, by the will of the people themselves, could devote itself exclusively and untiringly to what in reality was not popular art but which must have exercised a deep influence upon opinion and thought.

Democracy is rule by discussion and persuasion through word and argument. Freedom of speech and thought became the characteristics of the progressive democratic part of Greece, in contrast with the conservatism which even in cultural matters remained peculiar to the aristocratic communities. The ever-changing circumstances of society and city government, for which tradition could provide no precedent, stimulated independent thought. A knowledge of the world became necessary to the Greeks. Geographical descriptions of foreign lands and peoples were already known in the Ionian cities during their most flourishing period. Customs, morals, origins and history, were all discussed.

But the great step towards real historical study was taken by Herodotus of Halicarnassus, who was the first to attempt to place an historical episode (in this case, the Persian Wars) within a coherent framework of cause and effect. His work is still primitive in construction, still naive in its attempt to explain and understand, but brilliant in its appreciation of the interconnection of events. It is true that the East also had produced chronicles. Israel in particular possessed an historical literature in which Jehovah's guidance of his people formed the basic theme. But Herodotus and his Ionian predecessors created history in the European sense. He sought the explanation and development of things in themselves and in their structure. He was the continuer not of the chronicle but of the epic. In his works there is a conscious opposition between Greek and barbarian, a contrast between liberty and compulsion, and the military superiority of Greece begins to arouse an awareness of general superiority.

The Greeks not only discovered the world but attempted to understand it. They were still willing to accept many forms of knowledge from the East, in particular mathematics and astronomy, and never disguised this source. But at the same time they extended their own systematic scientific enquiries. The rather naive attempts of the Ionian natural philosophers who, sometimes with brilliant intuition, had sought the 'first principle' were followed by that more mature reflection which follows fearlessly wherever reason leads. The Eleatic school, made famous by the philosopher Parmenides, regarded the universe as a unity, an undifferentiated sphere, and denied the existence of change. Heraclitus of Miletus, on the other hand, recognised no other reality than eternal change. Anaxagoras started a new line of enquiry by postulating the infinite divisibility of matter; he believed that things were moved by mind (*nous*). All this fermenting life and thought was increasingly concentrated in Athens during the age of Pericles, that period of wonderful intellectual achievement between 480 and 430 when all talent and progressive ideas met in the city that Pericles called 'the school of Greece'.

This departure from tradition, which arose from scientific and philosophic enquiry and appeared as an 'Enlightenment', attracted those who wished to keep intellectually up-to-date. It was disseminated by the Sophists, able and learned men who publicised the results of scientific investigations

93
94

95
96

The power of Greece only achieved its full development after the failure of the Persians to conquer it. Darius I opened the struggle against the Greeks; his court is depicted upon a magnificent Apulian vase (**95**). In the centre, Darius, with a sceptre in his right hand, a sword in his left, listening to a speech and protected by a bodyguard. Beside him are five Persian notables. Above, the gods who would protect Greece (Zeus with sceptre and thunderbolt, helmeted Athena, and winged Nike); on left, Artemis with hind and Apollo with swan; on right, a figure symbolising Asia. **93.** Persian archers confronted Greek hoplites. A 5th-century relief from Susa gives us a picture of the Persian warrior. The first great battle between the Persian forces and the citizen-soldiers of Athens and Plataea was fought on the plain of Marathon (→ 94). **96.** A burial mound there commemorates the fallen Athenians.

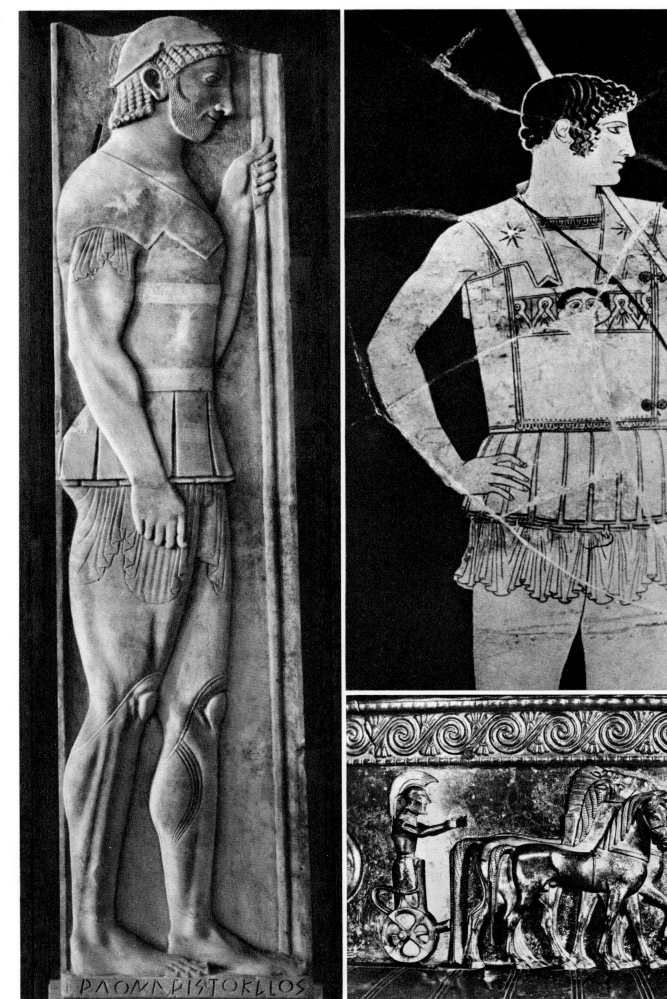

98

97
99

ΙΡΑΟΝΑΡΙSTOKLLOS

94 (Previous page). Aerial view of the battlefield of Marathon and environs: 1. the 'Dog's tail' (Cynosura), a small spit of land behind which the Persians anchored their fleet for protection from the wind and current. Hence they marched to the marshy plain. After hearing of the landing the Athenians occupied the hills on the southeastern side (2) and thence they marched against the Persians who had taken up position in the centre of the plain (3). The fallen Athenians, traditionally one hundred and ninety-two, were buried in a mound which still exists today (→ 96). Many preserved paintings and sculptures depict Greek soldiers and Greek military equipment. **97.** Greek hoplite with cuirass, greaves, and helmet, depicted upon the 'Aristion stele' found in an Attic burial mound. **98.** Soldier armed with spear; decoration of his armour includes a Gorgon's head. **99.** Greek hoplites on foot and in war chariots.

100

100. After the earlier catastrophe to the Persian fleet around the stormy south cape of the peninsula of Athos (still shunned by seafarers), Xerxes prepared for his campaign of 480 by mechanical works, including the cutting of a canal through the peninsula in order to avoid the cape. The existence of this canal, mentioned by Herodotus, was long doubted. It was however noticed that in the spring a strip of this isthmus showed a richer vegetation (the earth dumped into the canal was looser and thus more porous), and three hundred gold Darics were discovered in what was probably the canal bed. The photograph shows the peninsula viewed from the north. In the foreground the flat section with modern Nea Rodo. The canal probably crossed here. In the background, the abrupt peak (6,350 ft. high) near the tip of the peninsula, where a republic of monks (still semi-autonomous) has been established since the Middle Ages.
(For caption to following page see page 57.)

Marathon afforded a pause in the struggle. A new invasion under Xerxes in 480 brought the opponents face to face in the pass of Thermopylae, and the Greeks, consisting mainly of a Spartan army under Leonidas, suffered defeat. Thereupon the Persians captured Athens itself. **103.** The pass of Thermopylae, now considerably enlarged by alluvial deposit; the dotted line shows the approximate position of the ancient shore line. 1. 'Burial mound of Leonidas'; 2. warm springs from which the pass derives its name. **104.** The Persians owed their victory to treachery. They were informed of a path over Mount Callidromus by which they could circumvent the Greeks. Probable position of the path. **105.** The struggle was decided in favour of Greece at the naval battle of Salamis. The narrow strait seen from the place where Xerxes probably watched his defeat. **106.** The Persian general Mardonius was later defeated at Plataea; this completed the Greek victory. The battlefield near the city, with remains of walls.

107
108

109

Friezes from the Treasury built by the inhabitants of the once rich island of Siphnos (→ 4) ca. 530 B.C. in the sanctuary of Apollo at Delphi. They give a striking illustration of the Greek method of waging war. The artists of these reliefs chose their subjects from the struggle between gods and giants, the latter being represented as hoplites. **101** (on page 55). Detail from north frieze. Strikingly illustrates the force which these classical artists could impart to their work. The relief shows a hoplite, who has retained only his helmet, struggling with a lion. **102.** Another detail: Apollo and Artemis pursuing a heavily-armoured, fleeing hoplite. The hoplite is protected by a helmet, cuirass, and round shield; his weapons are spear and sword. **107–9.** Other fragments from the same series. **107.** Group of giants. **108.** Giants with the goddess Athena. **109.** Horses yoked to the chariot of the Dioscuri on the occasion of the carrying off of the daughters of Leucippus. The whole of this small Ionic temple is of great interest in exemplifying the transitional style of the period (→ 153).

FORTIFICATIONS AND FORTIFIED TOWNS

Wars among the Greek city-states led many cities to protect themselves by erecting defence works and fortifications at strategic points. A number of these military constructions have survived the centuries and give a good idea of the Greek defence systems. **110.** In the narrow pass of the Cithaeron range, on the road from Eleusis to Thebes, still lie the extensive ruins of the fort of Eleutherae. Eight solid towers, probably built in the 4th century, survive on the north side. **111.** At the foot of the fortifications on Mt. Ithome in the Peloponnese still stand the remains of the walls which transformed Messene into a redoubtable stronghold in the 4th century (→ also 67). The walls (**112**) are constructed in an extremely skilful manner. **113.** At Aegosthena on the Gulf of Corinth fifteen towers and a large section of the wall have been preserved. It was a fortified resting place for travellers from the Peloponnese to the north (→ for site, see also 10).

in lectures and classes and who thus became the founders of all later higher education. They attracted many young men from the upper classes as pupils who listened eagerly to their teachings. They taught the art of debate and triumphantly denounced traditional conceptions as mere convention, proposing new standards and ideas based upon pure reason. This teaching naturally provoked a fierce reaction from older and more conservative Athenians, who maintained that the Sophists were teaching the young to see everything upside down. And in truth this teaching was extremely dangerous, despite its undeniable merits such as the diffusion of general knowledge and the arts of rhetoric and sound reasoning. For whenever the theory of the Sophists was put into practice it soon looked as if the only true human motives were selfishness and love of pleasure, while the formal training in argument and oratory could be used to cloak cynicism and immorality in the garb of simplicity and reason, not least in political matters.

While public opinion sometimes reacted by condemning and banning the Sophists as a threat to public morals — measures which naturally had little effect — a man arose in Athens who recognised the danger and sought to combat it by rational means. This man was Socrates. He agreed with the Sophists that common opinion and tradition are often confused and conflicting, but at the same time he maintained that they are not completely arbitrary. By closely questioning his fellow-citizens he tried to penetrate to general truths, the ideas which are the basis of these beliefs. In his view standards of conduct should be deduced from general conceptions of right and wrong, just and unjust, ugly and beautiful, true and false, rather than from the natural impulses of the individual. He was firmly convinced that no one does wrong of his own free will but only through ignorance. Even though the people considered him as a Sophist *par excellence*, who dared to criticise everything, including their beloved democracy, he nevertheless provided the foundations for the Greek answer to the scepticism of the Sophists.

This stormy development was reflected in political life, in debates in the Council and Assembly, in the problems discussed by the dramatists in the theatre, in the daring theories of the philosophers, in the success of the Sophists — in short in the whole pattern of Greek thought, which in its maturity attempted to base life upon a foundation of reason.

CRISIS AND CATASTROPHE

The philosopher Heraclitus said truly that struggle is the father of all things. In nearly every field the conflict of opinions gave birth to more just conceptions. But in politics the radical spirit of the Greeks, their dislike of compromise and their stubborn clinging to what they regarded as natural right, had catastrophic results. In the age of Pericles itself Greece was divided into two ideologically opposed camps. The democratic cities joined Athens, the oligarchical cities sided with Sparta, while within nearly every city a minority, whether of democrats or oligarchs, opposed the dominant group. The clash came in 431 with all the ferocity which usually accompanies ideological struggles in which war is linked with civil tensions.

A quarrel between Corinth and its colony Corcyra, with an appeal by the latter to Athens for help, and the revolt from Athens of another Corinthian colony, Potidaea, precipitated the outbreak of the Peloponnesian War (431-404), which Pericles had foreseen and against which he had built up Athenian resources. Since Athens was not strong enough to risk a pitched battle against the combined land forces of the enemy, the strategy which Pericles advocated was for the population of Attica to withdraw behind the strong walls of Athens when the Peloponnesian army invaded Attica, which it proceeded to do every summer, and then to use the Athenian fleet to deliver a series of counter-blows. Thanks to its supremacy at sea Athens held its own against the enemy in the first part of the war, which lasted ten years. But in 430 Athens suffered an unexpected blow: a severe plague struck the over-crowded city and in the course of three years carried off about a third of the population. Pericles, himself a victim, died in 429. This loss proved irreparable: no other *strategos* ever succeeded as he had done in winning and holding the confidence of the people.

The Assembly now often ignored the *strategoi* who held the executive power and allowed itself to be swayed by irresponsible demagogues who proposed all sorts of wild plans and attributed their failure to the treachery of those charged with their execution. While attempts of the allies to revolt were crushed by force, the democracy changed from a system of organised confidence to a system of organised distrust which punished any opposition with senseless vindictiveness. Athens showed much energy in military operations, but leaders like Cleon failed to give the steady direction which Pericles had shown. The revolt of Mitylene was crushed with great severity; some successes were gained in Aetolia, and the seizure of Pylos provided a useful base of operations in the Peloponnese itself and led ultimately to the surrender of some Spartan troops; but the failure of an attempt to win back Boeotia and the successful revolt of Amphipolis, turned Athens to thoughts of peace. This was concluded in 421, but it was in reality little more than a truce. A renewal of hostilities was brought about largely by the activities of the extremely capable leader Alcibiades, who succeeded in gaining the people's enthusiastic support for his far-reaching and

ambitious plans. In 415 he won the assent of the Assembly to a great expedition against Sicily, undertaken in the hope of extending the power of Athens over Syracuse and the western Greeks. During his absence his enemies succeeded in arousing the suspicions of the people, and he was recalled. Instead of returning to Athens to be sentenced by the popular court, he fled to Sparta and urged more active prosecution of the war against Athens. With help from Sparta the Sicilian expedition was foiled: the commander Nicias failed to obtain the people's permission to withdraw, and in consequence the army and fleet were destroyed.

On the advice of Alcibiades the Spartans now proceeded to occupy the mountain fortress of Decelea in Attica. Athens was thus permanently threatened from the land side, and thousands of slaves went over to the enemy. The heaviest blow, however, was that Sparta with the help of Persian money built a fleet which assisted the discontented allies of Athens in Asia Minor to revolt. In Athens itself democracy began to totter after the Sicilian catastrophe, and an oligarchic *coup d'état* had a temporary success. But soon the energy of the people awoke anew; the oligarchs were overthrown and the war was continued. Alcibiades, who was unwilling to remain as an exile in Sparta, by skilful intrigue finally negotiated his return to Athens. Under his leadership some important successes were obtained. But the Persian prince Cyrus, who had been sent to Asia Minor with unlimited resources, was won over by the Spartan Lysander, who began to wear down the Athenian fleet. When Alcibiades saw that victory was impossible he again went into exile. The Athenian fleet gained one more victory, at Arginusae in 406; the victorious generals, however, were condemned to death by the people on a charge of neglecting to rescue some shipwrecked crews. In 405 the last Athenian fleet was attacked and destroyed by Lysander at Aegospotami. In the following year the city itself, besieged by land and sea, was forced to capitulate. The Delian Confederacy was dissolved; the walls of Athens were pulled down; the fleet was handed over; and the democracy was abolished.

The material and spiritual damage caused by this thirty years' war was incalculable. The old tradition by which Greek was bound to Greek by a certain tacit understanding disappeared for ever. Treachery and corruption were rife, and mercenary soldiers, who had appeared during the war, became a potential menace. With the help of such mercenaries Dionysius succeeded in setting himself up as tyrant of Syracuse, where he maintained an oppressive rule over his Greek subjects while carrying on a successful war against the Carthaginians.

In Greece Sparta was now the undisputed leader. In victory the Spartans proved brutal, tyrannical, and corrupt, and the former allies of Athens soon realised that they had merely exchanged the Athenian dominion for the harsh and arbitrary rule of Sparta. In 401 the Spartans had supported the attempt of their ally Cyrus to usurp the throne of Persia. This and their obligations to the Asiatic Greeks led them into war with Persia. At the same time a new conflict arose in Greece, for Corinth, Argos, and Thebes, supported by Persian money, used this opportunity to take up arms against Sparta. Athens, where the democracy had been restored, allied itself with them and rebuilt its own city walls. This action compelled Sparta to abandon the campaign in Asia Minor. In Greece neither side gained a decisive advantage. At length the Spartans abandoned the pretence of fighting for the freedom of the Greeks: in order to regain the favour of the Persian king they sacrificed the Ionians to Persia. Thus in 387 the Persian king was able to dictate the 'King's Peace': all Greek cities were to be free, or in other words powerless, and Sparta was to ensure the enforcement of this decree.

Until 378 the Spartans succeeded by means of brute force in repressing all opposition and any attempts by groups of cities to form new leagues for their self-defence. The reaction, however, became too strong. In 378 Thebes, which had been seized by the Spartans, expelled the occupying garrison; Athens joined the movement and formed a new Maritime League which was directed against Spartan oppression. After failing to defeat their enemies in battle, the Spartans tried to break the coalition by making peace with Athens and recognising the Maritime League, in the hope of preserving their own hegemony on land. But Thebes, though now isolated, continued the struggle, led by the brilliant general Epaminondas, and destroyed the Spartan army at Leuctra in 371. The Arcadians and Messenians rebelled, the Peloponnesian League collapsed, and Sparta's power was permanently crippled.

Thebes, however, did not long retain the leadership of Greece. After the death of Epaminondas in battle against the Spartans at Mantinea in 362 (→ 116, 117), it concluded peace and remained the strongest power in central Greece but hated by its neighbours, whom it held in severe subjection. Nor were the Athenians more successful in regaining their authority permanently. When they showed themselves inclined towards the old imperialism the allies rebelled in 357 and with Persian support held their own against the efforts of the Athenians to retain their supremacy. Thus the attempts to establish order in the world of city-states through the hegemony of one of them — Athens, Sparta, Thebes — had all failed. In the endless struggle Persian gold turned the scale. Only the fact that King Artaxerxes III had his hands full in reducing a widespread rebellion of the satraps,

114. Aegosthena provides a striking example of the external aspect of a small Greek city hidden behind heavy walls. **116-7.** Mantinea in the Peloponnese occupies a distinctive place in Greek civic architecture by reason of its circular plan. Nine gates probably gave access to nine roads to the city centre. The city was destroyed, and nothing survives except the foundations of the walls (→ 72), whose course and one hundred and twenty-six towers can still be distinguished, and some remains in the centre, including those of the agora, of temples, and of a theatre. In 362 B.C. a battle was fought near the city, at the foot of Mt. Skopi (see arrow), in which the great Theban commander and statesman Epaminondas, although victorious, lost his life. **115.** The walls of Posidonia (modern Paestum) in Magna Graecia (→ also 85), which are partly Greek, also give an impression of the appearance of a Greek city.

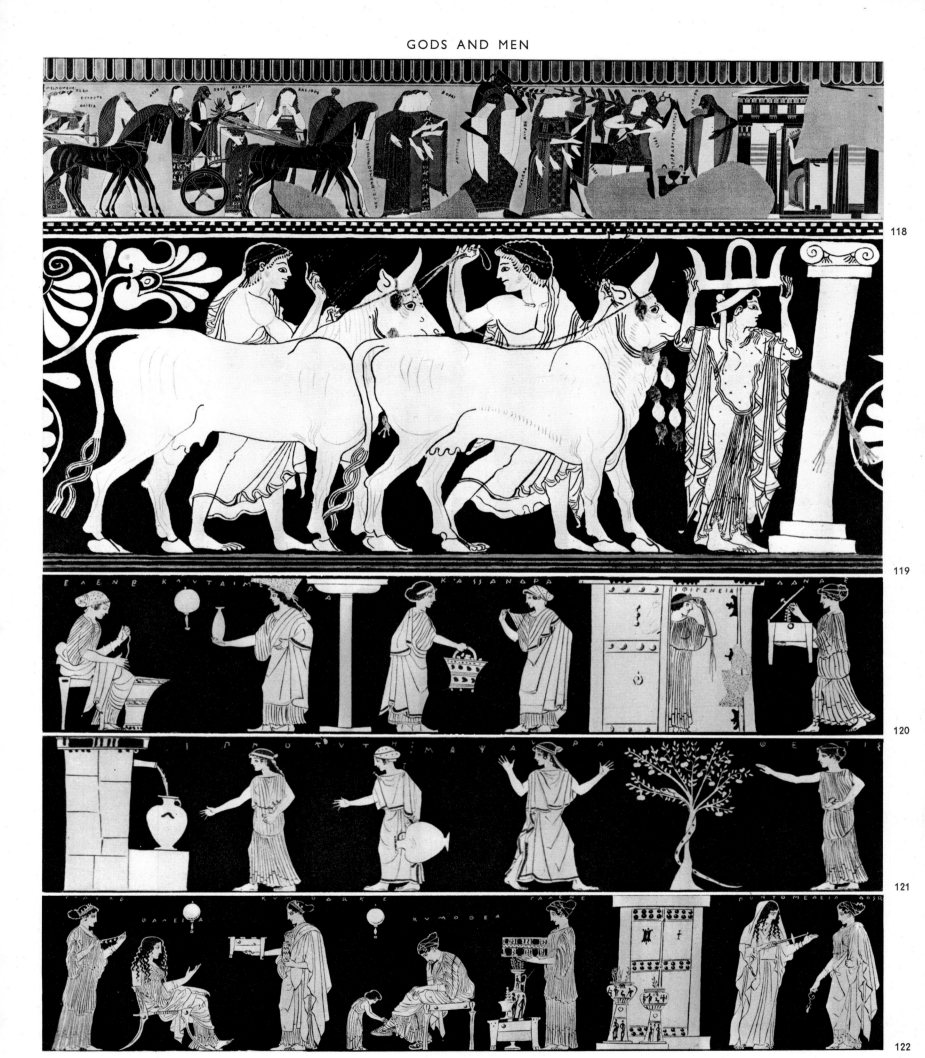

Public worship played a great rôle in Greek life. **118.** The border of a mixing-bowl shows, left to right: Zeus, the supreme god, with his wife Hera in a chariot surrounded by Muses; three of the Hours, goddesses of the seasons; Dionysus, god of wine and of many festivals; Hestia, goddess of the household hearth; Chariclo; Demeter, goddess of the fertile earth; Iris, messenger of the gods; the centaur Chiron; Peleus, the father of Achilles (for details on the gods see Map 24). **119.** Procession of cattle decked with garlands towards a place of sacrifice indicated by an Ionic pillar. **120-2.** Scenes from daily life. **120.** Women in a house with a court with Doric columns; to the right, a girl, winding a fillet about her head, stands in a doorway. **121.** Women with vessels by a fountain. **122.** Womens' quarters: ladies at toilet, having their hair attended to and being dressed. Two vases upon tall bases stand before a closed door.

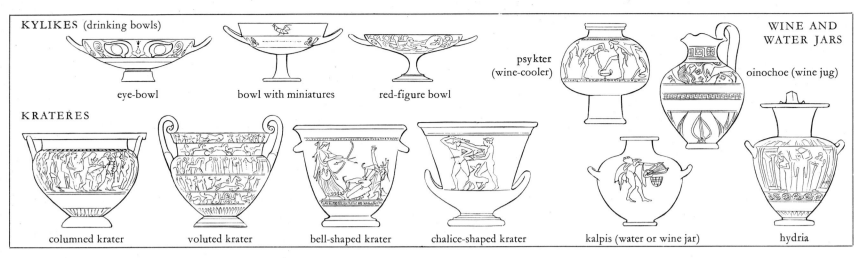

KYLIKES (drinking bowls)

eye-bowl · bowl with miniatures · red-figure bowl

psykter (wine-cooler)

WINE AND WATER JARS

oinochoe (wine jug)

KRATERES

columned krater · voluted krater · bell-shaped krater · chalice-shaped krater · kalpis (water or wine jar) · hydria

which had broken out under his weak predecessor Artaxerxes II, appeared to stand between Greece and complete subjection.

The situation in the West was not dissimilar. The Greek cities, divided among themselves, were unable to resist the invading Italian tribes, and Sicily seemed destined to fall into the hands of the Carthaginians. It was saved by the tyrant Dionysius of Syracuse, but only at the cost of the liberty of the Greeks. There was a remarkable interlude when after the death of Dionysius (367) his successor Dionysius II, under the influence of his brother-in-law Dion, called upon the philosopher Plato to assist in drawing up a just constitution. The project failed on account of the tyrant's mistrust of Dion, whom he banished. Dion returned and expelled Dionysius, but was himself assassinated for his attempts to realise an aristocratic ideal. Sicily remained in chaos until Timoleon, a Corinthian general, expelled the tyrants in 345, defeated the Carthaginians, and then (an unusual act for a Greek) laid down his power and restored the democracy. Yet after his death internal struggles broke out again until another tyrant, Agathocles, united the Greeks in the West for self-defence against Carthage. Meantime in Italy the Greek cities were hard pressed by the hill tribes in their hinterland and only the rich city of Tarentum preserved its independence by employing Greek mercenaries against the Lucanians and Samnites.

The Greeks themselves were dimly aware that the suicidal conflicts which ravaged Greece were a struggle for subsistence (*trophe*), and they complained of over-population. Wandering groups of mercenaries and robbers plagued the cities and became the willing tools of tyrants. It was fortunate for Greece that the professional soldiers, trained in the continuous wars, were in demand as objects of export, desired both by the king of Persia and by the rebellious satraps; typical of these were the Ten Thousand whose adventures were recorded by Xenophon.

The ravages of war were accompanied by a development in the economic situation, which though it did not produce an actual crisis nevertheless increased the tension. It has been observed (see page 34) that Greece owed its prosperity to its position as a border state and an exporter of high-grade articles. But by the dissemination not only of these products but also of the Greeks themselves around the shores of the Mediterranean it indirectly exported its techniques. This is usually considered as the beginning of the Hellenisation of the world, the glorious expansion of Hellenic culture over Western Europe. In Gaul, Thrace, southern Russia, and above all Italy the native tribes began to imitate Greek techniques and culture. On the other hand, the development of native production obviously encroached upon the markets of Greece, which began to lose its lead. This competition for a shrinking market was a significant factor in the internal struggles of Greece. Some political thinkers began to advocate the adoption of a leader, either a city as *hegemon* or a strong man who would restore order and unity so that a united Greece might attack and seize land and property from the old enemy Persia. Tyranny had already been established in Sicily, and in Greece similar aspirations were aroused in ambitious minds.

The remarkable thing is that it was not the former enemies, Persia and Carthage, who profited by the failure of the city-state world. In the West, still unnoticed by the Greeks, sharp-sighted though they were, the Roman republic in Italy was developing into a power which after 300 would overshadow the Greek world. In the East it was the kings of Macedon who suddenly appeared upon the scene and in a few short years changed the course of Greek history.

THE NEW POWER: MACEDON

Macedon had close connections with Greece from the earliest times. The ruling house was even considered to be Greek, that is, it was accepted as non-barbarian. The feudal structure which had existed in Greece in the eighth century survived in Macedon. The warlike aristocracy, led by a king as *primus inter pares*, lived in a perpetual state of internal feuds and external wars against the neighbouring Thracians and Illyrians. The coast was in

the hands of the Greeks, in whose struggles the king from time to time could play a part as a valuable ally. Greek technicians, scholars, and poets were welcome at the court in Pella.

About 360 B.C. the little kingdom faced a difficult situation. The king had been killed in the war against the Illyrians and his son was a minor; his nephew Philip, himself little more than twenty, acted as regent. He had been sent to Thebes as a hostage and had made acquaintance with Greek culture and, even more important, with the military reforms and tactics of Epaminondas. Now he began energetically to modernise his backward country. The Macedonian nobility was transformed into a well-trained heavy cavalry; the militia of farmers and shepherds, armed in the Greek manner, were organised in the Macedonian phalanx, which soon became famous. In this way those very elements which had rebelled against royal authority were pressed into service, and their warlike spirit was turned against external enemies. Above all, Philip discovered among his Macedonians the talented commanders who were capable of handling the weapon which he had forged.

The Illyrians and Thracians were defeated and the Thracian gold mines fell into Philip's hands; these provided him with a treasure which was to be the foundation of his diplomacy. The war between the Greek allies gave him the opportunity of taking the coastal towns under his protection. In 356 the heir to the throne was pushed to one side and Philip was recognised as king by army and people. A pretext for interfering in the affairs of Greece was afforded by the so-called Sacred War between Phocis and Thebes for the possession of the sanctuary at Delphi. The Phocians, their forces augmented by mercenaries whose wages were paid from the temple treasures of Delphi, conquered parts of Thessaly. When the Thessalians called upon Philip for help he repelled the Phocians and was elected generalissimo (*tagos*) of Thessaly. Next Olynthus, the last free Greek city in the north, long deceived by feigned friendship, was attacked and destroyed. Greece suddenly became conscious of being bounded on the north by a power which stretched from Thermopylae to the Hellespont.

Some of the Greeks saw in an alliance with the Macedonians an advantage for themselves and their cities; this was the view of the Athenian orator and politician Aeschines. Others, especially the intellectuals whose spokesman was the orator Isocrates, hoped to find in Philip the strong man who would bring peace and unity. Another Athenian orator, however, Demosthenes, realised that Philip constituted a great danger to Greece and to what the Greeks called liberty. By all the force of his oratory he tried to rouse his fellow-citizens to resist with all the means at their disposal and to end all quarrels among themselves. Athens indeed was already at war with Philip because of his occupation of the coastal towns; but the citizens were unable to appreciate the importance of this frontier struggle. The assistance which Demosthenes had advocated should be given to Olynthus was insufficient and sent too late.

In 346 a peace was concluded by which Philip's conquests were recognised. But when he extended his triumphal progress to Thrace and by occupying Phocis gained a foothold in Greece itself, the Greeks became alarmed. Demosthenes moved heaven and earth to effect an alliance of all the Greeks and at last succeeded in bringing about an agreement between Athens and Thebes. In 340 Philip attacked Byzantium, but the Athenian fleet appeared in time and compelled him to abandon the siege. He then turned against Greece itself. In 338 the forces of the Thebans and Athenians were decisively defeated at Chaeronea, thanks largely to the brilliant action of Philip's young son Alexander. Thebes was obliged to capitulate and received a Macedonian garrison; Athens, an impregnable fortress so long as the harbour remained open (and Philip had no fleet of any importance), prepared to resist, but was offered conditions so favourable that it submitted to Macedonian supremacy.

Under the leadership of Philip Greece was given a federal constitution. Meeting at the Isthmus of Corinth, the cities formed a new League in order

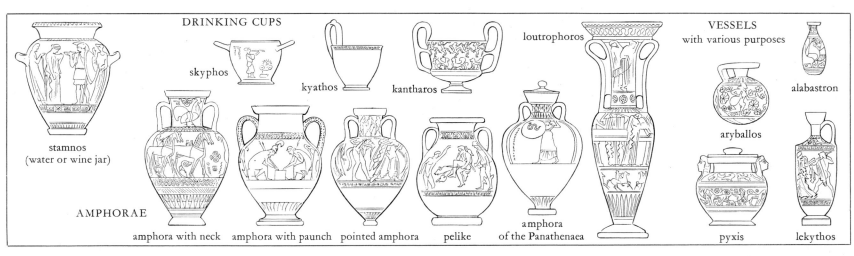

DRINKING CUPS

skyphos

kyathos

kantharos

loutrophoros

VESSELS
with various purposes

alabastron

aryballos

stamnos
(water or wine jar)

AMPHORAE

amphora with neck   amphora with paunch   pointed amphora   pelike

amphora
of the Panathenaea

pyxis   lekythos

to maintain peace among themselves. Philip was chosen as *hegemon*. Only Sparta refused to join; but it had become too unimportant for this to have any significance. The rôle of the independent city-state was now played out.

THE CULTURE OF THE FOURTH CENTURY
The background of the political and economic crisis of the fourth century was a radical alteration in Greek intellectual life. Statesmen were no longer servants of their city but were actuated more strongly by personal ambition. The popular assemblies and governments increasingly sacrificed traditional standards to their own sometimes short-sighted interests which rejected any scruples as old-fashioned. Personal questions had already occupied a prominent place in the work of the youngest of the great tragedians, Euripides. The teachings of the Sophists had also dangerously stimulated individualism. These trends had confused the political life of Greece. In the intellectual field the conflict of opinions promoted feverish activity and many-sided achievement.

ART. Sculpture maintained the technically perfect standard set by artists such as Phidias and Polyclitus. The subjects also remained the same. Sculptors continued to depict gods and heroes. But their aim was no longer the representation of the divine and superhuman but the expression of all that was essentially human, of beauty and grace. The Aphrodite of Praxiteles is no longer the goddess but perfect beauty in the form of woman; his Hermes is no longer the god but the enchanting early grace of youthful manhood (→ 179). Human beings too were now immortalised in marble and bronze, although in a stylised and idealised form. Lysippus became the great master of this form of portraiture; he was the only artist whom Alexander the Great judged worthy to make a statue of himself. Only fragments have been preserved of what appears to have been the most important building of the century, the Mausoleum of Halicarnassus, the monument erected to the memory of Mausolus king of Caria, which was decorated by the most famous artists of Greece. Its construction reflects the favour which this humanistic trend in art had begun to find farther East.

Contemporaries considered the paintings of Zeuxis and Apelles as in no way inferior to the works of the sculptors; owing to the fragile nature of the material none of these paintings has been preserved. Later imitations, in wall-paintings and mosaics, are only a poor reflection of the skill of the artists, but they show that they were well acquainted with the problems of perspective and composition.

LITERATURE. This changed mentality is even more evident in the written heritage. The work of Herodotus, the Father of History, was continued by the Athenian Thucydides, who described the Peloponnesian War in which he himself had taken part. Yet here the conception of history has completely changed. It is no longer a gripping narrative but a razor-sharp analysis based upon critical treatment of his sources. In this new historical method the unreliability of tradition is fully recognised; but this leads not to scepticism but to an attempt to arrive at some guarantee of truth through critical selection and strict reasoning. Xenophon, another Athenian, is at his best when describing his own adventure, the march of the Ten Thousand, but he also wrote the history of his own time (down to 362), reminiscences of his teacher Socrates, and even a romanticised biography describing the youth and education of Cyrus of Persia. His entire work shows him as a man who has broken through the confines of his city-state and who takes an interest in the rôle and training of rulers.

The political and social life of Athens is reflected in the works of the Attic orators. There we see how the weapon forged by the Sophists, the trained and skilful use of argument, attained its highest degree of perfection in the law courts and Assembly. The pamphlets of Isocrates provide a commentary upon fifty years of Greek history, and the passionate clinging to the ideal of the city-state finds its highest expression in the speeches of

Demosthenes (the *Philippics* or 'orations against Philip'), in which he defends his policy and attacks his enemies.

PHILOSOPHY. The Ionian natural philosophers had questioned the traditional ideas of the nature of the world. Their successors, the Eleatic school and Heraclitus, had posed the problem of the underlying causes of phenomena. The Sophists had introduced these revolutionary ideas into the education of the young, with disastrous results. Now that the traditional standards were no longer accepted, Greece looked for a new philosophy based upon reason.

Socrates had pointed the way to this. He had constantly sought for generally applicable principles which lie at the heart of human opinion underneath all confusion and error. The man who subjected everything to critical analysis and was the friend and guide of Alcibiades was considered an arch-Sophist by the people and in 399 was accused of refusing to honour the gods of the state and of corrupting the youth. He was condemned to death and executed, since he refused to take advantage of the opportunity to escape contrived for him by his friends. His death, which was as it were the test of his life and teaching, served only to confirm his influence upon his pupils, who continued in his footsteps.

The greatest of these was Plato, both a thinker and a splendid writer, who built up the critical method of his master into an all-embracing philosophical system. This he did by discussions in the Academy which he founded and by a series of incomparable written dialogues in which Socrates is represented discoursing with his friends and opponents. Seeking for generally valid conceptions as Socrates had done, he found them in the world of Ideas, the spiritual world which governs what to us is the world of reality. The soul, which proceeds from this world, derives from it the eternal knowledge which should dominate life and all activity if man is to develop his true nature and being and thus achieve happiness. Once man has contemplated these Ideas by his own intellectual effort, he can draw from them the rules for his own life and for that of the community, just as the mathematician develops his propositions directly from recognised axioms. By this doctrine Plato became the father of all idealist philosophy in the West.

In his great work, the *Republic*, subtitled 'On Justice', he plans a model community in which justice would reign. In this community each would do his part, that is, fulfil that task for which he is most fitted by nature. The mass of the people, who cling to material things, would pursue their function in order and peace, protected by the Guardians, an élite trained to lead and entirely devoted to the interests of the community. These Guardians would be allowed neither family nor possessions, these being the greatest incentives to selfishness. Property would be held in common and men and women live together in a free community. Children would be educated by the state without ever knowing their parents. Thus Plato hoped to breed a race of supermen who would support his system. Among them would arise the true sage, the philosopher-king, who would perceive the fulness of truth and by virtue of this insight would possess absolute authority and embody the living law. In a later work, the *Laws*, Plato makes the concession that if such truly wise men cannot be found or trained their function must be taken over by a comprehensive system of laws. This undoubtedly totalitarian system has been called a Utopia and has often been regarded as a purely artificial construction. It does indeed embody traces of the ancient Greek aristocratic ideas. But it is much more than a Utopia. It is the logically thought-out conclusion as to the governing of a community drawn from one infallible principle, the right of the expert to govern, which was for Plato an axiom, derived from his Greek milieu.

Plato's critical philosophy continued to be taught in the school which he himself founded, the Academy. His most gifted pupil, Aristotle, however, struck out in a different direction. After having acted as tutor to Alexander the Great, he founded the Lyceum in Athens and in it expounded his doctrine, which came to be called the Peripatetic. He took the teaching of Plato

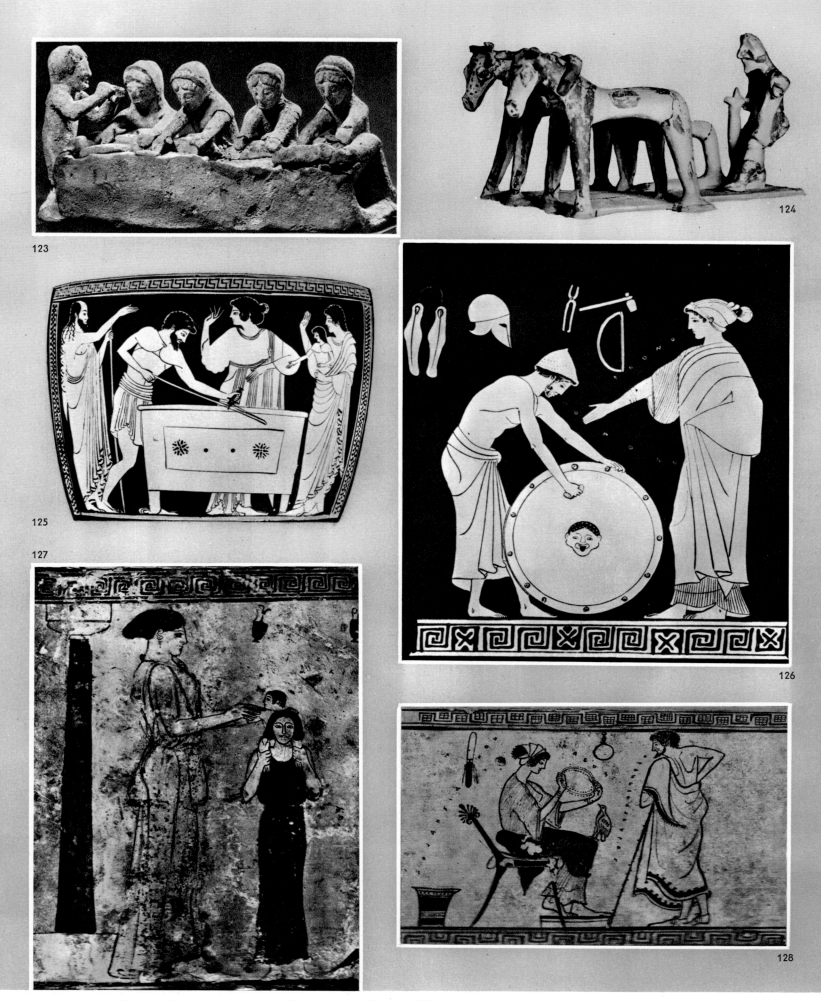

Two terracottas from Boeotia show us scenes from life in ancient Greece. **123.** Women kneading dough, moving in time to a flute-player. **124.** Farmer with a horse-drawn plough. Vase paintings, although mostly representing mythological subjects, provide a considerable amount of information concerning crafts. **125.** A carpenter bores a hole in the chest in which Danae and her child Perseus are to be cast into the sea. **126.** Hephaestus, shown as a smith, burnishing a shield for Thetis. He has his *himation* bound round his waist and wears the woollen or fur cap of a workman. On the wall hang completed greaves and a helmet of the Corinthian type; right: pincers, hammer, and saw. **127.** A woman lifts her child from the shoulders of a nursemaid. **128.** A man visiting in the women's room. The woman is dressed in a *chiton* and wears earrings and bracelets among her ornaments; she is holding a wreath.

129. Festivals in honour of Dionysus featured largely in Greek daily life. Fragment from a picture of a festival, showing a girl on a swing. 130. Activity in a bronze foundry. The metal, left, is melted in an oven; a stoker pokes up the fire. On the wall: horns, with votive tablets and models or already cast heads. In the centre, a smith; tools, etc., hang on the wall. On the right a smith works on the arms of a bronze statue which has already been cast but whose head has not yet been attached. 131. Mourning women at a tomb with a stele mounted on three steps. 132. Hermes brings a dead youth to Charon, who transported the dead across the Styx to Hades. 133. Parting of two persons, on a funeral relief. 134-5. Terracottas from Tanagra show us the fashionable women of the classical and Hellenistic periods. 134. Woman walking with her arms under her cloak. 135. Female figure. 136. Sepulchral steles in a cemetery in Athens.

as his starting point, but rejected the division between a world of Ideas and a so-called reality. In his opinion matter contained the potential to produce the latent form which is its highest realisation. He saw this development everywhere, but — contrary to our accepted ideas — it was determined not causally but finally, by the attraction of the form which compels matter to realise its potential. Unlike the markedly mathematically-minded Plato, he was historically inclined. He attempted to arrange and classify reality in an ascending series which finally attains the absolute form which he called god. This theory is expounded in the books called the *Metaphysics*.

As an organ for his thought he formulated the science of logic, whereby in the form of the syllogism all true reasoning can be compellingly formulated while faulty reasoning is exposed. He himself was a universal scholar with a grasp of all branches of the knowledge of his time. The studies of his school of collaborators and assistants produced a number of specialised branches of science such as zoology and botany as well as the history of literature and political science. These were carried on by his pupils as independent subjects. Both Plato's abstract constructive method and Aristotle's method of classifying and marshalling facts had a profound influence in classical times and in the Middle Ages; they even affected the technical formulation of the doctrine of the Christian Church.

After these two great philosophers and their schools other scholars continued to concentrate on mathematics, astronomy, the theory of harmony, and other branches of science. In spite of the scanty equipment at their disposal, they achieved far-reaching results. They were already familiar with the spherical shape of the earth and even wi h the idea of a heliocentric system as the likely explanation of some astronomical phenomena.

Ionian natural philosophy found a late exponent in Democritus, who advanced the theory that the universe was composed of atoms, of indivisible particles in space. Although this idea found little response during classical times on account of the meaninglessness which it implied in the *cosmos* (the ordered universe), it was later to be triumphantly acclaimed.

Greek culture had thus attained the climax of its achievement when the collapse of its own world, divided by frontiers and feuds, opened up a wider field for it. This was the time when the Greek mind, in the service of the Macedonians, was given the task of guiding the *oikoumene*, the whole inhabited world.

Hellenism

ALEXANDER THE GREAT

When after Chaeronea Philip had united Greece under his rule in the Corinthian League it was his avowed intention to proceed to liberate the Asiatic Greeks from the dominion of Persia. By the conquest of Persia he would acquire the living-space needed by the Greeks, as Isocrates and others had advocated, and at the same time he would be using a national war as a means to reconcile the Greeks to his supremacy. His advance divisions had already crossed the Hellespont into Asia when he was murdered in 336 by a Macedonian whose honour he had insulted. Despite his education in Greece he had remained at heart a dissipated Macedonian potentate.

Many Greeks expected and hoped that his kingdom would disappear with its founder. But his son Alexander, barely twenty years of age, immediately took up the reins. He appeared in Greece and assumed his father's office as *hegemon* and *strategos* of the League. A lightning campaign across the Danube and deep into Illyria restored order in the Balkans (see Map 26, p. 84). While he was there a rumour spread in Greece that he had been killed. Thebes took up arms and Athens and the Peloponnese prepared to follow its example. But with startling speed Alexander appeared at the pass of Thermopylae and took Thebes by storm. The city was destroyed and the inhabitants were sold as slaves. The unparalleled severity of these measures made it only too clear that the so-called alliance was in reality subjection. It also ensured the failure of the attempt which Philip had made to win over the Greeks. Henceforth Macedon was for Greece the arch-enemy to whose hegemony it never became reconciled. We are inclined to view Alexander's conquests as the triumph of the Greek spirit and culture. In point of fact it was the fervent hope of the Greeks that he might perish in Asia. But he had achieved his purpose. He wished to have his hands free for the campaign against Persia which he had inherited from his father but which he undertook in his own distinctive manner.

After the murder of the energetic Artaxerxes III the Persian throne was occupied by Darius III (Codomannus), who had not yet established his authority and showed himself a coward in moments of crisis. The plan of his Greek general Memnon to avoid battle in Asia and stir up rebellion in Greece by a naval campaign was rejected by the satraps of Asia Minor. As soon as Alexander had crossed the Hellespont they joined battle with him at the Granicus and suffered a crushing defeat. Alexander possessed superb cavalry, comprising Macedonians and Thracians, which he used not only to pierce the enemy lines but also to annihilate survivors in a fierce pursuit. The whole of Asia Minor fell into his hands. After the death of Memnon the Persian fleet which threatened his communications collapsed and there was no longer any question of a revolt in Greece. In 333 Alexander encountered the Persian army under the king himself at Issus. The Persians were defeated because at the critical moment Darius panicked and took to flight. Tyre was taken after a long siege during which Alexander had a mole built across the channel which separated the city from the land. In Egypt, which Artaxerxes had brutally reconquered a short time previously, Alexander was welcomed as a liberator. The oracle of Ammon greeted him as a son of the god. At the mouth of the Nile he founded Alexandria which was to replace Tyre as the chief port in the eastern Mediterranean.

In 331 the army turned eastwards. The Persian king's offers of peace were declined. At Gaugamela the motley Persian army was again defeated. Babylon, Susa, and Persepolis fell into the hands of Alexander, together with the treasures of the Persian Empire. Darius was deposed by his own satraps for his incompetence and murdered when it appeared that he might fall into the hands of his pursuers. Alexander proclaimed himself the successor of the Achaemenids and set out to conquer the eastern part of the Empire. He penetrated as far as the valley of the Indus, but when he wished to press on to the Ganges his exhausted troops refused to follow him any farther.

He returned to Babylon along the coast of the Persian Gulf and there began to organise his empire. At the same time time he planned a sea link with India, the circumnavigation of Arabia, and possibly the subjection of the West. These vast schemes were cut short by his death at Babylon in 323. His potential successors were a mentally unstable half-brother and, soon, a posthumous son. During his short fantastic career he had radically changed the face of the world.

Already at the crossing of the Hellespont he had abandoned the idea of a return to Macedon. It had soon become clear to his close followers that, unlike his father Philip, he did not think of himself merely as king of the Macedonians and *hegemon* of the Greeks. He dreamed of conquering the world not for Macedon but for himself. As his successes grew he ceased to think of himself as an ordinary man. He was a hero with a superhuman vocation. He accepted divine honours from the Orientals as if they were his due, and even from his own Macedonians he began to demand *proskynesis*, that is, that they should prostrate themselves before him. This provoked fierce resistance; even members of his immediate circle plotted against his life. He retaliated in barbarous style. His friend Clitus he murdered with his own hand; his best general Parmenion was dispatched by hired assassins. But although his soldiers might grumble and sometimes mutiny they always gave way when confronted with the immense personal magnetism of his presence. He possessed the intellect and the will-power to make the seemingly impossible possible. Even before his death he had become a legendary figure. There is no telling what he might have accomplished if he had lived longer. He himself had never even considered the possibility of failure, and he had taken no measures for the future in the event of his death.

THE KINGDOMS OF THE SUCCESSORS

Alexander's generals, extremely able and ambitious men hitherto dominated by a king who was younger than most of them, became rivals for power and soon were openly at war with one another. Some attempted to transform their satrapies into independent kingdoms; the ablest and most aspiring sought to win the entire empire (see Map 27, p. 84). The insignificant Philip III and the young Alexander disappeared from the scene, first by banishment and then by death. The distant provinces in the East became independent. The generals in control, who later adopted the title of kings, soon became Easternised but at the same time opened up northwest India to Greek influences. Their kingdoms and principalities survived for about 200 years, but in fact they had passed beyond the main Greek horizon.

The capable Ptolemy conquered and retained Egypt and the surrounding regions. Cassander proclaimed himself king of Macedon. Antigonus, the satrap of Phrygia, supported by his son Demetrius, fought for twenty years to gain the supremacy for himself. In 301 he lost his life at the battle of Ipsus against a coalition of rivals, of whom Seleucus was successful in gaining mastery over Syria and Mesopotamia (→ 210, 211).

Greece continued to rebel against Macedonian supremacy. An unsuccessful revolt after the death of Alexander cost Demosthenes his life. A decisive factor was that Athenian sea-power was eliminated by the Macedonian navy in 322. The mastery of the sea, retained since Salamis, was definitely lost now that the great powers disposed of means and man-power.

137. The Greek world possessed numerous local sanctuaries as well as those common to all. The island of Delos, a rock in the Cyclades only one square mile in area, occupied a special position. According to legend, Leto, pursued by the wrath of Hera, took refuge here and gave birth to Apollo and Artemis; it hence became a centre for the sworship of Apollo. The photograph shows the western side of the island, where the city of Delos lay. French excavations have revealed the extent of the complexes of temples, houses, and other buildings. 1. sacred lake; 2. agora of the Italians; 3. lion terrace with remaining lion statues (→ 138); 4. sanctuary; 5. sanctuary of the bulls, in which capitals are formed by sculpted, kneeling bulls; 6. temple of Apollo; 7. south agora; 8. old harbour; 9. houses and buildings of the city of Delos. **138.** One of the seven surviving archaic lions of Naxian marble. **139.** Damaged altar with phallic symbols in sanctuary of Dionysus.

140.

141
142
143

140. Roughly in the centre of Greece, according to Greek legend in the centre of the earth, and according to Strabo's description in a natural amphitheatre, lies the sanctuary of Delphi. It is enclosed to the north by the steep Phaedriadae ('shining rocks'), whose dust covered the sanctuary in the course of the centuries after destructive attacks and desecration. The photograph shows the group of buildings, barely 6 acres in extent: 1. stadium; 2. theatre; 3. temple of Apollo; 4. spring of Castalia. **141.** Consultation of the oracle by King Aegeus. The priestess, the Pythia, in a state of trance, utters sounds which are rendered as oracles by the priests. She holds Apollo's laurel wreath and a dish probably filled with water from the spring of Castalia. **142.** The *omphalos*, a navel-shaped stone covered over with a network pattern in marble, which marked the supposed centre of the world. **143.** Consultation of the oracle by Oenomaus. The *omphalos* stands in front of the priestess.

144. South of the sanctuary yawns the deep cleft the Plistus, in summer a narrow stream, in winter a rushing flood fed by rainwater from the mountains. From the temple of Apollo (ca. 1,870 ft.), can be seen Parnassus (8,067 ft.) above, and the valley, slightly above sea level, below. By its position this sanctuary is one of the most impressive of the Greek holy places. In the foreground is modern Kastri, rebuilt here after the original village which grew up about Delphi was pulled down at the end of the last century to facilitate the French excavations. **145.** View, from above the well-preserved theatre, of the temple of Apollo and the landscape of the valley which penetrates far inland. **146.** The Plistus (now the Xeropotamoi), after a winding course debouches into the Gulf of Itea rather more than twelve miles from Delphi. The Gulf is visible in the background at the end of the fertile plain with its thousands of olive trees.

Delphi today is little more than a collection of ruins, and the modern visitor has some difficulty in imagining the wealth and magnificence which were seen here throughout almost the whole of antiquity. **147.** The photograph gives a view of the small walled area which yearly attracted Greeks and non-Greeks from the whole classical world to honour Apollo and consult the oracle. Compare this photograph with that on the opposite page (→ **151**) in which the buildings and statues have been reconstructed. The most important points are: 1. temple of Apollo (present remains from 4th century); 2. temple terrace with statues; 3. Portico of the Athenians, erected after the victory of Salamis; 4. bouleuterium; 5. Treasury of the Athenians; 6. unidentified treasury; 7. Treasury of Syracuse; 8. of Potidaea; 9. of the Boeotians; 10. votive offerings of the Boeotians; 11. Treasury of Thebes; 12. of Siphnos; 13. of Sicyon; 14. exedra of the kings of Argos; 15. hall of the Spartans, established to celebrate Sparta's victory at the battle

of Aegospotami; 16. main entrance and direction of the spring of Castalia; 17. Treasury of Cnidos; 18. of the Aetolians; 19. column with sphinx of the Naxians; 20. Sacred Way through the sanctuary; 21. golden stars of Aegina; 22. monument of Aemilius Paulus, erected after the battle of Pydna (→ also 260-1); 23. the golden tripod of Plataea, later transferred to Constantinople where part still exists; 24. votive monument of the Rhodians; 25. Apollo; 26. place where charioteer was found; 27. monument of Alexander the Great; 28. theatre. French excavations have led to the identification of a number of monuments through the discovery of statues and reliefs. **148.** Excavation in 1893 of an archaic statue, probably representing Cleobis. **149.** Head of the charioteer, of which the discovery **(150)** in 1895 is also shown. **152.** Wall beside the Treasury of the Athenians with spaces for votive tablets. **153.** Reconstruction of the Treasury of Siphnos.

154

155
156

154. Many sanctuaries were dedicated to Asclepius, god of medicine, from whom countless sick people sought healing. The most important of the places dedicated to this god was in Epidaurus. The air photograph gives an impression of the extent of the complex, which contained not only temples and altars but also baths, inns, a stadium, gymnasium, theatre, and other buildings intended to render the pilgrim's stay agreeable: 1. temple of Asclepius; 2. tholos, a round temple, whose beauty was praised by Pausanias (→ 155); 3. altar; 4. baths with healing springs; 5. gymnasium; 6. stadium; 7. guesthouse; 8. theatre, still through its completeness the glory of Epidaurus; it was a place of relaxation on the fringe of the sanctuary, and was praised by the Greeks for its beauty. **155.** Reconstruction of the tholos and temple of Asclepius with part of the shelter for the sick. **156.** Family sacrifice upon an altar of Asclepius. Fragment of a votive relief.

157

158
159

157. Cos, a small island in the Sporades, with its cult of Asclepius, was from early times a famous centre of pilgrimage. It owed some of its importance to Hippocrates, the 'father of medicine', who was born on the island and laid the basis of his new medical theories during the treatment of those who sought healing in the water of the miraculous warm springs (6). The impressive remains of the sanctuary, built upon three terraces, still stand over against one of the hills which were formerly wooded but are now bare. Upon the oldest terrace (1) stood the temple (2) in which the temple treasures were kept. Between it and another temple (3) stood the altar(4) where gifts were offered and healing was sought. On the upper terrace stood a temple (5) of the 2nd century B.C. **158.** Relief showing Asclepius treating a sick person. **159.** Relief, probably from a votive tablet in honour of Asclepius, from someone cured of a disease of the foot. Many such expressions of gratitude can be found in all Greek sanctuaries.

160

161
162

163
164

Olympia, sometimes called the country-seat of the divine inhabitants of Olympus, lies in the Peloponnese, between the rivers Cladeus and Alpheus and Mt. Cronus. It derived its importance especially from the Olympic Games, held there for almost a thousand years. Earthquakes and floods have covered the area in and around the sacred dwelling-place of the gods, the 'Altis', with a thick layer of silt. **161.** View of the excavated area: 1. temple of Zeus which contained the majestic statue of the father of the gods; 2. temple of Hera (→ 172); 3. Treasuries; 4. Mt. Cronus; 5. Prytaneum; 6. Philippeum; 7. Palaestra; 8. Leonidaeum; 9. part of the wall of the Altis; 10. entrance to stadium; 11. bouleuterium. **163.** Foundations of treasuries. The sculptures of the temple of Zeus are among the supreme achievements of Greek art. **160.** Head of Athena. **162.** The statue of Apollo, marking an important stage in the development of art. **164.** Personification of the river Cladeus, admirable in its representation of attitude.

165-6. Typical features of Doric columns are heavy structure, absence of base, round echinus, and square architrave. The fluting, in a monolith (left) or in the drums (right), always accentuates the practical function. **168.** The Ionic style is lighter. The capital ends in graceful volutes. **169.** In this period the base and the abacus (**167**) became increasingly elaborate. **170.** The Corinthian column, evolved ca. 450, is at first distinguished mainly by capitals inspired by acanthus leaves. **171.** One beautiful type of column is that in the form of a female figure. Greek architecture developed from wooden buildings to stone constructions. **172.** The temple of Hera at Olympia, showing that stone columns gradually replaced wooden ones. **173.** The Doric temple of Aphaea in Aegina. **174.** The Parthenon, unsurpassed in beauty and proportion, represents the proud period of the greatness of Athens in the 5th century.

175

176

177

178

179

180
181

182

183

Greek sculpture developed from the archaic style to the matchless classical forms. **175-9.** Some phases of the development from early sculpture, usually characterised by rigid stylisation, to classical art (see also drawings on page 88). Typical is the 'archaic smile' (**175-6**). An improved knowledge of anatomy brought increased movement. The figures became more supple, as in the 'Fair-haired Ephebe' (**178**). The sculptures of the temple of Zeus at Olympia are the highest achievements of this still severe style (**177**). Statues and reliefs from the Parthenon (**180** → also 55) date from a period in which material and anatomy were completely mastered. Another example is the Nike of Paeonius (**181**). Fourth-century art, whose most important work is the Hermes of Praxiteles (**179**) whether it is the original or not, continued in this tradition. **183-4.** The temple at Bassae near Phigalia, owing to its isolated position, is one of the best-preserved buildings. Its sculptures (**182**) show the more lifelike form of the late 5th century.

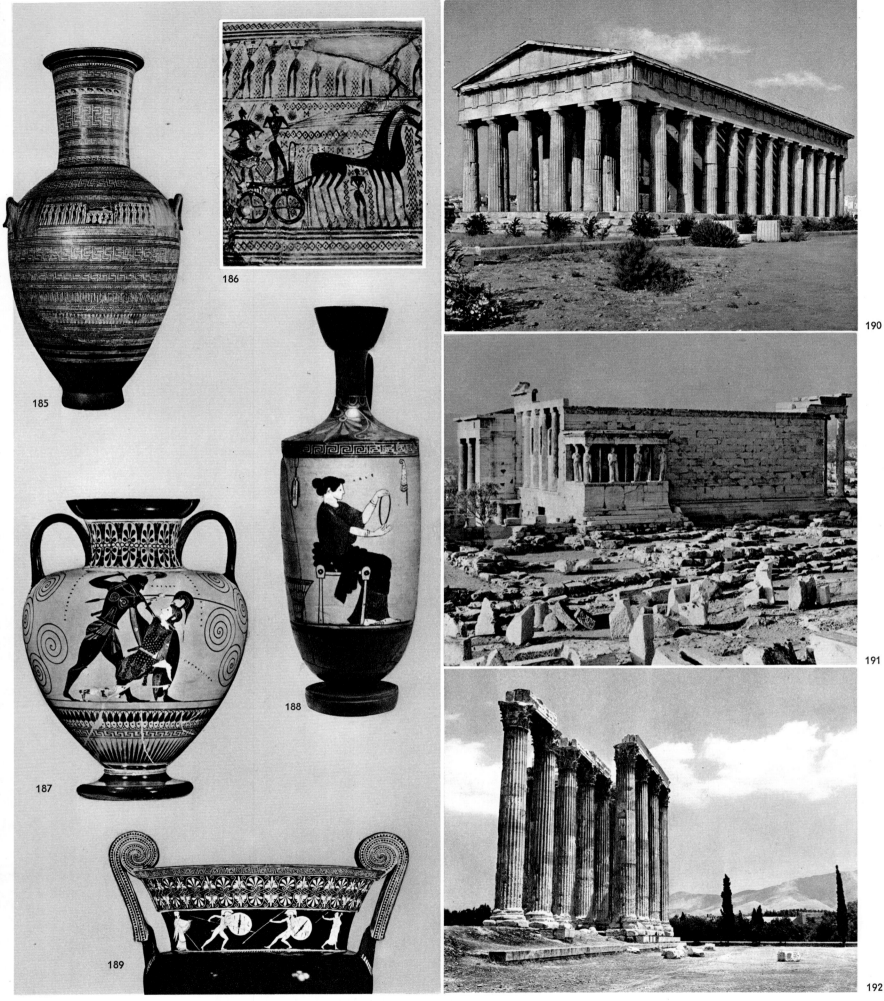

185

186

190

191

192

187

188

189

Greek pottery shows a great wealth of shape and decoration. The oldest pieces have geometrical patterns, sometimes consisting merely of geometrical motifs sometimes with animal and human figures (**185, 186**) executed in a similar style of flat silhouette. In early pottery the designs are worked in black upon a yellowish or reddish background. Later – in the red-figure period – the figures were formed from the red background colour. In the 'lekythos' vases the decoration was painted upon a layer of white. The achievements of Greek art are reflected in the vases which have been found in great numbers, especially in tombs. Other important temples (see pp. 75-7) of different periods and style are a Doric temple, dedicated to Hephaestus (**190**), the Ionic Erechtheum (**191**), and what remains of the Corinthian-style Olympieum (**192**), all in Athens. Some forms of Greek pottery and temples are illustrated on pp. 62, 63, 82, 89.

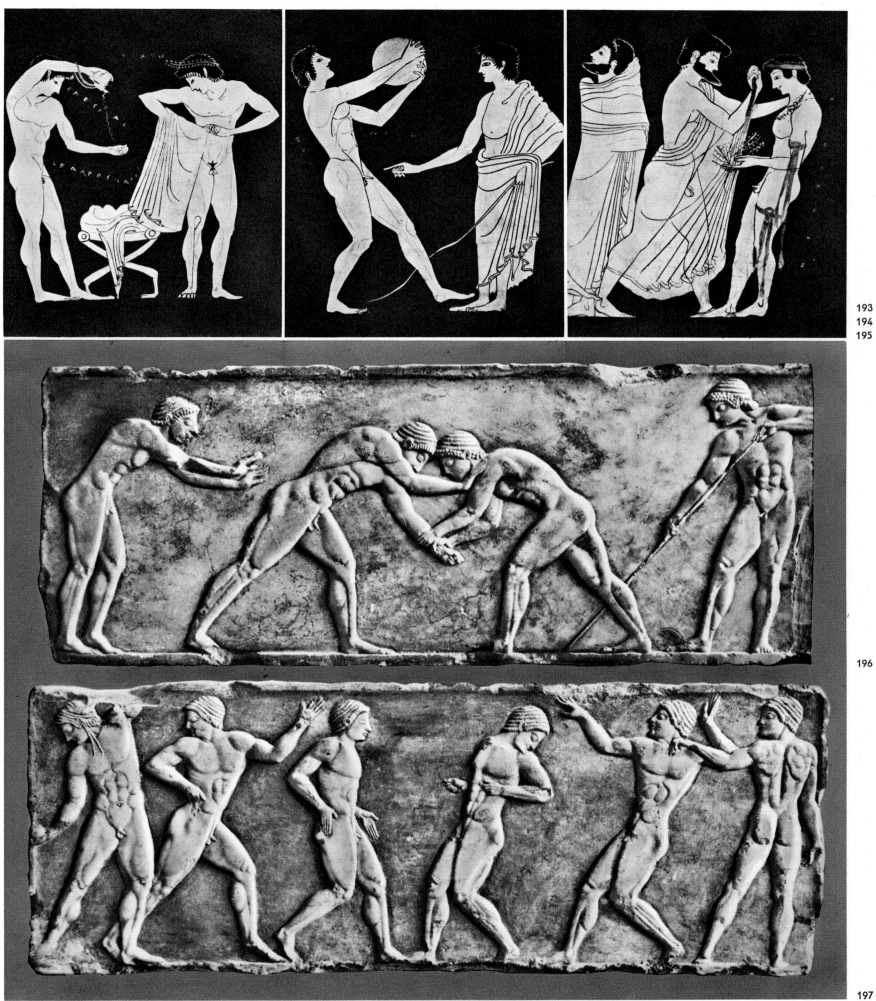

193
194
195

196

197

Numerous pictures on vases, reliefs, etc. show the prominent place occupied in Greek life by physical culture. Every city possessed gymnasiums and palaestra, where young men practised many branches of sport. **193.** Rubbing with oil and undressing before the competition, at which the athlete appeared naked (*gymnos*). **194.** Preparation for discus throwing under the guidance of a teacher. **195.** Binding of a victor's head with the wreath of victory. He holds myrtle branches in his hands and the bands of victory are already bound about his left arm and thigh. The sides of an archaic statue-base also provide striking scenes of sport. One side (**196**) shows various sports: a runner preparing for the start; two wrestlers measuring their strength; a spear-thrower making ready for the throw. The other side (**197**) shows an incident in a ball game between two teams. The player on the left is about to return the ball.

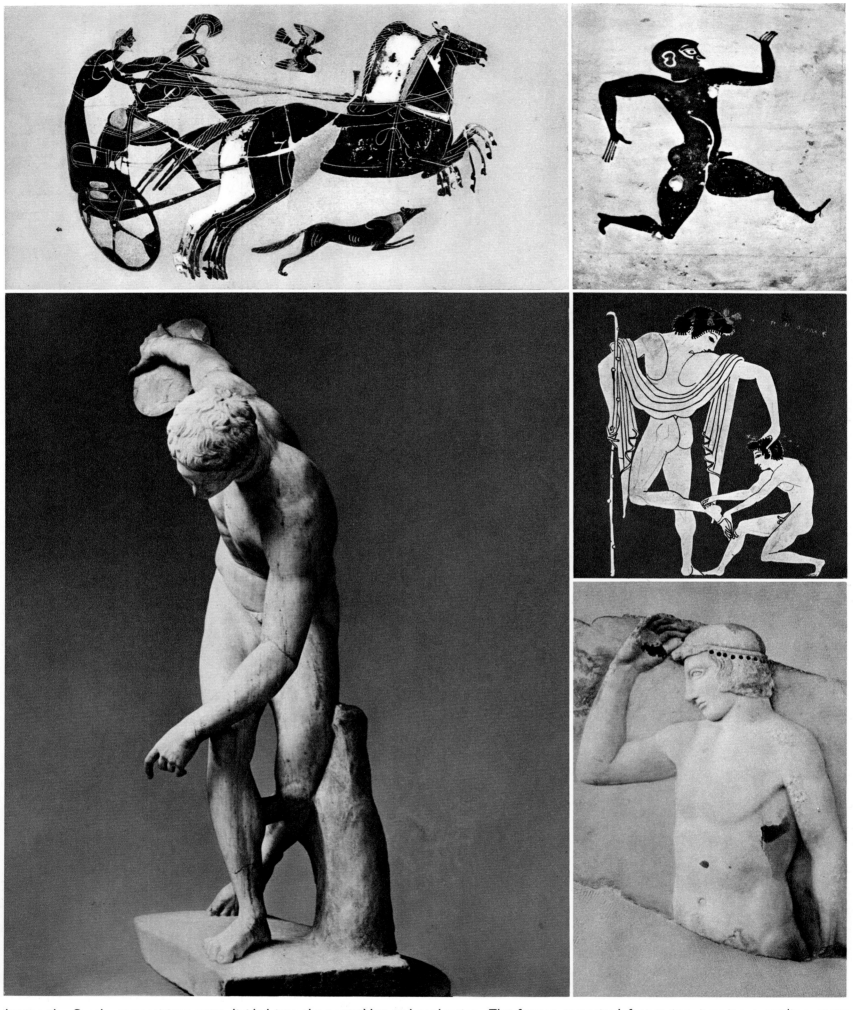

198
199
200
201

202

Among the Greeks competitions were divided into the pentathlon and pankration. The former comprised foot-racing, jumping, wrestling, spear and discus throwing, the latter boxing. **198.** Four-horse chariot with driver leaning forward, foot upon the pole. The horse-races, already described by Homer in the *Iliad*, took place with yoked horses. Chariot races were first introduced at the Olympic Games at Olympia. **199.** Competitor running at full speed. **201.** A common subject is the removal of thorns, splinters, etc. acquired through performing barefoot. **200.** Many famous sculptures were inspired by sport. The Discobolus of Myron, known only from copies, shows the moment at which the thrower prepares to hurl the discus with full force. This fine statue is justly renowned for its representation of attitude (see p. 192). **202.** Relief of a young victor. With his right thumb and index-finger he himself places the bronze wreath (now lost) upon his head.

203
204
205

206
207

It was a very great honour for athletes to take part in the main festivals, the Olympic at Olympia, the Pythian at Delphi, the Nemean at Nemea and the Isthmian near Corinth. **203.** The stadium at Delphi, fully 190 yards long, 30 yards wide at the centre. Here were held competitions in running, spear throwing, discus throwing and the long jump. The starting point was at the back (of the photograph), the finish in the foreground. **204.** The seats of the judges of the games in the stadium at Delphi are well preserved (see arrow on 203). **205.** Competitors' entry to the stadium at Olympia. **206-7.** Music also was an important factor in the daily life of the Greeks. The chief stringed instruments were the lyre and the cithara, the chief wind instruments the aulos (flute) and the syrinx (Pan-pipes). Two remarkable sculptures show the playing of music. **206.** Young man playing a lyre, on the side of the 'Boston Throne'. **207.** Flute player, side of the 'Ludovisi Throne'.

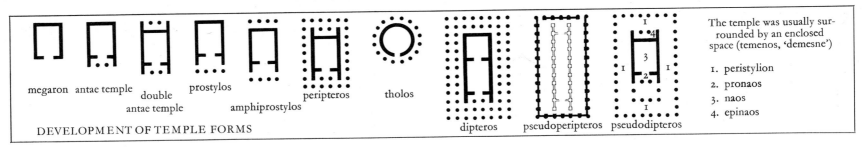

megaron antae temple double antae temple prostylos amphiprostylos peripteros tholos dipteros pseudoperipteros pseudodipteros

The temple was usually surrounded by an enclosed space (temenos, 'demesne')

1. peristylion
2. pronaos
3. naos
4. epinaos

DEVELOPMENT OF TEMPLE FORMS

far beyond the reach of the city-states. And yet resistance to Macedon persisted. Greece, although politically powerless, remained important to the Diadochi, who had to rely upon trained Greeks for their armies and administration.

Thus the successors of Alexander continued to dispute each other's influence in the Aegean area and to compete in declaring the Greek cities 'free' in order to gain their goodwill; but this 'freedom' in fact signified dependence upon the nearest 'protector'. Prosperity declined rapidly. Only a few ports, those which had become important links in the increasing traffic with the East, remained wealthy. Among these were Smyrna, Ephesus (→ 76), Byzantium, and above all Rhodes (→ 75), whose seamen had the reputation of being the best of their time.

Enormous damage was done when migrating Gallic tribes, called by the Greeks 'Galatians', stormed into Greece in 278 after having defeated and killed the Macedonian king Ptolemy Ceraunus. Even Delphi was plundered. Some groups crossed over into Asia Minor and on the Anatolian plateau founded a Galatian state which terrorised the surrounding country for almost a century. The band which had penetrated into Greece was destroyed by the Aetolians and the new king of Macedon, Antigonus Gonatas, who succeeded in restoring a state of comparative security and in obtaining the throne of Macedon for himself (278 B.C.) and his family.

After almost fifty years of war and rapid change equilibrium returned. Three great powers maintained their position: Egypt under the Ptolemies, Syria under the Seleucids (with Mesopotamia and, in theory, the lands as far as the Indus), and Macedon under the Antigonids. There also existed smaller states of secondary importance, the chief being the wealthy and well-governed city of Pergamum. The free cities of Rhodes and Byzantium prospered thanks to their geographical position and trade. They still tried to keep the seas open against the ever-increasing menace of piracy. Athens had lost every vestige of political power. It remained an important trading centre, but was chiefly renowned as a sort of venerable university town consecrated to the arts and sciences and full of curiosities from a great past.

In the struggle against the Macedonians and Galatians the Aetolians had come to the fore. In accordance with their ancient alliance, the states of central Greece united in self-defence. The Aetolians, however, were notoriously boorish and backward. Whenever they were not at war themselves they hired their men out as mercenaries to the highest bidder. Their league possessed no real *hegemon*: it was a federation of co-equal states and tribes, and in this form offered the only chance of liberty to the members.

In the Peloponnese the idea of federation was represented by the statesman Aratus, who made a league of Achaean cities the focal point of the struggle against the Macedonians. When he succeeded in expelling them from the citadel of Corinth, hitherto considered impregnable, the greater part of the Peloponnese joined the Achaean League. The way seemed clear for a stable free Peloponnesian federal state. But the Greeks were destined not to achieve unity, even in the form of an equal federation.

The Achaean and Aetolian Leagues became fierce rivals, and the growing unity in the Peloponnese was further disturbed by a bitter conflict between the League of Aratus and Sparta, which sought once again to realise its aspirations to leadership. Cleomenes III introduced sweeping reforms into the Spartan state and set up a new 'Lycurgan' régime. He created fresh citizens, redivided the land amongst them, and abolished the ephorate. This social revolution found great support throughout the whole of Greece, where social distress threatened to lead to repudiation of debts and redivision of land. The ancient Peloponnesian League began to revive, but it came into conflict with the conservative Achaean League. In this struggle Cleomenes showed himself by far the better general. The Achaeans were repeatedly defeated, and in this extremity Aratus repudiated his previous policy and rather than accept the superiority of Sparta invoked the help of the Macedonians, to whom he ceded Corinth, the gateway to the Peloponnese. Cleomenes was defeated at Sellasia in 222 by the superior Macedonian forces. For the first time in history Sparta was taken, and the supremacy of the Macedonians was restored, with the Achaean League as their ally.

At the peace congress of Naupactus in 218 the Aetolian ambassador spoke warningly of the 'cloud in the west'. The struggle between Rome and Carthage had broken out again, and clearly its result would be of decisive importance to Greece. The warning was of no avail. In 200 the Greeks, once again engaged in mutual conflict, called upon the Romans for help. The Romans came, and their coming was to prove permanent.

THE HELLENISTIC KINGDOMS IN THE THIRD CENTURY

On the mainland of Greece political and economic conditions became chaotic. Macedon was involved in a continuous struggle for hegemony in Greece, for the protection of the northern frontier against the invading barbarians, for the mastery of the Aegean Sea against Egypt, Pergamum, and Rhodes. Meantime the kingdoms in Africa and Asia achieved great prosperity and impressive external power.

Egypt. This country had fallen to the share of Ptolemy and his successors, who all bore the same name. The first three especially were able rulers and administrators. For them Egypt was a conquered territory, and all property belonged to the state. Following the ancient system of the Pharaohs (they called themselves the 30th dynasty), they organised their country as a domain in which Macedonians and Greeks became the ruling class and made up the army and the bureaucracy. With the Greek talent for organisation and commercial insight, they exported the products of the country under royal monopolies. The port of Alexandria became one of the largest cities and the greatest trading mart in the world (→ 220). The kings, the richest rulers of their time, employed their wealth in the upkeep of an army and a splendid court. Their gold often played a decisive part in intrigue and political conflict and furthered the ends of their diplomacy. At the same time they made Egypt, and especially Alexandria, a centre of learning and culture. In Alexandria was the great university and museum with its library containing in so far as possible all works written in Greek, where a staff of distinguished scholars studied all branches of knowledge.

Syria. The kingdom which Seleucus (→ 210) had acquired stretched from the Aegean Sea as far as India. Its centre lay in Mesopotamia and Syria. On the Tigris arose the new capital city, Seleucia, which supplanted Babylon. In Syria Antioch on the Orontes became the second-largest city after Alexandria and equalled it in splendour and magnificence.

This kingdom enjoyed little internal unity owing to its large extent and the extremely mixed population. Following the example of Alexander, who had initiated this policy on a large scale, Seleucus and his successors founded a number of Macedonian-Greek colonies in their territories. These were intended to serve as garrisons and administrative centres. Many old cities were also reorganised on the Greek model (see Map 28, p. 84). In these, the traditional ruling class of landowners, merchants, and intellectuals soon mingled completely with the Greek immigrants. Greek became the common language, and the Greek way of life was adopted by the cultured section of the population. Greek temples, theatres, stoas, schools, and gymnasiums transformed the external appearance of the cities (→ 215, 218). A new type, the Syrian Greek, emerged and provided many prominent figures in the artistic and intellectual life of the Hellenistic world. The country districts remained predominantly Aramaic.

Unlike the Ptolemies, for whom the Hellenisation of Egypt had been an unintentional consequence, the Seleucids deliberately endeavoured to bind together the varied multitude of their subjects by a cultural unity. In Syria they succeeded. The Hellenised population there was devoted to the ruling house, whose divine right (or rather, in the eyes of the Hellenistic Syrian, whose divinity) was taken as a matter of course. This policy, however, brought the Seleucid kings into sharp conflict with the Jews, who under the Persians had been granted an independent existence under the government of the high priests who ruled Jerusalem. For orthodox Jews Hellenisation meant repudiation of the law of Jehovah, and they grimly resisted the attempts of their latitudinarian leaders, who in order to win the favour of the kings wished to put an end to the isolated position of the Jewish people and to absorb the surrounding culture. The revolt of the Maccabees (168 B.C.) broke out against Antiochus IV Epiphanes, and after a heroic struggle they succeeded in defending their autonomy.

In the West, where Syria came into contact with the Mediterranean world, it was engaged in a perpetual struggle with Egypt for possession of the south part of Syria and the ports on the coast of Palestine. Unsubdued tribes in Asia Minor, Cappadocia, Pontus, Galatia, and the kingdom of Pergamum still threatened communications with the Aegean Sea, where Smyrna and Ephesus became great trading ports.

Competition for the throne among the Seleucids often led to grave internal crises. But the greatest danger came from the East. Among the peoples of Persia proper and among the nomads of the North, whom Alexander had temporarily subjected, unrest flared into national revolt. After 250 the Parthians, a tribe of still partly-nomadic feudal horsemen, under the dynasty

ZEUS   MARRIED

born in Crete, son of Kronos and Rhea, father of gods and men, god of thunder and lightning, maintainer of the moral order. Attribute: thunderbolt. Cult: originally localised in Crete; afterwards on all high mountains, especially Olympus, Mount Ida; also at Dodona (oracle), Olympia (the famous games).

HERA

sister and wife of Zeus, goddess of marriage and conjugal fidelity. Attributes: sometimes the peacock (sacred to her). Cult: on mountains and in strongholds; also in Argos, Mycenae, Sparta, Arcadia, Olympia, and Samos.

ARES

god of the brute force of war, with Eris, his sister, in his train. The dog, wolf, and cock are sacred to him. Cult: in Sparta, Thessaly, Boeotia, Athens (Areopagus), Achaia, Arcadia, and Elis.

HEBE

goddess of eternal youth, wife of Herakles after his reception among the gods.

HEPHAISTOS

god of fire and smith of the gods on Mount Olympus; with the Cyclopes he forges thunderbolts for Zeus. Cult: in Lemnos (forge on the mountain and later under Aetna in Sicily).

POSEIDON

son of Kronos and Rhea, brother of Zeus. God of the sea and the waters; rides in a chariot drawn by dolphins. The horse, bull, and dolphin are sacred to him. Attributes: trident and fish. Cult: in Thessaly, Boeotia, Peloponnesus, (Isthmus of Corinth), Calauria, Thera, Elis, Arcadia, Attica, and Asia Minor (Mycale and Halicarnassus).

HESTIA

sister of Zeus, goddess of the hearth (religious centre of family life) and afterwards also of the state (the fatherland). The fire on the hearth had to burn perpetually.

HADES

brother of Zeus, lord of the Underworld. Attributes: two-pronged fork, sometimes a hood or helmet on the head. Cult: in Elis and other parts of the Peloponnesus and Asia Minor (as Chthonios).

ASKLEPIOS

son of Apollon, god of healing. Attributes: staff entwined by serpent (sacred to him), dog (symbol of vigilance). Cult: early in Thessaly, then central and southern Greece, particularly Epidaurus and Cos, where he was credited with miraculous cures.

ERINUES

goddesses of vengeance, daughters of Acheron (river in the Underworld) and Nux (night). They have talons, snakes as whips, and burning torches; they pursue the evildoer. Their names are Alecto (the never-ceasing), Megaira (the malicious), and Tisiphone (the avenger of murder). From respectful fear they were also known as the Eumenides (the kindly ones).

NIOBE

granddaughter of Zeus. Proud of her 14 children, she scoffed at Leto with her twins. Apollon and Artemis killed her children and turned her into a rock eternally weeping.

METIS
good counsel

PALLAS ATHENA

born from the head of Zeus after he had swallowed Metis who was expecting a child. Goddess of the arts, learning, wisdom, the science of warfare; patroness of the city of Athens. Attributes: olive tree, owl, dragon, sometimes small Nike (victory), and the Aegis (terrifying shield). Cult: in Thessaly, Megara, Phocis, Corinth, Arcadia (Tegea), Achaia, Elis, Laconica, Crete, Rhodes, Ionia.

LETO

gave birth in Delos to the twins Apollon and Artemis. Cult: usually with that of her children; also in Argos.

APOLLON

originally from Asia Minor; subsequently adopted by the Greeks and regarded as born in Delos. God of song, music, dance, games, poetry (leader of the nine Muses), medicine, travel; prophet. Attributes: lyre, laurel, sometimes bow and arrows. Cult: in Delphi and Bassae among other places.

ARTEMIS

twin sister of Apollon, goddess of hunting and fertility. Attributes: bow and quiver; hound, or deer; dressed as a huntress. Cult: in Arcadia, Laconica, (Caryae), Elis, Aetolia, Euboea, Attica, Ephesus, Magnesia (under various titles).

PERSEPHONE

goddess who makes seed germinate and thus grants food and life (other name Kore). Carried off by Hades, she spends one-third of the year in the Underworld. Cult: usually combined with that of Demeter.

DEMETER

sister and wife of Zeus, goddess of corn and agriculture and bringer of fertility. Attributes: ears of corn, torch, basket with flowers and fruit. Cult: in every agricultural community (festival of Thesmophoria) and especially in Eleusis (the mysteries) and Sicily.

THE MUSES

goddesses of song, later of all arts and sciences. Klio (history), Euterpe (lyric), Melpomene (drama), Thaleia (comedy), Terpsichore (dance) Erato (love poetry), Kalliope (epic), Poluhumnia (the sublime hymn) and Ourania (astronomy). They dwell on Olympus, Helicon, and Parnassus. Orpheus was a son of Kalliope.

MAIA

SEMELE

DIONUSOS

god of vine-growing and wine and hence of the Maenades (Bacchantes) and Dionysiac ecstasy. A Thracian god, localised at Thebes. Silenos was his teacher; his followers are satyrs, the forest god Pan, the Muses, and many nymphs. Attributes: ivy, vine tendrils, drinking cup. Cult: in Naxos, Delos, Chios, Aetolia, Attica (Dionysia), and Asia Minor.

HERMES

messenger of Zeus, god of commerce, travel, sleep, wind and air, sagacity, artifice, and eloquence, and conductor of shades to the Underworld. Attributes: wings on shoes, hat, or shoulders, herald's staff, traveller's felt hat. Cult: on the mountain of Cyllene, in Attica, Lemnos, Imbros, Samothrace, and at the numerous Hermae (square pillars with head of the god).

MNEMOSUNE

THE GRACES

goddesses of joy, the followers of Aphrodite. Aglaia (beauty), Euphrosune (joy), Thaleia (the blooming). Cult: at Orchomenus, Athens, Sparta, Elis.

EURUNOME

THEMIS

divine justice, daughter of Ouranos (heaven) and Gaia (earth), goddess of law, justice, and order. Attributes: blindfolding bandage, scales, sword. Cult: Delphi (before Apollon).

DIONE

APHRODITE

goddess of love and beauty. Adopted from the East (cf. Astarte); considered by the Greeks as daughter of Zeus and Dione. Sparrows, doves, and swans were sacred to her; also the myrtle, rose, lime tree, and poppy. Cult: in Cyprus, Cythera, Cnidus, and Cape Eryx (Sicily). By Anchises she became the mother of Aeneas.

THE HOURS

the ever-youthful goddesses of the seasons. Eunomia (good government), Dike (right), and Eirene (peace). Later also goddesses of fate.

THE FATES

the goddesses of fate Klotho, Lachesis, Atropos. They determine the life and death of man. Attributes: Klotho, spindle or scroll (book of fate); Lachesis, staff of fate, globe; Atropos, shears, wax tablet, or sundial.

ZEUS   MARRIED
father of mortals (heroes, demigods)

ALKMENE

HERAKLES

national hero of the Peloponnesus, very popular throughout the whole of Greece; famous for his legendary strength. Hated by Hera, he performed the Twelve Labours for Eurystheus (including killing the Nemean lion and the Hydra of Lerna, taming Cerberus, catching the Arcadian stag, cleaning the Augean Stables). Received as a god in Olympus and married to Hebe. Cult: throughout Greece, especially in the Dorian lands, and later in Italy.

DANAË

PERSEUS

hero popular in mythology for having among other achievements beheaded Medusa, one of the Gorgons (winged monsters with iron claws and snakes for hair). Cult: in Argos, Mycenae, Seriphos, and even in Egypt.

LEDA

EUROPA

ELEKTRA

MINOS

king of Crete and after his death judge in the Underworld together with his brother Rhadamanthus.

DARDANOS

born in Arcadia; later settled in Phrygia, and at the foot of Mount Ida built the city of Dardania (later the famous Troy).

HELENA

one of the most famous women of ancient Greece. Married to Menelaus king of Sparta, she was abducted by Paris (Alexander) son of Priam king of Troy. This was the cause of the Trojan War.

DIOSKOUROI

the twins Kastor and Poludeukes, respectively patrons of horse-taming and boxing. They are devoted to each other; protect the people, and avenge wrongs. Cult: in Sparta, Messenia, and Argos, and later throughout practically the whole of Greece.

THE GODS OF THE GREEKS

—— Marriages of Zeus

—— Children of Zeus

HERA God or goddess

DANAË Demigod, hero, mortal

The names of divinities are given in Greek spelling

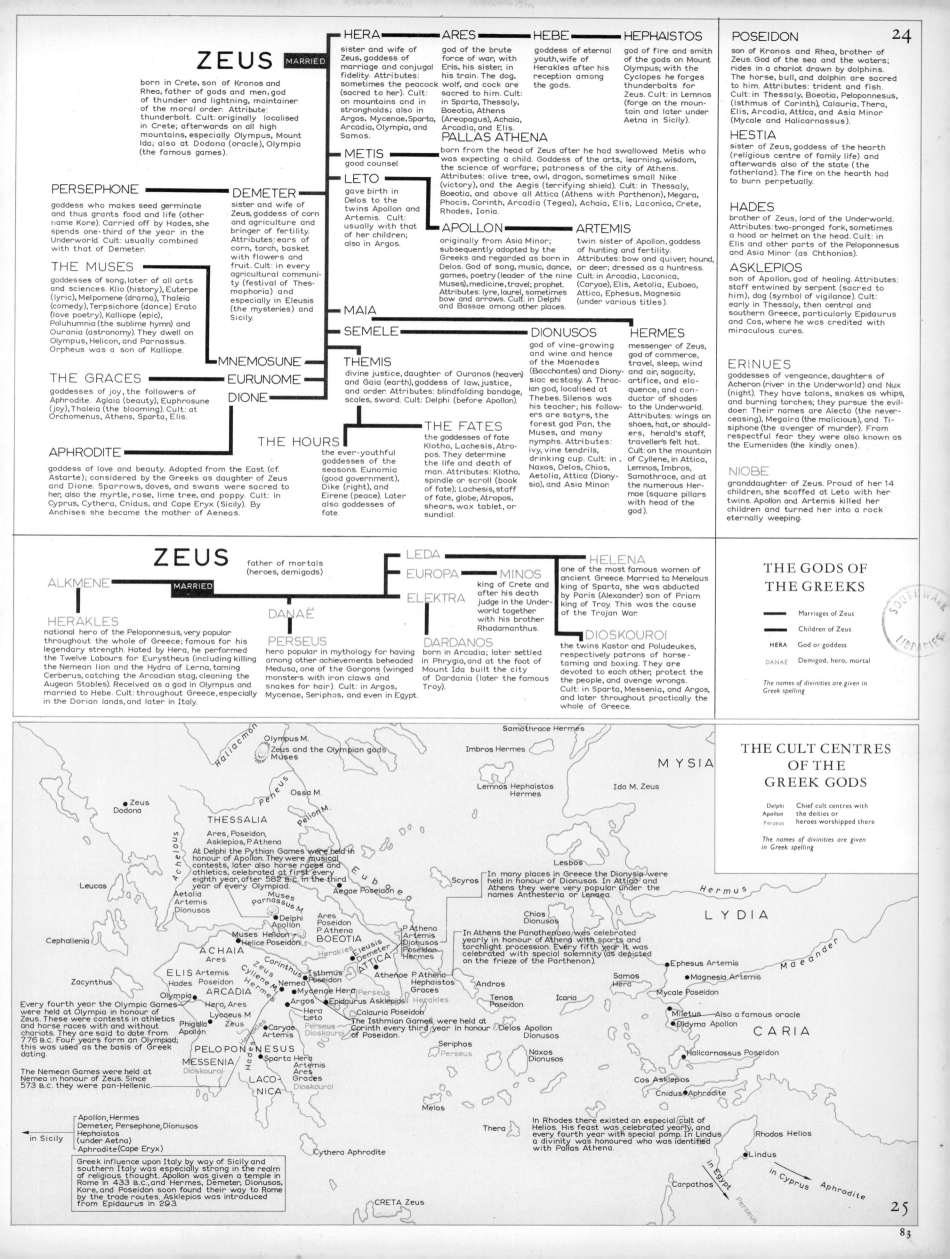

THE CULT CENTRES OF THE GREEK GODS

Delphi
Apollon   Chief cult centres with the deities or
Perseus   heroes worshipped there

The names of divinities are given in Greek spelling

At Delphi the Pythian Games were held in honour of Apollon. They were musical contests, later also horse races and athletics, celebrated at first every eighth year, after 582 B.C. in the third year of every Olympiad.

In many places in Greece the Dionysia were held in honour of Dionusos. In Attica and Athens they were very popular under the names Anthesteria or Lenaea.

In Athens the Panathenaea was celebrated yearly in honour of Athena with sports and torchlight procession. Every fifth year it was celebrated with special solemnity (as depicted on the frieze of the Parthenon).

Every fourth year the Olympic Games were held at Olympia in honour of Zeus. These were contests in athletics and horse races with and without chariots. They are said to date from 776 B.C. Four years form an Olympiad; this was used as the basis of Greek dating.

The Nemean Games were held at Nemea in honour of Zeus. Since 573 B.C. they were pan-Hellenic.

The Isthmian Games were held at Corinth every third year in honour of Poseidon.

In Rhodes there existed an especial cult of Helios. His feast was celebrated yearly, and every fourth year with special pomp. In Lindus a divinity was honoured who was identified with Pallas Athena.

Greek influence upon Italy by way of Sicily and southern Italy was especially strong in the realm of religious thought. Apollon was given a temple in Rome in 433 B.C., and Hermes, Demeter, Dionusos, Kore, and Poseidon soon found their way to Rome by the trade routes. Asklepios was introduced from Epidaurus in 293.

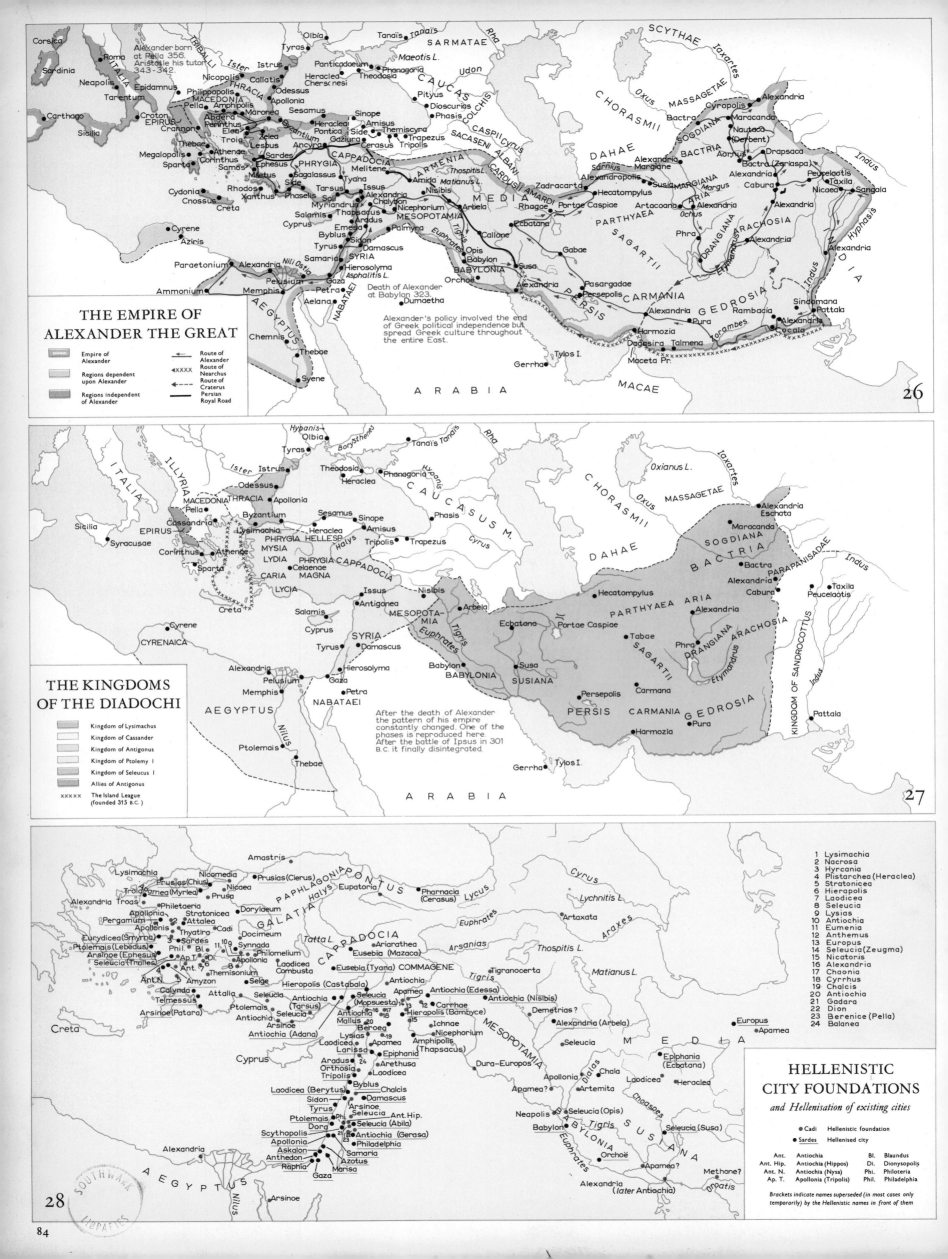

of the Arsacids, drove a wedge between Mesopotamia and the eastern Syrian satrapies which consequently became separated from the Seleucid kingdom and soon no longer lay within the horizon of the West. After 200 the Parthians were a serious menace to Mesopotamia, precisely in the period when Syria was defeated in the West by the Romans and lost all its territory in Asia Minor.

Asia Minor, geographically the centre of the empire carved out by Alexander, became during this period an extremely rich and prosperous region. The ancient towns on the Ionian coast, Smyrna and Ephesus, which served as the ports of a hinterland extending as far as Elam, grew larger and wealthier than ever before. The kingdom of Pergamum successfully held its position amid the struggles of the great powers. The capital developed into a centre of science and art which rivalled even Alexandria. Rhodes likewise profited from its central position ($\rightarrow$ 75) and became the trade centre of the Aegean. Rhodian seamen were considered the best of their time and often commanded the fleets of other states such as Egypt, Syria, and Macedon.

CHANGES IN ECONOMIC CONDITIONS

Alexander's conquest of the East brought about a radical change in the Greek world, comparable with the influence upon the structure of Europe of the discoveries of the fifteenth and sixteenth centuries A.D. The hoarded treasure of the Persians was brought into circulation to finance campaigns, the building of new cities, and the construction of roads. The lands which had been opened up offered work and prosperity to thousands of Greeks and Greek-trained soldiers, officials, technicians, teachers, and businessmen.

Greece, in view of its advanced stage of technical and commercial development, might have entered on a period of economic domination such as had been anticipated by those who saw a war of conquest against Persia as the salvation of the tottering economy of Greece. But Alexander and his successors had conquered their kingdoms for themselves, settled in them permanently, and took with them large numbers of talented citizens. This large-scale emigration need not in itself have been a disaster for Greece, as is shown by the earlier period of emigration, which had extended Greek territory and made a flourishing trade and industry possible. Now, however, while perhaps solving the problem of overpopulation, the Macedonian conquests aggravated the tendency to export Greek skills which has already been mentioned. The lands which profited from this became technically and economically emancipated from Greece. The organisation and exploitation of the resources of Egypt, inaugurated by the Ptolemies in accordance with Greek methods and mentality and expressed in the stupendous flourishing of Alexandria as the centre of this activity, betokened for Greece, whose granary and purchaser of wine and oil Egypt had been, a greatly weakened position, reflected in the rising prices of corn.

The competition of local industry must soon have made the Greeks realise that costs were too high. We again hear of poverty among the workers, rising prices, and the increasing influence wielded by those who had capital to convert into land. A symptom of this crisis appears in the slogans which advocated land partition and repudiation of debts, of which Cleomenes, for example, was able to take advantage. Disorganisation and wars made the situation worse. The population declined; deliberate limiting of the number of children became common among those who wished to maintain their family property at whatever cost.

Cultural standards, however, were kept up. The schools of philosophy in Athens and elsewhere flourished, and theatres and games retained their former splendour. The 'New Comedy' which arose in Athens and was the direct precursor of European drama was well able to bear comparison with earlier literary achievements. The Greeks themselves called Menander the second Homer. Science and art continued to develop.

The political and economic situation gave cause for alarm. General impoverishment visibly increased. It is a disputed question whether Roman domination was really the cause of the final decay of Greece or whether the causes were already present within Greece itself. They would certainly appear to have been, and it is impossible to tell whether Greek energy and commercial sense, left to themselves, would have been able to surmount this crisis. The marked revivals during the comparatively brief periods of peace in the third century suggest that such ability existed. The rule of the Romans, which through lack of understanding unintentionally aggravated and perpetuated the economic condition of Greece through misgovernment and exploitation, was in any case the final blow. It also broke the Greek spirit and transformed the once proud, aggressive, and independent Greek into the *Graeculus*, the 'Greekling', used by the Romans for his knowledge and skill but despised for his servility.

While ancient Greece, with its culture developing into a world civilisation, itself dwindled into insignificance, the East presented a different picture. There the Graeco-Macedonian rulers developed enormous activity by means of which a sense of enterprise and organising skill achieved impressive results. The wars of the Diadochi and the recurrent struggles among their successors for frontier regions and inherited territories occasioned only slight disturbances in their extensive dominions and brought about concentrations of men and materials from which much profit could be derived. The foun-

dation of colonies and the building of fortresses, temples, and palaces provided work and remuneration for countless numbers. A fine career was possible in army or administration, especially in taxation and monopolies.

This world, for which Droysen coined the arresting term 'Hellenism' (the word means 'Greek-speaking and Greek-minded'), sometimes appears startlingly modern. The towns, laid out according to plan, with well-paved roads, stoas, temples, parks, and aqueducts, far surpassed in wealth and splendour anything that Greece had ever possessed. Greatest of all was Alexandria, with its harbour on river and sea, visible far out to sea in consequence of the marble lighthouse 520 feet high ($\rightarrow$ 220) on the island of Pharos, built by an architect from Rhodes at the point where the sea current and the current of the Nile meet and prevent the silting up of the harbour. The extremely diverse population of more than half a million included an important Jewish colony. The whole city was overshadowed and dominated by the palace and the university buildings.

The canal linking the Nile and the Red Sea, which had been built by Darius, was once more in regular use. Larger and larger ships sailed the seas from India to the Straits of Gibralter. Banks and a sort of transfer accounting system, developed from principles already known in Babylon and Greece, facilitated trade. The towns in Syria and Asia Minor where the overland trade and caravan routes terminated flourished in the same manner. Science and art were at their peak. Everywhere there took place a cultural and commercial development not to be surpassed or even equalled in Europe until after the Renaissance.

It is not surprising that in modern times, when archaeology and the deciphering of papyri have brought this world again to life, many have considered Hellenism as the greatest period in Greek history. Yet this outward splendour cannot conceal the fact that the internal structure of these kingdoms remained extremely precarious. The palaces and cities owed their wealth and culture to the toil of a population who were almost slaves, tilling the land of the rich and noble, living upon the margin of existence, oppressed by taxation and obligatory services which weighed all the more heavily the more rational and efficient the exploitation became. There was no question of raising the standard of living for these masses. The civilisation of Hellenism and the benefits of prosperity were enjoyed by the upper classes alone. When the kingdoms were attacked by Rome their powers of resistance proved slight as soon as their mercenaries had been defeated. For the native populations Roman rule meant only a change of masters.

THE ROMAN CONQUEST

The gradual extension of the power of Rome will naturally be treated in the section on Roman history; here only a few main points need be touched on. At the time of the Second Punic War, when Hannibal had brought Rome to the extremity of peril, Macedon had attempted to advance itself at the expense of the Romans. After 200 Rome, whose assistance had been invoked by the Greeks for the liberation of their country, attacked the Macedonians and expelled them from Greece. When in 172 the Macedonians renewed the war, now supported by the sympathy of the Greeks, who had soon grown weary of the Roman protectorate, they were crushingly defeated at Pydna (168); the Macedonian monarchy was abolished, and in 147 the country was annexed by Rome ($\rightarrow$ 261).

In 192 Syria under Antiochus III the Great, who had acquired his proud surname by restoring the kingdom of his predecessors to its full extent, went to war with Rome over the supremacy of the Aegean Sea and was defeated and expelled from Asia Minor. Pressed in the east by the Parthians, who about 160 conquered Mesopotamia, and in the west systematically thwarted and weakened by the Romans, Syria dragged out a wretched existence amid continual strife for the throne until all that was left of what had once been so great a kingdom was annexed by Pompey in 64 B.C.

The Ptolemies survived longer by means of accepting the protection of Rome. The later kings entirely lacked the energy of the founders of the dynasty and ruled by the grace of the Romans, puchased by the payment of large gifts. The last queen, Cleopatra, by her personal influence over Caesar and Antony was still able to play a rôle in history. After the defeat of Antony she saved herself from captivity by a voluntary death, and Egypt was incorporated into the crown domain of the Caesars.

In Greece as elsewhere the administration of the Romans at first resulted in serious economic injury, especially when in the time of the civil wars the great men of Rome plundered the provinces without mercy in order to obtain means for the strengthening of their own power in their intestinal strife. But when order returned under the Emperors the prosperity of Asia, Syria, and Egypt quickly revived. They were the richest districts of the Empire. The Romans took over much of the Hellenistic organisation, and elsewhere also adapted it to the institutions of the Empire.

HELLENISTIC CULTURE

Greek culture was deeply rooted in Greek tribal and urban life. Although some of the great poets rose far above the thought and activity of their *milieu*, to achieve what may in truth be termed universal humanity, the tribe and the city-state remained the basis and inspiration.

The political development begun under Philip II of Macedon (**208,** coin of Philip) and completed under and after Alexander the Great, carried Greek culture to the farthest parts of the then-known world. Alexander the Great (**209**) prepared the way; his successors in the new kingdoms continued his policy. A few notable figures were Seleucus I (**210**), Ptolemy I Soter (**211**), Attalus I (**212**), and Mithridates the Great (**213**). Existing cities were expanded, and flourished. **214.** Theatre of Miletus with harbour, now silted up. **215.** The magnificent temple of Apollo in Didyma, one of the best-preserved temple complexes in Asia Minor, was erected upon an earlier foundation. Columns and pillar bases (→ 219, opposite page) are richly decorated. **216.** In the middle of the 2nd century B.C. Attalus II gave Athens a stoa which flanked the Agora. Modern building on ancient foundations. **218.** Gerasa, a member of the Decapolis in Palestine, was one of the numerous Hellenistic city foundations.

219
223

220 221 222 224

Hellenistic art is characterised by its monumental quality on the one hand and on the other by its portrait and genre pieces. The 'Girl of Antium' (217, opposite page) still shows affinity with classical art. 223. The Nike of Samothrace is typical of the sculptural style about the turn of the 3rd and 2nd centuries. 221. A coin of Demetrius Poliorcetes, one of the Diadochi, shows Poseidon, and on the reverse (222) a Nike standing upon the prow of a ship which makes it possible to reconstruct the Nike of Samothrace. 220. Alexandria, named after its founder, was until late in ancient times one of the greatest and wealthiest cities. A coin shows the harbour lighthouse and a sailing ship. 224. Pergamum was an independent centre where a remarkable virtuosity in monumental building and sculpture endowed artistic forms with a rather inflated style. An altar dedicated to Zeus typifies the colossal and ostentatious style of this Hellenistic art.

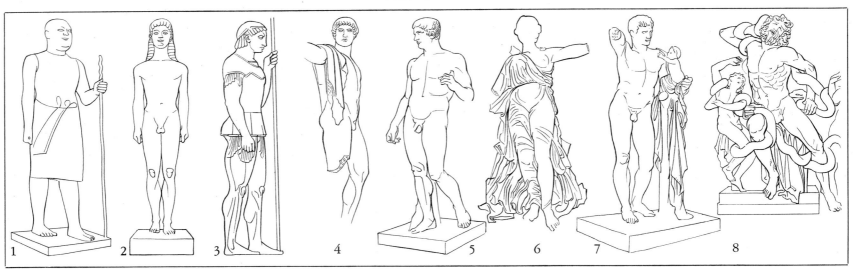

The frontal style of Egyptian sculpture (1) characterises archaic Greek sculpture up to ca. 500 B.C. Examples are the Greek 'kouros' (2) and the Aristion relief (3, → 197). The frontal style was followed by the 'contrapost' with the weight resting upon one leg. The Apollo of Olympia (4, → 162) is an important stage in this development. Further elaboration led to a striving after the ideal human form (5-6). After the Parthenon (→ 180) rigidity gave way to drapery and movement, as in the Nike of Paeonius, dating from the 4th century (6, → 181 and 223). This led in the Hellenistic period to richer and more exuberant forms. The Laocoon (8, a recent reconstruction; 1st cent. B.C.) is typical of this striving after pathos (→ also 224).

When, in the time of the Sophists and the Enlightenment, the ties of tradition were severed and it lost its compulsive power, when good and bad, ugly and beautiful, justice and injustice, appeared merely relative terms, the lofty intellects of Greece – Socrates, Plato, and Aristotle – attempted independently to construct a rationally justifiable philosophy of life from the nature of man himself, or at least to give a new permanent basis to traditional values. Yet they too had always taken as their starting-point man in the natural community of the family, village, or city. Aristotle had formulated this idea in his famous definition that man is a political animal. Without this community, he argued, man is either an animal or a god. In sculpture the gods of the city were depicted as essentially similar to the ideals of the citizens themselves. It was not the luxury of the rich but the prosperity of the city which was reflected in the construction of temple and theatre. In thought and speech the gap between Greek and barbarian was even more distinct. By the Macedonian conquests this culture of the city-state was called upon to take the lead in a new world where the city-state no longer played a dominant rôle, and where the Greek was compelled to feel his way in the *oikoumene*.

It was inevitable that radical changes should take place. Not unnaturally the Hellenistic intellectual world differed markedly from that of the earlier Greeks; rather it is surprising (and this indicates the self-contained power of Greek thought and feeling) that the difference was not considerably greater, and that the Hellenistic world remained as 'Greek' as it did. It is easy to forget that the rulers of this world were not Greeks but Macedonians together with Egyptians, Syrians, Babylonians, and Asiatics of every kind who, with the scattered Greeks, went to form the ruling upper class. What they had in common was Greek culture, which was taught in all the schools, and which soon dominated their behaviour and conscious thought.

RELIGION. It has already been said that Greek religion was essentially a cult of the city deities which influenced the life and actions of the citizens and whose favour had to be won and retained by perpetual rites. Such a cult must of necessity lose much of its value when the city-state disappeared. The Greek, separated from his own surroundings, was obliged, as it were, to stand alone face to face with gods who nevertheless elsewhere and everywhere continued to exercise their influence. Indeed, it had never been so obvious that the lives of all, no matter what their status, were governed by powers beyond human control, which raised one man to dizzying heights and as suddenly plunged another into the depths.

The thoughtful Greek had already been confronted with the fact that other gods were worshipped outside Greece. He had arrived at the conclusion that all these gods, although differing in name and ritual, symbolised nevertheless the same supernatural powers. Thus the way was paved for a far-reaching syncretism in the sphere of religion, all the more as Alexander's successors, who assumed the heritage of the former kings in the lands that they won, favoured this mingling of the Greek and native cults. The Syrians raised no objection to their Baal and Astarte being given the names of Zeus and Aphrodite; the ancient oracle of Ammon in the Egyptian desert was obviously for the Greeks an oracle of Zeus. Only the Jews protested against the identification of Jehovah with Zeus, and the equating of the temple in Jerusalem with other temples met with fierce resistance. On this account they were not absorbed by Hellenism.

Thus the early names of some of the Greek deities received new meaning and content, especially for those who accepted the new names with their Oriental significance and still retained their former religious loyalty. Whereas the cults of the Greek city-state had lost much of their significance now that the city-state no longer constituted the entire world of the citizen, Eastern religions, which spoke of temptation and redemption, gained a deeper significance in contrast with a life that must often have appeared meaningless. Kings and thrones might disappear, but the gods remained. Thus even among the Greeks Eastern religious influences penetrated, especially as they could be assimilated with the ancient Greek mysteries.

A surprising blend of early Greek conceptions and Eastern mysticism is found in the deification of the kings which was widely prevalent at this time. In the East the king was considered to be either the son of the god or the personification of the god himself. The Hellenistic kings inherited this tradition. Alexander, conscious of being one apart from his fellow men, had demanded divine honours even from the Greeks. He had met with fierce opposition from his Macedonians and from the Greeks, but this mentality quickly changed. For among the Greeks too the distance between man and god was not infinite. From the earliest times mighty men, the founders of families and cities, had been honoured after their death as heroes (or demigods, as we say, not entirely accurately, since the hero is undoubtedly a lower though still 'divine' power). It was also natural to the Greeks that Alexander after his death should be worshipped in Alexandria, as the founder of the city. Divine honours were also accorded later to rulers who were still living. By their position they were exalted above the lot of common man; they were raised above human law and rules of conduct, as those upon whose grace men felt themselves dependent. For the ruler himself this apotheosis constituted the legitimisation of his power in roughly the same manner as other princes saw themselves as the Anointed of the Lord or leaders appointed by God. The aureole of divinity elevated them above their subjects, Orientals as well as Greeks. From this time onwards their portraits appeared upon the coinage, which formerly had depicted deities or personifications of a city. The names which they adopted – Saviour, Benefactor, God upon Earth – reveal their pretensions. It is through these rulers that such honours were later transferred to the Roman Emperors.

Magic also, which was native to the East and cultivated as a secret art by the priests and soothsayers, could easily infiltrate into the working of Greek oracles and mystery ceremonies. The Greek Enlightenment, although by no means anti-religious, in general had been opposed to *deisidaimonia*, superstitious fear of the gods, ghosts, and spirits which was rife in Greece among the uneducated, but now even the intellectuals became contaminated with astrology, magic, and witchcraft – the more so since Stoic philosophy had recognised these elements in the religious life of the masses as legitimate spiritual phenomena that had been given a scientifically defined place in Stoic cosmology. From this time onwards the secret 'science' of the Egyptian priests, of Babylonian magicians and astrologers, obtained a mysterious attraction for the Greeks and for the West in general. This attraction was shown by the rapid spread of Eastern mystery-religions and the cults of Isis, Mithras, Sol Invictus, and others, which we find in the Graeco-Roman world at the end of the Hellenistic period.

We have already remarked that the Jews strongly resisted assimilation by Hellenism. Despite the glamour of Hellenistic culture, even the Jews of the Dispersion (Diaspora), more numerous than those living in Palestine itself, retained their exclusive monotheism; they recognised the one, true God exclusively in the God of their fathers and considered the gods of the heathen as idols. This rigid exclusiveness, coupled with a commercial activity which was striking even at this time, produced occasional outbursts of anti-semitism. In Alexandria there were conflicts between the prosperous Jewish community (which formed a separate economic unity in this city) and the Hellenistic population. Far from adapting themselves to Hellenistic culture, the Jews even gained proselytes among the Gentiles. To this end they undertook a translation of their sacred writings into Greek (the Septuagint), while in Alexandria especially educated Jews attempted in their writings to make the Jewish religion and tradition accessible to the Greeks. Philo Judaeus (1st century A.D.) is the best known of these Jewish apologists, and the books of the Maccabees, which describe the glorious struggle of the Jews in Palestine against the Hellenised Syrians, also originated from this circle. That the Greeks gained greater knowledge of the Jews resulted naturally in more interchange of ideas, but that Greek, especially Platonic, influence is evident in the thought and theories of Philo, for example, does not alter the fact that a man like Philo remained nevertheless essentially Jewish. Christianity was to be faced with the same problem, and profited by the methods of the Jewish apologists.

PHILOSOPHY. The philosophy of the intellectuals, who regarded the ancient mythology as a source of amusement for poets, and the religion of the people as the expression of irrational emotion that was of use only to the masses, was founded upon the ideas of Plato and Aristotle. These ideas, however, were adapted to the needs of a different society.

The classical philosophers had attempted to deduce the proper standards for a responsible individual and for communal life from the nature of the natural community of mankind. Now this natural community of the city-state had lost its authority, while the need for a reasonable moral foundation for human action was more imperative than ever. The Greeks had failed to replace the unit of the city-state by a higher notion of nation in which the individual might feel himself sheltered. The kingdoms in which they lived were obviously unnatural units formed by the play of circumstances. Even Aristotle, who had watched the formation of the empire of his pupil Alexander, had not attempted to analyse this new phenomenon in his political works. For him also the city-state remained the highest natural unity. The Hellenistic monarchs, who built up closely-reasoned juridical and administrative structures, based their existence and the duties of their subjects in the last instance upon the idea of divine right, borrowed from the East, or upon conquest. An opinion like that expressed by the enlightened despot Antigonus Gonatas, who called himself not the lord and master but the first servant of his people, was only rarely heard. The Greek when freed from loyalty to his city-state immediately turned to cosmopolitanism, world citizenship, that is, he proclaimed himself an autonomous and self-sufficient individual who had to maintain his position in the world with the aid of his own mind and his own right. He was no longer a social being but a rational being who upon a foundation of reason built up a philosophy which had happiness (*eudaimonia*) as its goal.

Epicurus maintained that this autonomous individual was capable of using his reason as a means of achieving physical happiness and pleasure. For him the universe consisted solely of atoms and empty space. Man was mortal, and death was the end of all. Without fear of gods or an afterlife, man should seek not coarse sensual pleasure but a life brought to a fine art. Politics, the service of the state, and marriage, were disturbing and dangerous to man's peace of mind. Friendship and harmony were the highest good. This philosophy found much support among both those who viewed life as a sport and a game of chance and those who lived in safe seclusion on their private properties.

In direct contradiction to it was the doctrine of the Stoics, established about 300 B.C. by the Cypriot Zeno, who taught that only virtue, based on knowledge, could make a man happy. The body was merely the instrument of the spirit. Outward possessions were valueless and could never bring permanent happiness. The wise man found happiness only in living in harmony with reason or nature, the divine spark in man. As a slave he was truly free; on the rack he was truly happy. Since virtue consists in activity, he devoted himself to the task imposed upon him by the world order. This conviction became for many a religion of duty, which the wise man performed without thought of material consequences. For the Stoic the natural law was identical with God. There was no essential difference between human and divine reason; Stoicism thus verges on pantheism. And since the apparently unreasonable was bound up with the reason which dominates all things, it was not difficult for the Stoics, by allegorical interpretation, to accept the traditional religion as a preliminary phase of reasonable insight. Signs and wonders were regarded as sometimes unfathomable portents of coming events.

Between these two extremes there existed a number of more moderate beliefs. The old Academy of Plato continued to exist, although it abandoned the true Platonic critical method for probabilism and scepticism. Its followers, however, seem to have recognised the laws of virtue, to which the Stoic attributed absolute truth. And although the professional philosophers quarrelled fiercely, they provided society with a pattern of morality and reasonable conduct in a generally accepted rational manner of life.

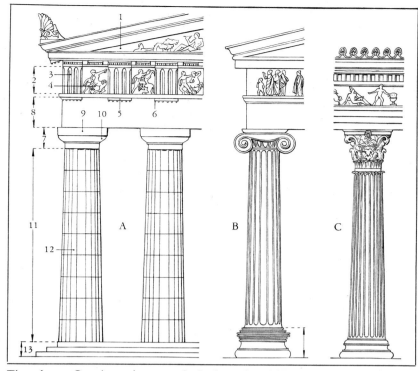

The three Greek architectural Orders (→ 165-74, 190-2). A. Doric, the earliest style, originated in Greece: 1. tympanon, the façade space, occurring at front and rear of the temple; 2. frieze; 3. triglyphs which carried the upper beam; 4. metope, square relief in the architrave (head beam) of the building; alternated with the triglyph; 5. regula, frame under the triglyphs; 6. guttae, small downward-pointing teeth on the regula; 7. architrave, the horizontal main beam resting upon columns or pillars; 8. capital, upper part of the column; varies according to Order; 9. abacus, square top; 10. echinus, round part of the Doric capital; 11. shaft; 12. fluting (usually 20 flutes), vertical grooves in the shaft, shallow in the Doric style and meeting in sharp ridges; 13. stylobate. B. Ionic Order, originated in Ionia ca. 600 B.C. The column stands on a base (14); flutes do not meet but are deeper (usually 24). Volute-shaped capital. C. Corinthian Order, variant of the Ionic, originated end 5th century B.C. Capital ornamented with stylised acanthus leaves.

LITERATURE AND ART. Literature became to a large extent *belles lettres*, in which beauty of form and elegance of expression, often comprehensible only to the educated élite, constituted the chief aims. The schools of rhetoric, which now extended throughout the whole of the Greek-speaking world, had a great influence. The works of the older writers became models to be imitated, with the result that the clever use of phrases and stock expressions and virtuosity of form often concealed a lack of content. The striking productions of the Alexandrian scholars reinforced this tendency to stagnation and mannerism.

It is remarkable that this brilliant Hellenistic world contributed so little that was really new. It was a continuation of the Greek world on a broader scale, based no longer on the city-state but on world-wide standards: yet it remained within the Greek sphere of ideas. It is noteworthy that while Greek scholarship flourished in Egypt it paid no attention to the monuments of Egypt itself, although the Greeks were familiar with Egyptian hieroglyphics. It ignored all that was barbarian. When Rome began to overshadow the Greek world the Greeks tried to Hellenise these new barbarians but took little notice of what was truly Roman, as for example the Latin language.

Monumental art, which drew on its Greek heritage and continued to use Greek techniques, developed in two directions – that of the splendid and colossal by which the kings displayed their wealth and power, and that of concentration upon the individual, upon portraits and *genre* pieces, upon the pathetic and the emotional, with the ever-present danger of lapsing into artificiality and forced effect. The most famous works which inspired European art during the Renaissance date from this period: the Laocoon, the Nike of Samothrace (→ 223), the Venus of Milo. The enormous altar of Pergamum (→ 224) displays this lavish magnificence, which seems to us almost dazzling; yet the sculptors of Pergamum were also capable of creating the strikingly individual type of the savage Galatians.

Hellenism was once considered a decline from classical purity and grandeur. This is certainly untrue. Hellenism was no decline but a change of *milieu*, of taste, and of manner of life, by which Greek culture became a learned civilisation which was internationally studied and imitated. It died away because it was not rooted in a truly living and productive soil. But it fructified others, both at the time of its greatness and later. Jews, Christians, Romans, and Arabs, all drew on its techniques and achievements

225
226
227

228

225. 'The Flaying of Marsyas', by an unknown sculptor, is a striking example of the way in which Hellenistic artists mastered their medium: they knew and were able to represent human anatomy. The art of portraiture (**226, 227**), formerly more idealised, assumed an often moving realism. Many heads of rulers, philosophers, orators, soldiers, and others, have been preserved; some are expressive of deep emotion. It is interesting to compare these with the even more realistic style of Roman bust portraiture (→ 262-6, 315-20, 329-36, 396-403). Owing to the nature of the material nearly the whole of Greek and Hellenistic painting has been lost; vase paintings, however, still convey some idea of its styles. The wall-paintings found in Herculaneum and Pompeii, often Roman copies of earlier works, give an impression of Hellenistic painting. **228.** 'The Feeding of Telephus by a Hind', one of the most important paintings from Herculaneum, now in the National Museum, Naples.

ROME: FROM CITY TO NATION

The Italian peninsula, excluding the Po valley, was inhabited after 1000 B.C. by Indo-European tribes (Umbrians, Sabellians, Oscans, and Latins), while Sicily was the home of the closely related Siculi. In Liguria part of the older pre-Indo-European population continued to survive in the desolate mountains. The Veneti had penetrated in the north-east, and the Messapians in the south, while Illyrian tribes, mingled with other peoples, are found along the whole of the east coast (Map 29, p. 93).

The country, down which runs the dominating mountain range of the Apennines, contains some extremely fertile plains but is mainly mountainous or hilly. Although by no means a natural unity, it offers less resistance to unification than the Balkan regions. The few natural harbours are situated on the west coast: just as Greece was oriented towards the east, Italy turned towards the west. Unlike the Greeks, however, the Italian tribes were not seafaring peoples; agriculture and cattle breeding were their chief means of subsistence. In ancient times, as today, Italy was among the most densely populated areas of the Mediterranean world. Its inhabitants were little conscious of any ethnic unity; the small agricultural settlements lived independently of each other, each jealously defending its pastures and ploughland against its neighbours. Sometimes, however, they joined together for worship at a central sanctuary.

The mineral wealth contained in the soil of Italy and the neighbouring islands was scarcely known to these tribes. It fell to immigrants, the Etruscans, to discover and exploit it, while the trade in the harbours of the south came into the hands of the Greeks from a very early period.

Italy was probably much more thickly wooded in antiquity than it is today. When the Romans later described the way of life of their remote ancestors, they gave with some justification a picture of a primitive people, industrious, frugal, and conservative, for whom hard work in the fields was only varied by hunting or war against their neighbours. Doubtless, being closely connected with the Greeks, as their language indicates, they were also not lacking in talents. But the circumstances of their life caused them to lag behind and kept them far removed from the cultural influences coming from the East.

229. The grim head of the bronze she-wolf on the Capitol in Rome. According to tradition she suckled the twins Romulus and Remus, who laid the foundations of a city which Romulus later called Rome and which was to expand far beyond the seven hills of its original settlement and to grow in might until it ruled the then-known world.

FOREIGN INFLUENCES

This agrarian world did not, however, develop in isolation: from earliest times it was dominated by foreign influences. From the eighth century B.C. onwards Greeks occupied the south and southwest coast (as far north as Cumae → 98), together with Sicily, whose population they gradually dominated (see Maps 31-4, p. 94). The northwest and central regions were controlled by the Etruscans, a mysterious people, whose origin and language still remain obscure. The most widely-held view is that, like the Greeks, they reached Italy by sea from the east before ca. 800 B.C. in the period that followed the general disturbance and migrations in the eastern Mediterranean. Arriving perhaps from Lydia and settling on the coast of Etruria, they spread as a ruling aristocracy throughout the whole of this area. By the sixth and fifth centuries some of them had crossed the Apennines and colonised the country south of the Po, around Bologna. Southwards their influence extended as far as Campania, while Elba and Corsica also came within their power. It was they who, together with the Carthaginians, limited the area available to Greek colonists for settlement.

We can gain some idea of their social and spiritual life from the great cemeteries which, like veritable cities of the dead, they were accustomed to build outside their city boundaries (→ 230-41). They achieved great prosperity by exploiting the fertility of their land and its mineral wealth, and carried on a flourishing trade with Greece. Greek together with Oriental influences predominate in their art, and their tombs are filled with articles imported from Greece. They adapted the Greek alphabet for their own use, but their language, though revealed in many an inscription, remains basically undeciphered, although a few names and words are known. The fact that it was almost certainly not Indo-European supports the theory of their eastern origin.

Their social structure was essentially aristocratic, although in early times each city probably had its own king. The twelve chief cities formed a loose league, sometimes perhaps with a common leader. Their way of life was luxurious and their religion strongly influenced by ideas of a future life, in which monsters and demons played an important part. The Greeks, who knew them to be warlike and cruel and feared them as sea rovers, named them Tyrrhenoi or Tyrsenoi, while the Romans, who were conscious of being indebted to them for many forms of religious and political life, called them Tusci or Etrusci. They themselves appear to have used the name Rasenna. They attained the zenith of their wealth and power during the sixth and fifth centuries B.C. After this time they were harassed from the north by the invading Gauls. In the south their power was checked by the battle of Cumae, in which their navy was defeated by Hiero of Syracuse (474). Rome regained its independence in 510 and Latium about this time also. By about 400 the Romans were ready to counter-attack and advance northwards against the cities of Etruria, and in the course of the next century they subdued the whole region. The Etruscan language and traditions lingered on until the beginning of our era. Etruscan influence upon Rome had been considerable, and Rome itself may be an Etruscan name.

FOUNDATION AND GROWTH OF ROME

Rome, according to tradition, was founded in 753 B.C. by Romulus, the son of Mars, upon the Palatine hill. Seven kings are said to have ruled over it, the last three of Etruscan origin, until in 510 B.C. the last of these foreign rulers, Tarquinius Superbus, a tyrant, was driven out by Brutus, liberty restored, and a republic established. Many of the recorded stories about early Rome are legendary. Unlike the Greeks, for whom the possession of the Homeric poems provided some kind of historical background, the early Romans possessed no written tradition. It was only in the late third century, when the city had become powerful, that Rome developed an historical interest in its own past, which was then reconstructed from meagre data. These comprised the official chronicles of the priests, lists of magistrates, the exploits of their ancestors proudly preserved by noble families, and some folk-legends, together with a few early documents such as treaties. It was from such unsatisfactory material that later Roman historians had to work when they came to reconstruct the early history of their country.

Rome was 'founded' in about the eighth century B.C. upon the group of hills which dominated a ford over the Tiber just below a small island in the river. This was also the point beyond which no vessels could proceed, and here a road running from north to south crossed with a 'salt route' which led from the Tiber estuary to the Sabines living in the hills to the east. At this spot small groups of shepherds and farmers, living on the scattered 'seven hills', united to form a larger community grouped around the oldest settlement upon the Palatine and to build a stronghold on the fairly steep and easily defensible Capitol (→ 350–1). The population was mixed, certainly including some Sabines, but was essentially Latin, akin to the peoples who inhabited the surrounding land and hills of Latium. Nascent Rome must soon have become a market centre for the neighbouring Latin towns, which were united in a league to maintain the cult of Jupiter Latiaris upon the Mons Albanus. The small town of Alba Longa, which originally controlled this cult-centre, was taken by Rome and destroyed. Rome then assumed the leadership, according to the legend, in the reign of Tullus Hostilius.

The social structure of Rome was still completely feudal. The *populus Romanus Quiritium* (the ancient name which always remained in official use) was composed of a number of families or clans (*gentes*). The heads of some of these clans, the fathers (*patres*), formed a Council of Elders, the Senate, which advised the king. The *patres* and their families, the patricians, had many dependent clients who owed loyalty and service to them as patrons. These formed a considerable part of the plebeians, who were full members of the early community; that is, they were Roman citizens but were excluded from certain privileges. The king (*rex*), who was chosen from the *patres*, was chief judge, leader of the army, and high priest; he was invested with supreme executive authority (*imperium*), sanctified by the gods through revealed omens (*auspicia*). This rather primitive organisation was called by the Romans their *res publica*, their 'public business' in contrast to their *res privata*, their private life, in which the *pater familias* maintained full rights over every member of his household (*familia*), rights which even included the power of life and death.

In the sixth century, when the Etruscans dominated central and northern Italy and saw that Rome was a strategic point on the road to the south, the Etruscan family of the Tarquins managed to seize the throne at Rome, supported perhaps by many of the plebeians. Under the Etruscan kings Rome became a much more powerful community and developed into a real city-state. Extensive earthworks gave protection, the valley between the hills was drained and became a commercial centre (the Forum), new religious ideas were introduced, and the great temple of Jupiter Optimus Maximus was built on the Capitol. Roman craftsmen began to imitate the technical skill of the Etruscans in metal and clay, industry and trade developed quickly, and the population increased: in brief, in the second half of the sixth century the early peasant community of Rome was swept into a much wider and more civilised world. But in 510 a rising of the patricians and their clans put an end to the domination of the Tarquins. Henceforth the very word *rex*, 'king', was abhorrent to the Romans, and Rome soon lapsed into a much more parochial state.

The Republic

THE BEGINNINGS OF THE REPUBLIC

Henceforward, in place of a king, two magistrates (later called consuls) were chosen from among the patricians to hold office for a year. The Senate (or *patres*) continued to act in an advisory capacity, but in fact became the dominant governing body. Public affairs, such as the choice of magistrates, legislation, war and peace, sentence of death, might theoretically be decided by the *Comitia* (popular assembly), but in fact the senators managed to impose their will on the assembly. This was partly due to the fact that the *Comitia* voted not individually but in groups (originally *curiae*, but later *centuriae*) which the heads of the clans, although numerically in the minority, succeeded in dominating. In its external policy the new *Res Publica Romana* formed an alliance on equal terms with the surrounding Latin towns, by which their private rights were shared, i.e. the right to contract a valid marriage and to possess land (the *ius connubii* and the *ius commercii*).

In the new Republic the plebeians, who had earlier been protected by the king, were left more at the mercy of the arbitrary decisions of the patrician magistrates and Senate. Thus the early part of the internal history of Republican Rome is characterised by a fierce struggle by the plebeians, first for protection and later for equality with the patricians. They were able to bring pressure on the patricians by threatening to withdraw from Rome altogether and thus deprive the state of labour and military support. Also their numerical superiority over the patricians increased, since the patrician families tended to diminish while the numbers of the plebeians grew because by a generous policy Rome absorbed into the citizen body many immigrants, including even people from some of the cities that it had subdued. Thus the plebeians came to include some wealthy and powerful members who were capable of assuming leadership in the struggle for equal rights. In the middle of the fifth century they compelled the patricians to recognise the officers (tribunes of the plebs) whom they had established for their own protection. Henceforth the persons of the tribunes were to be inviolable (e.g. not subject to arrest), and they could veto any action taken by a magistrate. Further, the plebeians forced the patricians to publish the laws in accordance with which they administered justice.

Even when these guarantees had been won, however, the struggle for equality continued and the plebeians fought for access to the magistracies. In 367 B.C. they secured that one of the consuls each year should henceforth be a plebeian, and they soon won entry to the other magistracies (those of praetor, quaestor, censor, etc.). Since the ranks of the Senate were kept filled by the censors, who normally chose former magistrates, the Senate gradually came to include a considerable number of plebeians, some of whom were as rich and distinguished as the aristocratic patricians.

Thus by compromise and common sense the Romans settled their internal social and political differences without bloodshed, unlike so many Greek cities whose internal development was all too often disfigured by civil war. At Rome, however, oligarchy was not abolished but received a new lease of life. A new élite grew up composed of patricians and plebeians, of families who through wealth and influence, through experience handed down from father to son (formal education was unknown in Rome) enjoyed the confidence of the people and regularly held the chief magistracies. These were the nobles (*nobiles*) and formed the governing class. Every young *nobilis* served in the army at an early age and then held a junior magistracy, so that, having gained a thorough knowledge of the affairs of state, he might in the end rise to the highest positions – praetor (who supervised the administration of justice), consul, and censor.

Unlike the Greeks, who had curtailed and weakened executive power and thereby secured greater freedom for their democratic Assemblies and leaders, the Romans allowed the magistrates to retain full *imperium* and found the safeguard to their liberty in the fact that magistrates held office for one year only (after which they could be called to account) and that each magistrate had a colleague who could check him. Further, from the beginning of the Republic the right of appeal to the people (*provocatio*) against the execution of a magistrate's sentence had been allowed. In contrast with the annually changing magistrates, the Senate was a permanent body and consequently its influence increased. In particular it gained control of financial and foreign policy, and although its resolutions were officially no more than recommendations, they were recommendations which the magistrates could not afford to ignore. The *Comitia* now voted in groups called 'centuries' (originally divisions of the population for military service); these were arranged by the censors on the basis of a scale of property qualifications which determined military obligations. The division was such that the first class (those who could provide themselves with full armour) and the knights (*equites*) together held a majority of the votes. Thus the rich could dominate the *Comitia*. The unpropertied citizens, the *proletarii*, were not debarred from voting but possessed collectively only one century, that is, one vote (out of probably 193).

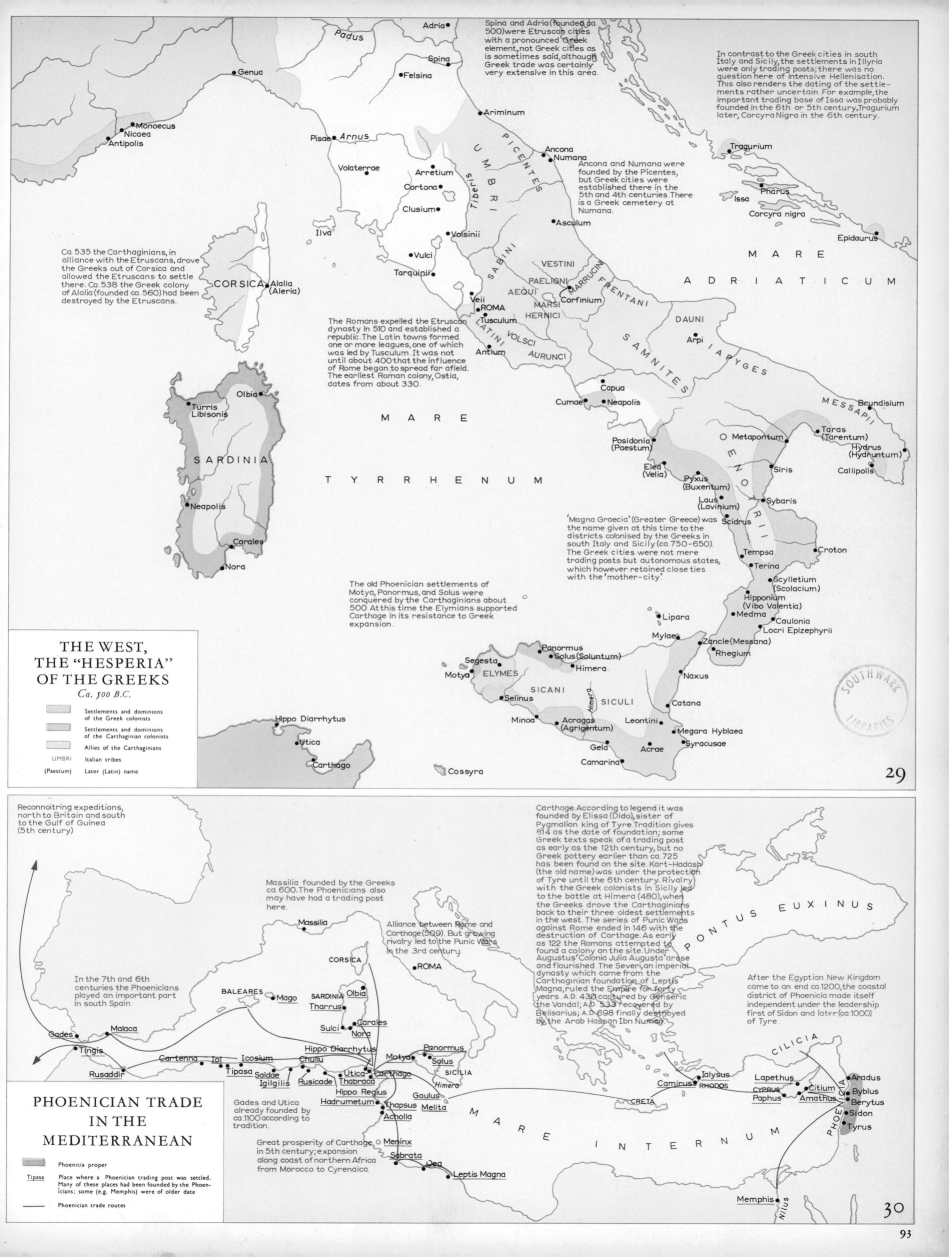

Map 29 — THE WEST, THE "HESPERIA" OF THE GREEKS
Ca. 500 B.C.

Legend:
- Settlements and dominions of the Greek colonists
- Settlements and dominions of the Carthaginian colonists
- Allies of the Carthaginians
- UMBRI — Italian tribes
- (Paestum) — Later (Latin) name

Spina and Adria (founded ca. 500) were Etruscan cities with a pronounced Greek element, not Greek cities as is sometimes said, although Greek trade was certainly very extensive in this area.

In contrast to the Greek cities in south Italy and Sicily, the settlements in Illyria were only trading posts; there was no question here of intensive Hellenisation. This also renders the dating of the settlements rather uncertain. For example, the important trading base of Issa was probably founded in the 6th or 5th century, Tragurium later, Corcyra Nigra in the 6th century.

Ancona and Numana were founded by the Picentes, but Greek cities were established there in the 5th and 4th centuries. There is a Greek cemetery at Numana.

Ca. 535 the Carthaginians, in alliance with the Etruscans, drove the Greeks out of Corsica and allowed the Etruscans to settle there. Ca. 538 the Greek colony of Alalia (founded ca. 560) had been destroyed by the Etruscans.

The Romans expelled the Etruscan dynasty in 510 and established a republic. The Latin towns formed one or more leagues, one of which was led by Tusculum. It was not until about 400 that the influence of Rome began to spread far afield. The earliest Roman colony, Ostia, dates from about 330.

'Magna Graecia' (Greater Greece) was the name given at this time to the districts colonised by the Greeks in south Italy and Sicily (ca. 750-650). The Greek cities were not mere trading posts but autonomous states, which however retained close ties with the 'mother-city'.

The old Phoenician settlements of Motya, Panormus, and Solus were conquered by the Carthaginians about 500. At this time the Elymians supported Carthage in its resistance to Greek expansion.

29

Map 30 — PHOENICIAN TRADE IN THE MEDITERRANEAN

Legend:
- Phoenicia proper
- Tipasa — Place where a Phoenician trading post was settled. Many of these places had been founded by the Phoenicians; some (e.g. Memphis) were of older date.
- Phoenician trade routes

Reconnoitring expeditions, north to Britain and south to the Gulf of Guinea (5th century)

Massilia founded by the Greeks ca. 600. The Phoenicians also may have had a trading post here.

Alliance between Rome and Carthage (509). But growing rivalry led to the Punic Wars in the 3rd century.

Carthage. According to legend it was founded by Elissa (Dido), sister of Pygmalion king of Tyre. Tradition gives 814 as the date of foundation; some Greek texts speak of a trading post as early as the 12th century, but no Greek pottery earlier than ca. 725 has been found on the site. Kart-Hadash (the old name) was under the protection of Tyre until the 6th century. Rivalry with the Greek colonists in Sicily led to the battle at Himera (480), when the Greeks drove the Carthaginians back to their three oldest settlements in the west. The series of Punic Wars against Rome ended in 146 with the destruction of Carthage. As early as 122 the Romans attempted to found a colony on the site. Under Augustus 'Colonia Julia Augusta' arose and flourished. The Severi, an imperial dynasty which came from the Carthaginian foundation of Leptis Magna, ruled the Empire for forty years. A.D. 430 captured by Genseric the Vandal; A.D. 533 recovered by Belisarius; A.D. 698 finally destroyed by the Arab Hassan Ibn Numan.

After the Egyptian New Kingdom came to an end ca. 1200, the coastal district of Phoenicia made itself independent under the leadership first of Sidon and later (ca. 1000) of Tyre.

In the 7th and 6th centuries the Phoenicians played an important part in south Spain.

Gades and Utica already founded by ca. 1100 according to tradition.

Great prosperity of Carthage in 5th century; expansion along coast of northern Africa from Morocco to Cyrenaica.

30

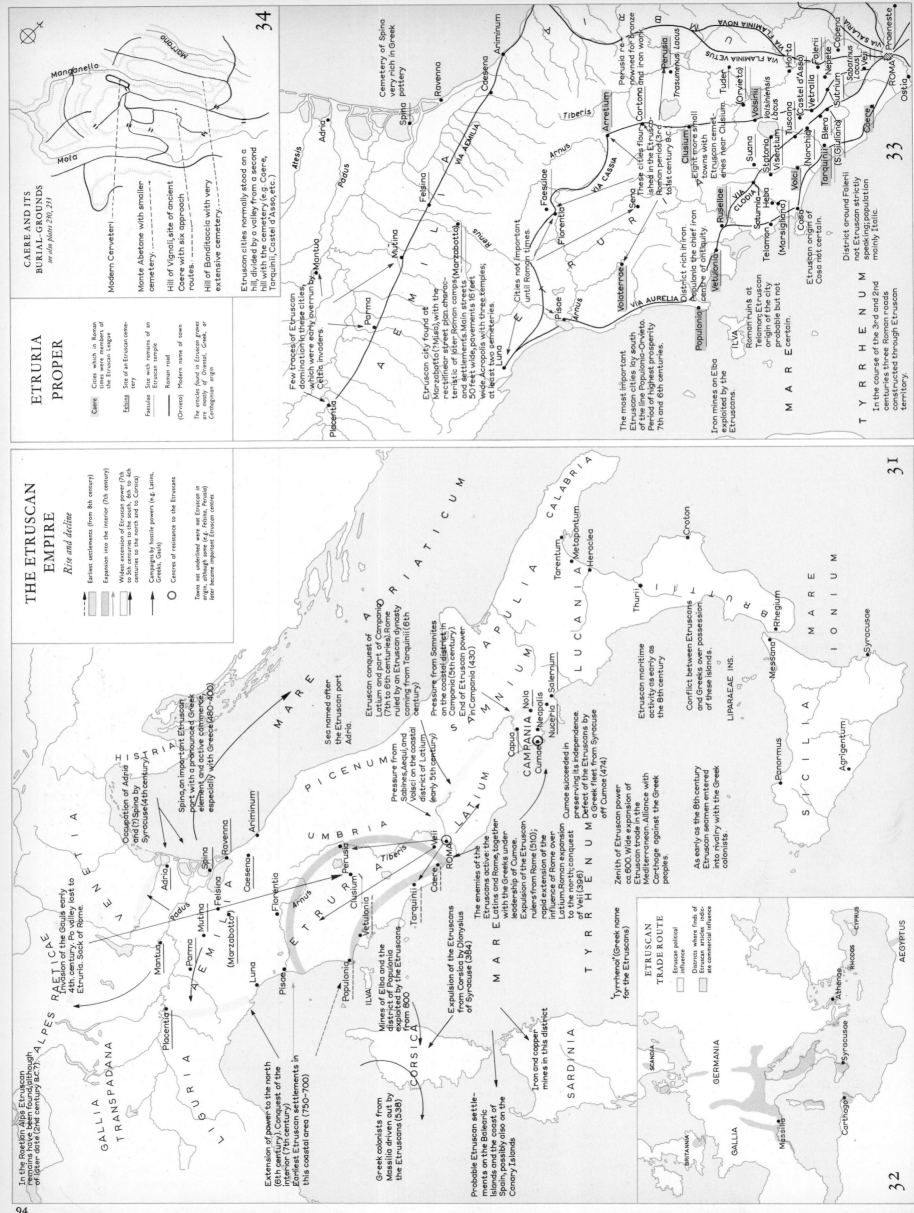

230
233

231
232
234

The Etruscans, who penetrated deeply into Italy from the coast, dominated Rome, and pressed southwards to Greek Cumae, built large cities. **230.** One of the most important was Caere, on the coast; modern Cerveteri occupies a small section of the plateau upon which the ancient city stood. The valley of the Manganello (centre) divides the city of the living from that of the dead upon the Banditaccia plateau to the right (see Map 34). **233.** Aerial view of the same area, with the modern city (upper left), the valley, and the hill with the cemetery and its numerous circular burial mounds. **231.** Tombs, hewn out of tufa and covered with earth mounds, in which the dead were laid, surrounded by funeral gifts. **232.** Streets with rock tombs convey the impression of a city of the dead even more than do the mounds. **234.** The walls of many towns in central Italy date from the Etruscan period. Gate, the Porta all' Arco in Volterra, of which the substructure is Etruscan.

235
236

The Etruscans, like the Greeks, disposed of well-armed, well-trained soldiers. After many campaigns they succeeded in conquering much of the Italian peninsula. **235.** Etruscan archer and spearman, accompanied by Nike with wreath. **236.** Battle scene on an Etruscan relief. Many shields, often more than 3 ft. in diameter, have been found in Etruscan graves at Cerveteri and elsewhere.

Rome gradually became the leader of the Latin League. During the fifth century the Romans and Latins had a stiff struggle against the expanding Sabellian highlanders, who also in this period were pressing hard against many of the Greek colonies in the south. In the north Rome had to face a hostile Etruria. The fourth century, however, saw the might of Etruria weakened by incursions of warlike Gauls who overran the Po valley and pursued their marauding expeditions as far as central Italy. Rome seized this opportunity in 396 to storm the Etruscan city of Veii, which guarded the southern flank of Etruria. In 390, however, Rome itself was overwhelmed and plundered by a Gallic host after a heavy defeat near the Allia. This day remained for all time in the Roman calendar as a *dies ater*, a day of disaster.

After the retreat of the Gauls, Rome was able to set itself up as the champion of central Italy against such threats from the north. It had now become a mighty city and proceeded to overshadow its Latin allies. After a war in which the latter made a last attempt to retain their independence, the league was dissolved. Some of the Latins were admitted into the Roman state with either full or limited Roman citizenship, while others remained allies as before though in practice they had sunk to a subordinate position.

Unlike Athens and Sparta, who had similarly succeeded in subjecting their allies, Rome converted many of its allies into Roman citizens, although at first with limited rights for some, and thus laid the foundations of a unity which the Greeks, with their conception of hegemony and of a natural barrier between the city-states, never attained. This difference of policy ultimately rests upon a difference of ideas. To the Greeks the city-state was a fact of nature and the gulf between the various states unbridgeable. To the Romans citizenship was a legal relation capable of expansion in great variation of form and status. As early as 350 the Roman citizens far exceeded those of Athens or Sparta in number and were distributed throughout a large area (Latium). In addition the other members of the confederacy that Rome had established were allied and economically bound up with Rome by *connubium* and *commercium* to such an extent that, far from desiring to break away, as did for instance the allies of Athens in the fifth century, they aspired to Roman citizenship. Thus were laid the foundations for a nation. The Romans, developing their own legal theories, had succeeded in avoiding the two rocks upon which the Greek city-state had always perished: they had built up a ruling élite experienced in political matters and enjoying the confidence of the people, and a governmental system that could be adapted to the needs of their growing territory; and they possessed a growing body of citizens capable of dominating first Latium and later all Italy, and assimilating it into one people and one state centred on Rome.

In the second half of the fourth century this Roman-Latin federation, after a fierce struggle against the group of Samnite tribes which equalled Rome in size and energy but was weaker in organisation, gained supremacy over the whole of central Italy, although only after suffering some heavy defeats. It immediately began to assimilate these people also, as the Latins earlier, by establishing colonies at strategic points and by the liberal granting of citizenship. Many Greek towns in Campania, especially Naples, gladly joined this federation, in which the members remained sovereign states and retained their local autonomy while becoming members of a larger union.

DEVELOPMENT OF THE ROMAN ARMY

In the fourth century the Romans developed to greater perfection the instrument of their expanding power: the legionary army. Every year

citizens were conscripted in turn for military service. Among the Greeks the great difficulty had always been that the distinction between citizen and soldier had never been clarified. Citizens, when serving in the army, still claimed freedom of expression and persisted in considering their commanders more or less as servants; lack of discipline had always been their weak point (Sparta had been able to maintain its superiority for so long thanks to its sense of discipline). But the Roman citizen during military service accepted even the severest discipline. In the field the magistrates held the supreme command (*imperium*) symbolised by the *fasces* borne before them by their lictors.

Camp was pitched and fortified every day anew according to a standard procedure, regardless of the heavy labour which this demanded of the soldiers. The battle order also was drawn up according to fixed rules, and the legions, which were divided into small units (maniples), carried out their tactical movements according to plan. Standard methods were devised to storm fortified places, which were often taken despite their reputedly impregnable positions. In routine and drill this citizen militia was the equal of the professional soldiers to whom the Greeks had been compelled to resort, while Italy provided a practically inexhaustible reserve of manpower to compensate for defeats. The fixed routine also made it possible for the consuls and praetors, who changed from year to year, to assume command; they had all been trained in this school and could relieve each other without difficulty. In 312 was laid the first of the great highways (the Via Appia) with which the Romans proceeded to unite their territory and thus facilitate the movement of their troops.

Thus equipped, Rome, hitherto almost unknown, suddenly appeared as a fresh power on the horizon of the Hellenistic world which the conquests of Alexander and his successors had created.

CULTURE

During the earliest period Rome did not develop a culture markedly different from that of the neighbouring Latin cities, and it remained essentially an agricultural peasant community. But to the south lay the Greeks (see Map 29, p. 93), to the north the Etruscans (see Maps 31–4, p. 94). It was from the most northerly Greek city, Cumae, that the Romans probably adopted their alphabet. Most of the Greek influences that reached early Rome came less by direct contact than through the mediation of the Etruscans, although some contact was made with Massilia, the Greek port in southern Gaul. What Rome owed to the Etruscans has already been briefly touched upon. The great temple of Jupiter was built by an Etruscan architect; the famous wolf which stood on the Capitol was Etruscan work (→ 229), and from the Apollo of Veii we can obtain an impression of the terracotta statues of the gods which adorned the oldest Roman temples. But despite its great cultural debt to the Etruscans, Rome remained basically a Latin city and hardly any Etruscan words were adopted into the Latin language.

RELIGION. The spiritual life of Rome was at first dominated by *religio*, the relationship between man and gods. In contrast to the Greeks who instinctively conceived their gods anthropomorphically, the early Roman felt himself surrounded on all sides by vague spirits which he could represent only by symbols. There were the spirits of the ancestors of the family; every house had its *lar*, the genius of the ancestor, and its *penates*, the household gods, which protected the possessions within the house. They were honoured

Another important Etruscan city was Tarquinii, whose 'Lucumos', the Tarquins, succeeded even in becoming kings of Rome. The tombs discovered there in the 18th century and afterwards nearly all have wall-paintings in them which reveal the artistic skill of the Etruscan painters. **237.** A man with wreath and drinking-bowl dances to the music of a double flute. **238.** A dead man with a drinking-bowl lying upon a bed; in his outstretched hand he holds an egg, a symbol of life. On the wall hang a wreath and an entwined sash. **239.** The burial mounds of Caere often contain sculpture. In one of the tombs the riches for the dead and the pillars are decorated with reliefs of everyday objects. **240.** A stone chair often stands beside the dead man's couch. **241.** In the background the hills of ancient Tarquinii and in front the valley which separates the city from the cemetery hill. Very few remains of the city have survived.

Excavations on the Germalus, the southwest angle of the Palatine (→ 353-8), have cast some light upon the dim origins of Rome. Remains of huts and holes for piles (243) have been discovered, dating from the beginning of the 8th century and the early 7th century B.C., the period in which Rome is believed to have been founded. The piles served as supports for the roof. In the middle was room for a fire; water was carried away by the channels. Judging from the remains which have been found, the huts had a perimeter of ca. 12 by 15½ ft. Traces of fire were plainly visible, especially on excavation, and indicated the position of the hearth. The form of the huts is similar to that of the numerous hut-urns which have been found in graves in Latium and Etruria and date from a somewhat earlier period (9th–8th cent.). **242.** From ca. 450 B.C. the Romans and Latins founded colonies in central Italy. Citizens were sometimes transferred to existing towns and given land. Strong 'Cyclopean' walls still surround many of these cities. Detail of the early city wall at Cori, south of Rome. In this little town, built upon a hill, are also preserved remains from later periods, including a temple of the first cent. B.C. on the highest point in the city. The mythological origin of Rome has always been an important subject in art. Thus a relief (245) from the beginning of the 3rd century A.D. shows Rhea Silvia by the Tiber while Mars descends to her surrounded by Cupids and torch-bearers. This is the moment when she will become the mother of Romulus and Remus, the founders of Rome. An altar (244) from Ostia, the port of Rome, shows the miraculous feeding of Romulus and Remus by the she-wolf alongside the recumbent god of the Tiber, who reclines with his left hand on a water pitcher. Two shepherds watch what is happening. Above the she-wolf the Palatine hill is represented symbolically, with the local god and the Roman eagle.

246

246. The Tiber rises on Mt. Fumaiolo (4,620 ft.) north of Arezzo. For the Romans it had an importance greater than that of any other river. Poets called it 'gentle Father Tiber', and sculptors depicted it as a recumbent, bristly-bearded river-god with a horn of plenty in his hand (**247**). Horace spoke of *flavus Tiberis*, 'the tawny Tiber', but the river acquires a deep yellow colour only when torrential rain loosens soil in the mountains and drives it down to the valley. Every year this silt advances the delta mouth nearly 4 yards seawards, so that classical Ostia is now about 3 miles from the coastline. The river is useful for shipping only in its lower reaches. During the Roman period it formed the link between Rome and the port of Ostia. The photograph shows the famous river at its source, in the region of Pieve Stefano, where is twists and turns through the narrow Apennine mountain country. Fed by numerous tributaries, after a course of nearly 250 miles through Tuscany, Umbria, Latium, the Campagna, and Rome itself, it debouches into the Mediterranean Sea, as the second longest river of Italy. Its two ancient mouths are now three miles inland; the more northerly, the Fossa Traiana, is kept open by dredging.

at a domestic altar which was in fact nothing but the hearth, in the centre of the early Roman atrium-house. At the same time all manifestations of nature were seen as the work of supernatural powers with whom the Romans had to live at peace. At birth, at marriage, at death, and before transactions of any kind, the favour of these spirits had to be gained by punctilious ritual. The fields were purified in solemn procession, the cattle blessed and protected by prayer and vow. The *pater familias* was naturally also the priest, and the religious equipment (*sacra*) of the family was carefully handed down to descendants.

Like the home and the family, the state also had its household gods. The *imperium*, the supreme command wielded by the Roman rulers, was perhaps originally a magic power which enabled the leader to bring prosperity and blessing to the community. All the transactions of the magistrates and all public affairs were in principle governed by the *auspicia*, the signs given by the gods through the flight of birds, intently observed by a priest (the *augur*), who stood beside the magistrate and explained their meaning to him. The army started for a campaign amid solemn ceremonies and returned with the same solemnity. Whenever Jupiter had granted victory to his people a triumph was celebrated in which the commander, wearing the dress of the god, rode in a chariot to the Capitol at the head of his army. Miraculous signs, and these included any abnormal event, were reported to the Senate and propitiatory ceremonies were held. Sometimes the official books of oracles, reputed to have been handed down from the Cumaean prophetess, the Sibyl, were consulted by a commission appointed for this purpose. Occasionally *haruspices* (Etruscan soothsayers who understood the art of reading the will of the gods from the entrails of sacrificial animals) might be consulted. Any irregularity was atoned for by sacrifice and feast.

In the ancient temple of Vesta in the Forum burned the eternal fire of Rome itself, guarded by the Vestal Virgins. In the Regia close by resided the *Pontifex Maximus*, head of the college of *pontifices* who supervised the

performance of religious ceremonies; this college acquired authority over all minor colleges.

In all religious rites the essential factor was the precise form of word and procedure. The slightest mistake rendered the ritual void; but on the other hand a ceremony completed without fault bound the god to grant his favour. It was a general custom among the Romans to make vows to the gods, but these took the form of a contract: *Do ut des* ('I give, in order that you may give'). Then if the god fulfilled the wish of the person making the vow, he in turn would fulfil the next promise which he made.

The Romans began early to identify the names of their deities with those of the Greek gods: for instance, Jupiter and Juno were equated with Zeus and Hera, Ceres with Demeter. Thus a real, if formal, religious sentiment developed, which made it possible and, for the Roman, logical, for this

247

248
249

250
251
252

After becoming a city-state, Rome freed itself from Etruscan domination, established a republic, and soon came into conflict with the neighbouring towns and tribes. The Etruscan cities, the Falisci, Volsci, Aequi, Samnites, and other tribes were gradually subjugated. **250.** Warrior from Capestrano, in the mountainous district of Picenum, in festive attire, with sun-helmet and girdle. Modern Ascoli Piceno (**252**), the former Asculum, possesses a bridge of the time of Augustus. **248.** Tomb-painting at Paestum showing Samnite soldiers with helmets, greaves, and corselets. **249.** View of the Caudine Forks near Benevento in Samnium, where during the great Samnite war the Samnites surrounded a Roman army and forced it to capitulate (321 B.C.). **251.** The Falisci were among the opponents most dreaded by the Romans. After their subjection and the destruction of their city the Romans allowed them to build another city on a new site (→ 253).

close interweaving of religious and political ceremonies to survive in Rome. The Greek historian Polybius later remarked with some astonishment that those religious scruples which had long been regarded by the enlightened Greeks as superstition and an obstacle to free speculation were for the Romans a source of power, a spiritual prop to the self-confidence that characterised Roman behaviour.

Law. This same formalism, encouraging discipline and order, marked Roman law from its beginnings. At the outset the Roman state confined itself to drawing up unvarying forms of procedure for dealing with legal disputes between citizens. According to strictly regulated norms – the close connection with religion appears from the fact that in early times it was the *pontifices* who drew up the procedure – the citizen could lodge his claims with the praetor, who, however, did not then administer justice himself but formulated and defined the chief points of the question at issue and then laid the case before a civil judge. The Romans did not produce a codified legal system apart from the Laws of the Twelve Tables (450 B.C.). These continued to constitute the basic code but were continually supplemented both by laws originating in legislation of the *Comitia* and by the law introduced by the praetors. Every year the praetor issued his edict regarding civil processes, wherein he defined which cases and what procedures he

would recognise, thus constantly creating new actions and new remedies.

In this way, in public and private affairs there gradually grew up a body of legal usages and precedents. This *mos maiorum* (ancestral custom) formed the basis of the individual laws and edicts, in essence strongly conservative, yet never fossilising into a rigid dogmatic system. It was precisely this wiry flexibility which made it possible for the institutions of a small city-state to expand and meet the needs of a large federal state without revolutionary upheavals (see pages 194 and Map 70, p. 183).

THE CONFLICT WITH THE HELLENISTIC WORLD AND WITH CARTHAGE

By the beginning of the third century Rome had united the whole of central Italy under its rule, and the internal conflict between patricians and plebeians had been resolved by the admission of all to public office, leading to the formation of a new class of *nobiles*. The power of Rome then expanded until it impinged upon the sphere of interest of the Greek cities in southern Italy, which till then had held their own successfully against pressure from the hill tribes in their hinterland. In particular, the wealthy and powerful city of Tarentum, which considered itself the champion of Magna Graecia had frequently employed Greek mercenaries to repel the Lucanians and the Samnites. In 280, fully resolved to call a halt in good time to Roman expansion, it provoked a quarrel with Rome and sent for Pyrrhus king of

253. Roman policy with regard to conquered cities and tribes during the early years of its expansion is strikingly illustrated by the fate of Falerii, the capital of the Falisci, and one of the twelve cities of Etruria, destroyed in 241 B.C. The inhabitants were compelled to abandon the strategic position of their city, built upon a height between the Monti Cimini and the river Tiber, and to construct at a short distance away on the plain a new dwelling-place, Falerii Novi, which was no danger to the Romans. The air photograph shows the sites of both cities. 1. The modern town of Città Castellana, on an eminence formed between steep river valleys, which here flow together, stands on the site of the original Falerii. A few miles away in the plain is Falerii Novi, also called Aequum Faliscum (2). Many remains survive, but the city was again abandoned in the Middle Ages in favour of the original site. Outside the city wall (→ 251) a cemetery with long corridors was hewn out of the rocks. After the wars with the Samnites and with Pyrrhus in south Italy and the crushing of the last resistance of the Etruscans, a united confederacy was achieved in Italy under the hegemony of Rome. Rome thus took its place among the Mediterranean powers, and in the following period was compelled to join issue with Carthage, which controlled extensive dominions abroad and by means of large-scale trade had become very wealthy.

Epirus, a war lord who had attempted to build up a kingdom for himself when the successors of Alexander were struggling for power. Since he had recently been driven from that part of Macedon which he had obtained, he gladly seized this new opportunity, seeing in it a chance to lay claim to the succession of Agathocles, tyrant of Syracuse.

The first clash between the Roman legions and the Greek professional army, at Heraclea in 280, went in favour of the Greeks. The Romans suffered a severe defeat and were driven back to the frontiers of Latium. Now for the first time, however, a noteworthy difference between the Hellenistic and Roman manner of fighting appeared. For the Hellenistic kings war was a game played for profit; for the Romans it was a struggle of life and death. Rome therefore rejected all offers of peace, having decided as a matter of principle that no negotiations could be undertaken with an enemy who had a footing on Italian soil. While Pyrrhus' mercenary army gradually shrank in numbers, the Romans could draw upon the reserves of a large population practised in the use of arms. After another 'Pyrrhic victory' at Asculum, where he again suffered serious casualties, Pyrrhus saw no use in continuing an obstinate war which offered no promise of gain. Instead he decided to champion the cause of the Greek cities in Sicily against the Carthaginians. While he was away the Romans recovered their lost ground; and when he returned to Italy the battle of Beneventum in 275, by which he had hoped to turn the tide, proved no decisive victory. The Romans had by now learnt enough of his tactics to hold their own at least in the open field. Pyrrhus abandoned his enterprise and returned to Greece, where he tried to conquer Macedon. He was killed in a street fight in Argos. Thus deserted, Tarentum and the other Greek cities were obliged to recognise Roman supremacy. They became the allies of Rome and retained a considerable degree of self-government. Thus by 270 the unification of the whole of Italy under Rome was an accomplished fact.

Carthage, founded by Semitic colonists from Tyre, had occupied the wealthy and powerful region of modern Tunisia and had dominated Numidia (Algeria). Expanding overseas, the Carthaginians had fought for centuries with the Greeks for the possession of Sicily (see Map 30, p. 93). With the extreme western tip of the island firmly in their hands, they had constantly tried to advance eastwards whenever the Greek cities, of which Syracuse was the most powerful, were divided among themselves. These struggles had compelled the Greeks time and again to entrust absolute power to one man and to accept the rule of a tyrant. Thus in the confusion following the departure of Pyrrhus a young and energetic ruler named Hiero had gained the throne of Syracuse. In order to restore peace and security to the island, he attacked Messana, where former Campanian mercenaries, the Mamertines, had established a robber state. The Mamertines appealed for help to both Rome and Carthage. The Romans thereafter captured Messana and forced the occupying Carthaginian garrison to withdraw. Thus began the struggle which led to the three Punic Wars (see Map 35, p. 103) and the complete destruction of the powerful Carthaginian empire.

The mercantile republic of Carthage possessed an excellent navy but was accustomed to rely largely on mercenaries for its armies. The Romans on the contrary were quite inexperienced in sea warfare. If they were to challenge the naval supremacy of Carthage, they must build a fleet; this they did by a magnificent effort. They constructed 160 ships, for which their Greek allies in south Italy helped to supply some of the crews. Further, these newly-equipped squadrons were commanded by consuls and praetors who were practised only in land fighting. Whereas on land in Sicily the Roman legions succeeded in driving the Carthaginians back to their coastal fortresses, they were at the outset complete beginners at sea. But by introducing grapnels and by placing legionaries on board, they changed naval battles into hand-to-hand fights in which the Carthaginian skill in manoeuvre was neutralised and the Roman soldiers could gain the upper hand. In this manner they won their first sea battle off Mylae in 260. They then risked an attempt to decide the war by a direct landing in Africa. This effort, however, in which they underestimated the strength of Carthage, ended in disaster. The sea, too, proved even more formidable than the Carthaginian navy: entire Roman fleets were wrecked by storms. The costly struggle dragged on for years, especially since in the young Hamilcar Barca the Carthaginians had found a commander whose ingenuity and energy were successful in repulsing the persistent Roman attacks on the Carthaginian bases in western Sicily, above all on the stronghold of Lilybaeum.

When it seemed that both sides had come to the end of their resources, Rome made one final effort. With the help of private individuals (who subscribed, as it were, to a war loan), a new fleet was equipped which in 241 defeated the Carthaginians off the Aegatian Islands and severed communications between Sicily and Africa. Carthage abandoned a struggle which had cost too much and lasted too long. Sicily was ceded to Rome and became the first overseas province.

But this long war was only the first act of the drama. While Carthage was handicapped by a serious revolt of its mercenaries, from whose pay this nation of merchants tried to recoup the losses suffered in the war, Rome took Sardinia and Corsica. The Tyrrhenian Sea now became entirely a Roman sea, and Carthage appeared permanently paralysed. It might remain a wealthy commercial state like Syracuse or Massilia, but it seemed to have been eliminated as a great power. That it did not in fact long remain humbled was due to the emergence of a few men of genius who concentrated their talents and energy on combating the superiority which Rome now exercised on land and sea. In this task, though they managed to carry their native city along with them, they received little encouragement from it. These men were Hamilcar, the undefeated commander in Sicily, and his sons.

After suppressing the revolt of the mercenaries Hamilcar turned to Spain and within a few years conquered the southern part of this prosperous country. Thus Carthage was compensated for the loss of Sicily by the annexation of this far richer province. An army was built up there, devoted to its commander and able to afford protection against any fresh Roman aggression. When Hamilcar was drowned in 229 his son-in-law Hasdrubal continued his work and advanced as far as the Ebro. When he was murdered in 221 the army chose Hannibal the son of Hamilcar as its commander-in-chief. The Romans had watched the revival of Carthaginian power with some anxiety, all the more since they were hampered by conflicts with the Gauls and in Illyria. They had secured Carthaginian neutrality by a treaty with Hasdrubal in which the Ebro was recognised as the northern limit of the Carthaginian sphere of influence in Spain. Now, however, their hands were freer. When Hannibal attacked the city of Saguntum, which lay south of the Ebro but was under Roman protection, they ordered him to leave it unmolested. Perhaps convinced that Rome was seeking a quarrel, and himself not unwilling to precipitate one, he continued the siege and finally took and destroyed the city. The government of Carthage refused to repudiate his action or hand him over as the Romans demanded. This episode led to the Second Punic War.

Rome, now mistress of the seas, counted upon being able to attack Africa and Spain. But these plans were foiled by the speed of Hannibal's magnificent march over the Pyrenees and Alps, without roads and through uncivilised tribes, into north Italy, where he arrived in 218. He won the support of many of the Gauls whom Rome had recently subjugated, and defeated the armies of the two consuls at Trebia. In the following year he continued his triumphal progress. Another Roman army was destroyed at Lake Trasimene in Etruria; central Italy was crossed; Fabius Cunctator, who was appointed to the temporary emergency office of dictator, by his policy of

The use of war-elephants composed an important element in Carthaginian military methods. **254.** Terracotta of an elephant carrying a 'tower'.

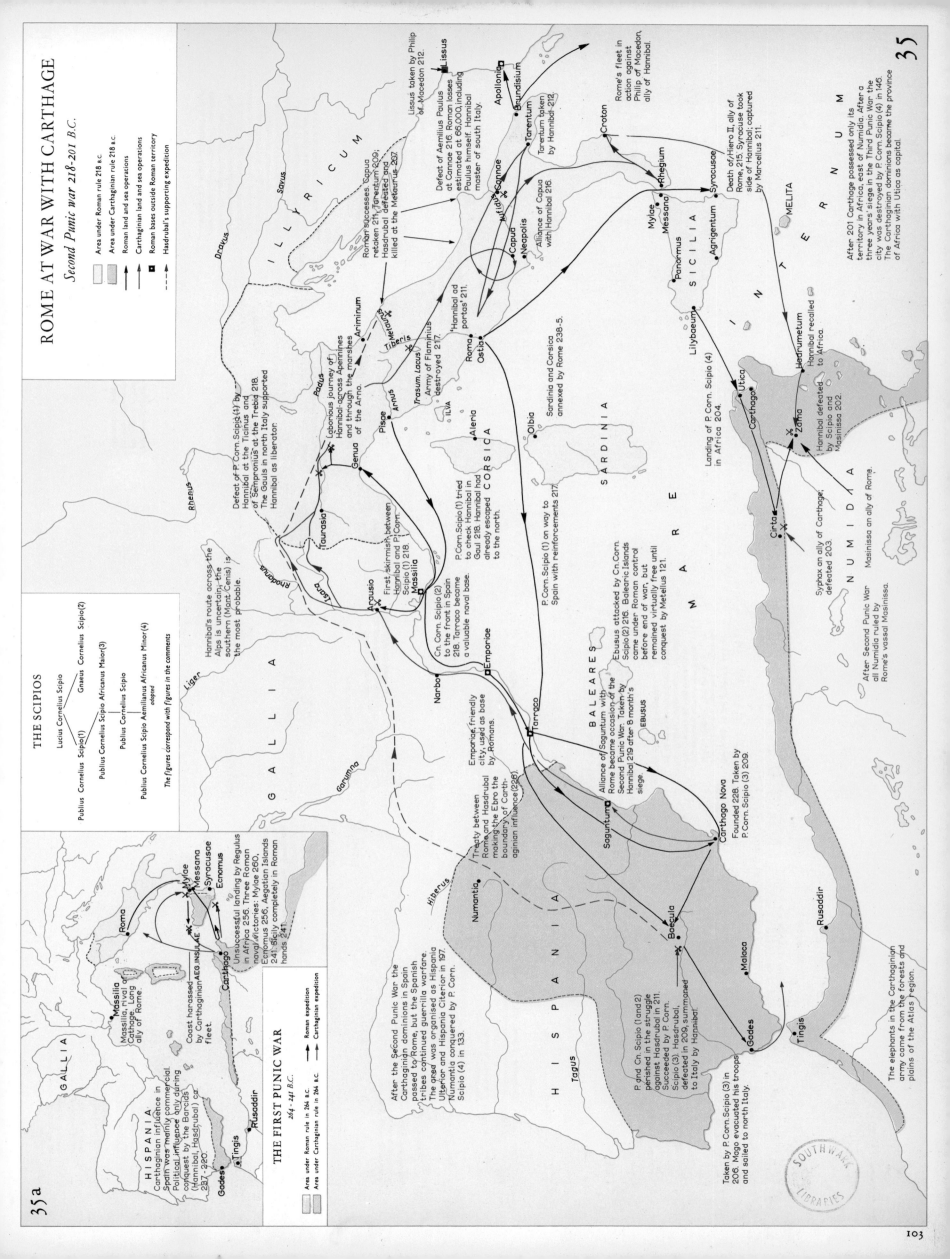

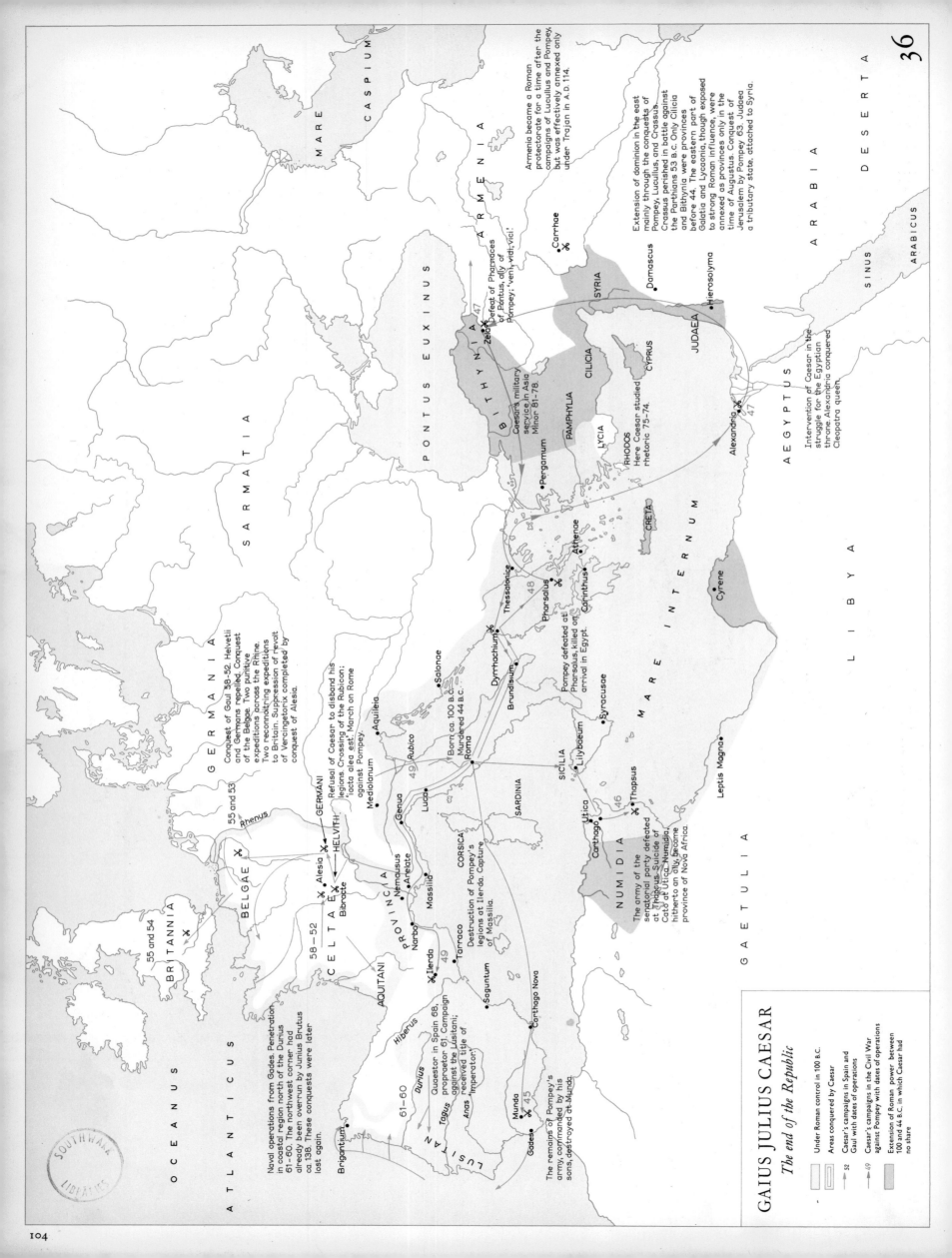

Rivalry with Carthage led to the three Punic Wars. **255.** An outstanding event in these was the battle in which the Carthaginians outflanked, sur-rounded, and annihilated the Romans under the command of the consul L. Aemilius Paulus near the village of Cannae, which stands on a hill near the valley of the Aufidus (now the Ofanto). The photograph shows the hill of Cannae with some loops of the Aufidus, by which lies the battlefield. The village of Cannae had already been destroyed by the Romans. **256.** A surprising discovery near the battlefield was that of mass graves containing skeletons which are possibly those of Roman and Carthaginian soldiers but which may be much later in date. **257.** On the hilltop stands an ancient column, erected in modern times to commemorate the battle, with the words from Livy (xxii, 54, 10): *Nulla alia gens tanta mole cladis non obruta esset* ('No other people would not have been crushed by the weight of such a disaster'). The photograph shows the battlefield and the Aufidus.

105

258
259
260

261

258. Rome's enemy Carthage was originally a Phoenician settlement, founded in the 8th cent. B.C. from Tyre in Phoenicia (see Map 30). After its destruction by Scipio Aemilianus in 146 B.C. it disappeared from the scene. On its restoration under Augustus it achieved new prosperity, especially as a transit centre for products from Africa. The present ruins result from the destruction of the city by the Saracen Hassan in A.D. 697. **259.** A great ally of the Romans in the Punic Wars was Hiero II, the powerful king of Syracuse. **260.** In the East the Romans expanded their Empire after their defeat of the Macedonians in the battle of Pydna. L. Aemilius Paulus, son of the consul defeated at Cannae, erected a trophy in the sanctuary of Delphi in memory of the victory (→ 147, 151). **261.** A few reliefs from the monument have been preserved. They show Macedonians (with round shields) fighting against Romans (with oval shields).

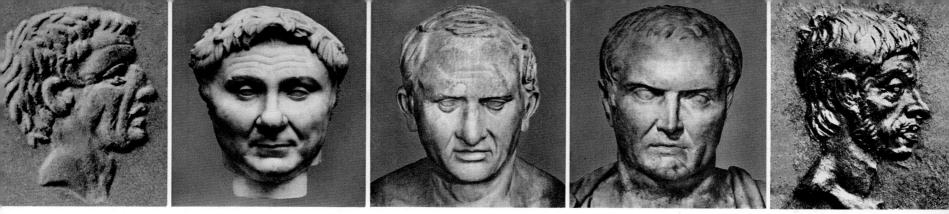

Some important figures of the Republican period. **262.** Lucius Cornelius Sulla (138-78 B.C.), a great statesman and restorer of the Republic. During his dictatorship a temple complex was built at Praeneste (modern Palestrina), of which a large part has been excavated (**267**). **263.** Gnaeus Pompeius Magnus (106-48 B.C.). **264.** Marcus Tullius Cicero (106-43 B.C.). **265.** Marcus Antonius (83-30 B.C.). **266.** Marcus Junius Brutus (85-42 B.C.).

avoiding battle only succeeded in winning time for another trial of strength. In 216 a Roman army of 80,000 men faced Hannibal at Cannae in Apulia and met disaster through the brilliant encircling tactics of the Carthaginian commander (→ 255-7).

Rome appeared lost. Its allies in southern Italy began to desert to Hannibal, first the important city of Capua, then Syracuse. In this crisis Rome owed its survival to the strength of its ties with its other allies, who for the most part remained faithful, and to the indomitable fortitude of the Senate, which even now rejected all thought of capitulation and continued the war despite the sacrifices required and the terrible devastation of southern Italy. Realising that none of their commanders was a match for Hannibal, the Romans avoided further pitched battles in Italy; instead they blockaded the disloyal cities and attempted to isolate Hannibal by harrying the enemy in Sicily and Spain.

In Spain Hannibal's brother Hasdrubal continued the struggle. In 211 he defeated in succession the two Roman commanders, the brothers Publius and Gnaeus Scipio, who both perished in the conflict. But the government in Carthage failed to press home its advantage. It sent reinforcements to Sicily and made an abortive attempt to seize Sardinia; but it left Hannibal, whose veterans diminished in numbers with every minor Roman success, without support. Having failed to win a swift and decisive victory, Hannibal now had to face the effects of the naval supremacy of Rome.

Step by step Rome regained lost ground. Capua and Syracuse were recaptured and so severely punished as to discourage other cities from revolt. A new commander, Publius Cornelius Scipio, was sent to Spain and succeeded in seizing the Carthaginian base of Carthago Nova by a surprise attack. In Italy the decisive moment came in 207. Hasdrubal managed to break through from Spain in an attempt to join his brother in Italy; but he was caught by the Romans near the Metaurus, his army was destroyed, and he himself was killed. In 204 Scipio, who meanwhile had ejected all the remaining Carthaginian forces from Spain, crossed to Africa. Victory followed victory until at last Carthage was obliged to recall Hannibal. In 202 Scipio, reinforced by the cavalry of the Numidian king Massinissa, won the final decisive victory at Zama. Strict organisation, inexhaustible energy and discipline, superior man-power, and the emergence of a general whose tactical reforms enabled the Roman legions once again to face Hannibal in a pitched battle had prevailed against personal genius.

Soon after peace was concluded Hannibal, threatened with extradition to Rome, was obliged to flee from his native city. Until his death in 183 he remained an exile, finding refuge first at the court of Antiochus of Syria, who failed to make adequate use of his services in his struggle against Rome, and then with Prusias of Bithynia.

Immediately after the Second Punic War, which made Rome undisputed mistress in the western Mediterranean, the Romans began to interfere in the affairs of the Hellenistic world. The cloud from the west spread over Greece and the east. The Romans, fully determined to prevent the emergence or existence of any equal power on their frontiers, intervened systematically in favour of any weaker party in order to forestall the threat of a stronger power.

At the invitation of Pergamum and Athens, victims of the aggression of Philip V king of Macedon, the Romans drove him out of Greece, which they then declared free, that is, the weak leagues and cities were left to administer their own affairs under a remote and benevolent Roman protectorate (196 B.C.). When a few years later King Antiochus III the Great of Syria invaded Greece, the Romans again intervened. They expelled Antiochus, pursued him to Asia Minor, and there inflicted a crushing defeat on him. Thus the whole of Asia Minor became subject to the power of Rome, who supported Pergamum as a client kingdom. In Syria revolt and rivalry for the throne were systematically fomented until the kingdom, hard pressed in the east by the Parthians, disintegrated completely. Egypt was 'protected' against Syria in such a manner that the later Ptolemies were conscious that they ruled only by the grace of Rome. War again broke out against Macedon, and after the victory of Pydna in 168 (→ 261) the monarchy was abolished. Rome now dominated the whole Hellenistic world.

THE CAUSE OF ROME'S SUCCESS

Within barely a century the Mediterranean world had found a new and permanent mistress. Ancient historians, and the Greek Polybius in particular, pondered over the reasons which made this rapid victory possible. They found the cause in the excellence of the Roman constitution. Whereas in Greece democracy and oligarchy had exhausted themselves in a death struggle, in the Roman 'mixed' constitution the royal power of the magistracy, the council of the nobles in the Senate, and the democratic activity of the people in the Comitia, balanced each other and provided a united basis at home for the development of power abroad.

The Romans had indeed built up a form of government which enabled them to make use of all their resources. Above all, they had succeeded in uniting Italy into a single federal state which when confronted by the onslaughts of Pyrrhus and Hannibal had given proof of a unity which could not be broken by attack from outside.

Rome thus possessed a war potential (a million fighting men in Italy) which far exceeded the forces of the Hellenistic kingdoms, where for years the state had relied less upon the armed citizen (as in the time of the Persian Wars) than upon the gold and mercenaries of the king. The genius of Hannibal had been pitted in vain against this solid bloc of Roman power. At first he pinned his hope upon the disaffection of the Italian tribes and cities, and when this hope proved false he had tried without success to build up a wide coalition against Rome. Fearing hostile alliances of this sort, the Romans were glad to see dissensions between potential foes. It was with the help of the Aetolian and Achaean Leagues that they defeated Macedon, and Macedon in turn did nothing to hinder the defeat of Syria. It has been said that the foundation of Roman policy was: 'Divide and rule.' In reality the divisions often existed already and Rome only had to exploit them.

Rome was not yet an aggressively imperialist power. It desired no territorial annexations, and made none in the East. When the Romans appeared aggressive, the motive was often fear, and they were seeking to safeguard themselves by weakening or destroying potential rivals. For them reverses (of which they suffered many, since their commanders and armies often showed more determination than skill) were no reason for surrender but an incentive to greater effort. Rome lost many battles but never a war.

ROMAN IMPERIALISM

After the defeat of Macedon at Pydna in 168, senatorial policy, which aimed at creating dependent states within the Roman sphere of influence, soon had to be modified. Rome, wishing to eliminate any threat of danger, could tolerate no disorder abroad which might weaken its interests, and was constantly obliged to intervene. This sometimes led to further annexation and the organisation of more overseas provinces.

When after the First Punic War Sicily was ceded to the Romans, they were confronted with the problem of how such a province should be organised. The policy which had been so successful in Italy, alliance with the Roman federal state, leading in many cases to assimilation, was not so suitable for Sicily with its Greek population, culture, and tradition. The Romans, who were far from original and gladly conformed to existing

267

The military skill of the Romans was one factor in the rapid expansion of the Empire. The army, originally one legion, developed into a body of many legions (see Maps 41-2). Sepulchral steles tell much about military organisation and army life. **268.** Soldier of Legio XIV Gemina. In his right hand a sling. **270.** Standard-bearer of the same legion. In his right hand a lance with an eagle resting upon thunderbolts, in his left an oval shield, on his breast decorations (two *armillae* and nine *phalerae*). **272.** Centurion of Legio XX Valeria Victrix. Roman engineers invented many devices for attack and defence. **269.** At the siege of Avaricum by Caesar this stronghold was taken by means of battering-rams mounted upon towers. **271.** Battering-ram with iron ram's head which made breaches in the walls. **273.** Army camp built as a bridgehead opposite Cologne by Constantine the Great in A.D. 310.

274
275

276
277

278
279

Trajan, one of the greatest commanders in the Imperial period, restored discipline and safeguarded the frontiers. His campaigns against the Dacians were one of his greatest achievements. The column erected in honour of this expedition (→ 280) gives a remarkable insight into various phases of the campaign. 274. Romans loading ships on the Danube in front of a Roman city with thick walls and an amphitheatre. 275. Dacians building fortifications against the Roman menace. 276. One of the technical triumphs of the Romans was the building of bridges across the Danube (→ 453). Roman soldiers on a simple bridge. 277. Weapons, uniforms, decorations, standards, etc., are often shown on the column. Standard-bearers and officers leave a camp and march across a boat-bridge. 278. Legionaries, protected by a roof of shields (testudo) attacking a Dacian camp. 279. Soldiers bringing siege weapons up to a fortress.

280. Detail from the column erected to commemorate the victory of Trajan over the Dacians. Starting from the bottom, the eight details show: the river-god Danube (extreme right) with boats and houses; Trajan addressing soldiers who are building a *castellum*; construction of a frontier fort; armed Dacians; crossing of the Danube; decapitation of Dacian chiefs; Trajan receiving barbarians; Trajan making a speech. **281.** To judge from many reliefs, the struggle in Germany and the region of the Danube made a great impression on the Romans. These wars were often viewed as a symbol of the struggle against the forces of evil, so that the scenes on sarcophagi do not always mean that the deceased actually fought in the campaign. The 'Ludovisi sarcophagus' gives scenes from the fighting. Fight between a horse-soldier and a barbarian. A soldier wearing a coat of mail looks on; another blows a tuba. **282.** The reliefs on the arch of Constantine also contain vivid battle scenes.

The vast conquests of the Romans, often in wild and lonely regions, obliged them to establish their frontiers wherever possible on natural barriers, which they reinforced with roads, ditches, walls, and forts. The Emperors of the 2nd cent. A.D., who devoted themselves particularly to the safe-guarding of the Empire by these means, fortified the Rhine defences against the Germans and built walls in Britain which ran across northern England and southern Scotland. The remains of Hadrian's Wall are the most impressive example of the Roman frontier defences now extant. Later Emperors perfected these fortifications. **283.** Roman soldiers building new wooden defences for a fort, while Trajan receives two Dacian chiefs. **284.** Building of a defence tower on the frontier. Teams of men bring and pass on baskets of stones. **285.** Dacians, always recognisable by their bristly beards and hair, captive within the walls of a prison camp and guarded by Roman soldiers.

286
287

288

The expeditions of Julius Caesar to Britain left no lasting results; the conquest was achieved only by later campaigns. The northern tribes retained their freedom and disturbed the life of their southern neighbours by their incursions. Against these tribes the Emperors Hadrian and Antoninus Pius built two walls, Hadrian's Wall and the Antonine Wall (see Maps 48, 48a); sections of the former still survive. **286.** Hadrian's Wall, here and there overgrown by trees, still runs across the border country of England and Scotland. **287.** Air photography has revealed many fortifications. This photograph shows the form of a Roman walled city, Silchester. The pattern of streets is still visible. **288.** A good example of a natural frontier with a fortified post is Richborough (Rutupiae) in Kent. The structure in the inner fortress is probably the foundation of a monument commemorating Trajan's settlement of the province (ca. A.D. 100). Later, protective fortifications were devised (ca. A.D. 280) against Saxon raiders.

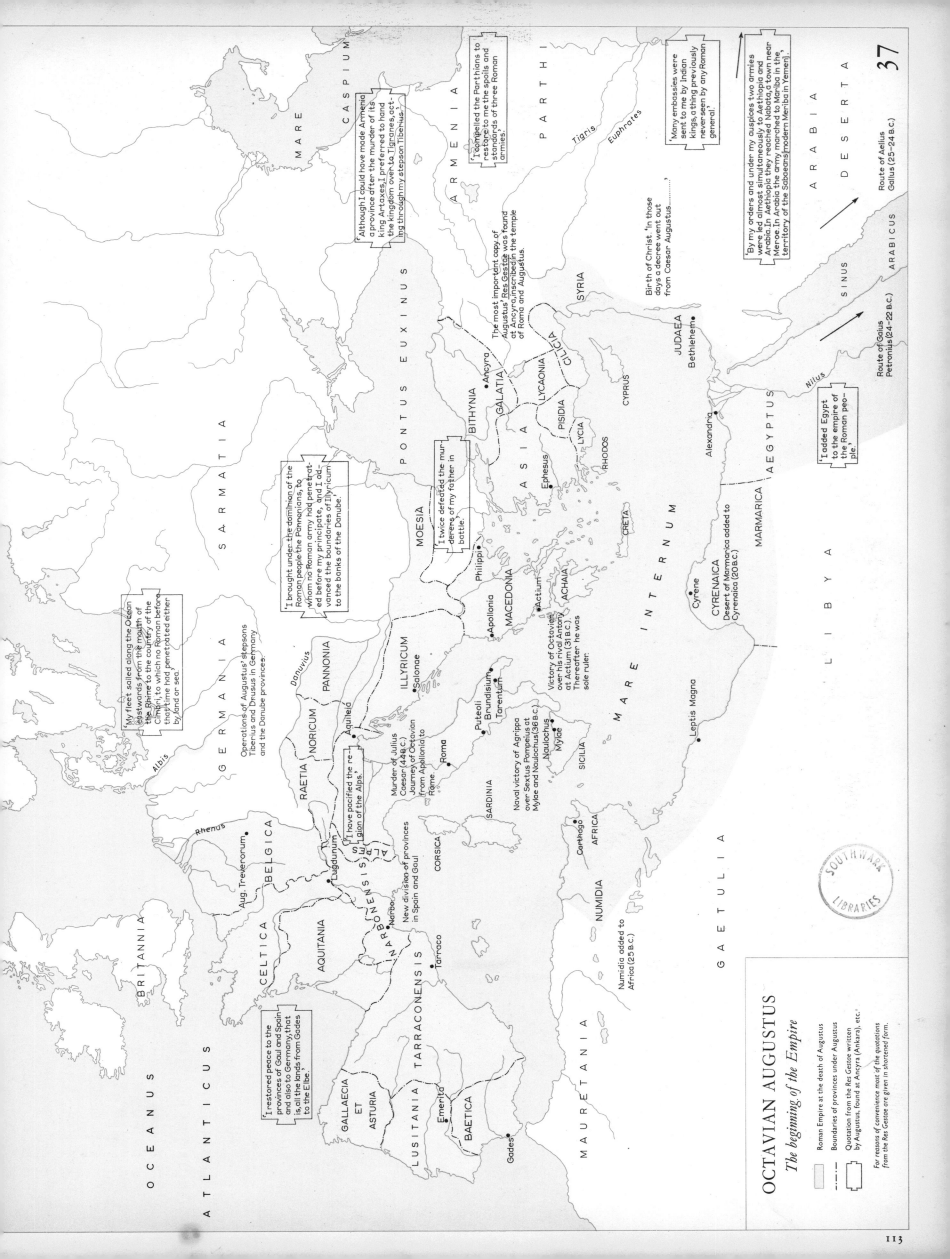

OCTAVIAN AUGUSTUS
The beginning of the Empire

Roman Empire at the death of Augustus

--- · --- Boundaries of provinces under Augustus

Quotation from the *Res Gestae* written
by Augustus, found at Ancyra (Ankara), etc.

*For reasons of convenience most of the quotations
from the Res Gestae are given in shortened form.*

OCEANUS

ATLANTICUS

BRITANNIA

GERMANIA

Operations of Augustus' stepsons
Tiberius and Drusus in Germany
and the Danube provinces.

'My fleet sailed along the Ocean
eastwards from the mouth of
the Rhine to the country of the
Cimbri, to which no Roman before
that time had penetrated either
by land or sea.'

Albis

Rhenus

Aug. Treverorum •

BELGICA

CELTICA

AQUITANIA

'I restored peace to the
provinces of Gaul and Spain
and also to Germany; that
is, all the lands from Gades
to the Elbe.'

NARBONENSIS
Narbo •

Lugdunum •

SARMATIA

'I brought under the dominion of the
Roman people the Pannonians, to
whom no Roman army had penetrated before my principate, and I advanced the boundaries of Illyricum
to the banks of the Danube.'

Danuvius

RAETIA **NORICUM**

PANNONIA

ALPES

'I have pacified the re-
gion of the Alps.'

Aquileia •

New division of provinces
in Spain and Gaul

Murder of Julius
Caesar (44 B.C.).
Journey of Octavian
from Apollonia to
Rome.

ILLYRICUM
Salonae •

CASPIUM

MARE

'Although I could have made Armenia
a province after the murder of its
king Artaxes, I preferred to hand
the kingdom over to Tigranes, acting through my stepson Tiberius.'

ARMENIA

'I compelled the Parthians to
restore to me the spoils and
standards of three Roman
armies.'

PARTHI

Tigris

Euphrates

PONTUS EUXINUS

Ancyra •

GALATIA

BITHYNIA

The most important copy of
Augustus' *Res Gestae* was found
at Ancyra, inscribed in the temple
of Roma and Augustus.

MOESIA

'I twice defeated the murderers of my father in
battle.'

Philippi •

MACEDONIA

Apollonia •

Actium •

ACHAIA

Victory of Octavian
over his rival Antony
at Actium (31 B.C.).
Thereafter he was
sole ruler.

ASIA

LYCAONIA

PISIDIA

CILICIA

LYCIA

Ephesus •

RHODOS

CRETA

SYRIA

JUDAEA
Bethlehem •

Birth of Christ. 'In those
days a decree went out
from Caesar Augustus........'

Alexandria •

AEGYPTUS

Nilus

'I added Egypt
to the empire of
the Roman peo-
ple.'

MARMARICA

Desert of Marmarica added to
Cyrenaica (20 B.C.).

Cyrene •

CYRENAICA

LIBYA

'Many embassies were
sent to me by Indian
kings, a thing previously
never seen by any Roman
general.'

'By my orders and under my auspices two armies
were led almost simultaneously to Aethiopia and
Arabia. In Aethiopia they reached Nabata, a town near
Meroe. In Arabia the army marched to Mariba in the
territory of the Sabaeans (modern Meriba in Yemen).'

ARABIA

DESERTA

Route of Aelius
Gallus (25–24 B.C.)

Route of Gaius
Petronius (24–22 B.C.)

ARABICUS

SINUS

ARABIA

37

TARRACONENSIS

Tarraco •

Numidia added to
Africa (25 B.C.).

NUMIDIA

MAURETANIA

GAETULIA

AFRICA
Carthago •

SARDINIA

CORSICA

Roma •

Puteoli •
Brundisium •
Tarentum •

Naval victory of Agrippa
over Sextus Pompeius at
Mylae and Naulochus (36 B.C.).

Naulochus •
Mylae •

SICILIA

Leptis Magna •

MARE INTERNUM

**GALLAECIA
ET
ASTURIA**

LUSITANIA

Emerita •

BAETICA

Gades •

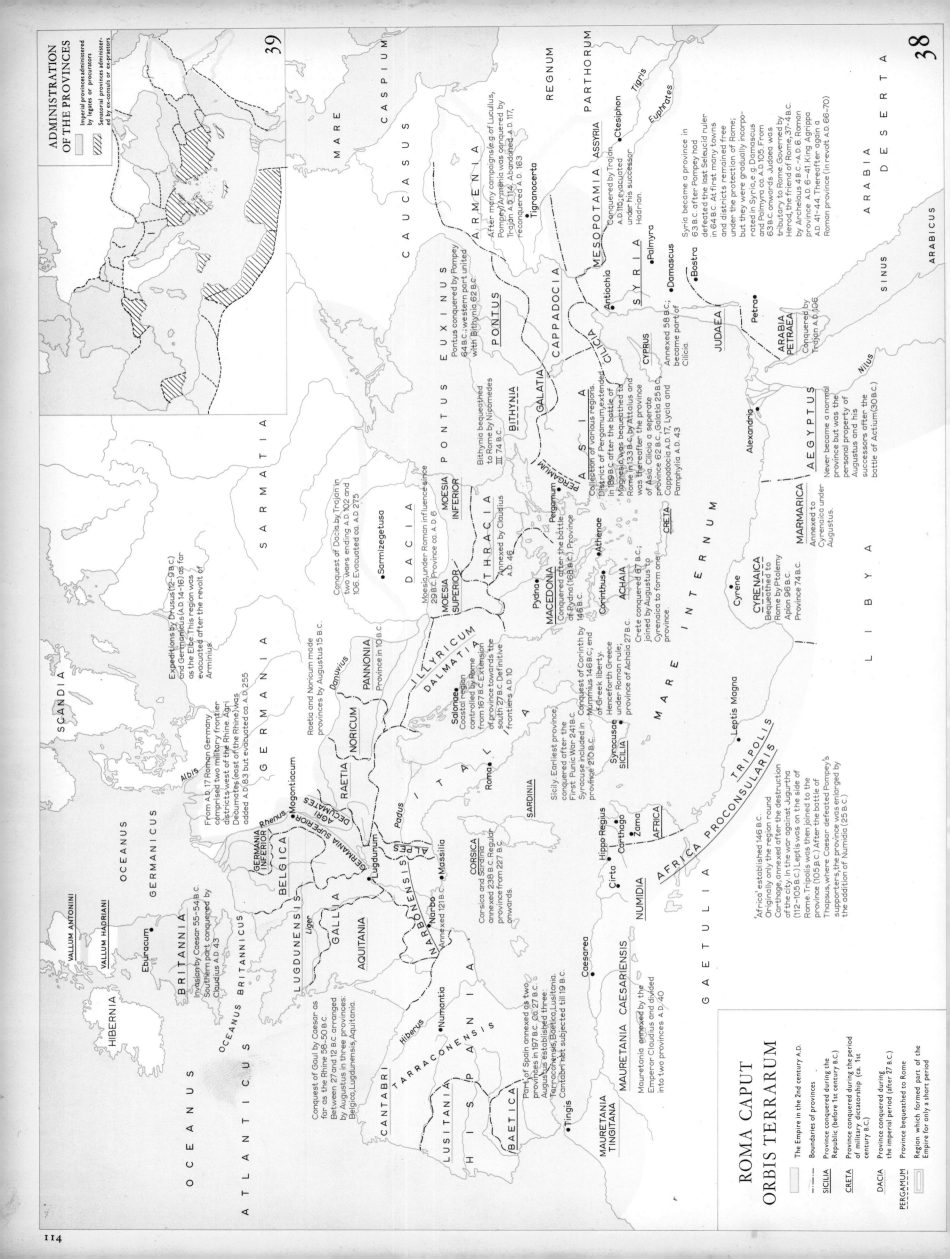

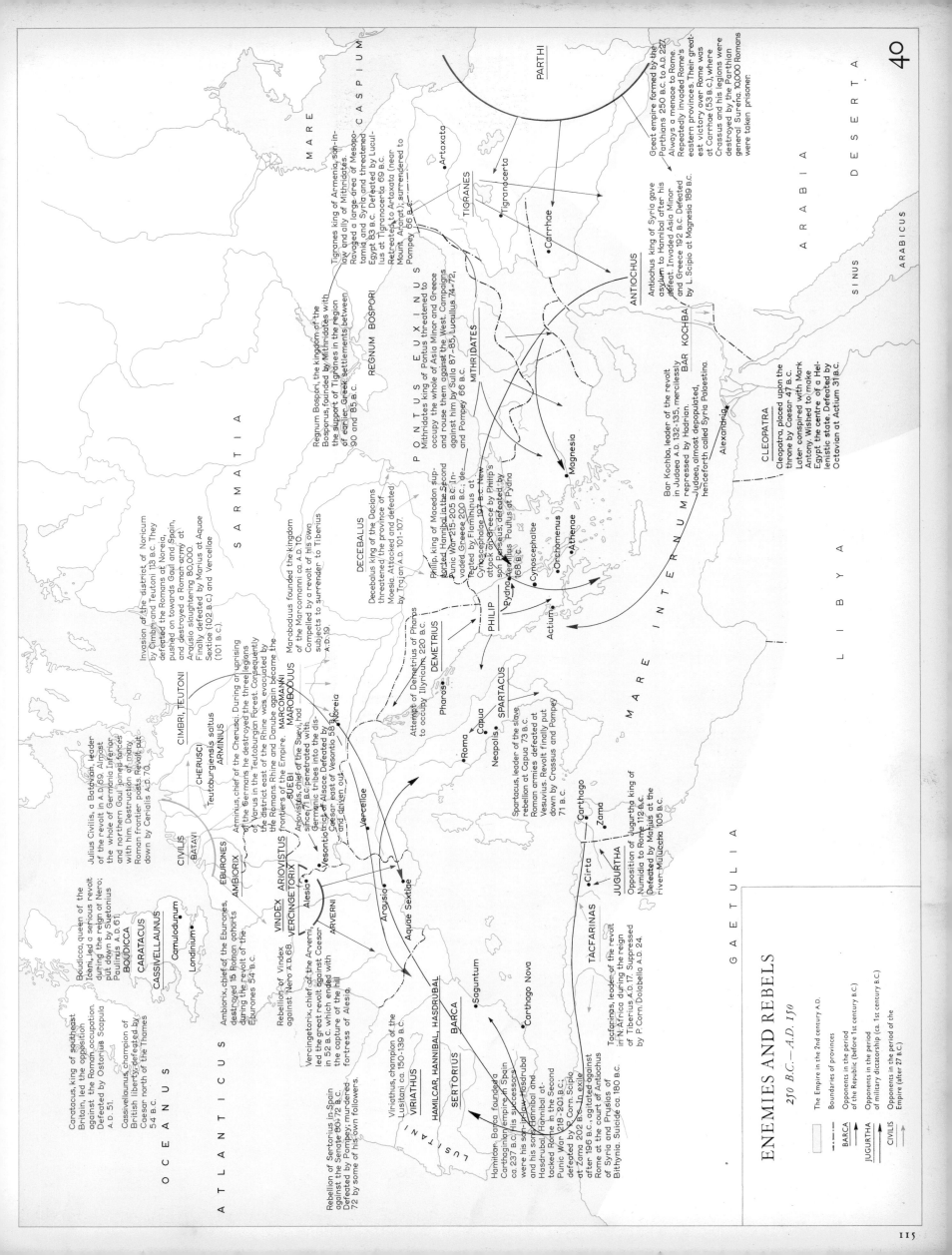

ENEMIES AND REBELS

250 B.C.—A.D. 150

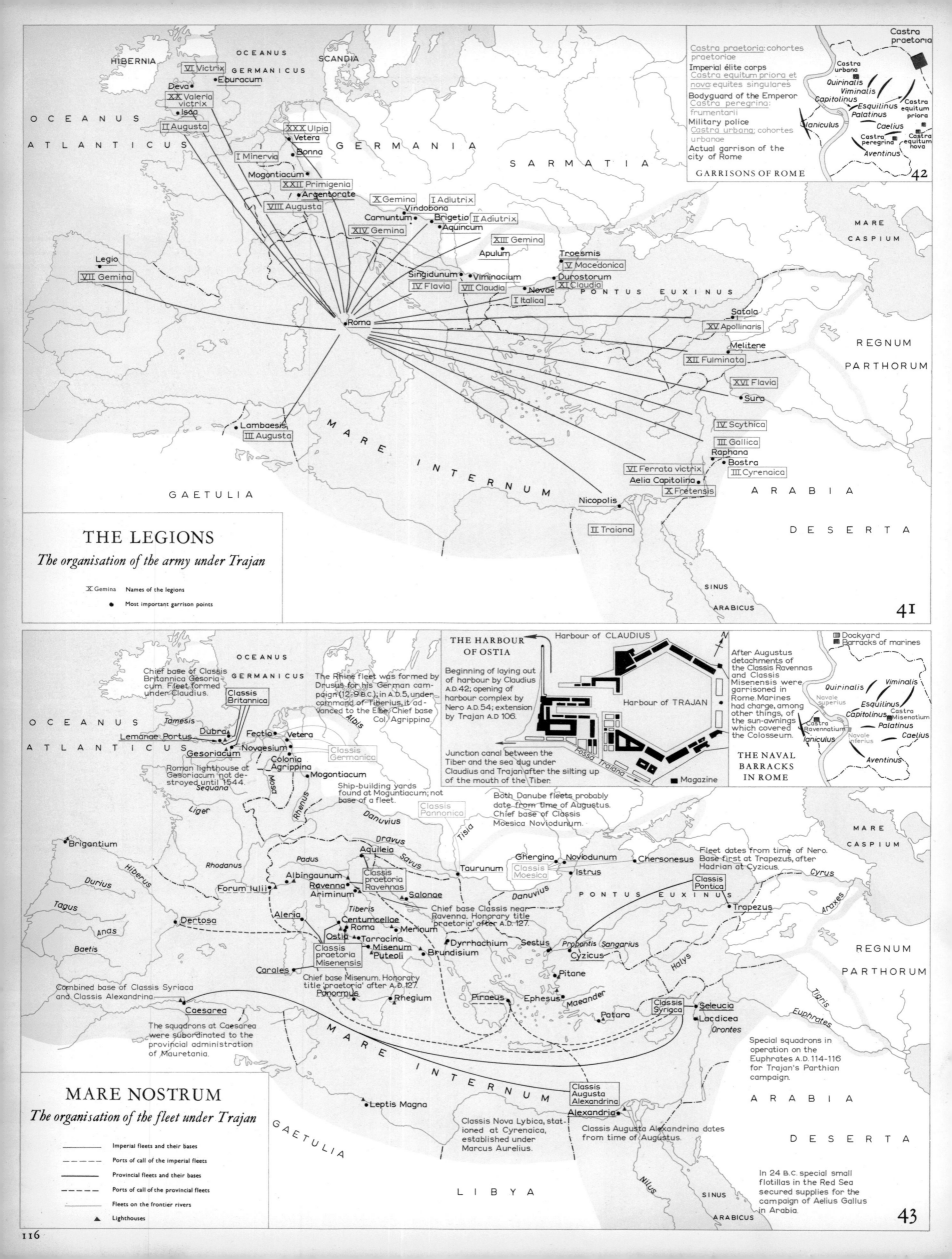

Map 41: THE LEGIONS

THE LEGIONS

The organisation of the army under Trajan

X Gemina — Names of the legions

• — Most important garrison points

Labels on map:

HIBERNIA · OCEANUS · OCEANUS GERMANICUS · SCANDIA

OCEANUS ATLANTICUS · GERMANIA · SARMATIA

V Victrix · Deva · Eburacum · Isca · XX Valeria victrix · II Augusta · XXX Ulpia · Vetera · I Minervia · Bonna · Mogontiacum · XXII Primigenia · Argentorate · VIII Augusta · X Gemina · I Adiutrix · Carnuntum · Vindobona · Brigetio · II Adiutrix · Aquincum · XIV Gemina · XIII Gemina · Apulum

Legio · VII Gemina

Troesmis · V Macedonica · Durostorum · XI Claudia · Singidunum · Viminacium · IV Flavia · VII Claudia · Novae · I Italica · PONTUS EUXINUS

Satala · XV Apollinaris · Melitene · XII Fulminata · XVI Flavia · Sura · IV Scythica · III Gallica · Raphana · Bostra · III Cyrenaica · VI Ferrata victrix · Aelia Capitolina · X Fretensis · Nicopolis · II Traiana

MARE INTERNUM

Lambaesis · III Augusta · GAETULIA

MARE CASPIUM · REGNUM PARTHORUM · ARABIA DESERTA · SINUS ARABICUS

Roma

41

Inset 42: GARRISONS OF ROME

Castra praetoria: cohortes praetoriae
Imperial élite corps
Castra equitum priora et nova: equites singulares
Bodyguard of the Emperor
Castra peregrina: frumentarii
Military police
Castra urbana: cohortes urbanae
Actual garrison of the city of Rome

GARRISONS OF ROME

Castra praetoria · Castra urbana · Quirinalis · Viminalis · Capitolinus · Esquilinus · Castra equitum priora · Palatinus · Caelius · Janiculus · Castra peregrina · Castra equitum nova · Aventinus

42

Map 43: MARE NOSTRUM

MARE NOSTRUM

The organisation of the fleet under Trajan

Legend:
— Imperial fleets and their bases
--- Ports of call of the imperial fleets
— Provincial fleets and their bases
--- Ports of call of the provincial fleets
Fleets on the frontier rivers
▲ Lighthouses

OCEANUS GERMANICUS · OCEANUS ATLANTICUS

Chief base of Classis Britannica Gesoriacum. Fleet formed under Claudius.

The Rhine fleet was formed by Drusus for his German campaign (12-9 B.C.); in A.D.5, under command of Tiberius, it advanced to the Elbe. Chief base Col. Agrippina.

Classis Britannica · Tamesis · Dubrae · Fectio · Vetera · Lemanae Portus · Novaesium · Gesoriacum · Colonia Agrippina · Classis Germanica · Mogontiacum

Roman lighthouse at Gesoriacum not destroyed until 1544.

Sequana · Liger · Rhenus · Mosa · Albis

Ship-building yards found at Moguntiacum; not base of a fleet.

Both Danube fleets probably date from time of Augustus. Chief base of Classis Moesica Noviodunum.

Classis Pannonica · Danuvius · Dravus · Tisia · Savus · Aquileia · Taurunum · Classis Moesica · Ghergina · Noviodunum · Chersonesus · Istrus

Fleet dates from time of Nero. Base first at Trapezus, after Hadrian at Cyzicus.

Brigantium · Hiberus · Durius · Tagus · Anas · Baetis · Rhodanus · Padus · Forum Iulii · Albingaunum · Ravenna · Ariminum · Aleria · Dertosa · Classis praetoria Ravennas · Tiberis · Centumcellae · Roma · Meriaum · Ostia · Tarracina · Misenum · Puteoli · Brundisium · Classis praetoria Misenensis · Carales · Panormus · Rhegium · Piraeus · Salonae · Dyrrhachium · Sestus · Propontis · Cyzicus · Pitane · Ephesus · Maeander · Patara · Sangarius · Classis Pontica · Trapezus · Halys · Classis Syriaca · Seleucia · Laodicea · Orontes

Chief base Classis near Ravenna. Honorary title 'praetoria' after A.D. 127.

Chief base Misenum. Honorary title 'praetoria' after A.D. 127.

Combined base of Classis Syriaca and Classis Alexandrina.

Caesarea

The squadrons at Caesarea were subordinated to the provincial administration of Mauretania.

PONTUS EUXINUS · MARE CASPIUM · Cyrus · Araxes · REGNUM PARTHORUM · Tigris · Euphrates · ARABIA DESERTA · SINUS ARABICUS

Special squadrons in operation on the Euphrates A.D. 114-116 for Trajan's Parthian campaign.

MARE INTERNUM

GAETULIA · Leptis Magna · LIBYA · Nilus

Classis Nova Lybica, stationed at Cyrenaica, established under Marcus Aurelius.

Classis Augusta Alexandrina · Alexandria

Classis Augusta Alexandrina dates from time of Augustus.

In 24 B.C. special small flotillas in the Red Sea secured supplies for the campaign of Aelius Gallus in Arabia.

43

Inset: THE HARBOUR OF OSTIA

THE HARBOUR OF OSTIA

Harbour of CLAUDIUS · Harbour of TRAJAN

Beginning of laying out of harbour by Claudius A.D.42; opening of harbour complex by Nero A.D.54; extension by Trajan A.D.106.

Junction canal between the Tiber and the sea dug under Claudius and Trajan after the silting up of the mouth of the Tiber.

Fossa Traiana

■ Magazine

Inset: THE NAVAL BARRACKS IN ROME

▨ Dockyard · ■ Barracks of marines

After Augustus detachments of the Classis Ravennas and Classis Misenensis were garrisoned in Rome. Marines had charge, among other things, of the sun-awnings which covered the Colosseum.

THE NAVAL BARRACKS IN ROME

Quirinalis · Viminalis · Esquilinus · Navale superius · Capitolinus · Castra Misenatium · Palatinus · Caelius · Janiculus · Navale inferius · Castra Ravennatium · Aventinus

289
290
291

292

The frontier (*limes*) in Syria, which Trajan had established at the beginning of the 2nd century, must have given rise to many problems of organisation, supply and defence. Although the military constructions have been buried in desert sand, the frontier is known in broad outline by means of air photography and excavation. Numerous forts spread out over hundreds of miles watched over the security of the main roads which traversed the entire region (see Map 49). **289.** The square fort Hân al-Hallâbât on the Syrian frontier. **290.** Across the desert still run traces of the wide roads which linked the forts and made rapid transport possible for legions and trade caravans. **291.** Part of the road between Antioch and Aleppo, 20 feet wide and made of hewn limestone blocks. **292.** The fort now called Qasr al-Hêr; the walls and towers have been in part preserved. The later use of these forts by shepherds contributed greatly to their destruction.

117

Reconstruction of the basilica of Trajan in Rome, built by Apollodorus of Damascus (early 2nd cent. A.D.). Right: ground plan.

precedent, simply continued the practice developed during the war. Every year a praetor was sent to such a province as military and civil governor. The Romans did not desire arbitrary rule; the praetor, now the governor, replaced the former ruler in the name of the Roman people. To him was paid the tribute formerly exacted by the ruling power; these burdens were often even lightened. He was responsible to the Roman people, who had entrusted him with his commission. At the end of his governorship he could be accused, but only in a Roman court. If the provincials had any complaints to make, they could lodge them only after his departure for Rome. This accorded with the conception of *imperium* as exercised in Rome itself. But in Rome the principle of collegiality and the possibility of appealing to the tribunes or to the popular assemblies afforded safeguards against magisterial oppression. Such possibilities were entirely absent in the provinces, where the *imperium* of praetor or consul was absolute throughout his whole period of office. Since a governor had no adequate staff of civil officials at his disposal the distribution of work and the collection of taxes were, as in Rome itself, farmed out to contractors who had to possess sufficient capital to advance the agreed sums. They would subsequently recover these amounts, together with their expenses, from the tax-payers.

Before reviewing the results of this system we must remark that the number of provinces increased rapidly. Sardinia and Corsica had been annexed in 238, after the First Punic War, and after the Second Punic War Spain was taken over as two separate provinces. In 149 a conflict was provoked with that powerless but still hated hereditary enemy Carthage. The city was destroyed (→ 258) and the territory annexed as the Roman province of Africa in 146. At the same time disturbances in Greece and Macedon, where permanent order had to be established, led to the creation of Macedonia as a province. In 133 the last king of Pergamum bequeathed his kingdom to Rome; it became the richest of the provinces, 'Asia'. About 121 Gallia Narbonensis was annexed as a province and became the link between the Gallic province in the Po valley (Gallia Cisalpina) and Spain. Syria was not incorporated until 63 B.C., and Egypt only in 30 B.C. This closed the Roman ring around the Mediterranean.

THE ECONOMIC CONSEQUENCES OF THE OVERSEAS CONQUESTS

For a century or so after the Romans had acquired their first overseas province (Sicily in 241 B.C.), their administration was generally efficient and upright. But this honourable condition did not remain untarnished. They may have honestly thought – their economic insight was still quite primitive – that they were imposing no heavier burdens on the provincials than had the former rulers. In actual fact their system proved ruinous for the provinces, since the profits, which were formerly spent within each province on the court, army, and officials, were now diverted to Rome. During the conquests, moreover, an immense amount of booty had already been carried away in the form of goods and slaves. Thus, even given honest methods of government, the provinces were bound to be slowly drained, as the capital amassed over the centuries flowed into Rome.

To make matters worse, however, corruption almost inevitably followed. The magistrates who went to the provinces had been obliged to bear the costs of their official career (for which they received no salary) and the usual expenses incurred in gaining popular favour at elections: distributions, games, even the outright buying of votes. Provincial administration offered them an opportunity to restore their fortunes by accepting gifts for favours

and benefits which it was in their power to confer. And, to quote a Roman's words, '. . . the stream of sacks that had to be filled was new each year'. The farming out of taxes (the tax-collectors were generally hated) was a catastrophe for the subject peoples. The contractors, mostly companies established in Rome, could extort considerable profit over and above their lawful due. Objections could be laid before the all-powerful governor, but he might be in league with the tax-collectors, and in any case would take care not to antagonise these mighty Roman capitalists in order to avoid incurring their vengeance in Rome when his term of office had expired, because after 123 B.C. they formed the court in which he would be tried if accused of maladministration. If for any reason obligations could not be met, cities and private individuals plunged into debt with money-lenders who to all purposes were the same capitalists who had farmed out the taxes. They demanded exorbitant interest (sometimes 40 per cent), and in fact a community which had once run into debt could seldom pay off the principal but had to go on paying an enormous, ever-recurrent interest. Despair sometimes led to revolt which was punished with reparations and even heavier taxes. Intrigue, swindling, and the buying of favours offered the only means of escape for the subjects. Thus did the Greeks, once so proud, become the despised *Graeculi* ('Greeklings').

For the Romans the result was corruption. In the provinces the hardened legions degenerated into rapacious garrison troops, more dangerous to the allies than to the enemy; officers and officials became accustomed both to extortion and place-seeking. These habits accompanied them when they returned to Rome. The stern discipline of ancestral custom, the cement which held together the ruling power of the Senate, began to weaken. Many Roman nobles increasingly sought only their own advantage when serving the state. In order to continue to secure this advantage they had to stand for higher office, and this caused them to spend increased sums of money and to extort more from their provinces in order to maintain their position. Rome grew increasingly rich on plunder and tribute from subject countries. This wealth, however, was not shared by all. To some extent the exploitation of the provinces had the same result as the Industrial Revolution in the eighteenth century. The capitalists became richer, the people poorer. The small Italian farmer, the backbone of Rome's military power, was ruthlessly torn away from his land to serve in foreign countries. He returned, if he survived, having lost the habit of agricultural work, discontented, to find his farm neglected and himself bankrupt. The corn which he grew himself could not compete with the grain imported from Sicily and Africa. He could sell his land to a rich tax-farmer who sought a good investment for his money and wished to take his place as a country squire and to gain social status. The ex-farmer could go to Rome or some other city to live as a proletarian upon the favour of a noble patron. For these nobles had need of the only thing he still retained: his vote in an election.

Large estates increased in number in many parts of Italy and engulfed the farms destroyed or abandoned in the Hannibalic War: they formed great ranches, worked by slaves, who had become numerous and cheap through Rome's many wars. The displaced Italian peasant was no longer needed even as a tenant farmer or worker, and industry which could have absorbed his labour scarcely existed. This gave rise to the paradoxical state of affairs – a mystery even to the Romans themselves – that the exploitation of the Empire ruined the Italian peasant class. The Italian allies also were involved in the same economic crisis. In their ranks, too, capitalists profited from the

The *Maison Carrée* at Nîmes (16 B.C.), the best-preserved Roman temple; built, following Roman custom, upon a podium.

opportunities for trade which, protected by Roman power, they promoted in the provinces, while many of their humbler citizens became proletarians. The fact, however, that they had helped Rome to found the empire and yet were deprived of the advantages of Roman citizenship aroused in them discontent and a spirit of revolt which began to undermine the loyalty that had withstood the onslaught of Hannibal. It was not that they desired separation from Rome; on the contrary, they began to demand Roman citizenship. This disruption of Italian economy and standards took place within a few decades. In vain did some old-fashioned statesmen, like Cato the Censor, endeavour to check the evils of extortion and corruption by public censure and by setting up special tribunals. Sterner measures were needed.

SOCIAL REFORM AND REVOLUTION

In the year 133 a high-minded young noble, Tiberius Sempronius Gracchus, took the initiative. As tribune of the plebs he proposed an agrarian law whereby the large property owners could be deprived of part of their estates, because in fact some that they were holding belonged to the state. This land would then be divided among the poor Roman citizens, and thus the class of small farmers in Italy could be revived. This proposal was naturally fiercely opposed in the Senate by the landowners. Gracchus, however, infected by a spirit of individualism which undermined the class unity of the nobles, brought his law before the popular assembly, caused another tribune who vetoed it to be deposed from office, and got his bill carried. In order to secure its efficient working, he had an agrarian commission of three men established, and served on this board himself. The senators, whether they desired social reform or not, considered Tiberius' methods revolutionary, and some feared that he might be seeking personal power. A few resorted to force, and during a serious riot Tiberius was killed. The Senate approved this action. For centuries Rome had been free from civil war and bloodshed - even the grim struggle of the patricians and plebeians had been settled without - it but now the murder of Tiberius Gracchus heralded a revolutionary age of civil disturbance.

The nobles were not all entirely selfish and they allowed the distribution of land in small allotments to continue, but it was of no avail, and the people continued to venerate Gracchus. In 123 his younger brother, Gaius Gracchus, was elected tribune and was re-elected to this office for a second year (122). During this time his political opponents might regard him as the uncrowned king of Rome. He succeeded in creating a rift between the Senate and the rich business men (the knights) who included the tax-farmers. He did this by transferring from senators to knights the control of the court which tried provincial governors, thus giving the knights considerable political influence. The people were won over by a corn law: each month a quantity of grain was made available to every citizen at a considerably reduced price; thus existing need was alleviated. Effective relief was to be provided by the founding of colonies in Italy and one outside on the site of Carthage. This measure, however, met with opposition, and even some of Gracchus' supporters began to weaken. He failed to secure re-election to a third tribunate for 121. A fracas developed into a serious disturbance, the Senate declared martial law, and one of the consuls brought out some troops who defeated the supporters of Gracchus. Gracchus himself fled and committed suicide. Once again the senatorial régime had been saved; but the hatred between the propertied and popular parties, between the conservative *optimates* and the *populares*, blazed more fiercely than ever.

The leadership of the *populares* (who were certainly no democrats) was seized time and again by ambitious nobles who wished in this manner to challenge the entrenched interests of the *optimates*, the dominant clique in the Senate. The conflict, which had arisen from a question of social reform, determined the future pattern of political life. The nobles, who controlled the Senate and secured most of the magistracies, had shown themselves capable of smothering an attempt at radical reform undertaken through legal channels. Now, whenever any unusual difficulty affected the normal smooth working of the government, the people might look for a strong man to whom special powers would be granted. A fit candidate for this rôle of 'the man trusted by the people' was soon found. After 110 B.C. Rome was threatened by serious military crises. In Africa the vassal king Jugurtha had risen in revolt and defied the Roman commanders, and the northern frontier was threatened by the migrating Germanic tribes, the Cimbri and the Teutoni. To meet this danger the people, contrary to all tradition, year after year chose as consul a capable soldier Marius, who was a *novus homo*, that is, not a member of the governing class by birth. He reorganised the army, replacing the drafting of unwilling recruits by the enlistment of volunteers of any class, a change which lightened existing burdens but later proved to have fatal consequences.

With this new type of army Marius conquered first Jugurtha and then the Cimbri and Teutoni. On his return he was consul for the sixth time and the most powerful man in Rome (100 B.C.), but he was no statesman and completely failed to find any solution to the internal tension. The tribune Drusus, who made a bold attempt to do so by promising citizenship to the Italian allies, was murdered. His death was the signal for a violent uprising of the allies (*socii*) throughout Italy (90). They fought in this Social War with such stubbornness that Rome, although finally the victor in battle, was compelled to grant them Roman citizenship. Thus the Roman nation henceforth included the whole of Italy.

This measure brought no immediate easing of internal tension, since both *optimates* and *populares* tried to attract the new citizens to their own side. While internal disputes increased, a new threat arose abroad. Mithridates, the mighty ruler of Pontus, had acquired a considerable empire around the Black Sea. The Romans, true to their old tactics, had systematically thwarted his increasing power. Mithridates now seized his chance and invaded the Roman province of Asia. Everywhere he was hailed as a saviour; Roman officials and merchants were slaughtered by his troops and the enraged populace. The revolt spread to Greece, where Athens chose the side of the king. Scarcely had Rome gained the upper hand in its war against the allies (the revolt still smouldered in Samnium) than the Senate had to appoint the consul Lucius Cornelius Sulla ($\rightarrow$ 262) to combat Mithridates. The people, however, transferred the command to its former war hero Marius. Now the results of the changed composition of the armies became apparent. The soldiers, recruited by Sulla and looking to him for reward and booty, remained more faithful to him personally than to the state. Sulla's legions marched on Rome and took the city by force; Marius was exiled and declared an outlaw. Sulla hastily settled affairs as he pleased and then left for Greece. Immediately after his departure, however, the struggle in Rome burst forth anew. Marius returned and massacred his political opponents, but died almost at once. For the next four years (87-84) Cinna, a *popularis*, ruled Italy while Sulla was defeating Mithridates. After making peace Sulla returned in 83 to Italy where the large armies of both parties met each other

The wide extent of the Empire, where armies often had to be moved rapidly to repulse an enemy attack and regular means of communication were necessary in times of peace, required a close-knit and well-maintained network of roads. The Roman engineers achieved work which has survived the centuries: these roads are still frequently used for traffic. **293.** The great roads of communication built by the Romans were normally completely straight. The Fosse Way, one of the great highways in Britain, stands out unchanged in the modern landscape. **294.** Road surface of the Via Flaminia. **295.** The use of the many mountain passes in the Alps dates from the time of the Romans. The Julier Pass (7 503 ft.) was an important communication route; it is still marked by two columns probably of Roman origin. **296.** The earliest main road in Italy was the Via Appia (340 miles) from Rome to Brindisi, where pillars (still standing) marked its end at the sea (see Map 53). Near Terracina Trajan had the Pesco Montano cut back to a height of 118 feet in order to facilitate road construction.

The world of the Pax Romana saw much traffic along the roads, which were marked with milestones and freely provided with places where travellers could rest and change horses (see Map 54). Not only did merchants travel throughout the whole Empire and even far beyond with goods for import and export (see Map 51), but other citizens also journeyed throughout the entire Mediterranean region either for business or pleasure. Travellers even used sleeping coaches covered by animal skins. In this way it was possible to travel in all seasons. The illustrations give some aspects of overland travel. **297.** Merchants with their pack-animals loaded with bales in a hilly region. **298.** Transport of wine in a sewn-up animal skin. The oxen are obviously having difficulty in drawing the wagon. **299.** Two-wheeled carriage. **300.** Four-wheeled coach for passenger transport. **301.** Two families on a journey, led by a Cupid. In front of the second coach a child learning to walk with walking wheels.

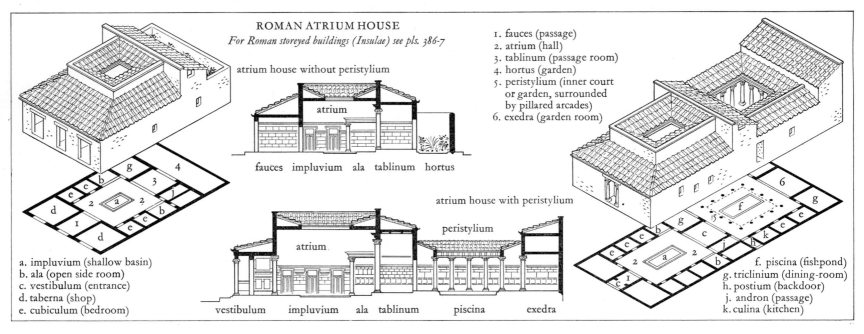

ROMAN ATRIUM HOUSE
For Roman storeyed buildings (Insulae) see pls. 386-7

atrium house without peristylium

atrium

fauces impluvium ala tablinum hortus

atrium house with peristylium

peristylium

atrium

vestibulum impluvium ala tablinum piscina exedra

1. fauces (passage)
2. atrium (hall)
3. tablinum (passage room)
4. hortus (garden)
5. peristylium (inner court or garden, surrounded by pillared arcades)
6. exedra (garden room)

a. impluvium (shallow basin)
b. ala (open side room)
c. vestibulum (entrance)
d. taberna (shop)
e. cubiculum (bedroom)

f. piscina (fishpond)
g. triclinium (dining-room)
h. postium (backdoor)
j. andron (passage)
k. culina (kitchen)

in civil war. Sulla triumphed. Thousands of his opponents were outlawed, and either fled to Spain, where the struggle persisted for years, or joined the pirates who, profiting from the prevailing confusion, were harassing shipping throughout the whole Mediterranean.

Having crushed all resistance by a reign of terror, Sulla, who was elected dictator, reorganised the constitution of the state. He aimed to make it impossible for tribunes, relying on the mass of the people, or for consuls, relying on their armies, to defy the Senate. He took measures to render the tribunes powerless and limited the authority of the consuls to unarmed Italy. They were to be merely the executive organs of the Senate, which became the government proper. As long as the powerful dictator lived no one dared to object. Yet as soon as he had voluntarily resigned his office (in 79) and died (78) the struggle broke out more fiercely than before, and the weak points in his reconstruction became evident. The Senate, now a body of 500 to 600 members, was too unwieldy, too divided, its members were too much concerned with the interests of themselves or of their families to form a homogeneous 'government'. Above all, now that the executive authority of the consuls was curtailed, it was difficult to check the power of provincial governors, who commanded armies which they themselves might have helped to recruit. Ambitious men sought the consulship as a gateway to a command in a province where they might need an army, if possible a special command with special powers, since it soon appeared that the senatorial republic, which had refused to accept a 'president' like Gracchus, none the less had to yield to an army commander with *imperium*, such as Sulla had been. Two men in particular soon came to the fore. These were Marcus Licinius Crassus, who won fame by crushing a dangerous slave revolt led by Spartacus and who dominated the money market of Rome by his immense wealth, and Gnaeus Pompeius (Pompey the Great) (→ 263), who subdued Sicily, Africa, and Spain for the Senate and was subsequently granted by the people a special command against the sea pirates with powers that extended over the whole Mediterranean. With his magnificent talent for organisation he swiftly accomplished this task (67 B.C.) and was afterwards given another special command, to end the war against Mithridates, which had broken out again in 74 and was still smouldering. He was given almost absolute power over all the eastern provinces. In this too he was successful. Mithridates was defeated and committed suicide. Pompey then settled affairs in the East on his own authority. Syria was annexed as a province and Judaea subjected. Meanwhile in Rome the energetic Julius Caesar was attempting, by means of political intrigue, to attain a position of power as leader of the *populares* (see Map 36, p. 104). The Senate began to view with alarm the power of these men who threatened to grow beyond the control of the Republic. It succeeded indeed, under the guidance of the accomplished lawyer Cicero (→ 264) in putting down the dangerous conspiracy of Catiline (63 B.C.). Yet the unity between senators and knights, that had been momentarily achieved by Cicero, was soon broken. When Pompey returned from the East in triumph and, contrary to the general expectation, disbanded his army instead of proclaiming himself dictator, the Senate could think of nothing better than to annoy and thwart the general, whom it now considered powerless. Caesar and Crassus were also annoyed by the Senate, and therefore these three powerful men made a private alliance to work together (the so-called First Triumvirate) which proved stronger than the Senate. They pursued their aim by means of political influence, money, and threats. Caesar was given a special command in Gaul, where in a triumphant struggle he subdued the whole country and secured the loyalty of his army to himself and himself alone. In face of this the central government was powerless; a central government in fact scarcely

existed any longer. In 55 Pompey and Crassus held the consulship. Thereafter Pompey had Spain as his province, and Crassus accepted Syria with the chance of a profitable war against the Parthians. He was, however, ignominiously defeated and killed by them at Carrhae.

Pompey, now directly faced with the growing might of Caesar, turned again to the *optimates*. In 49, when the Senate, relying on Pompey's support, ventured to recall Caesar from Gaul, civil war broke out. Caesar conquered Italy and Spain in a rapid campaign and afterwards followed Pompey to Greece where the latter had mobilised a large army. The decisive battle was fought at Pharsalus in 48 B.C.; it was a complete victory for Caesar. Pompey fled to Egypt but was murdered as he landed. The last Republican army was defeated in Africa in 46. Its leaders (the most famous was Cato, the implacable enemy of tyranny) committed suicide. Pompey's sons, who had organised an uprising in Spain, were defeated in 45 at Munda. Caesar was now undisputed master of the state. In 44 he was proclaimed lifelong dictator and was thought by many to be aspiring to royal powers. This was the end of the Roman Republic.

THE DEVELOPMENT OF ROMAN CULTURE

Romano-Italic culture had been influenced from the outset by the Greeks and the Etruscans. With the disappearance of Etruscan power and the Roman conquest of Greek southern Italy, the Greek element was intensified. Rome was flooded by Greeks who, in the beginning as slaves but soon as freedmen, became the accepted tutors of their masters. As Horace said: *Graecia capta ferum victorem cepit*. It was no longer merely a question of influence. Greek culture became an integral part of Roman life. In manner of living, architecture, painting and sculpture, poetry and prose, Greek models set the standard for all Romans who ventured to experiment in these fields. The more cultured Romans now began to write in Greek, and Rome became, and always remained, bilingual. The example of Cato the Censor, however, who in order to combat this Hellenisation and 'corruption of morals' wrote historical works in Latin, in the end prevailed, in the sense that Latin became the language of literature for Roman writers, although the literary forms were borrowed from the Greeks.

This Greek 'Enlightenment' had an adverse effect upon Roman religion. Greek mythology, with its aesthetic and imaginative character, penetrated the early animistic beliefs of the Romans, and, for the intellectuals at least, the colourful host of Olympian gods and Greek heroes replaced the mysterious world of spirits and powers (*numina*). Although the earlier beliefs, now regarded as superstition, retained a strong hold upon the ordinary Roman, especially in the countryside, the official state religion provided politicians with a means of influencing the masses. Religious ceremonies like divination and augury were used for political purposes. In one respect, however, the Romans remained true to character. Ecstatic cults, mystery religions and secret societies, were considered a danger to the state, and the Senate did not hesitate to suppress their excesses with the utmost severity.

True Roman judgment and taste can most clearly be discerned if the types of Greek literature which they imitated and the manner in which they adapted them are considered. Although the Romans were willing to learn from the Greeks, they would not surrender to them completely. In the field of literature, comedy (which imitated Greek New Comedy) was most in favour. Plot and intrigue were largely derived from Greek models (especially Menander), but the Roman writers introduced a typically Roman, while not always subtle, sense of humour. Plautus and Terence, the best-known writers, succeeded in avoiding mere translation and in infusing their works with a true poetic feeling. The epic must have been particularly

Roman glassware

Roman pottery and terra sigillata

attractive to the Romans in view of their mighty past. They possessed no real saga of their own, so that for them the epic became at first a poetic chronicle which despite the great poetic gifts of Ennius of necessity lacked dramatic unity. The Romans were also fond of historical plays; but as none of these has been preserved we can form only a vague idea of what they must have been like. There was little emphasis on individualism in the Roman character, so that at the beginning lyrical poetry was hardly represented at all.

In architecture both Etruscan and Greek models were followed. Arched constructions borrowed from the Etruscans remained characteristic of the Roman style. Although temples were built on Greek lines with rounded columns and architraves in the Ionic, Doric, or Corinthian manner, they retained the high Italic base which gave them a distinctive style. The purest expression of the Roman mind, however, was to be found in the functional constructions built of brick or concrete faced with stone. These included the enormous aqueducts by which spring-water was carried to the cities over hills and valleys, sometimes from distances of many miles (see especially → 455–8). Roads and bridges provide fine examples of the skill of the Roman engineers (→ 293ff, 453). Greek statues, paintings and mosaics were imported in quantity, originally as the spoils of war but later executed in Greece on commission to adorn the town and country houses of the Roman nobles. This mass-production threatened to smother true art.

Roman portraits display a completely different character. Of old the Romans had preserved death-masks of their forefathers and placed them in the entrance-halls of their homes as reminders of fame achieved and positions held. These served as models for the sculptors, who created individualistic portraits of great realistic power. The art of painting, too, though following Greek models and technique, soon showed a distinctively Roman spirit in the treatment of space and colour (→ 396ff, 228).

Early Rome had been an ugly, haphazard city built of clay, stone, and tufa. Slowly its centre at any rate became a city of marble, although its humble origins continued to be reflected elsewhere in the narrow, crooked streets which could never rival the regular, spacious planning of the great Hellenistic capitals. Nevertheless, for every Roman, filled with civic pride, it was the *urbs pulcherrima*, the most beautiful city in the world (→ 349ff).

While the external life of Rome was thus adapting itself to Greek cultural influences, the Roman outlook upon life also suffered a radical change under the influence of Greek philosophy. Greek views of life began to supplement and even to replace ancient Roman custom, which no longer appeared adequate when faced with the new and often puzzling problems which Rome's expanding horizon brought with it.

Roman life had always been governed by precedent, by the *mos maiorum*. The Roman ideal was *virtus*, manly virtue which comprised valour, loyalty to the family, the fatherland, and the gods, stern discipline and measured self-interest, and the preservation of *auctoritas* and *dignitas*. The reasonableness of this tradition was questioned by Hellenistic philosophers, especially the Sceptics of the New Academy, who maintained that it was possible to refute the validity of any tradition and to justify the opposite. When this brilliant art of debating was first heard in Rome the Senate, at the suggestion of Cato the Censor, had made haste to expel the men who were thus undermining Roman morality (155 B.C.). But their ideas fell upon fertile ground, especially among the younger generation, who went to Greece for education and study. The practical results of these theories soon became apparent. Ambition and self-interest, luxury, self-indulgence, and the neglect of duty rapidly grew common. In this spiritual crisis, comparable with that experienced in Greece in the time of the Sophists and the Peloponnesian War, the nobler Romans turned to the teachings of those of the Greek philosophers (Plato, Aristotle, and above all the Stoics) who had tried to give virtue a foundation in reason. In the 'good' lauded by these philosophers the Romans readily recognised the old Roman *virtus*; they gladly compared the moral attitude of their forefathers with the ethical teachings of the Greeks. It was not that they themselves wished to study philosophy as such. They desired rather to find in it foundations for the traditional Roman state, society, and conception of life. The Greek historian Polybius taught them that the balanced Roman constitution was the best, the Greek Stoic philosopher Panaetius that virtue and not self-interest must rule their actions now as it had done in the past. In the revolutionary period after the Gracchi philosophical slogans became more and more current. Each faction founded its practical policy upon an ideological basis. These ideologies were essentially justificatory arguments rather than a basis for political theory. For this reason they often appear to us, living in a later age, as not being meant seriously. For those involved, however, they provided a justification of their actions.

During the last fifty years of the Republic these intellectual movements produced Romans, trained in Greece, who set down their ideas in writing for a reading public. Practical statesmen took up their pens in order to justify their actions and attitude. We still possess the *Commentaries* of Julius Caesar, in which with incomparable clarity of language and thought he sketched for his contemporaries his own portrait as the great commander, the extender of Rome's empire, and the misunderstood patriot, caught up against his will in the civil war. The historian Sallust wrote monographs on typical crises during the previous hundred years (the war with Jugurtha, the conspiracy of Catiline) in order to expose the inefficiency and corruption of the governing coterie which he hated. The poets recorded in their lyrics their feelings and experiences as the image of their times. Catullus, although following Greek models, gives authentic glimpses of the emotional life of the gilded youth of Rome about 60 B.C. Lucretius composed his didactic poem *De Rerum Natura* ('On the Nature of Things') as an exposition of the materialist doctrine of Epicurus; yet in fact it reflected his personal intellectual struggles and his views of life and death. Poetry and literature became fashionable in Rome as they had been the fashion in Greece for centuries. Yet through all the rhetoric and artistic polish there sounds a note of bitter seriousness which inspired these writers in an attempt to find an intellectual prop in the chaos of their times and the disappearance of familiar values.

The man who may be said to personify this entire age is Marcus Tullius Cicero, the great orator who fashioned the Latin language into an instrument capable of reproducing all the rules of Greek rhetoric. By his oratory he dominated his audiences in both law courts and Senate house, and through them he attempted to influence Roman policy. In this he did not succeed, for his weapons were too weak when pitted against force and arms. Yet at the same time, when his political rôle was played out, he was able to sketch for his fellow-citizens with his pen his ideals of state and culture. He recommended the Greek philosophers, in whose writings he himself had found support and guidance and which he was the first to adapt for Latin readers. No philosopher himself, he was a man who throughout his whole life sought in philosophy the principles and foundations of his own conduct and that of others. He was the first consciously to tackle the problem of how a supranational culture, such as the Hellenistic culture had become, could be reconciled with the national heritage and way of life. This remains a burning question for Europeans today; and in this sense Cicero may be said to have been the first European.

It was during the Empire that the Romans first maintained a vast fleet (see Map 43); its efficient organisation made *mare nostrum* a reality for the whole Roman world. The two chief bases were Misenum and Classis. **302.** The port of Misenum. A row of piles (*pilae*) still reveals at low water the position of two piers (*moles*). Spaces hollowed out in the rocks (see arrows) served to house naval stores. Cape Misenum (**306**) at the foot of which lay the greatest naval base of the Tyrrhenian Sea. To provide the fleet with fresh water the Romans hewed out an enormous underground reservoir of tufa stone (**304**) fed by an aqueduct. **303.** The coasts were marked by lighthouses. A striking example of this is found on a sarcophagus, upon which is depicted the personified city of Ostia bearing the lighthouse of the harbour in her hand. **305.** Entrance to Classis, the base in the Adriatic. **307.** Warship with beak and oars, with legionaries on board.

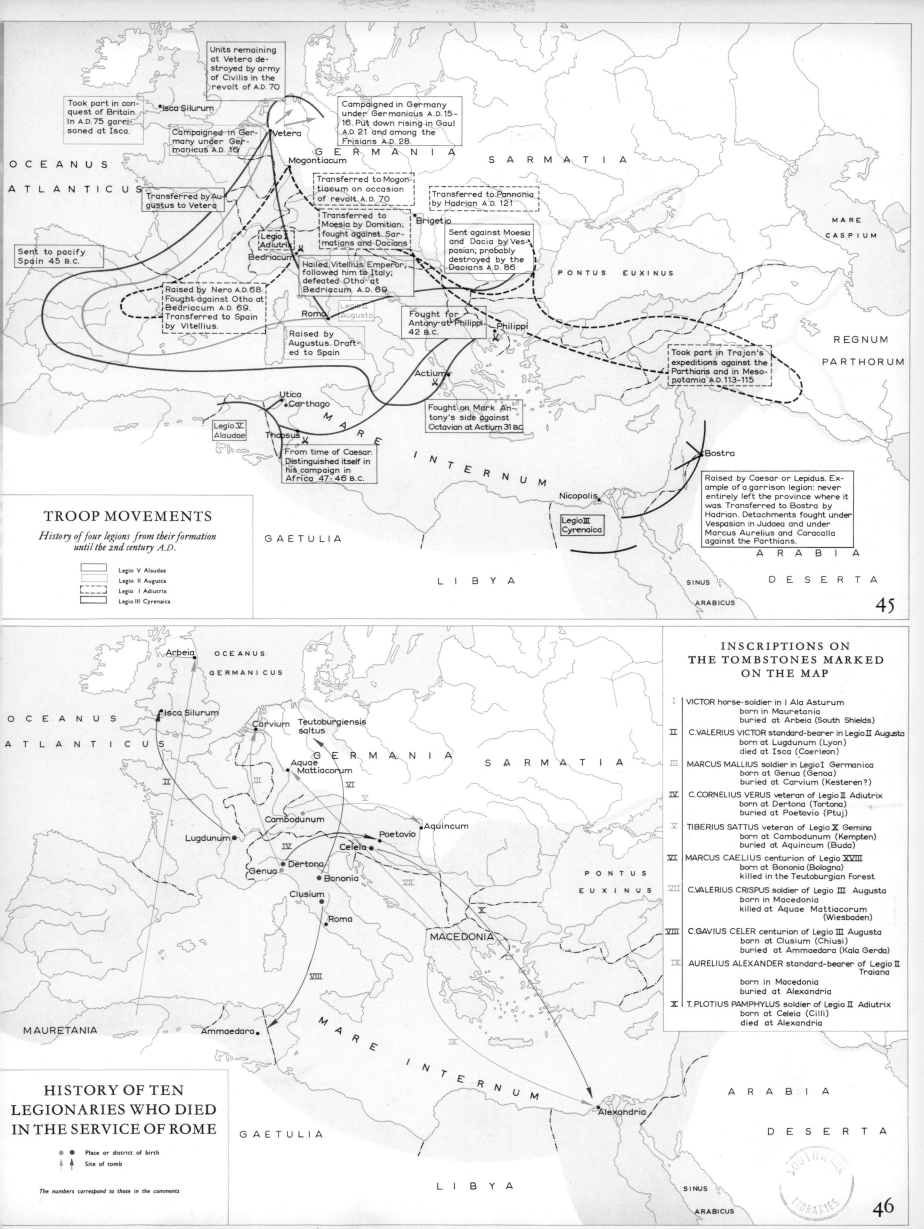

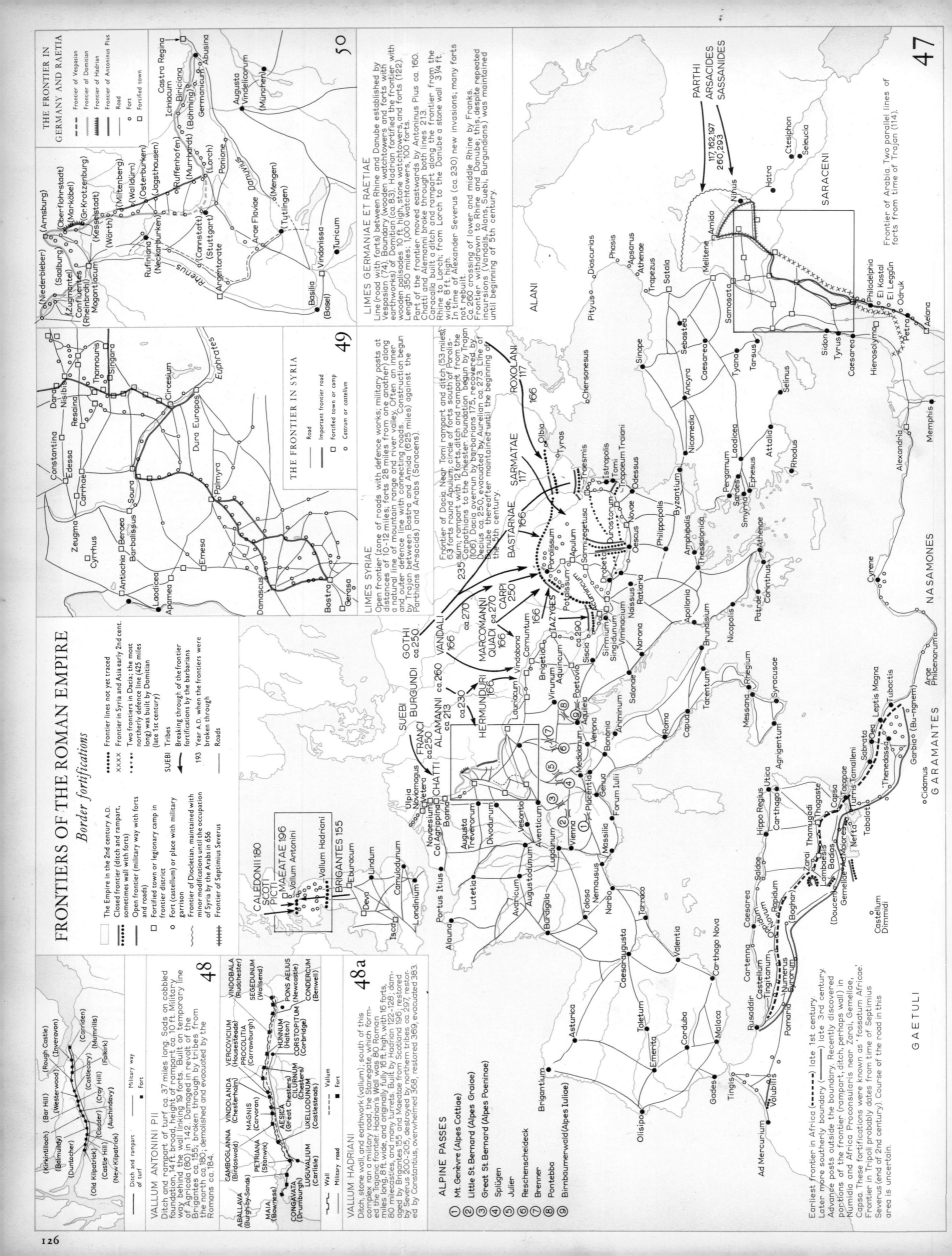

FRONTIERS OF THE ROMAN EMPIRE
Border fortifications

	The Empire in the 2nd century A.D.
	Closed frontier (ditch and rampart, sometimes wall with forts)
	Open frontier (military way with forts and roads)
□	Fortified town or legionary camp in frontier district
○	Fort (castellum) or place with military garrison
	Frontier of Diocletian, maintained with minor modifications until the occupation of Syria by the Arabs in 656
	Frontier of Septimius Severus

.....	Frontier lines not yet traced
xxxx	Frontier in Syria and Asia early 2nd cent.
····	Two frontiers in Dacia; the most northerly defence line (425 miles long) was built by Domitian (late 1st century)
→	Breaking through of the frontier fortifications by the barbarians
SUEBI	Tribes
193	Year A.D. when the frontiers were broken through
	Roads

THE FRONTIER IN GERMANY AND RAETIA 50

———	Frontier of Vespasian
····	Frontier of Domitian
⋙⋙	Frontier of Hadrian
—·—·	Frontier of Antoninus Pius
	Road
○	Fort
□	Fortified town

47

LIMES GERMANIAE ET RAETIAE

Line (road or frontier) between Rhine and Danube established by Vespasian (74). Boundary (earthworks) of Domitian (ca. 83). Hadrian fortified the frontier with wooden palisades 10 ft. high, stone watchtowers and forts (122). Length 350 miles; 1,000 watchtowers, 100 forts. Part of the frontier moved eastwards by Antoninus Pius ca. 160. Chatti and Alemanni broke through both lines 213. Caracalla built a ditch and rampart along the frontier from the Rhine to Lorch; later the Danube a stone wall 3/4 ft. wide, 8 ft. high. In time of Alexander Severus (ca. 230) new invasions; many forts not rebuilt.
Ca. 260 crossing of lower and middle Rhine by Franks. Frontier- withdrawal to Rhine and Danube; this, despite repeated incursions (Vandals, Alans, Suebi, Burgundians) was maintained until beginning of 5th century.

LIMES SYRIAE 49

Open frontier (zone of roads with defence works; military posts at distances of 10-12 miles; forts 28 miles from one another) along a natural line of mountain range and river valley. Often an inner and outer defence line with connecting roads. Construction begun by Trajan between Bostra and Amida (625 miles) against the Parthians (Arsacids) and Arabs (Saracens).

Frontier of Dacia near Tomi rampart and ditch (53 miles); 63 forts round Apulum; circle of forts south of Porolissum; rampart with 12 forts, ditch and rampart from the Carpathians to the Dniester. Foundation begun by Trajan (106). Dacia overrun by barbarians 175, recovered by Decius ca. 250, evacuated by Aurelian ca. 273. Line of Danube thereafter maintained until the beginning of the 5th century.

THE FRONTIER IN SYRIA 49

———	Road
■	Important frontier road
□	Fortified town or camp
○	Castrum or castellum

VALLUM ANTONINI PII 48

Ditch and rampart of turf ca. 37 miles long. Sods on cobbled foundation, 14 ft. broad, height of rampart ca. 10 ft. Military way behind the wall linking 19 forts. Built on temporary line of Agricola (80) in 142. Damaged in revolt of the Brigantes ca. 155, broken through by tribes from the north ca. 180; demolished and evacuated by the Romans ca. 184.

	Ditch and rampart of turf
■■■	Military way
■	Fort

VALLUM HADRIANI 48a

Ditch, stone wall, and earthwork (vallum), south of this complex ran a military road, the Stanegate, which formed the Trajanic frontier. Hadrian's Wall was 80 Roman miles long, 8 ft. wide, and originally fully 16 ft. high, with 16 forts, 80 milecastles, and many turrets. Built by Hadrian 122-128, damaged by Brigantes 155 and Maeatae 196, restored ca. 207, destroyed by northern tribes ca. 297, restored 369, evacuated 383.

———	Wall
—·—·	Military road
■	Fort

ALPINE PASSES

① Mt. Genèvre (Alpes Cottiae)
② Little St. Bernard (Alpes Graiae)
③ Great St. Bernard (Alpes Poeninae)
④ Splügen
⑤ Julier
⑥ Reschenscheideck
⑦ Brenner
⑧ Pontebba
⑨ Birnbaumerwald (Alpes Iuliae)

Earliest frontier in Africa (————) late 1st century
Later more southerly boundary (————) late 3rd century
Advance posts outside the boundary. Recently discovered portions of the frontier (rampart, ditch, perhaps wall) in Numidia and Africa Proconsularis near Zarai, Gemellae, Capsa. These fortifications were known as 'fossatum Africae.' Frontier in Tripoli probably dates from time of Septimius Severus (end of 2nd century). Course of the road in this area is uncertain.

126

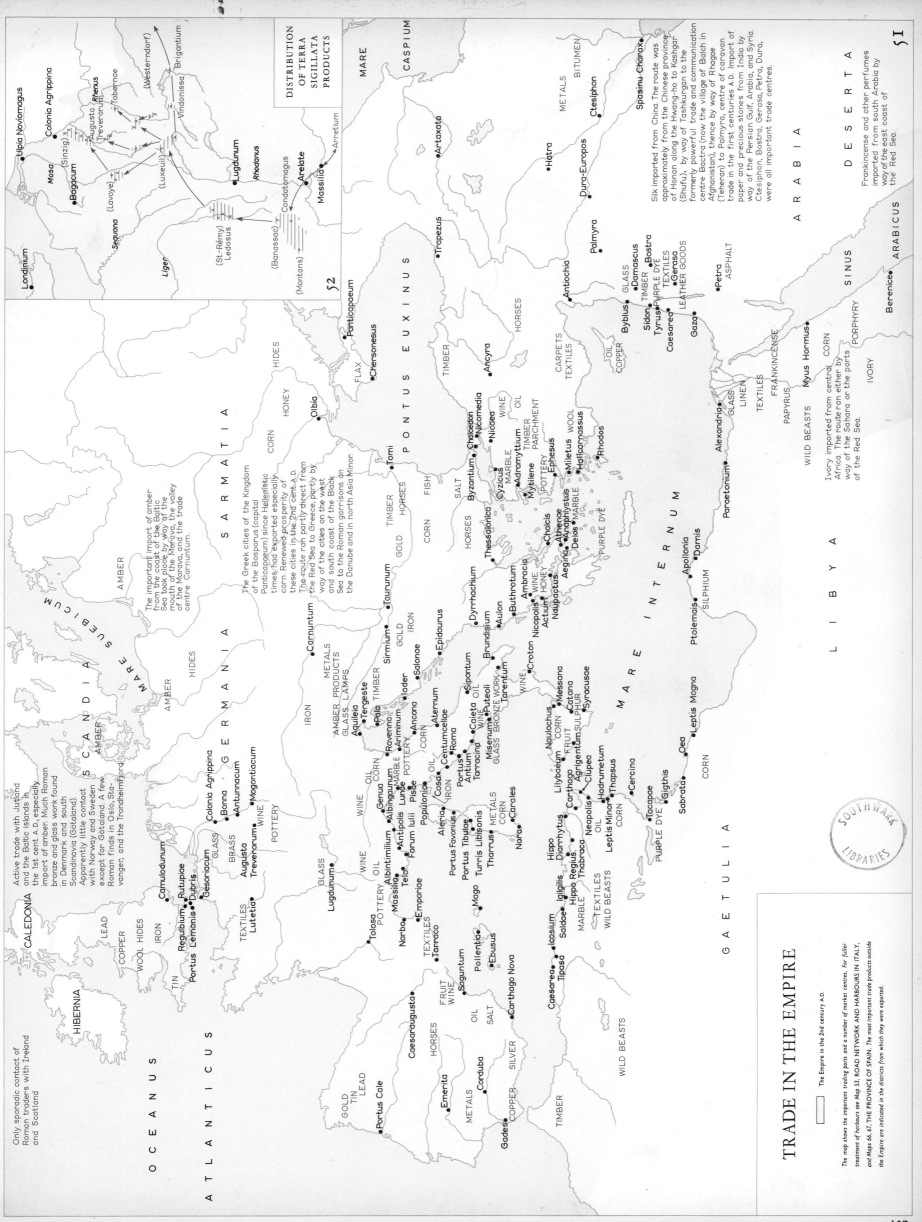

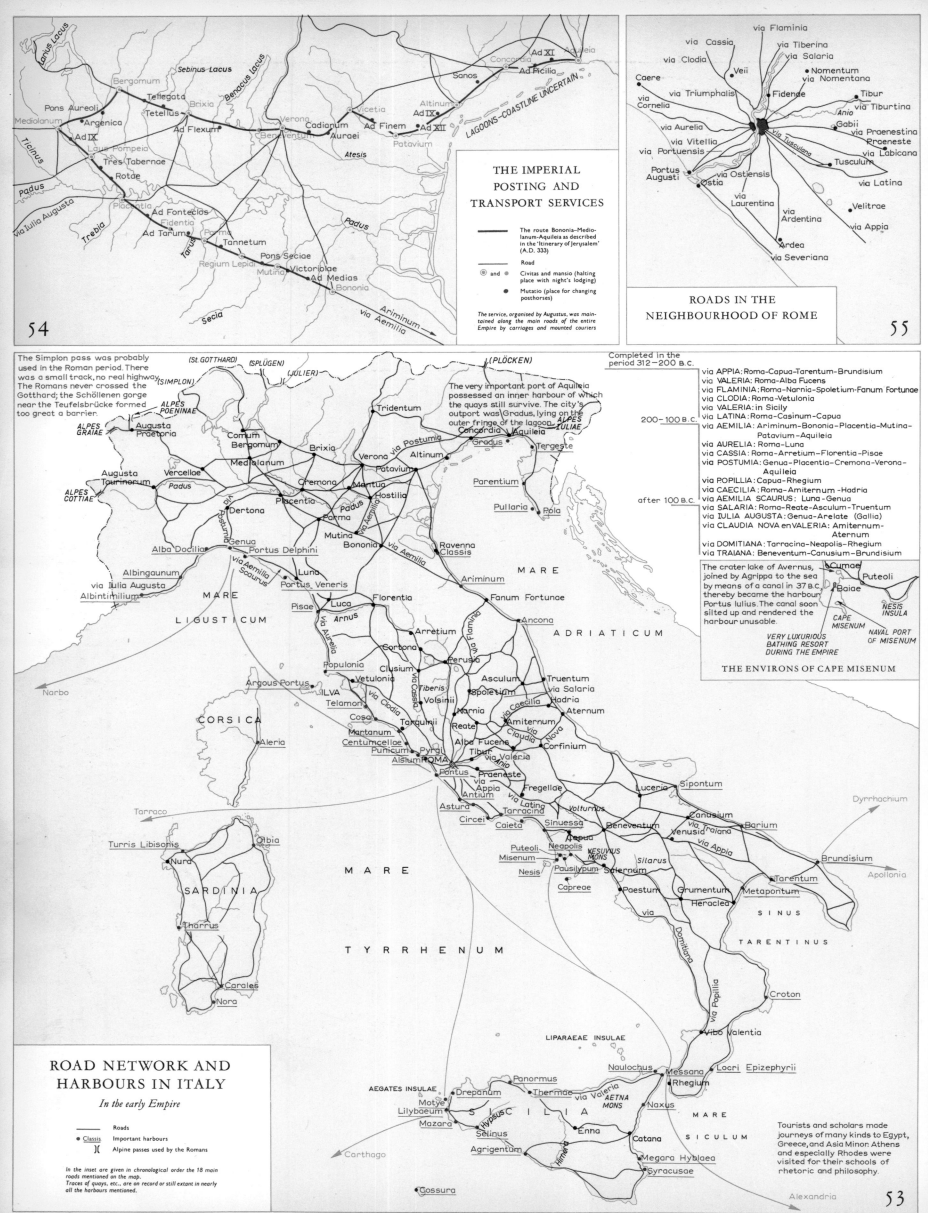

308. Three sailing ships in a rough sea. Left: a look-out tower; right: a lighthouse. 309. Large trading vessel, perhaps Phoenician, with sails hoisted. 310. Tow boat for transporting wine. 311. The departure and return of the merchant fleet were favourite themes in Roman sculpture. Upon a large relief showing the port of Ostia is depicted the return of a large sailing ship. On the poop the captain offers sacrifice as thanksgiving for their safe return. Behind the ship stands Neptune, and statues of various gods can be seen in the harbour. On one of the bases a team of four elephants is depicted; it is perhaps the Emperor Claudius, the founder of the port (see Map 43, inset), who stands in the chariot. The relief excels in the reproduction of many important details: the construction of the ship, the rigging, the boats in front of and behind the vessel, the sails, etc., can be clearly distinguished.

Arch of Titus at Rome   Arch of Constantine at Rome   Porta Nigra at Trier

From Republic to Empire

THE CIVIL WAR

Caesar manifestly wielded autocratic power, but it is uncertain whether he also aspired to the title of king. In a brief time he introduced many reforms and a wide range of legislation. He reformed the Roman calendar, which had become confused, by introducing the solar 'Julian' calendar. He suppressed the political clubs that had disrupted political life; he adorned the city with new buildings (the Forum Iulium, a basilica, and a public library); he drained marshland and improved municipal administration in Italy; he tightened up provincial administration; he was liberal in grants of Roman citizenship to provincials; and to meet the needs of his veterans and the poor in Rome he planned at least twenty overseas colonies which provided new homes for some 100,000 citizens. He prepared a great 'national' war against the Parthians to avenge Carrhae, perhaps hoping to increase the loyalty of his supporters and encourage the submission of his opponents. Yet he was regarded by many as a tyrant, and a conspiracy was formed which was joined even by enemies whom he had pardoned and by former adherents who felt overshadowed by their new master.

On the Ides of March 44 B.C. the dictator, conscious of the hatred surrounding him but from a curious sense of fatalism refusing to take measures to ensure his safety, was murdered in the Senate by a group of senators led by Brutus and Cassius. Cicero, a convinced Republican, immediately championed the cause of liberty. But it soon appeared that tyranny had not vanished with the tyrant. The Senate was helpless against Mark Antony, who was supported by Caesar's veterans. Then Caesar's great-nephew, the young Octavius (who after his adoption as Caesar's son under his will became Gaius Julius Caesar Octavianus) entered the lists against Antony. He considered himself Caesar's designated successor in political as well as private life. In 43 the opponents were reconciled by the mediation of Lepidus, and the three together, forming an alliance, forced through a measure giving this second Triumvirate full powers 'to reorganise the state'. Their first step was to issue extensive proscriptions, and their victims included even Cicero. In 42 Brutus and Cassius, who had assembled an army in the East, were defeated at Philippi, and both committed suicide. The members of the Triumvirate divided up the Roman dominions among themselves. Antony, the true victor of Philippi, retained the wealthy East; Lepidus received Africa; Octavian was given Spain and Sardinia and the task of finding land in Italy for the veterans who had been promised this as their pension. The land of many Italian cities was unceremoniously taken from the owners and parcelled out.

Throughout the following years, however, Octavian, whose cold-blooded cruelty during the proscriptions had aroused repulsion, developed into a ruler capable of restoring order and prosperity. At the same time he contrived to shift the blame for the sufferings caused by the civil war onto the shoulders of his colleagues and to pose as the champion of Italy and the West. Himself no great soldier, he found in Agrippa a commander of unswerving loyalty. Maecenas seconded him in his attempts to restore Italian culture. The services of the insignificant Lepidus were soon dispensed with, and Octavian took over his army and territory. Peace was re-established in the West, which declared for Octavian. In the meanwhile Antony, involved with Cleopatra queen of Egypt, launched a campaign against the Parthians which ended in disaster. The subsequent tension between Antony and Octavian led to direct conflict culminating in the destruction of Antony's fleet at the battle of Actium in 31 B.C. He fled to Egypt with Cleopatra, and his army, thus deserted, surrendered. Antony committed suicide in Alexandria, and his example was followed by Cleopatra when she saw that she could expect no mercy from Octavian (see Map 37, p. 113).

OCTAVIANUS AUGUSTUS

For the third time one man was master of the whole Roman world (30). Sulla had restored the sovereignty of the Senate. Caesar had made all authority in Rome dependent upon himself, and this Rome had not tolerated. What would be the choice of his adopted son and successor? In the Senate meeting of 13 January 27 B.C., Octavian announced his intention of restoring the Republic, and resigned all his special offices. In gratitude for this gesture the Senate accorded him a new name – Augustus, 'the exalted'. From this time he used the title Imperator Caesar Augustus. At the same time the Senate granted him new powers including the administration of a large number of the provinces which were those where most of the armies were situated. This great military command, together with his civil powers as consul, made him in effect the head of the restored Republic. Augustus wished to steer a middle course between Sulla and Caesar. Acting with sincerity, he restored the Republic, retaining the Senate and magistrates but adding a central ruler in his own person. Since he had supreme authority over the provinces in which armies were stationed, and these armies were henceforth commanded by his legates, the danger of independent army commanders was removed.

In Rome he held the office of consul for several successive years, but when this proved unpractical, partly through the difficulty that he always had a nominally equal colleague, he contented himself with a grant of tribunician power (*tribunicia potestas*) which made his person inviolable and gave him wide powers of veto. Though he did not hold the office of tribune of the plebs, his tribunician authority made him in a sense the protector of the people. He carefully regulated admission to the senatorial and equestrian orders, the two groups which were to supply the men to help him to administer the Empire. The magistrates were in effect chosen by the Senate (officially so under his successor Tiberius), often on the recommendation of the First Citizen (*Princeps*) – Augustus' official title.

As a result of these measures the popular assembly ceased to carry any weight at all. This was all to the good, for these assemblies were unrepresentative and irresponsible, and it was essential that the demagogy and mob violence of preceding decades should be eradicated at all costs.

The intention was that the Senate and *Princeps* should cooperate in administering the state, with the *Princeps* acting as chief magistrate. In fact the powers granted to Augustus were for limited periods and had to be renewed every five or ten years. That this arrangement led none the less to autocracy can be explained by the impossibility of creating procedure by which the *Princeps* could be replaced by selection either after a fixed period of office or after his death. When Augustus first assumed power he

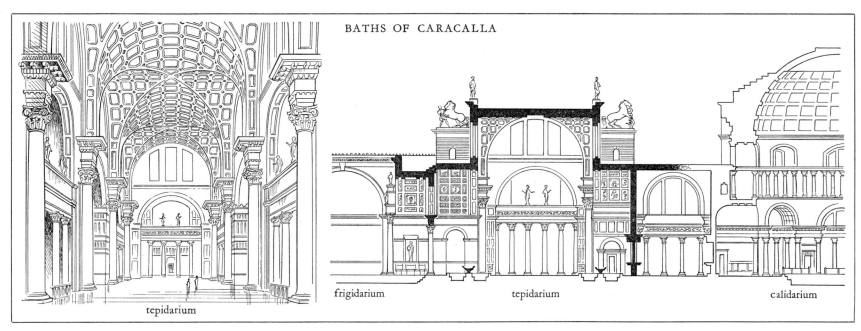

BATHS OF CARACALLA

tepidarium

frigidarium   tepidarium   calidarium

overshadowed all others in authority. If this was ever challenged, civil war would be inevitable. Thus Augustus took care that throughout his long reign there should always be a potential successor designated by himself. In order to render competition impossible he was obliged to keep all key positions in the hands of his family, relations, or loyal friends. Obviously then the Senate could be granted no real right of opposition, since violent protest against the opinions of the *Princeps* might appear as treason. Although the Senate might comment upon the ruler's policy, it was in fact completely powerless to intervene. Later, weaker successors of Augustus intensified this tendency and deliberately intimidated the ranks from which any possible pretenders might come, namely the senatorial nobility; so that the Senate, instead of continuing to collaborate fully in the government, became an instrument without a will of its own.

These developments, however, lay in the future. For the time being the Empire breathed again with the return of peace, order, and justice, which brought with them increased prosperity. A stop was put to the exploitation of the provinces, now under the supervision of Augustus' financial agents or procurators. Rome became the centre of a far-flung administrative system and was enlarged by Augustus into a magnificent city. The country towns followed suit as best they could. Despite the social reforms which Augustus introduced, there was little fundamental change in society, though the cessation of war began gradually to affect the slave economy: in the course of time slaves became more expensive and therefore tended to be treated better. The common people in Rome, who could no longer trade upon their right to vote, were humoured by distributions of free corn and by amusements ('bread and circuses'); the number of public holidays rapidly increased (see Map 59, p. 163, → 435–40). The Romanisation of the West continued apace, for some Emperors were extremely liberal in granting Roman citizenship. This period can truly be regarded as one of peace and prosperity.

The culture of the age of Augustus

In the tumultuous period of the revolution Roman culture had come of age. Orators, poets, and prose authors, writing in Latin, had taken their place beside their masters the Greeks. In the hopeful years of returning confidence, of newly-won security, literature flourished as never before. The imitation of Greek forms remained indeed the ideal of the Augustan poets, and they sought to equal the Greeks; yet they had their own thoughts, ideals, and sentiments.

Augustus himself, together with Maecenas, was a great patron of the arts. To their support nearly all the poets of this time owed their relatively care-free existence. A national poetry immortalised Roman ideals; a national historiography drew a picture of the past which may fall short of modern standards of historical criticism in some respects but which filled the Roman with pride and a feeling of vocation. These writers, who felt themselves prophets of the New Age, supported with conviction the ideals of *virtus* and *pietas* which Augustus sought to realise.

Many of these ideals proved illusions. The very essence of the Principate, which directed the people and worked and thought for them, gradually deprived them of initiative and undermined that public spirit which Augustus tried to arouse. The return of prosperity brought with it a privileged class which wasted its time in watering-place and country estates, indulging in luxurious and artistic pleasures. In art the technical perfection of language and form remained, but even in the later years of the reign of Augustus a noticeable lack of 'high seriousness', not to speak of frivolity, became manifest; the struggle for an ideal disappeared. Augustus found himself compelled to promulgate stern laws against the avoidance of marriage and the birth control practised precisely by that ruling class which according to his system was to govern the Empire. These laws had little permanent effect. Augustus even had to banish his own daughter and granddaughter on account of their scandalous conduct.

Yet the reorganisation carried out by the first *Princeps* bore fruit in another less spectacular field. The public spirit of Rome lived on in the service of the Empire in the staff of countless officials and soldiers who devoted their lives to this service, a body which for two centuries bore unrelieved yet with growing efficiency the burden of administering and defending the Empire. More than the glittering courtiers and the brilliant orators and writers, they were the true backbone of the Empire. By their efforts provinces were developed and communications improved by roads and bridges (see Maps 51–3, p. 127f). At first in the numerous cities of Italy and afterwards throughout the whole Empire there lived a Romanised class of local magistrates, merchants, soldiers, and citizens. More than literature, centred as it was about the increasingly corrupt life of the capital, the inscriptions, the remains of flourishing towns, the roads, bridges and aqueducts, testify to this aspect of the principate. It should never be forgotten that behind the everyday life of Rome, behind the pomp and corruption of the court, the public service of the state continued, firmly based on the foundations which Augustus had laid after many years of discreet labour.

The Empire

Tiberius

When Augustus died in A.D. 14 he was succeeded, without much opposition, by his stepson Tiberius (→ 318) who had been his designated heir. Wellnigh automatically the succession of the First Citizen by selection was thus replaced by the dynastic principle. It was taken as a matter of course that the Julian-Claudian house should have the right to the Principate. Provided that the would-be successor commanded the support of the army, recognition by the Senate was a formality. In the relationship created by Augustus,

whereby the *Princeps* controlled all forms of imperial power, decided upon war or peace, administered the finances of the imperial provinces, safeguarded Italy's food supply, and through his tribunician power possessed the right of speech and veto in the Senate and elsewhere, the Senate played a very secondary rôle. Any contribution of theirs was subordinated to the will of the *Princeps*, and his actions might at best be commented upon but seldom criticised. Despite all this, however, the Senate, from whose ranks

A number of mosaics at the trading centre of Ostia, where import and export gave rise to great activity, give a striking picture of Roman trade. The wares brought in were dealt with at a commercial exchange in the centre of the city, where seventy offices of merchants were grouped around a central court. Floor mosaics in front of the offices represent scenes of harbour life, and at the same time provided information to visitors about the nature of the trade, the course of the shipping lines, etc. **312.** Transfer of amphoras from one ship to another. **313-4.** Modern inventions such as oxygen apparatus for underwater swimming have made it possible to locate many ships which sank during the Roman period. Many ships have been found with their cargo of amphoras still on board. From the shapes, stamps of the makers, etc. of the recovered jars much can be deduced about the date of the pottery, the wares carried, and the routes followed.

The portraits of Roman Emperors offer a splendid gallery of statues, busts, effigies, etc. The portraits differ according to period and the importance and character of the Emperor depicted. A few striking figures from the long series of Emperors are: **315.** Gaius Julius *Caesar*, predecessor of the Emperors. **316.** Gaius Julius Caesar Octavianus *Augustus*, on a cameo made after Actium, and (**317**) as pontifex maximus. **318.** *Tiberius* Claudius Nero Caesar. **319.** Tiberius *Claudius* Drusus Nero Germanicus. **320.** *Nero* Claudius Caesar Drusus Germanicus. **321.** Titus Flavius Sabinus *Vespasianus*. **322.** *Titus* Flavius Sabinus Vespasianus. **323-7.** Reverse of coins showing events from the lives of the Emperors or general subjects. **328.** Titus Flavius *Domitianus* Augustus. **329.** Marcus Ulpius Nerva *Traianus*. **330.** Publius Aelius *Hadrianus*. **331.** Titus Aurelius Fulvus Boionius Arrius *Antoninus Pius*. **332.** Lucius Aurelius *Commodus*. **333.** Marcus Aurelius Antoninus Bassianus Caracallus (*Caracalla*). **334.** Gaius Aurelius Valerius *Diocletianus* Iovius. **335.** Flavius Valerius *Constantinus*. **336.** *Constantinus II.*

315
316
317

318
319
320

321 322 323 324 325 326 327 328

329
330
331
332

333
334
335
336

the provincial governors and army commanders were recruited, remained, together with members of the imperial house itself, the only group from which possible rivals might emerge. Even with the first change of ruler the legions on the Rhine had toyed with the idea of proclaiming their leader, the prince Germanicus, as Emperor in opposition to Tiberius. But Tiberius was an extremely able and experienced governor, although suspicious and solitary by nature. He reacted to this latent threat by stamping out anything which might be viewed as rebellion. His suspicions were merely strengthened by the all-too obvious flattery and submission of the apprehensive Senate. During his reign the notorious *delatores*, professional informers, became more common: thus relations in Rome were poisoned and the history of the court was dominated by successive trials for treason caused by intrigue and plots to win the Emperor's favour. Members of ancient families and even the sons of Germanicus (he himself had died in A.D. 19, poisoned by Tiberius according to the general but erroneous opinion) were sacrificed to his suspicions, fanned by his only confidant the Prefect of the Praetorian Guard Sejanus, who was himself, however, aspiring to the succession. After the unmasking of the conspiracy of his former trusted friend, Tiberius spent his last years in lonely bitterness and a pitiless reign of terror.

The dynasties of the first two centuries

The army, which automatically accepted the dynastic principle, followed the Senate in proclaiming the young Gaius (Caligula) as Emperor. His short reign became such an orgy of debauchery as to suggest that he was not completely sane. After his murder Claudius was put forward by the Praetorian Guard and ascended to the throne. He was well-intentioned and by no means incompetent, but eccentric, a man who commanded little respect and allowed too much influence to his freedmen servants, his favourites, and his wives. Agrippina, his fourth wife, had him poisoned in order to ensure the succession of her son Domitius Nero by a former marriage (→ 320). The name of Nero has become a household word on account of the atrocities that he committed through sickly suspicion and insane pride. He was, in fact, the murderer of his mother, wife, stepbrother, and advisers. Revolt finally flared up in the provinces and, abandoned by all, he committed suicide when he realised that he could not escape his pursuers. So ended the Julian-Claudian dynasty, under which the old aristocracy had been decimated by fifty years of terror and deprived of any real power.

It was at this moment that what Tacitus calls 'the secret of the Empire' came to light, namely the fact that, despite all outward constitutional forms, the ultimate sanction of the Principate was military force and that since the Senate no longer controlled the armies real power lay in the hands of the soldiers. One after another the large armies on the frontiers, inspired by *esprit de corps* and hope of reward, proclaimed their commanders as Emperor irrespective of their abilities. Civil war raged for three years (68–70). Galba, elevated to the throne by the troops from Spain, was murdered in Rome by the Praetorian Guard whose candidate Otho committed suicide after being defeated by the German armies of Vitellius. Vitellius, however, was opposed by the legions of the Danube and of the East, who chose as Emperor Vespasian (→ 321), the commander who at that time was occupied in crushing the revolt of the Jews. After a short but bloody struggle in which Rome was stormed and the Capitol burned he won the day. Happily for Rome he was an able, thrifty, and sober man who succeeded in restoring

discipline and maintaining order in the Empire. The rising of the Batavians, who under the leadership of Civilis had seized their opportunity and had been successful so long as the Roman legions were fighting among themselves, was now put down without much difficulty. The Jewish revolt ended with the destruction of Jerusalem. Now that the Empire passed into the hands of the Flavian house, future stability seemed assured since Vespasian had two sons. But after his death and that of his son Titus (→ 322), who only ruled for two years, there appeared once again, by virtue of the dynastic right, a ruler whose throne had not been gained by his own merit. This was his younger son Domitian (→ 328), who attempted to make good his lack of authority by terrorist methods. The times of Caligula and Nero returned until the day in 96 when Domitian was murdered by his own entourage who felt themselves perpetually menaced.

The Senate now availed itself of its constitutional rights and appointed as *Princeps* the old and widely admired lawyer Nerva. But Nerva succeeded in maintaining his position only by adopting as his son and successor the popular and able general Trajan, who succeeded him in 98 and inaugurated a new era. In a series of glorious campaigns the enemies of Rome, the Dacians on the Danube and the Parthians on the Euphrates, were defeated and driven back. Dacia was annexed as a province and Mesopotamia conquered. Under Trajan's rule the Empire attained its widest expansion (see Maps 41–4, p. 116, 47–50, p. 126). It was fortunate for Rome that neither he nor his successors possessed natural heirs. Thus the idea was finally realised that the *Princeps* should designate as his successor the most able of those around him. Hadrian (→ 330), Antoninus Pius (→ 331, 347), and Marcus Aurelius (→ 340–342, 345) owed their high position not to any law of succession or hazard of birth but to the choice of their predecessors, who adopted them as sons and heirs. Under their able and expert rule this century of the so-called senatorial Emperors, the Emperors by adoption, became the most brilliant period of the Roman Empire. Although upholding their authority autocratically, they had no need of terror. The Senate and Empire recognised their authority of their own free will. Fear of opposition and pretenders to the throne no longer existed. The internal structure of the Empire was systematically consolidated and extended.

Internal development

While contemporary historians devoted themselves mainly to recording events at the court and to the corruption and intrigues at Rome, together with the military exploits on the frontier - traditionally the chief material of the historian - radical changes were taking place in the internal life of the Empire. These changes are revealed only by indirect tradition or from archaeological remains and inscriptions.

We must not, therefore, be misled by stories of abuses and corruption at court. Life in the Empire continued undisturbed and enjoyed almost two centuries of peace in which to develop, while government and administration directed from Rome continued to function more and more efficiently. The restoration of peace and order by Augustus was the basis of this renewal of widespread prosperity. Not only was Rome enlarged into a city of marble (→ 354–5, 363), but in all parts of the Empire temples, theatres, and amphitheatres testified to the prosperity of the cities (see Maps 68, 71, pp. 166, 184). The road network, originally constructed for strategic purposes, rendered even isolated areas accessible and created an economic unity protected on land and sea by unceasing Roman watchfulness (see Map 51, p. 127).

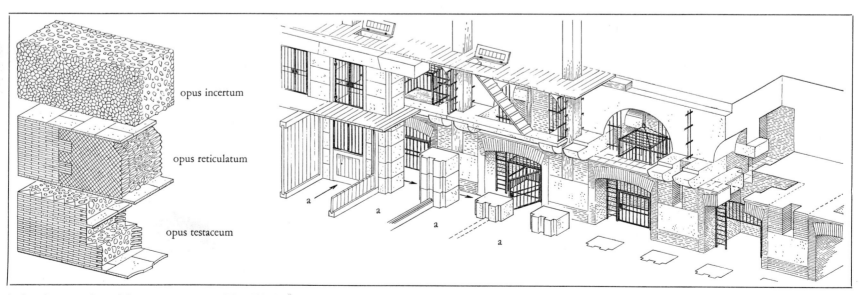

Left: three styles of Roman masonry. The filled-in core between the walls was called *opus caementicum*. Right: cages for wild animals under the Colosseum. They were brought in by way of an entry (a); after the cage had been hoisted to a higher floor, they could be driven into the arena by a gangway and hatch. There were safety nets between the stakes behind the hatch.

opus incertum

opus reticulatum

opus testaceum

Rome indeed continued to lay heavy burdens upon its subjects, but oppression by governors and tax-farmers was no longer tolerated by the imperial government. Justice and equity were upheld by appeal to the Emperor, whose imperial jurisdiction was aided by able lawyers. It is true that the frontier provinces still fell under the military administration of the legates of the Emperor, but these men worked with other officials who regulated financial affairs. During Augustus' reign the 'census', the gigantic task of compiling a land and population register as a basis for taxation, was undertaken and completed over a number of years (→ 434). Everywhere cities were built or enlarged after the Graeco-Roman pattern (→ 380, 385) while landowners had large villas in the country.

The cities were to a large extent self-governing. It was considered a duty for the leading citizens to hold civic office and to contribute from their private resources to the embellishment of their city. From the ranks of these local aristocracies were drawn many of the knights who occupied the higher posts in civil and military administration. An official civil service (unknown in the Republic) was thus formed. Though not without the faults of bureaucracy, this machinery ensured orderly administration. While Emperors like Nero or Domitian committed excesses in Rome the Empire continued to function thanks to the routine work and sense of duty of these public servants, knights and senators alike. It was not without reason that even in the farthest corners of the Empire temples were built and dedicated in gratitude to the goddess Roma and the Emperor as the symbols of the *pax Romana*.

The frontiers were protected by the legions, reinforced by the *auxilia*, auxiliaries recruited from the less Romanised tribes (see Map 41, p. 116). Frontier wars, though frequent, seldom disturbed or threatened the internal peace of the Empire, especially after Trajan had brought the Dacians and the Parthian menace under control. Only towards the end of the second century did Rome again become conscious of danger threatening from beyond its frontiers. The Empire had by now reached its natural boundaries. Where river, mountain or desert failed to provide a natural bulwark, open ground was protected by frontier works (*limites*); these consisted of military roads and where necessary ditches and palisades or even earth or stone walls; at intervals there were forts. At a short distance behind the frontiers the legionary encampments, which developed into strong fortified points, completed the system of frontier defence (see Maps 47–50, p. 126, → 283–4, 286–92). Permanent fleets guarded the coasts and checked piracy. Safe communication was possible from the Euphrates to Britain and from the Rhine as far as Morocco under the shadow of the Roman eagle (see Maps 43–4, p. 116, → 305–7).

The western provinces – Gaul, Spain, the Rhineland, and Britain – were quickly opened up and exploited in accord with normal Graeco-Roman methods. Land was reclaimed and systematically cultivated, mostly by large landowners who lived either on their estates or in the rapidly developing towns (see Maps 66–7, p. 165). The eastern territories, already cultivated for centuries, were recovering from the havoc of the civil wars and the mismanagement of local rulers. Many of these small principalities were gradually transformed into provinces directly administered by the Romans. There too the rural population continued its primitive mode of existence, while the rich, who adopted Graeco-Roman culture, lived in the cities. A certain differentiation and specialisation of production developed. Italy exported wine and earthenware, Gaul cattle and horses, Spain gold and silver, Africa and Egypt corn, Greece works of art, Asia wool and textiles, Britain tin and lead. Slaves were still imported from the frontier regions. In general, however, imports were not yet essential to the provinces, which relied for the most part upon their own agricultural production. Trade was largely limited to supplementing home produce and to luxury articles which could be transported at a comparatively low cost (see Maps 51–2, p. 127, → 297–300). Only for Italy was the importation of corn vital, and especially for Rome where the provision of food was in the hands of the Emperor, who could draw upon the cornfields of Egypt, Sicily, and Africa. The harbour of Ostia was enlarged under the Emperor Claudius in order to handle the corn fleets (see Map 43, p. 116, → 303, 311). But in general a considerable quantity of goods was interchanged within each province, and trade between the provinces became increasingly important.

Rome became a city whose population is estimated at roughly a million. Thousands were attracted there by the imperial court and the rich senatorial nobility. Since a large section of the urban population performed no really productive work, the government logically and justifiably provided for the masses that the capital had attracted by public assistance. The most questionable aspect was that this aid was also used to gain the favour of the mob, who were kept in a good mood by the provision of bread, games, and amenities (for example, the public baths, the Thermae). The custom of winning the loyalty of the soldiers and in particular the Praetorian Guard by regular gifts of money was also fraught with danger. This became obvious during the 'year of the four Emperors' following the murder of Nero, when the pretenders bid against each other and the soldiers sold their loyalty to the highest bidder. But in general the Empire appears to have been able without undue strain to afford the cost of army, administration, court, and capital.

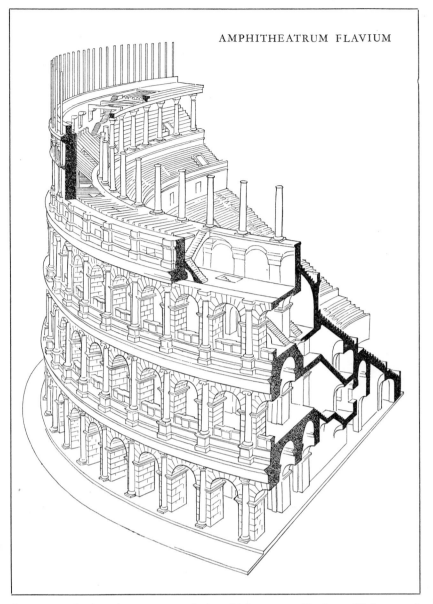

AMPHITHEATRUM FLAVIUM

Segment of the three-storeyed Amphitheatrum Flavium (Colosseum) in Rome. For the underground section see page 134.

THE CULTURE OF THE IMPERIAL AGE

During the first two centuries A.D. a universal Graeco-Roman culture grew up, extending from the Crimea to Spain and from Britain to the Euphrates. In the West Latin was spoken, in the East Greek (although even in the East Latin was the official language of the Empire). Throughout the whole Empire, on a large scale in Rome and the other important cities, and in the smaller towns in proportion, there sprang up theatres, public buildings, aqueducts, houses, and villas which all showed a general similarity and reflected the common Graeco-Roman way of life. By far the greater part of the remains of the art of antiquity to be seen in our museums today dates from this period, when the whole of what then constituted the civilised world was filled with buildings and works of art which imitated those of the earlier classical period. For this imperial culture was essentially an acquired culture, in both East and West, inculcated by teaching and example. Ancient Greece, where it had flourished spontaneously, and whose characteristic stamp it bore, had sunk again into insignificance. Athens, its leading city, had become a university town, even a museum town, where the remains of its former glory were preserved and contemplated with respect. In Athens, as in Alexandria, were flourishing schools of philology, mathematics, and astronomy, which continued the rational and abstract studies so dear to the Greek mind.

The mathematical and physical sciences, however, failed to discover the techniques which would allow them to be widely applied in improving material conditions. Society, founded of old upon slavery and serfdom, felt no need of improved techniques and implements. The demand never arose. Ships, tools, methods of transport, once devised, showed a remarkable lack of development, just as the striving for stability and the preservation of what had already been achieved were the real characteristics of this entire period. In literature this aspiration was displayed in the tendency towards imitation and archaism. Latin writers had always striven to equal the literary achievements of the ancient Greeks. Now they themselves, Cicero and his contemporaries, became models for later writers. There

337

338
339
340

341
342
343

The glory of the victorious Emperors was proclaimed to the farthest corner of the Empire by setting up triumphal arches and monuments. **337.** The inscription on the triumphal arch in Benevento erected in honour of Trajan mentions his campaigns against the Dacians. **338.** *Adventus Augusti*, the return of the triumphant Emperor. He is accompanied by a lictor, a standard-bearer, and a bodyguard and welcomed at the gates of Rome by the goddess Roma, the Senate (bearded man), and the people (beardless man). **339.** The Emperor Trajan crowned by Victory. **340.** Sacrifice by Marcus Aurelius in front of the temple of Jupiter, Juno, and Minerva on the Capitol in Rome. A boy hands him a casket with incense. Beside him is the flamen dialis with a felt cap on his head (→ also **366**). The bearded man in the toga behind him is the Senate personified. **341.** The victorious Emperor surrounded by officers and soldiers receives the submission of conquered barbarians.

DIVO·AN TONINO·ET

DIVAE·FAVSTINAE·EX·S·C

342 (opposite page). The triumphant Emperor. Marcus Aurelius in the triumphal chariot before a triumphal arch. Victory places a wreath upon his head. **343** (opposite page). Members of the Emperor's bodyguard. **344-5.** The Emperor, greeting the people with a characteristic gesture. Rear and front view of the only intact classical equestrian statue. **346.** Many Emperors were deified after their death. A fragment of the architrave of a temple dedicated to Antoninus and Faustina in the Forum still bears the inscription: 'To the deified Antoninus and the deified Faustina'. The Emperor and his wife are shown upon a relief (**347**) being carried heavenwards by a naked, winged genius. In his hand the genius holds a globe, symbol of power. **348.** The decline of imperial power is strikingly illustrated on a Persian rock relief: Valerian, defeated and taken captive by the Persian King Sapor I, kneels before his conqueror.

Tradition indicates the Palatine Hill as the site of the first settlement from which grew the later 'eternal', mighty, and sacred city of Rome (→ 353, 8). Archaeological investigation has not been able either to confirm or refute this tradition. The discovery, however, of Iron Age huts (→ 243) has demonstrated that people lived on and around the Palatine from the beginning of the 8th century. The original settlements united into a larger grouping after the Etruscans had built upon the Capitoline Hill. Thereafter the city slowly grew, although it in no way rivalled the Greek cities in the East. Rome's monumental greatness only began under Augustus, who constructed many great buildings and divided the city for administrative purposes into fourteen *regiones* (see Map 56). The later Emperors continued to enlarge this nucleus, adding their own forums, palaces, baths and temples.
350. The heart of earliest Rome is the Palatine Hill with its two peaks, Germalus (A) and Palatinus (B). This area formed a rough square and was hence called 'Roma Quadrata'. Next to it lay the Capitoline Hill (C), the acropolis of early Rome. It rises 193 ft. above the surrounding plain and is about 1,500 ft. long. 1. Curia; 2. Forum of Trajan; 3. Colosseum; 4. palaces on the Palatine; 5. Circus Maximus. The white line shows the district represented in Plate 352. **351.** Oblique view of roughly the same area as the preceding photograph, which was taken from vertically overhead. 1. Curia; 2. Forum of Trajan with market halls; 3. direction of the Colosseum; 4. Palatine; 5. Forum Romanum with numerous buildings; 6. Capitoline Hill.
349. A photograph taken from a height of 40,000 ft. shows the extent of the whole of classical and almost the whole of modern Rome. The white line indicates the area, in places still discernible, enclosed by the walls built by the Emperor Aurelian (A.D. 270-275) around the city of his day. Many of the city gates have been preserved or are still recognisable. 1. Porta Flaminia (Piazza del Popolo); 2. Porta Pinciana; 3. Porta Salaria; 4. Porta Nomentana (Porta Pia); 5. Porta Labicana (Porta Maggiore); 6. Porta Asinaria (Porta San Giovanni); 7. Porta Latina; 8. Porta Appia (Porta San Sebastiano); 9. Porta Ostiensis (Porta San Paolo); 10. Porta Aurelia. Seven low hills determined the aspect of the landscape in which the city was founded. A. Palatinus (167 ft.); B. Capitolinus (193 ft.); C. Aventinus (160 ft.); D. Caelius (160 ft.); E. Esquilinus (101 ft.); F. Viminalis (184 ft.); G. Quirinalis (154 ft.). In many places the old form of the city has been preserved in the new. Some striking features are: 11. Mausoleum of Hadrian (Castel Sant' Angelo); 12. Stadium of Domitian (Piazza Navona); 13. Circus Maximus; 14. Amphitheatrum Flavium or Colosseum; 15. Baths of Diocletian (with the modern Piazza Esedra); 16. Baths of Caracalla; 17. Castra Praetoria. These ancient buildings standing in the midst of the modern busy city give a strong sense of the continuity of its history.

352. Two events made the Palatine the most important of the seven hills, first the 'foundation' of the city in one of its caves, and later the choice of it by the Emperors for the site of their palaces. Cicero, Catiline, Octavian, and others had already had houses there. The Emperors added their increasingly richer and more stately dwellings to those of their predecessors, and imposing ruins are named after e.g. Tiberius, Nero, Domitian, Severus. The photograph shows the south side of the hill, which now gives a good impression of the extensive, sometimes labyrinthine, building caused by the city's ever-increasing expansion. In some places the Palatine was even artificially enlarged by high constructions which served as foundations for new buildings. After the Empire had been divided into an Eastern and Western section under Diocletian, this building activity came to an end. The palaces were kept up for brief visits by Emperors who resided elsewhere, but were not further enlarged or decorated. The sack of Rome on

several occasions, such as that by Alaric in 410, ushered in the decline which developed in the course of the centuries (especially in the period of the Renaissance), not least owing to the habit of using the palaces as quarries to provide precious marble and great hewn stones for new buildings; only the bricks remained. 1. Exedra of Domus Augustana (→ 354, 2); 2. Domus Augustana (→ 353, 6); 3. baths of Severus (→ 353, 3); 4. palace and garden of Domitian (→ 353, 4); 5. wings of the palace of Septimius Severus; 6. palace of Domitian or Flavian palace (→ 354, 3); 7. corner of the basilica of this palace; 8. Basilica of Maxentius or Constantine; 9. temple of Mars Ultor (→ 361-2); 10. church of S. Lorenzo in Miranda, built in the temple of Antoninus and Faustina (→ 346); 11. market halls of Trajan; 12. roof of the Curia (→ 374); 13. Arch of Septimius Severus (→ 375); 14. column of Trajan. The Forum Romanum lies hidden in the valley behind the high trees growing on the Palatine.

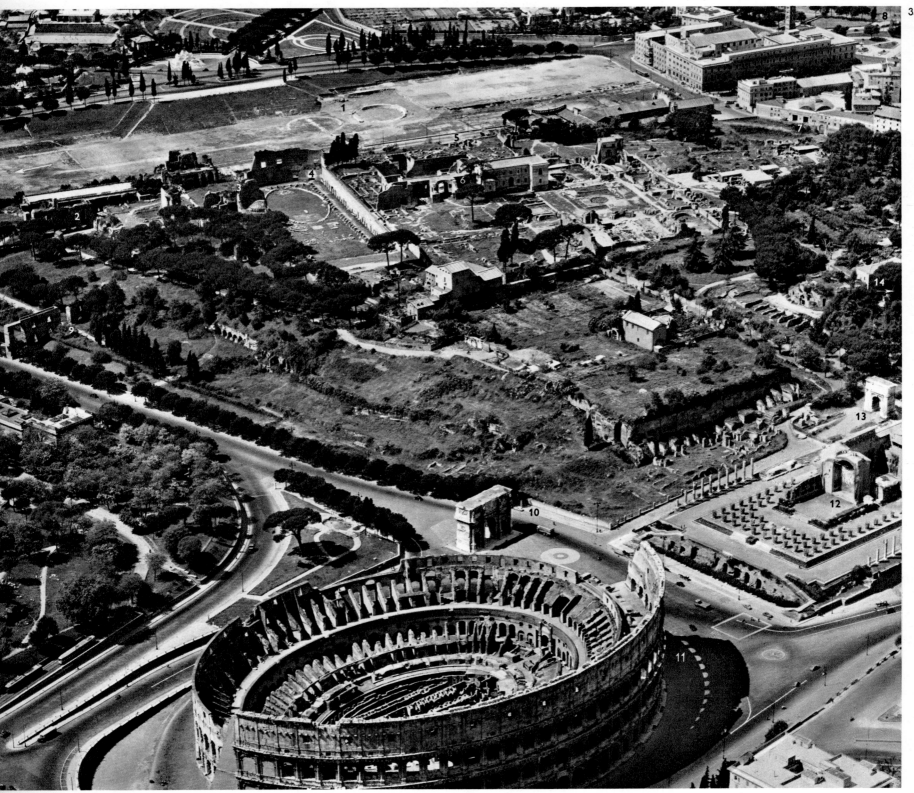

353. The Palatine Hill, with the ruins of the imperial palaces, viewed from the northeast, in the photograph bounded by the Circus Maximus (1 and→ 354, 1). The palaces and other buildings, viewed from the back, in contrast with Plate 352, are: 2. wings of the palace of Septimius Severus; 3. baths of Severus; 4. palace and garden of Domitian; 5. exedra of the Domus Augustana; 6. Domus Augustana; 7. earliest Latin settlement on the Germalus (→ 243); 8. bend of the Tiber; 9. remains of an aqueduct which carried water from the Caelius over the valley between the Caelius and the Palatine (it was a development of the aqueduct of Claudius and was built by Domitian to carry water to the palace and baths); 10. Arch of Constantine; 11. Amphitheatrum Flavium or Colosseum; 12. temple of Venus and Roma; 13. Arch of Titus; 14. to the Forum Romanum. **354.** Fragment of a model of Rome in the Museo della Civiltà Romana near Rome, showing the Palatine. 1. Circus Maximus with the spina; 2. exedra of Domus Augustana (→ 352, 1); 3. high constructions intended to enlarge the surface of the Palatine and which served as foundations for palaces (→ 352, 5); 4. centre of the Palatine with various palaces; 5. Amphitheatrum Flavium (→ 353, 11); 6. the aqueduct carrying water from the Caelius to the Palatine (→ 353, 9). **355.** Another section makes it possible to envisage the original conditions on and around the Forum Romanum. It also gives a good impression of the densely-crowded built-up area in the neighbourhood of the Forum, which was destroyed by breaches through it in modern times. 1. Temple of Claudius; 2. Amphitheatrum Flavium, with the Subura, a quarter inhabited by the populace, in the background; 3. baths of Trajan; 4. Arch of Constantine, set up ca. 315 after the victory of Constantine; 5. Palatine with section of Domus Augustana; 6. Arch of Titus; 7. temple of Venus and Roma (→ 353, 12), originally site of the colossal statue of Nero which was removed by Hadrian; 8. temple of the Dioscuri; 9. basilica of Maxentius or Constantine, a vast edifice exceeding all earlier buildings of the sort in compass and capacity; in the apse probably stood the colossal statue of Constantine, of which the head and some fragments have survived (→ 335); 10. Arch of Septimius Severus, set up by the Senate in honour of the Emperor in 203; 11. the Tiber; 12. the Capitol with the temple of Jupiter; 13. northeastern side of the Capitoline and the arx with the temple of Juno Moneta; 14. The imperial forums laid out respectively by Vespasian (Forum Pacis), Augustus (Forum Augusti), and Trajan (Forum Traiani). Behind them the Basilica Ulpia and temple of Trajan. The models show Rome at the beginning of the fourth century, when the city had attained its greatest extent and wealth. Later, the residence of the Emperors in other centres led to a cessation of building activity and in the end to a gradually progressive decay of the city.

356
357

358
359

360
361

The Forum Romanum was for centuries the heart of Rome. The small area contained many temples. After the fall of the Empire it was abandoned and eventually used as grazing ground. **356.** Therefore in 1772 Piranesi entitled this etching of it 'Campo Vaccino', and the name remained in use until the beginning of this century. **357.** This photograph of ca. 1890 shows the situation partly altered by excavation. The left and right sides are still covered by buildings and roads. **358.** Modern aspect viewed from the Palatine, and (**359**) looking towards the Capitoline. The Curia is just visible to the right. **360.** The Forum Boarium on the Tiber, with temple of Vesta (left), remains of the 'House of Crescentius' (centre), and temple of Fortuna Virilis, is an almost intact remnant of Rome. **361.** Remains of the temple of Mars Ultor, built by Augustus in his forum. The wall, in which the trace of the roof can still be seen, was a protection against fire. **362.** Reconstruction of the temple and surrounding buildings.

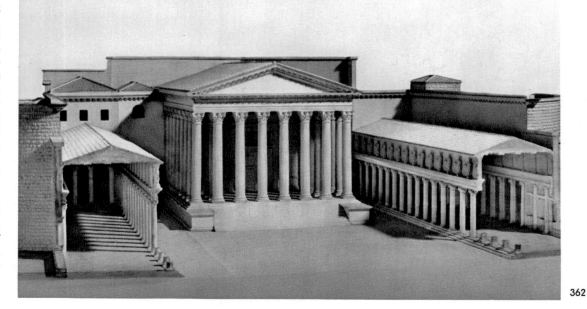

362

144

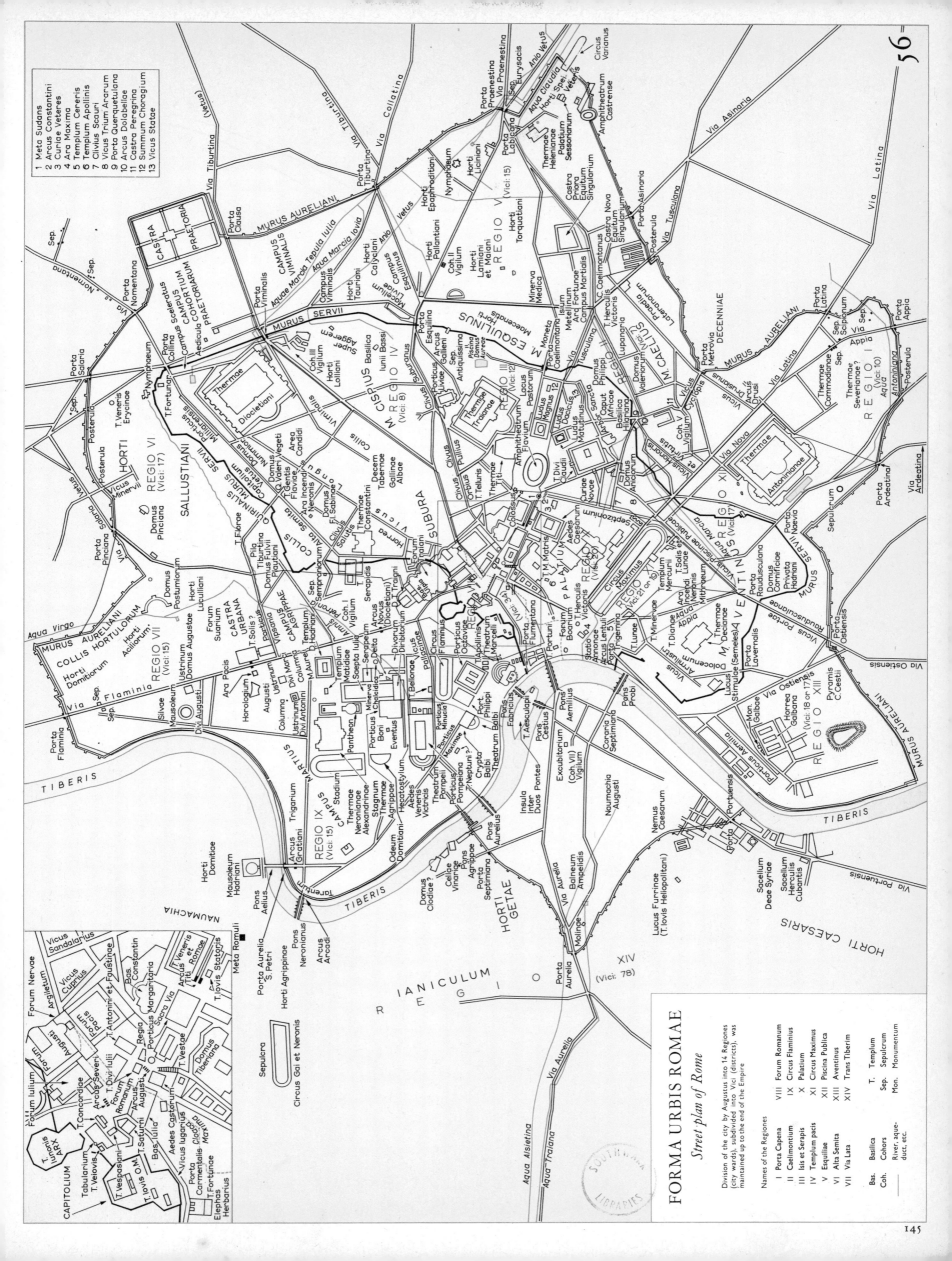

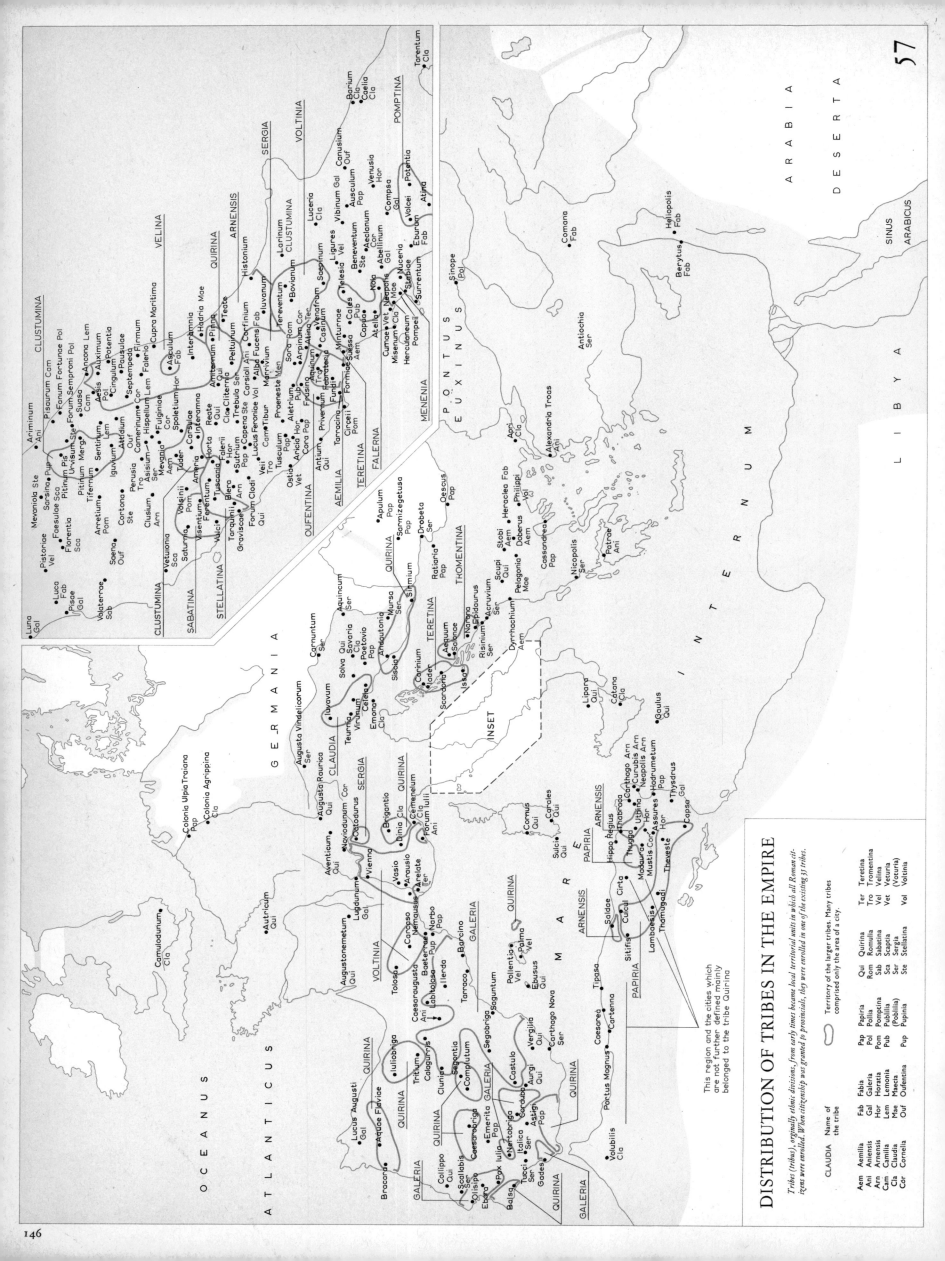

DISTRIBUTION OF TRIBES IN THE EMPIRE

Tribes (tribus), originally ethnic divisions, from early times became local territorial units in which all Roman citizens were enrolled. When citizenship was granted to provincials, they were enrolled in one of the existing 35 tribes.

CLAUDIA Name of
the tribe

Territory of the larger tribes. Many tribes
comprised only the area of a city.

This region and the cities which
are not further defined mainly
belonged to the tribe Quirina

Aem	Aemilia	Fab	Fabia	Qui	Quirina	Ter	Teretina
Ani	Aniensis	Gal	Galeria	Rom	Romulia	Tro	Tromentina
Arn	Arnensis	Hor	Horatia	Sab	Sabatina	Vel	Velina
Cam	Camilia	Lem	Lemonia	Sca	Scaptia	Vet	Veturia
Cla	Claudia	Mae	Maecia	Ser	Sergia	Vol	(Voturia)
Cor	Cornelia	Ouf	Oufentina	Ste	Stellatina		(Voltinia)
				Pap	Papiria		
				Pol	Pollia		
				Pom	Pomptina		
				Pub	Publilia		
					(Poblilia)		
				Pup	Pupinia		

146

were figures of outstanding merit like Seneca, and some of genius like Tacitus, who attained a personal stature despite the pressure of the schools of rhetoric and the classical models. In the second century, however, classicism reigned triumphant, seeking its inspiration only in imitation.

The same phenomenon can be observed in the Greek East. There too the rhetorician and the philologist took the lead and dictated the rules of composition and thought. They rejected the *koinè*, the common language of the cultured Greek which had developed during the Hellenistic period. With great ability and zeal they turned again to the Attic and Ionic dialects of their forefathers without realising that rigidity of form and style might expose the content to fossilisation. Books and writings, poems and orations, once a living part of the community, now became an elegant form of literature, a game, even though taken seriously, for the cultured and initiated which became more and more divorced from the true thoughts and aspirations of the people. The difference between the spoken and literary languages became so great that in many cases one may reasonably doubt whether ordinary people understood this literature at all. The fierce intellectual conflict, which in Greece had inspired the concept of freedom and democracy and subsequently the systems like that of Plato which aspired to an ordered life and society, was silenced. Such ideas no longer had any force in the imperial world.

During the Hellenistic period the Greek mind had struggled to adapt itself to the new world round about. It had attempted to solve the problem of how the individual must behave in the world in order to preserve his liberty and happiness. Various solutions found passionate champions. There was a sharp contrast between Epicurus, who had sought happiness in a reasoned zest for life, and the Stoics, who based their ideas upon devotion to duty resting upon sovereign reason. Their theoretical controversies lived on in the schools, where logic, physics, and ethics were made subjects for study and composition. But in public opinion these controversies were no longer vital. A generally accepted code of morals and behaviour was adopted by rhetoricians and philosophical popular preachers, usually in a modified and eclectic form. The original orthodox Stoicism lived again in a few noble figures who found a new religion in its dogmatic severity. The slave Epictetus, the imperial adviser Seneca, and the Emperor Marcus Aurelius found in it the moral support which enabled them to accomplish their appointed tasks. Stoicism provided a moral code of devotion to duty and conduct which gave form and substance to the framework of the Empire and directed Roman law, which had now become the law of the world, into channels of reason and humanity.

Pompeii gives us a picture, one might say a momentary glimpse, of the life and activity in a prosperous country town in the first century A.D. This town, buried in ashes and lava after a violent and totally unexpected eruption of Vesuvius in A.D. 79, has been brought to light by excavation. We see the houses of the rich, the workshops of the labouring population, and the *grafitti* scribbled on the walls by schoolboys, by candidates for the local elections, and by those advertising the fights in the amphitheatre. The whole scene suggests a high standard of life and culture. The same picture, which is reflected in Pliny's letters, is found again, though less complete, in the ruins in the deserts of Algeria and Syria, where towns once flourished in lands which are now deserted and desolate (→ 384–5) and where a few legions maintained the *pax Romana* in regions that were no longer menaced from without.

Trade was carried on by the Empire far beyond its boundaries, with India and 'free' Germany. The discovery of the regularity of the monsoons by a certain Hippalus (under Augustus?) led to the establishment of a direct sea-route from Aden to India. Even silk from distant China reached the Empire by way of the caravan routes or along the sea route from India to the Red Sea (see Map 51, p. 127). Ptolemy's map of the world gives some idea of the range of this commercial expansion. This world enjoyed two centuries of stability at home and abroad, of peace and prosperity, of order and justice. The wars with the Parthians and Dacians were fought far away, and to the mass of the fifty million subjects the marvels and intrigues of the court, the glory and corruption of the capital, were only distant rumours.

SIGNS OF DECAY

Despite this peaceful and splendid façade, we, who know what followed, can detect traces of inner weakness in the imposing structure. With the termination of hostilities slaves became more difficult to obtain, but this did not lead to a revival of a vigorous agricultural population. The large estates, the *latifundia*, continued to monopolise much of the land, now farmed by tenant farmers or *coloni*, many of whom lived on the verge of starvation and handed over the fruits of their labours to the landowners who normally lived in the city. They thus helped to furnish the rich with luxurious houses and retinues of servants, and to provide public buildings and theatres. In other words, the profits derived from the land were employed for non-productive ends. Even to contemporaries it was clear that the Italian peasant population which had conquered the Empire no longer really existed as an independent body. '*Latifundia perdidere Italiam*' sighed the elder Pliny before the end of the first century A.D. In the course of time this situation also spread to the provinces. In Greece the numerous cities, the cradles of Greek culture, were gradually overshadowed by the large estates owned by absentee landlords. The same happened in Africa, Spain, and Gaul. The busy traffic and lively trade carried on throughout the Empire did little to help the agricultural worker. Roman and Italian merchants were gradually eliminated from the East during the first century, and Oriental trade fell into the hands of Orientals. Further, luxury articles were imported from beyond the frontiers, and these imports were not balanced by exports in goods; they were paid for with gold, while the gold mines in the west were becoming exhausted in the second, and those in the Balkans in the third century. In short, the economic position of the Empire was unstable; it was in fact living above its means. It is obvious that any major disturbance would be catastrophic, since the economic expansion which might have cushioned the blow could not be stimulated again. As early as the first century A.D. we hear of a decline in the rural population, of abandoned fields which malaria soon rendered completely irrecoverable. Even after

363. Detail from a relief on the sepulchral monument of the Aterii (→ also 441, 452) shows a number of buildings along the Via Sacra. Identifications are disputed, but it is believed that from left to right are depicted: unknown triumphal arch of Titus (viewed from the side and from the front), and a temple of Jupiter Stator. **364.** The 'Forma Urbis' is a marble plan, dating from the 3rd century A.D., formerly set on a wall, and shows parts of the city. The fragment given here depicts the Porticus Liviae and the course of adjacent streets. The surviving fragments do not cover the whole of the city.

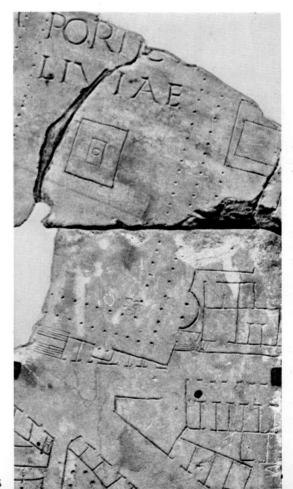

365. On the Arch of Trajan at Beneventum are depicted the most important figures of the Roman state religion: Jupiter (with sceptre and thunderbolt), Juno (with veil), Minerva (with helmet), Hercules (with club), Bacchus (with vine wreath), Ceres (with wreath of ears of corn), and Mercury (with herald's staff). **366.** Fragment of the Ara Pacis (Altar of Peace) of Augustus at Rome with two flamens (with pointed felt caps) and a man with an axe. **367.** An ox is being led to the place of sacrifice by two *popae* (sacrificial assistants). **368.** Offering being made by a general, while assistants give the victim the fatal blow. In the provinces many other gods and goddesses played a rôle. **369.** Epona, goddess of horses, venerated especially in Gaul and in the Danube regions. **370.** The Persian Mithras, whose worship spread widely, slaying the bull from which new life springs. **371.** Sacrifice to Attis, consort of the Phrygian Cybele.

372
373
374
375

The Senate played an important rôle in early Roman history, especially in foreign and financial affairs. Its permanent constitution gave it a marked advantage over the temporary elected officials. In Imperial times its power depended upon the power of the ruling Emperor; later it was no more than his instrument, used to proclaim decrees. **372.** Septimius Severus, seated upon a dais, presents his son and heir Caracalla to the members of the Senate. **373.** Detail from a relief found in the Tabularium in Rome showing the Senate symbolised by an old, bearded man wearing toga and tunic and with a staff in his hand. Next to him is a representation of the Roman people, a young man, naked to the waist, holding a horn of plenty. Together they formed *Senatus Populusque Romanus*. **374.** The Senate House (Curia), built by Caesar on earlier foundations and in its present form for the most part dating from the time of Diocletian (end of 3rd to beginning of 4th century A.D.). **375.** View of the triumphal arch of Septimius Severus through the doorway of the Curia.

149

376. Two magistrates, followed by servants and escorted by three lictors with fasces, lead a procession of sacrificial animals headed by trumpeters. A priest carries a dish, while the *victimarii* restrain the frightened animal. 377. Victorious commanders or magistrates with *imperium* were sometimes granted a triumph, or solemn entry into Rome. A relief from a temple of Apollo gives a striking picture of a portion of such a triumph. Chained prisoners walk in front, followed by trumpeters and *victimarii* with sacrificial animals. 378. Two lictors with fasces on their shoulders precede a chariot carrying the magistrate holding his sceptre. Behind the mule-drawn chariot walk men with a sedan chair. 379 (following page). Symbol of mighty, world-ruler Rome is the winged Victoria, goddess of victory, statues of whom were erected widely throughout the Empire. A relief from Leptis Magna.

380

381
382

383
384

Pompeii, excavated from the thick layer of ash and pumice-stone left by the eruption of Vesuvius in A.D. 79, is one of the most important archaeological sites. Although Greek ideas influenced the construction of Pompeii, its state at the time of its destruction provides a good picture of life in a Roman provincial town. **380.** The air photograph gives an impression of a burnt-out city. In the upper part of the photograph the city centre. 1. Forum with temples of Jupiter (2) and Apollo (3); 4. basilica (→ 382); 5. *macellum* with market halls. In the centre, now covered with trees, the Forum Triangulare with the large theatre (6) and the Odeum (7), a palaestrum (8) and some temples. **381.** The Forum with the temples of Jupiter and Apollo. **382.** The pillar bases give an impression of the extent of the basilica (→ 380, 4). **383.** Street with stepping stones between the pavements. **384.** Most towns possessed arches on the main roads. Triumphal arch on the Decumanus Maximus at Volubilis in Mauretania.

385. The extensive ruins of Colonia Marciana Thamugadi (modern Timgad in Algeria) give a clear picture of the layout of a Roman town. Many temples, basilicas, theatres, and streets often covered by arcades have been excavated from the sand. The city was a centre of Roman life; the inscription on the forum, *venari, lavari, ludere, ridere, hoc est vivere*, indicates the pleasant life enjoyed by many in these prosperous regions. In Ostia, the port of Rome, many finds have contributed to our knowledge of trade, buildings, religious life, etc. **386.** Ostia had a type of house different from those in Pompeii; they were large, tall blocks of flats. Ruins of one of the many houses which served as the basis for a reconstruction (**387**). **388.** Entrance gate with tympanum and two columns at Epagathiana, one of the greatest warehouses for grain and other imported goods in Ostia. **389.** The Via della Fontana, one of the best-preserved streets.

successful wars like those of Trajan, which yielded much booty, the resources of the Empire were exhausted. Arrears of taxes had to be remitted, and yet in Rome the Dacian booty was used to pay for the erection of grand buildings, with Trajan's column as the crowning glory (→ 280). At the same time the Emperors looked with suspicion on all private clubs and political associations which in some cases they banned. After the misery of war many of the provincials would willingly have agreed that all responsibility for finance and public services should be increasingly transferred from their own hands to the imperial administration, since the collection of taxes, for which the nominally independent 'communities' remained responsible, was becoming increasingly difficult. The municipal offices, which were considered honourable positions, and had been eagerly sought by the rich who personally contributed to their cost, were now becoming burdensome and unpopular.

Italy and the neighbouring peaceful provinces, which a few centuries before were able and prepared to repel foreign threats unaided, were now disarmed in order to prevent any local resistance or pretender from threatening the imperial authority. While the scattered middle classes in the cities could take no united action, the Empire passed into the hands of the army and the administrators. This was the circle which produced the Emperor Trajan, a Spaniard, and Antoninus, a Gaul by origin, though both men were of course completely Romanised. While the Roman state was enlarging its frontiers the Roman people, who should have formed the backbone of this state, lost all political influence. While the bond between state and people continued to weaken and Roman citizenship became increasingly of social rather than political value, the gulf between the ruling upper class and the masses widened. Literature was confined to *belles-lettres*; science and philosophy were the monopoly of professional scholars. Opinions on public affairs and the interests of the community were now heard only within official council-chambers, while for their part these authorities were but mildly interested in the opinions current among the mass of the common people.

While the native religions of many states and tribes within the Empire might appear to have lost their hold (thus Druidism had been repressed), deeper religious feelings were always dormant beneath the surface. In particular many Oriental religions, which promised to the believer deliverance and salvation in this world and in the world to come, spread quickly throughout the Empire. Isis and Mithras found many adherents, while Sol Invictus and Jupiter Dolichenus, although bearing Latin names, were in reality Eastern sun gods. It was in the company of such religious sects that Christianity spread from Judaea to all parts of the Empire.

It is not within the province of this survey to discuss the origin and nature of Christianity; we may merely record its emergence. It was a new faith, propagated by its adherents with fierce conviction. It was in direct contradiction to the humanistic and rationalistic bases of Graeco-Roman thought. It preached not self-sufficiency or the cult of the personality, but a doctrine of sin and grace, of reconciliation with God and a new life here and hereafter, of a belief in a Holy God which must of necessity condemn all anthropomorphic mythology and ecstatic mysteries as nonsense or as the work of the devil. It developed an organisation which far transcended the normal associations of society and those tolerated by the Empire among its subjects, and for this reason it soon clashed both with this society and with the imperial authorities. The Christians, who were preaching the fatherhood of God and the brotherhood of man, were certainly not inclined toward revolution, but the authorities misconceived their message and regarded their 'otherworldliness' as a sign of 'hatred of the human race', as Tacitus put it. In other words their attitude of mind was irreconcilable with the current humanistic culture of those who regarded themselves as civilised rulers. Matters came to a head when it was found that the Christians would refuse to sacrifice to the Genius of the Emperor as a normal act of loyalty to the state, and that they clung to their community of the Church even after the Emperor had declared this 'rabble' illegal. The first persecution had occurred when Nero used the small Christian community in Rome as scapegoats for the great fire for which popular rumour blamed the Emperor himself. Thereafter the conflict smouldered, since the autocratic Empire was virtually outlawing an ever-increasing section of its population. Even enlightened men like the Emperor Marcus Aurelius showed no understanding of the Christian mentality. Even when the movement had reached the intellectual circles, and Christian apologists attempted to defend and commend their religion to the authorities in writings, the latter saw only blind obstinacy and revolt which must be combated by force and persecution. Not that the Romans persecuted for religious reasons (indeed they were normally tolerant of foreign cults, provided that such toleration was mutual), but when on religious grounds a Christian refused to sacrifice, religion and politics had become involved in a tragic nexus.

CRISIS AND RESTORATION

The clouds began to gather during the reign of the Emperor Marcus Aurelius (→ 340-2, 344). A war against the Parthians led to a great victory, but the returning army brought the plague with it to the West. For years the disease raged, causing incalculable loss and the death of countless numbers. Then, while the sorely-tried Empire longed for peace and fewer troubles, the Danube frontier was pierced by a German attack which at one time endangered even the northern frontier of Italy. The Emperor himself took the field and with the utmost difficulty managed to repel this menace. The Danube provinces, however, were so ravaged and depopulated that he was compelled to recolonise the deserted regions with German prisoners of war. And, just when the Danube frontier had been repaired, although the danger of fresh attacks was by no

390. Comparison of a relief of a small mountain town, with houses, wall, and gates, and Castelnuovo di Porto (**391**) north of Rome, one of the many towns built upon the mountain slopes, shows that there has been little change in the construction of these places. Despite modifications throughout the centuries, the basic Roman town-plan can still be detected in numerous European towns which date back to the Roman period. **392.** The centre of Florence, bounded by the cathedral and the Palazzo Vecchio, corresponds roughly to the old Florentia. The *cardo* and *decumanus* have been preserved. **393.** Verona also shows traces of the Roman town.

Great and small events in the daily life of the Romans are particularly well represented in the carvings upon sarcophagi. **394-5.** A relief depicts a few scenes from childhood: Cupids playing with hoops and children playing at horses; boys and girls playing with nuts, in a game of tug-of-war, and drawing on a board. Roman portraiture attained a very high level and has left us many striking heads of men and women. **396-9.** Portraits of a girl (2nd cent. A.D.) and two women (1st cent. A.D.). **400-01.** Men of the Republican period. **402-03.** A subtle portrait, characteristic of the middle of the 2nd century. This head is especially striking in the treatment of the hair. **404.** A family meal; the man reclines on a couch, the woman sits with a child upon a chair. Food upon a small table. **405.** Toilet of a woman sitting in a cane chair, attended by female servants; one of them holds a mirror before her.

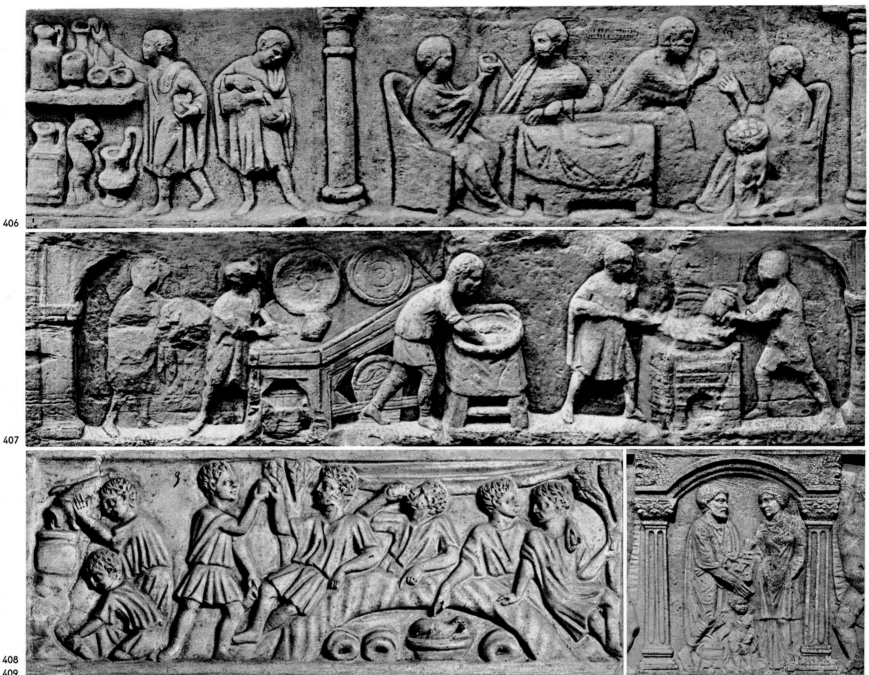

406

407

408
409

A sepulchral monument preserved at Igel, near Trier, contains scenes giving a picture of family life. **406.** Two slaves in the wine cellar filling goblets which they offer to a married couple. On the table, a plate with fish; the woman has a fruit basket on her lap. Women usually sat at table; men reclined (→ 404). **407.** Another relief on the same monument shows activity in the kitchen: two servants are stoking a furnace; another brings a pan of water, another takes flour from a sack, and a fifth kneads it into dough on a table. The reliefs are in the coarser provincial style of the 3rd century A.D. Some of the scenes depicted are interesting in revealing difference of conditions; others strike an unexpectedly modern note. **408.** To judge from numerous representations, much cheerful drinking went on in the city inns; at Ostia and Pompeii many have been preserved complete with bar. **409.** The marriage contract, *dextrarum iunctio* (the joining of the right hands), is often depicted. The man carries a scroll as symbol of marriage. **410.** Love scene between Cupid and Psyche. Representation on a sarcophagus at Isola Sacra in the Tiber at Ostia (→ 446)

410

411

412
413

In the cities business was transacted in the streets, where the merchant displayed his wares or carried on his trade in small shops (*tabernae*). Caesar assisted the tradesmen by building shops along his forum, and Trajan built behind his a large shopping centre with several storeys, the 'Mercati Traiani' (→ 351, 2). **411.** Interior of a draper's shop under an open gallery. Assistants are displaying a piece of cloth to customers. Numerous reliefs on sepulchral monuments give a more vivid picture of details of the practice of various trades than verbal descriptions could supply. **412.** Goldsmith fashioning a long object with a flat hammer on an anvil. Near him lie lumps of metal; above him hang scales for weighing the required quantities of gold. **413.** The smith L. Cornelius Atimetus, standing before his furnace with a pair of bellows while a workman hammers the glowing iron into the required shape. Various tools hang on the wall.

414
415
416

417
418

419

414. Finds at Ostia and Pompeii show how many eating and drinking places there were in Roman towns. Relief with a 'wine cafeteria' in which the vendor behind the bar pours into a bowl wine which is received in a pitcher by a client. The picture probably shows a market stall standing in a row of others. **415.** Relief, probably representing Juno Saponaria preparing soap; it has also been interpreted as the divine patroness of apothecaries. **416.** Money-changer in his 'bank'; his right hand rests upon his coins. **417.** Equally striking is the vegetable seller (kale, garlic, onions, etc.) behind her trestle table in the market. **418.** Bust of the butcher Tiberius Julius Vitalis, depicted at work upon a pig's head. **419.** A lively market scene shows a woman selling game and fruit; the two monkeys perhaps allude to the Eastern origin of the merchant. Below, two rabbits in a hutch. One customer is being served; two others, awaiting their turn, are engaged in animated discussion.

means eliminated, Marcus Aurelius died. He left behind him a son, the nineteen-year-old Commodus (→ 332), into whose hands the hard-pressed Empire was entrusted (see Map 47, p. 126).

This highly incompetent ruler rashly concluded peace on the northern front and hastened back to Rome. There followed a period of debauchery and corruption comparable with Nero's reign and then the murder of the Emperor. Now the struggle for the throne burst forth in full violence. The Praetorians openly sold the imperial dignity to the highest bidder. In the provinces the armies revolted and proclaimed their commanders Emperor, tempted alike by extravagant rewards and promises. Victory was finally won by Septimius Severus, a stern and capable man of African origin (→ 372). He was, however, intolerant of the traditions of the Principate and considered himself solely as a military despot. On his deathbed he is said to have exhorted his two sons to work in concord, enrich the soldiers, and despise the rest of the world. But his sons were not united. Caracalla murdered Geta and proved to be a cruel ruler. He allowed his troops to sack Alexandria; confusion and unrest prevailed everywhere during his reign. Rome, however, he enriched by the Baths of Caracalla, perhaps the greatest building of the city, overwhelmingly extravagant and magnificent. He too was murdered, as were his successors, the Praetorian Prefect Macrinus and the sun-priest Heliogabalus, who was connected with the house of the Severi. The last member of this house, Alexander Severus, survived longer, supported by his able Praetorian Prefect, the great lawyer Ulpian. Yet he too, through his weakness, fell prey to his own soldiers, together with Ulpian.

Thirty years of wild confusion followed. With fatal regularity the armies proclaimed their commanders Emperor - semi-educated army leaders anxious only to guard themselves from ever-threatening overthrow or death. The Empire was terribly ravaged and plundered by its own armies. The exhausted population sometimes reacted with savage peasant revolts which in their turn aroused equally bloody reprisals. Some provinces remained independent of the Empire for years under their own 'emperors', while the frontiers were overrun by barbarian invasions now that the legions were caught up in the struggle for the throne.

In the East the Persians of the New Empire, formed by the Sassanian kings who had overthrown the Parthian kingdom, crossed the frontiers. The Germanic Goths plundered the Balkans, Greece, and Asia Minor by land and sea. The Emperor Valerian was even captured by the Persians in 260 and died in captivity, while in the West his son Gallienus was engaged in perpetual conflict with his own rebel generals. The results of this catastrophe were permanent. In the first place, Rome for ever lost its military supremacy. The superiority of the Roman legions over their barbarian opponents had been based upon organisation and discipline and not upon any essential difference or superiority of equipment such as the fire-arms which later enabled Europeans to dominate less advanced peoples. Owing to the network of roads and the system of fortifications, the Roman regular army, highly trained and uniformly distributed throughout the whole empire, had always been able to move troops and supplies to a threatened point within a reasonable time even when a barbarian incursion broke momentarily through the frontier defences. As a rule the training of these troops lasted years, during which the recruits were moulded into soldiers who gained a professional outlook and exchanged their national loyalties for an all-embracing *esprit de corps* that was symbolised by their oath to the Emperor. For these soldiers Republic and Senate had become empty terms. They had little connection with the ordinary population, which for two centuries had been systematically rendered defenceless by the Emperors.

The situation which had threatened in A.D. 69 after the death of Nero developed further after the fall of Commodus. The troops' loyalty to the Emperor gave way to their loyalty to their corps and immediate commanders, from whose eventual accession they anticipated considerable advantage, relying upon the extravagant promises of the pretenders. For them the civil population was merely a defenceless mass, to be plundered if the occasion arose. During this struggle for imperial power the army became completely disorganised. Any would-be Emperor called into his service as many troops as possible from the area where he held sway; since trained soldiers were not easy to obtain, he recruited the wild and warlike tribes on the frontiers, often prisoners sent there by the Emperors in an attempt to combat depopulation. Since, however, the pretenders were dependent upon the favour of these mercenaries, there was no question of maintaining former discipline and laborious training. Soon even the centurions, upon whom the cohesion of the army had always depended, had disappeared. With their own arms, in their own units, with their own commanders, barbarian warriors soon filled the ranks of the legions, which were thus transformed from disciplined troops into savage bands of fighters, not dissimilar from the wild barbarians who menaced the frontiers, and whose fellow-tribesmen had often served in the Roman army and thus acquired an elementary form of military discipline. To make matters worse, it was precisely at this period that these foreign enemies of Rome joined forces. The Franks, Alamanni, Juthungi, and Marcomanni, although still comparatively few in number, were none the less stronger than the small tribes which up till now had inhabited the frontier region (see Map 69, p. 183).

The Goths even formed a kingdom which stretched from the Danube to south Russia. The Sassanians, successors of the Parthian Arsacids, whose rise coincided with a revival of the old Zoroastrian religion, were much more dangerous and fanatical foes than the Parthians had ever been. At its widest extent their empire stretched from Syria to India, and from Iberia in the north to the Persian Gulf in the south. Reviving the old Persian tradition, they sought to conquer the whole of Asia. That they did not accomplish their aim after the crushing defeat of Valerian can only be ascribed to the resistance of Rome's vassal king, Odenathus of Palmyra. He now became the real master of the eastern half of the Empire and only made pretence of continuing to recognise the authority of Rome.

420

421

422

423

Domestic architecture attained a very high level among the Romans. Houses in Pompeii and elsewhere show the types. **420.** Plan of the 'House of the masks', a Hellenistic-Roman house in Delos. **421.** Peristylium in the 'House of the Cupids' in Pompeii. Houses were often decorated with mosaics and paintings. **422.** Mosaic with Dionysiac scene in Delos. **423.** *Hypocaustum*, the central heating system, by which warm air was produced under a floor raised upon pillars and conveyed to the rooms above by channels in the marble-covered walls (**424**). The inhabitants of a Roman villa must have enjoyed more solid comfort than was known again until comparatively recent times.

424

425

426

A large sarcophagus from northern Gaul, now in Rome (**427**), with many country scenes, provides much information about agriculture in Roman times. Horses, cows, and a flock of sheep are assembled in wooded surroundings, while peasants gather vegetables and milk the sheep. On the upper rim Cupids disport themselves in carriages drawn by lions and deer. Peasants with holdings of land paid the owners both in money and in kind. **425.** Peasants paying rent in cash. They wear the local dress of the neighbourhood of Augusta Treverorum where the sarcophagus was found. **426.** Peasants bringing their landlord dues in kind. From left to right: a basket of fruit, a cock, eels, a goat, fish, and a hare. The landlord receives the payment in front of his house, the door of which is screened by a curtain hanging in folds. The representation of attitudes and expressions renders this little scene highly realistic.

427

430

The numerous amphitheatres throughout the Empire and especially in a large centre like Rome created a great demand for wild animals of every kind to give variety to the gladiatorial shows. Map 59 shows the exertions which the Romans made to supply the demand for thousands of animals. A great number of mosaics in an imperial villa at Piazza Armerina in Sicily depict tense moments in these hunts for antelopes, wild boars, hippopotami, wolves, tigers, panthers, etc. **428.** Fight between men armed with a spear and a great stone and an angry wild boar. **429.** Carrying off the boar after it has been overpowered. **430.** Men dressed in short tunics bring an ostrich and other creatures aboard ship along a gangway. **431.** Fragment of a sarcophagus showing Hercules combating the Hydra and subduing the Arcadian stag. He was sometimes accounted the patron of gladiators.

431

The economic situation was deplorable. Trade and communications suffered considerably, cities and land were laid waste, and the currency was devalued to such an extent that everywhere people resorted to barter and payment in kind: this resulted in the slowing down and paralysis of trade and production. Taxes increased and, since a new Emperor did not feel bound by the measures of the predecessor he had overthrown, they were often levied anew and were augmented by fines that were imposed for the support, even if unwilling, that had been given to his opponent. Money was of course needed to reward his soldiers and to buy off external enemies.

The governing classes in the provincial cities who had once aspired to membership of the local Senate (the *curiales*) were held responsible for these perpetual increases in taxation and often had to make good any deficit. Thus membership of the *curia* became a burden and might lead to financial ruin. When candidates could no longer be found, membership of the *curia* was made compulsory, and increasingly strong measures were taken to prevent evasion of duty. The exhausted peasant population, the *coloni*, were tied to their land and became serfs. The rich increasingly abandoned the decaying cities and settled on their country estates or villas; these were often fortified as a safeguard against robbers or the plundering soldiers of any chief or Emperor who happened to be marching past. The break-down of communications and the fact that many provinces lost contact with Rome for years signalled the end of imperial unity. The provinces were reduced to a state of autarchy which greatly lowered the standard of living. This state of emergency was further complicated by the fact that these warrior Emperors, themselves often semi-civilised and fanatical, began to persecute the rapidly spreading Christian religion, while many Romans felt that their present calamities were due to this defection from their national gods. Thus the Empire, stricken by internal decay, tried to re-impose unity upon an increasing number of its subjects by means of terror. The result was that this Empire, now represented by plundering soldiery and extortionate officials, was in the eyes of the provincials no longer merely a stranger, as earlier, but an object of hate and fear.

Nevertheless the internal structure was sufficiently solid to weather even this crisis. After 265 a group of exceedingly able and energetic officers from Pannonia and Illyria managed to regain authority over the disorganised armies. It is true that nearly all these powerful figures were ultimately murdered by their own soldiers and officers, but the murderers no longer succeeded in obtaining power. The successor came from the same circle as his predecessor and continued his good work. Claudius II succeeded in averting the Gothic menace by a great victory at Naissus; Probus drove the Germans back across the frontiers; and Aurelian restored the Empire

to its former dimensions by eliminating the principality of Palmyra which, under Zenobia, the widow of Odenathus, dominated the eastern half of the Empire. Palmyra, a city which owed its prosperity to the caravan trade, was captured and, after a second revolt, destroyed.

Aurelian and his successors were also murdered, but Diocletian (→ 334), elected by the army in 284, finally succeeded in consolidating the work of this series of warrior emperors. He ruled the Empire with a firm hand for twenty years.

Just as Augustus had once shaped his Principate in the light of his experiences of the preceding revolutionary period, Diocletian now consolidated the situation which had gradually arisen during a half century of anarchy. The system which he created is usually known as the Dominate (rule of the *dominus*).

THE DOMINATE

The system of Augustus, the constitutionally established *Respublica Romana* with the *Princeps* as chief magistrate, was abandoned and replaced by the military monarchy which already existed *de facto*. The prince now ruled by something approaching divine right: he was a direct representative of the gods and received divine honours from his subjects. Diocletian took the title Jovius, just as Aurelian had already assumed that of Lord and God, and required obeisance (*adoratio*) from his subjects. Following the example of the Eastern despots, and especially the Sassanians whom the Romans had learned to fear, he remained as remote as possible. Strict rules governed court procedure, and only with difficulty could anyone gain access to the Emperor who occupied such an exalted position. Further, Rome had long ceased to be the real capital, even though it was still considered as the first city of the Empire and the choice of Emperor had to be ratified by the Senate there. The Emperors had long ago transferred their court to their headquarters, which lay closer to the threatened frontiers at Trier, Milan, or Antioch (see Maps 69 a-d, p. 183). Diocletian took up residence in Nicomedia, between the Danube and Euphrates frontiers, and adorned it with magnificent buildings. From here he governed the Empire by his decrees. The completely devalued currency was reformed by a new monetary system based on the gold piece or *aureus*. To prevent fresh inflation prices were stabilised under threat of severe punishment for infringement. But since no measures were taken to guarantee the supply of goods at these fixed prices, this attempt at a planned economy was soon abandoned. The Empire was subdivided into smaller provinces, which in turn were joined to form larger units, the dioceses. The aim is clear: the military and administrative system had to be tightened: the official machinery had to be

432

433   434

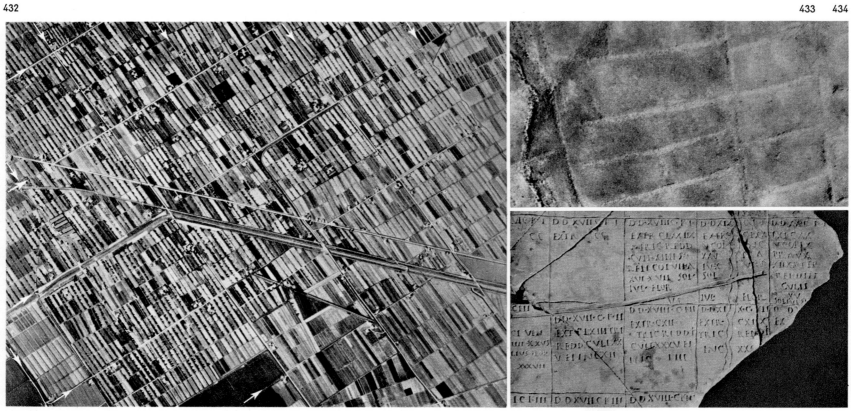

432. The Roman system of dividing up land (*centuriatio*, see Map 58) has survived in many places, including Italy. This air photograph from the modern province of Emilia shows the course of the roads dividing the various allotments, which mostly measured 20 by 20 *actus* (800 by 800 yards). **433.** Aerial survey has also revealed many traces of Roman agricultural methods in Algeria. The photograph shows the remains of walls designed to combat sand drift and erosion. **434.** A land register found in Orange in 1949 shows the partition of land by Roman *gromatici* (land surveyors). Here too they based their division upon *cardo* and *decumanus*; for example, DD is D(extra) D(ecumanus). The photograph shows a section with the river La Berre (the vertical, curved line) which is crossed by the road of Agrippa. This road comes to an end beyond Logis de Berre in a mountainous region difficult of access. The modern road departs here from the old plan and branches right towards Donzère.

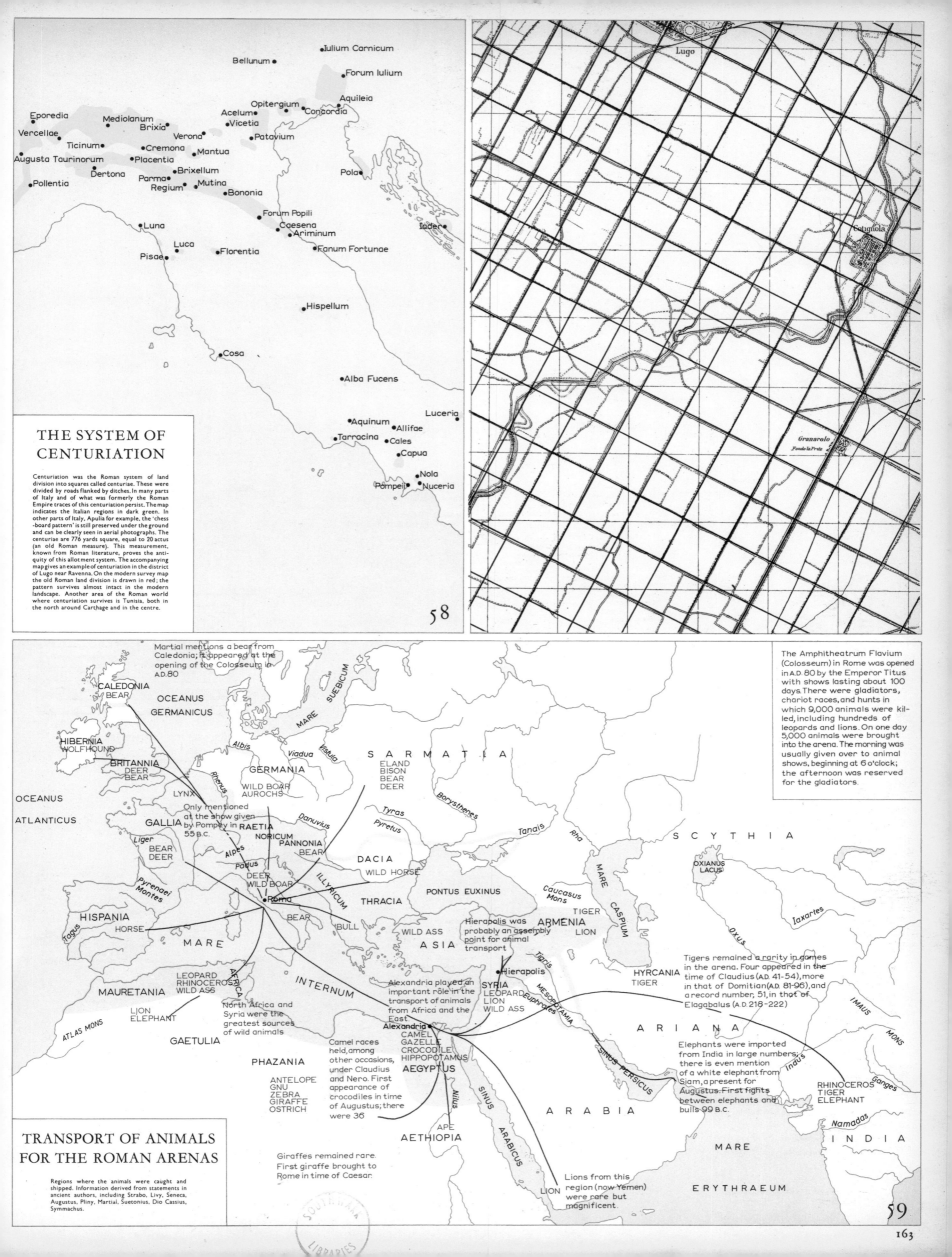

THE SYSTEM OF CENTURIATION

Centuriation was the Roman system of land division into squares called centuriae. These were divided by roads flanked by ditches. In many parts of Italy and of what was formerly the Roman Empire traces of this centuriation persist. The map indicates the Italian regions in dark green. In other parts of Italy, Apulia for example, the 'chess -board pattern' is still preserved under the ground and can be clearly seen in aerial photographs. The centuriae are 776 yards square, equal to 20 actus (an old Roman measure). This measurement, known from Roman literature, proves the anti- quity of this allotment system. The accompanying map gives an example of centuriation in the district of Lugo near Ravenna. On the modern survey map the old Roman land division is drawn in red; the pattern survives almost intact in the modern landscape. Another area of the Roman world where centuriation survives is Tunisia, both in the north around Carthage and in the centre.

58

Bellunum
Iulium Carnicum
Forum Iulium
Opitergium
Aquileia
Eporedia
Mediolanum
Acelum
Concordia
Brixia
Vicetia
Vercellae
Verona
Patavium
Ticinum
Cremona
Mantua
Augusta Taurinorum
Placentia
Pola
Dertona
Brixellum
Pollentia
Parma
Mutina
Regium
Bononia
Iader
Luna
Forum Popili
Luca
Caesena
Pisae
Florentia
Ariminum
Fanum Fortunae
Hispellum
Cosa
Alba Fucens
Luceria
Aquinum
Allifae
Tarracina
Cales
Capua
Nola
Pompeii
Nuceria

Lugo
Coturnola
Granarolo
Fonds la Prate

TRANSPORT OF ANIMALS FOR THE ROMAN ARENAS

Regions where the animals were caught and shipped. Information derived from statements in ancient authors, including Strabo, Livy, Seneca, Augustus, Pliny, Martial, Suetonius, Dio Cassius, Symmachus.

Martial mentions a bear from Caledonia; it appeared at the opening of the Colosseum in A.D. 80

The Amphitheatrum Flavium (Colosseum) in Rome was opened in A.D. 80 by the Emperor Titus with shows lasting about 100 days. There were gladiators, chariot races, and hunts in which 9,000 animals were kil- led, including hundreds of leopards and lions. On one day 5,000 animals were brought into the arena. The morning was usually given over to animal shows, beginning at 6 o'clock; the afternoon was reserved for the gladiators.

CALEDONIA BEAR
OCEANUS GERMANICUS
HIBERNIA WOLFHOUND
BRITANNIA DEER BEAR
LYNX
OCEANUS ATLANTICUS
Only mentioned by Pompey in 55 B.C.
GALLIA
BEAR DEER
GERMANIA WILD BOAR AUROCHS
SARMATIA ELAND BISON BEAR DEER
SCYTHIA
OXIANUS LACUS
DEER WILD BOAR
RAETIA NORICUM PANNONIA BEAR
DACIA WILD HORSE
HISPANIA HORSE
Roma
BEAR
BULL
ILLYRICUM
THRACIA
PONTUS EUXINUS
ARMENIA LION
HYRCANIA TIGER
TIGER
MARE CASPIUM
ARIANA
PYRENAEI MONTES
ASIA WILD ASS
Hierapolis was probably an assembly point for animal transport
Tigers remained a rarity in games in the arena. Four appeared in the time of Claudius (A.D. 41-54), more in that of Domitian (A.D. 81-96), and a record number, 51, in that of Elagabalus (A.D. 218-222)
MAURETANIA LEOPARD RHINOCEROS WILD ASS
LION ELEPHANT
AFRICA
North Africa and Syria were the greatest sources of wild animals
Hierapolis
SYRIA LEOPARD LION WILD ASS
MESOPOTAMIA
Alexandria played an important rôle in the transport of animals from Africa and the East
Elephants were imported from India in large numbers; there is even mention of a white elephant from Siam, a present for Augustus. First fights between elephants and bulls 99 B.C.
GAETULIA
Camel races held, among other occasions, under Claudius and Nero. First appearance of crocodiles in time of Augustus; there were 36
Alexandria CAMEL GAZELLE CROCODILE HIPPOPOTAMUS AEGYPTUS
ARABIA
RHINOCEROS TIGER ELEPHANT
INDIA
PHAZANIA ANTELOPE GNU ZEBRA GIRAFFE OSTRICH
APE AETHIOPIA
MARE ERYTHRAEUM
Giraffes remained rare. First giraffe brought to Rome in time of Caesar.
LION
Lions from this region (now Yemen) were rare but magnificent.

59

163

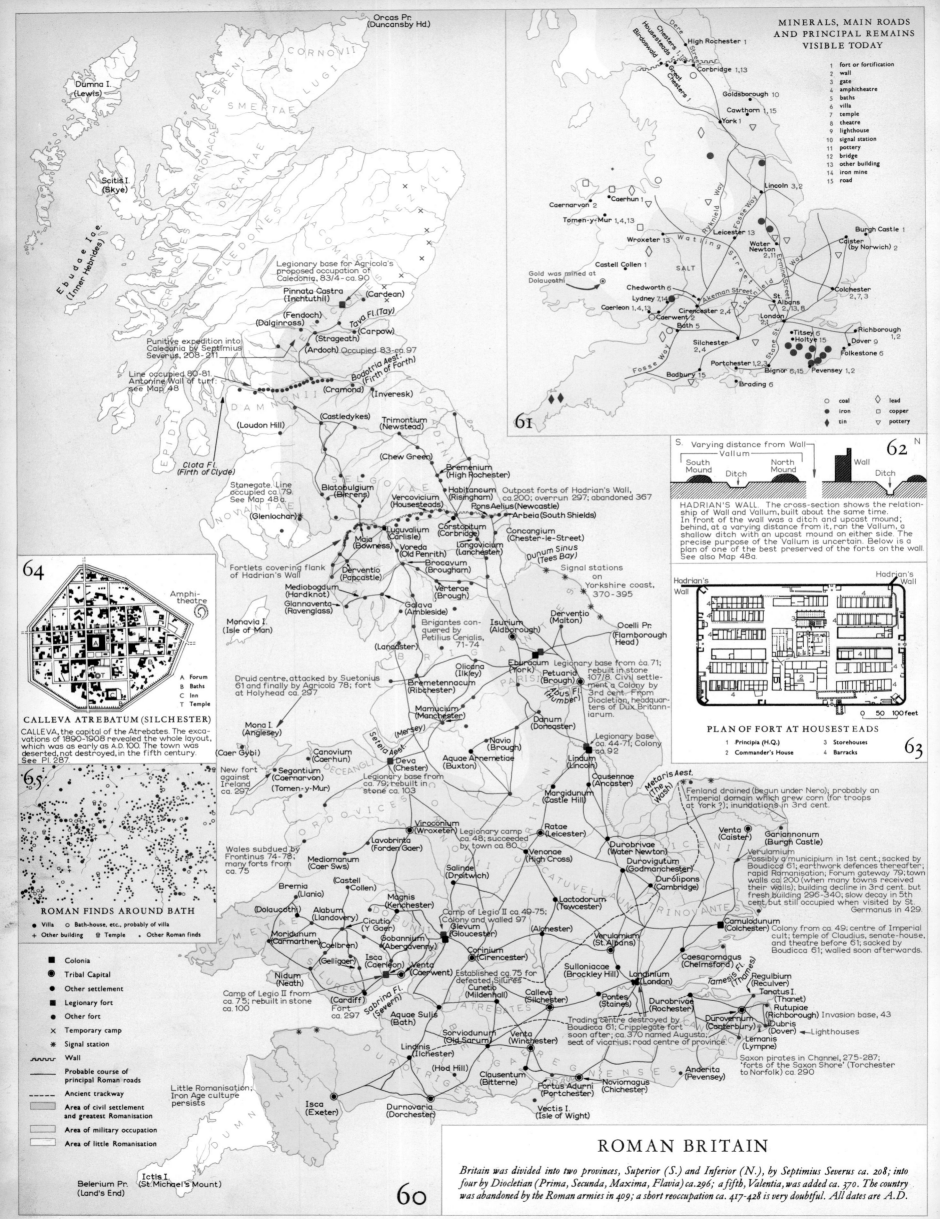

ROMAN BRITAIN

Britain was divided into two provinces, Superior (S.) and Inferior (N.), by Septimius Severus ca. 208; into four by Diocletian (Prima, Secunda, Maxima, Flavia) ca.296; a fifth, Valentia, was added ca. 370. The country was abandoned by the Roman armies in 409; a short reoccupation ca. 417-428 is very doubtful. All dates are A.D.

MINERALS, MAIN ROADS AND PRINCIPAL REMAINS VISIBLE TODAY

1 fort or fortification
2 wall
3 gate
4 amphitheatre
5 baths
6 villa
7 temple
8 theatre
9 lighthouse
10 signal station
11 pottery
12 bridge
13 other building
14 iron mine
15 road

○ coal   ◇ lead
● iron   □ copper
◆ tin   ▽ pottery

HADRIAN'S WALL. The cross-section shows the relationship of Wall and Vallum, built about the same time. In front of the wall was a ditch and upcast mound; behind, at a varying distance from it, ran the Vallum, a shallow ditch with an upcast mound on either side. The precise purpose of the Vallum is uncertain. Below is a plan of one of the best preserved of the forts on the wall. See also Map 48a.

PLAN OF FORT AT HOUSESTEADS
1 Principia (H.Q.)
2 Commander's House
3 Storehouses
4 Barracks

0 50 100 feet

CALLEVA ATREBATUM (SILCHESTER)
CALLEVA, the capital of the Atrebates. The excavations of 1890-1908 revealed the whole layout, which was as early as A.D. 100. The town was deserted, not destroyed, in the fifth century. See Pl. 287.
A Forum
B Baths
C Inn
T Temple
Amphitheatre

ROMAN FINDS AROUND BATH
● Villa
○ Bath-house, etc., probably of villa
+ Other building
⌂ Temple
· Other Roman finds

■ Colonia
◉ Tribal Capital
● Other settlement
■ Legionary fort
● Other fort
× Temporary camp
✳ Signal station
〰 Wall
— Probable course of principal Roman roads
--- Ancient trackway
Area of civil settlement and greatest Romanisation
Area of military occupation
Area of little Romanisation

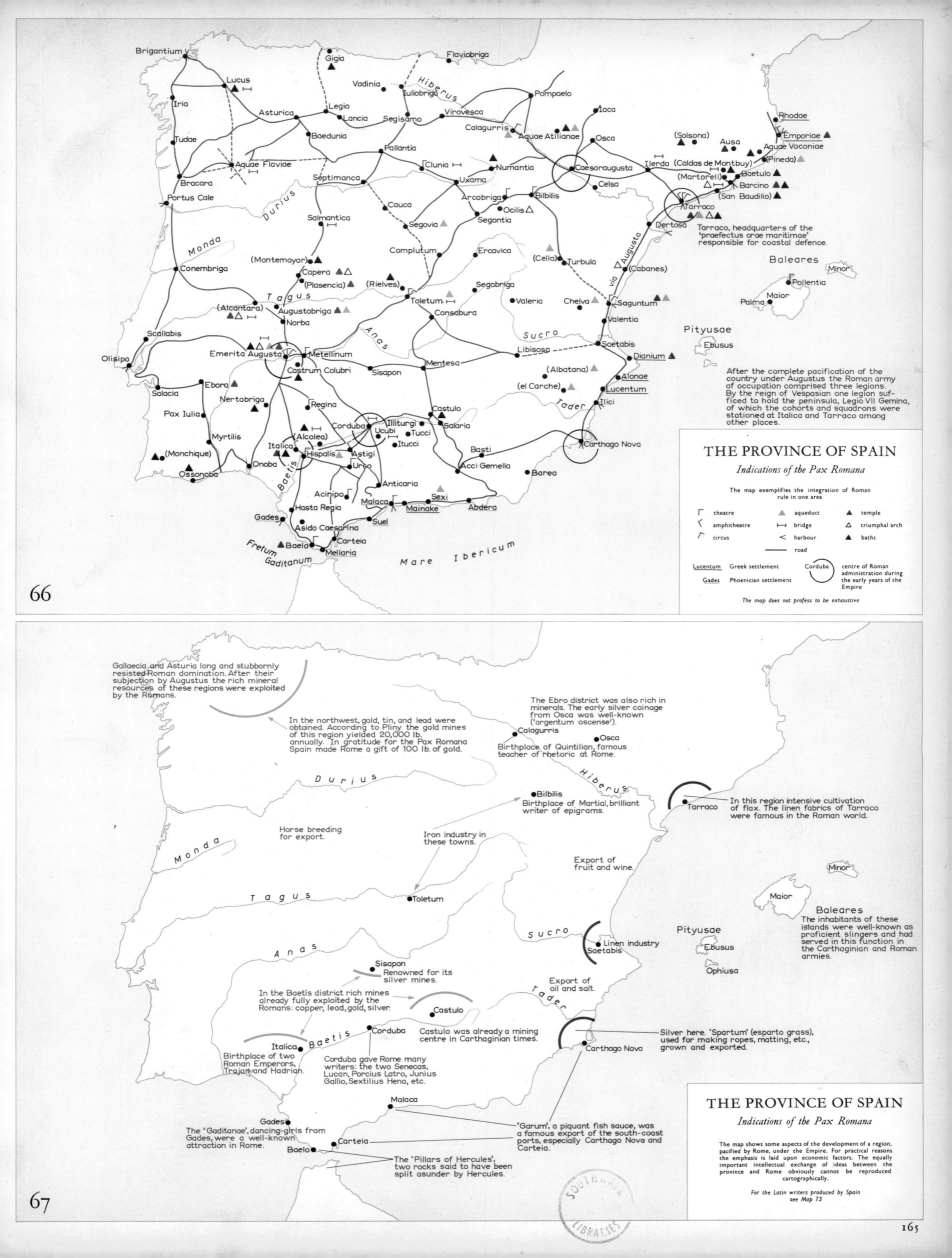

Map 66 — THE PROVINCE OF SPAIN

Brigantium · Lucus · Iria · Asturica · Legio · Lancia · Tudae · Baedunia · Gigia · Vadinia · Iuliobriga · Segisamo · Virovesca · Calagurris · Aquae Atilianae · Osca · Iaca · Pompaelo · Flaviobriga · Rhodae · Emporiae · Ausa · Aquae Voconiae · (Solsona) · (Pineda) · (Caldas de Montbuy) · Ilerda · (Martorell) · Baetulo · Barcino · (San Baudilio) · Tarraco · Dertosa · Aquae Flaviae · Septimanca · Pallantia · Clunia · Numantia · Uxama · Caesaraugusta · Celsa · Bilbilis · Bracara · Portus Cale · Cauca · Arcobriga · Ocilis · Segontia · Salmantica · Segovia · Complutum · Ercavica · (Cella) · Turbula · (Cabanes) · Conembriga · (Montemayor) · Capera · (Plasencia) · (Rielves) · Toletum · Segobriga · Valeria · Chelva · Saguntum · (Alcantara) · Augustobriga · Norba · Consabura · Valentia · Scallabis · Emerita Augusta · Metellinum · Castrum Colubri · Sisapon · Mentesa · Libisosa · Saetabis · Dianium · (Albatana) · Alonae · (el Carche) · Lucentum · Olisipo · Ebora · Nertobriga · Regina · Castulo · Salaria · Ilici · Salacia · Pax Iulia · Corduba · Illiturgi · Ucubi · Itucci · Basti · Carthago Nova · Myrtilis · Italica · (Alcolea) · Hispalis · Astigi · Urso · Anticaria · Acci Gemella · Barea · (Monchique) · Onoba · Acinipo · Sexi · Ossonoba · Hasta Regia · Malaca · Mainake · Abdera · Gades · Asido Caesarina · Suel · Carteia · Baelo · Mellaria

Tagus · Durius · Monda · Anas · Baetis · Sucro · Tader · Hiberus · via Augusta

Baleares — Minor · Maior · Pollentia · Palma · Pityusae · Ebusus

Fretum Gaditanum · Mare Ibericum

Tarraco, headquarters of the 'praefectus orae maritimae' responsible for coastal defence.

After the complete pacification of the country under Augustus the Roman army of occupation comprised three legions. By the reign of Vespasian one legion sufficed to hold the peninsula, Legio VII Gemina, of which the cohorts and squadrons were stationed at Italica and Tarraco among other places.

THE PROVINCE OF SPAIN
Indications of the Pax Romana

The map exemplifies the integration of Roman rule in one area

- theatre
- amphitheatre
- circus
- aqueduct
- bridge
- harbour
- temple
- triumphal arch
- baths
- road

Lucentum — Greek settlement
Gades — Phoenician settlement
Corduba — centre of Roman administration during the early years of the Empire

The map does not profess to be exhaustive

66

Map 67 — THE PROVINCE OF SPAIN

Gallaecia and Asturia long and stubbornly resisted Roman domination. After their subjection by Augustus the rich mineral resources of these regions were exploited by the Romans.

In the northwest, gold, tin, and lead were obtained. According to Pliny the gold mines of this region yielded 20,000 lb. annually. In gratitude for the Pax Romana Spain made Rome a gift of 100 lb. of gold.

The Ebro district was also rich in minerals. The early silver coinage from Osca was well-known ('argentum oscense').

Calagurris
Birthplace of Quintilian, famous teacher of rhetoric at Rome.

Osca

Bilbilis
Birthplace of Martial, brilliant writer of epigrams.

Tarraco
In this region intensive cultivation of flax. The linen fabrics of Tarraco were famous in the Roman world.

Horse breeding for export.

Iron industry in these towns.

Toletum

Export of fruit and wine.

Saetabis
Linen industry

Sisapon
Renowned for its silver mines.

In the Baetis district rich mines already fully exploited by the Romans: copper, lead, gold, silver.

Castulo
Castulo was already a mining centre in Carthaginian times.

Export of oil and salt.

Silver here. 'Spartum' (esparto grass), used for making ropes, matting, etc., grown and exported.

Carthago Nova

Corduba
Corduba gave Rome many writers: the two Senecas, Lucan, Porcius Latro, Junius Gallio, Sextilius Hena, etc.

Italica
Birthplace of two Roman Emperors, Trajan and Hadrian.

Malaca

Gades
The 'Gaditanae', dancing-girls from Gades, were a well-known attraction in Rome.

Carteia

Baelo

The 'Pillars of Hercules', two rocks said to have been split asunder by Hercules.

'Garum', a piquant fish sauce, was a famous export of the south-coast ports, especially Carthago Nova and Carteia.

Monda · Durius · Tagus · Anas · Baetis · Sucro · Tader · Hiberus

*Baleares
The inhabitants of these islands were well-known as proficient slingers and had served in this function in the Carthaginian and Roman armies.*

Minor · Maior · Pityusae · Ebusus · Ophiusa

THE PROVINCE OF SPAIN
Indications of the Pax Romana

The map shows some aspects of the development of a region, pacified by Rome, under the Empire. For practical reasons the emphasis is laid upon economic factors. The equally important intellectual exchange of ideas between the province and Rome obviously cannot be reproduced cartographically.

For the Latin writers produced by Spain see Map 73

67

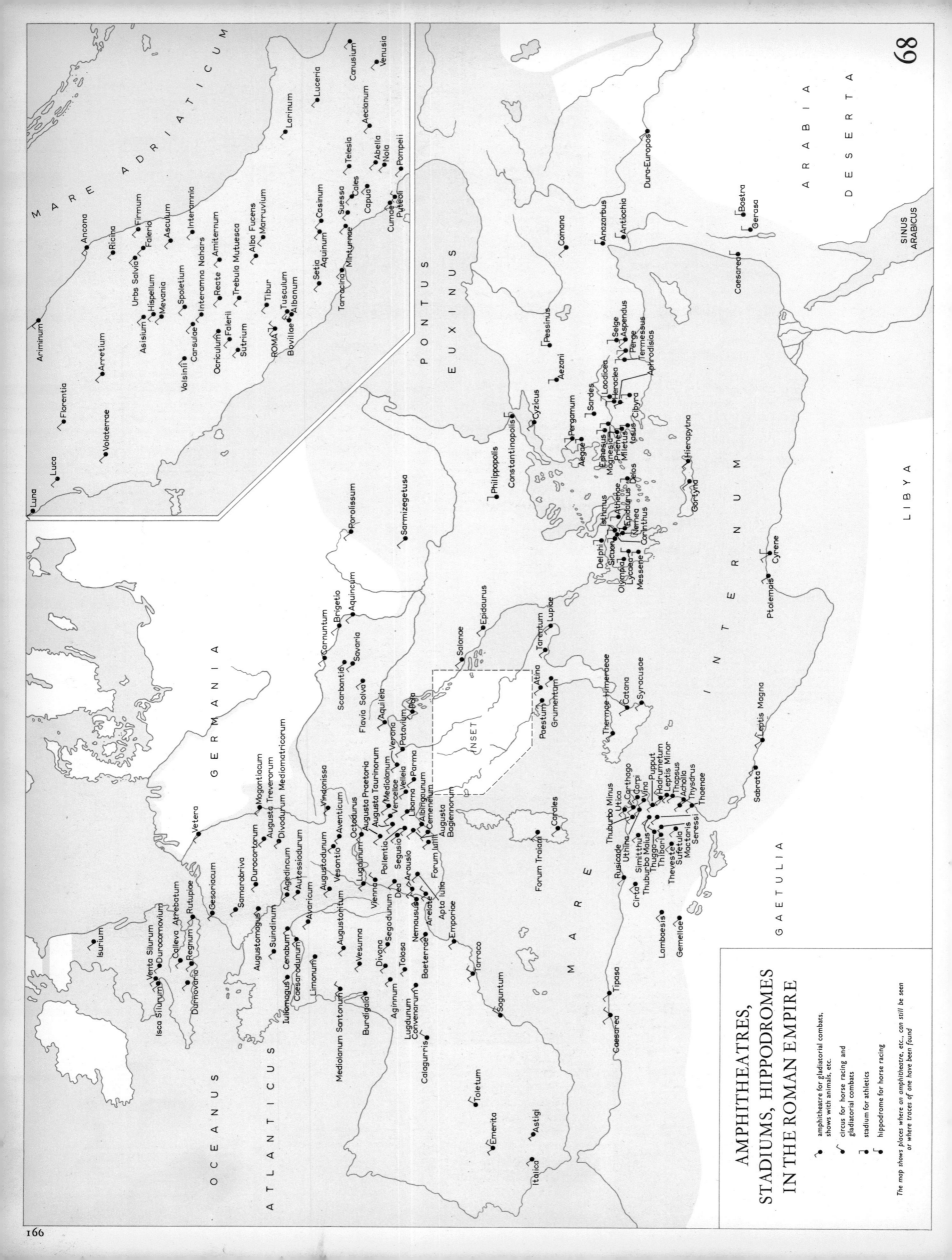

435
436

437
438

439
440

The policy of the rulers in both Republic and Empire aimed, among other things, at making and keeping the non-politically-minded people happy by providing them with food and games. The many representations of *ludi circenses* and the numerous remains of amphitheatres still show the important place occupied by these games. **435.** The amphitheatre in Pompeii, partly protected from the sun by an awning. **436.** Model of the Colosseum in Rome. The fourth storey has brackets to support beams which formed the frame for a sun-blind which was drawn over the spectators by sailors. **437.** Charioteer with two-horse team. **438.** *Bestiarii* fighting with a lion and lioness in a circus. **439.** Gladiator with oblong shield, short sword, and helmet with visor. **440.** Race of four-horse teams. The spina is decorated with monuments, including a column with a Victory and two columns with seven dolphins, one of which was removed after each lap.

167

441

442
443
444

Many burial places have been preserved throughout the entire Roman Empire. Besides local variations, it was a general rule that graves were outside the towns, assembled together in cemeteries or laid out in sepulchral monuments or mounds along the roads. **441.** A fragment of the sepulchral monument of the Aterii shows a moving scene of mourning. Women, accompanied by a flute player, lament around a dead woman lying on a high bed. **442.** The 'Tomba Rabirii' on the Via Appia near Rome. Many monuments from the later republican and early imperial times are still preserved along this road. **443.** Roman road near ancient Glanum in Provence with a sepulchral monument (right) and triumphal arch (left) dating from the time of Augustus. In the background the ruins of the city near the modern Saint-Rémy. **444.** Large sepulchral tower, the 'tomb of Cicero', beside the road to the south, near Formia.

447

445. In Pompeii also tombs stood ranged along many of the roads into the city. The best preserved are those outside the Herculaneum gate, in the sepulchral styles of the Hellenistic and Roman periods. **446.** In Ostia, a large cemetery with streets of tombs has been excavated on an island in the Tiber, the 'Isola Sacra'. A peculiarity of this is that behind the large tombs there are burial places for the poor, whose ashes were buried in the ground in urns. **447.** A marble sarcophagus from the end of the 2nd century shows a dead person upon his couch during a sacrificial meal. A servant offers him drink. In his left hand he holds a kantharos, in his right a ribbon the other end of which is held by a Cupid, invisible here. Before the couch stand a table, distorted to give a better view of the chicken, bread and knuckle of meat, and a straw-covered flask in the style of the modern Chianti bottles. On the right Mercury, the god of trade and traders, draws near with his purse in his hand.

169

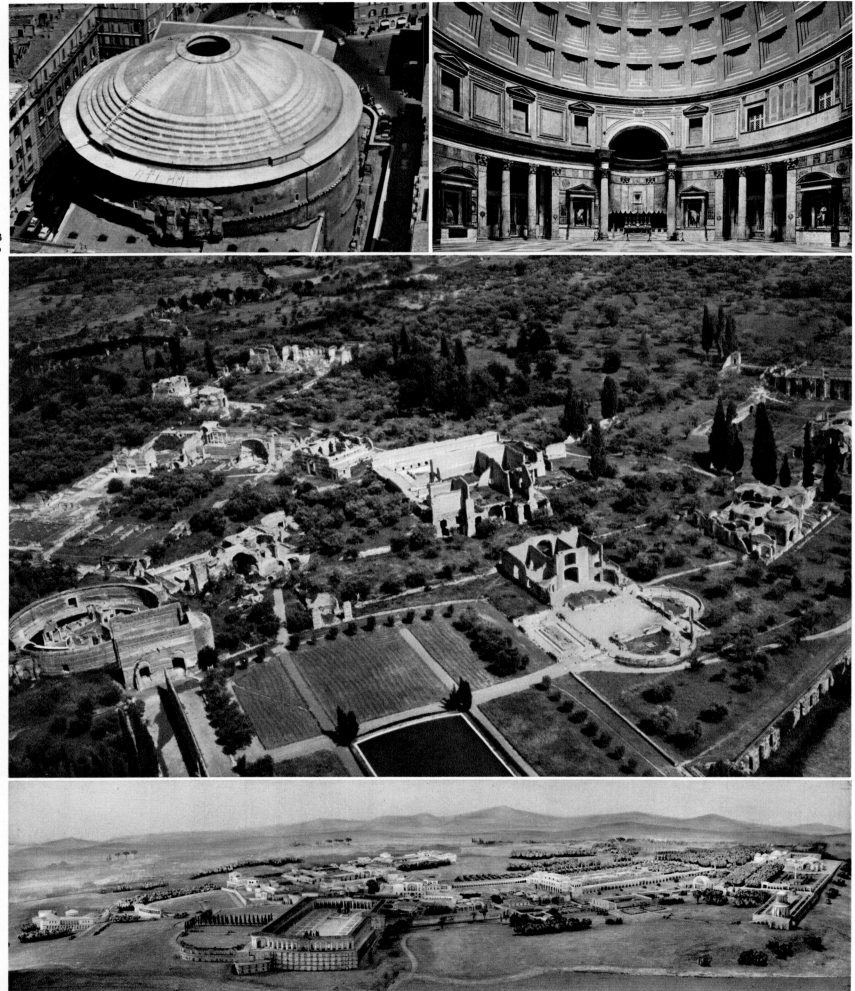

448
449

450

451

Architecture attained a high level among the technically-minded Romans, as is still evident from the numerous monumental ruins in Europe, Asia, and Africa. By the construction of the arch and the development of the vault they were able to realise ambitious projects, only equalled or surpassed in our time. New materials such as concrete helped to make this progress possible. One of the many examples is the Pantheon in Rome, whose enormous span of 140 feet was not surpassed until the nineteenth-century Crystal Palace in London. **448-9.** Exterior and interior of the Pantheon in Rome. **450.** The grand manner in which the Romans built their cities and palaces is apparent from – among other examples – the villa of Hadrian at Tivoli, whose imposing ruins still convey an idea of its former dimensions. **451.** Reconstruction of this villa. **452** (following page). A sepulchral monument shows one of the Roman technical appliances, a crane for heavy objects, operated by a tread-mill.

everywhere visible; in the hierarchically constructed bureaucracy with the Emperor at the head of both civil and military administration, these spheres must be kept clearly distinct. Everything, indeed, fell under state control. The *coloni* were tied to the land and craftsmen to their guilds and trades: the state had to have essential supplies and services at its disposal. The rich were condemned to hold local office, in other words to guarantee the tax returns. The only advantage of the new regulations was that these taxes could now at least be calculated. The army and the petty officials became the true masters of the Empire; welfare and prosperity attended only those who managed to win the favour and protection of one of these two great masters.

The curse of the preceding century had been that generals with armies on the frontiers had revolted against the authority of the distant Emperor and sometimes maintained their position successfully for several years. The Emperor could only be in one place at a time and was unable to send against a pretender a deputy upon whom he had conferred the necessary powers without being almost certain of having another rival Emperor on his hands. Diocletian attempted to combat this danger by what amounted to a universal distribution of imperial authority. As his colleague in the West he appointed his brother-officer Maximian, who like himself acquired the title Augustus, together with the name of Hercules. Each Augustus appointed a Caesar as a subordinate to help him in his task: Galerius in the East, Constantius Chlorus in the West. It was intended that in due course both Augusti should resign and be replaced by their Caesars, who in their turn would designate new Caesars. Imperial authority was thus represented in four places by men whose right to succession was definitely established and who had thus no motive for defection or revolt. Indeed, so strong was Diocletian's position that neither his junior colleague nor any of the Caesars rebelled against this joint arrangement—so long as he lived and continued in power.

The unity of the Empire would clearly be strengthened if its peoples could be led to give allegiance to one universally accepted religion, especially since the imperial cult had declined in prestige. Aurelian, who realised that the pagan world was moving nearer to monotheism, had established as a new state religion the worship of the Sun, as the Universal Deity who was revealed in the manifold individual cults. Diocletian, no less conscious of the unifying benefits of a state religion, was more conservative: he based it on Jupiter and the Graeco-Roman tradition. He was suspicious of all cults that might divide his subjects (thus he issued an edict against Persian Manichaeism) and towards the end of his life allowed himself to be persuaded, especially by Galerius, who was a fanatical pagan, to attempt to establish spiritual unity within the Empire. The Christian Church, which had grown rapidly and in many regions had begun to win over the majority of the population, was again persecuted. Churches and property were destroyed, the sacred books had to be handed in and burnt, Christians were barred from the army, civil service and municipal posts, and the clergy especially were harshly persecuted. Sacrifice in accordance with the requirements of the imperial cult was made obligatory: refusal was punishable by death. This was the longest and bloodiest of the persecutions, yet it resulted only in bitterness and confusion. Soon even pagans objected to obviously innocent persons being done to death. The courage of clergy and lay people aroused respect and even won new converts. The Caesar Constantius Chlorus refused to execute these decrees.

In 305 Diocletian laid down his imperial office and retired to Dalmatia where he had built a magnificent palace at Spalatum near Salonae. It now forms the centre of the town of Split.

His fellow Augustus Maximian also abdicated, and the two Caesars were promoted to the rank of Augustus. This artificial system failed, however, when Constantius died and his troops proclaimed his son Constantine as Augustus without consulting Galerius who, as the elder Augustus, had the right to designate a successor. Maxentius, the son of Maximian, feeling himself overlooked, now seized power in Italy. A bitter struggle followed. Maximian attempted to take up office again but was dissuaded by the old Diocletian who acted as intermediary but refused to return to office himself. He left Italy to his son and went to his son-in-law Constantine who, convicting him of revolt, condemned him to death. The next year Galerius died, but on his deathbed he revoked the decrees against the Christians. Only in the East was the persecution continued by the ruling Caesar Maximinus Daia.

In 312 Constantine marched against Maxentius who in the battle of the Pons Milvius, a bridge over the Tiber north of Rome, lost both his life and the battle. During the campaign Constantine had already placed the monogram of Christ on the shields of his soldiers, and many years afterwards he affirmed to Eusebius that before the battle he had seen a Cross of light athwart the afternoon sun and the words 'In this conquer' written in the sky. In 313 he, together with his Eastern colleague, Licinius, proclaimed the Edict of Milan which allowed the Christians freedom of religion. Although he was only baptised upon his deathbed in 337, it had long been clear that the Emperor considered himself a Christian. In 324 Licinius, who had remained faithful to paganism, was defeated and deposed by Constantine. The first Christian Emperor was now sole ruler of the Empire.

THE CHRISTIAN EMPERORS

Constantine ably and vigorously continued the work of Diocletian, but he abandoned the system of Augusti and Caesars and used his sons as regents. Although the frontiers remained unstable and the wars against the invading Germans and the Persians continued to smoulder, he succeeded in restoring order and prosperity to the Empire. It remained, however, a state ruled by force, in which bureaucracy and military authority banished all freedom. In order to strengthen the Empire's defences Constantine reinforced the local garrisons (*limitanei*), which formed a frontier army, with a new field army (*comitatenses*), composed of picked troops which could be used in threatened areas under the

453. The Romans achieved many prodigious feats in bridge-building: relief of a bridge over the Danube, more than half a mile long and supported by twenty pillars. **454.** A bridge built across two cliffs over the Lys in the Val d'Aosta. An aqueduct **(457)**, still in use, shows the system by which Roman towns were supplied with water. Water descending from higher ground was received in an aqueduct which directed it in a gently-sloping channel to its destination. Most conduits ran underground in lead pipes; only in cases of necessity was the water conveyed by way of expensive structures raised upon arches. **455.** The quantity of water thus transported was enormous. **456.** The channel of the aqueduct over the Gard, for example, is nearly 6 feet high and over 3 feet wide. Heavy flat roofing stones protected it against pollution. **458** (following page). The remains of the aqueduct in the Oned Rhumel in a desolate part of the Atlas range prove that Roman engineers were not intimidated by difficult ground.

command of the Emperor or one of his sons. These were, however, no longer Roman legions, but troops of German and Sarmatian mercenaries who, with their own commanders, their own equipment, and their own tactics, now formed the nucleus of the army. Constantine saw to it that even the highest military ranks were open to these non-Roman, semi-civilised barbarians, probably in the conviction that these generals at least would never aspire to the throne. Yet it would soon appear that although none of these Germans might themselves be capable of becoming Emperor they were well able to create one. But Constantine's own authority and that of his dynasty was for the time being sufficiently strong to keep this threat at bay.

In 330 the new era was, as it were, symbolised by the foundation of a new capital, the New Rome, Constantinople, magnificently situated upon the Bosporus, at the junction of all roads leading east and west. It became the economic and military heart of the Empire. The Christian Church was now relieved of all pressure and, with the Emperor's favour, soon attracted the great mass of the population. There arose, however, the problems of the relationship between Church and Emperor and of the unity of the Church. It was precisely this unity which was threatened by the fierce struggle between Arius and Athanasius concerning the doctrinal conception of the person of Christ. In 325 Constantine convoked the Oecumenical Council of Nicaea in order to settle this dispute. He himself occupied the position of chairman but, as 'bishop of those without the Church', as he himself put it, he largely confined himself to the execution of the Council's decisions, not without the aid of temporal power. Arius was defeated; his doctrine was declared heretical and his followers dismissed from their posts. These measures, however, did not restore peace and unity. Later rulers, themselves tending towards Arianism, tried to nullify the work of Nicaea and appointed non-orthodox priests to high ecclesiastical functions. These attempts had no permanent effect upon the faith of the people and its leaders, above all upon the holy monks. Only in the East did the Emperor retain a considerable influence in church affairs; there a caesaro-papism developed whereby the Emperor also became head of the church.

In the West imperial authority was much weaker, the Church retained a greater degree of independence, and the bishop of Rome, now termed the Pope, acquired increasing authority.

Paganism was dying. Now that it lacked state support, the temples and religious ceremonies fell into disuse. The Emperor Julian, who succeeded to the throne in 355, tried to reverse the Christian revolution and returned to paganism, but his attempts to revive the old religion were in vain. Yet the old gods were still worshipped in the countryside and on the frontiers among the uncivilised barbarian tribes, and a circle of pagan nobles and writers remained faithful with romantic enthusiasm to the ancient glory and the ancient traditions. The schools of philosophy in Athens where Neo-platonism predominated continued the struggle until they were closed by the Emperor Justinian. The Roman Senate too only abandoned its old traditions after stubborn resistence. When the Emperor Theodosius proclaimed Christianity as the state religion and banned pagan sacrifice and worship (380), many nobles, heirs of the old Roman families, protested fiercely but in vain. The altar of Victory, for centuries the symbol of Rome's victorious progress through history, was removed from the Senate-house in 382.

With great devotion these pagan writers applied themselves to the preservation of the ancient literature and learning. They may have lacked the ability to create independent work of great importance, but their care in copying and making extracts from the ancient literary treasures has preserved for later generations much that is precious.

Life and thought were now governed by a completely different pattern. For, even though Christian writers and scholars, laymen and clergy alike, might still use the forms of classical culture and follow its method of logic and thought, the classical world of ideas had none the less become alien to them.

THE BARBARIAN INVASIONS

In the middle of this period of transition, the Empire restored by Constantine received a blow from which it never recovered. In the year 375 the nomadic Huns, who for more than a century had been moving westward from the frontiers of China, reached the Volga. The dominant tribes in southern Russia, the Goths and the Alans, gave way before the pressure of the wild Mongolian horsemen. The Ostrogoths settled in what is now Hungary, the Visigoths, long in close contact with the Roman Empire—they had been converted to Arian Christianity by Bishop Ulfilas, himself

459. Many causes led to the decline of Rome from its unique position of power. The statues of the goddess of Victory (→ also 379) which the conquerors had erected everywhere throughout the Empire toppled and were buried by silt and sand. 460 (following page). On the ruins of Roman civilisation grew the new culture of the Eastern Empire and Byzantium, which struck off along fresh paths yet retained many characteristics of the older Empire. For a thousand years it exercised an important influence upon world history. The diptych of the Emperor Anastasius, who died in 517 (a stiff official portrait strikingly different from the reliefs, busts and coins of the earlier Emperors), typifies the last phase of a development which led from the rise of a new civilisation in Crete to the two focal points of Greece and Rome whose outstanding achievements in the one case of origination, in the other of diffusion, have determined the aspect of Western culture up to the present day.

a Goth—asked permission to enter the Roman Empire. Valens, the Emperor in the East, who perhaps saw fresh recruits for his army in this strong and warlike tribe, granted their request. When, however, the maintenance of these Goths created difficulties and the local authorities seized their possessions in exchange for food, they turned to arms and took what they needed by force; soon marauding bands infested the whole of the Balkans. Valens then declared war against them, but in the battle of Adrianople (378) his army was destroyed and he himself was killed.

Theodosius the Great did succeed, after years of struggle, in restoring a degree of order and reached a settlement with the Visigoths, but at the cost of allowing them to settle as *foederati* (allies) within the Empire. But the Danube frontier was lost for ever, and the so-called federated tribes formed in fact national units within the frontiers. Over them the Emperor had only nominal authority.

After Valentinian II, Emperor of the West, had been murdered by his Frankish commander Arbogast who had then assumed power with the help of a puppet Caesar appointed by himself, Theodosius succeeded in defeating him and in uniting the Empire once more under one ruler. But the whole could no longer be managed by one man. Even before he died Theodosius decided that his son Arcadius should inherit the East and the young Honorius the West. With this the division of the Empire became an established fact, although the fiction persisted that both Emperors were colleagues within the same Empire.

In point of fact the two halves soon became deadly enemies. Weak-willed Arcadius left the government to his favourites. These incited Alaric, the ambitious king of the Visigoths who was virtual ruler of the Balkans and had carried his marauding raids as far as Greece, to turn against Italy where their rival, the Vandal Stilicho, ruled for Honorius. Stilicho succeeded in defeating Alaric, but to achieve this victory he had been compelled to withdraw troops from the Rhine frontier. Numerous tribes – Franks, Burgundians, and Vandals – now poured into Gaul. When Honorius, harassed by suspicion and the fear of heresy (Stilicho was an Arian), ordered his death, his German troops deserted and left the way open for Alaric, who laid the whole of Italy under contribution and in 410 took and sacked Rome. After Alaric's death in southern Italy, the Visigoths made for southern Gaul where they founded a separate kingdom which soon included north-east Spain. Honorius and his followers, safely entrenched in impregnable Ravenna, could only look on helplessly while their commanders carried on the struggle (see Map 69, p. 183).

By about 450 the downfall of the Empire seemed imminent. The Huns, who had settled in the Danube and Theiss area, suddenly developed, under their leader Attila, an enormous power of expansion. First, they subjected the surrounding tribes from Germany to the Caucasus. Then came the turn of the Empire. The East was the first to suffer; the Balkan countries were terribly ravaged. The Emperor had to consent to pay a yearly tribute to the king of the Huns, who was perfectly conscious that Constantinople would in any case prove too much for his cavalry. It is extremely significant than many subjects of the Empire preferred to pay tribute to the barbarian than submit to the systematic extortion and curtailment of liberty imposed upon them by Roman bureaucracy.

In 451 Attila turned against the West. His advance, however, was checked on the Marne on the Catalaunian Fields by the Roman general Aetius at the head of an army of Romans, Visigoths, and Burgundians. The following year, Attila invaded Italy but was unable to take Milan. His sudden death in 453 put an end to his Empire and the menace of the Huns.

During this same period the Vandal Gaiseric (Genseric) seized Africa from the Romans (429). He occupied Carthage and established a pirate state which did incalculable damage. The fleets of East and West attempted in vain to dislodge him. In 455, after Valentinian III had murdered his commander Aetius out of jealousy and left Italy without a ruler, Gaiseric landed at Ostia and plundered Rome. The glory of the Eternal City now faded: the population rapidly declined, the great buildings fell into ruin. For another twenty years one impotent Emperor succeeded another, appointed and deposed by the German chief Ricimer. In 476 the German Odoacer killed the general Orestes (formerly secretary of Attila) and deposed his son who was ruling under the name of Romulus Augustulus. He sent crown and sceptre to Constantinople, and adopted the titles of *patricius* and of king of the Germans in Italy. This act, in itself insignificant, is usually considered the closing point in the history of the Western Roman Empire. The Emperor of the East did indeed nominally retain the crown of the West, and Justinian even succeeded in regaining the whole of Italy, Africa, and parts of Spain (550). But the Empire no longer existed in the proper sense of the word. The Eastern section, having freed itself from the domination of foreign mercenary leaders and having restored its defences, fused into a new unity in which the Greek way of life, Christianity, and imperial tradition went to form the new Byzantine Empire which survived until the Mohammedan capture of Constantinople in 1453.

But while East Rome flourished for nearly a millennium longer, the West meanwhile rapidly disintegrated into the national tribal states which inherited parts of it and which had to create for themselves upon the ruins a new existence and a new mode of life. But amid this dissolving world the survival of Roman law and the Latin language, the Roman Church and the Holy Roman Empire show   that the tradition of Rome in the West was still alive.

THE HERITAGE
OF CLASSICAL CULTURE

The fall of the Roman Empire was the outward manifestation of the fact that classical culture, that manner of life and thought originating in Greece and adapted to a non-Greek world, had perished. This was evident even before the breaking of that iron ring of legions which had held together in security the lands where this culture had flourished. Germans inherited the ruins, while the Christian Church continued to propagate the idea, in the spiritual domain, of an universal empire, now as the *corpus Christianum*. Church and empire, the two conceptions which dominated the Middle Ages, had their origin in this ancient world. In the schools and their teaching, in church language and theology, methods and ideas survived, transformed, sometimes even deformed, which derived from the classical world. They provided points of departure and contact for the revival in the Renaissance, which might dream of a renewal of the world of the ancients viewed as an ideal but which was in reality the beginning of a new era and the basis of that culture which we now know as the Western European or Atlantic. This culture differs greatly from its model, but nevertheless it bears both internal and external traces of its origin.

Whenever the nations of Europe reflect upon the common link which distinguishes their culture from that of other peoples, they find that it is the teachings of Greece and Rome, together with Christianity, which have determined the fundamental differences in thought and feeling. We are so steeped in the ideas of classical antiquity that many regard these foundations as so natural to us that they tend to forget that they are merely inherited.

The Graeco-Roman world and culture are things of the past. Their works, however, live on, sometimes as models, and they survive as living teachers for all who are conscious of having inherited this classical tradition. In this manner Greece and Rome have become intrinsic parts of Western European life. Without them the modern world could not have acquired its present form. What is more, in the ancient world deeds were done and ideas formulated which, however much a part of their native life and environment, outlived this origin and inspired all mankind.

Homer not only was a great poet in his own day and the father of European literature, of immeasurable historical importance for all who came after him, but he remains a poet whose work still appeals immediately to anyone sensitive to poetry, even if he may know no Greek and is unfamiliar with the Greek world of 2500 years ago. Sophocles' tragedies still convey a message to those who are conscious of the tragic greatness of man and his conflicts. Plato not only was a great thinker, but he remains an active force today, whose ideas still command respect and study.

All these works, and the examples could be multiplied almost indefinitely, belong to the imperishable treasures of our culture. They are the heirlooms which this period has left us: classical art and literature and Roman law deserve their separate place in this book, outside the historical survey. Nevertheless the effect that these heirlooms make upon our minds is also determined by the inner intellectual training which each of us, although unconsciously, has undergone from a tradition that originated in Greece. This tradition is one of freedom and justice.

The charters of the Western world, from the Declaration of Independence to the Charter of the United Nations, proclaim that liberty is the inherent and inalienable right of every man. From a purely historical point of view, however, the original status of man was not liberty but a servitude that linked him to a tradition and group, without which life and culture were impossible. History begins not with liberty but with despotism, and wherever man was unwilling or unable to accept a higher authority he remained a savage. Throughout the early world despotism and culture flourished side by side.

The only exception to this rule was in Greece. There, from experience and the nature of the people themselves, came the realisation that liberty does not consist in being free from authority but in possessing a law by which the liberty of each individual and section of the community is at the same time guaranteed and restricted by the rights of others. Even though Greece progressed no further than postulating the liberty of the citizen, while ignoring as yet the rights of non-citizens, women and slaves, it had nevertheless given birth to an idea which has proved irradicable and which still today remains to be fully realised.

The existence of community and state depends upon law, the generally accepted rule. So arises the question of the best and most just method of governing the community. It is not by chance that Greek terms are still employed today in the basic conceptions of politics, because this search for a community governed by reason originated in the small city-states of Greece and was preserved by the farmers, craftsmen, and fishermen who fought for freedom and succeeded in repelling Persian despotism. Even though these small cities destroyed each other in their fierce disagreement as to how this liberty and this justice should be realised, the Western world has followed in their footsteps and still seeks, although in completely different circumstances and on a vastly larger scale, the solution to the problem of a free world ruled not by arbitrary decision but by law, which transforms the chaos apparently inherent in unfettered liberty into a cosmos. This external political development and strife was naturally sustained through the spirit of partnership in good and evil. It is also evident that there were parallel developments in other spheres of life, inextricably entwined with outward progress, either stimulating and sustaining or curbing and being curbed.

Tradition, in Greece, was overborne by reason. Here for the first time reigned freedom of thought, freedom of speech, and freedom of knowledge. It seems to us a matter of course that a person should be able to say and think what he pleases; lack of such freedom would appear unbearable oppression. Yet such liberty is not a natural gift but a right which had to be fought for. Originally word and thought were governed by the fixed laws of tradition which appeared sacred and immutable. Woe to the man who infringed this tradition: he was cast out, if he was lucky enough to escape death. Heretics and freethinkers always tend to be feared and hated. Yet here too freedom is not merely the opposite of subjection. The sculptor or architect, although not bound by strict hieratic rules and free to express his original conception, normally follows almost automatically the works of his predecessors and teachers, building upon their model. Thus a Greek style developed, free yet bound by that ideal of beauty present in the mind of all craftsmen.

These were the masters who taught Europe to *see*. Not that their form of expression was necessarily the natural one or their art the only possible art. When, during the Middle Ages, the influence of Greece and Rome faded and became merely a vague memory, later artistic creations showed that European man was and is capable of giving form to quite another vision. The fact that Greek art appears to us so natural is due to the strong influence of Greek example and the Greek theory that the essence of things must be given ideal expression. Later successors transformed this classical conception into a classicism which aspired to the highest possible in imitation of the Greek model; and although this was certainly not in the spirit of the teachers themselves, yet it impressed this spirit deeply upon Western art, which remains incomprehensible if this factor is overlooked.

The same is true of literature. Epic, lyric, drama, tragedy, and comedy, all still bear their Greek names. They were all conceived and developed in Greece in forms that became standard. For here too freedom of expression means neither freedom from restraint nor arbitrary subjective expression, but work in accordance with the rules of art, just as the scientist today freely employs disciplined methods but aims at a goal above and beyond the facile and familiar. For the Greek poet and writer these rules were neither a constraint nor a hindrance but rather aids which he freely and willingly could and did use in order to profit by the experience of his predecessors. When, in our day, traditional forms tend more and more to disintegrate and the artist prefers chaos and experiment, with purely associative impulses, this does not imply a condemnation of Greek restraint and sobriety, but means merely that the intellectual problems of our time are proving too much for the artist, that he lacks the force and stability to dominate his problems as the Greek mastered his in firm lines and competent designs. We imply here no criticism of modern artists who are still experimenting in style, but merely note that precisely by that experiment they are unconsciously following in the path of Greece, which equally sought, and found, its own individual style. Greek art in no way developed from the imitation of a model – for pastiche and imitation, however skilful, are always a symptom of decline – but from pursuing a stylistic ideal which was approached by constant technical discipline.

Freedom is a dangerous possesion. We have already remarked – and this fact was particularly evident in the survey of Greek historical development – that the world of the Greek *polis* became a victim of its own ideal of freedom carried to excess. The same danger certainly threatened public and private morality when in the fifth century B.C. the new critical spirit showed signs of abandoning discipline as well as tradition. Searching for rules of conduct based not upon convention but upon nature, the Sophists regarded only self-interest and self-indulgence as the natural motives of man. Socrates, Plato, Aristotle and their pupils prevailed against this nihilism. They implanted in the European mind the realisation that behind the chaos of appearance, behind the apparently arbitrary nature of human life and thought, there lies a natural, innate law and necessity. They saw that the material world, for all its unpredictability, is none the less ruled by the spirit. It is thus that they became the fathers of all idealistic philosophy in the West.

Since their time the aim of knowledge for the West has been system, the heroic attempt to arrange and explain all phenomena in such a way that every fact can find a place and fulfil an accountable function. This was the Greek solution, whose influence prevails to the present day, regardless of whether it is the only correct or possible one. Even a person who contests its correctness must agree that man is just as much a pupil of those whom he combats as of those whom he follows.

Up till now we have, not without reason, spoken of Greece and the Greek influence, since our intellectual heritage is mainly and essentially Greek. Rome played a rôle which was different, although perhaps of equal consequence, and by adopting Greek culture preserved it and transmitted it to the West. Moreover, it gave this heritage a distinctive character. While the Greek mind pondered upon the human problems of individual and community and in practice pushed its conclusions to their ultimate limits, thereby perishing in an implacable ideological struggle, the sober and sensible Roman organised this disrupted *polis* world into an Empire which, however it originated, was in principle founded upon justice. Later Greek theorists saw in Rome the concrete realisation of the dreams of their most noble spirits. The Roman Empire gave to Europe its structural and cultural unity. The Romans profited by Greek wisdom in every field, yet without becoming completely Hellenised. They always remained themselves. Their commanders, statesmen, orators, and writers frequently had recourse to Greek theory, yet their practice remained Roman.

For the first time in history a nation was confronted with the problem which since then has remained acute for every European up to the present day: how to combine a supranational culture with individual independence. We moderns, historically inclined, may sometimes tend to lay too much stress upon Roman lack of originality, and to criticise their habit of imitation. This is essentially unjust, for the Romans were not concerned with preserving Greek culture or all that was typically Greek. Their aim was to extract and adapt all that might be useful in solving their own problems. By giving Greek gold the imprint of Roman coinage, without realising or intending it, they kept its value in circulation. Greece and Rome, side by side with Israel, undoubtedly have their place among our spiritual ancestors, not only in the sense that their legacies are among the precious possessions of our spiritual heritage, but above all because something of their spirit survives in all of us. We all bear their stamp.

Nevertheless the intellectual achievement of the ancient world is ours by inheritance and not our own creation. That which is inherited can also be lost; there is sufficient indication in our day that even this cultural heritage is threatened. That our culture should suffer change is inevitable; no classicism, which thinks to have discovered in the past the abiding standard, can prevent this. Yet it would be an incalculable tragedy should our culture sever itself from these roots from which it has grown.

Greek and Latin Literature

The spirit of a people lives in its literature. There its soul speaks, its heart beats. If we imagined the disappearance of all that archaeology has revealed by excavation and interpreted of the ancient world, the loss would be immeasurably great. Contact with classical culture would be injured but not severed. If, however, the literature were to disappear, all primary contact would be lost. The remains of architecture, sculpture, and painting would reveal to us something of the richness, the beauty, the skill of a mysterious people, but no Agamemnon would ride in his war chariot through the Lion Gate of Mycenae rich in gold, no Socrates would stroll with his friends from the Piraeus to Athens, no Pericles make a speech over the graves of the Athenian soldiers, no Horace meditate as he wandered along the Via Sacra, no victorious general ride in triumph through the streets of Rome towards the Capitol. Literature is the very life of a nation and deserves its place in an atlas which aims at explaining and illustrating the most important aspects of the classical world, even though this literature appeals not to the eye but to the ear and although its essence evades visual presentation. An atlas thus is not the place for a history of literature, yet it may offer room for a few glimpses of the literary heritage, which may either be illumined by illustrations or give meaning to them. Word and image complement each other. The great figures of literature loom like statues from a distant past – figures from the beginnings of epic, from drama, lyric poetry, and prose.

THE EPIC

The first image which meets us is that of Homer, the wise, blind singer of legend, as he was protrayed by the fancy of later generations. He journeys throughout the eastern Greek world, and in the courts of princes or at great festivals he sings of the mythical past, of the glorious deeds of the ancestor of the princely house, of the history of valorous forefathers, of the might of the gods. There were many of these poet-singers and their heroic sagas were numerous. For us, only the *Iliad* and *Odyssey* of Homer have survived. Who was Homer? Where did he live and when? Only the last question can be answered with any degree of certainly; he most probably lived in the eighth century B.C. For the further circumstances of his life we must fall back upon his works. These allow us to call him the first and greatest of European poets. The *Iliad* and *Odyssey* form such a glorious and perfect overture to European literature that no later epic can bear comparison with them. It is not by chance that only these two heroic sagas, of the many composed in the early Greek world, have survived, and not without reason that they have been called the Bible of the Greeks. For centuries they formed the basis of Greek education and culture. Quotations and scenes from the *Iliad* and *Odyssey* are found in the works of nearly every later writer and on countless vases and reliefs. Aeschylus modestly called his own tragedies fragments from Homer's dish. It would be difficult to overestimate Homer's influence, not only upon Greek, but upon all later European culture. A short consideration of both epics may help us to understand something of this influence.

The *Iliad* begins thus: 'Divine Muse, sing of the wrath of Achilles, son of Peleus, the unhallowed wrath which brought endless suffering to the Greeks, which sent the souls of many mighty heroes to Hades and left their bodies a prey for dogs and birds; thus was accomplished the will of Zeus. Begin thy song with the quarrel which brought discord between the son of Atreus, king of men, and the noble Achilles. Which of the gods provoked between them the bitter struggle? Apollo, son of Leto and Zeus.'

These opening lines at once tell us several things. First, the modest attitude of the ancient poet towards his art. He is not the artist; the Muse sings in him and he is merely the privileged instrument. In the second place we notice how Homer makes direct for his goal and places us immediately in the middle of the story. Without a word about the Trojan War and what gave rise to it, without any indication of time or place, the listener (or reader) is confronted with the true subject: the wrath of Achilles and his quarrel with Agamemnon and the endless suffering resulting from it – thus was accomplished the will of Zeus. This is the main theme of the *Iliad*, not the external event of a war, but the tragic conflict between two men which would bring death and disaster to many. It is for this reason that Achilles, who nourished anger, is the central figure, although he remains in the background for several books and one might be tempted to call the *Iliad* the epic of Agamemnon or of Hector. The figure of Hector especially is drawn by Homer with extraordinary warmth and feeling, so that in his fight with Achilles the sympathy of the modern reader is on his side and the stubbornness and cruelty of Achilles is to our mind only poorly compensated by his later more conciliatory attitude when in the last Book he returns Hector's body to his father Priam and the thought of his own aged and lonely father brings tears to his eyes. War is of necessity merciless, and this being so Achilles is shown us in the *Iliad* as a youthful, noble hero who during his short life performs deeds of almost supernatural strength and heroism but whose greatest victory is the subduing of his own anger and pride. This selfconquest of a heroic soul is the central theme and transforms the *Iliad* into a dramatic epic with a subordinate theme, the Trojan War with its thousand colourful scenes of courage and fear, wounds and death, quarrels and friendship.

Here we are continually struck by yet another quality of these two poems, perhaps the principal reason why every generation returns again to Homer: the graphic quality, the authenticity, the humanity of every page. Homer saw and lived through it all, and we see and live through it with him. All his characters – even the figures of the gods – are completely human in their vices and virtues. We feel ourselves one with them in their passions, thoughts, and feelings. Homer will never grow old because he has drawn from life man and all his emotions and because throughout the centuries man does not change but remains essentially true to himself. Each generation recognises itself in Homer.

This deeply human quality is especially clear and vivid in the *Odyssey*, an epic completely different in nature and subject from the *Iliad*. It is not a dramatic poem but a novel of adventure in verse. There is no doubt here concerning the identity of the main character. Odysseus is the great adventurer, the wanderer who overcomes all difficulties and dangers and is master of every situation. He loses all his ships and companions, is waylaid by the Cyclops, by Circe, by the Sirens, by Scylla and Charybdis, by Poseidon and many others, but after ten years of wandering added to his ten years of war, after a final struggle with the suitors in his palace, he returns triumphant to the arms of his wife Penelope and to his son Telemachus. A tale of perpetual enchantment, full of insight and wisdom, sparkling with the joy of life, the mirror of a human life lived to the full.

These two epic poems throw light upon obscure periods, both on Homer's own world and on the much earlier Mycenaean age in Greece in the thirteenth and twelfth centuries before Christ, the Greek heroic age, which reveals an aristocratic community in which only the nobleman is of any account. In the *Iliad* we see these nobles and heroes on the field of battle or at war-ravaged Troy. In the *Odyssey* a fuller view of life is revealed, of noble men and women at home in their palaces, of life at sea and in the country, of the wonderful characters and peoples met by Odysseus upon his adventurous journey. Homer's poems are two ever-flowing springs. He who drinks at them is certain of refreshment.

Homer's epic found no greater imitation than the *Aeneid*, the heroic poem of the Roman poet Publius Vergilius Maro (70–19 B.C.), born at Andes in the country near Mantua in northern Italy. He began the *Aeneid* in the year 29, a period which, as it were, called for such a poem. For over a hundred years Rome had been the scene of civil war, corruption, and unrest, until after the battle of Actium in the year 31 Octavian, later the Emperor Augustus, came to power and laid the foundations of a monarchy which ensured for Rome a few centuries of peace and prosperity. Rome breathed again and had time to reflect upon its past and present greatness. Temples and palaces were built, and art and letters found powerful patrons in Augustus and his minister Maecenas. Virgil, then forty years old, was a well-known figure in this literary circle, and partly at the suggestion of Augustus he glorified in his *Aeneid* Rome's greatness and its origin and past. The saga of Aeneas offered extremely suitable material. Aeneas was the son of Venus, a daughter of Jupiter, so that the family of the Julii (into which Augustus had been adopted) could pride itself on springing from Julus, the son of Aeneas, and through him from Venus and Jupiter himself. Virgil gave Rome its national epic upon which the youth of Rome was reared and in which every Roman could see a great present mirrored in a great past.

Virgil borrowed much from Homer. In the first half of the *Aeneid* he takes the *Odyssey* as his model, in the second the *Iliad*. The funeral games which are held on Sicily in honour of Anchises bear much resemblance to

461. Poet-singers travelled from one royal court to another, reciting their heroic poems. This is the world of Homer's epics.

those held for Patroclus in the *Iliad*. Aeneas' journey to the underworld is also strongly reminiscent of Book XI of the *Odyssey* in which Odysseus visits the abode of Hades. In addition, the reader of the *Aeneid* is reminded of Homer by many details and similes. In this respect Virgil does not differ from most of the Latin prose writers and poets, who were strongly influenced by Greece. It would however be both inaccurate and unjustifiable to consider Virgil merely as a talented imitator of Homer. Enriched and inspired by Homer, he has written a truly Roman work of art containing episodes which are entirely absent from Homer, such as the tragic love story of the Carthaginian queen Dido in Book IV. His hexameters, moreover, are magnificent, everywhere admired and nowhere surpassed. It is therefore not surprising that Dante, Petrarch, Torquato Tasso, Milton, Schiller, Vondel and many others should have admired Virgil and imitated his style. The undying quality of the *Aeneid* is proclaimed by Virgil himself at the close of the romantic adventure of Nisus and Euralyus, two youthful friends who offer their lives in the struggle. The poet ends the story of their heroic deed with the lines:

> *Blessed pair! If any power dwells in my verse,*
> *No day shall blot your name from mindful time,*
> *While on the Capitol's unshaken rock*
> *Aeneas' race still makes its home, while still*
> *Rome's father over Rome extends his sway.*

Upon his deathbed Virgil asked his friends to burn the manuscript of the *Aeneid*. Happily for mankind they ignored his request at Augustus' command.

DIDACTIC POETRY

Closely related to the epic is the poem intended for instruction, written in the same language and the same metre, the hexameter. Three names spring immediately to mind, one Greek and two Latin: Hesiod, Virgil, and Lucretius. Hesiod, a younger contemporary of Homer, a lesser poet certainly but none the less a rightly admired figure, was a farmer's son from Boeotia, reared in a humble, hard-working family. Besides the *Theogony*, an extensive genealogical work about the gods, he wrote a long didactic poem called *Works and Days*. The poet mentions the old myth of the Five Ages of the World. In the first or Golden Age men enjoyed perpetual happiness, without sickness or suffering, and died an easy death. The race of the Silver Age, after a promising youth, perished through impiety, that of the Bronze Age fell prey to war and mutual strife. The fourth generation was that of the heroes, which, after a heroic existence, was doomed to perish in war. The poet himself lived in the fifth, the Iron Age, weighed down by unwearying labour, menaced by care and trouble, when only daily effort and the avoidance of evil could make life bearable. Emphasis is laid upon agriculture. Hesiod enumerates the tasks of the farmer during the changing seasons, and adds numerous exhortations and precepts. The poem is sombre but charms by its sincerity and simple confidence in law and righteousness.

This work was the model for Virgil's *Georgics*, although there is no trace of real imitation. Urged by his friend Maecenas, Virgil wrote this poem on agriculture, which had fallen into decay through the civil wars: it was an occupation that was indispensable for the restoration of the state. The rehabilitation of husbandry could not have been better served than by the inspiring verses of a young poet already famous for his pastoral poetry (the *Eclogues*). Virgil divided his work into four Books. Each Book deals with a different subject, first arable farming, then tree growing, next cattle breeding, and finally beekeeping. Like Hesiod, Virgil exhorts the farmer to hard work and devotion to duty; but he surpasses his Greek predecessor in inspiration and poetic feeling. No less than in his later *Aeneid*, his verses captivate the ear by their magnificent ring.

More profound than either of these works upon agriculture is the poem of Lucretius (ca. 98–55 B.C.) 'On the Nature of Things' (*De Rerum Natura*). He was a disciple and admirer of the Greek philosopher Epicurus (ca. 300 B.C.), who sought human happiness in freedom from all sorrow and fear, above all from fear of the gods and of death. He taught that the universe, including the human body and soul, was mortal and composed of atoms. At death these atoms disintegrate and nothing remains. There is thus no cause to fear a hereafter. Lucretius eagerly propagated this doctrine by which he himself felt liberated. This passion often imparts to his verse an apostolic fire and a sense of lofty aspiration.

TRAGEDY

The genius of Greece is most fully seen in classic Attic tragedy, in which it could express itself simultaneously in word, song and mime, in an integrated 'drama' (literally a 'doing' or 'action'), not devised by human imagination but organically rooted in the cult of the god Dionysus and developed to record the life and suffering of heroic man. For Dionysus was not only the god of the vine. He was the god of the whole of nature, annually dying and being born again, the god of the eternal rhythm of life and death in which man too is caught up. In order to feel himself part of this natural process, man tries to raise himself above his ordinary, sober existence and in an ecstasy of wine, music, and dance, to feel himself one with the godhead. Man becomes beside himself (ecstasy), and feels the divine descending into him (enthusiasm). Man wishes to be for a time other than himself, and, disguised by a mask, he enacts in song and gesture the myth, the sacred story of the god. Already in the seventh century the dithyramb was sung, a choral song, alternating with a solo, dedicated to Dionysus. From this dithyramb tragedy gradually developed. One must assume that a need was felt for expansion and change. The enacting of the Dionysus story no longer sufficed, and other subjects were sought in the mythology of gods and heroes. Thus the dithyramb developed into the tragedy. The name tragedy (literally 'goat-song') still indicates its probable origin. The goat, symbol of fertility, was sacred to Dionysus, and the Dionysus singers sang their chorus dressed as goats, as satyrs. The name tragedy persisted even when all direct connection with Dionysus had been lost and the chorus of satyrs no longer appeared, although it was retained in the later, lighter satyric play which was usually performed in Athens as a fourth piece after the performance of a trilogy of tragedies.

To understand Greek tragedy one must realise the importance of the conception 'tragic' and the remarkable history of this word throughout the centuries. First applied to the satyr chorus dressed as goats or horses, it attained its most noble and fully developed expression in the tragedies of Aeschylus. What are 'tragic' and 'tragedy' in Greek drama? Among the ancients tragedy does not begin where suffering begins, but only where greater suffering than we can understand begins. This suffering, moreover, must not result from purely external circumstances, but must proceed from the nature of man himself. Aristotle said that the completely virtuous man, pursued by relentless adversity, is not a figure of tragedy. On the one hand man is subject to *moira*, blind fate, but as moral and religious consciousness deepens man has to assume

462. Earliest known portrait of Homer, on coin probably struck on the island of Ios in the second half of the 4th century. The poet is not yet portrayed as blind, as became customary in later times.

responsibility for his own actions and begins to relate conduct and fate. The doctrine of *moira*, logically thought out, cannot lead to tragedy, since man then acts according to a paralysing law of fatalism. Nor can tragedy arise from the idea that man determines his own fate by his conduct, since this leaves no place for suffering greater than we can understand. The conception of tragedy first arose from a fusion of these two conflicting ideas and attained its full majesty among the Greeks. Man is responsible for his own actions, but is nevertheless not able always to determine them himself or to predict the results arising from them. It is precisely the noble, heroic soul, exercising his humanity to the utmost, who is in danger of transgressing the limit. One step too far will bring about his downfall. He is struck by the thunderbolt of fate which passes by the common citizen. Tragic suffering always springs from some human defect, a fault, a delusion, a blind spot which brings about man's downfall and fills the spectator with fear and pity. This tragedy, with all its horror and impenetrability, has been immortalised by the Greeks in figures like Clytemnestra, Orestes, Oedipus, Antigone, and many others. They are driven on by pride, delusion, a sense of honour, and with a heavy heart we see them approach the abyss into which they will fall. It is characteristic that this fall is often sudden. In many tragedies the hero gradually climbs to a pinnacle, then suddenly crashes down. This crisis in the tragedy is called the *peripeteia*, the reversal of fortune. Tragedy in this sense generally forms the basis of the earlier dramas, but is more evident in some than in others – in the plays of Aeschylus and Sophocles more than in those of Euripides. The West has known four great tragedians, Shakespeare and three Athenians of the fifth century B.C. Each of the three Greeks can be said to represent a different period of this miraculous century. Aeschylus (525-456), the most forceful and powerful of the three, the creator of tragedy, is for us the symbol of that period in which the Athens of Miltiades and Themistocles fought its way forward, repelled Persia, and became a leading power. Sophocles (497-406), the pious and restrained poet, pursues his path of glory as tranquilly as Athens in the middle of the fifth century in the days of Pericles and Phidias. The doubt, disturbance, and discord of the end of this century are reflected in the works of the brilliant, sceptical, already somewhat decadent

figure of Euripides (480-406). Of roughly seventy tragedies which Aeschylus wrote, only seven have been preserved. The most famous are the *Persae*, *Prometheus*, and the *Oresteia*.

The *Persae*, produced in 472, is the only surviving historical play. It depicts the Persian court in 480, when King Xerxes has departed with his mighty army and fleet to bring Greece to subjection. This drama, in which a messenger and Xerxes himself in turn announce the destruction of the Persian fleet at Salamis, and which re-echoes with the doleful lamentation of king and chorus, must have deeply impressed the Athenians.

Prometheus has become for all time the prototype of the suffering rebellious spirit, who defies a higher and tyrannical power and protects mankind, to whom he gave fire and many other benefits. The *Prometheus* of Aeschylus inspired those of Goethe, Schlegel, Byron, and Shelley; it was also the model for an immortal song by Schubert to words by Goethe.

The *Oresteia* is the collective name of three connected tragedies, the only complete trilogy that we possess. They are, as it were, three acts of one mighty drama, produced in 458. The three tragedies are the *Agamemnon*, *Choephoroe*, and *Eumenides*. In the first play not Agamemnon, but Clytemnestra his wife, is the central figure. Love for her husband had turned to hate when, ten years before, on the departure of the Greek fleet to Troy, he sacrificed their daughter Iphigenia to his ambition. She is determined to avenge her wounded love by killing Agamemnon on his return, with the aid of her lover Aegisthus. The fall of Troy is announced in Argos by fire signals, and soon the triumphant Agamemnon appears upon the scene with his retinue and the prophetess Cassandra, daughter of Priam. He ascends the steps of his palace on a blood-red carpet, and is greeted by his wife with feigned joy. After he has entered his palace, quickly followed by Cassandra, cries are heard from within, the doors open, and Clytemnestra appears with a blood-stained sword in her hand; on either side lie the bodies of Agamemnon and Cassandra. Clytemnestra stands there as the symbol of vengeance, as a being of supernatural greatness and power. In icy calm she had accomplished the deed of cruel justice which will lead to her own tragic fall and that of Aegisthus. At the end of the play the chorus asks:

Ah, does Orestes still behold the light,
That with propitious fortune he may come,
And in full victory destroy this pair?

These words introduce the second drama, the *Choephoroe*, in which Orestes avenges his father by killing his mother. Eighteen years are presumed to have elapsed between the two plays. Orestes, who was still a child at the time of his father's death and was safely smuggled by his sister Electra to a neighbouring royal house, has now attained manhood. At Apollo's command he returns to Argos to kill his mother. This is required by the justice of the blood-feud. Anyone ignoring this demand has not paid what he owes to the shade of the murdered person and lives under a curse so long as he has not avenged his death. This idea of retribution determines Orestes' tragic fate and compels him to kill his own mother. The tragic situation is here complete – in the one case guilt towards the father, in the other towards the mother. No matter what he does, short-sighted man cannot escape guilt and destruction. Despite heroic deeds he remains subject to the eternal and mighty power of fate. Orestes' punishment will be madness, which seizes him as soon as the blood of his mother sticks to his hands, and, his deed accomplished, he realises its full horror. Doubt and restlessness destroy his confidence in himself; he is possessed by an overpowering fear. He feels himself pursued by the goddesses of vengeance, the Erinyes, and, driven by these same Furies, he flees from the stage. In the third drama, the *Eumenides*, this idea of retribution is condemned. Aeschylus expresses the more humane attitude of his time which abandons the old idea of vengeance, the stern law which merely added one crime to another. The avenger no longer himself kills the murderer but brings him to justice. If the court acquits him, the curse of the blood guilt is broken. Thus it happens with Orestes. By the intervention of Apollo and Athena he stands trial before a court of twelve judges upon the Areopagus in Athens. The Erinyes accuse him, Apollo defends him. Neither of the two parties is in the right, but both are justified from their own point of view. This is established by the fact that, in the verdict, there are six votes for him and six against. Divine intervention, now the only possible solution, comes with Athena's vote for his acquittal. There exists a forgiveness above the letter of the law. The Erinyes may not depart as wronged justice. They remain the symbol of the punishment of human guilt, but at the same time of a salutary and blessed power. The Erinyes, spirits of vengeance, become indeed the Eumenides, goddesses of good. This trilogy is the poet's finest achievement. It displays to the full his great range: loftiness of theme, profundity, poetical genius.

Aeschylus, the greatest of the three tragedians, was not the favourite of his contemporaries. This was the privilege of Sophocles, the darling of the Muses. With his more than one hundred and twenty tragedies, performed in groups of four, he won the first prize twenty-four times and never fell lower than second. It is understandable that the Athenians felt themselves closer to Sophocles than to Aeschylus. In Aeschylus, the main characters were either gods or people of almost supernatural power; Sophocles transported the spectators to the more normal world of men, the world of kings and princesses and warrior heroes. The number of actors was increased, the plot became more subtle and more tense. Of Sophocles, too, seven plays have been preserved, famous plays such as *Electra*, *Oedipus Rex*, *Antigone*. The last two draw on the mythical history of the Theban royal house, which also lived under a curse similar to that which destroyed the Pelopidae, the family of Agamemnon and Orestes. Oedipus, king of Thebes and beloved by his people, attempts to conciliate the anger of the gods and to free his city from a plague. To do this he must find the murderer of the former king, Laius, and banish him from the city. Gradually he discovers that he himself unwittingly killed Laius, that Laius was his father, and that, equally unwittingly, he has married his own mother and had children by her. On realising this he blinds himself and goes into exile. The structure of this tragedy is excellent, the sequence of events leading step by step to the dénouement. The characterisation is also first-rate. It is more a drama of human error than of human guilt, but guilt is not absent. The king has killed his father and married his mother; but he has done so in ignorance. Fate, and the curse of his house, bring about his downfall. The illusion of power and happiness in which he lives is shattered and the wise and honoured ruler becomes a wretched, cursed exile. The course of his life and its fatal turn are extremely moving, a warning example to every man who thinks himself happy. The chorus makes this clear in the last lines of the play:

> *See, this is Oedipus,*
> . . . .
> *Whose fortunes all the citizens beheld*
> *With envy! Into what a dire abyss*
> *Of sorrows has he fallen! Therefore call*
> *No mortal happy till you have beheld*
> *That final day when having passed the bourne*
> *Of life he is beyond the reach of pain.*

Towards the end of his long life of almost ninety years, Sophocles again made Oedipus the hero of a tragedy, the *Oedipus Coloneus*. It is as though the poet could not resign himself to the tragic fate of the noble Oedipus. This last play tells how the blind king, accompanied by his daughter Antigone, dies a mysterious death in Colonus, a village in Attica, in the presence of Theseus, king of Athens.

The curse upon the Theban royal house is not ended by the death of Oedipus. His children too are stricken. His two sons, Eteocles and Polynices, quarrel over the throne of Thebes. Polynices is driven out by his brother. He assembles an army abroad and, together with six other chieftains, takes the field against his own native city. The attack is repulsed. The two brothers kill each other in single combat and their uncle Creon becomes ruler. Under pain of death he forbids anyone to bury the body of the traitor Polynices which lies outside the city gate. This is the prologue to one of Sophocles' finest plays, the *Antigone*. The stern interdiction of Creon – according to the ancient Greeks the soul of the unburied finds no rest in the other world – is deliberately ignored by Antigone. There exist higher, divine laws which for Antigone prevail against a royal command. She steals out of the city at night and casts earth upon the body of her brother (a symbol of burial which satisfied ritual). Led before Creon, she avows and defends her action. Despite the appeals of his son Haemon, Antigone's betrothed, she is cast into a vault to await death. When however Tiresias, the blind soothsayer, goes to Creon and warns him of the anger of the gods at the pollution occasioned by the unburied body, Creon submits; he allows Polynices to be buried and orders Antigone to be set free. It is too late. She has already committed suicide, and his own son Haemon has killed himself. Creon's queen also stabs herself from grief. The king leaves the stage a broken man. The characters of Creon and Antigone are drawn with a master hand. Both are in the right to a certain degree, both are

guilty, both are 'tragic'. Creon fights for the rights of the state and is implacable towards the traitor who has violated them. Antigone obeys the dictates of her heart, the voice of her conscience. She would rather die than disobey the eternal, divine law of fraternal love and charity. Both are guilty of pride and obstinacy, both are figures of tragic grandeur. Antigone especially, in appearance a weak girl, yet possessing self-sacrificing courage and moral strength, is an unforgettable figure.

Euripides (480–406) was only a slightly younger contemporary of Sophocles. There is, however, an almost incomprehensible distance between these two tragedians. Intellectual development was rapid in the Athens of the fifth century, and it was thus possible for a wide breach to exist between a poet who was little affected by the trends of his time, like Sophocles, and his up-to-date contemporaries, many of whom were men of advanced ideas about religion and philosophy; they had a different attitude to life, and had abandoned the ancient belief in gods and heroes and the old, aristocratic way of life. Euripides shared these views. He was an advanced spirit, undoubtedly less gifted as an artist than his two predecessors, but possessing a more penetrating mind, a more sensitive nature, a more democratic and liberal outlook. Sophocles had already written of men, instead of gods and heroes, but only of the great ones of the earth—kings, queens and those of exceptional gifts. Euripides was the first to deal with society as a whole. In his tragedies not only kings, but also slaves, nurses, shepherds, and children appear. Nor is their rôle confined to walking on or bearing messages; they are thinking beings with an inner life of their own. He was consequently reproached with lowering the dignity of tragedy. This reproach is sometimes justified; but what the drama lost in dignity, it gained in greater appeal, humanity, and a wider range.

Euripides was a great judge of human nature. He was especially interested in the evil, morbid, sometimes almost demented inclinations of the human heart, above all of the female heart. The spectator witnesses with horror Medea's lust for revenge when, to avenge herself upon Jason, she murders their two children, and the fierce hatred of Electra for her mother Clytemnestra. Euripides was also the first to understand and portray the devouring, reckless passion which can afflict women, most vividly in the figure of Phaedra in the tragedy of *Hippolytus*, performed in 428. Hippolytus is the son of Theseus, king of Athens. Euripides portrays him as an upright young man, chaste, averse to all sensual love. He is an ascetic by choice, a follower not of Aphrodite, but of Artemis, the virgin goddess of the chase. When he reaches manhood his father marries again with Phaedra, a Cretan princess, who is about the same age as Hippolytus. Phaedra is seized by a burning love for her stepson. Everything about this woman is lovesick; she is demented, pale, and restless; she cannot sleep, she can neither eat nor drink; she is tormented by a frenzied desire which can find no satisfaction. In a moving scene she tells her need to her nurse, who cannot understand the depth of her mistress's feelings and exhorts her in vain to be calm. Her love, repulsed by Hippolytus with coldness and disgust, turns to a hate and bitterness, which Hippolytus' narrow-minded and impassive uprightness makes understandable. So it comes about that this woman, who is about to die for her love, decides upon a vile course of action. In a letter to Theseus she accuses Hippolytus of an attempt upon her honour and afterwards hangs herself in the palace. When Theseus returns and stands beside the body of his wife, he sees the letter grasped in her hand. He believes what he sees written there and, filled with anger and scorn for his hypocritical son, he prays his father Poseidon to kill Hippolytus. Poseidon frightens the horses of Hippolytus who is driving on the sea-shore; he is thrown from his chariot and carried home mortally injured. Artemis then descends from heaven and reveals to Theseus the truth and the innocence of his son, who dies in his father's arms. Although Hippolytus becomes the innocent victim of circumstance, Phaedra is and remains the central figure in this drama. She is a woman, noble-hearted by nature, but the victim of a fierce passion against which the only defence is her own conscience. She has no belief in the gods or any higher power to sustain her. The poet shows us how lonely and defenceless a human being can be when faced with the storms of life; he himself no longer found consolation in the gods.

Euripides was a many-sided spirit, at once thinker and poet. He served the Graces as well as the Muses, the goddesses of beauty as well as the goddesses of truth and knowledge. He was not always successful in keeping peace with both, but these lines from one of the choruses in his *Hercules Furens* show that this was his dearest wish:

> *Never will I desist from linking up*
> *Graces and Muses in fair fellowship.*
> *Without the Muses may I never live,*
> *But ever by their wreaths encompassed be!*

COMEDY.

In its original meaning the word 'drama' (a thing done or acted) applied not only to tragedy but also to comedy, likewise a creation of fifth-century Athens. Aristophanes (ca. 450–388) is the name of the brilliant author of some forty comedies of which eleven have survived. These plays provide us with an inexhaustible source of information about everyday life in the Athens of that time, and, to some extent, make up for the lack of other sources such as the newspaper, magazine, town-council report, or contemporary novel. The Old Comedy of Aristophanes mirrors the daily life of his century, above all its shortcomings and weaknesses. Politics and politicians, current events, war and peace, female suffrage, the education of the young, religion, literature, the famous personalities of the city – all these find their place in comedy, and whenever they incur the author's disfavour are held up to derision, a derision both merciless and frank. It would appear that on the Athenian stage no comment was too vulgar or too virulent to be made about either the living or the dead; the poet's humour and exuberance carried the audience with him.

Like tragedy, comedy comprised two component parts: chorus and play. In tragedy the chorus had retired increasingly into the background. In the earliest plays of Aeschylus, developed from the dithyramb, the chorus was the principal element, and even in the *Oresteia* the chorus plays an important rôle. Gradually, first in Sophocles, and to a greater degree in Euripides, action and dialogue gained in prominence while the chorus lost much of its significance. Aristophanes restored it to honour. This can be seen from the mere fact that many of his plays are called after the chorus: *The Birds, The Clouds, The Wasps, The Frogs,* and others. Only in his last plays does the chorus lose some of its importance. The hero occupies a special place in comedy, side by side with the chorus, and he is a very special sort of hero. The tragic heroes, no matter how great and powerful, were restricted by their humanity. The comic hero, on the other hand, is conscious of no restriction. He descends to the Underworld, crosses the Styx, flies to heaven on a dung-beetle, builds a city in the clouds. He triumphs over everything, he is a hero of laughter and folly. Yet this exuberance and fun are a cloak for gravity and seriousness. Aristophanes admired the *ancien régime* and hated demagogues like Cleon who persisted in continuing the war with Sparta. In his plays he wished to warn the Athenians, but was obliged to conceal his warnings under a layer of jokes if he wished to be heard. After all, his audience came to be amused. He knew, however, that laughter is capable of serving truth. A clear example is given in his play *The Peace*, performed in 421. An Attic farmer, tired of the miseries of war, mounts a dung-beetle and flies to heaven to ask Zeus to restore peace to Athens. When this does not succeed, with the help of his friends he frees the statue of the goddess of peace from the cave in which it is shut up and brings it in triumphal procession home to his city. The play is a comical and forcible plea for peace with Sparta, one of the most passionate desires of the poet. Peace was indeed concluded in that same year, the short-lived Peace of Nicias. The same underlying seriousness is to be found in the action of *The Birds*. The hero of this play founds in the realm of the birds and clouds a better fatherland, Cloudcuckooland, where he escapes the irritations of his earthly existence.

Aristophanes' characters are never types. On the contrary, his heroes overstep all conventions and cannot possibly represent anyone but themselves. Types appear for the first time in the New Comedy, of which Menander (ca. 343–292) is the foremost representative. Hitherto only fragments of his work have survived, but now we have a complete play, the newly discovered *Dyscolos* or *The Peevish Man*. New Comedy is also illustrated by the work of his Roman successors, the famous comic writers Plautus (254–184) and Terence (190–159). New Comedy undoubtedly reached Rome by way of the Greek cities in southern Italy. In the third and second centuries B.C. the Roman populace came into ever-increasing contact with these cities as a result of growing trade and especially through the Punic Wars, which drew thousands of Roman soldiers to southern Italy. The earliest Latin comedies were translations or adaptations from the Greek; the actors wore Greek costumes and the scene was set in a Greek city, usually Athens. The stage properties were extremely simple: a tent for the spectators with a screen background consisting of two houses with an alleyway or temple in between, easily mounted and dismantled. With these the leader of the troop (sometimes the author of the play), travelled through the country. Plautus travelled in this manner with his fair tent and made a name for himself by producing his own plays. Of these we possess roughly twenty. His characters are fixed types: the miser, the old father, the good and the prodigal son, the respectable girl and the cocotte, the greedy cook, the sponger and flatterer, the slave-trader, the cunning and resourceful slave. They wore a conventional mask with a white wig for the old men, a black wig for the young men, and a red wig for slaves. Convention also demanded that the right-hand exit should lead to the market, that on the left to the country or the harbour. The attraction of Plautus' comedies lies not in their logical construction of dramatic dénouement but in their *vis comica*, their comic thrust, their easy flow, the humour and speed of the various scenes, the freshness of language, the play upon words and the comic situation. Many of his plays inspired later writers: the *Aulularia* gave Molière the idea for his *Avare* and Hooft for his *Warenar*. Molière based his *Amphitryon* upon the *Amphitryo*, and Shakespeare's *Comedy of Errors* derives from the *Menaechmi*. Lessing took his *Der Schatz* from the *Trinummus*.

The literary legacy of Terence consists of six comedies. He was an African slave, bought and educated by a Roman senator. His plays lack the freshness and telling humour of Plautus, but excel in construction and literary form. In Terence the plot develops gradually and logically and leads to an exciting dénouement. His characters are also drawn with more care and greater psychological insight. The many quotations borrowed from his plays by later writers still testify to his knowledge of the human heart and to his worldly wisdom, especially evident in *The Brothers*. In this play two methods of education and their results are contrasted in a masterly and humorous fashion, that of the excessively stern and the excessively lenient father. His other plays are also rich in wisdom, and he possesses a fascinating style of narration.

THE LYRIC

Even in the very earliest times the Greeks were familiar with the song sung to the lyre. In the *Iliad* Homer tells how the ambassadors sent by Agamemnon find Achilles playing the sweetly-sounding lyre and celebrating the glorious deeds of the heroes; how the sons of the Greeks honour Apollo by their playing and song; how song re-echoes at the wedding feast; how at the vintage a boy accompanies his plaintive song upon the lyre. At all important events – birth, death, funeral, marriage, banquets, harvest, religious ceremonies – songs are sung, accompanied by the flute or the lyre, A distinction can be made between the sung and the spoken lyric. The metre of the sung lyric was extremely varied, and we only possess two forms of the spoken lyric, elegiac and iambic poetry. The elegy is a poem composed of distichs; a distich or couplet consists of two lines of verse, first a hexameter and second a pentameter. We possess only fragments of the work of the earliest elegiac poets.

We have, dating from the seventh century, some of the war songs of the Spartan Tyrtaeus and the love songs of Mimnermus of Colophon, and from the sixth century the didactic verses of the Athenian Solon and the drinking songs of Theognis of Megara. During the Hellenistic period (third century B.C.) Callimachus of Cyrene achieved fame by his prose and poetry (including elegiacs). He exercised a strong influence upon the Latin poets, especially Catullus and Ovid. The most important exponent of iambic poetry in the seventh century was Archilochus of Paros. His poems deal with many different themes: war, wine, fables, the personal life of the poet, all of which mark them as true lyrics.

For the sung lyric we must turn to Lesbos, an island which produced three great poets: the more or less legendary figure of Arion who lived in the seventh century and introduced the dithyramb to the court of Corinth, and two poets of the sixth century, Sappho and Alcaeus. Sappho, the most famous Greek poetess, gathered about her on Lesbos a group of young girls. With them she sang and danced in the cult of Aphrodite and the Muses. Great affection reigned among this group; in a hymn to Aphrodite Sappho expresses her sorrow that one of her pupils has left the circle. The first and last verses of this poem are:

> *Immortal child of Zeus, with rich-wrought throne,*
> *Weaver of subtle guile, I pray to you.*
> *Do not with sorrow and with moan*
> *My heart subdue.*
>
> *Come then and free me once again from woe!*
> *Fulfil for me my heart's desire, O Queen;*
> *Be my ally, as long ago*
> *You still have been!*

Of Alcaeus' poetry only fragments remain; they are also divided into verses. The metre of these two poets was repeatedly adopted by later writers, especially Horace.

Anacreon too was a famous lyric poet. He was born in Teos, off the coast of Asia Minor, about 570 B.C. For a time he lived at the court of Polycrates, tyrant of Samos, and later at other Greek courts. He composed many types of poetry: love songs, drinking songs, and hymns. Very little has survived; this is perhaps one of the reasons why many poems in a lighter genre were attributed to him in later centuries, the so-called Anacreontica. One of the most beautiful is given here:

> *O cricket, it is plain to see*
> *How happy this your life must be.*
> *When you had sipped a little dew*
> *To the tree's topmost bough you flew,*
> *And sitting there you now do sing,*
> *As blithe and merry as a king.*
> *Indeed, all things belong to you,*
> *All such as in the fields you view,*
> *And all to which the woods give birth.*
> *Honour to you men of this earth*
> *Pay, harbinger of summer days!*

And all the Muses sing your praise,
And Phoebus also holds you dear –
He it was gave you voice so clear.
Old age on you can work no wrong,
Wise, earthborn devotee of song;
Without pain, without blood – not far
From the estate of gods you are!

Pindar (ca. 578–438) occupies a very special place. He was born in Thebes of an ancient, noble Dorian family. Himself an aristocrat, he became the singer of the aristocracy in the last period of its power when, with the Persian Wars and the rise of Athens, democracy and the ideal of liberty began to triumph everywhere in Greece. Pindar ignored all this. His gaze was fixed upon the aristocratic past, and this alone he chose as the subject of his verse. He celebrated it in hymns, songs of praise and poems of several other types of which only short fragments have been preserved. The only complete poems we possess are more than forty victory songs, composed in honour of the victors in the Pythian Games at Delphi, the Isthmian at Corinth, the Nemean in Argolis, and the Olympic at Olympia. For centuries these games had been the privilege of the aristocracy. They alone had the time and money to practise for months in order to gain the prize in wrestling and on the race-track. In Pindar's poems the competition itself is merely secondary; he glorifies the noble victor as the representative of the ancient nobility and of a glorious past, but also as the man who honours the gods by his performance, the god in whose honour the games are held. He often incorporates in his poems instructive myths from a distant past which he interprets with words of wisdom and moral precept. Despite its beauty of language and distinction of subject, this poetry never became popular. There were two reasons for this: it was much too difficult and also too conservative and retrospective to satisfy later generations which eagerly looked to a new society.

Latin lyric poetry is represented by only two great writers: Gaius Valerius Catullus (84–54 B.C.) and Quintus Horatius Flaccus (65–8 B.C.). The Romans, even the poets, were more preoccupied with the state than with the individual, with practical matters and the community than with their own inner life. Unlike the Greeks, they were not accustomed to give expression to their most intimate feelings and emotions. Cicero called the lyric poets professional triflers and said that, even were he to live twice his allotted span he would have no time to read their works. This judgment may hold good for many Latin lyric poets of less value, and precisely on this account Catullus' work is the more striking.

Born in Verona, he settled in Rome at an early age and became one of a circle of young up-to-date poets, imitators of Callimachus and other Alexandrian writers, scornfully called by Cicero *cantores Euphorionis*, the singers of Euphorion, a poet of Alexandria. The book-learning and exaggerated verse technique of the Alexandrians in no way heightened the poetic value or lyric flow of their verses. Even Catullus is not immune from these faults, but he usually avoids any display of erudition. His poems glow with the emotion of a youthful, sensitive poetic soul. In his songs he reveals himself as one of the world's greatest lyric poets – his drinking songs, satirical songs, elegies, and above all in his love songs dedicated to Clodia, called Lesbia in the poems. The expression of the joys and sorrows of this love is extremely appealing, a purely poetic lyricism hitherto unknown in Latin literature.

One seeks in vain the emotional fire of the young Catullus (he died at the age of thirty) in the lyric poetry of Horace. This is perhaps because Horace was already thirty-five before he began to write, but also because he was of a completely different temperament. He was sober and staid in his judgments, opposed to any form of excess. There is another difference besides temperament: their choice of metre. Horace consciously avoided the Alexandrian models beloved of Catullus. He admired the classical Greek lyricists, Archilochus, Alcaeus, and Sappho, and prided himself on being the first Roman to employ the Aeolian song and the metres of Alcaeus and Sappho. This he did in four books of *Odes* (*Carmina*), of which Book 4 was published ten years later than the first three. Horace considered this his most important achievement. In the first ode of Book I he says that his greatest reward will be to be accounted among the lyric singers, and the last ode in Book III begins with the words: 'I have erected a monument more lasting than bronze.'

The subjects of the odes vary considerably. They contain many wise lessons: seek the golden mean; riches do not bring happiness; remember that life is short and transitory and death waits for all; enjoy the simple gifts of nature, avoid luxury; an easy conscience is the greatest treasure. He wrote patriotic songs, drinking songs, love songs, he celebrated quiet country life, he glorified Augustus' rule. His style is lapidary, his verse smooth, eloquent, and memorable; no poet has been more quoted, even to the present day. Besides odes he also wrote epodes, mostly in the iambic metre. Among these is the famous '*Beatus ille*' a glorification of country life with an ironical conclusion in which the person who has sung of nature with such enthusiasm reveals himself as a confirmed usurer. Horace also wrote in hexameters, both Satires and Epistles. He is one of those poets whose fame has endured in many lands, not least in England.

A few words more on the subject of the Roman elegy. Three names are worthy of mention: Albius Tibullus, Sextus Propertius (both born ca. 50 B.C.), and Publius Ovidius Naso (43 B.C. – A.D. 17). In his elegies Tibullus celebrated mainly love and country life; his verses are simple, without artifice, and with him the elegy attained a high degree of perfection. Propertius' love story in elegiac verse for his beloved Cynthia gives proof of passion and great talent, although his poetry is sometimes marred by learned allusions.

Ovid, however, was certainly Rome's most important elegiac poet. This is evident from the varied nature of his work. Besides love elegies (*Amores, Ars Amatoria, Remedia Amoris*), he wrote a collection of letters in the elegiac

463. It is still possible to use some of the ancient theatres. Scene showing the appearance of a chorus during a modern performance of the *Oedipus Rex* of the tragedian Sophocles in the still largely-intact theatre of Delphi (→ 147, 151). The orchestra, the area in front of the actors, is not entirely circular at Delphi as it is at Epidaurus (→ 467). By the orchestra was placed the scaena, a structure covered with wood, from which the actors entered the stage and to which they retired from it. This scaena was absent from the earliest theatres. The outlook over the valley of the Plistus was not so extensive for ancient as for modern spectators, being impeded by the temple of Apollo (→ 151).

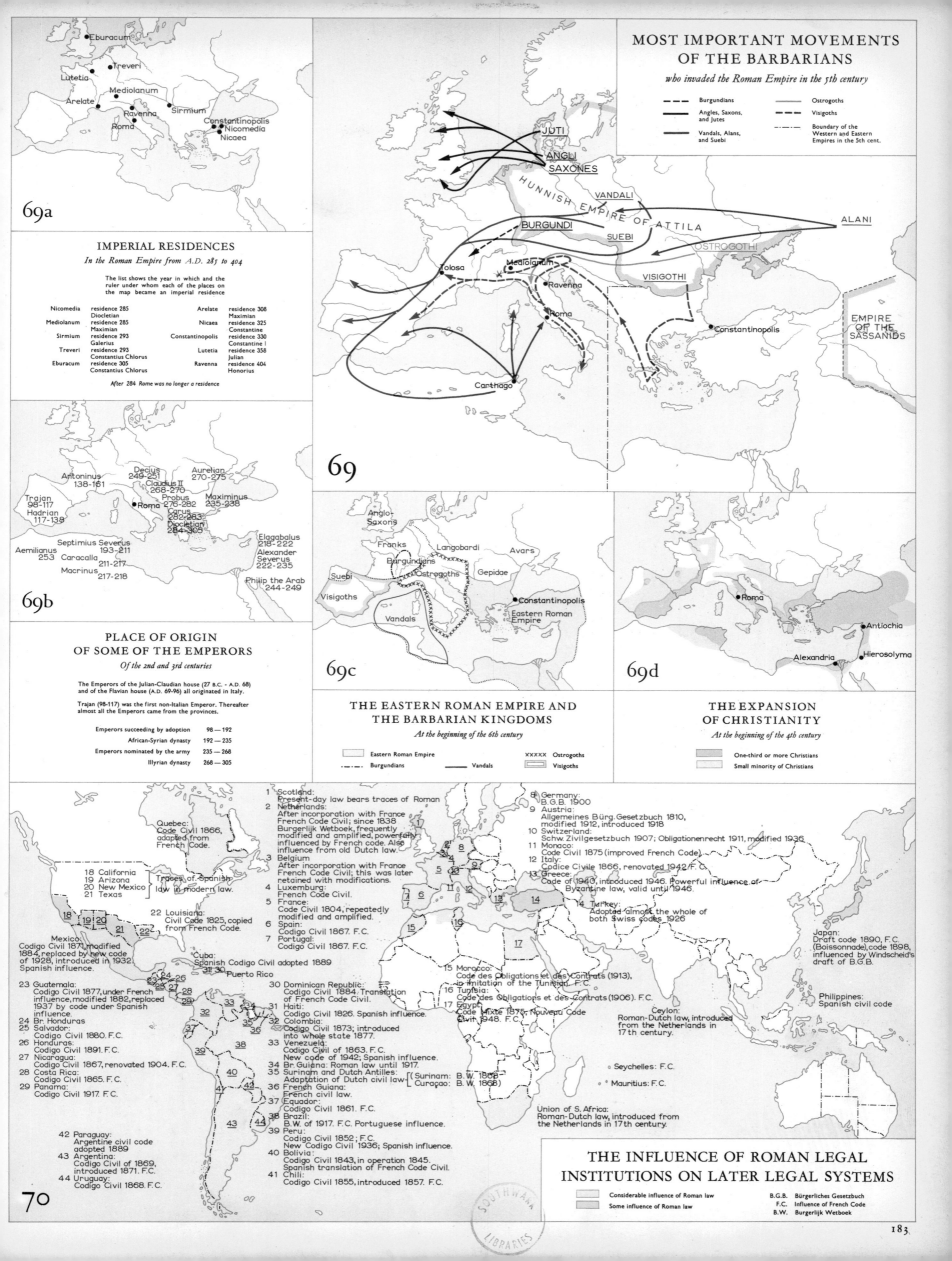

69a

IMPERIAL RESIDENCES
In the Roman Empire from A.D. 285 to 404

The list shows the year in which and the ruler under whom each of the places on the map became an imperial residence

Nicomedia	residence 285 Diocletian	Arelate	residence 308 Maximian
Mediolanum	residence 285 Maximian	Nicaea	residence 325 Constantine
Sirmium	residence 293 Galerius	Constantinopolis	residence 330 Constantine I
Treveri	residence 293 Constantius Chlorus	Lutetia	residence 358 Julian
Eburacum	residence 305 Constantius Chlorus	Ravenna	residence 404 Honorius

After 284 Rome was no longer a residence

69b

PLACE OF ORIGIN OF SOME OF THE EMPERORS
Of the 2nd and 3rd centuries

The Emperors of the Julian-Claudian house (27 B.C. - A.D. 68) and of the Flavian house (A.D. 69-96) all originated in Italy.

Trajan (98-117) was the first non-Italian Emperor. Thereafter almost all the Emperors came from the provinces.

Emperors succeeding by adoption	98 — 192
African-Syrian dynasty	192 — 235
Emperors nominated by the army	235 — 268
Illyrian dynasty	268 — 305

69

MOST IMPORTANT MOVEMENTS OF THE BARBARIANS
who invaded the Roman Empire in the 5th century

- Burgundians
- Angles, Saxons, and Jutes
- Vandals, Alans, and Suebi
- Ostrogoths
- Visigoths
- Boundary of the Western and Eastern Empires in the 5th cent.

69c

THE EASTERN ROMAN EMPIRE AND THE BARBARIAN KINGDOMS
At the beginning of the 6th century

- Eastern Roman Empire
- Burgundians
- Vandals
- Ostrogoths
- Visigoths

69d

THE EXPANSION OF CHRISTIANITY
At the beginning of the 4th century

- One-third or more Christians
- Small minority of Christians

70

1 Scotland: Present-day law bears traces of Roman
2 Netherlands: After incorporation with France French Code Civil; since 1838 Burgerlijk Wetboek, frequently modified and amplified, powerfully influenced by French code. Also influence from old Dutch law.
3 Belgium After incorporation with France French Code Civil; this was later retained with modifications.
4 Luxemburg: French Code Civil.
5 France: Code Civil 1804, repeatedly modified and amplified.
6 Spain: Codigo Civil 1867. F.C.
7 Portugal: Codigo Civil 1867. F.C.

8 Germany: B.G.B. 1900
9 Austria: Allgemeines Bürg. Gesetzbuch 1810, modified 1912, introduced 1918
10 Switzerland: Schw. Zivilgesetzbuch 1907; Obligationenrecht 1911, modified 1936
11 Monaco: Code Civil 1875 (improved French Code)
12 Italy: Codice Civile 1866, renovated 1942. F.C.
13 Greece: Code of 1940, introduced 1946. Powerful influence of Byzantine law, valid until 1946.
14 Turkey: Adopted almost the whole of both Swiss codes, 1926

15 Morocco: Code des Obligations et des Contrats (1913), in imitation of the Tunisian F.C.
16 Tunisia: Code des Obligations et des Contrats (1906). F.C.
17 Egypt: Code Mixte 1875; Nouveau Code Civil 1948. F.C.

Ceylon: Roman-Dutch law, introduced from the Netherlands in 17th century.

Japan: Draft code 1890, F.C. (Boissonnade), code 1898, influenced by Windscheid's draft of B.G.B.

Philippines: Spanish civil code

Quebec: Code Civil 1866, adapted from French Code.

18 California
19 Arizona
20 New Mexico
21 Texas
Traces of Spanish law in modern law.

22 Louisiana: Civil Code 1825, copied from French Code.

Mexico: Codigo Civil 1871, modified 1884, replaced by new code of 1928, introduced in 1932, Spanish influence.

Cuba: Spanish Codigo Civil adopted 1889
Puerto Rico

23 Guatemala: Codigo Civil 1877, under French influence, modified 1882, replaced 1937 by code under Spanish influence.
24 Br. Honduras
25 Salvador: Codigo Civil 1880. F.C.
26 Honduras: Codigo Civil 1891. F.C.
27 Nicaragua: Codigo Civil 1867, renovated 1904. F.C.
28 Costa Rica: Codigo Civil 1865. F.C.
29 Panama: Codigo Civil 1917. F.C.

30 Dominican Republic: Codigo Civil 1884. Translation of French Code Civil.
31 Haiti: Codigo Civil 1826. Spanish influence.
32 Colombia: Codigo Civil 1873; introduced into whole state 1877.
33 Venezuela: Codigo Civil of 1863. F.C. New code of 1942; Spanish influence.
34 Br. Guiana: Roman law until 1917.
35 Surinam and Dutch Antilles: Adaptation of Dutch civil law.
36 French Guiana: French civil law.
37 Ecuador: Codigo Civil 1861. F.C.
38 Brazil: B.W. of 1917. F.C. Portuguese influence.
39 Peru: Codigo Civil 1852. F.C. New Codigo Civil 1936; Spanish influence.
40 Bolivia: Codigo Civil 1843, in operation 1845. Spanish translation of French Code Civil.
41 Chili: Codigo Civil 1855, introduced 1857. F.C.

42 Paraguay: Argentine civil code adopted 1889
43 Argentina: Codigo Civil of 1869, introduced 1871. F.C.
44 Uruguay: Codigo Civil 1868. F.C.

Surinam: B. W. 1868
Curaçao: B. W. 1868

Seychelles: F.C.

Mauritius: F.C.

Union of S. Africa: Roman-Dutch law, introduced from the Netherlands in 17th century.

THE INFLUENCE OF ROMAN LEGAL INSTITUTIONS ON LATER LEGAL SYSTEMS

- Considerable influence of Roman law
- Some influence of Roman law
- B.G.B. Bürgerliches Gesetzbuch
- F.C. Influence of French Code
- B.W. Burgerlijk Wetboek

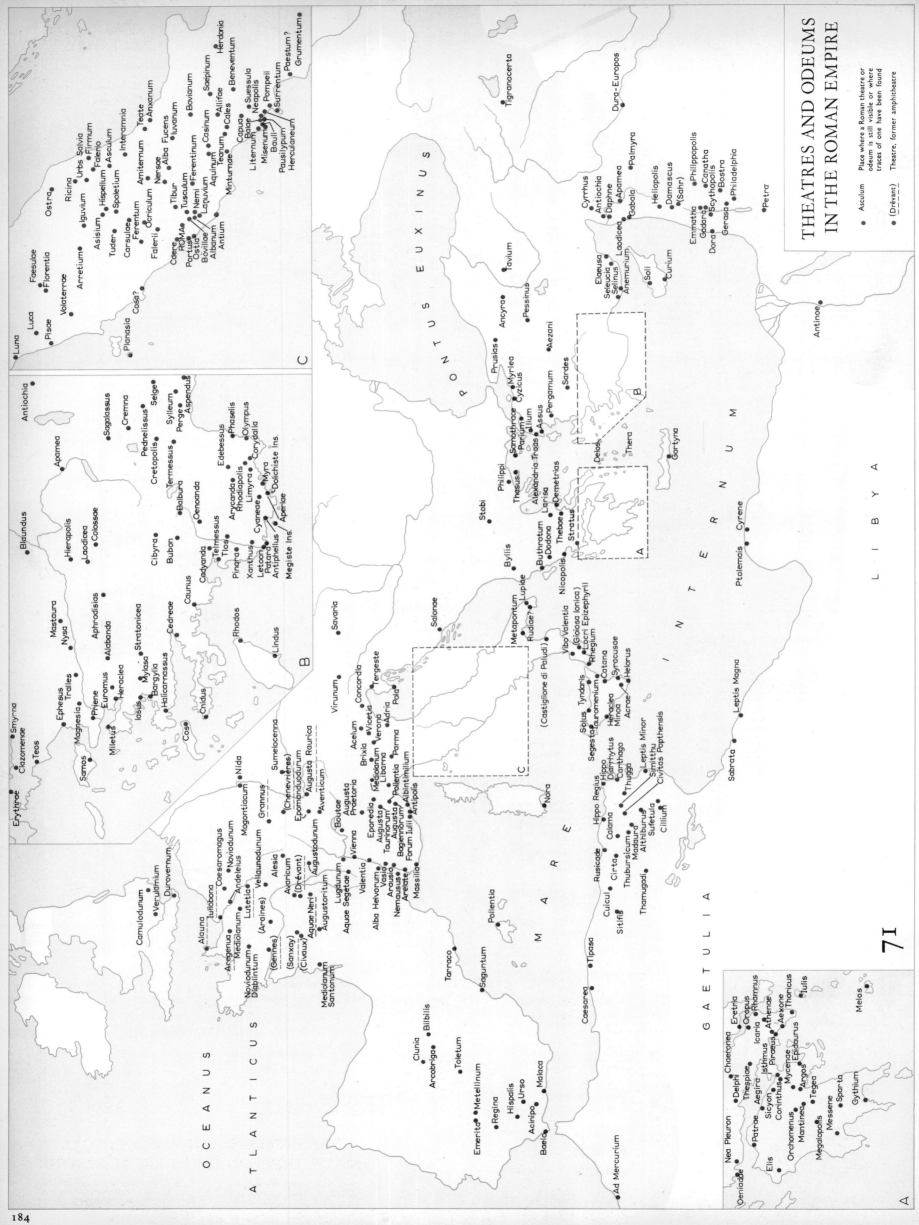

THEATRES AND ODEUMS
IN THE ROMAN EMPIRE

• Place where a Roman theatre or
  odeum is still visible or where
  traces of one have been found

(Drévant) Theatre, former amphitheatre

71

Map labels

OCEANUS ATLANTICUS

MARE INTERNUM

PONTUS EUXINUS

LIBYA

GAETULIA

Inset A (lower left)

Oeniadae
Nea Pleuron
Elis
Potroe
Delphi
Chaeronea
Orchomenus
Thespiae
Sicyon
Aegira
Isthmus
Corinthus
Mantinea
Megalopolis
Mycenae
Argos
Messene
Tegea
Sparta
Gythium
Eretria
Oropus
Rhamnus
Icaria
Athenae
Piraeus
Aexone
Thoricus
Iulis
Melos

Inset B (right)

Antiochia
Apamea
Blaundus
Hierapolis
Laodicea
Colosse
Sagalassus
Cremna
Pednelissus
Selge
Sylleum
Perge
Aspendus
Temessus
Cretopolis
Edebessus
Phaselis
Olympus
Corydalla
Balbura
Oenoanda
Aryconda
Rhodiapolis
Limyra
Myra
Dolichiste Ins.
Cibyra
Bubon
Telmessus
Cyaneae
Letoon
Apenae
Cadyanda
Tlos
Patara
Antiphellus
Xanthus
Pinara
Megiste Ins.
Mastaura
Aphrodisias
Nysa
Alabanda
Stratonicea
Cedreae
Caunus
Rhodos
Lindus
Smyrna
Ephesus
Tralles
Magnesia
Priene
Euromus
Heraclea
Mylasa
Iasus
Bargylia
Halicarnassus
Cos
Cnidus
Erythrae
Clazomenae
Teos
Samos

Inset C (upper right)

Luna
Luca
Foesulae
Florentia
Pisae
Volaterrae
Arretium
Planasia
Cosa?
Ostra
Ricina
Iguvium
Urbs Salvia
Firmum
Falerio
Asculum
Asisium
Hispellum
Spoletium
Interamnia
Tuder
Carsulae
Amiternum
Tecte
Anxanum
Ferentum
Ocriculum
Nersae
Alba Fucens
Iuvanum
Tibur
Tusculum
Bovianum
Nemi
Ferentinum
Casinum
Teanum
Sepinum
Cales
Beneventum
ROMA
Lapuvium
Aquinum
Capua
Herdonia
Caere
Ferelii
Antium
Minturnae
Atella
Suessula
Portus
Albanum
Litternum
Neapolis
Pompeii
Surrentum
Ostia
Bovillae
Misenum
Baiae
Paestum?
Pausilypum
Herculaneum
Grumentum

Main map place names

Camulodunum
Verulamium
Durovernum
Alauna
Iuliobona
Caesaromagus
Noviodunum
Mediolanum
Andelelus
Nida
Mogontiacum
Sumelocenna
Grannus
(Chenevières)
Epomanduodurum
Augusta Raurica
Aventicum
Virunum
Savaria
Concordia
Vicetia
Verona
Acelum
Adria
Tergeste
Pola
Stobi
Byllis
Apamea
Noviodunum
Diablintum
Alesia
Aregenua
Arecoricum
(Araines)
Lutetia
Vellaunodunum
Avaricum
(Drévant)
Augustodurum
Boutae
Augusta
Lugdunum
Vienna
Segetae
Eporedia
Mediolanum
Libarna
Brixia
Parma
Acelum
Augustoritum
(Gennes)
(Sanxay)
(Civaux)
Aquae Neri
Augustoritum
Aquae Segetae
Valentia
Alba Helvorum
Vasio
Augusta
Taurinorum
Augusta
Bagiennorum?
Pollentia
Albintimilium
Arausio
Nemausus
Forum Iulii
Antipolis
Arelate
Massilia
Mediolanum
Santonum
Cameven
Diabintum
Tarraco
Saguntum
Pollentia
Pollentia
Nora
Clunia
Bilbilis
Toletum
Arcobriga
Emerita
Metellinum
Hispalis
Regina
Urso
Acinipo
Malaca
Baelo
Ad Mercurium
Caesarea
Tipasa
Rusicade
Hippo Regius
Calama
Cuicul
Cirta
Sitifis
Thubursicum
Madaura
Thamugadi
Diarrhytus
Hippo
Carthago
Simitthu
Althiburus?
Sufetula
Cillium
Civitas Popthensis
Leptis Minor
Thugga
Sabrata
Leptis Magna
Ptolemais
Cyrene
Salonae
Metapontum
Lupiae
Rudiae?
Vibo Valentia
(Gioiosa Ionica)
Locri Epizephyrii
Rhegium
Catana
Solus
Tyndaris
Tauromenium
Segesta
Heraclea
Minoa
Acrae
Helorus
Syracusae
(Castiglione di Paludi)
Nicopolis
Buthrotum
Dodona
Thebae
Stratus
Demetrias
Larisa
Alexandria Troas
Assus
Pergamum
Sardes
Aezani
Delos
Thera
Gortyna
Antinoe
Philippi
Thasus
Samothrace
Panium
Ilium
Cyzicus
Myrlea
Prusias
Ancyra
Tavium
Pessinus
Cyrrhus
Antiochia
Daphne
Apamea
Palmyra
Seleucia
Elaeusa
Laodicea
Selinus
Anemurium
Soli
Curium
Gabala
(Sahr)
Heliopolis
Damascus
Emmatha
Gadara
Dora
Scythopolis
Canatha
Bostra
Philadelphia
Gerasa
Petra
Dura-Europos
Tigranocerta
Phillippopolis

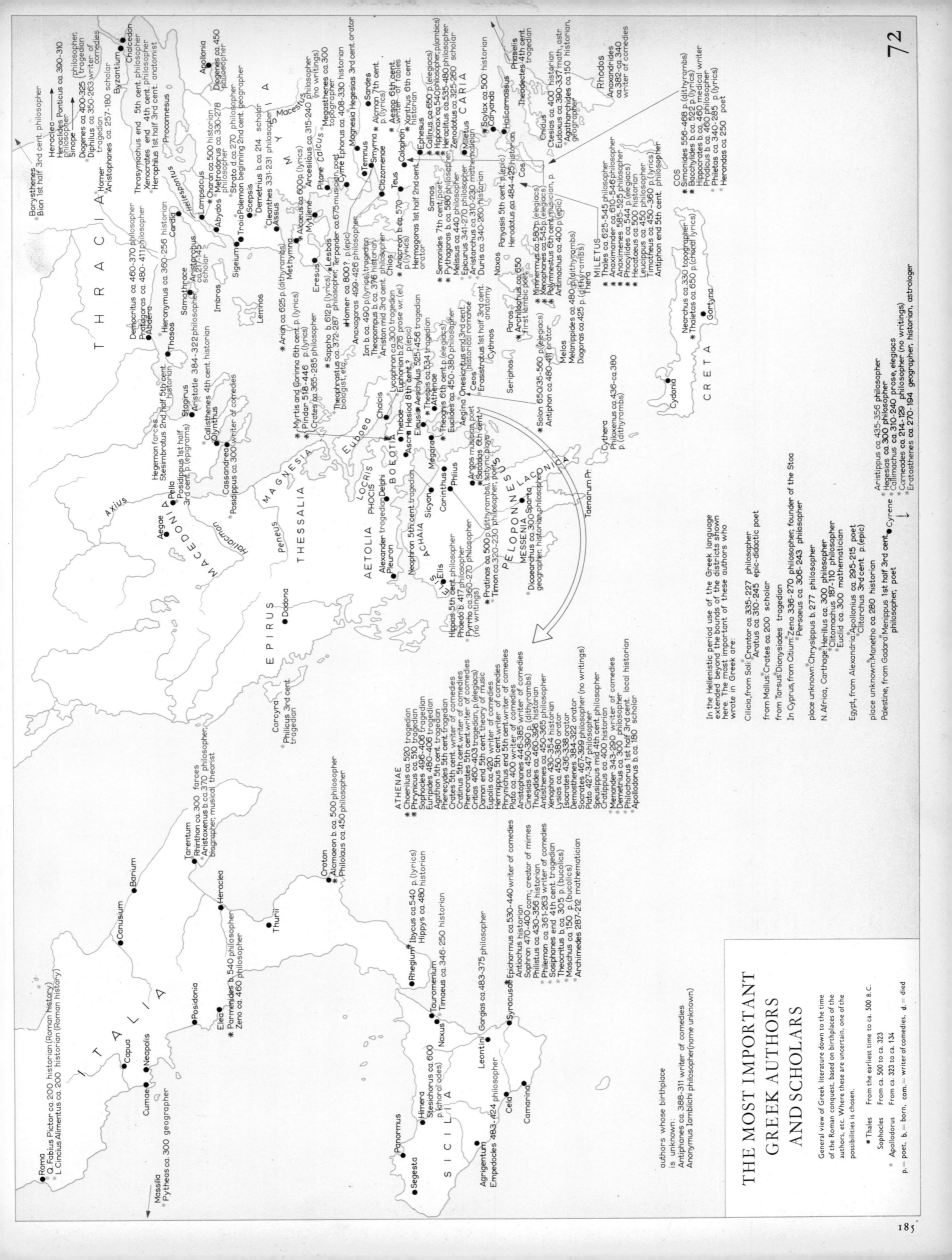

THE MOST IMPORTANT GREEK AUTHORS AND SCHOLARS

General view of Greek literature down to the time of the Roman conquest, based on birthplaces of the authors, etc. Where these are uncertain, one of the possibilities is chosen.

* Thales — From the earliest time to ca. 500 B.C.
* Sophocles — From ca. 500 to ca. 323
* Apollodorus — From ca. 323 to ca. 134
p.= poet, b.= born, com.= writer of comedies, d.= died

authors whose birthplace is unknown:
* Antiphanes ca. 388-311 writer of comedies
* Anonymus Iamblichi philosopher (name unknown)

In the Hellenistic period use of the Greek language extended beyond the bounds of the districts shown here. The most important of these authors who wrote in Greek are:

Cilicia, from Soli: Cranton ca. 335-227 philosopher
Aratus ca. 310-245 epic-didactic poet

from Mallus: Crates ca. 200 scholar

from Tarsus: Dionysiades tragedian

In Cyprus, from Citium: Zeno 336-270 philosopher; founder of the Stoa
Persaeus ca. 306-243 philosopher

place unknown: Chrysippus b. 277 philosopher
N. Africa, Carthage: Herillus ca. 300 philosopher
Clitomachus 187-110 philosopher
Euclid ca. 300 mathematician

Egypt, from Alexandria: Apollonius ca. 295-215 poet
Clitarchus 3rd cent. p. (epic)

place unknown: Manetho ca. 280 historian
Palestine, from Gadara: Menippus 1st half 3rd cent. philosopher; poet

Aristippus ca. 435-356 philosopher
Hegesias ca. 300 philosopher
Callimachus ca. 310-240 prose, elegiacs
Carneades ca. 214-129 philosopher (no writings)
Eratosthenes ca. 270-194 geographer, historian, astrologer

72

185

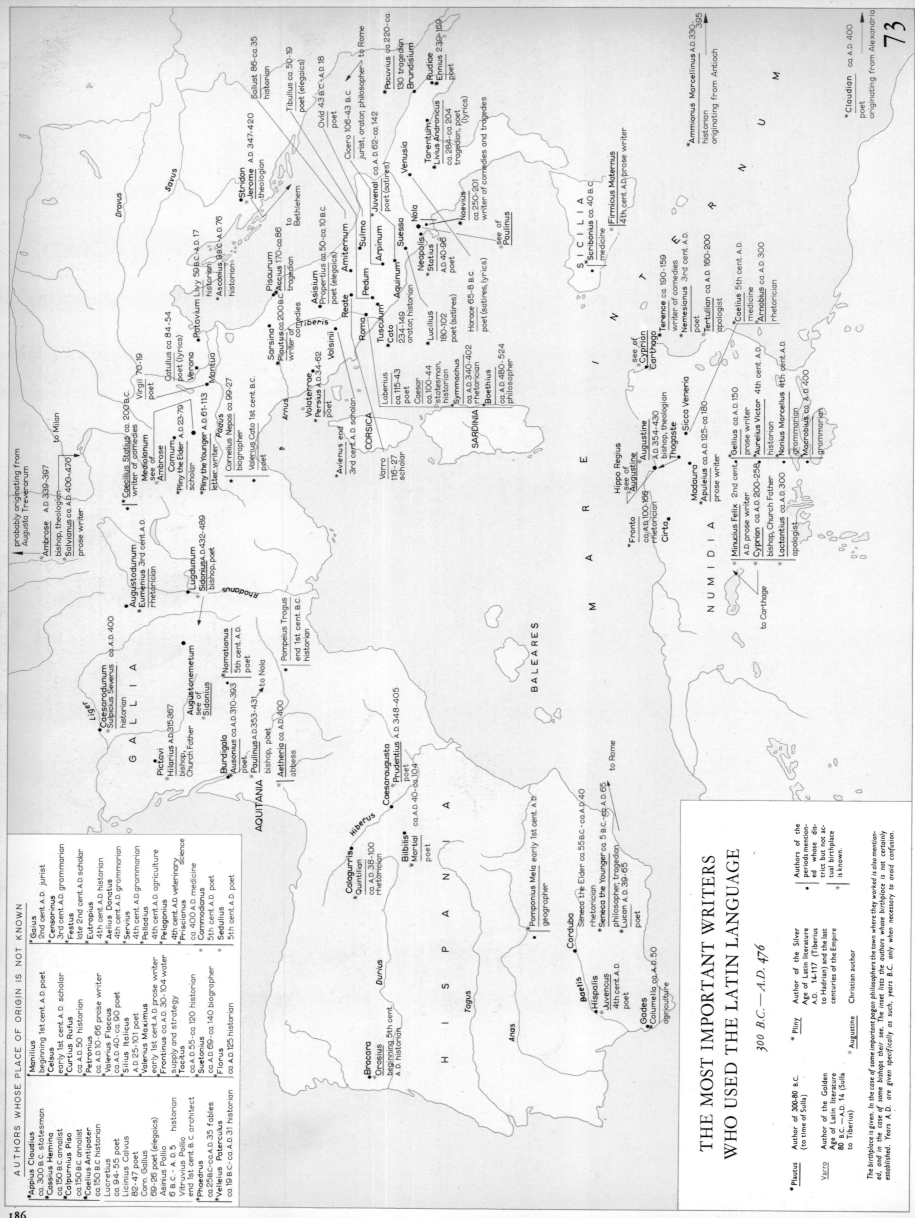

THE MOST IMPORTANT WRITERS
WHO USED THE LATIN LANGUAGE

300 B.C.—A.D. 476

In every place of any importance in the ancient world, theatres were built upon slopes and hills. The original form and construction date from the classical Greek period; the Romans made a number of modifications without abandoning the basic plan. **467.** The theatre of Epidaurus (→ 154) is one of the best preserved. The sixteen thousand spectators looked out over the circular orchestra and the scaena to a landscape which formed a natural background. **464.** Fragment of the 'Euripides relief', showing perhaps a scene from Euripides' *Heracles*, with the two main characters of Heracles and Megara. **465.** Scene from the New Comedy in front of elaborately constructed wings. **466.** Comic scene on a mosaic at Pompeii. **468-9.** The theatre of Epidaurus, where the auditorium with aisles, steps, and seats is built into a hill. The photographs were taken before and during a modern performance, for which the scaena (the stage building) was erected upon the ancient foundations.

187

metre, the *Heroides*, letters purporting to be from famous women of legend to their husbands or lovers, from Penelope to Odysseus, for example, or from Dido to Aeneas. All these writings bear the stamp of Ovid's education in the schools of rhetoric; they are often artificial, but at the same time they possess an undeniable poetic quality. So it is with all his writings. He had a natural talent for poetry such as is seldom found, but this very facility often led him astray and tempted him to exceed the limits of good taste. In this way he overwhelms and tires the reader with his continual self-pity in his *Tristia*, laments written in Tomi (modern Constanta on the Black Sea), whither he was banished by Augustus at the age of fifty. Some of the elegies in this collection are extremely beautiful, for example that in which he describes his departure from Rome. After mentioning one last collection of elegies, the *Fasti*, a calendar in verse of the first six months of the Roman year, we come to Ovid's most important work, the *Metamorphoses*. These are not elegiacs, but a poem in hexameters. In fifteen Books Ovid deals with about two hundred and fifty myths, nearly all of Greek origin, which have as their subject some form of transformation. Here Ovid is at his best. No other poet has such a flowing narrative style; the transition from one story to the other is sometimes laboured, sometimes natural, but always ingenious. We enter an enchanted world of fantasy, of gods and nymphs, centaurs and fauns, of tritons and mermaids, of flowers, springs, rocks, trees, animals who were once men and who were changed in shape through the power of the gods. It is only natural that this book, full of wit, fantasy, and humour, with its varied series of attractive myths, has continued to be read, re-read, and admired.

PROSE

Greek and Latin prose is so extensive, the number of writers so great that in such a short space there is room to mention only the most important authors, if one wishes to avoid a dry summary. Among the very greatest are the two Greek historians Herodotus and Thucydides. Each is great in his own manner, Herodotus as a master of narrative, Thucydides as an analytical historian. Herodotus was born ca. 485 in Halicarnassus, on the frontier between two worlds, the Asiatic and the Greek. At home in both, he was eminently suited to write the history of the great wars between Greece and Persia, the wars in which Greece freed herself from threat of Eastern domination and laid the foundation for the freedom of Western Europe. This struggle is the chief theme of his narrative, which was divided by later writers into nine Books, named after the nine Muses. It is, however, only with the fifth Book that he deals in detail with this subject; the first Books are devoted to the history and customs of the many lands which he visited on his travels: Lydia, Persia, Egypt, Greece, the Black Sea coasts, and Italy. He is a persistent investigator with an untiring curiosity, a collector of precious information from little known lands and periods. In his history this is faithfully, if rather indiscriminately, reproduced. From a literary point of view his anecdotes and short stories are the most important. His narrative style is gripping, simple, and lively. One has only to think of the colourful and charming tale of Croesus, the wealthy king of Lydia, who refused to believe Solon when he said that no man should be called happy before he was dead. He had to suffer a hard lesson before he was convinced; first the tragic loss of his favourite son, then the loss of his throne and all his possessions in a war with Cyrus, king of the Persians, and finally his own narrow escape from death on the pyre. The description of the Persian royal house is no less vivid; how Cyrus drove his grandfather Astyages, the last Median king, from the throne, thus becoming the founder of the Persian Empire which was to conquer the entire surrounding world with the exception of Greece. Herodotus devotes a whole book to the wonders of Egypt, and King Darius' campaign against Scythia is for him an occasion to expound the wonders of that country and its nomadic inhabitants. Nevertheless, the stories of all these lands and peoples concern him chiefly as an introduction to his great theme, the wars between East and West which in 479, after the battles of Salamis and Plataea, ended with a Greek victory over Persia, the victory of freedom over despotism.

Herodotus describes the wars which led to Athens' prosperity and greatness, Thucydides (ca. 460–400) the Peloponnesian War (431–404) which brought about the downfall of Athens. The difference between these two almost contemporary historians is remarkable. Thucydides was the first writer to take a critically scientific view of history. It was he who first employed the method which has continued in use until the present day: the careful investigation of all sources and the sharp distinction between truth and hearsay. His work contains no anecdotes, no curious ethnographical or geographical details. Thucydides confined himself to the political and military aspects of the period with which he was concerned. He himself said that he did not write to charm the reader with fabulous tales but to give a true picture of the events that had happened and of those that would sometime, in all probability, happen again in the same or a similar way; thus his work was written, not as a prize-essay to be heard for the moment, but as a possession for all time. When the war between Athens and Sparta broke out in 431 Thucydides was still a youngish man; he commanded an

Athenian fleet in 424, but was accused of negligence and was exiled. This gave him the time and opportunity for writing. His prose is stiff and difficult but always absorbing; it reflects the personality of a stern and serious-minded man, a clear and enlightened spirit, a sharp and critical intellect, a profound judge of humanity, a distinguished and truth-loving man. Especially dramatic and moving are his descriptions of the plague at Athens and the expedition to Syracuse with the tragic loss of the Athenian army and fleet. Amid the countless details concerning the war on land and sea he never departs from his main theme: the fall of Athens, brought about, as he says himself, by desire for power, originating in greed and ambition. The lively action of his narrative is constantly varied by speeches attributed by him to statesmen and army commanders. These are not set down exactly in the form in which they were delivered, but the main lines are faithfully reproduced. They are masterpieces of language and style and reveal the motives behind the facts. An outstanding example is the famous speech delivered by Pericles at the tomb of the men who fell in the first year of the war. In Thucydides the art of the historian reached its zenith. This combination of scientific method and great literary art is rarely found elsewhere.

After Herodotus and Thucydides Greece produced no more great historians. The Athenian Xenophon (ca. 430–354) did indeed attempt in his *Hellenica* to continue the work of Thucydides, which broke off with the events of 410 B.C. His capacities, however, appear to have been insufficient for the difficult task of giving deep insight into the confused situation in Greece at the end of and after the Peloponnesian War. He was better suited to writing his own memoirs of the expedition of the 10,000 Greeks with the Persian prince Cyrus to Cunaxa and their laborious retreat after his death. This book, the *Anabasis*, displays little artistic talent but makes its appeal through its directness, simplicity and clear description of detail.

From the Hellenistic period there has been preserved part of an elaborate history of the world in forty Books written by the Greek Polybius (ca. 201–120). This learned Greek came to Rome as a hostage and there became the friend of the younger Scipio whom he accompanied on his campaigns against Carthage and Numantia. He greatly admired the stability of the Roman constitution and was impressed by the manner in which, by expansion in the Mediterranean world, Rome had in so brief a time introduced a unity into world history. This was the main theme of his *History*, which dealt with the years 220–146 B.C. His style is not rhetorical but concise and rather monotonous. He took Thucydides as his model and was didactic in manner. His work was much utilised by later writers (e.g. Livy), who derived much material from this source.

The writings of Plutarch (ca. A.D. 46–120) who, indeed, did not claim to be an historian, are of a completely different kind. He was born in Chaeronea, a town in Boeotia, where he remained for the greater part of his life, occupying high posts and respected for his independence and humanity. He wrote biographies of famous Greeks and Romans, normally the biography of a Greek accompanied by that of a Roman with similar qualities, rounded off by a comparison of the two. The series began with Theseus and Romulus and ended with the Emperor Galba. He aimed, not at a complete history, but at painting portraits of great men as an example and lesson to humanity. His material is absorbing and the many anecdotes make the book most pleasant reading.

Among the Roman historians must be reckoned Julius Caesar, who was a man of letters as well as a great soldier and statesman. His two surviving works, the *De Bello Gallico* and *De Bello Civili*, excel in clarity and simplicity, untouched by sentiment or bombast. They give a clear account of his wars in Gaul and elsewhere and continually arouse in the reader the conviction of the superiority of the Roman Empire and of the Roman army under Caesar's command. A more rhetorical stylist and more philosophising spirit was Gaius Sallustius Crispus (86–ca. 35 B.C.). The greater part of his most important work, the *Historiae*, has been lost, so that we only possess two monographs from his hand: *Coniuratio Catilinae* and *Bellum Iugurthinum*. Sallust, disturbed by the corruption existing in Roman politics after the Punic Wars, found in these two subjects suitable material for demonstrating the corruption of the nobility and Senate. Influenced by Stoic philosophy, he taught that a return to ancient virtue and discipline was for the state the only remedy against moral and social decay. He wrote a terse, pithy Latin which served as a model for Tacitus and aroused great admiration among other writers, including Nietzsche.

This gift of saying a great deal in a few words was not possessed by the great historian Titus Livius (59 B.C. – A.D. 17). Educated in the schools of rhetoric, his narrative style is diffuse. He wrote a history of Rome in one hundred and forty-two Books, from the founding of the city down to his own time. A quarter of this work has been preserved. Livy is not a great critical historian; he paints too idealistic a picture of ancient Roman heroism and virtue in order to serve as an example to his own day, a period of moral laxity and self-seeking politicians. He is in the first place a moralist, to the detriment of his task as historian. Although his style is somewhat impersonal, his method of narration is none the less smooth and elegant, free from meaningless rhetoric. One can find in his work many an enthralling story, many an arresting description of a battle or a senatorial debate, many a telling speech. Throughout the whole of antiquity Livy was considered as the chief Latin historian.

For us nowadays the most prominent figure in Latin historiography is undoubtedly Cornelius Tacitus (ca. A.D. 55–129), one of the greatest writers that ever lived. His official career, begun under Vespasian, was interrupted during Domitian's reign of terror through which he lived, partly abroad, partly in Rome. These terrible years left an indelible mark upon his mind, and induced in him a pessimistic view of life and bitterness of spirit which made him a very sombre judge of the Emperors and society of his time. The situation was made worse by the fact that only after Domitian's death could he write freely and give vent to his indignation. We possess three short works by Tacitus: *Dialogus de Oratoribus*, a dissertation upon the decline of eloquence during his day; a biography of his father-in-law Agricola and his military career in Britain; and the *Germania*, a sketch of the origin and customs of the Germanic peoples. More important are his two great historical works, the *Historiae* and the *Annales*, which unfortunately do not survive in their entirety. The *Histories* cover the period from the death of Nero to the death of Domitian (A.D. 69-96) but only the account of the first two years survives. A considerable part of the *Annals*, which dealt with the events of A.D. 14-68, is also missing. In this last work Tacitus' talents as a writer attain their greatest maturity and perfection. His stern standards of moral conduct bring him into perpetual conflict with the corruption of the Senate and imperial court, which he exposes mercilessly and often sarcastically. His style is distinguished and apparently impartial, yet behind this impassivity one can sense the fervour of his convictions and his burning indignation. The writer's tension is transmitted to the reader. His style is extremely personal, at the same time concise, powerful, and poetic. He uses a minimum of words to convey the maximum of meaning, and the reader has continually to be on the alert. The *Annals* indeed sometimes appear more like a psychological novel than objective history. The figures of the Emperors, however, remain permanently etched in our minds: Tiberius, reserved, crafty, cruel, and hypocritical; Claudius, a weakling and a fool, bullied by women and freedmen; Nero, passionate, profligate, and cruel; Messalina, dissolute and shameless; Agrippina, evil and ambitious. Tacitus pays more attention to human failings than to human virtues. He describes not only the action but the motive behind it, a motive often even in itself. Historical reality is undoubtedly more complicated than Tacitus makes it appear, but his alert mind and literary talent render his work often sombre and moving and always absorbing.

During the classical period great prose writers are found not only among the historians but among the orators. Among the Greeks and Romans the art of rhetoric was held in high esteem and was taught in the schools. Many political figures showed themselves accomplished speakers, and oratory flourished in public debate and in the law courts. If we confine ourselves to the oration as a literary work of art, two great names spring immediately to our minds: the Athenian Demosthenes and Cicero the Roman.

Demosthenes (384–322 B.C.) won more fame by his political speeches than by his legal arguments. These speeches were mainly directed against Philip of Macedon and his growing power and threat to Greece. Between 350 and 340 B.C. Demosthenes attempted by his passionate speeches to incite the Athenians to take arms against Macedonian aggression until, in 338, Philip's victory at Chaeronea put an end to this policy. Sixteen speeches of this nature are attributed to him. They excel in logical construction and in their lively, yet sometimes pathetic, style. They display a sincere and ever-vigilant partiotism. Demosthenes' great political opponent was the orator Aeschines, who supported Philip. Demosthenes never had a good word to say for him, but continually accused him of treachery and corruptibility. We shall probably never be able to give a just and accurate judgment in this matter.

Among the countless Roman orators Marcus Tullius Cicero (106–43 B.C.) occupies the foremost place. A large part of his work has been preserved: fifty-six orations, three books on oratory, a few philosophical writings, and a great number of letters. He wrote a clear and effective Latin which was afterwards regarded as the model of pure Latin of the golden age of Roman literature and is still taught as the norm of 'classical' Latin. Cicero is undoubtedly a great stylist, extremely cultured but not in the least pedantic. On the contrary, his style is lively, sometimes impassioned, sometimes sarcastic, sometimes defiant. Nowhere else can one find such range of tone and variety of form. His writings, notably his orations and letters, have proved an inexhaustible source of knowledge for the political and cultural life of his generation. Although opinions about him have varied greatly throughout the centuries, he is still widely admired for his legal skill, his practised oratory, his brilliant style, and his vain yet healthy and uncomplicated personality.

It is exceptional to find philosophy which is at the same time great literature. Plato (427–347 B.C.) is a striking example of such a combination. He is not only a philosopher but also an artist, in his creative imagination, his power of characterisation, his gift for evoking the comic or tragic aspect of a situation, his mastery of language. In all his writings philosophical argument is indeed his real goal, but the literary form is so moving and poetic that one often forgets one is reading philosophy at all. Many of his twenty-five dialogues begin like a charming short story, graphic and vivid; a few pages later the reader is almost imperceptibly drawn into the philosophical argument. To take one example, the first pages of the *Protagoras*, when a youthful friend comes to wake Socrates in the early hours of the morning with the news that the great Sophist Protagoras has arrived in Athens and Socrates calms his elation with mild irony. How lively is the beginning of *The Republic* when Socrates meets a few friends at a religious celebration at the Piraeus and they cajole him into accompanying them to the house of the old Cephalus where discussions on the ideal form of government are to be held. How poetically described is the scene in the *Phaedrus* where Socrates walks with his friend alongside the brook outside Athens, how arresting the beginning of the *Phaedo* were the reader immediately feels himself caught up in the circle of friends who surround Socrates in his cell upon the last day of his life. How unforgettable is the end of this dialogue where the death of Socrates is described with such touching simplicity. Perhaps Plato's artistry and imaginative power are most clearly evident in the *Symposium* and the discussions on Eros held by those present. Each of the guests holds forth in his own manner: the physician is admonitory and pompous, Aristophanes witty and whimsical, the host and tragedian Agathon flowery and bombastic, Socrates wise and profound. Plato succeeds magnificently in putting himself in the place of every speaker and in adapting his language to each different personality. He is not only a philosopher but also a great writer, artist, prophet, and poet.

Rome produced no great philosophers or original thinkers. Cicero made Greek philosophy more accessible to the Romans though his philosophical writings, but his own contribution is relatively superficial and eclectic rather than original. The Romans were not given to theoretic speculation and were therefore most influenced by the Stoic doctrine, with its emphasis upon the practical virtues of obedience, self-control, and devotion to duty. The most important Roman follower of the Stoic doctrine was Lucius Annaeus Seneca (ca. 4 B.C. – A.D. 65). Besides a collection of his philosophical letters to his young friend Lucilius we also possess essays on anger, peace of mind, the brevity of life, and the happy life. The content of Seneca's work is rather monotonous and the same ideas are repeated again and again; only the virtuous are happy, poverty is better than wealth, death is not fearful but a liberation from all pain. His power lies in his endless variety of expression and artistry of form. The wealth amassed by this minister and courtier of Nero contrasts painfully with his doctrine. This cannot however be said of another Stoic writer, the Emperor Marcus Aurelius (A.D. 121–180). He left behind a diary, entitled 'To Himself', which he wrote during his campain against the Quadi in the Danube region. This book, written in Greek, expounds ideas similar to those in the essays and letters of Seneca, in particular the acceptance of death. It is of no great literary value, but bears the unmistakeable stamp of sincerity.

The letter as a literary genre is also found in classical literature. We have already mentioned Cicero's correspondence, an invaluable source of information concerning life in his time, a period of transition from republic to empire, of political unrest and civil war. We have also spoken of Seneca's letters, which greatly resemble his philosophical essays. A third Roman writer deserves mention here: Gaius Plinius (A.D. 62–113), a man of substance, born at Comum. He wrote in a much calmer period than Cicero, and his letters reflect the security which the wise rule of Trajan had restored to Rome after Domitian's reign of terror. His letters portray the colourful life of Rome: sittings of the Senate and law courts, the activities of the Roman *beau monde*. This style is refined, polished, elegant, and often racy. Especially famous are Pliny's two letters to Tacitus on the eruption of Vesuvius which in A.D. 79 overwhelmed the cities of Pompeii and Herculaneum. Pliny happened to be living with his mother in a villa in the neighbourhood. He gives a graphic description of the eruption and the subsequent panic. He also relates how his uncle, a writer and scholar, lost his life in this disaster. No less interesting is the letter which as governor of the province of Bithynia he wrote to the Emperor Trajan asking what measures to adopt against the Christian religion which had begun to gain ground in his province. This letter is one of the earliest documents concerning the Christian community and the Roman attitude towards it. Trajan's answer has also been preserved.

THE NOVEL. The novel makes a late appearance in Greek and Latin literature. This is understandable when one remembers that classical literature was essentially a national literature, and that the classical poet, writer, or artist was most concerned with the life of his fellow-countrymen and the state, of which he felt himself a part. The epic poet sings the glorious past of Greece and Rome, the tragedian makes alive the heroes and gods of the national mythology, the historian glorifies the past of his own people. Even a lyric poet like Pindar celebrated the national victors in athletic contests and war. In such literature, so closely bound up with city and people, there was scarcely place for the novel, which depicts personal and individual life, and the inner emotions of the human soul. Apart from a rare Greek novel of adventure or travel, the only work of fiction of which a considerable part has been preserved is the *Satiricon* of Petronius (died A.D. 66). This realistic novel of manners relates the adventures of three vagabonds who travel through southern Italy during Nero's reign. It reveals the interior of both common inns and rich houses. In it we meet beggars, thieves, poverty-stricken poets, and a wealthy *parvenu*, Trimalchio by name, whose banquet occupies a considerable part of that section of the book which survives. The *Satiricon* provides a realistic picture of the ethics and immorality of the period. It is crammed with entertaining scenes and telling parody. Petronius, originally one of the favourites of Nero's court, is undoubtedly a talented writer, and provides a rare store of everyday 'Vulgar' Latin.

Closely related is the book by Apuleius (born ca. A.D. 125). It is called the *Metamorphoses* or often *The Golden Ass*, since the main character, a certain Lucius, is transformed into an ass for his sins. After all kinds of peculiar adventures he is pardoned by the Egyptian goddess Isis and initiated into her mystery cult. It contains a very famous digression, the story of Cupid and Psyche, told in an elegant but sometimes rather artificial Latin. This tale inspired many later writers and artists, including Raphael in his wall paintings in the Villa Farnesina and the sculptor Canova in the famous group 'Cupid and Psyche' in the Villa Carlotta on Lake Como.

The second flowering of classical literature did not produce any new aspect, but a new phase was coming on, the literature of Early Christianity, which was written in a different style and which was imbued with a different spirit.

Classical art

It is possible to look at classical art in any or all of several different ways – through the eyes of the archaeologist, who may be most interested in typology or dating and value an object for its rarity or some unusual feature of technique; or through those of the historian, who scans ancient works of art as documents illuminating the political or social life of his period; or through those of the art historian, to whom trends, influences, transitions, techniques are of absorbing interest; or through those of the less specialised art-lover, who seeks the thrill of aesthetic experience that is largely independent of the date and background of the work but very much dependent on the date and background of the observer. Each of these ways is equally valid, and all that is necessary is to be clear which is being used. Misunderstanding is too often produced by failing to make explicit the viewpoint which underlies a set of judgments. The sensible thing is surely to spread our enjoyment as widely as we can by utilising the standards of as many viewpoints as we have time and inclination to master. The remarks which follow are written mainly from the point of view mentioned last above.

This attitude, however, is far from implying that no specialised knowledge is needed to appreciate classical art. True aesthetic pleasure is not always and everywhere obtained, and the lesser but still genuine rewards demand knowledge. The twentieth-century observer is at a lucky point in time to study classical art. The art of his own time reached, some fifty years ago, the end of just such a cycle of representational realism from Giotto to the Impressionists as can be studied in the development of Greek sculpture, and faced just such an *impasse* as confronted later Greek artists embarrassed by the perfection of their predecessors. They, too, had their Picassos and Braques in the anonymous mosaicists and ikon painters of Byzantium and Ravenna. With this experience behind us and with our renewed – perhaps over-sophisticated – pleasure in the primitive and naive, we should be better equipped than our grandfathers to appreciate the appeal of archaic Greek art and to place the mellow perfection of Praxiteles in a wider context.

It is often a delicate task to judge how much of the quality of early art is due to the adventitious appeal which it inevitably acquires when looked at through the glass of some thousands of years' subsequent experience. Are we justified in reading into a statuette of the great goddess an emotional intensity which the Cretan artist did not intend? Or did he put it there unwittingly – did he create, as artists have done since, better than he knew? And what of the colouring given by our knowledge of early religions? Such problems embarrass the critic; but perhaps it is wiser in this as in other things to take our pleasures where we find them, being scrupulous only not to offend by over-romanticising and over-sentimentalising the products of a particularly clear-eyed people.

MINOAN AND MYCENAEAN ART

The material development of the civilisation of Crete – the first great European civilisation known to us – has been fairly fully reconstructed by the archaeologists. It was a loose-knit mercantile empire which the legendary Minos controlled, and its long life is conventionally divided in three archaeological periods: Early Minoan (I, II, III), from ca. 3000–2000 B.C.; Middle Minoan (I, II, III), from 2000– ca. 1580 when many of the palaces were destroyed by earthquake; and Late Minoan, ca. 1580–1200.

The remains of Minoan art include pottery, metal-work, clay figures and statuettes, gems and seals, frescoes, and carvings. Most of these are of quite extraordinary interest to archaeologists and historians for technical reasons, and many, indeed perhaps most, make an equal impact by reason of their intrinsic value as works of art. The appeal of much of Minoan art to sophisticated twentieth-century eyes is immediate. Gracious charm, lightness and sureness of touch, and confidence of workmanship make an irresistible combination.

The frescoes, especially, with their supple yet strong line, their curious blend of liveliness and hieratic dignity, and their air of fashionable elegance (the temptation to use the word 'chic' is strong, and one of the frescoes is fancifully called 'La Parisienne') delight the eye (→ 19–21, 25). They portray scenes from the bull-sports, scenes of ceremony and daily life; and above all they and the vases show a keen impressionist eye for the appearance of the natural world whose animals, fishes, and birds look realistically out at us (→ 16, 22). Flowers toss in the wind and are (unusual in ancient art) recognisably, say, irises or carnations, and the leaf is shown fluttering from the tree.

The impressive representations of the snake goddess, symbol of a fertility-nature worship, and her male acolytes are well known in statue form and on seals (→ 17). We must, however, beware of any tendency to romanticise these remarkable and evocative figures. Space prevents the mention of the numerous other types of work unearthed at various sites on Crete and the mainland – the mirrors, the vases and cups, sometimes with gold repoussé like the magnificent bulls from Vaphio, the daggers, the toys – how many hundreds of years were to pass after the fall of Crete before toys were again made for exporting!

Cretan domination of the eastern Mediterranean was supplanted by Mycenaean about 1400. For the next 200 years the great cities of the mainland – Mycenae, Tiryns, Pylos, Orchomenus, and others – lorded it in the 'heroic' age mirrored in Homer (→ 27–51). Mycenaean metalwork, pottery, and carving reach an exceedingly high standard, though it is difficult on occasion to know what is Cretan in influence only and what is actually Cretan production. Especially fine are the bronze daggers elaborately inlaid in gold and silver and nielloed.

ETRUSCAN ART

Etruscan products can be dated between 750 and 100 B.C., and the best of them on the whole came from the hundred years following 550, when Etruscan power was at it height (see pages 91–2). The predominating influence was Greek, sometimes well-assimilated, but sometimes lying uneasily on national traditions from their warlike past and distant echoes from their Eastern origin (→ 99). Etruscan architecture, for instance, has little of the organic unity which characterises a Greek temple. It is massive, rambling, and, at its best, monumentally impressive (→ 232, 234, 239). Their statuary is incised, decorated, and painted terracotta, whose main attraction is that of the *primitif*; a good example is the Apollo of Veii (late sixth century). The important frescoes which adorned their walls survive in their necropolises and show the same curious blend of Greek convention and naive realism. The resulting flavour is not unpleasing (→ 235, 237–8). Their metal-work shows technical skill of a very high order. At its best Etruscan art is forceful and vigorously alive, echoing in an indefinable way the impact of this mysterious people upon history (→ e.g. 229).

ARCHITECTURE

By far the commonest remains of Greek buildings are those of temples, and it is of these we must speak. On pages 82, 89, 118–9, 122, 130–1, 134–5 are given some details of the orders of Greek architecture and the terminology of Greek and Roman building. To these the following general remarks may be added.

Two characteristics differentiate classical temples from most other holy edifices. They were designed not to worship in but to be a house for the god; and were planned from the outside in. In these respects they differed from Assyrian and Egyptian temples which preceded them and from Christian churches which succeeded them. In an Egyptian temple, for instance, the principal pillars were inside the structure, in a Greek temple they were outside (though, of course, there could also be pillars inside). In Assyria and Babylonia the inside walls were decorated with reliefs and carvings, in Greece the main ornamentation was outside on the pediments, friezes, *metopes*, and *tympana*.

From this it follows that a classical temple is small and usually placed on an eminence where it can be seen to best advantage, and that its beauty consists in the controlled proportion of the parts which combine to make an harmonious and satisfying whole whose unity is at once apparent to the eye. In this again it differs from Egyptian temples and Western cathedrals, which tend to achieve grandeur by size and magnificence of decoration, and to grow by cellular aggregation. To the end the Greek temple remained a strictly unified conception.

In the sunny Mediterranean lands the architect wished to construct a shrine that would enclose his deity in comfortable shade and coolness, though probably a hole was left in the roof so that the image was illumined by the morning sun. In colder northern lands the builders of the great cathedrals

470. One of the greatest Latin poets, Quintus Horatius Flaccus, lived for many years in the still rural Ustica (modern Licenza) in the Sabine mountains behind Tivoli, where the remains of his villa lie at the foot of the hills. In an epistle to Quinctius (*Ep.* i, 16) he writes of this spot: 'It is surrounded by a continuous row of hills, separated from each other only by one shady valley.' His 'Sabine farm' has become proverbial for a modest intellectual retirement. **471-2.** Masks from the Roman theatre. **473.** Remains of the theatre at Sabrata. **474.** Reconstruction of the stage at Sabrata. In the centre, the 'royal door' with side doors.

utilised the development of the arch to make their windows as large as possible to admit the maximum sunlight.

Simplicity, then, and proportion and grace are characteristics of classical architecture, and the subordination of the part to the whole, of decoration to design. By the end of the fifth century each part of the building was governed by principles of proportion and balance, worked out by centuries of trial and error. The ratio between the bottom and top of the column, between the circumference at the bottom and the height, between the diameter of the column and the interval separating it from the next, between the length and the breadth of the building, and so on down to the smallest detail of pediment, cornice, triglyphs, metopes, architrave, tympanum, frieze, etc. were known and used with only minor variations. Thus the effect of such masterpieces as the Parthenon (→ 174), Hephaesteum (→ 190), Propylaea (→ 59) and Erechtheum (→ 191) depends on a most subtle use of the 'standard' proportions, delicately distorted to compensate to the eye the effects of perspective in order to reinforce the impression of absolutely true geometrical symmetry. Horizontals, for instance, are given a very slight upward curve, perpendiculars lean slightly inwards, and columns are curved in along their length, producing an illusion of added height and strength.

It is apparent that an art of such refinement depends for appreciation on the connoisseur, able and eager to discern and relish tiny variations from the standard. This is indeed a serious limitation, and the rigidity of the conventions of Greek architecture ensured that, in spite of the fact that it had produced buildings of quite unequalled beauty of design and grace of execution, future development lay elsewhere, with styles which were flexible enough to welcome innovation. As in so much of classical art, its very perfection contained the promise of its decay, and the intellectual excitement which has kept Greek thought and literature alive to us for over 2000 years is not there to breathe life into it.

Mention, however, must be made of a number of developments made by Roman builders which were to prove of fundamental importance for the future. While much of Roman temple building was Italic modification of Greek styles, Roman builders and engineers, working largely in brick and concrete instead of limestone or marble, divised ways of exploiting the dome, the vault, and the arch. The importance of these elements for Western architecture needs no stressing. The earliest domed temple to be preserved is the Pantheon at Rome, probably the masterpiece of the Imperial architects (→ 448-9). With the exploitation of the barrel vault many of the features of the Romanesque cathedral appear – nave, aisle, apse, piers, vaults, half-dome. From the Roman civil basilica with its pillared nave and aisles came much of the traditional appearance of Christian churches. The use of the arch – known to but not developed by the Greeks – enabled the Roman builder to erect bridges and aqueducts (→ 448-9) of great length and sometimes incomparable beauty, as well as baths, theatres, amphitheatres, and the Imperial palaces. The dividing line between architect and engineer seems to have been always tenuous in ancient Rome and it is indeed inviting to argue, as some have done, that Rome's true contributions to the arts were the monumental structures of its engineers. Such are the justly famous and spectacular aqueduct of Pont du Gard (→ 456), the aqueduct at Segovia, and the magnificent bridge across the Tagus at Alcántara, 617 feet long, 26 feet wide, with a triumphal arch, built in A.D. 105 under Trajan.

SCULPTURE

The origins of Greek sculpture are obscure, but its development and its influence on European art are clear. Greek sculptors appear to owe little or nothing to their predecessors in Egypt and Crete, and the ideals and norms of perfection they evolved were essentially different. The aims of Greek sculpture can be simply stated: the perfect realisation of physical beauty in terms of idealised naturalism. The story of their quest and their success can be clearly outlined, but it should perhaps be emphasised that, though we know the names of a number of Greek sculptors, only one original work (the Hermes of Praxiteles) can be attributed with certainty to its creator. The rest survive in copies of Hellenistic or Roman date – copies moreover often carved in marble from originals built up in clay and cast in bronze. When questions of technique and style are under consideration this difference of materials and tools must be taken into account, as well as the possibility that the copyist has introduced 'improvements' and variations by accident or design. It should also be remembered that colour was often used on both stone and bronze to bring out details and drapery.

The earliest surviving seventh-century Greek statues of youths, maidens, and gods undoubtedly possess a charm and sometimes an elegance for twentieth-century eyes far in excess of their technical achievement (→ 123, 124, 148). Stiff and rudimentary though these are in their attempt at naturalism, they show from the beginning the two characteristic traits of Greek sculpture – its devotion to the human body and the search after a generalised ideal rather than the recognisable individual. Superficially reminiscent in some instances of Egyptian statues, they are quite different in intent. Egyptian statues, the product of a long, mature tradition, are deliberately stylised; the Greek are struggling to master appearances.

Between the seventh and the fifth centuries the parts and articulation of the body, the flow of drapery, and a variety of poses are slowly brought under the sculptors' control. The stiffness gradually relaxes – a leg is advanced, the figures are shown sitting, then as leaning, turning, or passing the weight from one foot to another (→ 162, 175-9). The progress that had been made by the fifth century can be judged from works like the Delphi charioteer (ca. 470 B.C. → 49-50) and the well-known Discobolus (Discus-thrower) of Myron (→ 200). Even this latter, however, in spite of its mastery of balance in movement, is conceived to be viewed from the front.

The ability to visualise in the round was perfected by the great sculptors of the classical period (480-332), many of whose names are known to us – Polyclitus who perfected the study of, and wrote a treatise on, the proportions of the human body, Phidias, who is reputed to have supervised and perhaps designed the sculptures of the Parthenon (the Elgin Marbles), Praxiteles, whose insinuating charm and voluptuous sentimentality endeared him to the Romans (→ 475) and whose Aphrodite of Cnidus became a model for later variations, Lysippus, who took some step towards individual portraiture.

In the fourth century too, the remaining poses were mastered, from repose to the extremes of violent action, and style became more and more polished. If the west pediment of Olympia (→ 162) is one of the supreme achievements of the fifth century, marked by poise and serenity even in action, the painted 'Alexander' sarcophagus with its emotional intensity can be taken as typical of the fourth. (This is one of the very few painted sculptures to come down to us.)

And so the classical period slips into the Hellenistic period (332-27 B.C.) and decadence, with its Dying Gauls, sensuous and erotic satyrs and fauns, and aged shepherdesses (→ e.g. 225; also 134-5, 217). The classical ideal of perfection was slackened to that of realism, and with this went a decline in technique, symbolised by the increasing use of the drill for details like hair and eyes (→ e.g. 332). But the signs of decay must not blind us to the very real achievements of the period. An age which could produce the Victory of Samothrace (→ 223), the Laocoon group (p. 88, Fig. 8), the altar of Pergamum (→ 224), the Hellenistic portraits (→ 226-7), and even the popular Venus of Milo was not devoid of originality or mastery.

One aspect of Greek sculpture deserves special mention: the carving of reliefs on the outsides of buildings, especially on pediments and friezes. Relief sculpture was brought to a high degree of perfection. Even as early as the sixth century its range of pose and movement greatly exceeded that of free sculpture (→ 85, 86), and this combined with the rigorous limitations of the space to be filled – especially of the awkward shallow triangle of the pediment – produced a style that was at once lively and constrained. The result at its best was an impressive hieratic dignity.

At first the relief was shallow and the figures were arranged in profile, at the same height, without overlapping. The corners of the pediment were often filled by carving figures at a reduced scale. Gradually, however, the relief was deepened, until it was in effect carved in the round, and at the same time the compositional relationships between the figures became more subtle and complex. The problem of the triangular corners was solved by contorting the pose and not by reducing the scale, and this frequently resulted in a happy blend of stylised artificiality and violent naturalism. Fortunately no attempt was made to master perspective (→ 55), and in spite of its undoubted ingenuity of attitude and composition, relief sculpture retained that attractive clash of increasing mastery of realistic detail set in a stylised frame in which successive episodes in a scene might be depicted in 'strip' technique. At its best, relief sculpture achieves a monumental simplicity with detail successfully subordinated to breadth of design. The counterpoint of a crowded frieze or pediment, with standing, fighting, falling, running, mounted, crouching, or prostrate figures contrasts strangely with the devotion of free sculpture to the single figure (→ 55, 101-2, 107-9, 180, 182).

It is easy to diagnose the cause of the decay of classical sculpture, apart that is from the disappearance of the city-state. Greek sculptors had set themselves an attainable physical ideal, and once the great masters of the fifth and fourth centuries had attained it there was nothing left for their successors but repetition, variation, and technical display, or the alternative of a complete break. They chose the former, and not until the spirituality of Christianity breathed life into the inheritance of the Empire did the needed break to a fresh, non-naturalistic style come.

It has long been common to regard Roman sculpture as a bathetic echo of that of Greece. It is true that after the Roman conquest of Greece a vast trade in the pillaging of Greek statuary and a thriving industry in its copying sprang up, thanks to the desire of the Roman middle and upper classes to decorate their villas with the evidence of prosperity. To this taste we owe a great part of our knowledge of Greek sculpture, as copies have sometimes survived where the original was destroyed from religious zeal or melted for metal or burned for lime.

But more must be said. Since the pioneer work of Wickholt in 1895 it has been customary to emphasise three ways in which Roman sculptors developed the style of their predecessors: by further extending the Hellenistic taste for representational realism, by improving the techniques of suggesting perspective backgrounds in reliefs, and by seizing on the anecdotal side of Greek and Hellenistic friezes and devising a grandiose style of narrative sculpture in continuous panels. There is indeed something specifically Roman in the way these narrative reliefs express an immanent sense of Rome's historical destiny. Outstanding examples are the reliefs on Trajan's column (→ 274–6, 279–80, 283–5, 453), Trajan's arch at Beneventum (→ 337, 339, 365), the arch of Titus, the column of Marcus Aurelius (→ 278), and the arch of Constantine (→ 282), all in Rome.

Also significant is the Roman taste for realistic individualised portraiture (→ 266, 396–403). Sometimes this native taste for realism predominated, leading to the extreme step of taking death masks and copying them in terracotta or marble; sometimes the more idealistic Hellenistic tradition predominated; and sometimes the two styles are successfully blended as in a well-known haed of Augustus (→ 317).

Apart from some outstanding exceptions, however, the general run of Roman sculpture, especially the minor sculpture of sarcophagi, tombstones, and so on (→ 244–5, 281, 303, 308, etc.), is of more interest to the student of Roman history and social life than to the student of art. The most fascinating aspect for the latter is the gradual transformation of the late classical manner into the eloquent stylisation of Romanesque.

PAINTING

Of Greek painting little can be said, for little is known and practically nothing survives. We know the names of artists like Polygnotus, Philoxenus, Zeuxis, and Apelles. Of the last we have the well-known story of his hiding to listen to comments on his work and overhearing a shoemaker criticising the drawing of a boot. Apelles modified the work, but, when the cobbler afterwards criticised the drawing of the leg, he burst out with the famous retort: 'Cobbler, stick to your last!' From this and other descriptions and anecdotes like the one crediting Zeuxis with cherries so realistically painted that the birds flew down to eat them, we can deduce that Greek painting was representational and descriptive. We know, too, that its main subjects were narrative anecdotes and portraits. The portraits of Alexander by Apelles, the only painter the conqueror sat to, were especially admired.

Greek vase painting (see pp. 62–3). Of the painting of vases, however, we have abundant records, and can trace the development of the various styles and phases in some detail. Pottery has been intensively studied and analysed as a means of dating archaeological finds, and under the scutiny of an expert even minute sherds can usually be dated with some precision and often reveal the chronology of a whole site. Here, however, there is space only for a brief description of the main styles of vase decoration.

Geometrical style. After the disappearance of the Bronze Age Minoan and Mycenaean cultures before that of iron, in the eleventh century, the first style of Greek vase decoration to emerge was the geometrical. As the name implies, the elements were regular shapes – circles, triangles, diamonds, hatched lines, key patterns. Though somewhat rigid in conception and execution, the best geometrical vases are surprisingly effective and satisfying, considering the simplicity of the elements, and show sensitive appreciation of weight and line in the disposition of the parallel bands of ornament (→ 185–6).

Black-figure. After an interval towards the end of the eighth and the beginning of the seventh centuries during which so-called 'oriental' motifs – sphinxes, lotus leaves, animal and human figures – were used, there developed in Corinth a new style in which the decoration was applied to the red clay of the vase in black paint, sometimes with the outline incised and details picked out in red or white paint (→ 64–6). The Attic school specialised in human figures and in the sixth century reached an extremely high level (→ 118, 187–8).

Red-figure. In the later sixth century the perfection of the black-figure technique was succeeded by the red-figure. In this the design is drawn on to the pot and the background filled in solid black. Fine details were added inside the silhouettes with black or with black diluted to give a warm brown over the red of the clay (→ 54, 98, 119–22, 189, 193–5, 201, 461).

The subjects of vase paintings were often scenes from mythology and many are spirited, charming, or humorous. The line is often sensitive and admirably contrived on the awkward shape of the vase side. The best vase painting must rank with the great achievements of classical art.

Roman painting. Our knowledge of Roman painting begins about the end of the second century B.C., when style and technique are already well developed. The earlier history is obscure, but wall-paintings of this date at Pompeii reveal qualities akin to the Roman contribution to sculpture: pleasure in the world of nature, a strong feeling for narrative, and an interest in the plastic qualities of the subject, in contrast to the two-dimensional treatment of Assyrian, Egyptian, and Greek artists. Most of the remains once decorated walls of houses in Rome, Pompeii, Herculaneum, Ostia, and elsewhere; they are, however, impressive rather than moving (→ 228).

The decoration of Roman pottery (*terra sigillata*; see Map 52, p. 127 and p. 123), while it sometimes reaches considerable refinement, especially where the clash of Roman and local styles produced an interesting amalgam,

cannot compare as significant art with its Greek counterpart.

MOSAIC

Mosaic is the construction of designs and pictures from small pieces of coloured glass, marble, or other material (*tesserae*). In Roman times the technique achieved considerable refinement, and mosaic pavements are among the most readily appreciable remains of Roman art. The two styles – the geometrical (*opus tesselatum*) and the pictorial (*opus vermiculatum*) were often combined in a central pictorial composition surrounded by borders of abstract patterns, and designs range from the pictorial notices to 'beware of the dog' which decorated many entrance floors to complicated compositions with elaborate perspective. Gradually these latter developed into decorative landscape designs and then into all-over patterns, and so into the non-representational style of Byzantium and Ravenna. Mosaic technique is exceptionally interesting, and some of the more complicated Roman examples contain over 150 tesserae to the square inch (→ 312, 422, 428–30).

Though Greek and Roman artists and craftsmen studied their business with care and intelligence – and often with genius – as is evidenced by the mathematical subtleties underlying the proportions of temples and vases, artistic matters were scarcely accorded that prominent place in serious discussion that was unhesitatingly bestowed on poetry, drama, philosophy, rhetoric, and politics. Compared with classical – especially Greek – thought, classical art lacks something – it lacks the attitude of fundamental questioning and intellectual daring which has kept classical thought a living force among us and which distinguishes, for examples the artistic ferment of the Italian Renaissance. It is perhaps significant that there was on Helicon no muse of sculpture or painting or architecture. Classical art was, by and large, of the body, physical, rather than of the mind, spiritual, descriptive and factual rather than imaginative and symbolic. Of these limitations and its own limited perfection it perished.

The legacy of Roman law

Detailed knowledge of Roman legal practice was gradually lost after the fall of the Western Empire, and not until a copy of the Digest (the principal section of the *Corpus Iuris*, the vast codification of Justinian) turned up in northern Italy in the eleventh century was a revival in knowledge and study possible in the West. In the fourteenth century the theoretical knowledge thus gained began to be applied in practice so universally in Continental Europe that the process became known as the *receptio* of Roman law.

One important result of the *receptio* was the similarity between the various derived codes, and though the professor of Roman Law is not now the international figure he was in the Middle Ages, the lasting family likeness between the national systems enables a Continental jurist to find his way easily in a neighbouring code. The two important secondary sources through which Roman law has shaped modern European practice and through it that of much of the Americas, South Africa, Egypt, Japan, and other countries are the French *Code Civil* of 1804 and the German *Bürgerliches Gesetzbuch* of 1900 (see Map 70, page 183). There are, of course, wide differences between these two codes, though each is avowedly based on Roman theory, since each is naturally an adaptation of the original to meet new circumstances and is an attempt to interpret Roman theory rather than an historical re-creation of Roman practice. The French codifiers derived much from Pothier, an eighteenth-century French juridical writer on Roman law; the compilers of the German code based themselves on the German teachers of Roman law (Pandectists) and their systematic textbooks. It should be emphasised, too, that modern European legal systems are not based wholly on Roman law. Canon law played its part, and the law of proof and the legal institutes typical of modern commercial society – shares, bonds, letters of exchange, insurance, partnership, and so on – were medieval creations.

It is comparatively easy to state in general terms the main concepts which jurists found of value in the example of Roman law. The most important was perhaps the idea of law as written reason, *ratio scripta*, employing the principles of natural justice. Nearly all students of both earlier and later date shared to a greater or lesser degree Savigny's view of law as securely founded on the *Natur der Dingen*, the nature of things, and in this light they shaped their own practice on Roman precedent. Again, Roman law was secular, and the distinction between legal and moral obligation (*ius* and *fas*) was established from the earliest times. This was of immense importance in freeing Roman law and its derived codes from theological considerations, and marks a sharp difference between such societies and those in which religion, morality, and law have been or still are considered inseparable. Roman law was free from ritual, magic, and cult: for example, right from the beginning, so far as we know, its law of proof did not involve ordeal, privileges of status, or the torture of citizens. It was a law which thought purely in terms of external fact rather than ethics or theology.

Thus the judgments pronounced in the courts of the secular Roman state, assembled in the *Corpus Iuris*, provided centuries later, at Bologna and elsewhere, the material for the legal thought of the teachers and students in the medieval world. In the Middle Ages the Roman law jurists took the lead in the struggle to free the individual from the ancient collective bonds of kindred and feudality and from irrational ritualistic practices such as trial by ordeal. In the twelfth and thirteenth centuries all this harmonised well with the interests and attitudes of an increasingly influential section of the community – the active and prosperous middle classes in the towns who were beginning to revolt against the economic and ideological structure of feudalism. In the *Corpus Iuris* the late-medieval jurist found the representation of a society which to be sure did not ensure personal freedom for every one (it recognised slavery) but in which order and law reigned without influence from the priesthood – in a word, of a purely secular society.

Another fundamental concept of Roman law – that jurisprudence arises essentially from the interpretation of written rules of edicts and laws, and that administration of law is interpretation and application to facts by the judge of the case formula – is to be explained by the circumstance that even in early Republican times the activity of the Roman jurists consisted in the exposition and interpretation of texts, in the earliest times of the Laws of the Twelve Tables (450 B.C.) and the most ancient case formulas, and later of the praetor's edicts. The fact that from the beginning of Roman legal history a written legal text existed in the Twelve Tables – and the creation by a small community of Latin farmers of a body of laws which found its sanction in a sense of justice and equity rather than in the authority of a divine or human lawgiver, was a remarkable achievement – decisively influenced the Roman juridical style of thought and method and through them the whole Continental European view of law and the administration of law in their broad principles down to the present day.

All this, of course, is not intended to imply that the Roman approach to law was the only or even the best one possible. English law and the law of the American and Commonwealth countries derived from it have taken their own independent course and built up systems which fitted the ways of thought and life of their society and fulfilled its needs. It remains none the less true that the majestic structure of Roman law is not merely of permanent interest as an academic subject of study to lawyers and historians all over the world; the normal, practical procedure of jurists throughout the greater part of Europe and many other parts of the world is a living growth still rooted in this precise yet flexible organism. For the peculiar character of the interpretation of legal rules which distinguishes Roman law lay in the remarkable combination of being tied to an authoritative text and the relative freedom as to what sense was attributed to this text. A jurisprudence could not have developed from the wholly free, arbitrary decisions of an absolute ruler, despot, or tyrant, who gave judgment on each case as it arose without rule or law, and even less from a complete enslavement to tradition, precedent, and a sacrosanct written text. It was precisely this combination of being free and being bound, the attribution of meaning within certain limits to which the Romans regarded themselves as restricted by legal texts, edicts, and formulas, which produced Roman legal practice and through it the modern Continental European concept of law.

The importance of Roman law in the shaping of Western culture lies as much in these fundamental concepts which it exemplified as in the fact that from it are derived large portions of the detailed working out of European and some other systems. Reason and equity (*ratio* and *aequitas*) are two of the mainsprings of Roman law, and though it was not alone in proclaiming their universal validity, it played its part in placing them permanently before us.

475. A classical motif which greatly influenced Renaissance artists was that of the Three Graces. Their office as attendants on Aphrodite enabled them to be used for the portrayal of female beauty. Of this group, employed in Hellenistic art and architecture, about 100 copies are known, excluding paintings.

INDEX

Modern equivalents to classical names are given in brackets following the headword. Where several variants occur they are distinguished by the words *earlier* or *later* or the language of the less familiar form, according as the variants represent differences in time or in nationality. For the sake of simplicity and uniformity, all towns are given the designation 'city', irrespective of their size or status. The names of provinces used wherever possible to identify places in the Empire are those of the organisation at its widest extent in the 2nd century A.D. (see Map 38).

ABBREVIATIONS

Fr. = French; Ger. = German; Gr. = Greek; Hell. = Hellenistic form; Lat. = Latin; Rom. = Roman

A

Abavalla (Burgh-by-Sands), fort on Hadrian's Wall in Britain: Map 48a

Abdera 1. (Adra), port on SE. coast of Baetica: Map 66
2. city on coast of Thrace: Maps 11, 16, 19, 26, 72

Abella, city in Campania: Map 68

Abellinum (Avellino), city on border of Campania and Samnium: Map 57

Abetone, Monte, hill near Cerveteri with Etruscan cemetery: Map 34

Abila, Hell. **Seleucia** (Tell Abil), city of the Decapolis in Syria beyond the Jordan: Map 28

Abus (Humber), estuary in N. Britain: Map 60

Abusina (Eining), garrison post on the northern boundary of Raetia, on the Danube: Map 50

Abydos, city in Phrygia, on the Hellespont: Maps 11, 15, 16, 19, 72

Academy, earliest school of philosophy in Athens, founded by Plato ca. 387 B.C.: pp. 63, 89

Acarnania, district in W. of central Greece: Maps 9, 11, 15

Acci Gemella (Guadix), city in S. of Tarraconensis, near border of Baetica: Map 66

Accius (170-ca. 68 B.C.), from Pisaurum, Rom. dramatist, author of 40 tragedies, mostly adaptations from the great Greek models: Map 73

Acelum (Asolo), city in land of the Veneti in Gallia Cisalpina: Maps 58, 71

Acesta, see SEGESTA

Achaeans, name for the Indo-European tribes who invaded Greece after 2000 B.C.: p. 21; Maps 3, 9; applied to one of the Greek tribes, originating in the S. of Thessaly: Map 15

Achaemenids, the earliest Persian dynasty, descended from Achaemenes: p. 66

Achaia, district on N. coast of the Peloponnese: Maps 1, 3, 9, 11, 15, 16, 25; after 146 B.C. name of the whole of Greece as a Roman province: Maps 37, 38

Acharnae, deme in Attica N. of Athens: Map 14

Achelous (Aspropotamos), river on the boundary of Acarnania and Aetolia: Maps 1, 3, 11

Achilles, one of the leading characters in the *Iliad*, the chief Gr. hero in the Trojan War, invulnerable except in the heel: pp. 177, 181

Acholla (Badria), place on W. coast of Africa Proconsularis: Maps 30, 68

Acinipo (Ronda la Vieja), city in Baetica: Maps 22, 66, 71

Acrae (Palozzolo Acreide), city in SE. of Sicily, Gr. foundation: Maps 16, 29, 71

Acragas, see AGRIGENTUM

Acre, see PTOLEMAIS

Acritas Pr., cape on the S. point of Messenia: Map 1

Acrite (Akri), island in the Aegean Sea, one of the Sporades: Map 1

Acrocorinthus, the citadel of Corinth: Plate 63

acropolis, the 'upper town' or citadel of a Gr. city, built upon a hill or height of natural strategic strength: Plates 56, 59, 73, 78; especially applied to the Acropolis of Athens, the steep rock with access from only one side, containing among other buildings the Parthenon, the sanctuary of the tutelary goddess of the city: p. 51; Map 13; Plates 53, 56, 57, 58, 59

Acruvium, city on coast of Dalmatia: Map 57

Acte, most easterly prong of the peninsula of Chalcidice: Map 1

Actium, cape (Punta) and town (Azio), on coast of Acarnania; off the cape Octavian defeated Mark Antony and Cleopatra in a naval battle 31 B.C.: pp. 130, 178; Maps 37, 40, 45, 51

Acumincum, city in Pannonia Inferior, on the Danube: Map 47

Adana, Hell. **Antiochia**, city in Cilicia: Map 28

Ad IX, XI, XII (i.e. 'at the ninth, eleventh, twelfth milestone'), names of various posting stages, with facilities for accommodation, on the Roman highways: Map 54

Ad Finem, posting stage in Gallia Cisalpina halfway along the route Patavium-Vicentia: Map 54

Ad Flexum, posting stage in Gallia Cisalpina near L. Benacus: Map 54

Ad Fonteclos, posting stage in Gallia Cisalpina on the route Parma-Placentia: Map 54

Ad Maiores (Henchir Besseriani), city in Numidia: Map 47

Ad Medias, posting stage in Gallia Cisalpina on the Via Aemilia between Bononia and Mutina: Map 54

Ad Mercurium, headland and fortress on the coast of Mauretania Tingitana: Maps 47, 51

Ad Picilia, posting stage in Gallia Cisalpina on the Via Postumia between Aquileia and Concordia: Map 54

Adramyttium (Edremit), city on coast of Mysia: Maps 1, 11, 51

Adria, Etruscan port in land of the Veneti: Maps 29, 31, 33, 71

Adrianople, see ADRIANOPOLIS

Adrianopolis (Edirne), city in Thrace, on the Hebrus: p. 175

Adriaticum or **Hadriaticum** or **Superum, Mare** (the Adriatic Sea): Maps 31, 53

Ad Tarum, posting stage in Gallia Cisalpina on the Via Aemilia where it crossed the R. Tarus: Map 54

Aeclanum, city of the Hirpini in Samnium, on the Via Appia: Maps 57, 68

Aegae 1. city near the coast of Lydia: Maps 18, 68
2. city on coast of Achaia, on the Sinus Corinthiacus: Map 1
3. city in Macedon, early residence of the Macedonian kings: Maps 11, 15
4. city in Euboea: Map 25

Aegaeum, Mare (the Aegean Sea): Map 1

Aegates Iae., islands W. of Sicily: p. 102; Maps 12, 35, 53

Aegatian Is., see AEGATES IAE.

Aegina (Egina), island with city of same name in the Sinus Saronicus: Maps 1, 9, 11, 14, 15, 17a, 19, 51, 72; Plate 173

Aegira. city on coast of Achaia: Map 71a

Aegisthus. paramour of Clytemnestra queen of Mycenae and in conjunction with her murderer of her husband Agamemnon; known from the tragedies of Aeschylus and Sophocles: p. 179

Aegium (Aigion), city in Achaia on the Sinus Saronicus: Map 11

Aegosthena (Porto Germano), place on N.W. coast of Megaris: Maps 1, 14, 17a; Plates 10, 113, 114

Aegospotami, river and small town in the Chersonesus Thracica, on the Hellespont, where the Athenian fleet was finally defeated by Lysander 405 B.C.: p. 59

Aegyptus, more or less modern Egypt without the peninsula of Sinai, which in ancient times belonged to Arabia Petraea: pp. 82, 85, 89, 107, 130, 188; Maps 23, 26, 27, 28, 32, 36, 37, 38, 59

Aelana ('Aqaba), port in Arabia Petraea, on the Red Sea: Maps 26, 47

Aelia Capitolina, see HIEROSOLYMA

Aelius Donatus (4th cent. A.D.) Rom. grammarian, author of school grammars and commentaries on Virgil and other writers: Map 73

Aemilia, district in Italy S. of the Padus, between Placentia and Ariminum: Maps 31, 33

Aemilianus, Marcus, Rom. Emperor A.D. 253: Map 69b

Aemilia Scauri Via, highway in N. Italy between Genua and Luna: Map 53

Aemilia Via, highway in N. Italy between Ariminum and Aquileia: Maps 33, 53, 54

Aemilius Paulus 1. **Lucius**, Rom. general; defeated Perseus of Macedon at Pydna 168 B.C.: Map 40
2. **Marcus**, father of LUCIUS, Rom. consul; perished at Cannae 216 B.C.: Map 35

Aeneas, Trojan hero, son of Anchises and the goddess Venus; fled from burning Troy with his father and little son, and under divine guidance after many wanderings landed in Italy, where, according to tradition, he became the ancestor of the Roman race: pp. 178, 188

Aeneid, Virgil's epic on the fortunes of Aeneas: p. 178

Aenianes, tribe in Thessaly: Map 15

Aenus (Enez), city on the coast of Thrace at the mouth of the Hebrus, according to legend founded by Aeneas: Maps 11, 16, 19

Aenus M., mountain in Cephallenia: Map 1

Aeolia, mythical island where the winds were kept shut in a rocky cavern by their king Aeolus: Map 10

Aeoliae Iae., see LIPARAEAE IAE.

Aeolians, people who invaded Greece from the north ca. 1600 B.C. and settled in Thessaly and other places: p. 31; Map 3

Aequi, people in Latium: Map 29

Aequum (Citluk), city in Dalmatia: Map 57

Aeschines (390-314 B.C.), Athenian orator; supported the cause of Macedon in opposition to Demosthenes: pp. 62, 189

Aeschylus (525-456 B.C.), from Eleusis, the first of the three great Athenian tragedians; author of more than 70 tragedies; introduced the second actor whereby the dialogue became independent of the

of the Sophists: Map 72
Antandrus, city on S. coast of Troas: Map 11
Anthedon, city on coast of Palestine: Map 28
Anthela, place near Thermopylae: Maps 15, 21
Anthemus, city in N. of Mesopotamia: Map 28
Anticaria (Antequera), city in S. of Baetica: Map 66
Antigone, daughter of Oedipus king of Thebes; buried her dead brother in defiance of the command of Creon, successor of Oedipus, and was sentenced to death by him; principal character in the tragedy of the same name by Sophocles: p. 180
Antigonea, city in Syria, on the Orontes: Map 27
Antigonids, successors of Antigonus, Diadochi kings in Asia Minor: p. 82
Antigonus 1. general of Alexander the Great and after his death king of a large part of Asia Minor; waged war against the other Diadochi; defeated and killed at the battle of Ipsus 301 B.C.: p. 66
2. **Gonatas,** son of Demetrius Poliorcetes, king of Macedon 283-240 B.C.: pp. 82, 89
Antimachus (ca. 400 B.C.), from Colophon, Gr. epic poet, author of the *Thebais*, etc.: Map 72
Antinoe *or* **Antinoopolis,** city in Egypt, on the Nile, founded by Hadrian: Map 71
Antiochia 1. (Antioch), city in Syria, on the Orontes, capital of the province, centre of Hellenistic culture: p. 82; Maps 38, 49, 51, 68, 69d, 71, 73
2. (Yalvac), city in Pisidia: Maps 18a, 57, 71
3. city in Commagene: Map 28
4. coastal place in W. of Cilicia: Map 28
5. city in Caria, on the Maeander: Map 28
6. city in E. of Phrygia: Map 28
7, 8, 9, 10, 11, 12, 13, 14, 15. Hell. for ADANA, ALEXANDRIA at the mouth of the Tigris, GERASA, HIPPOS, MALLUS, NISIBIS, NYSA, ORRHOE, TARSUS
Antiochus 1. the Great, Syrian king of the Seleucid dynasty (223-187 B.C.); afforded hospitality to Hannibal after his defeat at Zama: pp. 85, 107; Map 40
2. **Epiphanes,** son of THE GREAT, under whose tyrannous government (175-164 B.C.) the revolt of the Maccabees broke out: p. 82
3. Gr. historian from Syracuse (5th cent. B.C.) Map 72
Antiphanes (ca. 388-311 B.C.), Gr. writer of comedies: Map 72
Antiphellus, city on coast of Lycia: Map 71b
Antiphon 1. (late 5th cent. B.C.), from Miletus, Gr. philosopher, Sophist: Map 72
2. (ca. 480-411 B.C.), from Attica, the first of the so-called Ten Attic Orators: Map 72
Antipolis (Antibes), city on coast of Gallia Narbonensis, Gr. foundation: Maps 16, 29, 51, 71
Antissa, city on N. coast of Lesbos: Map 11
Antisthenes (ca. 450-365 B.C.), from Athens, Gr. philosopher, pupil of Socrates, founder of the school of Cynics: Map 72
Antium (Anzio), city on coast of Latium: Maps 29, 51, 53, 57, 71c
Antonini, Vallum (Antonine Wall), boundary fortification in modern Scotland, established by the Emperor Antoninus Pius in A.D. 142: Maps 38, 47, 48, 60
Antoninus Pius, Roman Emperor 138-161 A.D. by virtue of his adoption by Hadrian: pp. 134, 154; Maps 48, 50, 69b; Plates 331, 347
Antony, Mark (83-30 B.C.), friend of Caesar, member of the Second Triumvirate; later opponent of Octavian and defeated by him at Actium in 31 B.C., in consequence of which he committed suicide: pp. 85, 130; Plate 265
Antonius, Marcus, see ANTONY, MARK
Antunnacum (Andernach), city on the Rhine, on the border of Germania Inferior and Germania Superior: Map 51
Anxa, *earlier* **Callipolis** (Gallipoli), place on W. coast of Calabria, Gr. foundation: Maps 16, 29
Anxanum (Lanciano), city in NE. of Samnium: Map71c
Aornus (Tashkurgan, *earlier* Khulm) mountain fortress in Bactria, E. of Bactra: Map 26
Aous (Vijosë, *Gr.* Aoos), river in Epirus: Map 11
Apamea 1. (Qala'at el-Mudig), city in Syria, on the Orontes: Maps 28, 49, 71
2. (Diner), city on the border of Phrygia and Pisidia: Map 71b
3. (Birêgik), city in N. of Mesopotamia, on the Tigris: Map 28
4. city in S. of Mesopotamia, on the Tigris: Map 28
5. city in Susiana, N. of the Persian Gulf: Map 28
6. city in Media, near the Portae Caspiae: Map 28
7. Hell. for MYRLEA
Apelles (4th cent. B.C.), famous Gr. painter, patronised by Alexander the Great: pp. 63, 193
Aperlae, city on coast of Lycia: Map 71
Aphidna, deme in Attica, N. of Marathon: Map 14
Aphrodisias, city in Caria, dedicated to Aphrodite: Maps 18a, 68, 71b
Aphrodite, Gr. goddess of beauty and love; by the Romans identified with Venus: pp. 62, 88,181; Maps 24, 25
Aphrodite of Cnidus, a statue by Praxiteles (4th cent. B.C.), famous in antiquity and now known from later copies: p. 192
Apollo, Gr. god of the purifying light, of music and poetry; born in Delos; especially honoured as the god of the oracle at Delphi (Apollon Pythios), the proclaimer of the decrees of Zeus and purifier from the pollution of guilt; highly revered also by the Romans: pp. 177, 180, 181; Maps 24, 25; Plates 95, 102, 162
Apollo of Veii, an Etruscan painted terracotta of the 6th cent. B.C., found at Veii in 1916; generally regarded as the masterpiece of early Etruscan art: pp. 96, 190
Apollodorus (c. 150 B.C.), from Athens, author of philosophical, historical and mythological works: Map 72
Apollon, see APOLLO
Apollonia 1. (Marsa Susa), port on coast of Cyrenaica: Maps 16, 51
2. (Abulyont), city in Phrygia: Maps 18a, 28, 72
3. *earlier* **Sozopolis** (Sozopol), Gr. colony in Thrace, on W. coast of the Black Sea: Maps 16, 26, 27
4. city in Macedon, near W. coast: Maps 11, 16, 35, 37, 47
5. city in Mysia; Map 28
6. city on coast of Palestine: Map 28
7. city in SW. of Media: Map 28
8. Hell. for TRIPOLIS in Lydia
Apollonis, city in N. of Lydia: Map 28
Apollonius Rhodius (ca. 295-215 B.C.), from Alexandria, Gr. grammarian and epic poet, author of the *Argonautica*; taught rhetoric at Rhodes and later became chief librarian of the library at Alexandria: Map 72
Appia Via, the oldest and most famous highway in Italy, from Rome to Brundisium, called 'regina viarum'; construction was begun by Appius Claudius during his censorship 312 B.C.: p. 96; Maps 53, 55; Plates 296, 442
Apri, city in S. of Thrace: Map 57
Apsarus, city on E. coast of the Black Sea: Map 47
Apsus (Osum), river in Illyria: Map 11
Apta Iulia (Apt), city in Gallia Narbonensis, E. of the Rhodanus: Map 68
Apuleius (ca A.D. 125-ca. 180), from Madaura, Rom. prose writer, author of a fantastic romance, *The Golden Ass*, and other works: p. 190; Map 73
Apulia, district in S. Italy, bounded by Calabria, Samnium, and Picenum: Maps 3, 31
Apulum (Alba Iulia, *Ger.* Karlsburg), garrison town in Dacia: Maps 41, 47, 57
Aquae Aonemetiae (Buxton), city and spa in central Britain: Map 60
Aquae Atilianae (Sadaba), city in NE. of Tarraconensis: Map 66
Aquae Flaviae (Chaves), city in S. of Gallaecia: Maps 57, 66
Aquae Mattiacorum (Wiesbaden), city in N. of Agri Decumates, at the foot of the Taunus Mountains, famous for its medicinal springs: Map 46
Aquae Neri (Néris), city in NE. of Aquitania: Map 71
Aquae Segetae, city in SE. corner of Gallia Lugdunensis, on the Liger: Map 71
Aquae Sextiae (Aix-en-Provence), city in Gallia Narbonensis where Marius defeated the Teutoni 102 B.C.: Map 40
Aquae Sulis (Bath), city and spa in SW. Britain: Maps 60, 61, 65
Aquae Voconiae (Caldas de Malabellas), city in NE. of Tarraconensis: Map 66
Aquileia, important city and port on the boundary of the land of the Veneti and Istria, a strong fortified place; played a notable part against the invasions of the barbarians from the NE.; outstanding trade centre and renowned for its industries (e.g. glassware); destroyed by Attila A.D. 452: Maps 43, 47, 51, 53, 54, 58, 68
Aquincum (Budapest), frontier fortress in Pannonia Inferior, on the Danube: Maps 41, 46, 47, 57, 68
Aquinum (Aquino), city in S. of Latium: Maps 57, 58, 68, 71c, 73
Aquitani, people in SW. Gaul, conquered by Caesar's legates: Map 36
Aquitania, see under GAUL
Arabia, the modern Saudi Arabia, in antiquity divided into Arabia Felix (the fruitful strip along the Red Sea), Arabia Deserta (the desert district W. of Syria), and Arabia Petraea (the area E. of Palaestina as far as the Red Sea): Maps 23, 37, 38, 59
Arabicus, Sinus (the Red Sea): Maps 37, 38, 43, 59
Arachosia, district N. of Gedrosia, bounded on the E. by the Indus: Maps 23, 26, 27
Arachthus (Arta), river in Epirus: Map 11
Aradus *or* **Arvad** (Ruâd), city and port in Phoenicia, on a small island near the coast: Maps 26, 28, 30
Area Flaviae (Rottweil), garrison place in the district of Agri Decumates: Map 50
Arae Philaenorum (Ras el-Aàli), fort on the border of Cyrenaica and Tripolis: Map 47
Ararat M., mountain in Armenia: Map 40
Aratus 1. (271-ca. 213 B.C.), statesman and general: p. 82
2. (ca. 310-245 B.C.), from Soli, Gr. author: Map 72
Arausio (Orange), city in Gallia Narbonensis: Maps 35, 40, 57, 68, 71
Araxes (Araks), river in Armenia: Maps 23, 28, 43
Arbeia (South Shields), Rom. fort on NE. coast of Britain on the E. flank of Hadrian's Wall and the Tyne estuary: Maps 46, 60
Arbela, Hell. **Alexandria** (Erbil), city in Assyria: Maps 23, 26, 27
Arbogast, barbarian general of Theodosius I, chief minister of Valentinian II, whom he caused to be murdered A.D. 392: p. 175
Arcadia, district in the centre of the Peloponnese: Maps 1, 3, 9, 11, 15, 25
Arcadius, Eastern Roman Emperor A.D. 395-408: p. 175
Arcesilaus 1. (ca. 315-240 B.C.), from Pitane, Gr. philosopher, Academician, founder of the Second Academy: Map 72
2. name of 4 kings of Cyrene ca. 600-450 B.C.: Plate 89
Archilochus (ca. 650 B.C.), from Paros, Gr. poet, originator of iambic poetry: pp. 181, 182: Map 72
Archimedes (287-212 B.C.), from Syracuse, famous Gr. mathematician, inventor among other things of the law named after him: Map 72
Arcobriga (Monreal de Ariza), city in Hispania Tarraconensis: Maps 66, 71
Arctonnesus, promontory on S. coast of Propontis: Map 1
Ardea, city in Latium: Map 55
Ardeatina Via, road from Rome to Ardea: Map 55
Ardoch, site of Rom. fort in E. Scotland: Map 60
Aregenua, city in Gallia Lugdunensis: Map 71
Arelate (Arles), city in Gallia Narbonensis: Maps 57, 68, 69a, 71
Areopagus (i.e. 'the hill of Ares'), hill in Athens: Maps 13, 24; the oldest Athenian court, established upon this hill: pp. 42, 180
Ares, Gr. god of war; by the Romans identified with Mars: Maps 24, 25
Arethusa, city in Syria, on the Orontes: Map 28
Argenica, posting stage in Gallia Cisaplina, on the route Bergomum-Mediolanum: Map 54
Argentorate (Strasbourg), city in Germania Superior, on the Rhine: Maps 41, 50
Argolicus, Sinus (Gulf of Nauplia), bay S. of Argolis: Map 1; Plate 45
Argolis, district in NE. of the Peloponnese: p. 182; Maps 1, 11, 15
Argonauts (i.e. 'sailors of the Argo'), legendary Gr. heroes who sailed in the ship Argo to Colchis in search of the Golden Fleece: p. 21
Argos, 1. city in Argolis; in legend the realm of Diomede, in Mycenaean times one of the most important cities in Greece; also used as name for the district of Argolis, and by Homer as name of the Peloponnese or the whole of Greece: pp. 59, 102, 179; Maps 1, 9, 10, 11, 15, 17a, 18, 71a; Plates 68, 69
2. coastal place in Acarnania: Map 11
Aria, fertile district in E. of Ariana: Maps 23, 26, 27
Ariana, district N. of the Persian Gulf and the Arabian Sea, more or less the modern Iraq, Afghanistan, and Baluchistan: Map 59
Arianism, a system of Christian theology founded ca. A.D. 310 by Arius, condemned as heretical by the Council of Nicaea A.D. 325: p. 174
Ariarathea, city in Cappadocia: Map 28
Aricia (Ariccia), city in Latium on the Appia Via: Map 57
Ariminum (Rimini), city and port in N. of Umbria: Maps 33, 43, 51, 53, 57, 58, 68
Arion (ca. 625 B.C.), from Methymna, Gr. writer of dithyrambic verse: p. 181; Map 72
Ariovistus, leader of the Suebi: Map 40
Aristarchus 1. (ca. 310-230 B.C.), from Samos, Gr. mathematician; taught that the earth revolves round the sun and on its own axis: Map 72
2. (ca. 217-145 B.C.), from Samothrace, Gr. scholar, the most famous philologist of antiquity, known especially for his commentary on and textual criticism of Homer: Map 72
Aristippus (ca. 435-356 B.C.), from Cyrene, Gr. philosopher, pupil of Socrates, founder of the school of Cyrene: Map 72
Ariston (3rd cent. B.C.), from Chios, Gr. philosopher, at first a Cynic, later a Stoic: Map 72
Aristophanes 1. (446-382 B.C.), from Athens, Gr. writer of comedies, author of *The Clouds*, *The Wasps*, *The Birds*, and about 50 other plays: p. 181; Map 72
2. (ca. 257-180 B.C.), from Byzantium, Gr. scholar, responsible for editions of Homer among other works: Map 72
Aristotle (384-322 B.C.), from Stagirus in Chalcidice, famous Gr. philosopher, teacher of Alexander the Great, author of standard works on e.g. ethics and politics: pp. 63, 66, 88, 89, 123; Map 72

Aristoxenus (ca. 350 B.C.), from Tarentum, Gr. Peripatetic philosopher, author of biographies of Plato and Pythagoras, musical theorist: Map 72
Arius (ca. A.D. 260-336), from Libya, a priest of Alexandria, originator of the heresy which denied the complete divinity of Christ, condemned at the Council of Nicaea: p. 174
Arkalochori, place in central Crete; earliest traces from 3rd millennium B.C.: Map 4
Armenia, extensive mountainous region S. and SW. of the Caucasus: Maps 23, 26, 36, 37, 38, 59
Arminius, chief of the Cherusci; annihilated three Rom. legions under Varus in the Teutoburgian Forest A.D. 9: Map 40
Arnobius (ca. A.D. 300), from Sicca Veneria, Rom. rhetorician; after his conversion to Christianity author of apologetic works: Map 73
Arnus (Arno), river in Etruria: Maps 31, 33, 35, 53
Arpi, city in Apulia: Map 29
Arpinum (Arpino), city in Latium, birthplace of Cicero: Maps 57, 73
Arretium (Arezzo), city in Etruria: Maps 29, 33, 52, 53, 57, 68, 71c
Arsacids, Parthian dynasty named after its founder Arsaces (ca. 250 B.C.): pp. 82, 159; Map 47
Arsanias (Murat Suyn), river in Armenia, tributary of the Euphrates: Map 28
Arsinoe 1. *earlier* **Cleopatris,** city W. of the Nile delta, on the modern Bitter Lakes: Map 28
2. city in Phoenicia: Map 28
3. coastal place in W. of Cilicia: Map 28
4, 5. Hell. for EPHESUS, PATARA
Artacoana, city in Aria: Map 26
Artaxata, capital of Armenia: Maps 28, 40, 51
Artaxerxes 1. II, Memnon, king of Persia 404-358 B.C.: p. 62
2. **III,Ochus,** son of MEMNON, king of Persia 358-338 B.C.: pp. 59, 66
Artemis, Gr. goddess of the hunt, twin sister of Apollo; by the Romans identified with Diana: p. 180; Maps 24, 25; Plates 95, 102
Artemisium Pr., cape on the N. point of Euboea, scene of the naval battle between the Greeks and Persians 480 B.C.: Maps 1, 19
Artemita, city in SW. of Media: Map 28
Arvad, see ARADUS
Arverni, people in Gallia Celtica; have given their name to modern Auvergne: Map 40
Arycanda, city in Lycia: Map 71c
Ascalon (nr. 'Askalan), city on coast of Palestine: Map 28
Asconius (A.D. 3-88), from Patavium, Rom. writer: Map 73
Ascra, little town in Boeotia, residence of Hesiod: Map 72
Asculum (Ascoli), old capital of the Piceni in E. of Italy: Maps 29, 53, 57, 68, 71c; Plate 252
Asea, ancient fortress in S. of Arcadia, dating from 3rd millennium B.C.: Map 3
Asia, sometimes used for the continent in so far as it was known and for Asia Minor, but especially for a Roman province comprising originally the W. part of Asia Minor, later a constantly varying group of districts there: pp. 118, 119; Maps 37, 38
Asido Caesarina (Medina Sidonia), city in S. of Baetica: Map 66
Asine (Assine), 1. city on S. coast of Argolis: Maps 1, 3, 17
2. (Koroni) city on the SW. point of Messenia: Map 1
Asisium (Assisi), city in Umbria: Maps 57, 68, 71c, 73
Asklepios, Gr. god of medicine; specially noteworthy were his sanctuaries in Epidaurus and Cos; the snake was sacred to him; called Aesculapius by the Romans: Maps 24, 25; Plates 154-8
Asopus, 1. river in Boeotia: Map 22
2. coastal place on eastern tongue of Laconica: Map 1
Aspendus, city in Pamphylia: Maps 7, 16, 18a, 68, 71b
Assuras (Zanfour), city in Africa Proconsularis: Map 57
Assus (Assum), city on S. coast of Troas: Maps 1, 16, 18, 71, 72
Assyria, district E. of the Tigris: Maps 6, 38
Astacus, see NICOMEDIA
Astarte, Syro-Phoenician fertility goddess: p. 88
Astigi (Ecija), city in Baetica: Maps 57, 66, 68
Astura, place on coast of Latium: Map 53
Asturia, district in N. of Hispania Tarraconensis: Maps 37, 67
Asturica (Astorga), city in Gallaecia: Maps 47, 66
Astyages, king of Media 585-550 B.C., grandfather of Cyrus and deposed by him: p. 188
Astypalaea (Astypalaia), island in the Aegean Sea, one of the Sporades: Maps 1, 11
Atarneus, city near the coast of Mysia: Maps 11, 19
Atella, city in Campania: Map 57
Aternum (Pescara), city on the Adriatic Sea, on the boundary of Picenum and Samnium: Maps 51, 53
Atesis (Adige, *Ger.* Etsch), river in Gallia Cisalpina: Maps 33, 54
Athamania, district on the boundary of Epirus and Thessaly: Map 11
Athanasius (A.D. 295-373), from Alexandria, and its patriarch, theologian, the great opponent of the teaching of Arius: p. 174
Athenae 1. (Athens), capital of Attica, sacred to and named after the goddess Athena: legendary founder Theseus; earliest traces of habitation from Mycenaean times; spiritual and cultural centre of Greek world: pp. 39, 42, 56, 63, 85, 107, 119, 135, 181, 188; Maps 1, 3, 9, 11, 13, 14, 15, 17a, 18, 19, 25, 26, 27, 32, 38, 68, 71a, 72; Plates 53, 56, 57, 58, 59
2. (Atina), city on E. coast of the Black Sea: Map 47
Athenopolis (Saint-Tropez), city on coast of Gallia Narbonensis, Gr. foundation: Map 16
Athos M., headland in Chalcidice where the Persian fleet was wrecked 492 B.C.: p. 42; Maps 1, 11, 19; Plate 100
Atlanticus, Oceanus (the Atlantic Ocean): Maps 38, 43
Atina 1. (Atena), city in Lucania: Maps 57, 68
2. city in Latium: Map 57
Atlas M., mountain range in Mauretania: Maps 35, 59
Atrebates, tribe in Britain: Map 60
Attalea, city in Mysia: Map 28
Attalia (Antalya), city on coast of Pamphylia, founded by Attalus II: Maps 28, 47
Attalus III, king of Pergamum; made over his kingdom to Rome by will 133 B.C.: Map 38 (Pergamum)
Attica, district in E. of central Greece, with Ionian population; played a predominant part in the great age of Greece: p. 39; Maps 1, 9, 11, 14, 15, 19, 25; Plates 5, 9
Attidium, city in Umbria: Map 57
Attila, king of the Huns A.D. 434-453, called 'the Scourge of God'; ravaged the Eastern Empire 445-450; defeated at Châlons-sur-Marne by Aetius 451; penetrated into Italy 452, but spared Rome, it is said at the prayer of Pope Leo I: p. 175; Map 69
Attic Comedy, Gr. literary *genre,* divided into Old and New. Old flourished 5th cent. B.C.; chief representatives Cratinus, Eupolis, and especially Aristophanes: politics played an important part in the themes which it treated. New flourished 4th cent. B.C.; representatives Menander, Philemon, Diphilus; derived its subject matter from domestic life: pp. 122, 181
Aufidus (Ofanto), river in Apulia: Map 35; Plates 255, 257
Augusta Bagiennorum, city in W. of Liguria: Maps 68, 71
Augusta Praetoria (Aosta), city in NW. corner of Gallia Transpadana: Maps 53, 68, 71
Augusta Raurica (Augst), city in Germania Superior, on the Rhine: Maps 57, 71
Augusta Taurinorum, *earlier* **Taurasia** (Turin), city in Gallia Cisalpina, capital of the Taurini; the later name dates from the reign of Augustus: Maps 35, 53, 58, 68, 71
Augusta Treverorum (Trier), city in Gallia Belgica, capital of the Treveri; in the later years of the Empire one of its most flourishing and important cities: Maps 37, 47, 51, 52, 68, 73
Augusta Via, highway in Spain, from Carthago Nova to Tarraco: Map 66
Augusta Vindelicorum (Augsburg), city in Raetia: Maps 50, 57
Augustine (A.D. 354-430), from Thagaste, bishop of Hippo Regius, theologian, author of, among other works, the *Confessions* and *The City of God:* Map 73
Augustobriga (Talavera la Vieja), city in Lusitania, on the Tagus: Map 66
Augustodunum (Autun), city in Gallia Lugdunensis: Maps 47, 68, 71, 73
Augustomagus (Senlis), city in S. of Gallia Belgica: Map 68
Augustonometum (Clermont-Ferrand), city in E. of Aquitania: Map 57
Augustoritum (Limoges), city in Aquitania: Maps 68, 71
Augustus (i.e. 'the exalted'), title bestowed on OCTAVIANUS in 27 B.C. and subsequently assumed by the Emperors; under the Dominate, title of the senior two of the four tetrarchs: pp. 130, 171
Aulis, seaport on E. coast of Boeotia; from here the Gr. naval expedition to Troy sailed: Map 10
Aulon, coastal city on the Ionian Sea, on the boundary between Epirus and Macedonia: Map 51
Aulularia, comedy by Plautus: p. 181
Auraei, posting stage in Gallia Cisalpina on the Via Postumia between Vicetia and Verona: Map 54
Aurelian, Rom. Emperor A.D. 270-275, fortified Rome with a new wall, the greater part of which is still standing: p. 162; Plate 349; Maps 47, 69
Aurelia Via, highroad in Etruria between Rome and Luna: Maps 33, 53, 55
Aurelius Victor (4th cent. A.D.), from Africa, Rom. historian: Map 73
Aurgi (Jaén), city in Baetica: Map 57
Aurunci, people in the S. of Latium and Campania; exterminated by the Romans ca. 314 B.C.: Map 29
Ausa (Vich), city in the NE. of Tarraconensis: Map 66
Ausculum (Ascoli Satriano), city in the SW. of Apulia: Map 57
Ausonius (ca. A.D. 310-393), from Burdigala, Rom. poet: Map 73
Autessiodurum (Auxerre), city in Gallia Lugdunensis: Map 68
Autricum (Chartres), city in Gallia Lugdunensis: Map 57
Auximum (Osimo), city in the N. of Picenum: Map 57
Avaricum (Bourges), city in the N. of Aquitania: Maps 47, 68, 71
Avars, Mongolian people, living in the 6th cent. A.D. in the Danube plain: Map 69
Aventicum (Avenches), city in Germania Superior in the country of the Helvetii: Maps 47, 57, 68, 71
Aventinus M., one of the seven hills of ancient Rome: Maps 42, 44; Plate 349
Avernus Lacus, crater lake near Cumae where Virgil imagined the entrance to the underworld to be; Agrippa joined the lake to the sea with a canal, by which means it became, for a short time, the naval port of Portus Iulius: Map 53
Avienus (end of 3rd cent A.D.), from Volsinii, Rom. scholar: Map 73
Axius (Vardar, *Gr.* Axios), river in Macedonia: Maps 1, 11
Aziris (Wadi el Chalig), city on coast of Libya, E. of Cyrene: Map 26
Azotus (Esdûd), city on the coast of Palestine: Map 28

B

Baal (i.e. 'lord'), Syro-Phoenician deity: p. 88
Babylon, ancient capital of Babylonia, on the Euphrates; in 698 and 648 B.C. destroyed by the Assyrians, rebuilt after the downfall of the Assyrian empire, and ca. 600 B.C. the greatest and most beautiful city in the ancient world: p. 66; Maps 23, 26, 27, 28
Babylonia, district between the Tigris and the Arabian desert: Maps 23, 26-28
Bacchantes, see MAENADS
Bacchus, Rom. god of wine, identified with Dionysus: Plate 365
Bacchylides (ca. 522-ca. 450 B.C.), from Cos, Gr. lyric poet, nephew of Simonides; resided with him at the court of Hiero in Syracuse: Map 72
Bactra (Balkh), ancient powerful trading and commercial centre in Bactria, S. of the Oxus, situated on the 'Silk Road': Maps 23, 26, 27
Bactria, district in Asia, roughly equivalent to modern Afghanistan: Maps 23, 26, 27
Badbury, site in S. Britain with remains of Rom. road and burials: Map 61
Badias (Badès), city in Numidia: Map 47
Baecula, city in Baetica; the surrounding district is rich in silver mines: Map 35
Baedunia (La Baneza), city in Asturia: Map 66
Baelo (Bolonia), city on S. coast of Baetica: Maps 66, 67, 71
Baeterrae (Béziers), city in the S. of Gallia Narbonensis: Maps 57, 68
Baetica, see HISPANIA
Baetis (Guadalquivir), river in Baetica: Maps 43, 66, 67
Baetulo (Badalona), city on the N. coast of Tarraconensis: Map 66
Bagacum (Bavai), city in Gallia Belgica, capital of the Nervii; important trading junction: Map 52
Baiae (Baia), famous watering-place on the Sinus Cumanus, with many medicinal sulphur springs; in the time of the Rom. Empire it was notorious for worldly luxury: Maps 53, 71c
Balanea, city on the coast of Syria: Map 28
Balbura, city on the boundary between Caria and Lycia: Map 71b
Baleares Iae. (Balearic Islands), group of islands near the E. coast of Spain; the inhabitants were noted slingers and served as such in the Carthaginian and Rom. armies: Maps 30, 35, 66, 67
Balsa (Tavira), city on the S. coast of Lusitania: Map 57
Bambyce, see HIERAPOLIS
Banassac, town in SW. France, in ancient times a well-known centre for the production of terra sigillata: Map 52
Banditaccia, hill near Cerveteri, with a very extensive Etruscan cemetery: Map 34; Plates 230-3
Barbalissus (Meskene), city in Syria: Map 49
Barca (El Merg), place on the coast of Cyrenaica, Gr. foundation: Map 16
Barcides, distinguished family of Carthage to which Hasdrubal and Hannibal belonged: Maps 35, 40
Barcino (Barcelona), city on the E. coast of Tarraconensis: Maps 57, 66
Bargylia, city on coast of Caria: Map 71b
Baria (Vera), city near coast in the S. of Tarraconensis: Map 66
Barium (Bari), seaport in Apulia: Maps 53, 57
Bar Kochba, another name for Bar Koseba, leader

of the uprising in Judaea A.D. 132-135: Map 40
Basilia (Basel), city on the Rhine in the S. of Germania Superior: Map 50
Bassae, city in Arcadia, famous for its temple of Apollo: Maps 1, 18, 24; Plates 182-184
Bastarnae, German people: Map 47
Basti (Baza), city in the S. of Tarraconensis: Map 66
Batavi, German people from the delta of the Rhine: p. 134; Map 40
Batavians, see BATAVI
Bauli (Bacoli), city on the Sinus Cumanus: Map 71
Bedriacum, place in Gallia Cisalpina where in the 'Year of the Four Emperors' (A.D. 69) Otho was defeated by Vitellius, and later Vitellius was defeated by the troops of Vespasian: Map 45
Belerium Pr. (Land's End), cape in SW. Britain: Map 60
Belgae 1. tribe in N. of Gallia Transalpina: Map 36
2. tribe in Britain: Map 60
Bellunum (Belluno), city in E. of Gallia Cisalpina: Map 58
Benacus Lacus (Lago di Garda), lake in Gallia Cisalpina: Map 58
Beneventum 1. (Benevento) city in Samnium, capital of the Hirpini: p. 102; Maps 53, 57, 71c
2. (Castelnuovo di Verona) small place in Gallia Cisalpina on the route Verona-Brixia: Map 54
Berenice 1. important commercial port in the S. of Egypt on the Sinus Arabicus: Map 51
2. *earlier* **Euhesperides** (Bengazi), harbour on W. coast of Cyrenaica, Gr. foundation: Map 16
3. *or* **Pella,** city in Syria: Map 28
Bergomum (Bergamo), city in Gallia Cisalpina: Maps 53, 54
Beroea, *earlier* **Khalab** (Aleppo), city in Syria: Maps 28, 49
Berytus (Beirut), harbour in Phoenicia: Maps 30, 57
Bethlehem, city in Judaea, birthplace of David and Christ: Map 37
Bibracte (Mont Beuvray), hill fortress in Gallia Celtica, capital of the Aedui: Map 36
Bignor, site of Rom. villa in S. Britain: Map 61
Bilbilis (Calatayud), city in Tarraconensis: Maps 66, 67, 71, 73
Bion (3rd cent. B.C.), from Borysthenes, Gr. philosopher: Map 72
Biriciana (Weissenburg), fortress on the border of Germania Superior: Map 50
Bithynia, district in Asia Minor on the S. coast of the Black Sea: p. 190; Maps 28, 36-38
Blatobulgium (Birrens), outpost fort of Hadrian's Wall in Britain: Map 60
Blaundus, city in Lydia: Maps 28, 71b
Blera (Bieda), city in Etruria, on the Via Clodia: Maps 33, 57
Bodia, place on the boundary between Laconica and Messenia, where the beehive tombs of Mycenaean times were discovered: Map 3
Bodotria Aest. (Firth of Forth), estuary in N. Britain: Map 60
Boeae, city on the S. coast of the E. promontory of Laconica: Map 1
Boeotia, district in central Greece; fertile farmland: Maps 1, 9, 11, 19
Boethius (A.D. 480-524), from Rome, Rom. philosopher, counsellor of Theodoric; author of *De Consolatione Philosophiae*: Map 73
Boghaz-keui, see HATTUSHASH
Bonna (Bonn), boundary fortress on the Rhine in Germania Inferior: Maps 41, 47, 51
Bononia, in Etruscan period **Felsina** (Bologna), city in the N. of Italy; an important centre even before the Etruscan period: Maps 29, 31, 33, 46, 47, 53, 54, 58
Borysthenes (Dnieper), river in Sarmatia; also another name for Olbia, the Gr. settlement at the mouth of this river: Map 59
Bosporus, strait of Constantinople: p. 174; Map 11
Bostra (Bosra), city in Arabia Petraea: Maps 38, 41, 45, 49, 51, 68, 71
Boudicca, queen of the Iceni, led the uprising of ca. A.D. 60: Map 40
Boutae, city in the NE. of Gallia Narbonensis: Map 71
Bovianum (Boiano), city in Samnium: Maps 57, 71
Bovillae, city in Latium on the Via Appia: Maps 68, 71
Bracara (Braga), city in the S. of Gallaecia: Maps 57, 66, 73
Brading, site of Rom. villa in S. Britain: Map 61
Brauron, important deme on the E. coast of Attica: Map 14
Bremenium (High Rochester), outpost fort of Hadrian's Wall in Britain: Maps 60, 61
Bremetennacum (Ribchester), Rom. fort in NE. Britain: Map 60
Bremia (Llanio), Rom. fort in W. Britain: Map 60
Brigantes, powerful tribe in Britain with a capital at Eburacum: Maps 47, 48, 48a, 60
Brigantio (Briançon), city in the Alpes Cottiae: Map 57
Brigantium, 1. (La Coruña) city on NW. coast of Spain: Maps 43, 47, 66
2. (Bregenz) city in Raetia, on Venetus L.: Map 52
Brigetio (Oszöny), garrison town in Pannonia Superior, on the Danube: Maps 41, 45, 47, 68
Britain, see BRITANNIA
Britannia, more or less the modern England, Wales, and S. Scotland: Maps 32, 36, 38, 45, 60-5
Britannicus, Oceanus (the English Channel): Map 38
Brixellum (Brescello), city in N. of Aemilia, on the Padus: Map 58
Brixia (Brescia), city in Gallia Cisalpina: Maps 53, 54, 58, 71
Brocavum (Brougham), Rom. fort in N. Britain: Map 60
Brundisium (Brindisi), important port on E. coast of Calabria, port of embarcation for Greece: Maps 29, 35, 37, 43, 47, 51, 53, 73
Bruttii (Calabria), the SW. point of Italy: Map 31
Brutus 1. **Lucius Junius** (6th cent. B.C.), legendary first consul of Rome: p. 92
2. **Marcus Junius,** friend of Caesar, later one of his murderers: p. 130; Plate 266
Bubon, city on the boundary between Caria and Lycia: Map 71
Burdigala (Bordeaux), city in Aquitania, near the mouth of the Garumna: Maps 47, 68, 73
Burgundi, Ger. people from between the Oder and the Vistula; penetrated into Gaul in the 5th cent. A.D.: p. 175; Maps 47, 50, 69
Burgundians, see BURGUNDI
Buthrotum (Vatzindro), city on coast of Epirus, according to legend founded by Helen of Troy: Maps 51, 71
Buxentum, *earlier* **Pyxus** (Policastro), city on coast of Lucania, founded by the Greeks: Map 29
Byblus or **Gebal** (Jebeil), important seaport in Phoenicia: Maps 26, 28, 30, 51
Byllis, city in the W. of Macedonia: Map 71
Byzantium, *later* **Constantinopolis** (Istanbul), city on the Bosporus, according to legend founded by Byzas, a son of Poseidon; it was enlarged and became very prosperous under Constantine the Great, who resided there; capital of the Eastern Roman Empire: pp. 62, 88; Maps 1, 11, 16, 26, 27, 47, 68, 72

C

Cabura (Kabul), city in the N. of Arachosia: Maps 26, 27
Cadi, city in the W. of Phrygia: Map 28
Cadianum, posting stage in Gallia Cisalpina on the Via Postumia between Vicetia and Verona: Map 54
Cadyanda, city in Lycia: Map 71b
Caecilia Via, highway in central Italy between Rome and Hadria: Map 53
Caelia, city on the E. coast of Apulia: Map 57
Caelius 1. one of the seven hills of Rome: Maps 42, 44; Pl. 349
2. (5th cent. A.D.) Rom. medical author from Sicca Veneria: Map 73
Caenepolis, place on the coast of the W. spit of land in Laconica: Map 1
Caere (Cerveteri), ancient and powerful city in Etruria, member of the Etruscan League; has a very extensive cemetery: Maps 31, 33, 34, 55, 71c; Plates 230-233, 239, 240
Caerini, tribe in Caledonia: Map 60
Caer Gybi, site of Rom. fort in W. Britain: Map 60
Caesar, Gaius Julius (100-44 B.C.), famous Rom. general and statesman; conquered Gaul; defeated his rival Pompey and his supporters 49-45 B.C. and became sole ruler of the Roman state; murdered by conspirators led by Brutus and Cassius 15 March 44 B.C.: pp. 122, 123, 130, 188; Maps 36, 73; Plate 315. The name Caesar was used in the Principate as title of the Emperor, in the Dominate as title of the junior pair of the four tetrarchs: p. 171
Caesaraugusta (Zaragoza), city in Tarraconensis: Maps 47, 51, 57, 66, 73
Caesarea 1. *earlier* **Iol** (Cherchel), port on coast of Mauretania, Phoenician foundation; noted Rom. naval base: Maps 30, 38, 43, 47, 51, 57, 68, 71
2. (Kaisariye), port on coast of Palestine; after the fall of Jerusalem capital of Judea: Maps 47, 51, 68
3. city in Cappadocia, later capital of this province: Map 47
Caesarobriga (Talavera de la Reina), city in the E. of Lusitania, on the Tagus: Map 57
Caesarodunum (Tours), city in Gallia Lugdunensis, on the Loire: Maps 68, 73
Caesaromagus 1. city in Gallia Belgica: Map 71
2. (Chelmsford), city in E. Britain: Map 60
Caesena (Cesena), city in the E. of Aemilia, on the Via Aemilia, of Etruscan origin: Maps 31, 33, 58
Caicus, river in Mysia: Map 11
Caieta (Gaeta), cape with a city of the same name in Latium: Maps 51, 53
Calabria, district in the SE. of Italy: Map 31
Calagurris (Calahorra), city in Tarraconensis, on the Hiberus: Maps 57, 66-68, 73
Calama (Guelma), city in Numidia: Map 71
Calauria (Poros), island off the coast of Argolis: Maps 1, 15, 17a, 18, 25
Caledones, tribe in Caledonia: Map 60
Caledonia, ancient name for Scotland: Maps 51, 59
Caledonii, the inhabitants of Caledonia: Map 47
Cales, city in Campania: Maps 57, 58, 68, 71c
Caligula (i.e. 'Little Boot'), Rom. Emperor A.D. 37-41, son of Germanicus; spent his youth among his father's legions in Germany, where he was given his nickname: p. 134
Callatis, Gr. colony on W. coast of the Black Sea, in Moesia Inferior: Maps 16, 26
Calleva Atrebatum (Silchester), city in S. of Britain: Maps 60, 61, 64, 68; Plate 287
Callidromus M., mountain range in Locris: Map 21
Callimachus (ca. 310-240 B.C.), from Cyrene, Gr. writer of prose and elegiacs, prolific author and scholar; lived for a time in Athens and Alexandria: pp. 181, 182; Map 72
Callinus (ca. 650 B.C.), from Ephesus, the earliest Gr. elegiac poet, author of military songs: Map 72
Callipolis, see ANXA
Callisthenes (late 4th cent. B.C.), from Olynthus, Gr. historian: Map 72
Callone, city in Media on the Royal Road: Map 26
Calydon (Kalydon), city in Aetolia: Maps 11, 18
Calymna (Kalymnos), island in the Aegean Sea, one of the Sporades: Map 1
Calynda, city in the W. of Lycia: Map 28
Camarina, place on the S. coast of Sicily, Gr. settlement: Maps 12, 16, 29
Cambodunum (Kempten), city in Raetia: Map 46
Camboglanna (Birdoswald), fort on Hadrian's Wall in Britain: Maps 48a, 61
Camerinum (Camerino), city in Umbria: Map 57
Camirus, city on Rhodes: Maps 9, 11, 18, 30
Campania, district in central Italy, on the Tyrrhenian Sea; fertile and luxuriant land; capital Capua: Map 31
Camulodunum (Colchester), city in E. of Britain, *colonia* and centre of the imperial cult; sacked by Boudicca A.D. 61: Maps 40, 47, 51, 57, 60, 61, 71
Canarium (Caerhun), Rom. fort in E. Britain: Maps 60, 61
Canatha (Qanawât), city in the border territory of Syria and Arabia: Map 71
Candia, see HERACLEUM
Cane M., range of mountains on the coast of Mysia: Map 1
Cannae (Canne), village in Apulia, on the Aufidus, where the Rom. legions were destroyed by Hannibal 216 B.C.: p. 107; Map 35; Plate 255
Cantabri, people in NW. of Spain; went on resisting Rome for a long time after the rest of Spain was conquered: Map 38
Cantharus, see PIRAEUS
Cantiaci, tribe in SE. Britain: Map 60
Canusium (Canosa), city in Apulia: Maps 53, 57, 68
Capena, city in Etruria, just N. of Rome: Maps 35, 57
Capera (Caparra), city in Lusitania: Map 66
Capitol, temple with three *cellae*, consecrated to Jupiter, Juno, and Minerva, on southern, or Capitol, summit of the Capitoline; the sacred centre of Rome: pp. 92, 96, 99, 134, 177; Plate 355
Capitolinus, one of the seven hills of Rome, consisting of two summits, one crowned by the Arx, the other by the temple of Jupiter Optimus Maximus; together with the Palatine the earliest inhabited hill of the city; rich in history and tradition: p. 92; Maps 42, 44; Plates 349, 350, 351, 355
Cappadocia, district in Asia Minor, between Galatia and Armenia: Maps 6, 7, 23, 26, 27, 28, 38
Cappadox (Delice), river in Cappadocia and Galatia, a tributary of the Halys: Maps 6-8
Capreae (Capri), island in the Sinus Cumanus where Tiberius had a large villa: Map 53
Capsa (Gafsa), city in the SE. of Numidia: Maps 47, 57
Capua (S. Maria di Capua), important city in Campania, one of the most flourishing cities in ancient Italy: p. 107; Maps 29, 31, 35, 40, 47, 53, 57, 58, 68, 71c
Caracalla, Rom. Emperor A.D. 211-217, son of Septimius Severus: p. 159; Map 69b; Plates 333, 372
Carales (Cagliari), port on the S. coast of Sardinia: Maps 29, 30, 43, 51, 53, 57, 68
Carcaso (Carcassonne), city in W. of Narbonensis: Map 57
Carchemish, *later* **Europus** (Cerablus), a very early trading centre on the Euphrates, on the border of Syria; in the 14th cent. B.C. a powerful stronghold of the kingdom of the Hittites: Maps 6, 7
Cardean, site of Rom. fort in E. Scotland: Map 60
Cardia, city on the Chersonesus Thracica: Maps 11, 72
Cardiff, site of Rom. fort in W. Britain: Map 60
Cardusii, warlike mountain people in Armenia: Map 26
Caria, region in the SW. corner of Asia Minor between Lydia and Lycia: Maps 1, 9, 11, 19, 27
Carmana, city in Carmania: Map 27

CARMANIA — CLEOMENES III

Carmania, region to the E. of Persis: Maps 26, 27

Carneades (ca. 214-129 B.C.), from Cyrene, Gr. philosopher, founder of the New Academy: Map 72

Carnonacae, tribe in Caledonia: Map 60

Carnuntum (Petronell, *Ger.* Altenburg), important commercial centre and fortress city on the Danube: Maps 41, 47, 51, 57, 68

Carpathium, Mare, sea between Crete, Carpathos, and Rhodes: Map 1

Carpathos (Karpathos), island between Crete and Rhodes: Maps 1, 7, 8, 9, 11

Carpi 1. (Mraissa) city on the N. coast of Africa Proconsularis: Map 68
2. people in Dacia: Map 47

Carpow, site of fort (prob. Horrea Classis) in E. Scotland: Map 60

Carrhae (Harran), place in Mesopotania where Crassus was killed in the battle against the Parthians: pp. 122, 130; Maps 28, 36, 40, 49

Carsioli (Carsoli), city in the land of the Aequi, on the border of Latium: Map 57

Carsulae, city in S. of Umbria, on the Via Flaminia: Maps 57, 68, 71c

Carteia (Algeciras), port on the S. coast of Baetica, near the Fretum Gaditanum: Maps 66, 67

Cartenna (Ténès), city on the coast of Mauretania, founded by the Phoenicians: Maps 30, 47, 57

Carthago, *earlier* **Quart Hadasha** *or* **Kart Hadash** (Carthage), important Phoenician settlement on the coast of Africa Proconsularis, according to tradition founded ca. 810 B.C.; after three wars with Rome it was conquered by Scipio Aemilianus 146 B.C.; rebuilt as Colonia Iulia, it grew into the richest and most flourishing city in the province of Africa: pp. 102, 107, 118, 175, 188; Maps 16, 29, 30, 32, 35, 38, 40, 51, 57, 68, 69, 71, 72, 73; Plate 258

Carthago Nova (Cartagena), port in SE. of Spain, founded by the Carthaginians: Maps 35, 40, 47, 51, 57, 66, 67

Carus, Marcus Aurelius, Rom. Emperor A.D. 282-283: Map 69b

Carvium *or* **Carvio** (prob. Kesteren), place in the delta of the Rhine in Germania Inferior: Map 46

Caryae, city in Laconica with a famous sanctuary of Artemis: Map 25

Caryanda, city on the coast of Caria: Map 72

Carystus (Karystos), city in S. of Euboea: Map 11

Casinum (Cassino), city on the border between Latium and Campania, on the Liris: Maps 57, 68, 71c

Casmenae (prob. Spaccaforno), Gr. foundation in Sicily; the site is not wholly certain; the neighbourhood of Spaccaforno is most probable, but some authorities place it near Vittoria or Comiso: Map 16

Caspii, people on the W. coast of the Caspian Sea, S. of the Caucasus: Map 26

Caspium, Mare (the Caspian Sea): Maps 38, 43, 59

Cassander, governor of Macedon 319-301 B.C., opponent of Antigonus: p. 66

Cassandra, in Gr. legend the daughter of Priam; she was a prophetess condemned by Apollo never to be believed: p. 179

Cassandrea, *earlier* **Potidaea** (Pontidaia), city on the isthmus of the W. peninsula of Chalcidice: Maps 27, 57

Cassia Via, highway in Etruria from Rome to Pisae: Maps 33, 53, 55

Cassius 1. **Gaius,** together with Brutus leader of the conspiracy to murder Caesar (44 B.C.): p. 130
2. **Hemina** (ca. 100 B.C.), Rom. author, the first Rom. annalist to use Latin: Map 73

Cassivellaunus, leader of the British resistance to the Romans 54 B.C.: Map 40

Castabala, see HIEROPOLIS

Castanea, fortress on the E. coast of the Thessalian district of Magnesia: Map 19

Castel d'Asso, place in Etruria with an Etruscan cemetery; ancient name unknown: Map 33

Castell Collen, site of Rom. fort in W. Britain: Maps 60, 61

Castellum Dimmidi (Demmed), fortress in the S. of Numidia: Map 47

Castellum Tingitanum (Orléansville), city in Mauretania Caesariensis: Map 47

Castledykes, site of Rom. fort in S. Scotland: Map 60

Castra Regina (Regensburg), garrison city in N. of Raetia, on the Danube: Map 50

Castra Vetera, see VETERA

Castrum Colibri, place on the border between Baetica and Lusitania, near Emerita: Map 66

Castulo (near Linares), city in Tarraconensis, near the border of Baetica: Maps 57, 66, 67

Casos (Kasos), island in the Mare Creticum, between Crete and Carpathos: Map 1

Catalaunian Fields (prob. nr. Châlons-sur-Marne), in Gaul, scene of the defeat of Attila and his Huns by Aetius A.D. 453: p. 175

Catana *or* **Catina** (Catania), city on E. coast of Sicily, Gr. foundation: Maps 12, 16, 29, 51, 53, 57, 68, 71

Catilina, Lucius Sergius, spendthrift Rom. patrician, originator of a conspiracy unmasked by Cicero (63 B.C.): p. 122

Cato 1. **the Censor** (234-149 B.C.), from Tusculum, famous Rom. statesman and orator, the earliest Rom. prose author: pp. 119, 122, 123; Map 73
2. **the Younger** (95-46 B.C.), Rom. statesman; ardent republican and opponent of Caesar: p. 122; Map 36

Catullus (84-54 B.C.), from Verona, Rom. lyric poet: pp. 123, 182, 188; Map 73

Catuvellauni, tribe in Britain: Map 60

Cauca (Coca), city in the N. of Tarraconensis: Map 66

Caucasus M. (the Caucasus mountains): Maps 26, 27, 38, 59

Caudine Forks, a mountain pass near Caudium in Samnium, where 321 B.C. a Rom. army was surrounded by the Samnites and compelled to a disgraceful surrender: Plate 249

Caulonia, city on the E. coast of Bruttii, founded by the Greeks: Maps 12, 16, 29

Caunus, coastal place on the borders of Caria and Lycia: Map 71b

Causennae (Ancaster), city in E. Britain: Map 60

Cawthorn, site of Rom. forts in NE. Britain: Map 61

Cayster (Akar Çay), river in Lydia: Map 11

Cebrene, city in Troas, on the Scamander: Map 11

Cedreae, city on W. coast of Caria: Map 71

Celaenae, city in the S. of Phrygia, at the source of the Maeander: Map 27

Celeia (Celje), city in Noricum, between the Dravus and the Savus: Maps 46, 57

Celsa (Gelsa), city in Tarraconensis, on the Ebro: Map 66

Celsus (early 1st cent. A.D.), Rom. scholar, author of treatises on agriculture, rhetoric, and medicine: Map 73

Celtae, inhabitants of Gallia Celtica; called Galli by the Romans: Map 36

Cemenelum (Cimiez), coastal place at the SE. point of Gallia Narbonensis, S. of the Alpes Maritimae: Maps 57, 68

Cenabum (Orléans), city in Gallia Lugdunensis, on the Loire: Map 68

Cenchreae, city on the isthmus of Corinth: Map 1

Censorinus (3rd cent. A.D.), Rom. grammarian: Map 73

Centumcellae (Civitavecchia), seaport and naval base on the coast of Etruria: Maps 43, 51, 53

Cephallenia (Kephallinia), island in the Ionian Sea off the coast of Acarnania: Maps 1, 3, 9, 10, 11

Cephisia (Kiphissia), deme in Attica, N. of Athens: Map 14

Cephisus, river in Attica, W. of Athens: Map 14

Cerasus, Hell. **Pharnacia** (Kiresum), city in Pontus on coast of the Black Sea; the 'city of cherries' whence Lucullus sent the first cherries to Rome: Maps 16, 26, 28

Cercina (Kerkennah), island with city of the same name off the coast of Africa Proconsularis: Map 51

Ceres, Rom. goddess of agriculture, identified with Demeter, p. 99; Plate 365

Ceria (Keros), island in the Aegean Sea, one of the Cyclades: Map 1

Ceos (Keos), island off the coast of Attica: Maps 1, 11, 19, 72

Chaeronea, city in Boeotia, scene of the decisive battle 338 B.C. in which Philip of Macedon gained supremacy over Greece: pp. 66, 189; Maps 3, 11, 17a, 71a

Chala, city in Media: Map 28

Chalcedon (Kadiköy), city on the Bosporus, opposite Byzantium: Maps 1, 11, 16, 19, 23, 51, 72

Chalcidice, large peninsula on S. coast of Macedon with three tongues of land (Acte, Sithonia, and Pallene): Maps 1, 11, 15, 19

Chalcis 1. (Khalkis), city on the W. coast of Euboea and capital of the island; mother city of many settlements: Maps 1, 11, 15, 16, 19, 51, 72
2. city in Phoenicia: Map 28

Chalybon *or* **Beroea,** *earlier* **Khalab** (Aleppo), city in Syria: Map 26

Chaonia 1. region in the coastal district of Epirus: Maps 1, 11
2. city in Syria: Map 28

Charites, the three Gr. goddesses of beauty (Aglaia, Euphrosune, and Thalia); called the 'Graciae' by the Romans: see GRACES

Charon 1. (ca. 500 B.C.), from Lampsacus, Gr. historian: Map 72
2. ferryman in the underworld; carried the shades of the dead over the Styx: Plate 132

Charybdis, see SCYLLA

Chatti, Germanic tribe: Maps 47, 50

Chedworth, site of Rom. villa in S. Britain, with remains: Map 61

Chelonatas Pr., cape on coast of Elis: Map 1

Chelva, city near E. coast of Tarraconensis, near Saguntum: Map 66

Chennis, *later* **Panopolis,** city in Egypt, on the Nile: Map 26

Chersonesus 1. **Taurica** (Krim), peninsula with city of same name on N. coast of the Black Sea: Maps 16, 43, 47, 51
2. **Thracica,** peninsula on S. coast of Thrace: Maps 11, 19

Cherusci, tribe in Germany, in the district of the Albis: Map 40

Chew Green, site of minor fort in S. Scotland: Map 60

Chios (Khios), large island off W. coast of Asia Minor: Maps 1, 9, 11, 18, 25, 72

Choaspes (Kerkhab), river in Susiana and Media, tributary of the Tigris: Map 28

Choerilus (ca. 520 B.C.), Gr. tragedian: Map 72

Choirospilia, place in Leucas; earliest remains from 3rd millennium B.C.: Map 3

Chorasmii, tribe in E. of Caspian Sea: Maps 26, 27

Chrysia, city on S. coast of Troas: Map 18

Chrysippus (ca. 240 B.C.), from Cilicia, Gr. philosopher, one of the most famous Stoics: Map 72

Chullu (Collo), place on coast of Numidia, Phoenician foundation: Map 30

Churrians, people of ca. 2000 B.C., originating in the district of modern Kurdistan; in the 2nd millennium B.C. ruled the region of N. Mesopotamia east of the Hittite empire: Map 6

Cibyra, city on boundary of Caria and Lycia: Maps 68, 71b

Cicero (106-43 B.C.), from Arpinum, famous Rom. statesman, orator, jurist, and philosopher, and the greatest Latin prose author: pp. 122, 123, 130, 135, 189; Map 73; Plates 264, 444

Ciconians, tribe in Thrace: Map 10

Cicutio (Y Gaer), Rom. fort in W. Britain: Map 60

Cidamus *or* **Cidamae** (Rhadamès), fortress in the desert area of the Garamantes in Phazania: Map 47

Cierus, see PRUSIAS

Cilicia, district on S. coast of Asia Minor: Maps 7, 8, 23, 30, 36, 37, 38

Cillium (Kasserine), city on boundary of Africa Proconsularis and Numidia: Map 71

Cilurnum (Chesters), fort on Hadrian's Wall in Britain: Maps 48a, 61

Cimbri, people in N. of Germany; threatened the Roman frontier at end of 2nd cent. B.C.; defeated by Marius at Vercellae 101 B.C.: Maps 37, 40

Cimolos (Kimolos), island in the Aegean Sea, one of the Cyclades: Map 1

Cimon (ca. 470 B.C.), son of Miltiades, Gr. statesman and general: p. 42

Cincius Alimentus (ca. 200 B.C.), from Rome, one of the earliest Latin annalists; wrote in Greek: Map 72

Cinesias (ca. 450-390 B.C.), from Athens, Gr. poet, author of dithyrambs: Map 72

Cingulum (Cingoli), city in Picenum: Map 57

Cinna, Rom. consul, adherent of Marius: p. 119

Circe, legendary enchantress; in the *Odyssey* transforms the companions of Odysseus into swine: p. 177; Map 10

Circei *or* **Cercei** (S. Felice Circeo), city on coast of Latium: Maps 53, 57

Circesium (Bessireh), city in Mesopotamia, on the Euphrates: Map 49

Cirta (Constantine), most important city of Numidia, seat of the Numidian princes: Maps 35, 38, 40, 57, 68, 71, 73

Cithaeron M., mountain range on boundary of Attica and Boeotia: p. 11; Maps 1, 14, 22; Plate 110

Citium (Larnaca), city on S. coast of Cyprus: Maps 30, 72

Cius, Hell. **Prusias** (Gemlik), city in Phrygia, on the Propontis: Maps 11, 28

Civilis, Julius, Batavian, leader of the German revolt A.D. 69-70: p. 134; Map 40

Civitas Popthensis (Ksiba), city in Africa Proconsularis: Map 71

Cladeus, stream near Olympia; flows into the Alpheus: Plates 161, 164

Classis (Classe), port of Ravenna, important maritime base: Maps 43, 53; Plate 305

Claudian (ca. A.D. 400), from Alexandria, the last great representative of classical Latin poetry; wrote at the court of Honorius and Stilicho: Map 72

Claudia Via, highway in Italy between Amiternum and Aternum: Map 53

Claudius 1. **Appius,** called **Caecus** (ca. 300 B.C.), Rom. statesman and orator, author of verse aphorisms and legal and grammatical works which are the earliest recorded Latin literature: Map 73
2. **Tiberius,** Rom. Emp. A.D. 41-54; Britain was conquered during his reign: pp. 134, 135, 189; Plate 319
3. **Marcus Aurelius,** called **Gothicus,** Rom. Emperor A.D. 286-270, distinguished general; defeated the Alemanni and Goths at Naissus A.D. 269: p. 160; Map 69b

Clausentum (Bitterne), city in S. Britain: Map 60

Clazomenae, city on coast of Lydia: Maps 1, 7, 9, 19, 71b, 72

Cleanthes (331-231 B.C.), from Assus, Gr. philosopher, Stoic, pupil of Zeno: Map 72

Cleomenes III, king of Sparta 236-219 B.C.; abolished the obsolete laws of Lycurgus and gave Sparta a brief period of prosperity: pp. 82, 85

CLEON — CYTHERA

Cleon, Athenian demagogue, after the death of Pericles the political leader in Athens; killed at Amphipolis 422 B.C.: p. 181
Cleone, city in Argolis: Map 1
Cleopatra, the last queen of Egypt; carried on intrigues with Caesar and later with Mark Antony; committed suicide after the battle of Actium in 31 B.C.: pp. 85, 130; Map 40
Clisthenes (ca. 500 B.C.), Athenian legislator, leader of the opposition to the autocracy of Hippias and founder of Athenian democracy: p. 39
Clitarchus (ca. 280 B.C.), from Alexandria, Gr. epic poet: Map 72
Cliternia (Petrella), city in land of the Aequi: Map 57
Clitomachus (187-110 B.C.), from Carthage, Gr. philosopher, Academician, pupil of Carneades and after his death head of the Academy: Map 72
Clitus, general and friend of Alexander the Great, by whom he was put to death: p. 66
Clodia, Roman lady beloved by Catullus, by whom in his poems she was called Lesbia: p. 182
Clodia Via, highway in Etruria from Rome to Vetulonia: Maps 33, 53, 55
Clota (Clyde), river in N. Britain: Map 60
Clunia (Coruna del Conde), city in Tarraconensis: Maps 57, 66, 71
Clupea, *earlier* **Aspis** (Kelibia), city on E. coast of Africa Proconsularis, founded from Syracuse, after 146 B.C. a Rom. colony: Map 51
Clusium (Chiusi), important Etruscan city, member of the Etruscan League: Maps 29, 31, 33, 46, 53, 57
Clytemnestra, in legend, the wife of Agamemnon, whom she murdered on his return from Troy in conjunction with her lover Aegisthus; a leading figure in the *Oresteia* of Aeschylus: p. 179
Cnidus, city on W. coast of Caria, famous for its temple of Aphrodite: Maps 11, 15, 25, 71, 72
Cnossus (Knossos), city in Crete, in Minoan times capital of the island and residence of Minos; important excavations: pp. 21, 31; Maps 1, 3, 4, 4a, 9, 11, 18, 26; Plates 14, 15, 16, 18
Cocala, city on S. coast of Gedrosia, near the delta of the Indus: Map 26
Coelbren, site of Rom. fort in W. Britain: Map 60
Coelius Antipater (ca. 150 B.C.), Rom. historian, originator of historical monographs: Map 73
Colchis, district on E. coast of the Black Sea south of the Caucasus: Map 26
Collippo (S. Sebastiao do Freixo), city near W. coast of Lusitania: Map 57
Colonia Agrippina (Köln), frontier fortress on the Rhine, capital of Germania Inferior: Maps 43, 47, 51, 57
Colonia Iulia Carthago, name of Carthage when rebuilt in time of Augustus: Map 30 (Carthago); Plate 258
Colonia Ulpia Traiana, *or* **Vetera,** frontier fortress on the Rhine, in Germania Inferior: Map 57
Colonus, place in Attica, north of Athens, birthplace of Sophocles: p. 180
Colophon, city in the coastal district of Lydia: p. 181; Maps 1, 7, 8, 9, 11, 15, 19, 72
Colossae (Khonai), city in Phrygia: Map 71b
Colosseum *or* **Amphitheatrum Flavium,** amphitheatre in Rome built by Vespasian and Titus and opened in A.D. 80: p. 135; Maps 44, 59; Plates 350, 353, 355, 436
Columella (ca. A.D. 50), from Gades, Rom. writer on agriculture: Map 73
Comana, city in Cappadocia: Maps 57, 68
Commagene, the N. part of Syria, between the Taurus Mountains and the Euphrates: Map 28
Commodianus (5th cent. A.D.), Rom. Christian poet, author of *Carmen Apologeticum* and other works: Map 73
Commodus, Lucius Aelius Aurelius, Rom. Emperor A.D. 180-192: p. 159; Plate 332
Complutum (Alcalá de Henares), city in Tarraconensis: Maps 57, 66
Compsa (S. Andrea di Conza), city on boundary of Samnium and Lucania: Map 57
Comum (Como), city in Gallia Cisalpina, on Larius Lacus: Maps 53, 73
Concangium (Chester-le-Street), Rom. fort in NE. Britain: Map 60
Concordia, city in land of the Veneti, in the W. of Gallia Cisalpina: Maps 53, 54, 58, 71
Condatomagus (la Graufesenque), city on boundary of Aquitania and Narbonensis, famous centre of terra sigillata products: Map 52
Condercum (Benwell), fort on Hadrian's Wall in Britain: Map 48a
Confluentes (Koblenz), city in Germania Superior, at the confluence (hence the name) of the Rhine and the Moselle: Map 57
Congavata (Drumburgh), fort on Hadrian's Wall in Britain: Map 48a
Conimbriga (Coimbra), city in Lusitania, on the Monda: Map 66
Consabura (Consuegra), city in Tarraconensis, south of Toletum: Map 66
Constantina (Veran Sehir), city in N. of Mesopotamia: Map 49
Constantine 1. **I, the Great,** Rom. Emperor A.D. 306-337, after conflict with Maxentius (A.D. 312) and Licinius (A.D. 323) sole ruler of the entire Empire; recognised Christianity as the official religion of the Empire; moved the Imperial capital to Byzantium, which he renamed Constantinopolis (A.D. 330): pp. 171, 174; Map 69; Plate 335
2. **II,** son of **I,** Rom. Emperor A.D. 337-340: Plate 336
Constantinopolis, later name for BYZANTIUM: p. 174: Maps 51, 69
Constantius Chlorus, Rom. Emperor A.D. 293-306, father of Constantine the Great: p. 171; Map 69
Copais Lacus, lake in Boeotia, in antiquity renowned for its eels: Maps 1, 11; Plate 51
Copia, see THURII
Cora (Cori), city in Latium: Map 57; Plate 242
Corassiae Iae., group of islands S. of Samos, part of the Sporades: Map 1
Corcyra (Kerkira *or* Corfu), island off coast of Epirus, in the Ionian Sea: Maps 1, 3, 10, 11, 16, 17
Corcyra Nigra (Korčula), island off coast of Dalmatia, Gr. foundation ca. 500 B.C., thickly wooded with pine trees (whence its name 'black'): Map 29
Corduba (Córdoba), capital of Baetica: Maps 47, 51, 57, 66, 67, 73
Corfinium (Pentima), city in Samnium, capital of the Paeligni: Maps 29, 53, 57
Corinium 1. (Karin), city on coast of Dalmatia: Map 57
2. (Cirencester), cantonal capital of the Dobunni, in Britain: Maps 60, 61
Corinna (6th cent. B.C.), from Boeotia (probably Tanagra), Gr. lyric poetess, said to have been teacher of Pindar: Map 72
Corinthiacus, Sinus (Gulf of Corinth): Map 1; Plate 10
Corinthus (Corinth), important city, harbour, and centre of commerce, in N. of the Peloponnese, on the Isthmus of Corinth, famous for its wealth and luxury: pp. 59, 182, 193; Maps 3, 9, 11, 15-18, 25-7, 38, 47, 68, 71; Plates 60-3
Coritani, tribe in Britain: Map 60
Cornelia Via, road from Rome to Caere: Map 55
Cornovii 1. tribe in Caledonia: Map 60
2. tribe in W. Britain: Map 60
Cornus (S. Caterina), port on W. coast of Sardinia: Map 57
Corone (Koroni), coastal settlement in SE. of Messenia: Map 1
Coronea, city in Boeotia: Map 11
Corpus Iuris, the collection of all the Roman legal sources in existence ca. A.D. 530, codified by Tribonius and other jurists by command of the Emperor Justinian; comprises: 1. the Digests or Pandects; 2. the Codex; 3. the Institutions; 4. the Novels: pp. 193-4
Corsica, island in W. of the Mediterranean; played an important rôle in history when the Carthaginians established themselves there; later, with Sardinia, one of the earliest Roman provinces: pp. 102, 118; Maps 16, 29, 30, 31, 35, 38, 53
Corstopitum (Corbridge), fort and civil settlement near Hadrian's Wall in Britain, on the military road (Stane Gate) just S. of Hadrian's Wall and the N.-S. trunk road; important archaeological site: Maps 48a, 60, 61
Cortona, city in Etruria, near Trasimenus L.: Maps 29, 33, 53, 57
Corydalla, city near S. coast of Lycia: Map 71
Cos, island with city of same name off coast of Asia Minor, sacred to Asclepius: Maps 1, 3, 7, 9, 11, 18, 25, 71, 72; Plate 157
Cosa (Ansedonia), city and port in Etruria: Maps 33, 51, 53, 58, 71c
Cossura (Pantelleria), island between Sicily and the dominions of Carthage: Maps 29, 53
Cottiae, see ALPES
Cotyora, city in Pontus, on the S. coast of the Black Sea: Map 16
Cramond, site of Rom. fort in S. Scotland: Map 60
Cranii (Argostolion), city on the W. coast of Cephallenia: Map 11
Crannon (Krannon), city in Pelasgiotis, in the centre of Thessaly: Maps 11, 26
Crantor (ca. 335-227 B.C.), from Soli, Gr. philosopher, Academician, commentator of Plato: Map 72
Crassus, Marcus, member of the first Triumvirate (ca. 60 B.C.): p. 122
Crates 1. (ca. 450 B.C.), form Athens, Gr. author of comedies, one of the founders of the Old Attic Comedy: Map 72
2. (ca. 200 B.C.), from Mallus, Gr. scholar; wrote at the court of Attalus II of Pergamum: Map 72
Cratinus (ca. 5th cent. B.C.), from Athens, Gr. author of comedies, the earliest known and renowned founder of the Old Attic Comedy, author of at least 20 comedies: Map 72
Cratippus (ca. 400 B.C.), from Athens, Gr. historian; wrote a continuation to the history of Thucydides: Map 72
Credones, tribe in Caledonia: Map 60
Cremna, city in Pisidia: Map 71
Cremona, city in Gallia Cisalpina, on the Padus, established as a Rom. colony in 219 B.C. in the then recently subjected district: Maps 53, 58
Crenides, city in SE. of Macedon, near the border of Thrace; Philip built the city of Philippi on its ruins: Map 11
Creon, legendary king of Thebes; character in several plays by Sophocles: p. 180
Crete, island S. of Greece, with a flourishing civilisation 3000-1400 B.C. ('Minoan culture'): p. 190; Maps 1, 3, 4, 6-9, 11, 16, 25, 26, 30, 38; Plates 14-26
Creticum, Mare, sea N. of Crete: Map 1
Cretopolis, city in Pamphylia: Map 71
Crimisa Pr., cape on E. coast of Bruttii: Map 17
Crisa (Chryso), city in Phocis, near Delphi: Maps 15,19
Critias (460-403 B.C.), from Athens, Gr. author and politician, pupil of Socrates, uncle of Plato; after the Peloponnesian War one of the Thirty Tyrants; perished in the liberation of Athens: Map 72
Croesus, king of Lydia 560-546 B.C.; famous for his wealth: pp. 39, 188
Cronus Hill, hill in Elis, at the foot of which lay the demesne land of the temple of Olympia: Plate 161
Croton (Crotone), city on E. coast of Bruttii, Gr. foundation, famous for the school of the philosopher Pythagoras: Maps 12, 16, 17, 29, 31, 35, 51, 53, 72
Ctesias (ca. 400 B.C.), from Cnidus, Gr. historian, author of a history of Persia, a work on India, etc.; Map 72
Ctesiphon, city on the Tigris, fortress and residence of the Parthian kings: Maps 38, 47, 51
Cuicil (Djemila), city on the boundary of Numidia and Mauretania: Maps 57, 71
Cumae (Cuma), city on coast of Campania, earliest Gr. foundation in Italy, 8th cent. B.C.; legendary residence of the Sibyl: pp. 91, 96; Maps 16, 29, 31, 53, 57, 68; Plate 78
Cunaxa, city on the Euphrates, scene of the battle in which Cyrus the Younger perished in his rebellion against his brother Artaxerxes (401 B.C.): p. 188
Cunetio (Mildenhall), city in S. Britain: Map 60
Cupra Maritima (Cupra Marittima), city on coast of Picenum: Map 57
Curium, city on S. coast of Cyprus: Map 71
Curtius, Quintus (ca. A.D. 50), Rom. historian, author of a life of Alexander the Great: Map 73
Curubis (Korba), city on NE. coast of Africa Proconsularis: Map 57
Cyaneae, city in S. of Lycia: Map 71b
Cybele, Asiatic goddess, with an especial cult in Phrygia; worshipped as the great mother of all living things; identified with Rhea: Plate 371
Cyclades Iae., group of islands in the Aegean Sea: Maps 1, 3, 15
Cyclops, a one-eyed giant, featuring in the *Odyssey*, etc.; the Cyclopes were the assistants of Hephaestus in his work as a smith: p. 177: Map 10
Cydonia (Khania), city on NW. coast of Crete: Maps 1, 4, 11, 26
Cyllene, city and port on coast of Elis: Map 11
Cyllene M., mountain in Arcadia, traditionally the birthplace of Hermes: Map 25
Cyme, city and port on coast of Lydia: Maps 1, 9, 11, 15, 19, 72
Cynoscephalae, district in S. of Thessaly where Philip V of Macedon was defeated by Flamininus 197 B.C.: Map 40
Cynosura, small promontory in the Gulf of Marathon behind which the Persian fleet is supposed to have passed in the battle of 490 B.C.: Maps 14, 20; Plate 9
Cynuria, district on E. coast of the Peloponnese, between Argolis and Laconica: Map 15
Cyphanta, city on E. coast of Laconica: Map 1
Cyprian (ca. A.D. 200-258), bishop of Carthage, theological writer: Map 73
Cyprus, island in E. of the Mediterranean, rich in minerals (copper); early Phoenician settlement, later occupied by Greeks; successively under rule of Egypt, Persia, Greece, Macedon, the Ptolemies, Rome: Maps 6, 7, 8, 16, 23, 26, 27, 28, 30, 32, 38
Cyrenaica, the fertile district in Africa between Libya and Tripolis, more or less the present plateau of Barca: Maps 27, 37, 38
Cyrene (Cirene), capital of Cyrenaica, important commercial city, Gr. settlement: p. 181; Maps 16, 18, 26, 27, 38, 47, 68, 71, 72; Plates 87-91
Cyropolis, city in Sogdiana, near the Iaxartes: Map 26
Cyrrhus, fortified city in N. of Syria: Maps 28, 49, 71
Cyrus 1. founder of the Persian empire, reigned 550-529 B.C.: pp. 39, 188
2. **the Younger,** son of Darius II; rebelled against the legitimate heir, his brother Artaxerxes; perished at Cunaxa 401 B.C.: pp. 59, 188
3. (Kura), river in Armenia: Maps 23, 26, 27, 28, 43
Cythera (Kythira), island with city of same name S. of

Laconica, famous for its temple of Aphrodite: Maps 1, 9, 10, 11, 25, 72

Cythnos (Kythnos), island in the Aegean Sea, one of the Cyclades: Maps 1, 11, 19

Cytorus, city in Paphlagonia on S. coast of the Black Sea: Map 16

Cyzicus, flourishing city in Phrygia, on the S. coast of the Propontis: Maps 11, 16, 18, 43, 51, 68, 71

D

Dacia, district N. of the Danube, more or less the modern Transylvania and Romania: p. 134; Maps 38, 45

Dacians, people settled in Dacia: p. 134

Dagasira, city on S. coast of Gedrosia, on the Arabian Sea: Map 26

Dahae, Scythian people E. of the Caspian Sea: Maps 26, 27

Dalginross, site of Rom. fort in E. Scotland: Map 60

Dalmatia, the coastal district on the E. of the Adriatic Sea: Map 38

Damascus, very ancient city in Syria, junction of caravan routes: Maps 23, 26, 27, 28, 38, 49, 51, 71

Damnonii, tribe in N. Britain: Map 60

Damon (late 5th cent. B.C.), from Athens, Gr. musician, teacher and friend of Pericles: Map 72

Danae, mother of Perseus by Zeus, who approached her in the form of a golden shower: Map 24

Danum (Doncaster), Rom. fort in E. Britain: Map 60

Danuvius *or* **Danubius,** *earlier* **Ister** (Danube), river dividing Germany from Dacia, for centuries the boundary of the Empire in this area; the earlier name remained in use for its lower course: Maps 16, 26, 27, 37, 38, 43, 50

Daphne, city in N. of Syria, on the Orontes: Map 71

Dara, city in Mesopotamia, on the border of Armenia: Map 49

Dardanos, the legendary ancestor of the Trojans, founder of Dardania, the later Troy: Map 24

Darius 1. **I,** king of Persia 521-486 B.C.: pp. 39, 188; Plate 95
2. **III Codomannus,** king of Persia 336-330 B.C.; defeated by Alexander the Great at Issus 333 B.C.: p. 66

Darnis (Derna), city and port in Cyrenaica: Map 51

Dascylium, city in Phrygia, on the Propontis: Maps 11, 19, 23

Dauni, people in N. of Apulia: Map 29

Dea (Die), city in Gallia Narbonensis, E. of the Rhône: Map 68

De Bello Gallico, the account by Julius Caesar of his military operations for the pacification of Gaul: p.188

Decantae, tribe in Caledonia: Map 60

Deceangli, tribe in Britain: Map 60

Decebalus, king of the Dacians ca. A.D. 100: Map 40

Decelea, fortress in Attica, occupied by the Spartans 413 B.C., during the Peloponnesian War: p. 59; Maps 1, 11, 14

Delian Confederacy, league of Athens and all the Ionian cities in Thrace, Asia Minor, and the islands, with as its main object the protection of the Gr. cities in Asia Minor; its treasury was in the temple of Apollo in Delos: pp. 42, 51, 59

Delium, city in Boeotia, on the Euripus: Map 11

Delos, island in the Aegean Sea, one of the Cyclades; according to the legend, it was a floating island until Zeus moored it to become the birthplace of Apollo and Artemis; centre of cult of Apollo; site of treasury of the Delian Confederacy; very important centre of commerce: p. 42; Maps 1, 11, 18, 19, 25, 68, 71; Plates 137, 420

Delphi, sacred city in Phocis, at foot of Mount Parnassus, famous for the sanctuary and oracle of Apollo; in antiquity regarded as the centre of the earth: pp. 82, 182; Maps 1, 11, 15, 17a, 18, 19, 25, 68, 71a

Delphi Charioteer, a Gr. statue of ca. 470 B.C., interesting in showing the transition from archaic to classical Gr. sculpture: p. 192; Plates 149, 150

Demetae, tribe in Britain: Map 60

Demeter, Gr. goddess of agriculture and crops; especially worshipped in the Eleusinian Mysteries; by the Romans identified with Ceres: pp. 51, 99; Maps 24, 25

Demetrias 1. fortified city in Thessaly, on the modern Gulf of Volo: Maps 18, 71
2. city in Mesopotamia, on the Tigris: Map 28

Demetrius 1. called **Poliorcetes** ('the Besieger') (337-283 B.C.), son of Antigonus, king of Asia, p. 66
2. of Pharos, put in possession of Illyria by favour of the Romans 228 B.C.; later in opposition to Rome and expelled: Map 40
3. (ca. 200 B.C.), from Scepsis, Gr. author; wrote among other things an antiquarian work on the Trojan War: Map 72
4. (ca. 300 B.C.), Gr. author, orator, and statesman: Map 72

Democritus (5th cent. B.C.), from Abdera, Gr. philosopher, known for his atomic theory: p. 66; Map 72

Demosthenes (385-322 B.C.), the greatest Athenian orator, opponent of Philip of Macedon, against whom he composed his famous *Philippics*: pp. 62, 63, 189; Map 72

Dendra, place in Achaia: Map 3

Derbent, city in Bokhara: Map 26

Dere Street, Rom. road in N. Britain, between Hadrian's Wall and Antonine Wall: Map 61

Dertona (Tortona), city in Liguria: Maps 46, 53, 58

Dertosa (Tortosa), city near coast of Tarraconensis: Maps 43, 66

Derventio 1. (Malton), Rom. fort and civil settlement in E. Britain: Map 60
2. (Papcastle), Rom. fort in NE. Britain: Map 60

Deva (Chester), legionary fortress on W. coast of Britain: Maps 41, 47, 60

Diadochi ('the Successors'), generals of Alexander the Great who after his death divided and ruled his empire: pp. 66, 82; Map 27

Diagoras (ca. 425 B.C.), from Melos, Gr. poet, author of dithyrambs: Map 72

Dialas, river in Media, tributary of the Tigris: Map 28

Dianium, *earlier* **Hemeroscopeum** (Denia), cape and city on coast of Tarraconensis, of Gr. origin: Map 66

Diaspora ('the scattering'), name for the Jews living outside Palestine after the Babylonian Captivity: p. 88

Dichaearchus (ca. 300 B.C.), from Messene, Gr. scholar, pupil of Aristotle, geographer and author of a history of Gr. culture: Map 72

Dido *or* **Elissa,** legendary princess of Tyre, said to have been deposed and expelled by her brother Pygmalion and become the founder of Carthage; Virgil introduces her into the *Aeneid*: pp. 178, 188

Didyma (Yoran), city near W. coast of Caria, S. of Miletus, famous for the sanctuary and oracle of Apollo: Maps 3, 7, 9, 18, 19, 25; Plates 215, 219

Digests *or* **Pandects,** excerpts from the works of about 40 Rom. jurists, forming part of the *Corpus Iuris* of Justinian: p. 193

Dimini, very ancient fortress in Thessaly, finding place of pottery of the 2nd half of the 3rd millennium B.C.: Map 3

Dinia (Digne), city in E. of Narbonensis: Map 57

Diocaesarea, city in Cilicia: Map 18

Diocletian, Rom. Emperor A.D. 284-305; with him began the period of absolute monarchy and the division of the Empire into East and West; persecuted the Christians; abdicated the Empire; his palace on the Dalmatian coast at modern Split is famous: pp. 162, 171; Map 69; Plate 334

Diogenes 1. (ca. 450 B.C.), from Apollonia, Gr. philosopher: Map 72
2. (ca. 400-325 B.C.), from Sinope, Gr. philosopher, renowned Cynic: Map 72

Dion 1. (409-354 B.C.), brother-in-law and opponent of Dionysius tyrant of Syracuse: p. 62
2. (probably Tell el Ash'ari), city in Syria, one of the ten Gr. cities beyond the Jordan: Map 28

Dione, Gr. goddess, mother of Aphrodite: Map 24

Dionusos, see DIONYSUS

Dionysiades (4th cent. B.C.), from Tarsus, Gr. tragedian: Map 72

Dionysius 1. Gr. leader, later tyrant of Syracuse (405 B.C.), known for his successful opposition to the Carthaginian policy of expansion in Sicily: p. 59
2. tyrant of Syracuse 367-357 B.C. and 346-344 B.C.: p. 62

Dionysopolis, city in Phrygia: Map 28

Dionysus, *Gr.* **Dionusos,** Thracian god; for the Greeks the god of wine; by the Romans identified with Bacchus: pp. 51, 178-9; Maps 24, 25; Plate 82

Dioscurias (Sukhumi), commercial city on E. coast of the Black Sea, founded from Miletus: Maps 16, 26, 47

Dioskouroi, Gr. gods, the twin brothers Kastor and Poludeukes (*Lat.* Pollux), sons of Zeus, worshipped as patrons of seamen: Maps 24, 25

Diphilus (ca. 350-263 B.C.), from Sinope, Gr. writer of comedies, representative of the Attic New Comedy: Map 72

Divodurum Mediomatricorum (Metz), city in E. of Gallia Belgica: Maps 47, 58

Divona (Cahors), city in S. of Aquitania: Map 68

Doberus, city in Macedon: Map 57

Dobunni, tribe in Britain: Map 60

Docimeum, city in Phrygia: Map 28

Dodona, city in Epirus, famous for the oracle of Zeus, whose utterances were deduced from the rustling of the sacred oak trees: Maps 1, 3, 9, 11, 15, 25, 71

Dolaucothi, site of Rom. gold mining, in W. Britain: Map 61

Dolichiste, small island off the coast of Lycia: Map 71b

Dolopes, tribe in SW. of Thessaly; according to tradition took part in the Trojan War: Maps 1, 15

Domitian, Rom. Emperor A.D. 81-96, son of Vespasian and brother of Titus: pp. 134, 135, 189; Plate 328

Domitiana Via, highway in Italy between Tarracina and Rhegium: Map 53

Dora (El Burj), city on coast of Palestine: Maps 28, 71

Dorians, people who ca. 1200-1000 B.C. penetrated down from N. Greece and brought the Mycenaean culture to an end: pp. 31, 32; Map 3

Doris, small district in central Greece between Mount Parnassus and Mount Oeta; regarded as place of origin of the Dorians: Maps 1, 15

Doriscus, city in SE. of Thrace: Maps 11, 19

Dorylaeum (Eskisehir), city in N. of Phrygia: Map 28

Drangiana, region in centre of Ariana, W. of the Etymandrus: Maps 26, 27

Drapsaca, city in Bactria: Map 26

Dravus (Drave), river in Noricum and Pannonia: Map 43

Drepanum (Trapani), city and cape on NW. point of Sicily, Phoenician foundation: Map 53

Drerus, city in NE. of Crete: Map 18

Drobeta (Turnu Severin), city in S. of Dacia, on the Danube: Maps 47, 57

Drusus, Marcus Livius, Rom. tribune of the people 91 B.C.: p. 119

Dubris (Dover), port on SE. coast of Britain; had a Rom. fort and two lighthouses: Maps 43, 51, 60, 61

Dumaetha, city in Arabia Deserta: Map 26

Dumnonii, tribe in S. Britain: Map 60

Dunum Sinus (Tees Bay), inlet at the mouth of the Tees in N. Britain: Map 60

Dura-Europos (Salihiye), city in boundary district between Mesopotamia and Arabia, on the Euphrates; now in ruins: Maps 28, 49, 51, 68, 71

Duris (ca. 340-260 B.C.), from Samos, Gr. historian: Map 72

Durius (Douro), river in Spain: Maps 43, 66, 67

Durnovaria (Dorchester), city near S. coast of Britain, capital of the Durotriges: Maps 60, 68

Durobrivae 1. (Rochester), city in SE. Britain: Map 60
2. (Water Newton), city in Britain with important potteries: Maps 60, 61

Durocornovium, city in Britain: Map 68

Durocortorum (Rheims), city in Gallia Belgica, capital of the Remi: Map 68

Durolipons (Cambridge), city in E. Britain: Map 60

Durostorum (Silistra), garrison town in Moesia Inferior, on the Danube: Maps 41, 47

Durotriges, tribe in S. Britain: Map 60

Durovernum (Canterbury), city in SE. of Britain, capital of the Cantiaci: Maps 60, 71

Duroviguntum (Godmanchester), city in E. Britain: Map 60

Dyrrhachium, *earlier* **Epidamnus** (Durazzo), city and port in Macedon, Gr. foundation: Maps 16, 26, 43, 51, 57

Dystus, city in Euboea: Map 18

E

Ebora (Evora), city in Lusitania: Maps 57, 66

Eburacum (York), city in N. Britain: Maps 38, 41, 47, 6, 69

Eburones, Ger. tribe in Gallia Belgica between the Meuse and the Rhine: Map 40

Eburum (Eboli), city on boundary of Campania and Lucania: Map 57

Ebusus (Ibiza), island with settlement of the same name E. of Spain: Maps 35, 51, 57, 66, 67

Ecbatana (Hamadan), ancient capital of Media: Maps 23, 26, 27, 28

Ecnomus Pr., cape on S. coast of Sicily: Map 35a

Edebessus, city in Lycia: Map 71b

Edessa *or* **Orrhoe,** Hell. **Antiochia** (Ourfa), city in N. of Mesopotamia: Maps 28, 49

Egypt, see AEGYPTUS

Eion, city on S. coast of Macedon, at mouth of the Strymon; port of Amphipolis: Map 11

Elaea, city on coast of Asia Minor, on the boundary of Mysia and Lydia: Maps 9, 11, 15, 19

Elaeus, city on S. point of the Chersonesus Thracica: Map 26

Elaeusa, city on coast of Cilicia: Map 71

Elagabalus *or* **Heliogabalus,** priest of the worship of the Sun at Emesa in Syria; in A.D. 218, at the age of 13, proclaimed Emperor under the name of M. Aurelius Antoninus, on the pretext that he was the son of Caracalla: murdered A.D. 222: p. 159; Map 69b

Elam, district in Asia Minor north of the Persian Gulf: p. 85

Elea, see VELIA

Eleatic School, school of philosophy at Elea (5th cent. B.C.), founded by Xenophanes, Parmenides, and Zeno; the Eleatics supported the doctrine of the unchanging Being, in opposition to Heraclitus, who taught that of the eternal Becoming: pp. 51, 63

Electra 1. daughter of Agamemnon; revenged his murder in conjunction with her brother Orestes; leading character in plays by Aeschylus, Sophocles,

and Euripides: pp. 179, 180
2. daughter of Atlas and mother of Dardanus by Zeus: Map 24
Eleusis, city in Attica, famous for the mysteries celebrated there in honour of Demeter and Persephone; connected to Athens by the 'Sacred Way', the route followed by the procession: p. 51; Maps 1, 14, 17a, 18, 25, 72
Eleutherae, fortified settlement in Attica, on the border of Boeotia: Maps 14, 17a, 22; Plate 110
Elimea, district in S. of Macedon, on the border of Thessaly: Map 11
Elis, city in district of same name in W. of the Peloponnese: Maps 1, 3, 9, 11, 15, 25, 71a, 72
Elissa, see DIDO
Elymi, ancient tribe in the W. corner of Sicily: Maps 12, 29
Emerita *or* **Emerita Augusta** (Mérida), city in Lusitania, on the Anas: Maps 37, 47, 51, 57, 66, 68, 71
Emesa (Homs), city in Syria: Maps 26, 49
Emmatha city in Syria: Map 71
Emona (Ljubljana), city in SW. of Pannonia Superior: Map 57
Empedocles (483-424 B.C.), from Agrigentum, Gr. philosopher of the later school of natural philosophy: Map 72
Emporiae (Ampurias), city and port in Tarraconensis, Gr. foundation: Maps 16, 35, 51, 66, 68
Enna *or* **Henna** city in the interior of Sicily: Map 53
Ennius (239-169 B.C.), from Rudiae, Rom. poet, called 'the father of Latin poetry'; author of tragedies on the Gr. model, satires, an epic, etc.: p. 123; Map 73
Epaminondas (4th cent. B.C.), great Gr. statesman and general; procured for Thebes the hegemony of Greece for a short period: p. 59
Ephesus (Selçuk), very important city and harbour on the coast of Lydia, capital of the province of Asia, famous for the temple of Artemis: pp. 82, 85; Maps 1, 7, 8, 11, 15, 18, 19, 23, 25, 26, 28, 43, 47, 51, 68, 71b, 72; Plate 76
Ephorus (ca. 408-330 B.C.), from Cyme, Gr. historian: Map 72
Epicharmus (ca. 530-440 B.C.), from Syracuse, Gr. author of comedies, founder of the Doric-Sicilian comedy; wrote at the court of Hiero I: Map 72
Epictetus (ca. A.D. 100), Gr. freedman, teacher of the Stoic doctrines in Rome: p. 147
Epicurus (342-270 B.C.), from Samos, Gr. philosopher; founded the Epicurean school at Athens: pp. 89, 123, 147, 178; Map 72
Epidamnus, see DYRRHACHIUM
Epidaurus 1. *or* **Epidaurum** (Cavtat), city on coast of Dalmatia: Maps 29, 51, 57, 68
2. city on E. coast of Argolis, famous for the sanctuary of Asklepios: Maps 1, 11, 17a, 18, 25, 68, 71a; Plates 154, 155, 467, 468, 469
3. **Limera,** city on E. coast of Laconica: Map 1
Epidii, tribe in Caledonia: Map 60
Epiphania 1. (Hama), city in Syria, on the Orontes: Map 28
2. Hell. for ECBATANA
Epirus, district in N. of Greece, on the Mare Ionium: Maps 1, 9, 11, 26, 27, 28
Epomanduodurum, city in Germania Superior: Map 71
Epona, Gallic divinity, patron of horses: Plate 369
Eporedia (Ivrea), city in Gallia Cisalpina: Maps 58, 71
Erasistratus (ca. 275 B.C.), from Ceos, Gr. writer on medicine, esp. famous for his anatomy: Map 72
Eratosthenes (ca. 270-194 B.C.), from Cyrene, Gr. historian and geographer, librarian of the library at Alexandria: Map 72
Ercavica (Santaver?), city in the centre of Tarraconensis: Map 66
Erechtheum, temple on the Acropolis at Athens, dedicated to Poseidon, Erechtheus, and Athena; famous Porch of the Caryatids: p. 192; Map 13; Plates 59, 171, 191
Eresus, city on SW. coast of Lesbos: Maps 11, 72
Eretria, city and port in Euboea, on the Euripus: p. 39; Maps 1, 11, 15-19, 71a
Ergines *or* **Agrianus** (Ergene), river in Thrace: Map 11
Erinyes, *Gr.* **Erinues** (the Furies), Gr. goddesses of vengeance who pursued the wrongdoer (Alekto, Megaira, and Tisiphone): pp. 179-80; Map 24
Ermine Street, Rom. road in Britain: Map 61
Erymanthus M., mountain range on the boundary of Elis, Arcadia, and Achaia: Map 1
Erythrae 1. city on coast of Lydia: Maps 1, 9, 11, 15, 19, 71b
2. city in Boeotia: Map 22
Erythraeum, Mare (the Arabian Sea): Map 59
Esquilinus, one of the seven hills of the city of Rome: Maps 42, 44; Plate 349
Eteocles, son of Oedipus king of Thebes, brother of Polynices and Antigone: p. 180
Etruria, district in Italy, more of less the modern Tuscany: pp. 91-2, 96; Maps 31, 33
Etruscans, see ETRUSCI
Etrusci *or* **Tusci** *or* **Tyrrheni** *or* **Tyrsenoi,** people probably originating in Asia Minor; in 8th-7th cent. B.C. landed in Italy and settled especially in the district between the Tiber and the Arno (called Etruria after them); in the course of centuries subdued and incorporated by Rome; impressive traces of their culture survive; their language has not been deciphered: pp. 91-2, 96, 122; Maps 31-4; Plates 230-41
Etymandrus, river in Arachosia: Maps 23, 27
Euboea, island off coast of Attica and Boeotia: Maps 1, 3, 9, 10, 11, 15, 19, 24
Euclid (ca. 300 B.C.), from Alexandria, Gr. mathematician and physicist: Map 72
Euclides (ca. 450-380 B.C.), from Megara, Gr. philosopher, founder of the school of Megara which combined the doctrines of the Eleatics with propositions of Socrates; gave shelter to many pupils of Socrates who after his death were no longer safe in Athens: Map 72
Eudoxus (ca. 390-337 B.C.), from Cnidus, Gr. scholar; wrote on mathematics, astronomy, geography, medicine: Map 72
Euhesperides, see BERENICE
Eumenia, city in Phrygia: Map 28
Eumenius (3rd cent. A.D.), from Augustodunum, Rom. rhetorician: Map 73
Eupatoria (Erbaa), city in Pontus: Map 28
Euphorion (ca. 250 B.C.), from Chalcis in Euboea, Gr. author of elegiacs, etc. and many learned works in prose: p. 182; Map 72
Euphrates, river in Mesopotamia: Maps 6, 7, 8, 23, 26, 27, 28, 38, 43, 49
Eupolis (ca. 420 B.C.), prominent representative of the Attic Old Comedy, author of 20 plays: Map 72
Euripides (480-406 B.C.), Gr. tragedian, friend of Socrates: pp. 63, 179-81; Map 72
Euripus, strait between Euboea and Attica: Map 14
Euromus (Ayakli), city in Caria: Maps 18, 71b
Europa, Phoenician princess, abducted by Zeus in the form of a bull: Map 24
Europus 1. see RHAGAE
2. see CARCHEMISH
Eurotas, river in Laconica: Maps 1, 11; Plates 13, 69
Eurunome, Gr. goddess, mother of the Graces: Map 24
Eurydicea, Hell. for SMYRNA
Eurymedon, river in Pamphylia: Map 11
Eurypontids, Spartan junior royal house, descended from Eurypon: p. 34
Eusebia, 1. Hell. for TYANA
2. Hell. for MAZACA
Eutresis, place in Boeotia; earliest remains from 3rd millennium B.C.: Map 3
Eutropius (4th cent. A.D.), Rom. historian: Map 73

F

Fabius 1. called **Cunctator,** Rom. statesman and general; appointed dictator after the victory of Hannibal at Lake Trasimene 217 B.C.: p. 102
2. called **Pictor** (ca. 220 B.C.), one of the earliest Rom. annalists, author of a history of Rome down to the end of the Second Punic War; wrote in Greek: Map 72
Fabrateria, name of two small towns in Latium: Map 57
Faesulae (Fiesole), city in N. of Etruria: Maps 33, 57, 71c
Falerii, *later* **Falerii Novi** *or* **Aequum Faliscum** (Cività Castellana), fortified city N. of Rome, on the Via Flaminia: Maps 33, 57, 68, 71; Plates 251, 253
Falerio, city in Picenum: Maps 57, 68, 71c
Fanum Fortunae (Fano), city on coast of Umbria, terminus of the Via Flaminia; famous temple of Fortune: Maps 53, 57, 58
Fates, Gr. goddesses (Klotho, Lachesis, Atropos) who appointed the fate of men and spun the thread of their lives: Map 24
Fectio (Vechten), naval base on the Rhine, near Traiectus; used by Drusus and Germanicus in their operations in Germany: Map 43
Felsina, see BONONIA
Fendoch, site of Rom. fort in E. Scotland: Map 60
Ferentinum (Ferentino), city in Latium: Map 71c
Ferentum *or* **Ferentium,** city in S. of Etruria: Maps 57, 71c
Festus (3rd cent. A.D.), Rom. scholar: Map 73
Fidenae (Castel Giubileo), city in Latium, N. of Rome: Map 55
Fidentia (Fidenza), city in Gallia Cisalpina, on the Via Aemilia: Map 54
Firmicus Maternus (4th cent. A.D.), from Sicily, Rom. author of a work on astrology; later a convert to Christianity: Map 73
Firmum (Fermo), city in Picenum: Maps 57, 68, 71c
Flaminia Via, highway in Italy from Rome to Fanum: Maps 33, 53, 55; Plate 294
Flavia Solva, city in the border district of Noricum and Pannonia: Maps 57, 68
Flaviobriga (Castro Urdiales), port on N. coast of Tarraconensis: Map 66
Florence, see FLORENTIA
Florentia (Florence), city in Etruria, on the Arno: Maps 31, 33, 53, 57, 58, 68, 71c; Plate 392
Florus (ca. A.D. 125), Rom. historian: Map 73
Folkestone, site of remains of two Rom. villas, on S. coast of Britain: Map 61
Formiae (Formia), city on coast of Latium, on the Via Appia: Map 57
forum, Rom. city square or market place; esp. the Forum Romanum at Rome, at the foot of the Capitoline, surrounded by temples, basilicas, and municipal buildings: p. 99; Map 56 (inset), Plates 84, 87, 351
Forum Clodii (Materano), city in S. of Etruria, near Lacus Sabatinus: Map 57
Forum Iulii (Fréjus), important city and port on the coast of Gallia Narbonensis: Maps 43, 47, 51, 57, 68, 71
Forum Iulium (Cividale di Friuli), place in land of the Veneti in W. of Gallia Cisalpina: Map 58
Forum Popilii (Forlimpopoli), city in E. of Aemilia, near Ariminum: Map 58
Forum Sempronii (Fossombrone), city in N. of Umbria: Map 57
Forum Traiani (Fordongianus), city in Sicily; Map 68
Fossa Traiana, junction canal between the Tiber and the port near the mouth of the Tiber, constructed by Trajan A.D. 106: Map 43a
Fosse Way, Rom. road in Britain: Map 61
Franci, German people who established themselves in Gaul in the 5th cent. A.D.: pp. 159, 175; Maps 47, 50, 69
Franks, see FRANCI
Fregellae (Ceprano), city in Latium, on the Liris: Map 53
Frentani, Samnite tribe on E. coast of central Italy: Map 29
Frisia, district N. of the delta of the Rhine, more or less the modern Friesland, Groningen, E. and W. Friesland: Map 45
Frontinus (1st cent. A.D.), Rom. writer on aqueducts: Map 73
Fronto (ca. A.D. 100-166), from Cirta, Rom. rhetorician: Map 73
Frusino (Frosinone), city in Latium, on the Via Latina: Map 57
Fulginiae (Foligno), city in Umbria: Map 57
Fundi (Fondi), city in land of the Aurunci in Latium: Map 57

G

Gabae (Isfahan), city in SE. of Media: Map 26
Gabala (Jebelen), city on coast of Syria: Map 71
Gabii, ancient city in Latium, NE. of Rome: Map 55
Gadara (Umm Qeis), city in Syria, one of the ten Gr. cities beyond the Jordan: Maps 28, 71, 72
Gades, *earlier* **Gadir** (Cadiz), city in Baetica, early Phoenician colony: Maps 30, 35, 36, 47, 51, 57, 66, 67, 73
Gaditanum, Fretum (Straits of Gibraltar), strait between Spain and Mauretania: Map 66
Gaetuli, desert tribe in Gaetulia: Map 47
Gaetulia, extensive interior district of Africa S. of Numidia and Mauretania: Maps 38, 47, 59
Gaius (2nd cent. A.D.), famous Rom. jurist, author of the *Institutiones,* an introduction to jurisprudence: Map 73
Galatia, district in centre of Asia Minor: Maps 28, 36, 37, 38
Galatians *or* **Galli,** tribe in Galatia: pp. 82, 89
Galava (Ambleside), Rom. fort in NW. of Britain: Map 60
Galba, Servius Sulpicius, Rom. Emperor A.D. 68-9; assassinated after his defeat by his rival Otho: pp. 134, 188
Galepsus, city near S. coast of Thrace: Map 11
Galerius, Emperor of the Eastern division of the Roman Empire A.D. 305-11, in succession to Diocletian: p. 171; Map 69a
Gallaecia, district in the NW. of Spain: Maps 37, 67
Gallia (Gaul), more or less the modern S. Netherlands, Belgium, Luxembourg, France, W. Switzerland, Germany W. of the Rhine, and N. Italy; divided into Cisalpina S. and Transalpina N. of the Alps. In Caesar's time divided into Belgica (between the Rhine, Moselle, and Seine), Aquitania (S. of the Garonne), Provincia or Narbonensis (between the Pyrenees and Alps), and Celtica (the remainder of Gaul). Under the Empire the central district was called Lugdunensis; Aquitania was extended by the area between the Garonne and the Loire. Gallia Cisalpina was divided into Transpadana and Cispadana (respectively N. and S. of the Po): pp. 118, 122; Maps 31, 32, 37, 38

GALLIENUS — HERNICI

Gallienus, Rom. Emperor A.D. 261-268, son of Valerian: p. 159
Gallus, Cornelius (69-26 B.C.), Rom. elegiac poet: Map 73
Ganges, river in India: Map 59
Ganus (Gaziköy), city in S. of Thrace, on the Propontis: Map 11
Garamantes, desert tribe in Phazania: Map 47
Garbia, frontier fortress in the desert district of Tripolis: Map 47
Gariannonum (Burgh Castle), one of the 'forts of the Saxon Shore' in Britain: Maps 60, 61
Garumna (Garonne), river in SW. of Gaul: Map 35
Gaugamela, village in Assyria known for the battle fought there between Alexander the Great and Darius III of Persia 331 B.C.: p. 66
Gaul, see Gallia
Gauls, Celtic people living in Gaul: p. 102
Gaulus (Gozzo), small island near Malta: Maps 30, 57
Gaza (Ghazze), fortified city near the coast in S. of Syria Palaestina: Maps 26, 27, 28, 51
Gaziura, city in Pontus: Map 26
Gebal, see Byblus
Gedrosia, district N. of the Mare Erythraeum, between Persis and the Indus: Maps 26, 27
Gela, city on S. coast of Sicly, Gr. foundation: Maps 12, 16, 29; Plate 81
Gelligaer, site of Rom. fort in W. Britain: Map 60
Gellius, Aulus (ca. A.D. 150), from Africa, Rom. prose writer, author of an encyclopaedic work, the *Noctes Atticae*: Map 73
Gelo, tyrant of Syracuse 491-478 B.C.; successfully defended Gr. interests in Sicily against the Carthaginians: p. 42
Gemellae (El Kasbat), city in S. of Numidia: Maps 47, 68
Genseric *or* **Gaiseric,** founder of the kingdom of the Vandals in the 5th cent. A.D.: p. 175
Genua (Genoa), city and port on coast of Liguria: Maps 29, 35, 46, 47, 51, 53
Georgics, didactic poem on farming by Virgil (29 B.C.): p. 178
Gepidi, Ger. tribe; settled in Dacia in the 5th cent. A.D.: Map 69c
Geranea M., mountain range in Megaris: Map 1
Gerasa, Hell. **Antiochia** (Jerash), centre of communications and trade in the border district of Arabia and Syria Palaestina: Maps 49, 51, 68, 71; Plate 218
Germalus, one of the peaks of the Palatine in Rome: Plates 243, 350
Germani, people inhabiting NE. Europe: pp. 162, 171, 175; Map 36
Germania, the area between the Rhine, Vistula, and Danube, more or less the modern Germany, E. Poland, and Czechoslovakia: later two Roman provinces on the left bank of the Rhine were called respectively Germania Inferior (the district between the Rhine, the Scheldt, and the line Bonn-Bavai) and Germania Superior (a small area S. of Bonn and the district of the Lingones, Sequani, and Helvetii): Maps 32, 37, 38, 45, 59
Germanicum (Kösching), fortress in N. of Raetia, on the Danube: Map 49
Germanicus, Gaius Julius Ceasar (15 B.C.-A.D. 19), nephew and adopted son of the Emperor Tiberius; famous for his campaigns in Germany: p. 134
Germanicus, Oceanus (the North Sea): Maps 38, 43
Germans, see Germani
Gerontia (Joura), island in the Aegean Sea, NE. of Euboea: Map 1
Gerrha, city on NE. coast of Arabia, on the Persian Gulf: Maps 26, 27
Gesoriacum (Boulogne), city in Gaul, on coast of the English Channel; port of embarcation for Britain: Maps 43, 51, 68
Geta, brother of the Emperor Caracalla; succeeded jointly with him to their father Septimius Severus in A.D. 211, but was murdered by him A.D. 212: p.159
Ghergina, city in Dacia, near the delta of the Danube: Map 43
Gigia (Gijon), city near the N. coast of Asturia: Map 66
Gigthis (Bou Ghara), city on E. coast of Africa Proconsularis: Map 51
Giuliano, S., place in Etruria with Etruscan cemetery; ancient name unknown: Map 33
Gla, fortress in Boeotia dating from Mycenaean times, on Copais L. and formerly an island in the lake: Map 17 (inset A); Plate 51
Glannaventa (Ravenglass), Rom. fort on NW. coast of Britain: Map 60
Glanum (Saint-Rémy in Provence), city in Gallia Narbonensis: Plate 443
Glenlochar, site of Rom. fort in S. Scotland: Map 60
Glevum (Gloucester), place in S. Britain; A.D. 49-75 base of Legio II, colonia from A.D. 97: Map 60
Gobannium (Abergavenny), Rom. fort in W. Britain: Map 60
Goldsborough, site of Rom. signal station on NE. coast of Britain: Maps 60, 61
Gonnus, fortified city in land of the Perrhaebi in Thessaly: Map 18
Gordium (Gordion), ancient Phrygian capital in Galatia, on the Sangarius: Maps 6, 7
Gorgias (ca. 483-375 B.C.), from Leontini, Gr. philosopher, Sophist, pupil of Empedocles, famous rhetorician: Map 72
Gortyna *or* **Gortyn,** city in Crete; important finds from 3rd and 2nd milleniums B.C.: Maps 1, 4, 11, 18, 68, 71
Gothi, Ger. people originating from Scandia; in 3rd cent. A.D. migrated southwards and divided into Ostrogoths and Visigoths: pp. 159, 174; Map 47
Goths, see Gothi
Gournia, city in E. of Crete: Maps 4, 18
Gracchus, Tiberius and **Gaius,** Rom. brothers, social reformers; murdered by their opponents in respectively 133 and 121 B.C.: pp. 119, 123
Graces, Gr. goddesses of beauty (Aglaia, Euphrosune, Thalia): Maps 24, 25; Plate 475
Gradus (Grado), port of Aquileia, on the northerly gulf of the Adriatic: Map 53
Granicus, small river in Mysia where Alexander the Great defeated the Persians 334 B.C.: p. 66; Map 11
Grannus (Grand), place in SE. of Gallia Belgica: Map 71
Graviscae, city on coast of Etruria: Map 57
Grumentum (Grumento), city in Lucania: Maps 53, 68, 71
Grynium *or* **Grynia,** city and port in Lydia with sanctuary and oracle of Apollo: Map 7
Gythium (Gythion), city on S. coast of Laconica, Spartan naval base: Maps 1, 11, 71a

H

Habitancum (Risingham), outpost fort covering Hadrian's Wall in Britain: Map 60
Hades, Gr. god of the Underworld, son of Kronos, brother of Zeus; by the Romans identified with Dis or Pluto; also name of the Underworld as his kingdom: pp. 177, 178; Maps 24, 25
Hadria (Atri), city in Picenum: Maps 53, 57
Hadrian, Publius Aelius, Rom. Emperor A.D. 117-138, from Spain; adopted son of Trajan; a man of letters, legislator, and efficient administrator: p. 134; Maps 48a, 69b; Plate 330
Hadriani, Vallum, famous line of fortification established by Hadrian in N. Britain A.D. 122: Maps 38, 47, 48a, 60, 62, 63; Plate 286
Hadrumetum (Sousse), city on E. coast of Africa Proconsularis: Maps 30, 35, 51, 57, 68
Haemon, son of Creon, lover of Antigone; character in the *Antigone* of Sophocles: p. 180
Hagia Triada, city near S. coast of central Crete: Maps 4, 18
Hagios Kosmas, place on W. coast of Attica; earliest remains from 3rd millennium B.C.: Map 3
Haliacmon (Haliakmon), river in Macedon: Maps 1, 11
Halicarnassus (Bodrum), city on SW. coast of Caria; famous for the Mausoleum (tomb of Mausolus): pp. 63, 188; Maps 1, 7, 8, 9, 11, 15, 18, 19, 25, 51, 71b, 72
Halicyae, Rom. city in W. of Sicily: Map 12
Halonnesus (Hagiostrati), island in the Aegean Sea, S. of Lemnos: Maps 1, 11
Halpa (Aleppo), trade centre in Syria: Map 6
Halus, city in SE. of Thessaly: Map 11
Halys (Kizil Irmak), the largest river in Asia Minor: Maps 6, 7, 8, 23, 27, 28, 43
Hamilcar Barca, Carthaginian general; reduced the greater part of Spain under the dominion of Carthage ca. 237-229 B.C.: p. 102; Map 40
Hannibal (247-183 B.C.), Carthaginian general, son of Hamilcar; in the Second Punic War crossed the Alps and brought Rome into the most extreme peril; at last defeated by Scipio Africanus at Zama 202 B.C.: pp. 102, 107; Map 40
Harmozia (Hormuz), city on S. entry of the Persian Gulf: Maps 26, 27
Harpassus (Aksu), river in Caria: Map 11
Hasdrubal 1. son-in-law of Hamilcar Barca: p. 102; Map 40
2. son of Hamilcar; came to the assistance of his brother Hannibal in the Second Punic War, but was defeated and killed at the Metaurus 207 B.C.: p. 107; Map 40
Hasta Regia (Mesa d'Asta), city in S. of Baetica: Map 66
Hatra, strong desert fortress in Mesopotamia, frequently besieged in vain by the Romans, for example by Trajan A.D. 117: Maps 47, 51
Hattushash (Boghaz-keui), ancient capital of the Hittite empire from ca. 1800 to 1200 B.C.; great city with strong walls; important excavations leading to the discovery among other things of the royal archives with ca. 1200 clay tablets with cuneiform inscriptions; the name Hittites is derived from Hattushash: Map 6
Heba (Magliano), city in Etruria: Map 33
Hebe, Gr. goddess of youth, cupbearer of the gods: Map 24
Hebrus (Maritsa, *Turkish* Meriç), river in Thrace: Map 1
Hecataeus (ca. 500 B.C.), from Miletus, Gr. historian; wrote among other things an account of a journey throughout the world: Map 72
Hecatompylus (Damghan), ancient capital of Parthia and residence of the Parthian kings: Maps 26, 27
Hector, son of Priam, the most valiant Trojan hero in the Trojan War; killed by Achilles; leading character in the *Iliad* of Homer: p. 177
Hegemon, from Thasos, Gr. poet; belonged to the Attic Old Comedy; known for his parodies: Map 72
Hegesias 1. (ca. 300 B.C.), from Cyrene, Gr. philosopher, champion of hedonism: Map 72
2. (3rd cent. B.C.), from Magnesia, Gr. orator: Map 72
Helena (Makronisi), island off E. coast of Attica: Maps 1, 14
Helice, city near N. coast of Achaia; swallowed up by the sea in consequence of an earthquake: Maps 1, 25
Helicon M., mountain in Boeotia, sacred to the Muses: Maps 1, 25
Heliogabalus, see Elagabalus
Heliopolis (Baalbek), city in Syria: Maps 51, 71
Hellenica, historical work by Xenophon, designed as a continuation of Thucydides: p. 188
Hellespont, see Hellespontus
Hellespontus (Dardanelles), strait joining the Aegean Sea and the Propontis: p. 39; Maps 1, 19
Helorus, city on SE. coast of Sicily: Map 71
Helots, name for the conquered race kept as public slaves by the Spartans: p. 34
Helvetii, Celtic people inhabiting the district between the Rhine, the Rhône, and the Jura Mountains (more or less the modern Switzerland): Map 36
Hemeroskopeion, *later* **Dianium** (Denia), city on E. coast of Spain, colony of Massilia: Map 16
Hephaestia, city on N. coast of Lemnos: Maps 11, 71
Hephaestus, see Hephaistos
Hephaistos, Gr. god of fire, son of Zeus and Hera, husband of Aphrodite; by the Romans identified with Vulcan; his forge was reputed to be in Lemnos or under Mount Aetna in Sicily; his assistants were the Cyclopes: Maps 24, 24; Plate 126
Hera, Gr. goddess, sister and wife of Zeus: p. 99; Map 24
Heraclea 1. see Siris
2. Hell. **Plistarchea,** city on W. coast of Caria: Maps 28, 71b
3. (Vakif), city in Caria near the Honaz Mountains: Map 68
4. **Sintica,** city in Macedon, on theStrymon: Map 57
5. (Eregli), city in Bithynia, on the Black Sea: Maps 26, 27, 72
6. (Sebastopol), city in the Chersonesus Taurica: Maps 26, 27
7. city in Media: Map 28
8. island in the Aegean Sea, one of the Cyclades: Map 1
9. see Pelagonia
Heraclea Minoa, see Minoa
Heracleum (Iraklion), port on N. coast of Crete: Map 4
Heraclides Ponticus (ca. 390-310 B.C.), from Heraclea Pontica, Gr. philosopher: Map 72
Heraclitus (ca. 525 B.C.), from Ephesus, Ionian natural philosopher: pp. 51, 59; Map 72
Heraeum, city in S. of Thrace, on the Propontis: Map 11
Herakles, *Lat.* **Hercules,** Gr. demigod, son of Zeus and Alkmene; performed many heroic deeds, including the famous Twelve Labours; extremely popular in Greece: Maps 24, 25; Plates 365, 431
Herculaneum (Ercolano), city in Campania, on the Gulf of Naples; with Pompeii buried in ashes from the eruption of Vesuvius A.D. 79: pp. 189, 193; Maps 57, 71c
Hercules, see Herakles
Herdonia, city in Apulia: Map 71c
Herillus (ca. 300 B.C.), from Carthage, Gr. philosopher, pupil of Zeno: Map 72
Hermagoras (2nd cent. B.C.), from Temnus, Gr. orator: Map 72
Hermes, Gr. divinity, messenger of Zeus and god of trade; by the Romans identified with Mercury: Maps 24, 25; Plates 132, 179
Hermes of Praxiteles, a famous Gr. statue of the 4th cent. B.C.: pp. 63, 88 (Fig. 7), 192; Plate 179
Hermione (Hermioni), port on SE. coast of Argolis: Maps 1, 11
Hermippus (5th cent. B.C.), from Athens, Gr. author of comedies: Map 72
Hermunduri, Suebian tribe: Map 47
Hermus (Gediz), river in Lydia: Maps 1, 6, 7, 8, 11
Hernici, tribe in Latium: Map 29

Herodotus (ca. 484-ca. 425 B.C.), from Halicarnassus, Gr. historian, called 'the Father of History'; wrote on the Persian Wars: pp. 51, 188; Map 72

Herondas (ca. 250 B.C.), from Cos, Gr. poet: Map 72

Herophilus (ca. 275 B.C.), from Chalcedon, Gr. writer on medicine, renowned anatomist: Map 72

Hesiod (prob. 8th cent. B.C.), perhaps born at Cyme, lived at Ascra in Boeotia; Gr. poet, originator of didactic verse; wrote the *Works and Days*: p. 178; Map 72

Hesperia (i.e. 'the West'), Gr. name for Italy: Map 29

Hestia, *Lat.* **Vesta**, Gr. goddess of the household hearth, daughter of Kronos and Rhea: Map 24; Plate 118

Hestiaeotis, district in NW. of Thessaly: Maps 1, 15

Hibernia (Ireland): Maps 38, 51, 59

Hiberus (Ebro), river in Tarraconensis; in the 3rd cent. B.C. the boundary between the Roman and Carthaginian spheres of influence in Spain: Maps 35, 38, 43, 66, 67

Hierapolis 1. *earlier* Bambyce (Membij), city in N. of Syria: Maps 28, 59
2. (Pambuk Kalesi), city in Phrygia: Maps 28, 71b

Hierapytna (Hierapetra), city on S. coast of Crete: Map 68

Hiero 1. tyrant of Syracuse 478-467 B.C., patron of art and learning; Aeschylus, Simonides, and others lived long at his court: p. 91
2. tyrant of Syracuse 264-215 B.C., faithful ally of Rome: p. 102; Plate 259

Hieronymus (ca. 360-256 B.C.), from Cardia, Gr. historian; served under Alexander the Great and the Diadochi: Map 72

Hieropolis *or* **Castabala**, city in E. of Cilicia: Map 28

Hierosolyma (Jerusalem), city in Syria, made capital of his kingdom by David; later capital of Judaea; destroyed by Titus A.D. 70; after A.D. 130 Rom. colonia under the name Aelia Capitolina: p. 134; Maps 23, 26, 27, 36, 41, 47, 69a

Hilarius (A.D. 315-367), bishop of Poitiers, Church Father: Map 72

Himera 1. city on N. coast of Sicily, Gr. foundation; destroyed by the Carthaginians ca. 409 B.C.; rebuilt near by under the name Thermae Himeraeae: Maps 12, 16, 17, 29, 72
2. (Salso), river in Sicily, known for the battle fought there in 480 B.C. in which the Greeks defeated the Carthaginians: p. 42; Maps 30, 53

Hipparchus, son of Pisistratus, tyrant of Athens; assassinated 514 B.C.: p. 39

Hippias 1. son of Pisistratus; succeeded his father as tyrant of Athens; expelled 510 B.C.: p. 39
2. (5th cent. B.C.), from Elis, Gr. philosopher, Sophist: Map 72

Hippocrates (ca. 400 B.C.), from Cos, Gr. writer on medicine, regarded as one of the founders of medical science: Map 72; Plate 157

Hippo Diarrhytus (Bizerta), coastal settlement in Africa Proconsularis: Maps 29, 30, 51, 71

Hippolytus, son of Theseus, victim of the ill-fated passion of his stepmother Phaedra; leading character in the play of the same name by Euripides: p. 180

Hipponax (ca. 540 B.C.), from Ephesus, Gr. elegiac poet: Map 72

Hipponium, see VIBO VALENTIA

Hippo Regius (Bône), city and port on N. coast of Africa Proconsularis, Phoenician foundation: Maps 30, 38, 47, 51, 57, 71

Hippos (Qala't el-Hosn), one of the ten Hellenistic cities beyond the Jordan: Map 28

Hippys, from Rhegium, Gr. historian: Map 72

Hispalis (Sevilla), city in Baetica, on the Baetis: Maps 66, 71, 73

Hispania, the modern Spain and Portugal; after conquest by the Romans divided into Ulterior (west) and Citerior (east); the definite subjugation by Augustus was followed by a new division into Tarraconensis (northeast), Baetica (south), and Lusitania (west): pp. 102, 107, 118, 122; Maps 35, 37, 38, 66, 67

Hispellum (Spello), city in Umbria: Maps 57, 58, 68, 71c

Hissarlik, village in the district of Troas, near the hill containing the ruins of Troy: Map 5

Histonium (Istonio), city near the coast in land of the Frentani: Map 57

Historiae, historical work by Tacitus; deals in fourteen Books with the history of Rome from Galba to Domitian: p. 189

Histria (Istria), peninsula in the NE. of the Adriatic Sea: Map 31

Hittites, group of early peoples in Asia Minor and N. Syria, whose culture is known from, among other sources, excavations at Boghaz-keui; first appearance ca. 1800 B.C.; powerful empire ca. 1600-1200 B.C.: p. 31; Map 6

Hod Hill, Rom. fortlet in S. Britain: Map 60

Holtye, site in S. Britain with remains of Rom. road near by: Map 61

Homer 1. the greatest Gr. poet; all the circumstances of his life and authorship are subject of controversy; prob. originating in Asia Minor ca. 800 B.C.; reputed author of the *Iliad* and *Odyssey*; pp. 177, 178; Maps 10, 72; Plate 462
2. from Byzantium, Gr. tragedian: Map 72

Honorius, Emperor of the Western Roman Empire A.D. 395-423; in his reign Alaric and the Visigoths penetrated into Italy and sacked Rome: p. 175; Map 69

Horace (65-8 B.C.), from Venusia, Rom. poet, author of *Odes, Epodes, Satires, Epistles*; member of the circle of Maecenas: pp. 177, 182; Map 73; Plate 470

Horta (Orta), city in Etruria, on the Tiber: Maps 33, 57

Hortia, Rom. lady, beloved by Propertius, by whom she was called Cynthia in his poems: p. 188

Hostilia (Ostiglia), city in Gallia Cisalpina, on the Padus: Map 53

Hours, Gr. goddesses of the seasons (Eunomia, Dike, Eirene): Map 24

Housesteads, see VERCOVICIUM

Hunnun (Halton), fort on Hadrian's Wall in Britain: Map 48a

Huns, Asiatic people, originating from Mongolia; at the end of the 4th cent. A.D. penetrated into the Roman Empire under the leadership of Attila and established a great kingdom which broke up after his death A.D. 453: pp. 174, 175; Map 69

Hydrea (Hydra), island off E. coast of Argolis: Map 1

Hydruntum, *earlier* Hydrus (Otranto), city on E. coast of Calabria, Gr. foundation: Map 29

Hydrus, see HYDRUNTUM

Hymettus M., mountain in Attica SE. of Athens: Map 14

Hypanis 1. (Bug), river in Sarmatia: Map 27
2. river in the Caucasus: Map 27

Hyphasis (Bias), river in India: Map 26

Hypsus (Belice), river in Sicily: Map 53

Hyrcania, district SE. of the Caspian Sea: Map 59

Hyrcanis, city in Lydia: Map 28

I

Iaca (Jaca), city in extreme N. of Tarraconensis, at the foot of the Pyrenees: Map 66

Iader (Zadar), city on coast of Dalmatia: Maps 51, 57, 58

Ialysus, city in Rhodes: Maps 1, 3, 9, 15, 30

Ianiculus, that one of the seven hills of Rome which was beyond the Tiber: Maps 42, 44

Iapyges, people in N. of Apulia: Map 29

Iasus, city on W. coast of Caria: Maps 11, 68, 71b

Iaxartes (Syr Darya), river in modern Turkestan: Maps 23, 26, 27, 59

Iazyges, Sarmatian tribe: Map 47

Ibericum, Mare, sea SE. of Spain: Map 66

Ibycus (ca. 540 B.C.), from Rhegium, Gr. lyric poet: Map 72

Icaria 1. city in Attica at the foot of Mt. Pentelicus: Map 71a
2. (Nikonia), island in the Aegean Sea, one of the Sporades: Maps 1, 9, 11

Iceni, tribe in Britain; revolted A.D. 61 under their queen Boudicca and sacked Camulodunum, Verulamium, and Londinium: Maps 40, 60

Ichnae, city in N. of Mesopotamia where Crassus defeated the Parthians: Map 28

Iciniacum (Theilenhofen), fortress on the frontier of Germania Superior: Map 50

Icknield Way, Rom. road in Britain: Map 61

Icosium (Algiers), city on coast of Mauretania, Phoenician foundation: Maps 30, 51

Icta I. (St Michael's Mount), island off SW. coast of Britain: Map 60

Ictinus (5th cent. B.C.), from Athens, famous architect, designer of the Parthenon: p. 51

Icus (Chiliodromia), island in the Aegean Sea, NE. of Euboea: Maps 1, 11

Ida M. 1. mountain in central Crete, with the cave in which Zeus was said to have been hidden in infancy: Maps 1, 4
2. mountain in Troas: Maps 10, 25

Igilgilis (Djidjelli), city on coast of Mauretania, Phoenician foundation: Maps 30, 51

Iguvium (Gubbio), city in Umbria: Maps 57, 71c

Ilerda (Lérida), city in Tarraconensis, N. of the Hiberus: Maps 36, 57, 66

Iliad (i.e. 'the story of Ilium'), epic poem by Homer; describes an episode in the siege of the city by the Greek forces (the wrath of Achilles against Agamemnon in consequence of an injury done him): pp. 177, 178, 181; Map 10

Ilici (Elche), city near coast of Tarraconensis: Map 66

Iliturgi (Menjibar), city in E. of Baetica: Map 66

Illyria, see ILLYRICUM

Illyricum, the coastal district E. of the Adriatic Sea, more or less the modern Dalmatia, Bosnia, and Herzegovina: pp. 102, 162; Maps 37, 38

Ilva (Elba), island in the Tyrrhenian Sea: Maps 29, 31, 33, 53

Imaus M. (the Himalayas): Map 59

Imbros (Imroz), island in NE. of the Aegean Sea, off the coast of the Chersonesus Thracica: Maps 1, 7, 9, 11, 25

Inachus, river in Athamania, tributary of the Achelous: Map 11

India, more or less the modern India: Maps 26, 37, 59

Indus, river in India: p. 66; Maps 23, 26, 27, 59

Institutiones, text book providing an introduction to jurisprudence; forms part of the *Corpus Iuris* of Justinian: p. 193

Interamna Nahars (Terni), city in Umbria: Maps 57, 68

Interamnia (Teramo), city in S. of Picenum: Maps 57, 68, 71c

Internum, Mare (the Mediterranean Sea): Maps 35, 38, 43

Inveresk, site of Rom. fort in S. Scotland: Map 60

Iol, see CAESAREA

Ion (ca. 490 - ca. 422 B.C.), from Chios, Gr. poet and author of tragedies: Map 72

Ionia, coastal area of Lydia and the adjacent islands, where there were Ionian settlements: p. 39

Ionians, race which penetrated into Greece from the N. and settled for example in Attica: p. 31; Maps 3, 9

Ionium, Mare (Ionian Sea): Maps 1, 31

Ios, island with city of the same name in the Aegean Sea, one of the Sporades: Maps 1, 11

Iphigenia, daughter of Agamemnon, condemned to be sacrificed to Artemis; according to some versions of the legend rescued by her and carried off to Tauris; leading character in tragedies of Euripides: p. 179

Ipsus, city in Phrygia where Antigonus was defeated and killed 301 B.C.: p. 66

Iria (Padron), city near W. coast of Gallaecia: Map 66

Irrhesia (Piperi), island in the Aegean Sea NE. of Euboea: Map 1

Isara (Isère), river in Gaul, tributary of the Rhône: Map 35

Isca 1. (Exeter), cantonal capital of the Dumnonii in SW. Britain: Map 60
2. or Isca Silurum (Caerleon), legionary fort, base of Legio II in W. Britain: Maps 41, 45, 46, 47, 60, 61, 68

Isis, Egyptian goddess of life and fertility; later worshipped by the Romans also: pp. 88, 154, 190

Isocrates (436-338 B.C.), famous Athenian orator: pp. 62, 63; Map 72

Isopata, place in central Crete: Map 18

Issa (Vis), island off the coast of Dalmatia, Gr. settlement; important centre of Gr. influence in the Adriatic: Maps 29, 57

Issus, city in Cilicia where Darius III was defeated by Alexander the Great 333 B.C.: p. 66; Maps 26, 27

Ister, see DANUVIUS

Istria, see HISTRIA

Istropolis, see ISTRUS

Isurium (Aldborough), cantonal capital of the Brigantes in N. Britain: Maps 60, 68

Italica (Santiponce), city in Baetica, on the Baetis: Maps 57, 66, 67, 68

Itanus, city on E. coast of Crete: Map 1

Ithaca (Ithaka), island in the Ionian Sea off the coast of Acarnania; in legend, the home of Odysseus: Maps 1, 3, 10, 11; Plate 3

Itucci (Baena), city in E. of Baetica: Map 66

Iuktas, place in central Crete; earliest remains from 3rd millennium B.C.: Map 4

Iulia Augusta Via, highway in Gallia Cisalpina and Narbonensis between Genua and Arelate: Maps 53, 54

Iuliobona (Lillebonne), city in Gallia Lugdunensis, near the mouth of the Sequana: Map 71

Iuliobriga (Retortillo), city in Tarraconensis: Maps 57, 66

Iuliomagus (Angers), city in Gallia Lugdunensis: Map 68

Iulis, city in Ceos: Map 71a

Iulium Carnicum (Cédarchis), city in NE. of Gallia Cisalpina: Map 58

Iuvanum, 1. city in Samnium in the district of the Frentani: Maps 57, 71c
2. (Salzburg), city in Noricum: Map 57

J

Jason, prince of Iolcus in Thessaly, leader of the Argonauts; with the assistance of Medea stole the Golden Fleece: p. 180

Jerome, St (A.D. 347-420), from Stridon, lived later at Bethlehem; theologian, known especially for his Lat. translation of the Bible (the Vulgate): Map 73

Jerusalem, see HIEROSOLYMA

Judaea, kingdom in S. of Palestine, made a Rom. province A.D. 6; the Romans sometimes extended

Nola, city in Campania: Maps 31, 57, 58, 68
Nomentana Via, highway from Rome to Nomentum: Map 55
Nomentum, city in Latium NE. of Rome: Map 55
Nonius Marcellus (4th cent. A.D.), from Africa, Rom. grammarian: Map 73
Nora, city on S. coast of Sardinia: Maps 29, 30, 53, 71
Norba (Cáceres), city in Lusitania N. of Emerita: Map 66
Norchia, modern city in Tuscany, on the route of the Clodia Via; ancient name unknown: Map 33
Noreia (Neumark), city in Noricum where a Rom. army was defeated by the Cimbri 113 B.C.: Map 40
Noricum, district W. of Pannonia, bounded by the Alps, the Danube, and the Inn, more or less the modern Austria: Maps 37, 38, 40
Notium, city on coast of Lydia: Map 11
Novae (Swisjtow), garrison town in Moesia Inferior, on the Danube: Maps 41, 47
Novaesium (Neuss), frontier fortress in Germania Inferior, on the Rhine: Maps 43, 47
Novantae, tribe in Britain: Map 60
Noviodunum 1. (Soissons), city in Gallia Belgica: Map 71
2. (Nyon), city in land of the Helvetii, on Lacus Lemanus: Map 57
3. city in Moesia Inferior, near the delta of the Danube: Map 43
4. **Diablintum** (Jublains), city in Gallia Lugdunensis: Map 71
Noviomagus (Chichester), cantonal capital of the Regnenses in S. Britain: Map 60
Nuceria (Nocera), city in Campania: Maps 31, 57, 58
Numana, city in N. of Picenum, Gr. foundation of 5th-4th cent. B.C.: Map 29
Numantia (Cerro de Garray), strongly fortified city in Tarraconensis; bulwark of Spanish resistance to Rome 143 B.C.; captured by Scipio Aemilianus 133 B.C.: p. 188; Maps 35, 38, 66
Numerus Syrorum (Lalla Marnia), city in W. of Mauretania Caesariensis: Map 47
Numidia, coastal district in Africa; in the 2nd cent. B.C. more or less the modern Algeria; under Rom. rule reduced to the modern E. Algeria; capital Cirta: p. 102; Maps 35-8
Nura, port in NW. of Sardinia: Map 53
Nysa, city in S. of Lydia, on the Maeander: Map 71

O

Oceanus, in the opinion of the ancients, the ocean surrounding the whole world, out of which the sun and moon rose and in which they set: Map 10
Ocelli Pr. (Flamborough Head), cape on NE. coast of Britain: Map 60
Ocha M., mountain range in S. of Euboea: Map 1
Ochus, river in Parthia: Maps 23, 26
Ocilis, city in N. of Tarraconensis: Map 66
Ocriculum (Otricoli), city in S. of Umbria: Maps 68, 71c
Octavian, Gaius Julius Caesar (63 B.C.-A.D. 14), greatnephew and adopted son of Julius Caesar; member of the Second Triumvirate, later opponent of Mark Antony, whom he defeated at Actium 31 B.C.; he thus became the sole ruler of Rome and its first Emperor with the honorary title Augustus, which became the official name for later Emperors; his reign was a period of peace and prosperity for the Empire: pp. 130, 178; Map 37; Plates 316, 317
Octodurus (Martigny), city in district of the Alpes Poeninae, on the Rhône: Maps 57, 68
Odenathus (3rd cent. A.D.), distinguished citizen of Palmyra; made himself king of a kingdom of Palmyra established by him and eventually ruled the whole E. part of the Roman Empire; succeeded after his death 267 A.D. by his widow Zenobia: pp. 159, 162
Odessus (Varna), city in Thrace, on W. coast of the Pontus Euxinus, founded from Miletus: Maps 16, 26, 27, 47
Odoacer, king of the Heruli; deposed the last Rom. Emperor of the West, Romulus Augustulus, 476 A.D. and reigned as king of Italy until defeated and killed by Theodoric the Ostrogoth A.D. 493: p. 175
Odysseus, king of Ithaca; took part in the Trojan War; had an adventurous journey and return home after the fall of Troy; chief character in the *Odyssey*: pp. 177, 178; Map 10
Odyssey (i.e. the 'story of Odysseus'), epic by Homer; describes the wanderings of Odysseus on his way home after the fall of Troy: pp. 177, 178; Map 10
Oea (Tripoli), city on coast of Africa Proconsularis: Maps 30, 47, 51
Oedipus, king of Thebes; compelled by ill-fate, unwittingly killed his father and married his mother; chief character in two plays by Sophocles: pp. 179, 180
Oeniadae, coastal settlement in S. of Acarnania: Maps 18, 71a
Oenoanda, city in N. of Lycia: Map 71b
Oenoe, Attic deme, frontier fortress against Boeotia: Map 14
Oenophyta, place in Boeotia on the border of Attica: Map 11
Oenotrii, the earliest inhabitants of S. Italy, which in poetic style was called Oenotria (i.e. 'land of wine'): Map 29
Oenussae Iae., group of islands off the S. coast of Messenia: Map 1
Oescus, city in Moesia Inferior: Maps 47, 57
Oeta M., mountain range in S. Thessaly where Herakles was said in the legend to have burned himself to death; near the Sinus Maliacus forms the Pass of Thermopylae: Maps 1, 21
Oetylus (Itylon), city on W. coast of Laconica: Map 1
Olbia 1. (Terranova), port in NE. of Sardinia: Maps 29, 30, 53
2. (Nikolaev), city in Sarmatia, on N. coast of the Pontus Euxinus, near the mouth of the Borysthenes and the Hypanis: Maps 16, 26, 27, 47, 51
3. (Hyères), city near the coast of Gallia Narbonensis:, Gr. foundation: Map 16
Olicana (Ilkley), Rom. fort and settlement in N. Britain: Map 60
Olisipo (Lisbon), city in Lusitania, at the mouth of the Tagus: Maps 47, 57, 66
Olympia, small plain in Elis between the Alpheus and the Cladeus where the Olympic Games were held; the Altis (grove of Zeus) and its immediate neighbourhood contained many temples, statues, and public buildings, of which the most famous was the Olympieum (temple of Zeus Olympius) containing the colossal statue of Zeus by Phidias: pp. 51, 182, 192; Maps 1, 11, 15, 18, 25, 68; Plates 161-4, 172
Olympian gods, the most important Gr. divinities, living on Mount Olympus, ruled by Zeus: p. 122; Map 24
Olympic Games, athletic festival held every four years at Olympia in honour of Zeus by all the tribes and cities of Greece; legend gave Herakles as the founder; names of the victors are on record since 776 B.C.; the Games were forbidden by Theodosius the Great A.D. 394: p. 182; Plate 205
Olympus, city on E. coast of Lycia: Map 71
Olympus M. 1. mountain in N. of Thessaly, traditionally residence of the most important Gr. gods: Maps 1, 10, 19, 25; Plates 7, 8
2. mountain in Lesbos: Map 1
Olynthus, city on coast of Chalcidice, Gr. in origin; destroyed by Philip II of Macedon 348 B.C.: p. 62; Maps 11, 16, 18, 72
Onesicritus (late 3rd cent. B.C.), from Aegina, Gr. author; took part in the campaigns of Alexander the Great and wrote a historical romance about his adventures: Map 72
Onoba (Huelva), port on SW. coast of Baetica: Map 66
Ophiusa (Formentera), one of the Pityusae Iae.: Map 67
Opis, Hell. **Seleucia,** city in Babylonia, on the Tigris: Maps 26, 28
Opitergium (Oderzo), city in land of the Veneti, in W. of Gallia Cisalpina: Map 58
Oppidum Novum (Duperré), city in Mauretania Caesariensis: Map 47
Opus, capital of the district of the Locri Opuntii, on the Mare Euboicum: Map 11
Orcas Pr. (Duncansby Head), cape on N. coast of Caledonia: Map 60
Orchoe, *earlier* **Uruk** (Warka), ancient city in Babylonia, Maps 26, 28
Orchomenus 1. ancient capital of Boeotia; destroyed by the Thebans 367 B.C.; rebuilt by Philip of Macedon: Maps 3, 15, 17a, 18, 40; Plate 50
2. city in Arcadia: Maps 1, 71a
Ordovices, tribe in Britain: Map 60
Ordymnus M., mountain in Lesbos: Map 1
Oresteia, trilogy of tragedies by Aeschylus (*Agamemnon, Choephorole, Eumenides*) relating the tragic fortunes of the house of Atreus: pp. 179, 181
Orestes 1. son of Agamemnon, whose murder he revenged upon his mother Clytemnestra; tried and acquitted for this action by the court of the Areopagus at Athens; character in plays by Aeschylus, Sophocles, and Euripides: pp. 179, 180
2. general of Attila; placed his son Romulus Augustulus on the throne of the Western Roman Empire A.D. 474: p. 175
Orestis, district in SW. of Macedon: Map 11
Oreus (Oreoi), city on NW. coast of Euboea: Map 11
Oricum, coastal settlement in N. of Epirus: Map 11
Oroatis, river in N. of Persis: Map 28
Orontes (Nahr el 'Asi), river in Syria: Maps 6, 7, 8, 43
Oropus, city on the border of Attica and Boeotia, on the Euripus: Maps 11, 14, 17a, 18, 71a
Orosius (early 5th cent. A.D.), from Bracara, Rom. historian: Map 73
Orrhoe, see EDESSA
Orthosia, city and port on coast of Phoenicia: Map 28
Orvieto, rock fastness in Etruria; ancient name unknown: Map 33
Osca (Huesca), city in NE. of Tarraconensis: Maps 66, 67
Oscans, one of the earliest Latin peoples, settled in central Italy; driven back towards Umbria by the Etruscans: p. 91
Ossa M., mountain range in the E. of Thessaly; in legend the Giants piled M. Pelion upon it in an attempt to scale M. Olympus: Maps 1, 25; Plate 7
Ossonoba (Faro), port on SW. coast of Baetica: Map 66
Ostia, the port of Rome, at the mouth of the Tiber; probably founded late 4th cent. B.C.; fell to ruin late 4th cent. A.D.; now partly excavated: p. 135; Maps 29, 33, 35, 43, 55, 57, 71c; Plates 303, 386-9, 446
Ostiensis Via, road connecting Rome with Ostia: Map 55
Ostra, place in N. of Umbria: Map 71c
Ostrogoths, Ger. people originating in Scandia (Götaland); penetrated into the Roman Empire in the 5th cent. A.D. and founded a kingdom in Italy under Theodoric the Great: p. 174; Map 69c
Otho, Marcus Salvius, Rom. Emperor for a few months A.D. 69; defeated at Bedriacum by his rival Vitellius: p. 134
Othrys M., mountain in Phthiotis: Map 1
Ovid (43 B.C.-A.D. 18), from Sulmo, Rom. poet, author of the *Metamorphoses, Ars Amatoria, Fasti,* etc.; banished by Augustus to Tomi on the Pontus Euxinus, where he composed his plaintive *Tristia*: pp. 182, 188; Map 73
Oxianus Lacus (Aral Sea), large lake in the modern Turkestan: Maps 27, 59
Oxus (Amu Darya), river in the modern Turkestan: Maps 23, 26, 27

P

Pacuvius (ca. 220-130 B.C.), from Brundisium, Rom. tragedian: Map 73
Padus (Po), river in Gallia Cisalpina: Maps 31, 33, 35, 38, 43, 53, 54
Paeania, deme in Attica E. of Athens: Map 14
Paeligni, tribe in central Italy: Map 29
Paeonia, district in N. of Macedon: Maps 10, 11
Paestum, *earlier* **Posidonia,** city on coast of Lucania, founded by Greeks from Sybaris 524 B.C., destroyed by Lucanians ca. 400 B.C.; after 273 B.C. a Latin colonia; known for its still existing Gr. temples: Maps 16, 17, 29, 53, 68, 71c; Plates 84, 115
Pagasae, city in SE. of Thessaly, near the border of Magnesia: Map 18
Pagasaeus, Sinus (Gulf of Volos), gulf on E. coast of Thessaly: Map 1
Palaikastro, place near E. coast of Crete: Map 4
Palatinus, one of the seven hills of Rome, and certainly the earliest inhabited; according to tradition Romulus and Remus were here found and suckled by the she-wolf; later the hill of Imperial palaces and residences of patricians: p. 92; Maps 42, 44; Plates 349-54
Pale (Lixouri), city in W. part of Cephallenia: Map 11
Palladius (4th cent. A.D.), Rom. writer on agriculture: Map 73
Pallantia (Palencia), city in NW. of Tarraconensis: Map 66
Pallas Athena, Gr. goddess of wisdom, learning, arts and crafts, and military science; born out of the head of Zeus; patroness of Athens and especially revered in the Parthenon there; by the Romans identified with Minerva: Maps 24, 25; Plates 52, 95, 108, 160
Pallene, W. prong of land of Chalcidice: Maps 1, 19
Palma, city in Insula Maior (Mallorca), one of the Balearic Is.: Maps 57, 66
Palmyra (Tudmur), city in the Syrian desert, centre of caravan routes: p. 162; Maps 26, 38, 49, 51, 71
Pamphylia, district on S. coast of Asia Minor: Map 38
Panactum (Panakton), fortress in NW. of Attica, on the border of Boeotia: Maps 14, 17c
Panaetius (ca. 180- ca. 112 B.C.), from Rhodes, Gr. philosopher; friend of Laelius and Scipio Africanus in Rome, where he spread the teachings of Stoicism; succeeded Antipater as head of the Stoic school at Athens: p. 123
Panathenaea, festival held every four years at Athens in honour of Athena as patroness of the city: p. 42; Plate 55
Pandects, see DIGESTS
Pannonia, district bounded by the Danube and the line Sirmium-Poetevio-Carnuntum, more or less the modern W. Hungary; as a Rom. province divided into Pannonia Inferior and Pannonia Superior: p. 162; Maps 37, 38, 45
Panormus (Palermo), port on NW. coast of Sicily, Phoenician foundation: Maps 12, 29, 30, 31, 35, 43, 53
Pantheon, temple in Rome dedicated to Mars and

250

Picenum, coastal district in E. of Italy, between Umbria and Samnium: Map 31

Pictavi, see LIMONUM

Picti, tribe in Caledonia: Map 47

Pinara, city in Lycia: Map 71b

Pindar (518-446 B.C.), from Thebes, famous Gr. lyric poet, author of splendid odes in commemoration of victors at the Olympian, Nemean, and Pythian Games: pp. 182, 190; Map 72

Pinna (Penne), city in land of the Vestini: Map 57

Pinnata Castra (Inchtuthil), site of legionary fort in E. Caledonia, base for Agricola's proposed occupation of Caledonia: Map 60

Piraeus, port of Athens, built in the time of Themistocles and Pericles; contained three harbours (Munichia, Zea, Cantharus); 5th cent. B.C. the roads from Athens to Piraeus were fortified by the 'Long Walls': p. 42; Maps 1, 11, 14, 19, 43, 71

Pisae (Pisa), city in Etruria, near the mouth of the Arnus; at an earlier period an important port: Maps 29, 31, 33, 35, 51, 53, 57, 58, 71

Pisaurum (Pesaro), city on coast of Umbria: Maps 57, 73

Pisidia, district in S. of Asia Minor, N. of Lycia: Maps 8, 23, 28, 37

Pisistratus, tyrant of Athens 538-528 B.C.; an able ruler: p. 39

Piso, Calpurnius (ca. 150 B.C.), Rom. author and annalist: Map 73

Pistoriae (Pistoia), city in N. of Etruria: Map 57

Pitane, port on W. coast of Mysia: Maps 7, 43, 72

Pithecussa *or* **Aenaria I.** (Ischia), volcanic island in the Sinus Cumanus: Map 16

Pitinum 1. Mergens, city in N. of Umbria: Map 57
2. **Pisaurense,** city in N. of Umbria: Map 57

Pityus, city on NE. coast of the Pontus Euxinus: Maps 16, 26, 47

Pityusae Iae., group of islands E. of Spain: Maps 66, 67

Placentia (Piacenza), city in N. of Aemilia, near the confluence of the Padus and the Trebia: Maps 31,33, 47, 53, 54, 58

Planaria (Pianosa), small island in the Tyrrhenian Sea, S. of Elba; under the Empire used as a place of banishment: Map 71c

Plataea, city in Boeotia where the Greeks under the leadership of Pausanias defeated the Persians 479 B.C.: pp. 42, 188; Maps 14, 17, 19, 22; Plate 106

Plato 1. (427-347 B.C.), from Athens, famous Gr. philosopher, pupil of Socrates, founder of the Academy, originator of the doctrine of Ideas: pp. 63, 89, 123, 147, 189; Map 72
2. (ca. 400 B.C.), from Athens, Gr. author of comedies: Map 72

Plautus (ca. 200 B.C.), from Sarsina, Rom. author of comedies, inspired by the Attic New Comedy: pp. 122, 181; Map 73

Pleuron, city in Aetolia: Maps 18, 72

Pliny 1. the Elder (A.D. 23-79), from Comum, Rom. scholar, author of a *Natural History*: pp. 147, 189; Map 73
2. **the Younger** (A.D. 61-113), nephew of THE ELDER, from Comun, Rom. man of letters, friend of Tacitus; his extant works are a panegyric on the Emperor Trajan, under whom he was governor of the province Bithynia, and ten Books of letters which are a valuable source of information on the life and ideas of the age: p. 190; Map 73

Plistarchea, see HERACLEA

Plutarch (ca. A.D. 50-120), from Chaeronea, Gr. writer; lived for a time in Rome and was favoured by the Emperors Trajan and Hadrian; his best-known work is the series of parallel biographies of famous Greeks and Romans: p. 188

Pnyx, hill in the outskirts of Athens where the Popular Assembly was held: Map 13

Poetovio (Ptuj), strong fortress in Pannonia, on the Dravus: Maps 46, 47, 57

Pola (Pula), port on the SW. point of Istria: Maps 51, 53, 58, 71

Polemon (early 2nd cent. B.C.), from Troas, Gr. author of works on ancient monuments and inscriptions: Map 72

Poliochni, place near E. coast of Lemnos; earliest remains from 3rd millennium B.C.: Maps 3, 6

Pollentia 1. (Alcudia de Mallorca), city and port in Insula Maior (Mallorca), the largest island in the Baleares: Maps 51, 57, 66, 71
2. (Brà), city in Liguria: Maps 58, 68, 71

Pollio, Asinius (late 1st cent. B.C.), Rom. orator, historian, poet, and writer of tragedies; none of his works have survived: Map 73

Pollux, see DIOSKOUROI

Poludeukes, see DIOSKOUROI

Polyaegos 1. (Pelagonisi), island in the Aegean Sea, NE. of Eubosia: Maps 1, 11
2. island NE. of Melos, one of the Cyclades: Map 1

Polybius (204-122 B.C.), from Megalopolis. Gr. historian; brought to Rome as a prisoner after the conquest of Macedon by the Romans 168 B.C.; became an intimate friend of Scipio Aemilianus, whom he accompanied upon his expedition against Carthage; author of a history in forty Books, of much merit and value, which has unfortunately survived only in part: pp. 101, 123, 188

Polyclitus (5th cent B.C.), from Sicyon, famous Gr. sculptor: pp. 51,192

Polycrates, tyrant of Samos ca. 532-522 B.C.; under his rule Samos attained great wealth and prosperity: p. 182

Polygnotus (5th cent. B.C.), Gr. painter: p. 193

Polymnestus (6th cent. B.C.), from Colophon, Gr. poet: Map 72

Polynices, son of Oedipus, brother of Eteocles and Antigone: p. 180

Pomaria (Themcen), city in W. of Mauretania Caesariensis: Map 47

Pompaelo (Pamplona), city in NE. of Tarraconensis: Map 66

Pompeii, city in Campania, at the foot of Vesuvius M.; buried under ashes in the eruption of A.D. 79; now for a great part excavated: pp. 147, 193; Maps 17, 57, 58, 68, 71c; Plates 380-3, 421, 435, 445

Pompeius, Trogus (end of 1st cent. B.C.), from Gaul, a Celt in origin; Rom. historian, author of the *Historiae Philippicae* (designed as a history of the Macedonian monarchy, but in effect a universal history) of which Justin made a popular abridgment: Map 73

Pompey (106-48 B.C.), Rom. statesman and general; defeated Mithridates of Pontus; captured Jerusalem and made Syria a Rom. province; son-in-law and at first ally of Caesar, later his rival in their contest for power; defeated by him at Pharsalus 48 B.C. and treacherously murdered in Egypt on his escape there: pp. 85, 122; Plate 263

Pomponius Mela (1st cent. A.D.), from Spain, Rom. geographer: Map 73

Ponione (Faimingen), garrison post on the boundary of Raetia and Germania Superior: Map 50

Pons Aelius (Newcastle upon Tyne), Rom. fort near the E. end of Hadrian's Wall in Britain: Maps 48a, 60

Pons Aureoli, posting stage in Gallia Cisalpina on the route Bergamum-Mediolanum: Map 54

Pons Seciae (Rubiera), place in Gallia Cisalpina where the Via Aemilia crossed the Secia: Map 54

Pont du Gard, aqueduct of the, one of the most famous Rom. remains in France; built under the administration of Agrippa to bring water to Nîmes; has 3 tiers; length 902 ft.; total height 160 ft.: p. 192

Pontes (Staines), Rom. settlement in Britain, on the Thames: Map 60

Pontus, coastal district on S. coast of the Pontus Euxinus: Maps 28, 38

Pontus Euxinus (the Black Sea): Maps 1, 38, 40, 43

Popilia Via, highway in Italy between Capua and Rhegium: Map 53

Populonia, city on coast of Etruria, member of the Etruscan League; centre of iron trade: Maps 31, 33, 51, 53

Porolissum, city in N. of Dacia: Maps 47, 68

Portae Caspiae, mountain pass S. of the Caspian Sea, near Rhagae; of prime importance for communication between the E. and W. sections of the Persian Empire: Maps 26, 27

Portuensis Via, road connecting Rome with the port of Portus: Map 55

Portus, the port of Rome at the mouth of the Tiber; established by Claudius A.D. 42, extended by Trajan A.D. 106: Maps 43 (inset), 51, 53, 55, 71c

Portus Adurni (Portchester), one of the 'forts of the Saxon Shore', on S. coast of Britain: Maps 60, 61

Portus Argous (Portoferraio), city and port in Ilva: Map 53

Portus Cale (Oporto), port in Lusitania, at the mouth of the Durius: Maps 51, 66

Portus Delphini (Portofino), city and port in Liguria: Map 53

Portus Favonius, port on E. coast of Corsica: Map 51

Portus Itius, port on coast of Gallia Belgica: Map 47

Portus Lemanae (Lympne), port in SW. of Britain: Maps 43, 51

Portus Magnus (Saint-Leu), port on coast of Mauretania Caesariensis: Map 57

Portus Tibulae, port on N. coast of Sardinia: Map 51

Portus Veneris (Porto Venere), port in Liguria: Map 53

Poseidon, Gr. god of the sea; son of Kronos, brother of Zeus; by the Romans identified with Neptune: pp. 177, 180; Maps 24, 25

Posidippus 1. (ca. 275 B.C.), from Pella, Gr. poet, author of epigrams: Map 72
2. (ca. 300 B.C.), from Cassandrea, Gr. author of comedies, representative of the Attic New Comedy: Map 72

Posidium Pr., cape on S. coast of Ionia, near Didyma: Map 18

Posidonia, see PAESTUM

Postumia Via, highway in Gallia Cisalpina between Genua and Aquileia: Map 53

Potaissum, city in Dacia: Map 47

Potentia 1. (Potenza), city in N. of Lucania: Map 57
2. city in N. of Picenum: Map 57

Potidaea (Pontidaia), fortified city on the W. isthmus of the peninsula of Chalcidice; destroyed by Philip of Macedon 356 B.C.; rebuilt as CASSANDREA: Maps 1, 11, 15, 16, 19

Praeneste (Palestrina), very ancient city in Latium with a famous temple of Fortune: Maps 33, 53, 55, 57; Plate 267

Praenestina Via, highway from Rome to Praeneste: Map 55

Praesus, city in E. of Crete: Map 1

Praetorian Guard, bodyguard of the Rom. Emperors, instituted by Augustus; since the time of Tiberius garrisoned in the Castra Praetoria NE. of Rome: pp. 134, 135; Map 42 (inset)

Prasiae, city on E. coast of Laconica: Map 1

Pratinas (ca. 500 B.C.), from Phlius, Gr. poet, author of a satyric play; forerunner of tragedy: Map 72

Praxiteles (ca. 350 B.C.), from Athens, famous Gr. sculptor: pp. 63, 192; Plate 179

Priam, legendary king of Troy at the time of the Trojan War; character in the *Iliad*: p. 179

Priapus, coastal settlement in Phrygia, on the Propontis: Map 11

Priene (Kelebeç), coastal settlement on the boundary of Caria and Lydia: Maps 1, 9, 11, 15, 18, 68, 71b

Prinias, city in central Crete: Map 18

Priscianus (ca. A.D. 400), Rom. writer on medicine: Map 73

Privernum (Priverno), city in Latium: Map 57

Probus, Rom. Emperor A.D. 276-282: p. 169; Map 69b

Procolitia (Carrawburgh), fort on Hadrian's Wall in Britain: Map 48a

Proconnesus (Marmara), island in the Propontis: Maps 1, 11

Prodicus (ca. 400 B.C.), from Cos, Gr. philosopher, friend of Socrates and Plato: Map 72

Prometheus, Gr. hero who incurred the wrath of Zeus by giving mankind the gift of fire: chief character in a trilogy by Aeschylus, of which only one play (*Prometheus Bound*) survives: p. 179

Pronni, city in SE. of Cephallenia: Map 11

Propertius (ca. 50-10 B.C.), from Asisium, Rom. elegiac poet; belonged to the circle of Maecenas: p. 182; Map 73

Propontis (Sea of Marmara), gulf between the Pontus Euxinus and the Aegean Sea: Maps 1, 43

propylaea, a gateway building; esp. the Propylaea at the entrance to the Acropolis at Athens: pp. 51, 192; Map 13; Plate 59

Protagoras (ca. 480-411 B.C.), from Abdera, Gr. philosopher, a famous Sophist ('Man is the measure of all things'); lived and wrote at Athens; friend of Euripides and Pericles; one of the dialogues of Plato was called after him: p. 189; Map 72

Prudentius (A.D. 348-405), from Caesaraugusta, Rom. Christian lyric poet: Map 73

Prusa (Bursa), city in Bithynia: Map 28

Prusias 1. city in Bithynia, rebuilt from the earlier Cierus by King Prusias: Maps 28, 71
2. Hell. for CIUS in Bithynia

Ptolemais 1. (Tolmeta), city and port in Cyrenaica: Maps 51, 68, 71
2. Hell. for Acco (Acre), city on coast of Palestine: Map 28
3. city in Egypt, on the Nile: Map 27
4. city on coast of Pamphylia: Map 28
5. Hell. for LEBEDUS

Ptolemy 1. name of a Macedonian dynasty of kings of Egypt founded by Ptolemy I Soter (i.e. 'the Preserver'), a follower of Alexander the Great who obtained possession of Egypt after the death of Alexander 323 B.C. and reigned until 285 B.C.; the dynasty lasted until the death of Cleopatra 30 B.C.: pp. 66, 82, 107
2. **Ceraunus,** son of Ptolemy I king of Egypt; assassinated Seleucus king of Macedon and usurped his throne 280 B.C., but after a reign of a few months was defeated, taken prisoner, and put to death by the Galatians: p. 82

Ptous M., mountain range in Boeotia E. of Copais Lacus: Map 17

Pullaria (Brioni), island off the coast of Istria: Map 53

Punicum (S. Marinella), port in Etruria: Map 53

Punic Wars, the three wars between Rome and Carthage (264-241, 218-201, 149-146 B.C.); ended with the destruction of Carthage: pp. 102, 107, 188; Maps 30, 35, 38, 40

Pupput (Souk el Abiod), city on E. coast of Africa Proconsularis: Map 68

Pura, capital of Gedrosia: Maps 26, 27

Puteoli (Pozzuoli), city and port on the Sinus Cumanus; in the time of the Republic the most important trading port in Italy; later surpassed by Ostia: Maps 37, 43, 51, 53, 68

Pydna, city in Macedon where King Perseus of Macedon was defeated by Aemilius Paulus 168 B.C.: pp. 85, 107; Maps 1, 11, 38, 40; Plates 147, 260, 261

T

tragedian: Map 72

Theodosia (Feodosiya), Gr. settlement on the Chersonesus Taurica: Maps 26, 27

Theodosius the Great, Rom. Emperor A.D. 378-395, ardent opponent of paganism; repelled the menace of the Goths: pp. 174, 175

Theognis (end of 6th cent. B.C.), from Megara, Gr. poet: p. 182; Map 72

Theogony (i.e. 'the origin of the gods'), a work by Hesiod on the origin of the world and the gods: p. 178

Theophrastus (ca. 372-287 B.C.), from Eresus in Lesbos, Gr. philosopher, pupil of Plato and Aristotle; after the latter's death he presided over the Peripatetic school; also author of works on biology, mineralogy, etc.: Map 72

Theopompus (ca. 350 B.C.), from Chios, Gr. historian: Map 72

Thera (Santorin), a crescent-shaped volcanic island in the Aegean Sea, one of the Sporades: Maps 1, 11, 71

Therma (Saloniki), port on S. coast of Macedon S. of Chalcidice, later capital of the province: Maps 11, 19

Thermae *or* **Thermae Himeraeae** (Termini Imerese), city on N. coast of Sicily, founded by the Carthaginians 407 or 406 B.C. to replace Himera which they had destroyed in 409 B.C.: Maps 53, 68

Thermaicus, Sinus (Gulf of Thessalonica): Map 1

Thermi, city on E. coast of Lesbos, probably settled before 3000 B.C.: Maps 3, 6

Thermopylae, mountain pass in the N. of Greece near the Sinus Maliacus; famous for the stand made by the Spartans under Leonidas against the Persian invaders 480 B.C.: p. 42; Maps 19, 21; Plate 103

Thermum (Thermos), capital of Aetolia: Maps 11, 18

Theseus, legendary Gr. hero; killed the Minotaur, united Attica and made Athens the capital; worshipped as the national hero of Attica: pp. 21, 180, 188, 189

Thespiae (Thesbia), city in Boeotia at the foot of Mount Helicon: Map 71a

Thespis (ca. 534 B.C.), from Athens, Gr. poet, considered to be the inventor of Gr. tragedy: Map 72

Thesprotia, district in the S. of Epirus: Maps 1, 10, 11

Thessalia, district in the N. of Greece, E. of Epirus: p. 62; Maps 1, 3, 9-11, 15, 19; Plate 6

Thessaliotis, district in the centre of Thessaly: Maps 11, 15

Thessalonica (Thessaloniki), city in Macedon founded on the site of the earlier Therma; a flourishing commercial city owing to its being situated on the Egnatia Via: Maps 47, 51

Thessaly, see THESSALIA

Thetis, Gr. sea goddess, mother of Achilles: Plate 126

Theveste (Tébessa), city in E. of Numidia: Maps 57, 68

Thibari (Thibar), city in W. of Africa Proconsularis: Map 68

Thoricus (Thorikon), deme on E. coast of Attica: Maps 14, 71a

Thospitis Lacus (Lake Van), lake in Armenia: Maps 26, 28

Thrace, see THRACIA

Thracia, district between the Pontus Euxinus, the Aegean Sea, Macedon, and Moesia, more or less the modern Bulgaria: p. 62; Maps 1, 9, 11, 19, 38

Thrasymachus (ca. 430 B.C.), from Chalcedon, Gr. rhetorician and philosopher; a Sophist: Map 72

Thuburbo Maius (Henchir Kasbat), city in Africa Proconsularis: Map 68

Thuburbo Minus (Tébourba), city in Africa Proconsularis: Map 68

Thubursicum (Khamissa), city in Numidia: Map 71

Thucydides (ca. 471-ca. 400 B.C.), from Athens, famous Gr. historian, wrote a history of the Peloponnesian War: Map 71

Thugga (Dougga), city in Africa Proconsularis: Maps 57, 68, 71

Thurii, *later* **Copia,** Gr. settlement on E. coast of Lucania, founded ca. 443 B.C. by; Pericles as a panhellenic colony in the west: Map 31

Thyatira (Akhisar), city in the N. of Lydia: Map 28

Thysdrus (El Djem), city near E. coast of Africa Proconsularis: Maps 57, 68

Tiber, see TIBERIS

Tiberina Via, route along the Tiber from Rome to to the Grove of Feroniae: Map 55

Tiberis, river on which Rome stands; rises in the Apennines; called *flavus* (i.e. 'tawny') by Horace on account of the colour of the water: Maps 31, 33, 43, 53; Plate 246

Tiberius, Rom. Emperor A.D. 14-37, Augustus's stepson and successor; a capable ruler, but latterly notorious for his system of 'delations' and the resulting treason trials; lived in Capri from A.D. 27 to the end of his life: pp. 131, 134, 189; Map 43; Plate 318

Tibullus (ca. 50-19 B.C.), from Pedum, Rom., elegiac poet: p. 182; Map 73

Tibur (Tivoli), city in Latium, picturesquely situated near the waterfalls of the Anio; a favourite resort, with many villas: Maps 53, 55, 57, 68, 71c; Plates 450, 451

Tiburtina Via, highway from Rome to Tibur: Map 55

Ticinum (Pavia), city in Gallia Cisalpina, on the Ticinus: Map 58

Ticinus (Tessino), river in Gallia Cisalpina, tributary of the Padus: Maps 35, 54

Tifernum, city in Umbria, on the Tiber: Map 57

Tigranes (1st cent. B.C.), king of Armenia, son-in-law of Mithridates: Map 40

Tigranocerta, city in Armenia, founded by Tigranes: Maps 28, 38, 40, 71

Tigris, river in the modern Iraq: Maps 6, 7, 8, 23, 38, 43

Timaeus (ca. 346-250 B.C.), from Tauromenium, Gr. historian, author of a history of Sicily: Map 72

Timoleon, a Corinthian, Gr. statesman and general: freed Syracuse from the tyrant Dionysius II 344 B.C.: p. 62

Timon (ca. 320-230 B.C.), from Phlius, Gr. Sceptic philosopher and satirical poet: Map 72

Timotheus (ca. 450-360 B.C.), from Miletus, Gr. lyric poet: Map 72

Tingis (Tangier), port on W. coast of Mauretania Tingitana, Phoenician foundation: Maps 30, 35, 38, 47

Tipasa (Tefessad), city on the coast of Mauretania Caesariensis, Phoenician foundation: Maps 30, 51, 57, 68, 71

Tiresias, legendary Gr. soothsayer from Thebes; character in the *Oedipus Rex* of Sophocles: p. 180

Tiryns, ancient stronghold in Argolis with Cyclopean walls, dating from Mycenean times: Maps 3, 17, 18; Plates 45-9

Tisia (Theiss), tributary of the Danube between Pannonia and Dacia: Map 43

Titsey, site of Rom. villa in SE. Britain: Map 61

Titus, Rom. Emperor A.D. 79-81, captured Jerusalem A.D. 70 after he had taken over command of the East from his father Vespasian: p. 134; Plate 322

Tlos, city in Lycia: Map 71b

Tmolus M., mountain in Mysia: Map 10

Toletum (Toledo), city in Tarraconensis, on the Tagus: Maps 47, 66, 67, 68, 71

Tolosa (Toulouse), city in the S. of Gaul; in the 5th cent. A.D. capital of kingdom of the Visigoths: Maps 47, 51, 57, 68, 69

Tomen-y-Mur, site of Rom. fort and settlement in W. Britain: Maps 60, 61

Tomi (Constanza), city in Moesia Inferior, on W. coast of the Pontus Euxinus; founded from Miletus: p. 188; Maps 16, 47, 51

Torone, city on the central tongue of land of Chalcidice: Maps 1, 16

Toronaicus, Sinus (Gulf of Kassandra), gulf between the tongues of land of Chalcidice: Map 1

Trachis, city in the S. of Thessaly, near Thermopylae: Map 21

Tragia (Gaidaros), island in the Aegean Sea, one of the Sporades: Map 1

Tragurium (Trogir), city on the coast of Dalmatia: Map 29

Traiana Via, highway between Beneventum and Brundisium: Map 53

Trajan, Rom. Emperor A.D. 98-117, adopted son of Nerva; capable ruler and general, conquered Dacia: pp. 134, 135, 154, 189; Maps 43, 69b; Plates 280, 281, 283-5, 329, 453

Trajan, Column of, richly decorated pillar in the Forum Traiani in Rome, erected to commemorate Trajan's victory over the Dacians A.D. 107: Plates 274-277, 279, 280, 283-285, 453

Tralles (Aydin), city in the S. of Lydia: Maps 11, 28, 71b

Trapeza, place in central Crete; earliest remains from 3rd millennium B.C.: Map 4

Trapezus (Trabzon), port on S. coast of the Pontus Euxinus: Maps 16, 23, 26, 27, 43, 47, 51

Trasimeno, Lago, see TRASIMENUS, LACUS

Trasimenus Lacus (Lago Trasimeno), lake in central Italy, near Perusia, where Hannibal ambushed and annihilated a Rom. army under Flaminius 217 B.C.: Maps 33, 35

Trebia (Trebbia), river in Gallia Cisalpina, tributary of the Padus: Maps 35, 54

Trebula, see TREBULA MUTUESCA

Trebula Mutuesca, city in the land of the Sabini, near the Salaria Via: Maps 57, 68

Tres Tabernae (i.e. 'the three taverns'), posting stage in Gallia Cisalpina on the route Placentia-Laus Pompeia: Map 54

Treveris, name of Augusta Treverorum from the time of Diocletian (A.D. 284): Map 69

Triballi, tribe in Moesia Inferior: Map 26

Tridentum (Tridento), city in Gallia Cisalpina, on the Atesis: Map 53

Trimalchio, character in Petronius's picaresque 'novel' *Satiricon:* p. 190

Trimontium (Newstead), Rom. fort in N. Britain, at a crossing of the Tweed: Map 60

Trinacria, see SICILIA

Trinovantes, tribe in Britain: Map 60

Trinummus, title of a comedy by Plautus: p. 181

Tripolis 1. (Tarabulus) city on the coast of Syria: Map 28
2. coastal region in Africa, part of the province of Africa Proconsularis: Map 38
3. city in Pontus, on S. coast of the Pontus Euxinus: Maps 26, 27
4. city in the SE. of Lydia, on the Maeander: Map 28

Tritium (Tricio), city in Tarraconensis: Map 57

Triumphalis Via, connecting road between Rome and the Clodia Via: Map 55

Troas, the land of Troy, the NW. part of Mysia, bounded on the N. by the sea: Map 1

Troesmis, garrison town in Moesia Inferior near the Danube delta: Maps 41, 47

Troezen, town in Argolis: Map 11

Troia (Troy), city in Troas whose strong walls were said to have been built by Apollo and Poseidon; during the reign of Priam it was conquered by the Greeks after a siege lasting ten years (ca. 1180 B.C.); discovered at Hissarlik by Schliemann in 1868 and since then further excavated by Dörpfeld and Blegen; the excavations reveal nine settlements one upon the other; Homer's Troy is the layer described as VIIA: pp. 178, 179; Maps 3, 5, 6, 7, 9, 10

Tropaeum Traiani, monument erected in A.D. 108 at modern Adam Klissi in Romania to commemorate Trajan's victories: Map 47

Troy, see TROIA

Truentum *or* **Castrum Truentinum** (Porto d'Ascoli), place on the coast of Picenum: Map 53

Tubactis (Misurata Marina), place on the coast of Tripolis, on the Syrtis Maior: Map 47

Tucci (Martos), city in the E. of Baetica: Maps 57, 66

Tudae (Tuy), city near W. coast of Gallaecia: Map 66

Tuder (Todi), city in Umbria, on the Tiber: Maps 33, 57, 71

Tullus Hostilius, third of the seven kings of early Rom. history: p. 92

Turbula (Teruel), city in the E. of Tarraconensis: Map 66

Turicum (Zürich), city in the land of the Helvetii: Map 50

Turnu Severin, see DROBETA

Turris Libisonis (Porto Torres), port on NW. coast of Sardinia: Maps 29, 51, 53

Turris Tamalleni (Telmine), city on the border of Numidia and Africa Proconsularis: Map 47

Tuscania (Toscanella), city in Etruria, on the Clodia Via: Maps 33, 57

Tusci, see ETRUSCI

Tusculana Via, road from Rome to Tusculum: Map 55

Tusculum (Frascati), city in Latium, originally head of the Latin League; Cicero had a country-seat near here: Maps 29, 55, 57, 68, 71, 73

Twelve Tables, Laws of the, earliest codified system of Rom. law, established 451-449 B.C.: p. 101

Tyana, Hell. **Eusebia,** fortified city in the S. of Cappadocia: Maps 26, 28, 47

Tylus (Bahrein), island in the Persian Gulf: Maps 26, 27

Tymbres (Porsuk), river in the E. of Mysia: Map 11

Tyndaris (S. Maria di Tindaro), city on N. coast of Sicily, Gr. in origin: Maps 17, 71

Tyras 1. (Dniester), river in Sarmatia: Map 59
2. (Akkerman) city at the mouth of 1.: Maps 16, 26, 27, 47

Tyre, see TYRUS

Tyrrheni, see ETRUSCI

Tyrrhenum *or* **Inferum Mare** (the Tyrrhenian Sea): Maps 31, 33, 53

Tyrsenoi, see ETRUSCI

Tyrtaeus (7th cent. B.C.), Gr. elegiac poet, writer of patriotic poems and songs; lived and wrote in Sparta: p. 181

Tyrus (Soûr), port in Phoenicia; Tyrus and Sidon were the most important Phoenician cities: pp. 66, 102; Maps 23, 26-8, 30, 47, 51

U

Ucubi (Espejo), city in the E. of Baetica: Map 66

Udon, river in Sarmatia, flowing into the Caspian Sea: Map 26

Ulfilas (4th cent. A.D.), Arian bishop of the Visigoths; made a Gothic translation of the Bible: p. 174

Ulpia Noviomagus (Nijmegen), fortified settlement in Germania Inferior, in the land of the Batavi; raised to the status of a colonia by Trajan and hence called 'Ulpia': Map 47

Ulpian (ca. A.D. 200), famous Rom. jurist, friend and

became ruler of the kingdom of Palmyra; defeated and taken prisoner by Aurelian A.D. 272: p. 162

Zenodotus (ca. 325-260 B.C.), from Ephesus, Gr. scholar, known especially for his works on Homer: Map 72

Zeugma, city on the N. border of Syria, on the Euphrates: Maps 28, 49

Zeus, the supreme Gr. god, ruler of gods and men; his attribute is the thunderbolt; the Olympian Games were held in his honour: pp. 88, 99; Maps 24, 25; Plate 95

Zeuxis (ca. 431-400 B.C.), Gr. painter: pp. 62, 193

Zorambes (Dasht), river in Gedrosia: Map 26

Zoroastrianism, Persian religion founded by Zoroaster in very ancient times: p. 159

NOTES TO THE PLATES

Date of origin is given if reasonably certain. Museums, collections, etc., are indicated where known. The following abbreviations are used.

Mus. = Museum; Athens, A.M. = Athens, Acropolis Museum; Athens, N.M. = Athens, National Museum; Avignon, M.C. = Avignon, Musée Calvet; Berlin, Staatl. Mus. = Berlin, Staatliche Museen; Boston = Boston, Museum of Fine Arts; Cop. = Copenhagen, Ny Carlsberg Glyptothek; Uff. = Florence, Galleria degli Uffizi; Paris, B.N. = Paris, Bibliothèque Nationale; L. = Paris, Louvre; Rome, Gab. Fot. = Rome, Gabinetto Fotografico; Rome, Bar. = Rome, Museo Baracco; Rome, Cap. = Rome, Museo Capitolino; Rome, Civ. Rom. = Rome, Museo della Civiltà Romana; Rome, Lat. = Rome, Museo Lateranense; Rome, Ter. = Rome, Museo delle Terme; Rome, Cons. = Rome, Palazzo dei Conservatori; Rome, Tab. = Rome, Tabularium; Trier, L. = Trier, Landesmuseum; Vat. = Vatican City, Vatican Museums.

1 View to the north from the temple of Poseidon at Sunium. 2 Cornfield in Attica. 3 View of the island of Ithaca. 4 Island of Siphnos in the Cyclades. 5 Coast of Attica. In the foreground the temple of Poseidon on Cape Sunium. 6 Plain of Thessaly with the river Peneus. 7 Vale of Tempe with mouth of the Peneus in the Aegean. 8 Summits of the Olympus range. 9 Plain of Marathon looking S.S.W. from the burial mound. 10 Gulf of Corinth with site of former Aegosthena (modern Porto Germano). 11 View from the acropolis of Sparta; the former city area is now overgrown with olive trees. 12 Plain of Messene viewed from the north. 13 Plain of Laconica with Sparta. 14 Palace of Minos at Cnossus. 15 Sacred horn in palace at Cnossus. 16 Northern entrance of palace at Cnossus. 17 Serpent-goddess or priestess. Mus. Heraklion. 18 *Megaron* of the queen in palace at Cnossus. 19 Bullfight showing a man and two women. 15 in. 16th cent. B.C. Mus. Heraklion. 20 Fragment of a fresco from Cnossus. 21 Restored fresco showing women spectators, the 'Ladies in blue'. Ca. 1550 B.C. 22 Minoan jar from Gournia, 16th cent. B.C. 7½ in. high. 23 Representation of Minoan houses, from Cnossus. Ca. 1⅛ in. 24 Upper part of vase from Hagia Triada. Ca. 3½ in. high. 25 Cupbearer, partly-restored fresco from Cnossus; detail from procession. About life-size. 26 Palace at Phaestus in Crete. 27 Landscape around Mycenae. 28 Citadel of Mycenae, aerial view. 29 Citadel of Mycenae from the south. Reconstruction by Chipiez, deduced from existing ruins. 30 Entrance to the Lion Gate at Mycenae. 31 Lion Gate, exterior. Late Minoan, ca. 1400 B.C. 32 View from the Lion Gate in the direction of Argos. 33 Lion Gate, interior. 34 Shaft-tomb behind Lion Gate. 35 Excavations at Mycenae by Schliemann in 1876. 36 'Tomb of Atreus', interior. 37-9 Golden masks from Mycenae, ca. 11¾ in. high. Athens, N.M. 40 Golden beaker with spiral ornamentation, from Mycenae. Ca. 3⁷/₈ in. high. Athens, N.M. 41 Silver rhyton from Mycenae in shape of bull's head, with bronze ears, plated with silver and gold. Horns of gold-leaf. Total height ca. 11¾ in. Athens, N.M. 42 Representation of temple with sacred horns and doves, from Mycenae. Athens, N.M. 43-4 Golden ornaments with lion and butterfly, from Mycenae. Athens, N.M. 45 Citadel of Tiryns, east side. 46 West side. 47 Entrance to citadel of Tiryns. 48 Sally stairway on south side of citadel of Tiryns. 49 Detail of north corner of citadel of Tiryns. 50 Exterior of entrance to Mycenaean tomb at Orchomenus. 51 Mycenaean citadel at Gla. 52 Owl of Athena on tetradrachmon. 6th cent. B.C. 53 Aerial view of Athens. 54 Nike with wine-cup and drinking bowl, dressed in chiton with kolpos. Painting on the 'Nola amphora' from Suessula. Ca. 480 B.C. Boston. 55 Horsemen from procession of the Panathenaea. Fragment from north frieze of Parthenon. 3rd quarter of 5th cent. B.C. 56 Acropolis, seen from the Hill of the Muses. 57 Seen from the Agora. 58 Aerial view of centre of Athens. 59 Of the Acropolis. 60 Of Corinth. 61 Road from Corinth to Lechaeum, the old port of Corinth. 62 View from Acrocorinth of Corinth with in background the gulf of Loutraki. 63 Aerial view of Acrocorinth, near Corinth. 64-6 Fragments of pottery with various pictures, found at Corinth. Berlin, Staatl. Mus. 67 Walls of Messene in Messenia. 4th cent. B.C. 68 Theatre at Argos, excavated at the beginning of this century. 69 The river Eurotas near Sparta. 70 Aerial view of Argos with the acropolis Larissa. 71 Ruins of the temple at Tegea. 72 Acropolis of Mantinea (in foreground) seen from the plain of Arcadia. 73 Acropolis of Lindus in Rhodes. 74 Trireme hewn out of the rock at foot of acropolis of Lindus. 75 Harbour of Rhodes. 76 View from hills near Ephesus. 77 Probable temple of Hera at Metapontum (S. Italy). 78 Acropolis of Cumae. 79-80 Reverse and obverse of dekadrachmon from Syracuse. 81 Tetradrachmon from Naxos. Ca. 460 B.C. 82 Tetradrachmon from Naxos. Ca. 460 B.C. 83 View of Sybaris, perhaps the fourth city of this name in S. Italy. 84 Aerial view of Posidonia (Paestum), with the city centre. After centuries of prosperity the silting up of the river Sele drove the inhabitants from the city, which became overgrown and was not rediscovered until the laying of a road in the 18th cent. 85 Dancers, metope from the temple of Hera at the mouth of the river Sele near Paestum. End 6th cent. B.C. Paestum, Mus. 86 Soldier, metope from unidentified building at the mouth of the river Sele. Early 5th cent. B.C. Paestum, Mus. 87-8 Aerial view of Cyrene. 89 Dish of Arcesilaus, king of Cyrene. Ca. 6th cent. B.C. Paris, B.N. 90-1 'Venus of Cyrene', ca. 50 B.C. Rome, Ter. 92 Torso of Spartan warrior ('Leonidas'). Ca. 480 B.C. Sparta, Mus. 93 Archer of the Persian guard. 5th cent. B.C., from Susa. L. 94 Aerial view of plain of Marathon with the island of Euboea in the background. 95 Fragment of the 'Persian vase' found in a burial chamber at Canosa (Apulia) in 1851. Krater with volute handles. Nap. 96 Part of the burial mound of the Athenians in the plain of Marathon, with copy of the 'stele of Aristion' (see Plate 97). 97 Grave stele of a soldier in marble of Mt. Pentelicus, from inscriptions called 'stele of Aristion', executed by Aristocles. Height 7ft. 10½ in. Found in 1839 on a burial mound in Attica. Athens, N.M. 98 Fragment of the 'amphora of the Achilles painter'. Vat. 99 Fragment of the rim of the 'krater of Vix', found in 1952 in a Celtic burial mound at Vix (Côte-d'Or). The voluted krater is 42 in. high; diameter of base 40 in. Probably Etruscan, 6th cent. B.C. Châtillon-sur-Seine, Mus. 100 Aerial view of the peninsula of Chalcidice from the north with Mt. Athos in the background. 101 Fragments from reliefs on the north frieze of the Treasury of the Siphnians at Delphi. Parian marble. Found in 1894. Lion from a team driven by Cybele attacks a giant. End 5th cent. B.C. Delphi, Mus. 102 Another fragment from the same frieze. Apollo and Artemis shoot with a bow in the battle with the giants. A giant takes to flight, looking back as he does so; before him lies another giant who has fallen. Delphi, Mus. 103 Aerial view of the plain of Thermopylae seen from the south. 104 Aerial view of part of the mountain range near Thermopylae, roughly at the place of the path used by the traitor Ephialtes. 105 The bay of Salamis, between the island of the same name and Attica. 106 Battlefield of Plataea in Boeotia with remains of the walls of the city. 107-9 Fragments of the relief from Delphi (→ 101, 102). 108 Giants, Ares (left) with helm and shield. Delphi, Mus. 108 Hera bending over a fallen giant. Delphi, Mus. 109 From the south frieze. Horses of the Dioscuri from the rape of the daughters of Leucippus. Delphi, Mus. 110 Remains of the fortress of Eleutherae (4th cent. B.C.), from the southern entry to the gap of Kaza in the Cithaeron range on the road from Eleusis to Thebes. 111 Fragment of the walls of Messene (4th cent. B.C.). 112 Fragment of wall of Messene (4th cent. B.C.). 113 Towers of Aegosthena (now Porto Germano), ca. 31 miles north of Athens on the Gulf of Corinth. 114 Walls and towers of Aegosthena. 115 Walls and towers of Greek and Roman origin at Paestum. 116 View from the acropolis of Mantinea over the former city area. 117 Foundations of the towers of Mantinea in Arcadia. 118 Fragment of main frieze of the krater of Clitias and Ergotimas. Attic, 1st half 6th cent. B.C. Florence, Arch. Mus. 119 Festival procession to Ionian sanctuary for bringing a gift. In the foreground woman with ceremonial basket in elaborate Ionian chiton and himation. Boys bear branches; woollen garlands hang from the horns of the cattle. Scene on lekythos from Gela, ca. 500 B.C. Boston. 120-2 Fragments from 3 Attic pyxes with domestic scenes. Ca. 455 B.C. Br. M. 123 Kneading of dough. Boeotian terracotta, end 7th cent. B.C. L. 124 Man with horse-drawn plough. Boeotian terracotta, end 7th cent. B.C. L. 125 Making of chest for casting Danae and Perseus adrift. Left, King Acrisius of Argos, sceptre in hand; right, nurse with child. Black-figure hydria, ca. 490 B.C. Boston. 126 Hephaestus and Thetis, the former dressed as a workman, the latter with chiton and himation. Fragment from the Nola amphora of Suessula, ca. 480 B.C. Boston. 127 Domestic scene. A nurse hands a child to its mother. Lekythos from Eretria. 128 Woman wearing chiton receives a visit from a man. She has a wreath in her hands and a bird on her knee; a mirror hangs on the wall. Lekythos from Athens. 129 Swinging girl. Fragment from a skyphos, 5th cent. B.C. Berlin Staatl. Mus. 130 Ore foundry. Fragment of a dish, 5th cent. B.C. Found in 1835 at Vulci. Berlin, Staatl. Mus. 131 Two women at a stele. On a lekythos from Eretria. 132 Hermes bringing a dead man to Charon. 133 Funeral relief showing women. Ca. 330 B.C. Athens, N.M. 134 Female figure, both arms concealed beneath the himation. Terracotta from Tanagra, late-classical. L. 135 Similar figure, draped in a himation. L. 136 Two grave steles in the Dipylon burial-ground at Athens. 137 Aerial view of Delos with city and sanctuaries. 138 Archaic lions at the sacred lake of Delos. 139 Remains of a sanctuary of Dionysus in Delos. 140 Aerial view of the sanctuary at Delphi and modern Kastri. 141 King Aegeus before the oracle of Delphi; picture on dish of Kodros, ca. 430 B.C. Berlin, Staatl. Mus. 142 Omphalos (navel) found on the Sacred Way near the foot of Gela at Delphi. Surrounded by network of bands which actually covered the stone of the old oracle and is here carved in the marble. Delphi, Mus. 143 Fragment of a cista, a round box in which toilet necessities, etc., were kept. From Praeneste (Palestrina). Shown here is part of the Cista Barberini, early 3rd cent. B.C. Rome, Villa Giulia. 144 As 140. 145 View from theatre at Delphi over valley of the Plistus. 146 View from Delphi over plain towards the Gulf of Itea. 147 The sanctuary of Delphi in its present state. 148 Discovery of the archaic

statue of Cleobis or Biton at Delphi on 30 May 1893. Ca. 590 B.C. **149** Head of the charioteer, a greenbronze statue 5 ft. 10$^{7}/_{8}$ in. high, part of a team of horses, now lost, erected as a votive offering at Delphi. Ca. 470 B.C. Delphi, Mus. **150** Discovery of the charioteer in the temple of Apollo at Delphi on 1 May 1895. **151** As 147, but with reconstruction superimposed upon the original photograph. **152** Places for votive stones in the wall near the Treasury of the Athenians at Delphi. **153** Reconstruction of the front of the Treasury of the Siphnians at Delphi. Delphi, Mus. **154** Aerial view of the Asclepieum at Epidaurus. **155** Reconstruction of part of the sanctuary of Asclepieus with tholos at Epidaurus. **156** Fragment of votive relief of Asclepius found at Piraeus. End 4th cent. B.C. Athens, N.M. **157** Sanctuary of Asclepius on the island of Cos. Most buildings in their present state date from 3rd cent. B.C. **158** Relief showing sick man and Asclepius. Corinth, Mus. **159** Tombstone of Xanthippus; in his hand a foot as votive offering. May, however, be the tombstone of a shoemaker. Br. M. **160** Head of Athena, metope from the temple of Zeus at Olympia, 470–455 B.C. Found during German excavations 1875–81. Olympia, Mus. **161** Aerial view of the sanctuary at Olympia. **162** Apollo from the west front of the temple of Zeus at Olympia. The right leg is bent: important moment in the history of sculpture by departure from the usual frontal position. Olympia, Mus. **163** Foundations of one of the Treasuries at Olympia. **164** Figure usually called Cladeus as symbolising the divinity of one of the rivers near Olympia. Fragment from east front of temple of Zeus at Olympia. Olympia, Mus. **165** Doric column, monolith from temple of Apollo at Corinth. 6th cent. B.C. **166** Doric column from the 'Basilica temple' at Paestum. 575–550 B.C. **167** Coffered ceiling from the temple of Asclepius at Epidaurus. Epidaurus, Mus. **168** Ionic capital with graceful volutes and of beautiful workmanship, from north side of east portico of Erechtheum at Athens. 425–400 B.C. Br. M. **169** Pillar base from portico of Erechtheum at Athens. **170** Corinthian capital from temple at Epidaurus. Epidaurus, Mus. **171** Caryatid from southwest portal of Erechtheum at Athens. End 5th cent. B.C. Br. M. **172** Temple of Hera at Olympia, 650–625 B.C. **173** Temple of Aphaia in Aegina, 500–475 B.C. **174** Southeast front of the Parthenon at Athens, 450–425 B.C. **175** Part of woman's head, probably archaic, ca. 530 B.C. From the archaic temple of Artemis at Ephesus. Marble. Br. M. **176** Head of a young man of the Apollo type. Boeotian limestone. Found in the sanctuary of Apollo Ptoios in Boeotia in 1885. Archaic, 1st half 6th cent. B.C. **177** Head of Lapith woman(?), from the west front of the temple of Zeus at Olympia. Parian marble. 470–445 B.C. Olympia, Mus. **178** 'Blonde ephebe'. Transition from archaic to classical refinement. Ca. 480 B.C. Athens, A.M. **179** Head of Hermes found in the Hereum at Olympia in 1887. Parian marble. Height 7 ft. It is not certain whether the statue is an original by Praxiteles dating from the middle of the 4th cent. B.C. or a copy dating from the beginning of Roman Imperial times. Olympia, Mus. **180** East frieze of the Parthenon, probably with the gods Poseidon, Dionysus, and Demeter. By Phidias; Pentelic marble. Ca. 430 B.C. Athens, A.M. **181** Nike of Paeonius, found at Olympia in 1875. Parian marble. Original total height 7 ft. 1 in.; including lost wings 9ft. 6½ in. Ca. 421 B.C., after the Peace of Nicias. Cf. the Nike of Samothrace (Plate 223). Olympia, Mus. **182** East side of frieze of temple of Apollo at Bassae (Phigalia). Left, a Greek attacks an enemy; centre, fight between Greek and Amazon; right, wounded Amazon falls. Br. M. **183** Temple at Bassae, probably by the same architect as the Parthenon (Ictinus). 425–400 B.C. In the distance in the background Mt. Ithome. **184** Aerial view of temple at Bassae. **185** Krater of geometric period, 8th cent. B.C. Athens, N.M. **186** Fragment of 'Dipylon krater' with geometric ornamentation. Two soldiers in war chariots at the burial of a dead man. Attic, 8th cent. B.C. **187** Attic black-figure amphora, 540–530 B.C. Achilles defeats Penthesilea, queen of the Amazons. Br. M. **188** Grave lekythos. Girl, according to inscription called 'the beautiful', looks at a fillet. Athens, N.M. **189** Attic red-figure krater with picture of the death of Hector. Ca. 490 B.C. Found at Cerveteri. Br. M. **190** Hephaesteum at Athens, 450–440 B.C. **191** Erechtheum with Caryatids on the Acropolis at Athens, 425–400 B.C. **192** Olympieum at Athens, begun 475–450 B.C. **193-5** Scenes from palaestra on mixing-bowl, probably work of Euphronius, ca. 510 B.C. Berlin, Mus. **193** Hegesias anoints himself and Lycus undresses. **194** Preparation for throwing the discus. **195** Crowning of a victor. **196** Foreside of a statue base found near Dipylon in 1922. Attic, late 6th cent. B.C. Pentelic marble. Left, runner at the starting place; centre, wrestlers coming to grips; right, spearthrower lays a finger of his right hand on the loop of the spear-strap. Athens, N.M. **197** Left side of same base. Six young men in teams of three playing a ball game. Athens, N.M. **198** Fragment of amphora showing four-horse chariot. 6th cent. B.C. Berlin, Staatl. Mus. **199** Fragment of 'Fikellura amphora' of Rhodes, ca. 550–525 B.C. **200** Graeco-Roman copy of the bronze Discobolus of Myron. Br. M. **201** Hippomedon pulls a thorn from the foot of Tranion. From the same mixing-bowl as 193–5. **202** Relief of young victor setting the wreath of victory upon his head; the wreath was added in bronze to the marble relief. Votive offering of a victor. Found in 1915 in the temple of Athena at Sunium. Athens, N.M. **203** The stadium at Delphi. The spectators' seats at the right have disappeared. **204** Places for the judges in the stadium at Delphi. **205** Entrance to the stadium at Olympia. **206** Narrow side of the 'Boston throne', showing man playing a cither. Parian marble. Originating from Italy, mid 5th cent. B.C. **207** Side of the 'Ludovisi throne', found in 1887 in the former Villa Ludovisi in Rome. Parian marble. Originating from Italy, ca. 460 B.C. Rome, Ter. **208** Philip II of Macedon; coin. Br. M. **209** Alexander the Great, shown as the youthful Heracles with lion skin; silver coin. **210** Seleucus I of Syria; coin. Br. M. **211** Ptolemy I of Egypt. Br. M. **212** Attalus II of Pergamum. **213** Mithridates the Great; coin. Br. M. **214** View of Miletus from theatre; in background, silted-up harbour and bay. **215** Temple of Apollo at Didyma (Asia Minor). **216** Stoa of Attalus in the Agora at Athens; restored by the American School of Archeology in 1956. **217** Servant with sacrificial tray, known as 'the girl of Antium', found in 1878 near Antium. Parian marble. Probably mid 3rd cent. B.C. Rome, Ter. **218** Ruins of Gerasa (now Jerash) in modern Jordan. **219** Base of column in the temple of Apollo at Didyma. **220** Lighthouse and sailing-ship in port of Alexandria; coin of the time of Commodus. **221** Demetrius Poliorcetes ('the conqueror of cities'); coin. **222** Reverse of this coin with picture of a Nike on prow of a ship. **223** Nike of Samothrace. Ca. 190 B.C. L. **224** Fight between Amazons and giants from altar at Pergamum, erected by Eumenes II ca. 190 B.C. Now in Berlin. **225** Flaying of Marsyas by Apollo. Early 2nd cent. B.C. Rome, Cons. **226** Head of a man. Vat. **227** Head of Antinous of Hadda. Paris, Musée Guimet. **228** The 'Feeding of Telephus', the most important of the wall paintings in the basilica of Herculaneum. Left, allegorical figure of Arcadia. Behind her a satyr with a syrinx; Telephus is being suckled by a hind. Right, Heracles; behind him, Nemesis or Parthenos. Monumental quality, drapery, and forms of bodies are reminiscent of the plastic art of Pergamum. Nap. **229** Head of the Capitoline wolf, probably Etruscan. Rome, Cons. **230** Valley of the Manganello with (left) site of former Caere and modern Cerveteri. **231** Etruscan burial-mounds at Cerveteri. **232** Etruscan street of tombs at Cerveteri. **233** Aerial view of cemetery at Cerveteri, in which the hundreds of round burial-mounds are plainly visible. **234** City gate of Volterra. **235** Etruscan warrior. Fresco from grave at Cerveteri. 5th cent. B.C. L. **236** Etruscan relief with battle scene. 5th cent. B.C. Rome, Bar. **237** Dancing youth with kylix, from 'Tomb of the Leopards'. 6th cent. B.C. Cemetery of Tarquinii. **238** Recumbent man, from 'Tomb of the Lionesses'. 6th cent. B.C. Cemetery of Tarquinii. **239** Tomb with reliefs of household objects. Cemetery of Cerveteri. **240** Interior of tomb. Cemetery of Cerveteri. **241** View of Tarquinii. **242** View of the 'Cyclopean Wall' (wall of unhewn stone) at Cori south of Rome.? 6th cent. B.C. **243** Remains of the earliest settlement on the Germalus, the southwest corner of the Palatine in Rome, between early 8th and 7th cent. B.C. **244** Altar, found near the 'Guild Square' at Ostia. A.D. 124. Rome, Ter. **245** Relief on sarcophagus showing Rhea Silvia lying beside the Tiber. Ca. A.D. 210. Vat. **246** The Tiber near Pieve Stefano. **247** The god Tiber. Statue on the Campidoglio in Rome. 1st cent. B.C. **248** Samnite warriors with typical helms, greaves, and cuirasses in three pieces. From tomb at Paestum. Early 4th cent. B.C. Nap. **249** Caudine Forks, north of Benevento. **250** Warrior. From Capestrano in Picenum. Unique stone statue. 6th cent. B.C. Rome, Villa Giulia. **251** Wall and gate of Falerii Novi, founded by the Romans in 241 B.C. **252** Roman bridge of time of Augustus at Ascoli Piceno. **253** Aerial view of Cività Castellana (Falerii) and Falerii Novi. **254** Terracotta from Pompeii. War elephant. Nap. **255** Aerial view of battlefield of Cannae. Upon the hill, ruins of the village of Cannae. **256** Possibly graves of Roman and Carthaginian soldiers at Cannae. **257** Memorial column on top of hill near Cannae. The column erected in modern times is of antique origin. On the base is a sentence from Livy (xxii, 54, 10): *Nulla alia gens tanta mole cladis non obruta esset.* **258** Aerial view of Carthage. **259** King Hiero II of Syracuse with royal fillet; silver coin. **260** Reconstruction of triumphal monument of L. Aemilius Paulus, erected after the battle of Pydna 168 B.C. The inscription informs us that the consul took the monument from Perseus and dedicated it anew. **261** North side of the relief around the monument in Plate 260, showing battle between Macedonians (round shields) and Romans (oval shields). Delphi, Mus. **262** Lucius Cornelius Sulla, 138–78 B.C.; reverse of denarius. 1st cent. B.C. Berlin, Staatsmuntenkabinet. **263** Gnaeus Pompeius Magnus, 106–48 B.C. 1st. cent. B.C. **264** Marcus Tullius Cicero, 106–43 B.C. 1st cent. B.C. at. **265** 'Marcus Antonius', 82–30 B.C. 2nd half 2nd cent. A.D. Uff. **266** Marcus Junius Brutus, 85–42 B.C. 2nd half 2nd cent. A.D.; portrait on aureus. **267** Buildings of the Republican period at Palestrina (Praeneste). **268** Sepulchral monument of Publius Flavoleius Cordo of Modena, who died after 23 years of service. Belonged to Legio XIV Gemina, stationed mainly near Mainz. In his right hand he holds a sling. 1st half 1st cent. A.D. Mainz, Mus. **269** Model of siege of Avaricum (Bourges) by Caesar in 52 B.C. Avaricum (left) was protected by its natural position and by a wall of stones, earth, and wooden piles. Caesar had the steep slope raised by a palisade (*agger*) of wooden beams upon which were built two towers with bridges. To protect the soldiers alleys of boughs were constructed, covered by fresh pigskins against fire. **270** Sepulchral monument of Gnaeus Musius from Velleia, standard-bearer (*aquilifer*) of Legio XIV Gemina. In his right hand a lance with an eagle perched upon thunderbolts; his left hand rests upon an oval shield, likewise ornamented with a thunderbolt. Upon his breast two *armillae* and nine *phalerae*. 1st half 1st cent. A.D. Mainz, Mus. **271** Reconstruction of a battering-ram of the time of Caesar. Rome, Civ. Rom. **272** Sepulchral stele of Marcus Favonius Facilis, centurion (*centurio*) of Legio XX Valeria Victrix, which fought, among other occasions, during the conquest of Britain A.D. 43. Mainz, Mus. **273** Model of army camp at Deutz on the Rhine opposite Cologne, built in A.D. 310 by Constantine. Walls 65 ft. 7$^{3}/_{8}$ in. high, 13 ft 1½ in. thick; towers 52 ft. 5$^{7}/_{8}$ in. across, 65 ft. 7$^{3}/_{8}$ in. apart. **274** Weapons and baggage being loaded into ships. Column of Trajan, Rome. **275** Dacians laying fortifications. Column of Trajan, Rome. **276** Roman soldiers crossing a simple bridge-Column of Trajan, Rome. **277** Standard-bearers and officers (some wearing a lion skin like that of Hercules). **278** Soldiers attacking under a shield. Column of Marcus Aurelius, Rome. **279** Soldiers with siege implements. Column of Trajan, Rome. **280** Fragment of column of Trajan (118 ft. 1$^{3}/_{8}$ in. high) in Rome. The column shows scenes from Trajan's campaigns against the Dacians in A.D. 100-102 and 105-106. The base contained a golden cinerary urn. On top was a statue of Trajan, now replaced by one of St. Peter. **281** Barbarian fighting with Roman horse-soldier. Two soldiers look on while another blows on the tuba. Right upper corner of Ludovisi sarcophagus. 3rd cent. A.D. Rome, Ter. **282** Fragment of battle scenes on inner side of the arch of Constantine in Rome. 4th cent. A.D. **283** Trajan receives two Dacian chiefs while Roman soldiers lay fortifications. Column of Trajan, Rome. **284** Roman soldiers building a fort. Column of Trajan, Rome. **285** Dacian prisoners within the walls of a Roman camp. Column of Trajan, Rome. **286** Hadrian's Wall in northern England. **287** Shape of the Roman fortified town of Silchester. **288** Roman fort on the river at Richborough in Kent. **289** Square fort at Hân-al-Hallâbât, Syria. **290** Remains of a Roman road in the Syrian desert. **291** Road between Antioch and Aleppo. **292** Quasr-al-Hêr, northwest of Souhné, Roman fort in the Syrian desert. **293** The Fosse Way, one of the great Roman roads in Britain. **294** Road surface of the ancient Via Flaminia. **295** Probably Roman stones on the top of the Julier Pass (7,433 ft.) in Switzerland. **296** The Via Appia near Terracina. **297** Slightly-reconstructed version of a relief showing goods transport. Late period. Trier, L. **298** Wine transport on ox-cart. Rome, Ter. **299** Two-wheeled cart. Late period. Trier, L. **300** Roman travelling carriage from Vaison-la-Romaine (Provence). Gallo-Roman. Avignon, M.C. **301** Parents with child on a journey. The carriage is guided by a flying Cupid. Children with goose and a running-wheel. Late 1st, early 2nd cent. A.D. Rome, Ter. **302** The old port of Misenum (Campania). **303** Personification of Portus, port of Ostia. Fragment of sarcophagus. 3rd cent. A.D. Rome, Ter. **304** 'Piscina Mirabilis', colossal waterworks of the time of Augustus, dug out of a hill which closed off the old port to the east. 227 ft. long, 83 ft. 8 in. across, 49 ft. 2½ in. deep; capacity 16,478 cubic yards of water. **305** Mosaic in S. Apollinare Nuovo in Ravenna representing Classis, the most important port on the Adriatic Sea. **306** View of Cape Misenum. **307** Warship with legionaries. Vat. **308** Sailing ships in rough sea. Fragment of a sarcophagus. Cop. **309** Sailing ship, perhaps Phoenician, originating from sarcophagus from Sidon. 2nd cent. A.D. Beirut, Nat. Mus. **310** Towboat for transporting wine. Gallo-Roman. Avignon, M.C. **311** Representation of port of Ostia with ships, groups of statues, etc. 3rd cent. A.D. Rome, Mus. Torlonia. **312** Transhipment of amphorae. Mosaic in the 'Square of the Guilds' at Ostia. **313** Salvage of amphorae from sunken Roman ship. **314** Amphorae. Brindisi, Mus. **315** Julius Caesar. Rome, Cap. **316** Augustus. Fragment of cameo with allusion to the victory of Actium. Vienna, Kunsthist. **317** Augustus. Rome, Ter. **318** Tiberius; golden coin. **319** Claudius; tetradrachmon. The Hague, Kon. Kab. van Munten en Penningen. **320** Nero. Rome, Cap. **321** Vespasian. Br. M. **322** Titus. Br. M. **323** Reverse of coin of Claudius. Br. M. **324** Temple of Diana (reverse of 319). **325** Temple of Vesta (reverse of 321). **326** Conquest of Judaea (reverse of 322). **327** The Emperor Hadrian welcomed by Fortuna. Maastricht, Bonnefantenmus. **328** Domitian. Br. M. **329** Trajan. Ostia, Mus. **330** Hadrian. Rome, Cap. **331** Antoninus

Pius. Rome, Ter. **332** Commodus with the attributes of Hercules. Rome, Cons. **333** Caracalla; portrait on a sestertius. Berlin, Staatl. Mus. **334** Diocletian; portrait on an aureus. Berlin, Staatl. Mus. **335** Constantine I. Rome, Cons. **336** Constantine II. Rome, Cons. **337** Upper part of arch of Trajan at Benevento. Early 2nd cent. A.D. **338** The Emperor received in Rome. The globe in the hand of the goddess Roma is a falsification. This marble relief originally represented the Emperor Hadrian on his return from Syria in A.D. 117. Later his portrait was replaced by that of Marcus Aurelius. Early 2nd cent. A.D. **339** Inner side of ceiling arch showing Trajan and Victoria. Arch of Trajan at Benevento. Early 2nd cent. A.D. **340** Marcus Aurelius at a sacrifice. 2nd. cent. A.D. Rome, Cons. **341** Barbarians offering their surrender to Marcus Aurelius. 2nd cent. A.D. Rome, Cons. **342** Triumph of Marcus Aurelius. 2nd cent. A.D. Rome, Cons. **343** The Imperial Guard. 2nd cent. A.D. Rome, Tab. (see also 373). **344-5** Equestrian statue of Marcus Aurelius in the Campidoglio at Rome. 2nd cent. A.D. **346** Fragment of architrave from temple of Antoninus and Faustina in the Forum at Rome. 2nd cent. A.D. **347** Fragment of relief on base of a column erected in honour of Antoninus and Faustina on their deification. 2nd cent. A.D. Vat. **348** Valerian kneels before Sapor I (reigned A.D. 241—272). Rock relief in the province of Fârs in Iran. 3rd cent. A.D. **349** Aerial view of Rome taken from a height of 40,000 ft. **350** Vertical aerial view of the centre of Rome. **351** Oblique aerial view of the centre of Rome with the Capitoline and Forum Romanum. **352** Oblique aerial view of the Palatine Hill in Rome. **353** And from the northeast. **354-5** Model of ancient Rome. Rome, Civ. Rom. **356** Forum Romanum from an etching, 'Veduto di Campo Vaccino', 1772, by Piranesi. **357** Forum Romanum from a photograph of the late 19th cent. Rome, Gab. Fot. **358-9** Forum Romanum as it is today. **360** Ancient buildings in the Boarium in Rome. **361** Forum of Augustus in Rome. **362** Reconstruction of temple of Mars Ultor after I. Gismondi. Rome, Civ. Rom. **363** Fragment of tomb of the Aterii. End 1st cent. A.D. Rome, Lat. **364** Fragment of Forma Urbis, from reconstruction in Palazzo Braschi, Rome. Early 3rd cent. A.D. **365** Relief with Roman gods and goddesses upon the arch of Trajan at Benevento. Early 2nd cent. A.D. **366** Relief with gods and goddesses in Ara Pacis in Rome. 1st cent. A.D. **367** Sacrificial animal, led to the place of sacrifice by popas. Side of sarcophagus, Camposanto, Pisa. **368** Sacrifice offered by general. Uff. **369** Epona on horseback. Trier, L. **370** Mithras killing the bull. Early 2nd cent. A.D. Statue by the Athenian sculptor Criton. Ostia Antica, Mus. **371** Sacrifice by a priest of Cybele to Attis, who stands under a pine tree. 3rd cent. A.D. Ostia Antica, Mus. **372** Septimius Severus and Caracalla before the Senate. End 2nd cent. A.D. Rome, Pal. Sacchetti. **373** Detail from a marble panel found beneath the Palazzo della Cancelleria in Rome. 2nd cent. A.D. Rome, Tab. **374** Curia in Forum Romanum, Rome. **375** View through door of Curia, Rome. **376** Procession of magistrates. 1st cent. A.D. Vat. **377** Triumphal procession. Probably 1st cent. A.D. Rome, Cons. **378** Procession of magistrates. 4th cent. A.D. Aquileia, Mus. **379** Victoria, Leptis Magna. Early 3rd cent. A.D. **380** Aerial view of Pompeii. **381** Aerial view of the Forum. **382** Interior of the basilica at Pompeii. **383** Street in Pompeii. **384** Decumanus Maximus with triumphal arch at Volubilis (Morocco). **385** Aerial view of modern Timgad (Algeria). **386** Ruins of storeyed house in Ostia. **387** Reconstruction of storeyed houses in Ostia. **388** Horrea Epagathiana in Ostia. **389** Road, the 'Via della Fontana', in Ostia. **390** Relief showing mountain town, found in Lake of Nemi. Avenzano, Mus. Torlonia. **391** View of Castelnuovo di Porto on the Via Aurelia near Rome. **392** Vertical aerial view of the centre of Florence. **393** Vertical aerial view of Verona. **394-5** Panal on sarcophagus with playing Cupids and children. 3rd cent. A.D. Rome, Lat. **396** Portrait of a girl, full-face. 2nd cent. A.D. Rome, Ter. **397** Portrait of a girl, profile. **398** Portrait of a woman, perhaps Agrippina. 1st cent. A.D. Rome, Ter. **399** Portrait of a woman, perhaps Julia, daughter of Titus. 1st cent. A.D. Rome, Cap. **400** Bust of a man. Republican period. L. **401** Bust of a young Roman. Republican period. Rome, Bar. **402-03** Bust of Volcacius Myropnous. Ca. 160 A.D. Ostia Antica, Mus. **404** Sepulchral stele of L. Herennius Praesens. 2nd cent. B.C. Avignon, M.C. **405** Relief from a sepulchral monument from Neumagen showing four maids attending to the toilet of a lady of quality. 3rd cent. A.D. Trier, L. **406-07** Various scenes on frieze of sepulchral monument at Igel near Trier. 3rd cent. A.D. **408** Eating and drinking vessels of men on couch, including a dish with fowl. 3rd cent. A.D. Vat. **409** Relief on sarcophagus showing *dextrarum iunctio*. End 2nd cent. A.D. Isola Sacra, Ostia. **410** Cupid and Psyche. Fragment on sarcophagus. 2nd cent. A.D. Ostia Antica. **411** Interior of draper's shop. 1st cent. A.D. Uff. **412** Goldsmith at work. 1st cent. A.D. Vat. **413** Smith at work. 1st cent. A.D. Vat. **414** Relief with wine cafeteria. Gallo-Roman. Dijon, Mus. **415** Relief with goddess as patroness of apothecaries or Juno Saponaria. Épinal, Mus. **416** Money-changer. 2nd cent. A.D. Rome, Palazzo Salviati. **417** Vegetable seller. Ostia Antica, Mus. **418** Bust of butcher Tiberius Julius Vitalis. Rome, Villa Albani. The inscription 'Marcio always drunk' was added later. **419** Poultry and vegetable seller. End 2nd cent. A.D. Ostia Antica, Mus. **420** 'House of the Masks' in Delos. Ca. 2nd cent. B.C. Graeco-Roman. **421** 'House of the Golden Cupids' in Pompeii. **422** Mosaic from 'House of Dionysus on the the Panther' in Delos. Graeco-Roman. **423** Hypocaustum in bathhouse at Baden-Baden, Germany. **424** Central-heating channels in wall of house in Ostia Antica. **425** Rent payment in money. 3rd cent. A.D. Trier, L. **426** Rent payment in kind. 2nd half of 3rd cent. A.D. Fragment of sepulchral monument at Igel. **427** Sarcophagus with rural scene. Mid 3rd cent. A.D. Rome, Ter. **428-30** Fragments from a large series of mosaics found in an extensive villa at Piazza Armerina (Sicily) which may have belonged to the Emperor Maximian. Probably 2nd half of 3rd cent. A.D. **428** Hunting a wild boar. **429** Carrying away captured wild boar. **430** Game being loaded into ship. **431** Left, Hercules fighting the Hydra; centre, Hercules bringing the boar to his taskmaster King Eurystheus, who creeps away in fright; right, Hercules capturing the Arcadian stag. Hercules was sometimes considered the patron of gladiators. Fragment of a sarcophagus. Uff. **432** Traces of centuriatio in the province of Emilia. **433** Traces of walls against shifting sand, etc., in Algeria. **434** Fragment of a land register found at Orange. Orange, Mus. **435** Amphitheatre at Pompeii, showing what has been taken for the conflict between the inhabitants of Pompeii and Nocera in 59 B.C. (following the statement of Tacitus, *Annals*, xiv, 17). Nap. **436** Model of the Amphitheatrum Flavium in Rome, called the 'Colosseum' after the enormous statue of Nero as sun-god. Built by Vespasian and opened by Titus in 80 A.D. The three storeys were constructed with arches and columns in the three styles. It seated 45,000 spectators. Model by Gismondi. Rome, Civ. Rom. **437** Charioteer in two-horse chariot (*biga*). One of the horses is decorated with the head of a Gorgon from Herculaneum. Nap. **438** *Bestiarii* in circus fighting with lion and lioness. Two columns with seven eggs; an egg was removed after each round. Terracotta relief. Rome, Ter. **439** Sepulchral monument of a gladiator. Originating from Ephesus. Judging from the four wreaths, he had won four victories. Rome, Ter. **440** Chariot race with four-horse teams (*quadrigae*) round finishing post and obelisk. The spina is decorated with monuments, including one with two columns and two dolphins; after each round one dolphin was removed. Vat. **441** Mourning. Relief on the sepulchral monument of the Aterii. End 1st cent. A.D. Rome, Lat. **442** 'Tomba Rabirii' on the Via Appia in Rome. **443** Sepulchral monument of the Julii (high tower, right) in Saint-Rémy (formerly Glanum), Provence, with triumphal arch; consists of a base upon which stands a square building with round towers in which statues of the deceased were kept. Period of Augustus. **444** 'Tomb of Cicero', near Formia. **445** Street with tombs outside the Herculaneum gate at Pompeii. **446** Tombs of the poor in Isola Sacra near Ostia. **447** Deceased at sacrificial meal. A.D. 180-190 Ostia, Isola Sacra, *in situ*. **448-9** Dome and interior of the Pantheon in the Campus Martius in Rome, erected by Marcus Agrippa under Augustus, dedicated 27 B.C., rebuilt by Hadrian and Septimius Severus. Total diameter 184 ft.; interior diameter 138 ft.; diameter of the opening in the dome 29 ft. 6 in. **450** Aerial view of the villa at Tivoli built by the Emperor Hadrian. 2nd cent. A.D. **451** Model of the villa of Hadrian at Tivoli, by Gismondi. Tivoli, Villa Adriana. **452** Fragment of the sepulchral monument of the Aterii, showing a crane for lifting heavy objects. End 1st cent. B.C. Rome, Lat. **453** Trajan offering sacrifice before a bridge, probably near Turnu-Severin in Romania. Fragment of the column of Trajan, Rome. **454** Model of bridge over the Lys in Val d'Aosta. Rome, Civ. Rom. **455, 457** Course of aqueduct in plain of Thermopylae. **456** Watercourse in the Pont du Gard near Nîmes. The bridge, in three storeys, supports an aqueduct over the river Gard. Probably built by Agrippina. **458** The Oued Rhumel gap in Algeria with ruins of a Roman aqueduct. **459** Fallen Victoria at Leptis Magna (Libya). **460** Byzantine diptych showing the Emperor Anastasius. Ca. A.D. 517. On the lower part bears with their opponents during a *venatio* in an amphitheatre in Constantinople. In the late-classical period *venationes* (combats with wild beasts) replaced the gladiatorial games which had been forbidden. The diptych was destroyed by fire in Berlin during the Second World War. **461** Rhapsodist singer during a performance. Fragment from an Attic red-figure amphora found at Vulci. 480 B.C. Br. M. **462** Homer, earliest known representation, from the island of Ios. 2nd half 4th cent. B.C. Only existing specimen. Diameter $\frac{3}{4}$ in. **463** Performance of Greek drama in the theatre at Delphi. **464** Fragment of 'Euripides relief' from Constantinople. **465** Fragment of comic scene. Angry father leaves house with a stick to receive his drunken son. Ca. 170 A.D. 175. **466** Comic scene. Two credulous women on a couch (*kline*) consult a fortune-teller who is just about to recite her formulas over a goblet. Mosaic from Pompeii. Nap. **467** View from the back row over the theatre and landscape of Epidaurus. **468** Aerial view of Epidaurus. **469** Aerial view of Epidaurus during a modern performance of a Greek drama. **470** View of Horace's villa in ancient Ustica near Tivoli. **471** Two tragic masks. Relief on sarcophagus. Rome, Ter. **472** Stage masks. Relief from Pompeii. In the background, a temple. Nap. **473** View from theatre at Sabrata. **474** Reconstruction by C. Guidi of the theatre at Sabrata. Early 2nd, late 3rd cent. A.D. Rome, Civ. Rom. **475** The Three Graces. Fragment of a group. Roman copy, probably after an original by Praxiteles.

ACKNOWLEDGMENTS

A. B. C. Press, Amsterdam 463 — Aerofilms Ltd., London 87, 88, 286, 287, 293 — Air Ministry, Rome 253, 255, 349, 350, 351, 352, 353, 380, 381, 392, 393, 432, 448, 450 — Alinari, Fratelli, Florence 97, 143, 178, 179, 180, 207, 217, 228, 239, 245, 248, 250, 260, 268, 270, 272, 274, 275, 276, 277, 279, 283, 284, 285, 307, 308, 309, 310, 311, 315, 316, 317, 329, 330, 332, 336, 340, 347, 362, 363, 365, 366, 370, 372, 390, 394, 395, 396, 398, 406, 407, 412, 413, 414, 416, 418, 421, 426, 435, 437, 438, 439, 440, 441, 451, 452, 453, 465, 472, 474 — Anderson, S. A. D., Rome 449 — Antiquarium, Ostia Antica 371 — Bibliothèque Nationale, Paris 89 — Brink, R. E. M. van den, Laren 16 — British Museum, London 175, 182, 187, 188, 189, 201, 208, 210, 211, 213, 221, 222, 321, 322, 323, 325, 328, 461 — Brunner, E., Braunwald (Switzerland) 458 — Combier, L., Mâcon 258, 443, 466 — Commission des fouilles archéologiques, Paris 434 — Deutsche Zentrale für Fremdenverkehr, Frankfurt-am-Main 423 — Direzione generale dei monumenti e gallerie pontificie, Vatican City 98, 226, 264, 376, 408 — École française d'Athènes, Athens 148, 150 — Gabinetto Fotografico Nazionale, Rome 338, 341, 342, 343, 357, 378, 402, 403 — Galleria degli Uffizi, Florence 265 — Giraudon, Paris 224 — Grollenberg, L., O. P., Nijmegen 291 — Heyden, A.A. M. van der, Amsterdam 1, 2, 3, 9, 10, 11, 12, 27, 28±, 29, 30, 31, 32, 33, 34, 36, 37, 39, 40, 41, 45±, 46±, 47, 48, 49, 50, 53±, 55, 56, 57±, 58±, 59±, 60±, 61, 62, 67, 69, 70±, 71, 72, 78, 91, 92, 96, 101, 102, 103±, 104, 105, 106, 107, 108, 109, 110, 111, 112, 113, 114, 116, 117, 133, 136, 140±, 142, 144±, 145, 146, 152, 153, 154±, 156, 158, 159, 160, 162, 163, 164, 165, 166, 167, 168, 169, 170, 171, 172, 174, 177, 181, 183, 190, 191, 192, 199, 202, 204, 205, 225, 229, 230, 231, 232, 234, 240, 241, 242, 243, 244, 246, 247, 249, 251, 252, 257, 261, 269, 271, 273, 280, 281, 282, 294, 295, 296, 298, 301, 302, 303, 304, 305, 306, 312, 314, 335, 337, 339, 344, 345, 346, 354, 355, 358, 359, 360, 361, 367, 368, 374, 375, 382, 383, 386, 388, 389, 391, 397, 410, 411, 415, 417, 419, 424, 427, 431, 436, 442, 444, 445, 446, 447, 454, 455, 456, 457±, 467, 471. Photographs marked ± were taken with the co-operation of the Royal Hellenic Air Force — Hirmer, Collectie 81, 82 — Hötte, H.H., Baarn, wrapper photograph, 51 — Hubregt, A. V. H., Maarn 77, 83, 115 — Inspection des antiquités, Rabat 384 — Institut français d'archéologie de Beyrouth, Beirut 292 — Koninklijke Kabinet van Munten, Penningen en Gesneden Stenen, The Hague 319, 324 — Louvre, Paris 93, 123, 124, 134, 135, 186, 223, 235, 400 — Ministry of Information, Athens 68, 149, 203, 422 — Musée Archéologique, Châtillon-sur-Seine 99 — Musée Calvet, Avignon 299, 404 — Musée Guimet, Paris 227 — Museo Barraco, Rome 236, 401 — Museo delle Terme, Rome 90, 331 — Museo Nazionale, Naples 95, 254 — Museum at Cannae 256 — Museum at Epidaurus 155 — Museum at Heraklion, Crete 15, 17, 19, 20, 21, 22, 23, 24, 25, 42, 43, 44 — Museum of Fine Arts, Boston 206 — National Museum, Athens 176, 185, 196, 197 — Nuovo Museo, Paestum 85, 86 — Ny Carlsberg Glyptothek, Copenhagen 263 — Otterbeek, J.L.M., Hilversum 76, 214, 215, 219 — Palazzo dei Conservatori, Rome 377 — Rheinisches Landesmuseum, Trier 297, 299, 369, 405, 425 — Richter, E., Rome 84, 320, 399, 401 — Ripartizione Antichità e Belle Arti del Comune di Roma, Rome 364 — Royal Hellenic Air Force, Athens (Copyright Elsevier, Amsterdam) 4, 5, 6, 7, 8, 13, 14, 63, 73, 75, 94, 100, 137, 147, 157, 161, 184, 420, 468, 469 — Soprintendenza alle Antichità della Sicilia Orientale, Syracuse 428, 429, 430 — Staatliche Münzsammlung, Berlin 79, 80 — Stampa Angeli, Terni 267 — Stibbe, C., Amsterdam 26, 74, 138, 139, 173, 216, 470 — Tadema, A. A., Heemstede 379, 459, 473, 475.

PLATES REPRODUCED FROM BOOKS

Antike Denkmäler 35, 64, 65, 66 — Baradez, J., *Vue aérienne de l'organisation romaine dans le Sud-Algérien* 433 — Furtwängler, A., and Reichhold, K., *Griechische Vasenmalerei* 118, 119, 120, 121, 122, 125, 126, 129 — Furtwängler, A., and Riezler, W., *Weissgründige Attische Lekythen* 127, 128, 131, 132 — *Die Schönsten Griechenmünzen Siziliens* 81, 82 — Poidebart, A., *La Trace de Rome dans le désert de Syrie* 289, 290 — Sazo, S. de, *Mon album des Profondeurs* 313.

MAPS

A. R. A. van Aken 14, 29, 30, 31, 32 (from data in catalogue of the Mostra Etrusca, 1955), 33, 34, 35, 36, 37, 38, 39, 40, 41, 42, 43, 44, 45, 46, 47–50 (from data supplied by J. M. H. Fernhout, 52 (from data supplied by Oswald D. Pryce), 53, 54, 55, 59, 66 (from data supplied by P. de Palol and G. Guinea), 67, 69, 70, 73 — P. Calasanctius Cap. 1, 2, 3, 4, 5, 6, 7, 8, 9, 10, 11, 12, 13, 14, 15, 16, 17, 18, 19, 20, 21, 22, 23, 24, 25, 26, 27, 28, 72 — F. Castagnoli 51, 58 — L. Cozza 56 — G. Forni 57, 68, 71. — H. H. Scullard 60-5 (much of the material on Maps 60 and 61 is based on the Ordnance Survey Map of Roman Britain, 3rd Edition, and grateful acknowledgment is made to the Controller of H. M. Stationery Office)